D0205864

Edmund Gosse

ANN THWAITE

Edmund Gosse

a literary landscape, 1849–1928

The University of Chicago Press

Sources of Illustrations

Illustrations are reproduced with the kind permission of their copyright owners. Most come from the family collection for which I thank Jennifer Gosse. For 2 and 3, I thank Edmund Barr Gosse; 7 the owners of Sandhurst; 18 and 36 the Brotherton Library, Leeds University; 5, 8, 38, 39, 40, 41, 42, 51, 52, 53, 54, 59, 60, 61, 62 the Syndics of Cambridge University Library; 26, 27, 35 National Portrait Gallery; 48 Shirley Turner. For the Beerbohm cartoons (19, 25, 55 and two in text) I have to thank Sir Rupert Hart-Davis and Mrs Eva Reichmann.

The University of Chicago Press, Chicago 60637
Secker & Warburg Limited, London W1V 3DF

© 1984 by Ann Thwaite
All rights reserved. Published 1984

Phototypeset by Rowland Phototypesetting Limited
Bury St Edmunds, Suffolk
Printed in Great Britain

92 91 90 89 88 87 86 85 84   1 2 3 4 5

Library of Congress Cataloging in Publication Data

Thwaite, Ann.
  Edmund Gosse: a literary landscape, 1849–1928.

  Includes bibliographical references and index.
  1. Gosse, Edmund, 1849–1928—Biography.   2. Authors,
English—19th century—Biography.   I. Title.
PR4725.G7Z84   1984   828'.809   83–18076
ISBN 0-226-80136-5

Contents

List of Illustrations

Illustrations in the text

For Anthony inevitably and for Alice
but also for my friends

'Friendship has been like sunlight and like sleep'
Father and Son

Introduction

THE MOST POTENT image of Edmund Gosse for me is the 1857 portrait of the boy at his father's side, which appears over and over again in editions of *Father and Son* and was faithfully reproduced by the actors in Dennis Potter's television version of the book. The other prevalent image of Gosse is of the elderly man of the Beerbohm cartoon, staggering back in mock surprise at the sight of the bust of himself presented to him on his seventieth birthday in 1919. This is the Gosse of Osbert Sitwell's 'courteous revelation' in *Noble Essences*, and the cartoon formed the cover of the Penguin edition of John Gross's *The Rise and Fall of the Man of Letters*. Some of the most eminent men in England are gathered round him. The list of signatories to his birthday greetings included Barrie and Bennett, Chesterton and Conrad, Graves, Hardy, Housman, Kipling, Pinero, Sassoon, the two Archbishops, two former Prime Ministers, and numerous peers of the realm, including Curzon, Londonderry, Lytton.

How did the one – the pale boy so rigorously reared, so much encouraged to ignore the values of the secular world – become the other, the man whom H. G. Wells called 'the official British man of letters'? It also interested me to investigate the justice of twentieth-century reactions against Gosse. T. S. Eliot said 'the place that Sir Edmund Gosse filled in the literary and social life of London is one that no one can ever fill again, because it is, so to speak, an office that has been abolished'. But it seemed, the more I looked into it, that Gosse had held that office well, and performed functions that still need to be performed by those who care about literature.

Geoffrey Grigson told me how, to him as a young man in the twenties, Gosse's *Sunday Times* articles seemed 'too long, too urbane, and tiresome; and that everyone of our Eliot generation said so'. Anthony Powell remembered quoting Gosse as an authority when he was a very young man in 1926 or 1927 and being laughed at by two slightly older contemporaries: 'I suppose it was pretty generally known that he was unreliable.' And yet, Powell said, there was the fact of his 'unassailable prestige' – because he had known so many of the great Victorians. Indeed, it seems as if he had known everyone. 'Gosse's genius for knowing people was extraordinary,' George Saintsbury once said.

John Gross has described Gosse as the 'one belletrist of his generation whose name still means something to the world at large'. Is that how Gosse is now to be described – as a 'belletrist'? It seems a terrible fate for the author of *Father and Son*. My parents' shelves were full of Gosse. I remember my disappointment as an adolescent in the 1940s at finding that his *Modern English Literature* ended with Tennyson. But then I went on to read *Father and Son*. It was one of the formative books of my youth, just as *The Secret Garden*, about whose author I wrote my previous biography, had been one of the formative books of my childhood. As it happens, Edmund Gosse and Frances Hodgson Burnett were born in the same year, 1849, and their paths crossed and recrossed in the London of the 1890s.

In 1918, hardly foreseeing that in the 1980s it would be set as an A-Level examination text, Gosse told George Moore that *Father and Son* was 'already almost forgotten'. He had no great hopes of immortality and his reputation certainly suffered a severe decline after his death. The attitudes of Ezra Pound and Virginia Woolf replaced the chorus of praise that celebrated his seventieth birthday. It has become customary to deride him. I give two recent examples. The life of Edward Garnett, published in 1982, has several references to Gosse (unindexed and inaccurate, incidentally), all of them derogatory; a typical note on Gosse in the 1982 selection of Robert Graves's letters calls him a 'notoriously conservative, inaccurate yet nevertheless influential critic'. It seemed time for a reassessment, more than fifty years after his death and the immediately subsequent publication of the official *Life and Letters*.

There have been regular suggestions that Gosse, far from being the pillar of the establishment Bloomsbury abhorred, had in fact been involved in the Wise forgeries and had been a secret homosexual, as well as being malicious, snobbish and a hopelessly unreliable scholar. He certainly had 'a genius for inaccuracy' in Henry James's phrase. But he possessed far rarer qualities than accuracy. Raymond Mortimer attempted to set the record straight in the *Sunday Times* in 1949, a hundred years after Gosse's birth. 'How trivial are the inaccuracies for which he was attacked compared with the felicity of his style, the width of his allusions, above all with the gusto of his bookishness.' Thirty-five years later this tribute sounds dated. We do not use words like 'felicity', 'gusto' or even 'bookishness', without reservations and inverted commas. But I have shared Mortimer's pleasure in reading Gosse's criticism.

As for those other suggestions, they seemed worth investigating further. At least I knew I had Gosse on my side in trying to get at the truth. In 1897 he wrote in a letter, 'If biographers would only see how much they enhance the qualities of their subjects by admitting peculiarities and even failings.' He disliked the feeble waxworks produced by pious Victorian biographers. He knew that the characters that interest us are those whose weaknesses we recognize in ourselves and in our friends, the victims not the heroes. Like his father, Gosse despised the 'goody-good lives of good men'. But it hardly seems fair if the weaknesses and vanities survive and the strengths and virtues are forgotten.

In trying to get at the facts I had one particular problem. Gosse described himself as a 'tainted source' when someone was compiling a bibliography of his work. How much more so can this be said with regard to his own biography. Not only did his memory betray him. He also changed things deliberately very often to make a better story. On the whole I have favoured the unpublished rather than the published version, as the unpublished is often in a letter written at the time and likely to be more accurate. But it is possible that some of Gosse's own inaccuracies have persisted into this book, alongside, inevitably, some of my own.

Edward Marsh tells, among many other good Gosse stories in *A Number of People*, how one of his assailants, 'the redoubtable Dr Furnivall', was eventually 'seized with remorse and told his victim that in the darkness of the night the words JUSTICE TO GOSSE had appeared on the wall in letters of fire'. I had no such Belshazzar-like visitation; but the message seemed equally clear. I wanted to look at him directly, this man who appeared over and over again playing bit parts in the biographies of other people, part of the furniture of Victorian and Edwardian England. He even crops up in contemporary fictions, to give authenticity to imaginary characters: in Anthony Powell's *A Question of Upbringing*, in Malcolm Bradbury's *Stepping Westward*, in a Michael Innes short story, in a recent first novel – *My Life Closed Twice* by Nigel Williams. But he was in danger of becoming a caricature, and a caricature less accurate than Beerbohm's.

This is obviously not the Gosse who was a close friend of such different people as Swinburne, Robert Louis Stevenson, Hardy and Henry James. Nor is it the man who introduced Ibsen to England and first drew attention to Gide; the devoted neighbour of Robert Browning who also encouraged the young Robert Graves. The real Gosse has been in danger of being lost.

On the whole, I have concentrated on the characters in Gosse's story in whom there is most interest. I have had to ignore some people whom Gosse knew well and to pay less attention to others than some would wish. Otherwise my text could hardly have been contained in one volume. There are a number of people who played a larger part in Gosse's life than this book suggests. Students of, for instance, Clement Shorter, James Fitzmaurice Kelly, Evelyn Baring (Lord Cromer), Gordon Bottomley, J. G. Frazer, J. H. Shorthouse, Maurice Hewlett or Frederic Harrison may look in vain for any light on Gosse's relations with them. I can only apologize and plead lack of space. In 1920, Gosse told Dover Wilson: 'Papers accumulate so maddeningly that I have got into the bad habit of destroying them as soon as they have served their purpose.' But he was too much of a biographer himself ever to destroy a letter which might have any conceivable interest in years to come. His archive, scattered as it now is in libraries in several countries, must be one of the largest ever left by one man. The problem of compression has been immense.

Elizabeth Bowen, in a preface to a 1965 collection called *Critics who have influenced taste* (which includes Frank Swinnerton's essay on Gosse), takes us to task if we think of critics as 'failed artists' – but Gosse was manifestly that. For many years, the thing that mainly mattered to him was being a poet. His failure to be 'among the English poets' hurt him as much as Churton Collins's notorious attack on his criticism. In fact, his life, in some ways so static, was full of crises and agitation and emotional adventures, as well as of worldly success and pleasures. Collins, T. J. Wise, A. C. Benson and Virginia Woolf all in their different ways made him their victim; but finally, as Gosse agreed with Haldane in 1918, 'No man is the victim in reality of anyone but himself.'

Gosse's best memorial is of course *Father and Son*. When he had finished reading it in November 1907, H. G. Wells wrote to Gosse, 'This is a book I would ill-spare as any book and I perceive I only begin to know you . . . One could go on with a good appetite to the rest of your autobiography.' Many people must have wondered, as Wells did, what happened after that. Gosse never wrote his own autobiography beyond that moment when, as a tall young man, he chose to mix with the Pre-Raphaelites rather than the Plymouth Brethren. He seemed to emerge again fifty years later as a garlanded elderly gentleman, Aldous Huxley's 'bloodiest little old man', Virginia Woolf's 'dapper little grocer'. How, apart from everything else, had he so shrunk? I wanted to find out.

I thought at one stage I might begin my own book in 1867 with Gosse starting work at the British Museum, in order to avoid the problem of rewriting *Father and Son*, a daunting idea. But there is so much material from these early years, unused by Gosse himself, that far from feeling the problem of rewriting his book, I had some difficulty in finding space even for the more important events in it. My early chapters are designed to be read alongside *Father and Son*. If there are readers of this introduction who have not yet read that book, they might well get hold of a copy now. (Penguin have recently brought out a new edition in their English Library series.) Then they will surely want to know, as I wanted to know, more about the 'truth' behind that book, and what happened next.

How did the young man who had thrown off 'the yoke of his dedication' cope with his new life in London? James Hepburn, a recent editor of *Father and Son*, suggests that Gosse, in coming to London and thinking to find freedom, in fact 'escaped into a smaller life'. It is an interesting thought. But it remains remarkable that this under-educated youth, coming to the city with few connections and little money, so soon found himself able to give as his references for a job he coveted the names of three of the greatest poets in England: Tennyson, Browning and Matthew Arnold. How did he eventually become the confidant of the Prime Minister, consulted about who should be the next Poet Laureate, whether Meredith should be buried in the Abbey, whether Yeats should have a Civil List Pension? This is the story not only of one literary life, but of matters concerning several generations of writers.

Ann Thwaite
Low Tharston
Norfolk, 1983

Messages Human and Divine

THE CHILD THOUGHT he was not wanted. Fifty-seven years later, in his most famous book, Edmund Gosse wrote, 'the advent of a child was not welcomed but was borne with resignation'. In another place he called himself 'a helpless and unwelcome apparition'. He imagined his parents, that austere middle-aged couple, made uneasy by his intrusion into their scholarly devout lives in a small quiet house in Tottenham, his father disturbed by infant cries as he bent over his microscope (in the slide a smear of dirty water from Hornsey Road Ponds), his mother interrupted in her work of saving sinners, the two of them no longer able to find their pleasure chiefly in an analysis of the prophetic books of the Bible.

Edmund Gosse spent a good deal of his life making himself feel loved, wanted, admired, appreciated. He needed an audience and applause as much as any actor. He was impatient of solitude and afraid of it. It was as if he needed to make up for the long quiet hours he remembered, without playmates or stories, his face pressed against the window to catch whatever glimpses he could of a racier world.

In fact, his infancy, as we shall see, was wrapped in a lavish love and parental concern unusual for the period. His parents were indeed middle-aged and ardent seekers after God's truth, but they were as passionate lovers as any more worldly couple and their passionate concern for each other included their child. 'It is a very sweet thing, dear William, to love and to be loved.' So wrote Philip Henry Gosse to his brother on 3rd May 1849, five months after his marriage to Emily Bowes and five months before the birth of his only son, Edmund William, who was to be the cause of so much devoted anguish. 'I could wish for no greater earthly blessing for you, dear William,' he continued, 'than as kind, as gentle, as good a helpmeet as the Lord has given me.'

It had taken P. H. Gosse, natural historian, a long time to find the woman he loved. He was born in 1810, the son of an ill-assorted pair, Thomas Gosse and Hannah Best. Thomas himself was born in 1765, the eleventh child of William Gosse and Elizabeth Corbin of Ringwood in Hampshire. Edmund Gosse, Francophile, used to claim his ancestry was French – that the Gosses had been Huguenots, who came over at the time of the revocation of the Edict of Nantes in 1685, but there are Gosses in Ringwood from the very first Parish Register in 1561.

William Gosse was in the woollen trade and was prosperous enough at one stage, but he left nothing for Thomas when he died in 1784. The boy, who had shown artistic talent, had by then spent several years at the Royal Academy Schools – Sir Joshua Reynolds had taught him; William Blake had been a fellow pupil. But Thomas's skill was a trade and a craft, not an art. On his father's death he apprenticed himself to a London mezzotint engraver but his real pleasure was in translating the Greek poets. Then on the 22nd July 1790 – he often recalled the date – he saw a clear vision of Christ in majesty rising above the junction of Fleet Street and Chancery Lane. His new religious conviction was to confirm in him a spirit of acceptance with his lot which lasted the rest of his life. He had no success in the eyes of the world but no sense of failure either. He decided to make his living as an itinerant painter of miniatures and travelled England on foot, looking for customers. He carried with him little more than his Theocritus, his Bible and the tools of his trade, but he was clothed with the armour of righteousness and nothing could harm him or alter his convictions.

Thomas was nearly forty-two when he met Hannah Best, a sort of companion-maid in a Worcester household where he was 'taking likenesses'. She was twenty-six and as dark and determined as he was fair and ineffectual. He continued his peripatetic life; she eventually set up home with their four children in Poole in Dorset, where he would spend not more than a tenth of his time. Poole was full of Gosse relatives, all, as Philip recorded, 'much above us in wealth and position'.

Thomas was a writer as well as a painter. Dull religious epics in blank verse and sacred emblematical essays flowed from his pen. He lived in the hope that one day he would persuade someone to publish something. Hannah Gosse waged ruthless war against 'that cursed writing', and against his reading too. Philip recalled as a child seeing his father on many occasions hide a book under his little green baize desk when hearing his wife's footsteps. He would snatch up his paintbrush and ivory; Philip would not tell tales.

The whole household, for all its vagaries and uncertain income, was firmly stayed upon the Rock of Ages. 'Whosoever is fixt on Him can never be moved.' Hannah brought her family up in 'reputable sub-gentility'. Thomas's earnings never exceeded £100 a year; Hannah supplemented that by taking in lodgers. She was resourceful and hardworking and trained her children to be the same. Saturday afternoons were the only time for play. But Philip's memories of his schooldays suggest a much freer, rougher boyhood than his son was to have. When he learnt to whistle (after weeks of shaping his lips and pretending when his brother William whistled), the tune was certainly 'Jesu, lover of my soul'. But 'rude, doggerel rhymes' were as familiar as hymns.

Philip was an industrious student; he claimed that he never 'miched' or missed a day's school. But sometimes his mother kept the boys at home for a whole term, to save school fees, setting them to study on their own in a back garret and keeping a sharp eye on them. They were allowed to read anything they liked. It was Emily, Edmund's mother, not his father, who would deprive the son of fiction.

Philip showed unusual cleverness and Hannah was determined he should know some Latin. She knew the value of education though she had little herself. After William, aged fourteen, had sailed off to Carbonear in Newfoundland for service in the firm of his uncle, Hannah contrived, with one less mouth to feed, to let Philip have a year at a boarding school in Blandford. He acquired in that one year a good fundamental knowledge of Latin and the elements of Greek. He read both languages until the end of his life. He started writing poetry. And he developed his interest in natural history, which had been encouraged all his childhood by his Aunt Susan, mother of Thomas Bell FRS, who was later instrumental in getting Philip's first books published. Susan Bell, his father's sister, had herself been a teacher. It is claimed that she was the first person to preserve invertebrate animals alive out of the sea. She died in 1829, long before the apparent invention of the aquarium, the credit for which is usually shared between Philip Gosse and Robert Warington.

Philip left school reluctantly at fourteen. He studied on his own for a while and then had a clerk's job on the Poole quays but lost it. Eventually, again reluctantly, he followed William to Newfoundland. He signed on for six years, for his board and lodging and £20 a year, as a clerk in a whaling merchant's counting house at Carbonear. He was just seventeen.

Philip writes of having experienced his 'entrance into virility' on board ship and confessed that his youthful lusts threw back for years the work of God in his soul. 'For a while they drowned my divine convictions and it was of God's special mercy that they did not drown me in destruction and perdition.'

There was certainly nothing pious or priggish about the young Philip Gosse, though he undoubtedly obeyed his mother's final injunction to read his Bible daily. Years later William wrote and asked if he were as fond of a joke as ever. He had listed a 'jest book' among his favourite childhood reading and he had taken with him to Carbonear his manuscript pages of jokes 'copied out of *Joe Miller*, with which I expected to take captive the laugh of the office'. Jokes did not necessarily rule out a consciousness of sin. Dancing was perhaps more dubious than telling jokes. Certainly 'the elegant accomplishment' had been forbidden by his parents' 'Puritan prejudices' and he longed to learn.

There was a great deal to learn. In the early days in Newfoundland he wrote a novel, or at least a story. He drew everything he saw. He learnt to dislike the Papist Irish. He fell briefly into debt over a shillingsworth of cinnamon. He fell in love and never said a word. He kept a journal. He gazed at an engraving by Bartolozzi of Venus bathing. He kept a poetry anthology. He made his own violin and an Aeolian harp.

1832, his son eventually considered, was probably the most important year of Philip's life. He was twenty-two. At an auction on the 5th of May he bought Adams's *Essays on the Microscope*. 'How much happiness, which chequers my earthly existence, may have depended on the laying out of ten shillings at a book sale.' The book turned him from a dilettante collector into a scientist. A few weeks later his spiritual condition was entirely altered as well. The threatened death of his sister, at home in Poole, made him turn to God. In his own words: 'I cannot say that I was born again as yet, but a work was commenced . . . which culminated in regeneration.' He remembered the last time he swore. He discovered with profound relief, on his joyful first return to England that summer, that his sister had recovered. He returned to Newfoundland 'the day before Sir Walter Scott died'. It was during this period that he developed the conviction 'that it was proper to exclude from his companionship all those whose opinion on religious matters did not coincide with his own'. It seemed he had forgotten about the publicans and sinners. The resulting isolation had a disastrous effect on his temperament.

In 1835, after fulfilling his contract in the counting house at Carbonear and having used his leisure to learn more about the entomology of Newfoundland than anyone had known before, he moved on into Canada and tried to farm, teaching and writing in the winters. But he was not a farmer. Tired of a diet of buckwheat and pigsmeat and the hard lonely work which brought so little reward, in 1838 he moved south to Alabama where he got a job as a schoolmaster at Mount

Pleasant. His pupils became a 'volunteer corps of collectors'. The butterflies delighted him but slavery sickened him. It sickened him, too, that the pious people with whom he mixed, the Methodist preachers among them, accepted slavery as calmly as 'the most dissolute and savage overseer, flicking his boots with his cow hide on the verandah of a rum-shop'.

Slavery had much to do with his abrupt departure. Resigning his job, he spent Christmas on board a steamer on the Alabama River in high spirits, sharing in a splendid turkey, 'his curious objection to everything which in any way suggested the keeping of Christmas as a festival, not having yet occurred to him'. It was on his return voyage to England, after an exile of twelve years, that he first overcame his shyness and questioned his fellow travellers about the condition of their souls. 'This habit,' Edmund recorded, 'he preserved till the end of his life.'

Philip Gosse began to view life solely as 'a dressing-room for the theatre of Eternity', a curious analogy considering his puritanical attitude to the theatre. But in the dressing-room he had to earn a living. He was by now too old to be considered a candidate for the Wesleyan ministry. He was almost literally starving (in his London garret he ate a herring as slowly as possible for his only meal of the day), when his cousin Thomas Bell recommended the manuscript of *The Canadian Naturalist* to a publisher. It was the first of a long line of books that are still prized and collected.

The 1840s were years of continuous self-education for Philip Henry Gosse. As he wrote and taught to earn his living, he turned himself into a learned as well as a practical naturalist. He also developed his own peculiar theology, praying each day that he might be 'one of the favoured saints who shall never taste of death, but be alive and remain until the coming of the Lord'. It was Habershon's *Dissertation on the Prophetic Scriptures* which first convinced Philip of the imminent advent of Christ. Alec Waugh, long afterwards, mocked the constant state of excited expectation this induced: 'My grandmother recalled how Philip Henry Gosse would stand in the doorway, austere, solemn, confident, unwinding an interminable worsted scarf from about his neck and saying to her mother, "Well, Cousin Ann, still looking daily for the coming of the dear Lord Jesus? Are not all the prophecies indeed fulfilled?" The ominous decision would then go forth that the Lord would accomplish the number of his elect on Saturday afternoon at about three o'clock. When Saturday afternoon came and waned to evening, without the expected event occurring, a new text was found to justify the delay.'

V. S. Pritchett has reminded us not to pity the extreme puritan too much. 'However much he may bore others, he never suffers from boredom himself.' Certainly P. H. Gosse was never bored. He thought there was no happier way to wait for the second coming than in busying himself with scientific investigation. In 1844 he was sent by the British Museum of Natural History to work in Jamaica as a collector. He preached on alternate Sundays at a coffee plantation called Content. Living at Bluefields, with a group of Moravians, he wrote and illustrated the magnificent *Birds of Jamaica* and added twenty-four new species of mammalia, reptiles and fishes to those already known.

His father, Thomas, died in Philip's absence and, on his return, Hannah kept house for him. He was now meeting regularly with a group of dissident Christians at Hackney. So much has been said (and some of it by Edmund Gosse) about the Brethren's reputation for 'bigotry and unlovely prejudice' that it is worthwhile to look more closely for a moment at the ideals informing that small group of Christians, which contained both of Edmund Gosse's parents. For it was at a meeting in Hackney, probably in Ellis's Rooms, Well Street, that Philip Gosse met Emily Bowes.

The Brethren's negations were numerous. They had no ritual, no appointed ministers, no government, no hierarchy of any kind. Their manner of worship was the most democratic possible. They believed in the corrupting power of the world – that they mixed with the unsaved at their peril, that snares and delusions lay on every hand and it was essential to avoid all things 'not becoming to saints', which could include fashionable clothes, dancing, gambling, the theatre, worldly literature and of course lust and evil thoughts. For Brethren, there could be no revenge, no affirmation, no vote; baptism by total immersion was for believers, not babies.

Most essential of all was their conviction that the saving blood of Jesus is the only means of access to Heaven, that good works, charity and humility would get one nowhere without it, so that it followed that these virtues in the unsaved were thought little of by those who *were* saved. They believed that the Scriptures should be followed implicitly and exclusively, that the Holy Ghost could interpret the Bible directly to the saved.

Their beliefs may seem crippling and limiting to us, their practice leading to intolerance and misery. But it is easy to see the attraction of that group of Christians gathered informally together in the room in Hackney, round a plain deal table, breaking a loaf of bread and passing the cup of wine from hand to hand each Sunday, each one feeling himself equal and free to speak. There were also 'Scripture readings' one night in the week, where the Brethren discussed the true meaning of Christ's words with erudition and insight. Most of this exclusive company could read the original Greek as they pored for hours over a few words ('the just shall live by faith') and there was 'unrestrained freedom of discussion and perfect loving confidence'. Edmund would later look sadly at 'this Utopian dream of a Christian socialism, with all its simplicity, naïveté and earnest faith'. But Philip's excitement at the revolutionary movements in Europe and Chartist demonstrations at home was not because he imagined any palliation in the lot of the great majority of mankind. For forty years he always linked the news of political crisis with the possibility of the Second Coming.

Edmund Gosse said that it was in 1847 that his father joined the Brethren. But on 21st October 1848, in a letter to his brother William describing Emily Bowes, Philip says that for 'the last seven or eight years', she has been 'in communion with us who break bread at Hackney'. So it seems likely that they met before Philip went to Jamaica. By 1848 'natural esteem has ripened into love'. Emily was all that Philip could have hoped for. She possessed 'in a very high degree, an elegant and cultivated mind, and a heart trained by many years of acquaintance with God to subjection to His will'.

Emily Bowes was of American descent, though she had been born in Wales. Both her parents came from Boston. Her mother, Hannah, was the daughter of the Rev. John Troutbeck; her father, William Bowes, was the grandson of Nicholas Bowes, an early graduate of Harvard. Strangely, Edmund Gosse did not discover his American connection until after his father's death in 1888 and after his only visit to America. Telling his old Boston friend, Oliver Wendell Holmes, of his discovery, he wrote enthusiastically about finding that he had the true blue blood of Boston, unadulterated from colonial times, flowing in his veins. 'I am prouder than if I had traced myself back to belted Earls.' It sounds like a line from *Little Lord Fauntleroy* but he undoubtedly meant it.

William Bowes, Edmund's grandfather, had 'lost a fortune on the turf', Edmund told another American friend, George Armour, in a letter many years later. (In public, in the *Life of Philip Henry Gosse*, William had merely 'inherited a large property and spent it, nearly to the last penny'.) This was in 1814, when Emily was eight, and she and her two younger brothers, Edmund born 1808 and Arthur born 1813, were brought up in 'the most humble manner'. Fortunately there were kind friends. Her godfather arranged an annuity which brought in a 'clear annual sum of twenty-five pounds for her maintenance and education'. In her own memories, begun after a sermon which encouraged a frequent and minute enquiry into our past lives (in order of course to help us to do better in the future), Emily considered her own education 'idle, irregular', but her application and attitude were such that she mastered Hebrew and German, as well as Latin and Greek.

At nine, she was already a Sunday School teacher and showing extraordinary devoutness in the bosom of a worldly family. Her favourite reading was 'a little book called *Incitement to early piety*'. But, in a painting of her at that age, she looks full of determination and character, mischievous rather than meek. And she loved making up stories, an instinct she never quite suppressed although her governess told her such invention was wicked. Her son long after fantasized that the world might have lost a good novelist – 'a little older than Mrs Gaskell'; but the best-selling Narrative Tracts, to which she turned her pen after her marriage, do not suggest quite such a remarkable talent.

'I cannot recollect a time,' Emily wrote, 'when I did not love religion,' but she recognized too vividly her own frailty. Her early experience of the sudden reversal of fortune made her find it difficult to trust in God and she was forever 'fearing poverty, destitution, starvation even in the midst of friends and affluence'. She did not have as much to try her as Edmund suggested in *Father and Son*. She went as governess when she was eighteen not to the 'savage Irish nobility' but to the family of a pleasant English clergyman, the Rev. John Hawkins of Compton, near Faringdon in Berkshire. Certainly it was with money she earned at Compton that she paid for her brother Edmund to study at Cambridge, but not apparently until 1835, and she did not give up working when Edmund had taken his MA at the age of thirty. Instead she moved on to a slightly less arduous household. The Hawkinses by then had twelve children; she had been with them for fourteen years. In 1838, she took charge of the five orphan daughters of Sir Charles Musgrave of Brighton. After three years, as her brothers were both working as teachers, it seemed reasonable to return home to London to care for her parents in their declining years.

Emily was 'happy and contented, thankful to Providence for making us a united family', she wrote to an American cousin, Sarah Stoddard, in 1841. She certainly had no thought of marriage. But she went each Sunday to the meeting house in Hackney. She described the group to Sarah Stoddard. They did not belong to any sect. They 'endeavoured to revive the love of the early Christians by persuading all who love the Lord Jesus to meet together without quarrelling about their little differences, taking the Bible only as their rule of life, the Holy Spirit as their teacher and God as their only head and master'.

Looking at her own character with the same candour she applied to everything, Emily criticized her 'wicked pleasure in reading of wickedness'. She also despised her 'inclination to dissemble, to conceal her own opinion and pretend to adopt that of those I wish to please'. Long after, her son was to be accused of the same fault. In fact she had strong opinions of her own and a 'will like tempered steel'. And if she had any doubts, they were not visible to an outsider. She seemed to have perfect faith, to trust entirely in her Lord and to believe He was with her every hour. She 'would ask Jesus to guide her to a pin if she wanted one', a young milliner recalled after her death. She 'sparkled with joy when unexpectedly brought into contact with those who loved her Lord or when recognising some expression of His ever-watchful care'. Indeed, she sparkled a good deal. 'Her figure was slim and tall, her neck of singular length and grace', her hair a bright auburn, piled fashionably high, her eyes clear and blue looking directly from a pale, freckled face. She had published two books of religious poetry. 'She was sympathetic – gentle, quick, eminently intelligent.' She had a lively, sociable temperament. She was talkative and tolerant, with a crowd of devoted female friends.

Philip, on the other hand, living alone with his mother after those adventurous years abroad, had fallen into a habit of almost hermit-like seclusion. He refused most invitations. He was shy, he was poor, he hated small talk. He would shut himself away from his mother's prattling tongue and work on his books. He spent a great many solitary hours at the British Museum. The *Birds of Jamaica* was followed rather surprisingly by a manual to the British Museum collection of Egyptian antiquities, showing how they illustrate scripture, and by *Mammalia*, the first in a series of five natural history books for the SPCK. In 1848 he was writing on *Popular British Ornithology*. In designing and colouring the illustrations (more than seventy birds) he worked almost entirely from the collection at the Museum, a practice he was later to reject.

There is a clear indication of the speed at which he worked. He began his bird book on September 16th and finished on 21st November 1848. On September 17th he proposed to Emily Bowes. In 1836 she had concluded her early reminiscences by renouncing 'all the sinful lusts of the flesh'. Marriage of course was different: 'the twain shall be one flesh'. But their surviving courtship letters give little evidence of the overwhelming love they would come to feel for each other. On September 20th Philip was asking 'My dearest Miss Bowes' when he could tell her parents how they felt. Should he get to know her better first? But no: 'If what I desire be, as I think, of God, he will bring it to pass.' Two months later, the day after he had finished *Popular British Ornithology*, on Wednesday forenoon, 22nd November 1848, Philip Henry Gosse was married to Emily, only daughter of William and Hannah Bowes of Upper Clapton; the ceremony performed by

Robert Howard in the presence of the Registrar at Brook Street Chapel, Tottenham, Middlesex. There was a wedding breakfast at the Howards' house in Bruce Grove and then Emily and Philip went home to Philip's little house at 13 Trafalgar Terrace, part of Mortimer Road on one side of De Beauvoir Square, Tottenham. Hannah Gosse had tactfully gone off to stay for a week or two with her niece Mrs Ann Morgan of Clifton, leaving them in seclusion and quiet for a while. But she would return and there would be problems.

In October Philip had written to William, 'Dear Mother will still reside with us and I hope will be both willing and able to be comfortable; as it will be our wish to make her so.' By December he was not quite so sanguine. 'It is rather too early to say how Mother will be able to get on with us; she does not seem to have any prejudice against her daughter-in-law, but you know her infirmity of temper. We hope, however, things may go smoothly.' In fact, as Edmund surmised years later, there was a good deal of the prejudice of a woman who, possessing no intellectual resources herself, looks with suspicion on those who do.

By May, Philip was glad to report that Hannah was planning a long visit to Poole. 'Our honeymoon is not over yet and we intend to keep it up for an indefinite period.' Emily was pregnant and was spending a great deal of time annotating an interleaved copy of the Hebrew Bible.

In June, Philip Gosse at long last bought himself a microscope. It was seventeen years since he had first read Adams's *Essays on the Microscope* in Newfoundland, the book that had had so much influence on his scientific studies. He had worked with magnifying slides but he had never had a proper microscope. Now he had one and on 11th June 1849 he made his first examination of a rotifer or wheel-animalcule, that minute form of life which was to be the subject of one of his most important contributions to human knowledge. At different stages of his life he was obsessed with birds, butterflies, ferns, orchids, sea-anemones and stars, and each one in turn gave way to a new enthusiasm. But he never tired of rotifers. Edmund would record that 'they danced under his microscope when he put his faded eye to the tube for the last time in 1888'.

Philip Henry Gosse was still excited by the novelty of his microscope (his small garden full of open pans for infusoria, three separate stagnations of hempseed, poppy seed and hollyhock seed waiting to be examined) when his son was born on 21st September. In his diary he wrote simply 'E. delivered of a son. Received green swallow from Jamaica.' This was certainly the order of events. But in a letter to William in Southampton he is a little more forthcoming: 'I write in pain and weariness to say that my beloved Emily was safely delivered of a fine boy today at noon. She had a severe time and was delivered by the aid of instruments. She and the babe are doing well.' He was to be called Edmund William, after his uncles, and was always known to his parents as Willy.

Emily was not so sure he was a fine boy. It had been an alarming birth. She wrote in her diary a few weeks later: 'When he was born he seemed quite dead and uttered no cry, being put into a warm bath and other means being used, after a time he uttered a faint cry – but the medical attendants expected he would go off in convulsions: his chest and head and face were much out of place.' Philip remembered all the anxiety and attention given to Emily, and Edmund's life saved by one of the 'attendants', an anonymous old woman, who awoke in him 'a spark of vitality' when everyone else had given him up for dead.

Starting so badly, he soon became as handsome as any other baby and the 'firm healthy child' was said much to resemble his uncle Arthur, though Emily herself was glad to see a likeness to his father Philip Henry. She always called her husband Henry. Emily's diary throws some interesting light on child-rearing methods of the time: 'Our first battle' (this is at six weeks old) 'seems to be as to whether he will lie down awake or be put to sleep in arms – may I persevere at proper and reasonable times in teaching him this lesson . . . In consequence of his never taking the breast and my being weak and in need of rest, he slept first with nurse Yorke till October 9 and then with Mrs. Thompson till October 20. On Sunday October 21 he first slept with me and I found he woke at 11 – at 2 and at 5 for food, after which he would sleep no more but required nursing the rest of the morning. I was soon able to break him of this and now he generally sleeps till breakfast time – all the earlier part of the night in his little crib . . . Bringing him up by hand, we are continually told his food does not agree with him, but hitherto he has had nothing but milk and water which he seems to enjoy and he grows fast without being fat.' He was first out in the garden when he was four weeks old on 19th October 'and has been out since whenever the weather has been fine'.

'We have given him to the Lord,' Emily continued, 'and we trust he will early manifest him to be His own if he grow up.' At the Room, the Brethren 'prayed for us and for our child that he may be the Lord's'. It was the first act of a dedication which was hardly less solemn than that of the infant Samuel, though no bullocks were slain, nor flour and wine offered at the temple.

Emily had hoped that old Mrs Gosse might be softened by Edmund's birth and that the breach between them might be healed. Hannah Gosse had returned to the house sometime before the birth, after her long visit to Poole. But she would never be happy with them. She felt lonely and neglected in her own sitting-room, as Emily sat with Philip Henry in his study and the two of them pored over the standard German book on rotifers: Ehrenberg's *Die Infusionsthierchen*, Emily's German and Philip's knowledge of the subject working marvellously together.

Hannah Gosse sat in the next room wanting company and 'much discontented with Henry's conduct from the time he was engaged'. Naturally she had thought to have him to herself and the baby was small consolation. She had had grandchildren before – her youngest son, Tom, had been married for years and two of *his* small sons (one called after his uncle Philip Henry Gosse) had died before reaching their fourth birthdays. On the 16th November she left them, and Catherian (Kate) Jones, a new young servant, arrived.

The archives contain many memorials of this happy domestic time. There are two outlines of Edmund's right hand, lovingly traced by his father at 'ten weeks old' and 'five months and one week old'. 'Baby's length' on the second date was given as '25¾ inches'. Edmund was proving an even more interesting focus of scientific study than the rotifers or the green swallow *Hirundo euchrysea*, which had arrived on the same day. There is Philip's painting of the swallow and there too a rather more crudely painted portrait of the baby, presumably by Emily, in a lacey bonnet and a dress with blue ribbons, crawling on blue booteed feet towards a bright striped ball.

He was certainly given credit for being a remarkable baby – already at two months old Emily wrote, 'He grows tall and plump and fairer and larger. He smiles and even laughs . . . He discovered the moon last night and watched it very attentively.' Soon he would shout poems in its praise.

They spent a quiet winter and spring, leaving the house very little. But fortunately for the record, Emily's aunt was taken ill at Leamington that summer and Emily was called to her deathbed. Aunt Bowes was William's only sister, an eccentric 'spoiled by temptations of flattery and prosperity'. She had never married and there was a small fortune for her heirs. 'May I find her alive,' Emily prayed dutifully on the train journey. 'May I have the opportunity of putting Jesus before her. May she receive Him even at the last hour as a little child. Lord save her soul.' Scribbling in her journal on the train, she thought fondly of her family at home: 'Keep me from gossip and foolish talk. Keep me from foolish talking to H. May we grow in grace. May we set a good example to Baby . . . Keep us from covetousness, from the love of money, from desiring what is not ours. May this money come to us, or not, as would be best for us and may we be content with thy appointment. Save her soul O! Lord and then we will be content that others should have her money.'

In Tottenham Philip Henry had been left in charge of his small son, with Kate to help him. 'He has been outrageously good,' the father reported smugly. 'Having taken a ride in his carriage, circumradiating the garden many times, is now gone peacefully to sleep. I shall let Kate have him for the night, as it seems a delightment to her.'

At his desk upstairs Philip was working on *Fishes* for the SPCK. The postman called with a letter from Emily ('My sweet little baby . . . how I do long to see him and his father. My own love how lonely you must feel tonight – and how much I am sure you must wish me back . . . I do not like to go to bed. I shall be so lonely.') Kate brought the letter up and then in a moment up she came again.

'You know,' said she, 'the chair in the hall?'

'Yes,' said P. H. Gosse.

'Baby walked alone all the way from there to the street-door.'

The scientist dropped his work, took his rule and rushed downstairs. He 'measured the distance and found it six feet! And then,' he wrote to Emily, 'I induced him to try again and he several times made several steps but he was excited and could not get on so well. Dear little fellow! It is so funny to see him. How he balances himself and straddles wide, to get a good broad foundation, then he staggers two or three steps forward and plump! down on his little bottom.' The tone is very similar to that of the popular scientist observing the cockle's progress: 'And as to what the brilliant organ is going to do, that we see. For the long taper foot being thrust to its utmost, feels about for some resisting surface – that stone, half buried in the sand, for instance; which no sooner does it feel than the hooked point is pressed stiffly against it, the whole foot by muscular contraction is made suddenly rigid and the entire creature – mantle, siphons, foot, shell and all, – is jerked away . . .'

Emily's prayers in her diary throughout 1850 and 1851 are a good indication of the sort of familiar problems that worried her. 'May I become an early riser. May I become neat and orderly. May Baby be obedient. May I not be too sleepy to pray at night. May we not put it off too late. May Kate be converted. May H. and I be used to her soul's good. May I not spoil her. May I have firmness and decision. May I get my things in order. May I keep them in order. May we have needful cash. May we not incur more debts.'

Emily *had* inherited some money from her aunt Sarah Bowes, but it was unwisely invested, as Edmund recorded in *Father and Son*, remembering the name of the Cornish tin mine, Wheal Maria, so curious in his childish ears. 'Did you invest any money in the mines?'

Emily wrote to William Gosse in 1852. 'I hope not, as we see no very immediate prospect of getting any return.' And in 1854, Philip wrote to William: 'It was indeed an unfortunate day when we were persuaded to engage in mining speculation:– I suppose £2500 would not cover the losses of myself and Emily's two brothers through this.' They visited the two brothers, Edmund and Arthur, regularly, and it was on one of these visits that the speechless infant Edmund, alone in their dining-room, watched as a dog came in through the window and stole the leg of mutton which was waiting to be carved. It was his earliest memory. 'So that was what became of the mutton,' they exclaimed years later. 'It was not you who, as your uncle Arthur pretended, ate it up in the twinkling of an eye, bone and all.' The uncles' losses of both fortune and mutton were typical. They seemed dogged by ill-luck; both would die early.

Fortunately P. H. Gosse's books were selling extremely well. All the work on rotifera, the hundreds of hours spent translating Ehrenberg, not to mention the hours of Bible study and of pleasant foolish talking, and the hours of observing Edmund, had not meant that Philip's more remunerative work had been neglected. The book, the *Birds of Jamaica*, had been wrongly costed. 'The numbers will only turn me in about 1/9 each and, as there are four plates, it gives only 5¼d each bird,' – hand-coloured birds, they were. Philip was more careful after that.

There were four books published in 1851, including the splendid *A Naturalist's Sojourn in Jamaica*. It was in this book that P. H. Gosse defined his position as an observer of *living* creatures: 'Natural history,' he declared, 'is far too much a science of dead things; a necrology. It is mainly conversant with dry skins, furred or feathered, blackened, shrivelled and haystuffed; with objects, some admirably beautiful, some hideously ugly, impaled on pins and arranged in rows in cork drawers; with uncouth forms, disgusting to sight and smell, bleached and shrunken, suspended by threads and immersed in spirit . . . These distorted things are described; their scales, plates, feathers counted; their forms copied, all shrivelled and stiffened as they are; . . . their limbs, members, and organs measured, and the results recorded in thousandths of an inch.' But Gosse would look at living animals, their ingenious resources, their 'sayings and doings'. Darwin was among the many who praised his approach.

It was time for him to raise his eyes from the tiny living rotifera in his microscope slides and observe some English wildlife on a larger scale. High time, in fact. In December 1851, Emily wrote to William: 'Henry's illness began about the last week in November. The disease is nervous, partly caused by indigestion and partly by study and I greatly hope that by attention to diet and relaxation from study, his health may soon be better.' Hannah came to look after Edmund while they had a brief holiday in Freshwater. But an entirely different pattern of life was needed.

In February Edmund and his parents set off for Devon. Devon was decided upon because of the rockpools and the favourable tides. P. H. Gosse had decided to study marine zoology. It was a decision that was to have a far-reaching effect. In April, leaving his wife and child happily settled at Bank Cottage, St Marychurch near Torquay (the village where he was eventually to live for more than thirty years), Philip went off to explore other sea shores which form the basis of *A Naturalist's Rambles on the Devonshire Coast*. The letters that survive their brief separations are full of love and full of Edmund.

Emily started a letter the moment Philip left her. The two-year-old Edmund kept on saying 'Where Papa?' When his mother suggested he should get up from his rest and dine with Mamma, he added 'and Papa'. When he realized he wasn't there, Edmund said, 'Papa got Basket? Papa got 'ings?', remembering how often he had seen Papa going off with his basket and collecting-jars to the rock pools below St Marychurch. Walking out that afternoon, Edmund picked white violets for his father and Emily enclosed three in her letter, 'though they will be fading, they will be sweet as he found them and I picked them. I need not tell you how I think of you and every tread that sounds like yours out of doors makes me sad to think it cannot be you'. She thought of that consoling verse from the Psalmist: 'There shall no evil befall thee, neither shall any plague come near thy dwelling.'

Philip in Ilfracombe, writing to Emily, thanked his sweet son for his violets and his kisses. 'I do long to kiss him again and you too, my own love. O my sweet beloved one, my helper, my comforter, my joy, my love, I wish I could just now throw my arms round your neck and kiss your dear mouth. And kiss my sweet little Willy's dear mouth too . . . Give him as many as he will patiently take now, as sent from me. And, O my darling, imagine that this paper embodies a thousand kisses and a thousand wishes of affection for your own sweet self.'

The first plague to visit their dwelling was only measles. By then the dwelling was in Weymouth and Philip was briefly in London. Emily was devoting most of her time to her child, and his imagination and vocabulary flourished in her loving care. There was no question of him being seen and not heard. It is worth giving one of his dictated letters to his father nearly in full, for it is a remarkable tribute to Emily's patience and to her knowledge that every small word would delight the absent father. It is not often one has a glimpse into the stream of consciousness of a Victorian three-year-old with measles.

July 11, 1853

My dear Papa,

I should like to see you again. We been for a walk. I wish to see Papa again . . .

Dear Papa I didn't kiss my hand to you but you kissed your hand to me and I cried. (What will he say Mamma if he has such a sad letter?) Papa I should like you to hear the books I read in bed. Mamma told me a story of Jesus dying on the cross. I wish to see you again. Dear Papa I wish that somebody could preach to the people to make them good. I want you to come back and preach to the people. Dear Papa do you know that I went out with you one day to get some snails. Dear Papa I want to see you again (that I haven't put, have I?) I know I shall like to see you again. Dear Papa I should like to see you again. Dear Papa I'm going to be a good boy. I shall love Mamma, dear Papa. My dear Papa I should like to see you again. Did you give my love to Uncles, Papa? and Grandmamma, did you send my love to Grandmamma? . . . I want you to come back and tell me that hymn dear Papa, "I shall not 'ant". "The Lord is my shepherd, I shall not 'ant". Papa do you know I seed a donkey one day when I goed out to get snails. Dear Papa there came a dead fish now directly. It was a pike I thought. Mary brought it up in her hand. Dear Papa I'm going to pray for you this night, pray to take care of you. Dear Papa you pray for me when you're in the omnibus.

Dear Papa I want to see you.

I don't like to be by myself, dear Papa. I must send this letter to the post when I'm done. I'm going to take this letter to the post that we writed to you my dear Papa . . .

George came up to play with me today. I played at animals down upon the floor and shells down upon the floor. Dear Papa, Mamma has brought me home some strawberry. Thirty hundred I think we got. I've got spots and pimples and fleas all over me. Dear Papa did you have a nice bed and some nice tea? Dear Papa I went in Mamma's bed and I sleeped all the night with her. I am very well dear Papa. Dear Papa I haven't been to a walk today because of my spots . . . I played with pussy while Mamma was gone to fetch strawberries. Dear Papa I want you to come home. When are you coming? I didn't like to be by myself but I was to do it. Mary was in the bedroom while I was playing with pussy. Dear Papa I didn't like to be by myself when I was by myself, when Mamma went to get the strawberries.

from little Willy Gosse at Weymouth and Mamma.

Dear Papa I'm going to have my tea and I'm going to have my strawberries and I can't write any more.

Emily added:
'Farewell for the present, my own sweet love.
Do not expect another letter tonight.'
Next day she added,
'Willy is much better today . . . The rash is thick out and he is a sad figure but as merry as a grig and as good as gold. Willy talked last night of his pimpernels and said he was covered with fleas and bruises.'

In *Father and Son*, perhaps to underline the contrast of the time before and after his mother's death and to emphasize the effect of the sea on him in that September of 1857, Edmund suggests that most of his early childhood was spent in a small dark house in north-east London and makes little of 'certain visits, made with a zoological purpose'. In fact, from the time of his earliest memories, the Gosse family spent almost as much time by the sea as in London. His third year, as he does tell us, was spent in Devon, mainly at Marychurch and Ilfracombe. In 1853 they were at Weymouth in Dorset from April till December. In 1854 they spent two months at Tenby in Wales. The following year they were in Dorset and Devon from March till September.

As Edmund recorded, they were indeed 'always cheerful and often gay' – but he was not, as he suggested, withdrawn from every outside influence, like Princess Blanchefleur, the Saracen slave girl, in her marble tower. It was only in the London winters that he was left so much to his own devices. It was then that he retreated to the attic, hungry for diversion, and found the pages lining the lid of the tin trunk. It was then that he took up natural magic and delicious speculations in superstition and idolatry and experiments in prayer, but also the 'ardent adventures' of a more normal childhood. Years later he would tell Robert Louis Stevenson how he remembered hunting 'upon the forest-track behind the sofa-back'. He remembered too how inextricably bound were the two sides of his parents' life – work and prayer, nature and God – and how natural it seemed for his mother to interrupt the family prayers one day to ask his father, 'Do you think that can be *Boletobia fulginaria*?' when it seemed it might be that very rare moth, flying in through the open window.

It was certainly in London that Edmund first became aware that his father was not all-powerful. But it was also in London that his father gave him cunning geography lessons, developed as a schoolmaster a dozen years before. And his mother beguiled him with a special present. Holding him up in her arms, she told him to touch one of the golden tulips high on the parlour wall-paper. 'This shining tulip shall be yours,' she said, marking the flower with a tiny scarlet mark. 'This will be your own, your very own.' And Edmund loved that paper tulip, so he said, more than all the real toys and real flowers 'that lavish love had strewn before me'.

So were their winters, quiet, private, self-contained, full of prayer and absorbed work. Sometimes the silence would be broken after hours by Philip Henry's voice from the microscope, 'Emily! Emily!' And she would take Edmund into the study to share some new discovery. But the summers were different. At the sea, life had frequent drama and excitement and people. Each childhood summer is graphically described in the pages of P. H. Gosse's books. The child is always there, just as God is always there, not often mentioned but never forgotten. We see Edmund eating sea anemones in the interests of scientific experiment ('my little boy voted that " 'tinny [*Actinia*] was good" and loudly demanded more, like another Oliver Twist'). We watch him eating wild strawberries and pulling off the petals of a dogrose in a Devon lane while blue butterflies dance around him. We see him, as the tide comes in, making a pool for a colony of *Purpurae*. 'He related very gravely his apprehensions of being drowned, when he had to wade through the water, which was actually over the soles of his shoes!'

Weymouth Edmund remembered mainly from missing a steamer excursion to Swanage when, at the last minute, 'a coal popped out of the sitting room fire in our lodgings and slightly burned me'. In a letter to Thomas Hardy (when they were both old men) Gosse gives a clear picture of what his father was up to in Weymouth – dredging with Jonas Fowler from Whitrose to Church Hope and from St Aldhelm's Head to Portland Bill. He was 'collecting specimens for the newly-formed aquariums and sending them to the Zoo in Regent's Park and the Crystal Palace and elsewhere'. On 5th September 1853 he started a salt water tank of his own in Weymouth lodgings with a tolerant landlady. This was the first private aquarium ever made, Edmund claimed. He had it himself later, 'until about 1893 when it fell to pieces'.

Philip Gosse told Charles Kingsley, who shared his enthusiasms, that he had collected over 4000 specimens – living animals and plants – in the season of 1853. When he returned to London, Kingsley offered to send specimens from Devon. On December 23rd, Gosse wrote to Kingsley from 58 Huntingdon Street, Islington (the larger and more comfortable house of *Father and Son*), that his first task was to adapt 'a sort of conservatory, which I mean to use as an Aquarium, filling it up with several Tanks and Vases for Marine Natural History. We are but just "moved in" but as soon as I can get my fittings ready, I shall feel greatly obliged by anything you can send'. On 5th January 1854 Gosse joyfully acknowledged a hamper full of 'the splendid treasures of the deep', and on February 2nd he wrote: 'It is a grand gala day for Mrs. Gosse as well as myself, when we get an opportunity of examining a consignment from the sea; such an array of pans and bowls, of vases and tubs comes out and the whole house is on the tiptoe of expectation.' He regretted one splendid crab, *Echinus miliaris*, which had come up from Dorset with them and might have been a comfort to him yet if it had not been overlooked in the unpacking and remained lodged on the side of a jar where it unfortunately starved. Such dramas Edmund undoubtedly shared in. He was 'wild about animals' as Emily recorded in her diary, continuing 'often says what is not true'.

Emily wrote down for Edmund a letter to a small friend which shows a typical enjoyment of names (a junior version of the Victorian obsession with classification):

My dear little Mary,
   I am going to have some paints as soon as my uncle Edmund or uncle Arthur will bring them me. I expect red, yellow and brown and black and green and blue and white. Why I have those paints is because I am going to paint the Lion, Tiger, Panther, Wolf and Bear, Elephant, Rhinoceros, Baboon, Giraffe and Ass and Squirrel and Cow, Goat, Zebra and hundreds more. The Eagle, Owl and Hawk and Stork and Ostrich and Duck and a few more birds, among them there is a goldfinch and a jay, I am glad to say . . . And a gudgeon and a ling and a pike and a porpoise and whale.

Soon he would be able to write letters himself. A brief note dated 10th March 1855 is proudly annotated 'the first letter ever written by my Boy without assistance of any kind'. It reads simply: 'Dear Papa I want to see you very much Edmund William Gosse.' His reading was already excellent. (His first spoken word had apparently been 'book'.) Already in 1852 – before he was three – he had been able to recognize the sweet name of Jesus. What was he to read? His mother was convinced of the hideous dangers of fiction. In *Father and Son* Edmund considers his situation must have been 'almost unique', but in fact his mother's attitude was not unusual. W. T. Stead (whom Edmund was

25

to know well) put it like this: 'the Novel was regarded as a kind of Devil's Bible, whose meretricious attractions waged an unholy competition against the reading of God's word'.

In the *Pocket Aesculapius or Everyone his own Physician* (my copy of the 25th thousand was published in 1840) John Abernethy warned against 'that most deadly mental poison, Novels and Romances', not on scriptural grounds, but because they 'excite the imagination and give sails to minds that rather require ballast'. The imagination is often suspected of leading man away from God and one does not have to go very far for scriptural authority to misinterpret: 'The imagination of man's heart is evil from his youth' (Genesis 8.21) and the even more familiar 'He hath scattered the proud in the imagination of their hearts'. The prohibition was part of a narrowing and a fear which hardly seems reflected in the copious records we have of the small family. But Philip, as Edmund grew, became more and more anxious about the sails which would carry his lamb away from him, remembering, I suppose, his own early experience. ('It was of God's special mercy' that he had narrowly escaped drowning 'in destruction and perdition'.) Philip was prepared to accept whatever Emily decided would help to keep their child safe in his dedication.

Facts, however secular, were never seen as a threat. He was allowed an almost daily diet of the *Penny Cyclopaedia*, whatever it discussed. He was familiar with hummingbirds but had never heard of fairies. He knew about wolves – and not just the ravening kind that come in sheep's clothing – but had never heard of Little Red Riding Hood. So he tells us. But of course his main reading was in the Scriptures. He had inevitably been listening to pretty stories about David and Solomon – and Jesus – for years. By 14th February 1854, aged four and a half, 'Willy can read fluently though not always correctly in the testament,' his mother noted in her diary. Next day she 'walked with Willy and Papa down Hemingford Road. W. wilful, perverse and fretful'. But his development was generally satisfactory. The month before he had asked his mother, 'What is a sin offering?' Emily explained it and Edmund remarked, 'I suppose now that Jesus has died, they don't kill the animals anymore.' He was pleased of course.

'Precocious intelligence!' the fond mother observed in her diary. No bullocks need be slain, but the child was as truly the Lord's.

They were in London at the time and their life was far more sociable than Edmund suggests in *Father and Son*. The tracts Emily was writing in these months are full of actual incidents and people she was meeting: 'I knew a gentleman . . .' 'the husband of a young lady of my acquaintance.' There was a lot of calling in Emily's diary – some of it obviously of a charitable nature ('With Willy called on Mrs. Wiggins –

lent her salve'). Some of it was concerned with the tracts, but sometimes surely it was purely sociable. On 17th March 1854, a Friday: 'With Willy called on the Heaths. Saw Louisa . . . on the Bergers, saw Mr. Jukes. On C. Pearse and Mother and Mrs. Grosvenor.' It is hard to believe there were no children in any of these households and it is certainly not literally true, as Edmund later suggested, that he had never played with other children in his first seven years.

Philip was now working too intensively to have much time for Edmund. 'I am pressing my book hard to get it out by the first week of May. I propose to entitle it *The Aquarium*: an unveiling of the wonders of the deep sea.' This was the book, more than any other, which started the mid-Victorian passion for sea-shore collecting. The Oxford English Dictionary gives P. H. Gosse the credit for coining the word 'aquarium', and social historians of the period (illustrating their comments with cartoons from *Punch*) record a world gone mad in the pursuit of four-angled squirters (*Cynthia quadrangularis*), Torbay bonnets (*Pileopsis hungaricus*) and bimaculated suckers (*Lepidogaster bimaculatus*) – not to mention starfish, sea anemones and octopuses.

VALUABLE ADDITION TO THE AQUARIUM.

Tom (who has had a very successful day) presents his Sisters with a fine Specimen of the Cuttle-Fish (*Octopus vulgaris*).

Gosse had had the excellent idea of giving classes on the seashore, and Charles Kingsley gave early publicity in his *Glaucus or The Wonders of the Shore*: 'That most pious and most learned naturalist, Mr Gosse . . . proposes to establish this summer a regular shore class . . . and I advise any reader whose fancy such a project pleases to apply to him for details.' And Thomas Huxley wrote appropriately that 'he would have much pleasure dredging up a client or two for you'. Gosse was overwhelmed with applications from ladies and gentlemen eager to combine pleasure with instruction. Edmund recalled 'a long desultory line of persons on a beach of shells – doubtless at Barricane [near Ilfracombe]. At the head of the procession, like Apollo conducting the Muses, my father strides ahead in an immense wide-awake, loose black coat and trousers, and fisherman's boots, with a collecting-basket in one hand, a staff or prod in the other. Then follow gentlemen of every age, all seeming spectacled and old to me, and many ladies in the balloon costume of 1855, with shawls falling in a point from between their shoulders to the edge of their flounced petticoats, each wearing a mushroom hat with streamers'. These 'enthusiastic nymphs' conducted small Edmund along the beach, jumping him over 'the perilous little water courses that meander to the sea' and letting him stoop to collect in his pink frock the profuse and lovely shells at his feet.

Philip Gosse was offering 'a fund of intellectual delight that would never satiate'. There was no longer any need for gentlemen 'in a marine village to lounge by the hour together in the news room', nor for young ladies to sit about among the rocks reading the dreaded novels, nor for anyone 'to wander to and fro with listless and vacant countenances'. Gosse had awoken as he wished, but far more than he wished, a passion for collecting. Years later he commented, 'the ladies and dealers together have swept the whole coast as with a besom'.

The works of the Lord, in all their glory, were to disappear with alarming rapidity into the baskets and aquaria and rubbish bins of the multitude. But 'Happy truly is the naturalist! He has no time for melancholy dreams. The earth becomes transparent; everywhere he sees significance, harmonies, laws, chains of cause and effect endlessly entwined, which draw him out of the narrow sphere of self into a pure and wholesome region of joy and wonder.' Even in Hornsey Road Pond there were ten-spined sticklebacks. In rockpools there was treasure more rewarding than might be mined in California or Australia. One might even find *Pycnogonia crustacean*, with a stomach in his legs and no body.

P. H. Gosse's books are a satisfying mixture of the erudite and the trivial, crowded with people as well as natural history. Edmund later remarked with justice: 'Man was the animal he studied less than any other, understood more imperfectly and, on the whole, was least interested in.' But in these years with Emily everything interested him – even the way people cope with that tantalizing indecision about the weather when an outing is planned and 'the sandwiches are cut and mustarded' and a small boy keeps asking 'When will it be fine, Mamma?' When they went out – this was on the Tenby holiday – they were 'uproariously merry', a whole crowd of them trying to cross a bog, looking for marsh pennywort, osmundroyal, water bedstraw, bog-myrtle and asphodel – and getting white hose and lavender-coloured boots 'grievously bemired'. Or picnicking by the castle at Manorbier, with champagne and lectures on cromlechs. There was little sign of the recluse Philip had been and would be again.

The bog-myrtle did remind him of the virtues of affliction: 'a lowly shrub, like a minute willow, but most fragrant especially when the leaves are bruised; a beautiful emblem of the Christian, who often needs to be pounded in affliction's mortar, before the odour of his graces will flow out'. But affliction seemed far away that happy summer.

Both Emily and Philip were becoming immensely successful. *The Aquarium* was the most profitable of all his books. The following year a thousand copies of P. H. Gosse's *A Handbook to the Marine Aquarium* (for those who could not afford *The Aquarium* at 17 shillings) sold within a few weeks of publication and a second edition was rushed out. There was apparently money to spare for supporting a missionary to the poor. Emily's 'Little Book on Education', as she called it, was published under the title *Abraham and his Children*. ('May it save souls. May it be favourably reviewed,' Emily prayed realistically. 'May it soon come to a second edition.') Her tracts were already distributed in their tens of thousands. 'Gosse's Tracts may be ordered . . . sample packets price 6d. 120 Assorted. Price 1s. Or 5s. per 1000.' Eventually one title alone would sell half a million copies.

Philip was in great demand as a lecturer. He gave learned papers at the learned societies and in June, 1856, he was elected a Fellow of the Royal Society. 'But what would all this be worth,' he wrote to his brother William, 'if I were not a member of another Royal Society, even of that Society of Kings and Princes for whom Jesus died? This is the true honour, to be an heir of God and a joint heir with Christ and this, through grace, has long been mine.'

He needed all his spiritual strength and the happiness of that true honour, for when they returned to Tenby in the summer of 1856 Emily still smiled but she sat on the rocks and did not scramble over them as she had two years before. There was a gnawing pain in her breast. She talked to anyone who came near her and gave away her tracts and listened to their problems, but the pain never went away.

Edmund had had some presentiment of disaster the previous winter. 'I specially recollect sitting on a Sunday morning upon a cushion at her knees, one of her long, veined hands resting upon mine, to learn a chapter of the Gospel of Matthew by heart; and, while her soft voice read out the sacred verses, suddenly seeing something in her large eyes and wasted features, which gave me a premonition that I should lose her. Most clearly I recall the terror of it, the unexpressed anguish. It is the more strange, because I am sure that this was in the winter, and before any one had guessed that she was stricken with mortal disease.'

One day Emily said to Philip, 'How very happy we are! Surely this cannot last.' Each day was lapped in love. She had reason to believe, she wrote to a friend, Anna Shipton, that her small son 'was indeed a child of God'. Her tracts were being distributed 'even to the most distant parts of the globe' and she had evidence of the 'sound conversion to God' of a number of people who had talked with her. If there was any danger, it was of spiritual pride. On her birthday she had written in her diary, 'May I be kept lowly, trusting, loving!'

In April 1856 she felt a lump in her breast, consulted her doctor and was told immediately it was cancer. Edmund remembered his mother returning from the doctor and telling Philip the news as he rose to greet her in the room where Edmund apparently slept. 'He says it is cancer,' she murmured, though Edmund could not bring himself to use the word, writing about it fifty years later.

'What is cancer?' the boy asked next morning at breakfast; his parents looked at each other and could not answer him. Christ cares not for earthly happiness, they thought. Temporal joy may give way to eternal, if it be His will. Lay not up for yourselves treasures on earth. Though He slay me, yet will I trust in Him.

They consulted specialists and a new treatment was suggested. There was an American, Jesse Weldon Fell, practising in London, who claimed to have found a new cure for breast cancer, treating the tumours by applying the essence of a root supposedly first used by North American Indians on the shores of Lake Superior. 'The cancer is slowly killed and then thrown off from the healthy flesh,' Philip wrote to his brother. The Gosses saw photographs of patients in different stages of treatment and the inspiring, if grim, sight of one woman at the actual moment when her tumour (dark, hard and apparently dead) was being separated by Dr Fell with his fingers from the white living flesh surrounding it. He claimed a success rate of 80 per cent. The Gosses sought God's advice and agreed that Emily should undergo the treatment. They were full of faith – a faith that could not be damaged whatever resulted. 'God cannot belie himself and He has nowhere promised to grant His children all their foolish hearts would like, but what He judges best for their real welfare. He has promised wisdom, but not success.' God could not lose. Whatever resulted they convinced themselves would be His will. The end that He had in view was in fact 'the removal of His beloved child to His own presence in Paradise'.

But first there was temporal hope. There was a summer at Tenby when it seemed all might be well. Edmund's seventh birthday was spent 'in an ecstacy of happiness on golden sands under a brilliant sky'. Then there was a long, long winter of pain and weariness.

In the first stages of the treatment, Emily travelled regularly from Islington to Pimlico and never missed a chance to offer her tracts and the promise of eternal bliss. 'Sometimes my fellow-passengers are of an encouraging kind . . . Sometimes their very looks repel one's advances.' The tracts themselves are full of scenes in railway-carriages and omnibuses. To everyone she had a word of grace and courtesy, undeterred by the scornful refusal of some and the stolid indifference of others. Edmund watched as she talked to complete strangers ('He calls none "strangers" who come to Him') and the boy listened as they warmed to her interest and told her of the problems that beset them. In the doctor's waiting-room she moved among the band of pale sufferers proclaiming the tidings of salvation.

In October it was decided to take lodgings in Cottage Street, Pimlico, near Dr Fell's surgery. There Emily and Edmund ('her faithful companion and assiduous nurse') lived from 10th October until 24th December, the painful monotony of the days relieved only by visits to the doctor, by dull meals and Philip's comings and goings. (He had to get back to his microscope.) 'Willy has been a little ministering angel to her all through the affliction living with her constantly,' he wrote to his brother. 'I do my work at Islington and go over to them every afternoon.'

The mother and son were alone together 'through dreary days and still more dreary nights' which left their indelible impression on the temperament as well as the memory of the boy. He read to her endlessly – from the Bible, of course, but also from B. W. Newton's *Thoughts on the Apocalypse* and from the turgid pages of Mr Elliot's *Horae Apocalypticae*. Seldom, surely, has a small boy been made so conscious of suffering. Emily Gosse tried hard to practise what she had preached: in one tract she had urged travellers not to worry about the discomforts of a journey, because the journey is short and they are nearly home. But as the drastic treatment continued, it was harsh pain rather than discomfort, and no fortitude or resolution could stop

Edmund from seeing that his mother's eyes continually brimmed with tears. Looking back, Edmund saw himself as his mother's 'sole and ceaseless companion'. It was not actually so. In his memorial to his wife, Philip paid tribute to Mrs Hislop, 'our beloved friend and sister in Christ whose love and service at Pimlico, nothing could exceed'.

In this Memorial, Philip Gosse describes the medical procedures with his customary scientific exactitude: the removal of the skin by nitric acid, the scoring of the tumour, the pressing into the parallel cuts of narrow strips of linen rag covered with a purple mucilaginous substance, which gradually destroyed the tumour. 'It was brought to a woody hardness,' he wrote. 'When the tumour eventually fell out of its cavity, it resembled nothing so much as a blackened penny bun.' There was some relief from the 'removal of the dead weight and the intermission of the gnawing medicaments' but the disease had gone too far. After further excisions, at last Dr Fell had to admit: 'Oh, 'tis in your blood.'

Philip brought Emily back to Islington on Christmas Eve. His cousin, Mrs Morgan, came up from Clifton to help nurse Emily. She was put under the care of a homeopathic physician, Dr John Epps, whose gentle treatment alleviated her final pain. She knew she was dying. She was not afraid of death but she wished she could have shared with Philip the rest of his earthly pilgrimage. She knew, he said, how often she had checked and counteracted the earthly tendencies of his heart and its inclination to love the present world. *She* was the strong one and it was *her* inspiration that later drove Philip, entrusted by her with Edmund's salvation, into strange severities and eccentric prohibitions.

A little before ten on Sunday evening, 8th February 1857, Emily Gosse murmured 'I'm going home – I must go home!'

'Yes,' Philip replied. 'What a blessing that you have a home to go to!'

She immediately added, though indistinctly, 'And a hearty welcome!' It was the title of one of her tracts: *A Home and a Hearty Welcome*.

After a while she said, 'I shall walk with Him in white. Won't you take your lamb and walk with me?' The last sentence she repeated, not sure that Philip understood her. 'I believe, however,' he wrote afterwards, 'she alluded to our dear little boy.'

They could hear her murmur, 'Open the gates! Open the gates and let me in!' She was ready to go. At one o'clock in the morning, she died.

2

A Nursery for his Soul

IN THE SMALL house in Islington, Edmund had been spared little of the anxiety and the grief. He had become conscious too early of 'that torrent of sorrow and anguish and terror' which flows under all our feet. His father knew that Emily had merely gone before him into a room where he would surely follow. There was no bitterness; his faith never wavered. But tears would flow down his cheeks as he held his motherless son in his arms. One family, the three of them still dwelt in Christ, 'though now divided by the stream, the narrow stream of death'.

Edmund at seven years old was fully conscious of all that was expected of him. His dedication had been renewed at his mother's deathbed. But now his father had lectures to give; Mrs Morgan took him back to Clifton with her. Two weeks after his mother's death, his father wrote to him from Edinburgh:

> My own sweet boy,
> I seem to love you better than ever . . . and now that beloved Mamma is gone to be with Jesus, you are all that is left to me. I pray much that the Lord will make you a true believer. Your sins can be washed away, only by the precious blood of Jesus . . . O remember all the words of dearest Mamma, how she read to you, and taught you and prayed for you. I trust you will be obedient and cheerful to dear Cousin, who is so kind to you; and also obliging and kind to your young cousins. Do not think of self, but try to make others happy, and then you are sure to be happy yourself . . .

Poor Edmund. With this letter – perhaps it came in the same post – there was a letter of sympathy from a woman called Hester Rhodes. She urged the boy 'to be a sweet comfort to the heart of your afflicted father. May you be daily ripening for that bright and glorious and happy world where you will meet your beloved mother and be with her forever'.

At Clifton, fortunately, the atmosphere was relaxed and warm. It was, as Edmund would recall, 'a blessed interval in my strenuous childhood'. There were a lot of adolescents – Mary, John, Henry, William and Alice – including Ann, aged fifteen, who was to become the grandmother of Alec and Evelyn Waugh. Alec remembered his grandmother telling how Edmund, in his holland suit, knelt excitedly before a case of stuffed birds and exclaimed with high-pitched enthusiasm, 'Cousin, you have here a remarkable specimen of the Golden Oriole.' She was touched by the eagerness which would always be one of his greatest charms.

Edmund remembered walks with his tall cousins waving like trees above him, noisy evenings (one of the boys taught him how to fire a pistol out of the attic window) and occasional excursions into the country. He wrote a happy letter to his father about the Zoological Gardens ('I think I liked the best of all the New Holland Emu and two Barnacle Geese') and going down the Zigzag and watching the tugs on the Avon. 'I love you very much,' he wrote, 'and think of you very often,' adding optimistically at the end 'I hope you will come and stay here the whole of the year.'

But it was not to be. He was with the Morgans for less than four weeks. On the 19th March he returned to the quiet house in Islington. These are the long empty hours of childhood he would recall so vividly in *Father and Son*. In memory he felt he was living, not just behind a window, but isolated, cut off, in a bell-jar. People moved beyond the window; life went on. The boy saw everything: the milkman, the anti-Papist onion seller, the fat sailor beseeching all and sundry to 'watch and pray', the Punch and Judy show, the pedlar with his bag full of trinkets. But he remembered himself as entirely cut off from the life of the world. When he was not gazing out of the window, his cheek cold against the glass, he was shut up in his father's study, observing the aquaria, drawing, reading the old *Penny Cyclopaedias* – and studying the Scriptures.

Just occasionally, he recalled, the father and son would walk down the Caledonian Road and, getting as far as the canal, near Horsefall Basin, would stand together on the bridge, watching the ducks and the vermilion and azure barges gliding by. He thought of this time as a long time, but in fact it was only six weeks after his return from Clifton that Sarah Andrews joined the household. This was the Miss Marks of *Father and Son*, the 'thoroughly good and honest woman, not intelligent and not graceful, but desirous in every way to do her duty'. She was certainly determined to please, not just because it was in her nature to try to do so but, particularly, as became clear later, because she harboured hopes of becoming the second Mrs Gosse. We have various clues to her character beyond the picture in *Father and Son*. Was she perhaps one of those acidulated women he wrote of years later who intimidated everyone by an assumption of direct communication with God? Certainly Edmund spent a lot of time trying to be good for her, rather than ignoring her existence. He said she was bustling and nervous, not particularly refined, not quite 'a lady'. Years later, describing someone else to his wife, Edmund wrote: 'I imagined a broken-down 'umble retainer of the Sarah Andrews species: instead of that, a young woman, completely a lady . . . quite alert and self-possessed and bubbling over with fun.' The definite implication was that poor Sarah Andrews was none of these things.

Eventually her unrefined expectations would come to grate on P. H. Gosse, but she certainly did more than her duty. One of the things she encouraged Edmund to do was to keep his first diary. Sixty years later, he noted: 'The entries in ink I dictated to Miss Andrews. The names in pencil are in my own handwriting.' In fact, it had started as a birthday book and the pencil names are birthdays (including 'May 24 Sunday Queen Victoria') – but the ink entries reveal a crowded social life, not suggested in *Father and Son*. In July 1857, for instance, Edmund stayed a few days at Tottenham; he went with Miss Andrews to Twickenham. He had tea with the Hislops, playing with Arthur and Eddy. He drank tea several times with dear Grandmamma and he went to Reigate to see the Bergers. At Reigate he was 'surprised to find a little French young lady in the summerhouse' and some caterpillars of the Peacock butterfly on the nettles. Another day he got some leaves for his silkworms. Mrs Hislop, Lucy and Eddy visited them in Huntingdon Street – more than once – and he went with Miss Andrews to visit her sister, Mary. So it went on.

But on 1st September Edmund recorded that Papa had gone to see a house. By the 10th, the books were being packed and the study and back-parlour carpets taken up. On September 23rd, two days after Edmund's eighth birthday, they left London for Devonshire. On Friday 25th September 1857 they moved into their new house – Sandhurst, St Marychurch, near Torquay.

And it *was* new, brand new, a solid handsome house, flanked by two enormous elms, standing in a sea of red mud. Ten years before, St Marychurch had been a very small village. Now, because of its 'proximity to the fashionable town of Torquay', it was expanding. It was about a mile and a half to the north, 'an ancient but not picturesque assemblage of white-washed cottages and small shops, close to the sea-cliff but out of sight of the sea'. Higher than Torquay, on clear days there was a view of Dartmoor. Bathing machines were just beginning to invade 'its savage coves and creeks'. New villas were rising in all directions.

Billings Devon Directory for 1857 lists, among the attractions of the area, Kent's Cavern, where early traces of human remains, not to mention the extinct hyena, had recently been found, and the marble quarries at Petit Tor 'where so many of the beautiful Devonian fossils are found'. Fossils were in Philip Gosse's mind. He had just sent his new book *Omphalos* off to the printers. This was the book which he felt should settle once and for all the conflict between religion and science – between the short chronology which a strict interpretation of the Bible suggested, and the enormous antiquity of the earth beginning to be suggested by the geologists. Philip Gosse came up with the Law of Prochronism, which argued that the course of nature is cyclical and that, creation occurring at one moment in that cycle, everything bore witness of an illusory past. As Adam had a navel, though he had never had an umbilical cord, as there were full-sized trees growing in the Garden of Eden, so everything at the moment of creation must have retrospective marks. In an amazing flow of rhetoric – a sort of strange poetry – Gosse proved to his own satisfaction that God had planted fossils in the rocks. It was not to deceive us into thinking the world had begun differently from the way Genesis tells us. It was not to test the faithful or fool the scientists. It was simply because at that dramatic moment of creation, when God created the heaven and the earth, 'the world presented, instantly, the structural appearance of a planet on which life had long existed'. The world, he said, had been created at a precise moment, 'as precise as the moment in which I write this word'.

Already depressed and saddened by Emily's death (and by the shocked reception of his frank memorial of her last days on earth), he was now hurt and dismayed by the reactions to a theory he had confidently expected could appeal to atheists and Christians alike. He had become used to flattering praise for his books, but his disappointment was not that of a man who cares for fame and fortune; it was that of a man who cares for truth, thinks he has found it and finds the world unimpressed. P. H. Gosse was attacked on all sides. His friend and admirer Charles Kingsley – hardest blow of all – was 'staggered and puzzled'. He wrote that *Omphalos* had actually made him doubt the Creation. Gosse's inadvertent *reductio ad absurdum* had made Kingsley doubt 'and I fear it will make hundreds do so'. He could hush up his conscience at the single thought of Adam's navel – but he could not believe 'that God has written on the rocks one enormous and superfluous lie'. He would not for a thousand pounds put *Omphalos* in his children's hands. 'It was more like to make infidels than to cure them.'

Of course there were people who took the wild surmises seriously. My own copy was presented as a prize for Proficiency in Botanical Science by a Fellow of the Zoological Society. A few copies were certainly sold; but most were destroyed, and Philip Gosse's reputation was irretrievably damaged, even more than Edmund's would be thirty years later. It was *Omphalos*, as much as Emily's death, that hardened Philip's heart and drove him into rigid patterns of fanaticism and fear. Edmund, after Philip's death, would note that his father, 'invulnerably cased in fully developed conviction upon every side', now hardly modified his habits of thought for the rest of his life. Sometimes it seemed he dared not think.

The world, the changing world, was an even more sceptical and dangerous place than he had believed. It would require all his vigilance, all his cunning, to keep their lamb within the fold and safe from the ravening wolves. Darwin, two years later, presented all the evidence, not only against the literal interpretation of Genesis, but also against a benign Creator. Part of his creed was the overturning of an idea most precious to Gosse – that nature proclaimed the glory of God. It is no coincidence that in these years, the late 1850s, Philip Gosse came more and more frequently, as Edmund observed in *Father and Son*, to be angry with God. There was from time to time a suspicion that all the sacrifice, all the devotion, might not have been worth it. But such doubts only fuelled his determination to pursue a life of dedication. Emily's voice was always in his ears: 'Take our lamb and walk with me.' *She* knew; she believed. And to her faith Philip clung.

At least Philip could return to the observation of species. Darwin himself had been asking for his evidence of crustacean battles: 'Can you tell me, you who have so watched all sea-nature, whether male crustaceans ever fight for the females?' There was also the interesting possibility that molluscs might be carried long distances on a duck's foot. There were plenty of experiments that could be carried out in Marychurch. He had often spoken to Darwin at meetings of the Royal Society and the Linnean Society. But now he cut himself off from London. He did not hear Darwin deliver his paper on the origin of species.

In the Sandhurst garden, Edmund helped Papa in planting climbers. One of the Hannafords – the Burmingtons of *Father and Son*, whose household was to figure largely in Edmund's Marychurch life – 'gave us a rose tree and several little plants'. Trees were established. But that first winter was a hard one. The house was damp, under-furnished and underheated. Under his pile of blankets, Edmund trembled. They were new to the community and there was much curiosity and suspicion to contend with. Uninvited but unresisted, Philip Gosse had preached the word of God at Marychurch only two days after their arrival to a tiny band who met at the Public Room, a group of 'simple rustic souls' who had no connection with any national religious body. The meeting place, like the Room in Hackney, was 'without ritual, choral adjunct or outward adornment', with nothing to beguile young Edmund – no stained glass, of course, or vestments, or what Kingsley called 'stage-acting in the house of God'. Nothing but the smells of horses rising through the floor-boards from the stables below.

But the 'saints' in Marychurch were very different from the erudite text-unravellers in Hackney. A group of more learned Christians, including Dr J. E. Gladstone, cousin of the future Prime Minister, met regularly each week at Sandhurst to study the Scriptures, but Philip Gosse saw the brethren in the Room as rural innocents striving to come to God but easily led astray. It was all the more important that the newcomers should do nothing, absolutely nothing, that did not redound to the credit of Jesus – so there were to be no secular songs, no Christmas puddings (that 'flesh offered to idols'), no indulgences or treats which could possibly be misinterpreted.

Emily had once written that it was 'the jovial companion, the glass of grog, the foolish song that keep the poor sinner from reaching the haven of rest'. Father and son watched daily for the personal return of Christ and it was unthinkable that they should not be ready for Him. Act after act was taboo, for fear it might lead others into sin. And even when they were together, discussing with relish the details of the carpet-bag murder, Philip must have remembered Emily's voice, in one of her tracts, scorning those who find time to verse themselves 'in all the shocking details of crime and misery'.

It seemed at times that most things were forbidden. Sundays were, of course, particularly hedged with restrictions. Not one moment of the sacred day should be spent 'in secular occupations or mere amusements'. Yet there is plenty of evidence of pleasure in the early Marychurch years. The house itself became more and more attractive: outside the clematis climbed more luxuriantly up the verandah; the gardens and greenhouses and aquaria were full of rich delights. Inside there were brilliant cases of tropical insects and in winter the leaping flames of good fires.

Philip became absorbed in his great work which was eventually to be *Actinologia Britannica*. He had been observing sea anemones for years. Now he began a full-scale study of the British Sea Anemones and Corals, adding no fewer than thirty-four new species by his own personal investigation. He enlisted the support of other collectors throughout the British Isles. Day after day the morning post on the breakfast table included one or two little boxes 'of a salt and oozy character'. But most of his researches were based on local observation.

Day after day, too, the middle-aged widower and the small boy combed the rock pools at Anstey's Cove, at Oddicombe, at Petit Tor, or took longer excursions to Maiden Combe northwards or Livermead to the south. Edmund was 'his constant and generally his only companion'. Philip carried a large wicker basket. Edmund carried a glass jar in a wicker case and a green gauze net. Even as a child Edmund was aware of his father's eccentric appearance, in clothes which grew to look as if they might have been 'bequeathed to him by some ancient missionary long marooned, with no other garments, upon a coral island'.

Sometimes they would see other collectors inspired in all probability by Gosse's own books. Indeed on one occasion Edmund remembered coming across a party of ladies 'who were cackling so joyously over a rarity they had secured that our curiosity overcame our shyness, and we asked them what they had found. They named a very scarce species, and held it up to us to examine. My father, at once, civilly set them right; it was so-and-so, something much more commonplace. The ladies drew themselves up with dignity and sarcastically remarked that it *was* the rarity, and that "Gosse is our authority."'

P. H. Gosse was at his best on these expeditions, stirred by the chase, treating the boy as a useful apprentice and even as a friend. 'He had no other friend,' Edmund said. And yet really they could never be friends. They were always father and son. It was probably of these regular expeditions that Edmund was thinking when in a poem, years later, he looked back on a childhood 'dowered with such wealth of pure delights and natural influence'. Father and son would hang together over the rock pools, eager for new discoveries. On 29th June 1859 Edmund Gosse, aged 9¾, added a new genus to the British fauna: *Phellia murocincta*, the walled corklet. He prided himself on being an embryo scientist, but they were both liable to unscientific feelings. Once they found a young eel grasped and partly swallowed by an *Anthea cereans*. 'My little son, who was with me,' wrote P. H. Gosse, 'begged for the life of the first and I drew it by force from the green embrace.'

Sometimes they would dredge in Tor Bay, hiring a small trawler. Charles Kingsley, whose differences over *Omphalos* had not severed their friendship, was with them on one special day – it was 11th August 1858 – when they hauled up the first specimen ever observed of the diadem anemone: *Bunodes coronata*.

When Philip Gosse was away lecturing, Edmund wrote enthusiastic letters to keep him in touch with developments at home. The letters often begin with extravagant affection: 'My 1000000000 dear Papa', 'My veeeeeerry dear Papa', 'My *very excessively* dear Papa', 'my extremely precious Papa'. And they end with such flourishes as 'I remain your very very very (12 times) indeed indeed loving son' or with '121 kisses from your loving son'. One is covered with dots of the pen. 'Papa, what are these? Willy kisses.' The letters have a tremendous dash and confidence, as if the writer knows whatever nonsense he writes it will be well received.

Edmund also does not seem to be worried about admitting to worldly pleasures. There seems to have been no question at this time anyway of 'laying the matter before the Lord', as in the memorable case in *Father and Son* when the Lord was asked whether or not Edmund was to go to the Browns' party. On 16th February 1859 he writes: 'I enjoyed myself very much at the Miss Willses yesterday among the young ladies. We played at Lotto, and Bell and Hammer and Solitaire and I saw the gymtastics [sic] and held them too.' And three days later: 'The Miss Bibbins have just called; I am (D.V.) going to tea on Monday evening at their house'.

Violets enclosed in one of the letters remind us of the letters Emily dictated for him six years before. Edmund comments on his reading ('*The History of Insects* is not so interesting as *The Conquest of Peru*') and his writing ('My book has got as far as T. Quercus') but most of the news is of the cats, the garden and the inhabitants of the aquaria. The cats are re-christened with fantastic names ('Mr Eatmouse-when-he-can-find-them' etc), 'the broad beans are coming up Magnificently' and 'the *Acontia* of our *Adamisia* are snow white', followed by six exclamation marks. As for the aquaria: 'the *Lerianthus lyodii* is very well' but '*Bolocera egis auratus* has fatally burst!' The letters also record the arrival of Grandmamma Hannah Gosse, who joined the household in the spring of 1858 and remained with them until her death in 1860, though this is not mentioned in *Father and Son*.

Miss Andrews reported that the 'dear old lady' seems very happy 'and is most grateful for all that is done for her'. Edmund told his father that she had been admiring the house, 'especially the kitchens', but years later he remembered she could be as scornful and vehement as ever. Though 'filled with respect for her son', she could not resist, on seeing his new tropical fern house, lately fitted up in the Sandhurst garden, from commenting, 'I wonder . . . that you care to keep a parcel of fern.' It seemed to her of no more significance than the bracken that had grown everywhere in Dorset. Philip's interests remained alien to her to the last.

Hannah's presence made little difference to the quiet house. 'For hours and hours, my grandmother would be sitting at her patchwork, silent, in her padded chair; my father, almost motionless, in his study below her; and I equally silent, though not equally still, free to wander whither I would in house and garden,' Edmund remembered. But often he *was* still, shut away in the box-room, obsessed with his book, his own eccentric variation of his father's work, a record of slightly imaginary animals, meticulously drawn and described. This was 'the hush in which you could hear a sea-anemone sigh'. And in that hushed house, working on his 'grotesque monographs', Edmund learnt virtues that would stand him in good stead all his life – he learnt to concentrate his attention, to define the nature of distinctions, to see accurately and to name what he saw. He learnt also to finish the piece of work he had in hand.

A letter from Sarah Andrews to P. H. Gosse on Good Friday 1858 gives a vivid picture of the loving pressures on Edmund to be 'good' – the pressures which made him sometimes long 'to be a godless child':

I must now tell you something which I fear will pain you about dear Willy. I have wanted him to tell you himself but he prefers me to do so. Susan told me he was very good on Monday but Tuesday he was so naughty and disobedient that she told him she should tell both you and me. I feel it my duty not to keep you in the dark, as I wish the dear child to feel deeply the sin of his act of disobedience to your commands in the sight of God. By God's help, I have endeavoured to bring his mind to think much of it, and ask the Lord to help him to be a better child. The punishment I gave him yesterday was not to go into the greenhouse or to see the animals; but today he has been very good and has had his usual amusements. My heart was too full to tell you this yesterday, as I felt much grieved, the dear child having said things in passion which might have made much mis-chief between the maids and myself, but thank the Lord he has given us all much peace and has not allowed Satan to have power . . . How delighted we all shall be to have you home. Susan and Kate desire their duty to you. Accept much Christian love from

> Yours respectfully,
> Sarah Andrews.

Willy was always soon forgiven. ('Be ye kind one to another, tender-hearted, forgiving one another, even as God for Christ's sake hath forgiven you.') The bond between father and son was strong and physical. Philip wrote to Edmund in 1858: 'With what pleasure will you sit on my knee and throw your arms round my neck, when it pleases the Lord to bring me back to you; and how joyfully shall I press you to my heart.' Edmund wrote to Philip in 1859: 'There are only 2 days more, after today, when I hope to sit on your knee and hear you talk. As Miss Andrews said yesterday "Oh that will be joyful" and so it certainly will be.' Miss Andrews's own joy in Philip Gosse's pres-ence was not to last much longer.

Years later, in his biography of Coventry Patmore, Edmund would write of that strange Christian parent and 'the ceaseless oscillation of his spirit between severity and tenderness'. He must certainly have been thinking of a parallel with his own father. Now, to his father's satisfaction, Edmund appeared to be growing in grace as well as physical stature. He had been shrimp-like; now he began to fill out. Spirit, body and mind were all developing rapidly. His education was haphazard. Miss Andrews had long given up any attempt to teach him. He learnt what he wanted to learn and what his father was prepared to teach him – no mathematics, no modern languages at this stage, but lots of botany, zoology, geography and of course religious knowledge. His father started him on Latin from a book which had belonged to old Thomas Gosse and the 'grim arrangements of con-junction and declension' were redeemed because they had something to do with Virgil. P. H. Gosse remembered verses he had learnt in

Newfoundland or Alabama and the sound of the Latin was Edmund's further revelation of the beauty of poetry. His infant ears had already delighted in the lesser euphony of the hymn writers, the clashing verses of James Hyslop's *Cameronian's Dream* (found by chance in the Pimlico lodgings) and the strange cadences of Isaiah and Revelation.

Philip Gosse devised one educational exercise which irked Edmund at the time but which he was later to be glad about. He would be sent out on some specific walk – say 'up the lane to Warbury Head and round home by the copses'. And he had to observe and record, in language as full as he could, everything he had seen on the excursion. 'It forced me to observe sharply and clearly, to form visual impressions, to retain them in the brain and to clothe them in punctilious and accurate language.'

It was at this time that Philip convinced himself that his son was adult in his knowledge of the Lord and ready for the immense privilege of breaking bread with the saints at Marychurch. In *Father and Son*, Edmund tells in detail the story of his public baptism. The ceremony was performed by Leonard Strong at the larger meeting house in Warren Road, Torquay. It was, Edmund said, 'dazzling beyond words'. He was the actor in the centre of the stage. It was the most important event in his whole childhood. Everything seemed to have led up to it; afterwards there could only be a falling away. In some ways, not realizing this, the father relaxed. The son was safe in his heavenly Father's arms. He was caught and caged, secure, protected. There was no need any longer, it seemed, for such extreme vigilance.

Other factors the following year contributed to an easing of the strains on Edmund. At the end of February 1860 his grandmother, Hannah Gosse, died in her 81st year. On the day of her funeral, Leonard Strong called on old friends of his, the Curtises in Upton Cottage, Torquay. He found there a middle-aged East Anglian visitor, Eliza Brightwen. She tells the story:

> Mr Strong came into the cottage and said, 'I am just come from the Cemetery, where I have been conducting the funeral service over Mr Gosse's mother.'
>
> I at once asked, 'What Mr Gosse? Is he the noted naturalist?'
>
> 'Yes,' said Mr Strong, 'and he lives in St Marychurch, close by you . . . He is the minister of a small church at the east end of that village.'

Miss Brightwen knew P. H. Gosse to be an eminent naturalist but had no idea where he lived. Her curiosity was awakened and she and Mr Curtis decided to go to one of his meetings.

'After the meeting was over, my friend and I walked with Mr Gosse and his little son as far as Sandhurst gate.' He told them they would be welcome at the weekly Scripture readings at the house. 'We returned to the cottage well pleased with the minister and his courteous and kind manner to us as strangers . . . He was in the full vigour and swing of his useful life, ardent and enthusiastic in every movement.' Often after this, through the summer months of 1860, she would watch father and son 'running and jumping down the declivities of the rocks, till they reached the pebbly shore'. Gosse knew she was also interested in natural history and lent her books. Sometimes he took his microscope and specimens to the cottage. Sometimes she and some young friends would go down to the beach with them. He would bring out 'new and curious and lovely creatures' and his audience would gather round and exclaim 'How beautiful! How wonderful!' and afterwards agree they had spent a delightful morning.

If Edmund was worried that she was a 'Pedobaptist', fortunately Eliza was not aware of the fact. She made herself popular with him by commenting appreciatively on the maritime empire he was moulding out of clay at the edge of the village horse-pond. It was his pleasure to create islands, archipelagoes, harbours, bays, peninsulas and isthmuses. She showed a most intelligent interest.

On September 3rd Eliza Brightwen left Torquay to join an aunt and uncle at Frome in Somerset. Three days later, she received a letter from P. H. Gosse 'proposing and urging, in strong terms, that I should become his wife', Eliza recorded. 'This certainly was no little surprise to me. However after a week or two of consideration and consulting my friends, I accepted the offer of his hand.' She must have seen, as Edmund saw, not the apparent austerity that sometimes repelled strangers and even friends ('Be sober, be vigilant; because your adversary the devil, as a roaring lion, walketh about, seeking whom he may devour'); Eliza Brightwen saw rather 'the immeasurable tenderness passing across the great brown lustrous orbs of his eyes. His smile was rare, but when it came it was exquisite'.

Eliza's family were wealthy Quakers; she was connected with the famous banking family, the Gurneys of Norfolk, kin of Elizabeth Fry and Anna Sewell, the author of *Black Beauty*. Her uncle was John Brightwen of Thorpe, from whom she would inherit a considerable amount of money. The family, not surprisingly, were opposed to the match but on 18th December 1860 they were married: Philip, aged fifty, widower, and Eliza, aged forty-seven, spinster.

Edmund describes, in a letter to Philip and Eliza ('My beloved Parents') written on their silver wedding day, that first evening twenty-five years before:

How well I remember the setting out of the new lamp, the gift of the brethren at the Room, in the unfamiliar drawing-room – poor Sarah Andrews alternately weeping and scolding around, all in her bonnet if I remember right, as a symbol of her fugitive status – and then the noise of the carriage arriving in the dark, and the flutter of my shyness as the gracious new Mamma came in – in a grey silk dress, I think, am I wrong? and kissed me – the beginning of so sweet a life for me, under fresh and unspeakably favourable auspices.

Eliza gives her own side of the story:

I had a hearty welcome from my dear little stepson. My beloved husband and he made me quite at home, telling me many of their old traditions and amusing family stories, with much fun, and we had quite a merry breakfast. I soon found out that Mr Gosse had a good deal of humour and fun when quite in the intimacy of his home, not withstanding that to his circle of friends and neighbours he was grave and somewhat stern, as became one who had taken the position of pastor.

Later, P. H. Gosse was to rebuke himself for the amount of humour and fun they indulged in, worrying about the ill effects of 'unseemly levity' on Edmund's development.

Eliza's coming opened up a wider life for the son; but for the father, it seemed to encourage him all the more to keep himself to himself, to cut himself off from the world. As the home became more comfortable, he was more and more reluctant to leave it. In 1862 he began 'the culture of tropical orchids' and the boiler and heating pipes for the rare plants transformed the temperature of the house as well.

Eliza urged him to renew his old contacts in London but, after *Omphalos*, he could not face his fellow-scientists, though he could still exchange useful letters about observable phenomena. His letters about butterflies and orchids went all over the world. Eventually the Sandhurst garden contained no fewer than five hot-houses or conservatories. God had been good to him, temporally as well as spiritually. The second marriage, like the first, was a very happy one. And P. H. Gosse continued to rejoice in 'the inconceivable perfection and glory of the Divine handwork'. Nothing Darwin or anyone else could say would shake his belief in works of nature as 'ever fresh proofs of His all-pervading care, of His wondrous skill and wisdom, of His glorious majesty and power'.

Eliza soothed, loved and honoured P. H. Gosse and became 'the most indulgent of Edmund's protectors'. She was a mildly cultured woman, kindly and tolerant. In early life she had been a pupil of Cotman and she painted rather well – landscapes in the Norwich tradition. She brought with her books and pictures which opened windows for her young stepson. The boy had never seen Greek sculpture until one day Eliza received a gaudy gift book of some kind, with a few steel engravings of statues of the Greek gods. His father, questioned in excitement, dismissed the so-called gods as shadows cast by the vices of the heathen. He had no feeling for the visual arts, in spite of his own skill as a recording artist. Eliza shared Philip's love of poetry and encouraged Edmund's. Her sister Maria was married to a brother of the Palgrave who was working away at that very moment on his *Golden Treasury*; later she would send him Edmund's first book of poems. Eliza herself kept a commonplace book, an album of verses, copying out Byron, Scott, Milton, Tennyson.

Edmund called his stepmother 'one of the most lovable of all mankind'. But she could stand up for herself and for Edmund. Her individuality could be bruised but not permanently damaged. There was a fuss over her carnelian brooch which offended the eye of a zealous member of the brethren. 'One must fasten one's collar with something, I suppose,' she said, refusing to be browbeaten. Years later Edmund's daughter would remember Eliza as 'coquettish in her dress and caps', wearing good silks and fine laces.

One odd surviving letter from Mary Grace Hannaford suggests the surveillance Eliza had to survive in the early years of her marriage:

My darling Mr Gosse,
I have observed an evident advance in holiness in your dear partner, her prayers are deeper . . . Now perhaps you are the honored instrument of this growth in grace, therefore if the Lord witholds fruit in one way he gives it you in another, so be *strong* and of good courage, knowing that your labour is not in vain in the Lord excuse pencil as I write lying down . . .

Mary Grace (could she really have been the 'delightful creature' Edmund suggests in *Father and Son*?) had been a bosom friend of Sarah Andrews and had seen her displacement with regret. Sarah had gone by the time of the census in April 1861, so it is reasonable to assume she left very soon after Philip's remarriage. There is an advertisement in the evangelical paper *The Revival* for 6th July 1861:

A CHRISTIAN LADY, who for over three years and a half has had the superintendence of a widower's family, wishes for a re-engagement of somewhat similar character, where she may serve the Lord Jesus.

References permitted to Mr P. H. Gosse, Sandhurst, Torquay, who will be happy to answer any enquiries, and to whose care enquiries addressed S.A. may be sent.

Both Edmund and Philip remained in contact with Miss Andrews for many years, exchanging letters and visits and helping her out financially.

Edmund had started school in the summer term of 1860, apparently as the result of a direct approach from Nicholas Meneer, a young schoolmaster soliciting custom. He was running a small school in Trafalgar Villa, Westhill Road, St Marychurch which boasted in its 1859 advertisement in the Torquay Directory that pupils were 'prepared for Oxford and Cambridge examinations, the Public Schools and for Commercial and Agricultural pursuits'. Moreover it claimed that the fact that 'none of the Candidates sent from this School failed to Satisfy the Examiners, is a fair proof of the sound training imparted to the Pupils'.

P. H. Gosse was impressed and remained so. Edmund enjoyed this school and made a crowd of friends, the 'unconverted boys' with whom he spent idyllic holidays in a blaze of sunshine. He remembered 'descents of slippery grass to moons of snow-white shingle, cold to the bare flesh; red promontories running out into a sea that was like sapphire' and 'our happy clan climbing, bathing, boating, lounging, chattering all the hot day through' – 'a glorious life among wild boys on the margin of the sea'. It was his first awareness of his own gregariousness.

It was in the summer of 1861 that Eliza took her new stepson, aged eleven, to visit her family in Norfolk. 'My kind stepmother swept me along in the swirl of her flounces and I found myself in such clover as I have never dreamed of . . .' They paid a sort of state visit to the Gurneys at Earlham in the large Brightwen barouche. 'It was, as I now find, but a distance of a few miles from Thorpe to Earlham, yet, half-sunken among the crinolines of the ladies and drawn with dignity through the breadth of Norwich and out into the country, the expedition seemed endless in its delight.' Many years after this visit, reviewing Augustus Hare's book on the Gurneys, Edmund felt 'drenched with virtue, drugged with respectability, repelled by their intense gentility, piety and propriety' ('not a black sheep in the whole comfortable, curly flock'). But in 1861 he was enchanted by his visit to Earlham, his first visit to the sort of house he was always to delight in.

That autumn he returned not to Trafalgar Villa School but to Mont Videre House where Nicholas Meneer had moved. This was 'the larger and more distant school' of *Father and Son*. There survive a few

47

examples of Edmund's work under Meneer and they are not particularly encouraging. But one essay he wrote in February 1861 at Trafalgar Villa has already a Gosse-like quality. It is on 'the Contrast between the Town and the Country'. Eleven-year-old Edmund comes down very strongly for the country. 'Persons who have never been in London often greatly wish they were there but they soon find the difference: they get up early – but they do not hear the lark nor see the lambs in the meadows – but they do hear their next-door neighbours snoring and look at two rows of straight dingy houses.' So much for Huntingdon Street, Islington – but the master has crossed out those realistic neighbours snoring and destroyed the nice balance of the sentence. All the same, Edmund loved him.

Philip admired the schoolmaster too but was worried about Edmund's friends. He had tried an experiment of providing him compulsorily with a suitable companion – young George Fewings, brother of Elizabeth Fewings, the cook at Sandhurst, and son, it would seem, of the washerwoman (called Mrs Pewings in *Father and Son*) who had been accused of intemperance but had seen the error of her ways and returned to the fold. George was exactly Edmund's age and had indeed stolen some of Edmund's thunder by being convincingly converted by Edmund's baptism and joining him very soon afterwards as a baptised believer of unusually tender years. Philip took him on as a gardener's boy and encouraged, with a typically classless attitude, the friendship between the two young brethren. But of course it didn't work. They had little in common.

Edmund's chosen friend at Marychurch was Mansel Dames – known as Frank – a fellow pupil at Meneer's school, who was to remain a close friend until he went off to India, having passed into the Civil Service nineteenth in the whole of England. This was the boy of *Father and Son* whose tastes were 'singularly parallel to my own', who scoured the horizon with him for books of prose and verse. But he was not a believer. Years later P. H. Gosse was still worrying away at Dames's soul: 'He is growing into a man, and if successful, will soon have to go away to India, that scene of worldliness and temptation, and I fear he is as yet out of Christ.'

Their shared tastes in books were causing problems too. It was a long time since Edmund had been able to be confined to *Parables from Nature* and the *Penny Cyclopaedia*. Even in Philip Gosse's 'swept and garnished library' a few traitors had lurked. Edmund had furthered his taste for fiction from the pages in the lid of the old skin trunk in Islington to *Tom Cringle's Log* by Michael Scott and Hannah More's *Coelebs in Search of a Wife*. His father had offered him *Tom Cringle's Log* for the geography: 'You'll find all about the Antilles there,' he said.

Edmund suggested 'it was like giving a glass of brandy neat to someone who had never been weaned from a milk diet'. It was a pagan world and gave Edmund perhaps his first real sensation of a life not bound by the Law and the Prophets.

Hannah More was of course an exemplary Evangelical and her novel was much devoted to religion and morals, but Edmund lingered over 'pictures of frivolous society and even perilous intrigue', which were indicating what should be avoided. He remembered the book long afterwards with affection for its tempting knowledge of a naughty world and said that he would not disturb his memories of it by reading it again. 'If I were alone with *Coelebs* on a desert island, I would not read it,' he wrote, which was ridiculous: such was his appetite for print, he would have devoured the instructions on a tin of cocoa if there had been nothing else to read.

Philip and Eliza were becoming confused and illogical about what Edmund should read and should not read. Under the surviving elms he read anything that he could get hold of. He was starting to write poetry but had barely heard of Shakespeare. He would say in *Father and Son* that Philip prided himself on never having read Shakespeare in his life. Edmund thought he had first heard the name of Shakespeare on the lips of James Sheridan Knowles – he who had been the most prominent playwright of the day before yesterday and in old age had come to Torquay as a Baptist minister. In fact, Philip did echo Shakespeare from time to time.

'Hark, hark the lark at heaven's gate sings!' he quoted on an early morning walk on Dartmoor. Similarly, Philip Gosse would quote from Scott's novels – even beginning the Preface to *Omphalos* with a telling analogy from *Ivanhoe* – but forbidding Edmund to have anything to do with them. Poetry was almost equally dangerous – for Edmund's vulnerable spirit. Eliza's knitting needles clattered nervously when Edmund innocently read aloud from *Hero and Leander*.

'The downward path is easy,' Philip was fond of repeating. Some major effort had to be made in order to save the lamb from straying. There was always the danger that thorns would grow up and strangle the good seed. There was ever-present the awful possibility that the cares and riches and pleasures of the world would stop the seed from bringing forth good fruit. The decision was made that Edmund should be sent to boarding school. By an ill chance, Philip had heard of a school in Teignmouth – Thorn Park Classical and Mathematical School in Coombe Vale Road – whose principal was Thomas Edgelow. Leonard Strong's two sons, Robert and James, went there and the establishment purported to be peculiarly wrapped in sanctity.

In December 1862 Edmund went to Exeter to have his first try at

'Junior Cambridge' and attained third class honours, including a distinction in Zoology and passes in Religious Knowledge, English, Latin and Mathematics. He was only just thirteen and the performance was considered very creditable, but perhaps it was the mere pass in Religious Knowledge that finally influenced his father to remove him from Nicholas Meneer's tuition. He wrote an immensely tactful letter just before Christmas.

> We feel very grateful for all the fatherly care you have taken of him and desire to express our thorough satisfaction with the progress he is making in learning. I do not think any master could get on boys better than you do or could have his heart more in his work: and surely I have never known a master who so succeeded in winning the love and confidence of his pupils.

But the trouble was that Willy was not finding any spiritual companionship at Mont Videre. 'He does not find one boy who is of the slightest help to him spiritually.' P. H. Gosse admitted his son was probably not trying very hard to win his fellows for Christ. 'He loves play as much as any boy and he is carried away by the general tone, which without being morally evil is earthy.' The father saw a dulling in the son's spiritual life and, against Willy's own desire, he had decided to send him to another school 'in which a good many of the elder boys are converted to God and among whom there is a recognised Christian circle whose influence is manifest for blessing'. The boy would be in 'a nursery for his soul'. In fact, Thorn Park's Christian virtues seem to have been illusory, but Philip remained in the dark about the school's singular lack of piety.

'I want Willy's soul to prosper above all things else,' P. H. Gosse wrote to Thomas Edgelow, agreeing to pay £50 a year for boarding five nights a week, for all tuition, laundries and all incidental expenses. 'It is my desire that his talents may be hereafter used in the Lord's service and I would have his studies and his fellowship all to be ancillary to this object.' He was to start French immediately and to get on with Greek, particularly the New Testament.

So the child of many prayers left his father's immediate care. The school was conventional, dull, suffering from what could only be called an intellectual drought. Edmund was lonely and unhappy – but not bullied. He slipped into the common adolescent poses of carelessness, dissidence and ennui. A letter written in the summer of 1863, when he was nearly fourteen, gives startling proof of this, comparing very poorly with his letters of four years before. Even his stepmother, indulgent as she had always been, was disappointed in him. Most of the time he remained and felt inconspicuous. Once, just once, he made his schoolfellows take notice when, on a sudden impulse, he locked a master in a classroom and took the consequences. Once, just once, he remembered a master paying him some more welcome attention – on a cliff-top walk – when he confided in the boy his enthusiasm for Thomas Carlyle. 'There was something startling in the fervour of the revelation. I was surprised – since I was idle and inconspicuous in the classroom – at the compliment of being singled out from the herd of boys to receive this exalted utterance, and I was deeply and permanently impressed.'

The master may well have been a man called Anderson, who was reported to have said on his early death-bed that he had hoped to see young Willy Gosse prominent – 'He was very wayward but he was the most sympathetic of my pupils.' Thomas Edgelow, himself, was not very impressed with him. Writing to P. H. Gosse in June 1864, he lamented the boy's 'extreme forgetfulness – when told of his carelessness he appears conscious of his fault . . . but alas he forgets . . .' 'There is a large amount of superficial work in his exercises', but he 'generally evidences a fair share of attention, industry and knowledge'.

Edmund was reading poetry with avidity. It was when he first read Keats's *Endymion* that he said to himself, 'I, too, will be a poet.' What he called 'the passion for rhyming' became part of his life. It was a quiet time in poetry. Mrs Browning and Clough were recently dead. Tennyson had published nothing since *The Idylls of the King*. Matthew Arnold appeared to have given up poetry. Robert Browning had been silent since the cold reception of *Men and Women*. Certainly Christina Rossetti had just brought out *Goblin Market* but the Pre-Raphaelites were hardly yet shaking the literary world. Young poets could dream that it was waiting for them.

At Thorn Park Classical and Mathematical School, Edmund Gosse scribbled away and dreamed. His poems in his notebook were annotated with where he wrote them: 'in the classroom in morning school', 'at Prayers one morning at school' and so on. He never wrote copiously. Years later, amazed at A. C. Benson's fluency, he would say that his own poetry 'oozed drop by drop' even in his youth. His notebook for 1866 is not crammed – one poem in January, three in March – two of them written 'in chapel one Sunday'. May was rather more productive and included one poem, 'written in bed at home', which he sent optimistically to *Chambers's Magazine*. 'It was, of course, refused,' Edmund wrote later. 'Who could stand the second verse?' Who indeed could stand the first?

> I know a fairy bower
> Hung round with eglantine
> Where blushing roses flower
> And ivy tendrils twine.
> There on this summer's eve
> I come alone to think
> And airy tissues weave
> Till misty shadows sink.

Most of the verse is similar routine stuff with echoes ('My aching brain frets in its narrow prison-house of clay') and acknowledged homage ('Elegy on the anniversary of the burial of Shelley'). There is only one poem which has any real biographical interest. 'In Disappointment' (15th May 1866) is glossed 'I keep this as a record of my feelings at the time of much unpleasant feeling being caused at school by the revelations, perhaps utterly false, of W. A. Stradling', of whom we know nothing else. Edmund stressed in *Father and Son* that he 'formed no close associations' at school, that he had known nothing there of 'the magnetism of humanity which has been the agony of mature years', that he could look back on none of the fragile loves most men recall with tenderness and passion. But at sixteen he regretted in a careful copperplate that

> . . . he who seemed so kind
> Could beneath a placid brow
> Such a cruel heart allow
> And so base a mind.
> Yet my love I cannot banish
> Though respect must sadly vanish . . .

It was the first experience of love and friendship betrayed.

The stillness of his life, the very lack of stimulus and intensive teaching, seemed to allow his mind to make its own useful preparations for life. Edmund developed his own delight in words; he formed his own habit of intensive reading. 'I often wonder how the people live who have no literature to sink into and rest,' he would say sixty years later in a letter to Siegfried Sassoon. Books were already a sanctuary as well as a joy. He saved his fares from Teignmouth to Torquay on Saturdays, taking the ferry and walking the long six miles along the coast and spending the saved money on books, lamenting years later that there had been no cheap editions available – no Dick's Shakespeare or Everyman's sixpenny library.

At school everything was not dull. He was taught German by Isabel

Becker, half-English, half-German, and totally unconventional. Edmund described her: 'Erratic and independent herself, she is not surprised by any whim or eccentricity in another.' There is a note in Edmund's handwriting recording the fact that she took him on a trip to Hamburg, but I can find nothing else about that. On his nineteenth birthday, she gave him a silver fruit-knife inscribed with his name, and some books which had belonged to her dead fiancé, the master who had hoped to see Edmund prominent one day. Their friendship continued for years after Edmund left school. She wrote him 'gigantic' letters and encouraged his poetry. She wrote to one of his friends, John Blaikie, in 1868: 'Gosse's sonnet I understand perfectly as I do all his writings . . . He is as open and clear in his words as in his character.'

It must also have been at this time that Edmund met another unusual woman: Elise Otté. She had been born in Copenhagen and her widowed mother had married Benjamin Thorpe, the philologist, while he was studying Anglo-Saxon in Denmark. Her stepfather gave her an extraordinary education – she learnt most of the modern languages, but also Anglo-Saxon and Icelandic. When she was still very young, Elise was able to help Thorpe with his translations but she found him a pedant and a captious taskmaster. In 1840 at the age of eighteen, she escaped to find work as a governess in Boston and attended lectures at Harvard in geology, physiology and anatomy. Later she worked in Frankfurt and with her stepfather again in London (translating German and Scandinavian folk tales and Icelandic sagas). In 1849, the year of Edmund's birth, she joined the household of G. E. Day, Professor of Anatomy at St Andrews. She worked on scientific translations for members of the faculty there. In 1863 she moved with the Days to Torquay where she met the Gosses. It was undoubtedly Elise Otté who began Edmund's interest in Scandinavian languages. He recorded that the second Danish war in 1864 – the year he was fifteen – was the earliest foreign event in which he took an interest. Elise Otté had a profound effect on him in many ways. 'She lived wholly in the pursuit of knowledge,' he was to write of her, but there was nothing dry or dull about her. 'Her sympathy with all that was modern, audacious and liberal never failed her.' He made no lasting friendships among his schoolfellows at Thorn Park but he would know Elise Otté until the end of her life.

At home in Marychurch things were more comfortable. In 1864 Eliza Gosse inherited some money on trust. Under her uncle's will, she had the income from £9000 for her lifetime. As she said, it 'was valuable as giving my husband more rest and enabling him to have more leisure; so that he did not need any longer to work, either in writing or in lecturing'. P. H. Gosse never lost his interest in everything and continued his varied scientific experiments and investigations, but there was no incentive for him to present his findings to the world. By 1865 he had ceased to be a professional writer, though of course many of his books were still in print. And he had even more time available for worrying about Edmund's soul.

The father longed for the son to be everything he had himself desired to be, without any of his own shortcomings. Philip thought that when Edmund preached his first sermon, he would feel he had kept faith with Emily, that he would be able to say, 'My poor work is done. Oh! Lord Jesus, receive my spirit.' His terrible conviction was that those who were not saved were damned. This was what gave such urgency to his demands on Edmund, such vigilance to his scanning of his spiritual well-being, such intense concern that the boy should remain within the cage of his own narrow dogma.

He believed, though it is difficult to believe it of one so tender-hearted, that God would punish with eternal pain and damnation all those who did not come to Him through the saving power of Christ's blood. In life, P. H. Gosse 'could not bear to witness the pain or distress of any person, however disagreeable or undeserving', but he was prepared to believe that in death millions of faithful Moslems, Hindus, Buddhists and Roman Catholics, together with the worshippers at St Mary's, St Marychurch, would suffer eternal damnation in a lake of fire and brimstone. And he hoped passionately that he and Edmund would never taste death but, at the rapidly-approaching Second Coming, they would rise together 'to meet the Lord in the air!'

Nevertheless, Philip rejected Edmund's polite suggestion that he should not return to school for his last year, in order to be at his father's right hand when Christ came. P. H. Gosse had to insist, of course, that it is our duty to carry on as usual, knowing we will be instantly united with our loved ones (provided that they also are saved) on the glorious day. Indeed he was already making active plans for Edmund's future career. There was no question of earning a *living* as a pastor to a group of brethren – that was inevitably a spare-time vocation. A suggestion had already been rejected that Edmund should join a bank at Great Yarmouth under the aegis of Eliza's brother, Thomas Brightwen. It was just as well. No excitement in commercial circles apparently exceeded that of 10th May 1866 when the allied family bank of Overend, Gurney and Company Limited suspended payment, with liabilities in the region of eleven million pounds. Now the possibility of work in the Civil Service was discussed. It was thought, for some reason, that the Civil Service was less likely than banking to divert the soul from God.

At this period, getting any sort of place in the Civil Service, however humble, involved the exercise of patronage and influence. P. H. Gosse wrote to his old friend, Charles Kingsley, now Professor of History in the University of Cambridge, who he thought would have the right sort of connections. Kingsley went to enormous trouble for the son of his old companion, though they had had little contact in recent years. 'The more I differed from your conclusions in *Omphalos*,' Kingsley wrote on 31st December 1865, 'the more I admired the moral courage and conscientiousness which dared to say what it thought at such a time.' Kingsley wrote about Edmund to Theodore Walrond, who was one of the Civil Service examiners and happened to be married to Kingsley's niece. It was he who suggested the British Museum:

> I should think the best thing you could do for young Gosse would be to ask Lord Cranworth, whom I believe you know well, to nominate him as 'Junior Assistant' in the British Museum. He, as Lord Chancellor, is one of the three Principal Trustees of the Museum, the Archbishop of Canterbury and the Speaker of the House being the others . . . This is one of the few places in the Civil Service at all worth having which are open to a youth of seventeen – the examination is slight . . . and is not competitive. The pay I understand is poor and promotion slow but it is nearly the only department in which a man of literary or scientific tastes would find anything to gratify them or even keep them alive.

Kingsley promised to write to the Lord Chancellor if Gosse 'thought of the British Museum', but he asked for a full account of Edmund, his talents and achievements. Kingsley suggested the father brought the son to see Sir Anthony Panizzi, the Chief Librarian – a necessary preliminary to a formal application. Fortunately Kingsley also knew 'the likely Lord Chancellor if the Tories get in' – so there were 'two strings to our bow'.

On 27th November 1865, Philip took Edmund to London to see Kingsley and Panizzi. Edmund left an unpublished fragment describing this visit, written years later, but as he gets the date so wildly wrong (he says it was 'early in the autumn of 1866') it is difficult to trust his memory. He describes the cockcrow start (after 'long ejaculations of family prayer'), and his feelings of 'vague distress' and fear at the unknown. They travelled first class, as Philip always did. At Newton Abbot a young woman joined them and a label on her luggage announced her to be 'Miss Christabel Coleridge'. Edmund was consumed with curiosity, wondering if 'she was of the poet's family'. No one spoke a word and she got out at Exeter, where her place was taken by an elderly gentleman. The two men started talking and the boy found himself listening to the sort of conversation he had heard so many times as a small boy travelling with his mother. Now his feelings were different. Without much preliminary, Philip Gosse 'advanced the Cross of Christ. He eagerly enquired whether our new acquaintance had found peace on the bosom of his Saviour'. The answer was curt. The elderly gentleman withdrew to his corner of the carriage, buried himself in a book and took no further notice of them.

Edmund was full of trepidation and confusion.

I sank back upon the dusty velvet, sick with vague distress and despair, and I felt, as I had often before had occasion to feel, that all the doors of social intercourse were shut in the face of my insignificance. It seemed to me, as we were whirled towards the dim exuberance of London, that everything which life could offer me, all the amenities, all the developments, would be checked and nipped by this resolute nonconformity and that everything which faced me in the prospect of an independent career, was doomed to be frustrated by the irresistible and formidable faith of my Father. It is remarkable that this conviction produced, not rebellion, but only hopeless depression, a resignation to the inevitable gloom.

They entered London in a fog and slept badly at a small hotel near the Strand. They had stayed there the year before, with the crumbs and the bluebottle flies, when P. H. Gosse had spoken at the Freemasons' Hall at some enormous evangelical conference, and Edmund had been distressed to hear another speaker call Shakespeare 'a departed sinner'. Now, in November 1865, Kingsley arrived and breezily urged young Edmund 'to look more of a man'. He did his best to cheer them up but both father and son seemed solemn and ill at ease. They walked to the British Museum together, and Philip pointed out to Kingsley and the boy the grimy window in Great Queen Street from which, in the dreariest hour of his life, twenty-five years before, he had looked down upon the roaring midnight debauchery of Drury Lane. Oh what sloughs and pitfalls lay in wait for Edmund, he thought, and how hard it would be to walk in God's way. The boy himself could hardly believe he could be happy away from home; he saw himself as vulnerable as a soldier-crab without a shell, pale and soft and lost.

The first sight of Panizzi, the Chief Librarian, and of the British Museum did nothing to dispel the feelings of despair that had gripped Edmund on the journey to London. But matters seemed to be out of his own hands. Panizzi was alarming – a 'dark little old Italian, sitting

Father and son, 1857

Hannah and Thomas Gosse, Edmund's grandparents (from miniatures painted by
Thomas himself)

Emily Bowes: Edmund's mother as a
young woman

Edmund as a small child

Huntingdon Street, Islington, London (above)

Sandhurst, St Marychurch, Devon (below)

Edmund aged 10, 13, 16 and 19

Eliza Gosse, *née* Brightwen

Philip Henry Gosse

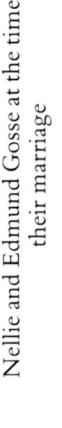

Nellie and Edmund Gosse at the time of their marriage

Edmund

Laurence and Anna Alma-Tadema

Edmund posing for the Epps sisters

like a spider in a web of books' with an eye that Edmund felt gauged his weakness like a gimlet. Kingsley told Philip that 'much will depend (and so much the better for him morally) on your boy's exertion during the next year', but the negotiations continued.

Throughout 1866, as Edmund worked at school in Teignmouth on the course that had been decided would best equip him for his lowly office, dozens of letters and commendations, promptings and soundings out, references and certificates buzzed back and forth among the high and mighty. Charles Kingsley wrote to the Lord Chancellor; then, fortunately, a lady guest of Kingsley's turned out to be not only an old friend of the Speaker of the House of Commons but also a great admirer of P. H. Gosse's books. The Hon. Edward Egerton MP also agreed to talk to the Speaker about Kingsley's protégé. On 25th June 1866 William B. Lushington, nephew of Lord Cranworth, wrote to Theodore Walrond, suggesting Kingsley write to both the Archbishop and the Speaker. Kingsley wrote to Dean Stanley because 'I know the Archbishop only slightly and could not ask him myself'. Kingsley reminded everyone that the candidate is 'the son of Mr Gosse . . . who . . . has deserved well of his country for popularizing natural history so gracefully as well as so soundly'. Urging his qualifications, Kingsley suggests 'the lad seems to have remarkable talents of the very kind which are suited in the British Museum. He has distinguished himself in local examinations; has shown spontaneously great facility for statistics, geography, cataloguing etc and is now (by Panizzi's advice) making himself a good modern linguist'.

By July, there was a new Librarian. There was also a new Lord Chancellor, and Kingsley was annoyed to find it was Lord Chelmsford, 'whom I don't know the least . . . But I shall be in town the end of this week and will fish for him. I don't doubt we have mutual friends'. All should be well, he thought, as 'we can consider ourselves pretty sure of the Speaker and the Archbishop'. He begged Gosse to send back the Archbishop's and the Speaker's letters as his daughters wanted them for their autograph collection.

P. H. Gosse had of course written to Thomas Edgelow at Thorn Park School urging him to do his part in securing Edmund's future career:

I have procured him a grammar and a dictionary of the Swedish . . . I do not of course expect that your masters should *teach* him this language being out of the ordinary course. All I ask is that you will arrange his studies so that he will have six hours each week to devote to his Swedish books. Another point is his handwriting. This is at present inelegant, even scrawling; a neat handwriting would be indispensable in the office we are seeking. You write a neat hand yourself. Can you not *teach* my boy handwriting? . . . You should set him good copies, see to his mode of holding the pen, to the formation of his letters, especially capitals and criticize the copy with him when it is done.

The father, in fact, threatened to remove Edmund at the end of the next quarter unless there was some improvement in this respect – but really he would like him to stay at school until he was seventeen and eligible for the job. 'I had made Willy draw me up a syllabus of his previous studies and the hours devoted to each. In this I have *crossed* such as I wish him henceforth to forego.' He suggested how Edmund should spend the twelve hours gained.

Edmund had had splendid results, as Kingsley had noted, in the December 1865 Senior Cambridge examinations. He had passed with first class honours; in English he was third in the whole of England and in German fifth. Now he had a good last year at school, the year he was sixteen, reading avidly, improving his languages as well as his handwriting. At one stage, he went through a period of religious fervour, mingled and confused with emotions aroused by Shakespeare and Keats, as much as by Wesley and the Bible. In one moment of exaltation, he begged that the Lord Jesus would come and take him to Himself before he had gone out into the world and been led into temptation. But the Lord did not come – and he knew, though it would be many years before he admitted it, that for him the Lord would never come. Certainly no divine intervention would save him from the Reading Room at the British Museum.

When Edmund finally came to fill in his application, in very neat handwriting, on his seventeenth birthday, he was able to write:

> I can speak English
> German
> I can write French
> I can read Greek
> Latin
> Italian

I have a rudimentary acquaintance with Danish [which presumably included Swedish] and Hebrew.

I have a somewhat extensive knowledge of English literature, English history, Geography, Euclid and Arithmetic.

They were impressive enough qualifications for someone who was to be little more than a copying clerk. He certainly knew a great deal more about the culture and languages of the modern world than if he had gone to one of the great public schools. It was at this period that J. A. Symonds, who would become his friend, lamented that the boys at Harrow, who knew the difference between Apelles and Pindar and could write a good essay on the wars of Sulla and Marius, did not know whether Dryden, Sir Joshua Reynolds, Claude Lorraine and Wordsworth were celebrated for painting or for poetry.

On 13th December 1866 Charles Kingsley at last wrote to P. H. Gosse 'I heartily congratulate you and your lad.' Thirteen and a half months after the first enquiry, on December 11th, Edmund William Gosse, aged seventeen, had been elected at a meeting of the Trustees of the British Museum to fill an empty vacancy. His appointment as a Junior Assistant or Transcriber on probation began on 22nd January 1867. It would be confirmed as a permanent appointment in twelve months' time if Mr Gosse gave satisfaction.

In September, anticipating success, P. H. Gosse had written to Anne Buckham, an old friend in Tottenham, asking if she could find lodgings for Willy. She replied to suggest she could not do better than to receive the dear boy herself. For a guinea a week he could have a comfortable bedroom and take his meals with her. She was very fond of young people. The house, 6 The Terrace, White Hart Lane, was 'a little out of the high road, quite country and the railway omnibus sets down at the end of the lane'. Miss Buckham assured her 'dear Brother in the Lord' that there would be many who would welcome the dear Boy to Tottenham 'especially as he is one united to us in Christian fellowship'.

And so Edmund came to London, vulnerable, apprehensive, but full of his own energies and considerable ambitions. He realized there was one thing he had not left behind with the childish things in Marychurch. His dedication had come with him. He was still caged in the bars of that special cage, and in his ear he always heard – if no longer with the background of the roaring sea – his father's voice, echoing his mother's: 'Come my lamb and walk with me.'

Sometimes he could hear Christ's own clear voice: 'Lo! I am with you always, even to the end of the world. Come unto me all ye that are heavy laden and I will refresh you.' It was still in the Scriptures, not in the world, that he would seek for answers to justify himself and to arm himself against his father. But he was beginning to know that his ways would be other ways.

3

The Assassin behind the Tree

THE FATHER WAS relieved to have found the son such respectable lodgings. Anne Buckham and her other lodger and friend, Mary Ann Baker, were Brethren – members of the Brook Street Meeting. They had known Edmund's mother. Miss Buckham was fifty-seven and Miss Baker nearly seventy; it was the older woman who became Edmund's particular friend. But both were 'most charming and very gentle'. Edmund lived with them for nearly eight years and they treated him like a favourite nephew – sharing his interests, listening to his poems and translations, keeping an eye on him. There was no doubt that the Tottenham house was a home from home. Edmund always referred to them as his aunts.

Miss Baker particularly interested him. 'Riches and position in society would have been hers had she been content to be *in* the world.' As a small child, years before in Bristol, she had been a pupil at the famous female academy run by Hannah More – the author of that overstimulating fiction *Coelebs in Search of a Wife*. (And Hannah More's childhood nurse had tended the dying Dryden. Edmund was always to enjoy that sort of connection.) When Miss Baker was herself dying, in her eighty-ninth year, she could still repeat the whole of the Gospel of St John without hesitation. Miss Buckham would go to bed early but Edmund and Miss Baker sat up late at night talking over supper in the kitchen, with the cats, and not all their talk was of God – though in her memorial notice she was said to have 'spent her life in prayer and praise' and to have 'needed no other book but the bible'.

This was comforting for Philip Henry Gosse at home in Marychurch, worrying ceaselessly about the world, the flesh and the devil and their designs on his beloved son. In theory, conduct meant little to Philip Henry Gosse. 'Vision, the condition of grace, was everything.' But in practice, of course, he tried to examine Edmund's conduct. The Museum itself was a possible den of iniquity. Philip wanted to know absolutely everything about it. He asked Edmund for a sketch plan of the various offices. 'Your room, I see, looks into a "street"; yes, but what street? If this is Montague Street, as I think, I can pretty well understand your whereabouts.' Philip knew the Museum well, of course, from all those silent hours of studying birds nearly twenty years before. But Edmund, naturally, would not be silent. The world and its beguiling conversation would be with him. 'I am glad you like your companions,' Philip wrote to Edmund in February 1867, a few weeks after he had begun work. 'Tell me plainly, is their conversation such as you can listen to without defilement? I do not mean, is it other than secular? This I could not expect; political, metaphysical, argumentative, jocose, bantering, all this it might be, of course; but tell me whether it is lascivious . . . I know what office talk was when I was young.' He remembered Poole and Newfoundland, and trembled.

Philip's letters were full of advice about the most trivial things – advice one might have thought he could have given Edmund years before. Telling him to write and thank Charles Kingsley for all his help, he said 'Begin your letter at least one third down on the first page.' He suggested Edmund should keep an 'orderly record of letters received' and complete accounts of everything he spent. He should, of course, give a tithe to the Lord. 'It might seem to you that £9 a year would be a great deal for you to give away; but I am sure you would be no poorer in the long run.' 'Whatever you can lay by at the year's end . . . I will double it.' The father asked the son to keep a journal and send regular instalments home. ('A very useful task,' Edmund admitted, 'but extremely irksome.') Philip criticizes the boy's handwriting. He observes his punctuation is 'very loose and defective'. He wants him to write more fully. 'You spoke one week of being out every evening. What sort of "out"?' He chides him for 'insufficient stamping' and for not writing more frequently: 'A great many kind inquiries always besiege us on Sundays about you. We felt rather cheap, last Sunday, to have to say "We have not heard from him now for over a week!"'

In another letter Philip suggested that Edmund might find a book on Etiquette in that enormous catalogue he was working on. 'Look it over in the dinner hour. You would pick up many hints worth knowing – with much rubbish doubtless.' But above all, of course, the letters were crammed with worries about the state of Edmund's soul. 'My solicitude has never been that you should not love *me* (of that I had no doubt) but that you should not love *God*. Who should give a child holy counsel but a father?'

Through this interrogation, this assault by counsel, advice and criticism, Edmund remained apparently perfectly good-tempered.

Philip admitted 'I do not sugar my words but treat you as a manly antagonist, who can stand hard knocks.' And Edmund could. His letters in reply bear no trace of the fearful boy he recorded years later, cowering on the dusty velvet in the railway carriage. At this stage, he felt he had nothing to hide. ('Your account of your evenings is quite satisfactory. We are glad you devote an evening to German.') But he never took criticism lying down. He stood up to it, answered it, and accused his father in his turn when he seemed to go too far; but always with a loving tone. Philip had to apologize more than once for his letters. 'Pardon me if my arrows are too sharply pointed.' 'I am sorry that you found one drop of bitter in my last. You must not think that, whenever I suggested any improved mode of doing anything, I am displeased with what is done. As your father (and you know, a somewhat critical one), I freely suggested some things worth knowing, now that you are a growing man. Let me say once for all that it would greatly hamper me in giving you fatherly counsels of suggestions in practical matters if I thought you would feel shamed, as if I had imputed fault. All that you have done since you have been in London . . . has given me the most entire satisfaction . . . and has elicited my constant thanksgiving to God for having given me a son in every respect so good.' 'It is a delight to me to talk with a child so loving and so beloved.'

It was ten years since his mother's death. 'If she can look down and see you now, I think she adoringly owns that her prayers have been answered.' Edmund had read the words in one of her own tracts to good avail:

> Young men, who are expecting soon to leave the quiet and restraint of your parents' home, let me say a word to you.
>
> Perhaps you are looking forward with eagerness to the uncontrolled liberty before you, anticipating with delight the pursuit of pleasure, without the necessity of giving account to anyone of your conduct. Pause and reflect! 'The wages of sin is death; but the gift of God is eternal life.'

'"He that begetteth a wise child shall have joy of him." This I have found true and know I shall find true,' Philip wrote, 'O keep close to God, and He will preserve you from the paths of the destroyer. My son, if sinners entice thee, consent thou not . . . Let me find you pure in heart, simple in manners, undefiled with tobacco-smoke, or anything else, untouched by any of the abominations of modern puppyism.' He should never forget that the Coming of the Lord draweth nigh.

At times, of course, the boy did forget. And the Department of Printed Books in the British Museum was full of puppyish sinners – fellow assistants, transcribers and copying clerks. One of Edmund's main jobs from 9 am to 4 pm was to copy out slips of author's names and works into the great manuscript catalogue. In 1867, Edmund wrote years later, the Department 'was not the admirably equipped and neatly disciplined institution which students know and value to-day'.

Great laxity prevailed among the assistants and librarians, whose standard of accuracy was low, and their zeal that of the Church of Laodicea. If attempts were made to stir these drones, the reply was obvious that they were so meanly paid and so villainously housed that neither activity nor assiduity could be expected from them. Into this dull hive I was thrust, a young bee as idle as the best of them; I have nothing to say here of the queer, even grotesque conditions of life in that mysterious fortress or cage of steel and leather in which my days were spent. But one advantage, unforeseen by those who appointed and those who neglected me, pursued my official indolence.

When the small amount of work demanded from the slaves, by slave drivers even lazier than themselves, had been performed, we transcribers in the Printed Book Department enjoyed an almost unlimited leisure. Cricket was not unpractised in the remoter galleries; less audacious spirits cultivated the pencil or the jew's-harp. My own diversion was reading, ceaseless devouring of the printed page. I believe that the Library is nowadays – I am sure very properly – closed to youths of 17 or 18, but there was no-one then to check me or say me nay. Through the long silent afternoons, immersed in the curious odour of slowly decaying calf-skin, I would stand in the Upper Gallery of the King's Library or among the Garrick Plays, absorbing with ceaseless appetite the obscurer parts of seventeenth-century literature.

Edmund found the work as the years went by infinitely tedious and the physical conditions often distressing. In summer he baked palely like a crumpet in that singularly horrible underground cage, made of steel bars. There were the fire-proof steel floors under the steel ceilings with the steel ladders in between. Outsiders had a romantic view of his work, with such congenial colleagues, among such treasures – but hour after hour he would have to trace with a stencil, half a dozen times, the title of each new book. And afterwards the slaves remembered 'the unpleasant severity, the official discourtesy and the irritating surveillance, the pedantry and red tapeism of those weary, alien, sodden years at the Museum'.

That last phrase was Théophile Marzials', and he was to become a close friend. *He* was certainly a sinner. It was Marzials who made hay once while the Superintendent was out of the Reading Room. The Superintendent was the Rev. Frederick Laughlin, eventually dismissed from the cataloguing staff for threatening to use a revolver against a colleague in the Department. He had gone out and his juniors were amusing themselves in various ways (those jew's-harps perhaps) when he unexpectedly returned. Marzials had climbed to an upper gallery and was not aware of it. Marzials leant over the railing 'looking with his wide aureole of golden hair like the Blessed Damozel, and smiled. There was no response. Dead silence save for the droning quills. Leaning still further out, he boomed down on the workers below, "Am I or am I *not* the Department's darling?" ' Laughlin gave him one look and Marzials fled. Edmund could hear his footsteps on the metal stairways, echoing until they seemed to fade away into infinity.

Marzials was a composer and a poet – later he became addicted to Dr Collis Browne's Chlorodyne and to boys: 'With Jack today and Tom tomorrow,' J. A. Symonds would report. Marzials loved Edmund and sometimes set his poems to music. Later Marzials and Gosse would go together to visit William Bell Scott through whom Edmund would meet the Pre-Raphaelites, but that was not yet. In 1867, his friends were the other junior assistants, especially Dorset Eccles and Charley Walker. Neither of them cared much for poetry. 'Walker is strongest in a brilliant vein of diableries and persiflage, which is much opposed to poetry.' Diableries, indeed. But to Edmund's relief, Walker was 'very nearly a Nonconformist'. He could tell his father that one night, after a long walk across the stubble fields (so nearly in the country was White Hart Lane), before they parted, they had prayed together, just the two of them. So acceptable was Walker that Edmund would actually take him to Marychurch to stay at Sandhurst in the summer of 1869. 'An ungodly person I could not receive as a guest,' Philip wrote, 'but with Walker there would be no objection.' Walker 'is one who loves the Lord, besides being your friend'.

Edmund was still seeing a good deal of his old unconverted Marychurch friend, Mansel Dames, the one who had been at Mr Meneer's school with him and was to go to India in October 1870. He now lived in Clapham and the son sent his father the following account of a visit in the hot summer of 1868. A few days earlier he had suggested he looked up each day at 'the leaden firmament, with a horrible expectation of being served up with greens and potatoes'. 'What an oven the earth is.'

Last evening I went to the Dameses at Clapham. They have a very nice quiet little house far away from any noise but the universal shriek of the myriad railways that interlace just there . . . In one large room upstairs the three boys sleep and there was set up a spare bed for me, but the heat was far too intense for sleep.

At last M. and I got out of the window into the gutter and dangled cautiously over the parapet. The situation would have been breezy but there was no breeze. It would have been cool but the stones had not forgotten the sun. Still it was the breeziest and coolest possible and we sat there a long time entertaining Clapham with a lively delineation of desolate albatrosses blown on to some unfriendly shore, or anything else, except ghosts whom the liveliest fancy could not imagine in Clapham. It was an interesting thing to sit there in the clear summer night and see London flaring in the North and maniac lights dashing along attached to invisible trains and the dull sky enlivened by occasional flash fireworks from Cremorne . . . After a while the albatrosses crept home and were lost to Clapham, and soon after to consciousness.

The father's comment was: 'You two boys sitting in night shirts on Dames's housetop must have been an edifying spectacle in the small hours. I am thankful you did not take the short cut into the street.' There was no word of reproach or disapproval.

On the other hand, when Edmund describes in detail an August weekend visit to Dorset Eccles's home at Thornton Heath, the father is in anguish. There was Edmund spending the Lord's Day in the house of a known and professed infidel. 'It seems hard,' he wrote, 'to requite your love and confidence by reproof.' But again and again he does. In an essay on Samuel Butler many years later, Edmund Gosse wrote: 'It is true that a boy who writes to his father and mother . . . is constrained to resign himself to certain innocent hypocrisy. Very few children are able to send to their parents, and very few parents are able to endure from their children, a perfectly sincere description of their crude sentiments during adolescence.'

Of course Edmund censored his revelations ('We are in ignorance of all the details of your daily life, except what you yourself tell us'). But really he was amazingly frank and his father did find it hard. The Eccles weekend was full of 'roses and raptures'. They sat around talking over the midday meal. 'I do not know a more congenial place for talk than a dinner-table with four people sitting round it.' He would feel that all his life, though usually with more than four. 'The chief characteristic of the day' at Thornton Heath 'was its *dolce far niente* character, a rare treat to one whose Sundays are usually so tiring.' In the afternoon they lay in the sun with Mrs Eccles, his friend's young wife, whispering silvery nothings to the babies. They killed wasps and ate greengages.

It seemed small consolation that that Sunday morning he had been to the parish church with Mrs Eccles (finding, to his Nonconformist taste, the sermon stilted and conventional) and that he sat up late at night, when the Eccleses had gone to bed, studying the 1st Epistle to the Thessalonians and praying.

His father thanked him for writing so fully. 'It is very sweet to think that we see our darling boy as he is, and not, like the moon, only his show-side.' But he went on: 'I want to see you cherishing the same feelings of sensitive honour, gratitude and love towards the Lord Jesus that you do towards me. You would not dine with my enemies, however witty and well-behaved.' He told him again and again that his first duty was to be true to Christ. He must not care about what men thought of him. But of course he always did. The boy saw it was his duty in this world 'to soften men's hearts and not to harden them'. Bravely, he called his father's theology narrow and his father replied: 'Is it narrower than God's? Does it not seem narrow to you because you have imbibed the lax, broad notions of such fascinating writers as Kingsley, instead of making the written Word your only standard of truth?' It was impossible to argue with him but Edmund went on trying. He would accuse his father from time to time of not listening to other people's views, but P. H. Gosse was 'more formidable in argument than the Numidian lion'.

Edmund went on, for many years after leaving home, for far longer than he suggests in *Father and Son*, trying to work out his own form of belief. He did not really want, as he suggests in *Father and Son*, 'to be a godless child'. In fact he longed to believe and accept. What he could not believe and accept was that Christ wanted him to live the sort of life his father suggested was the only way to keep himself unspotted by the world. We tend to think of the Victorian period as a time of religious devotion, when it was easy to remain in the fold. But P. H. Gosse was not alone in seeing enemies on every hand. *The Sunday at Home*, a family magazine for Sabbeth reading, in one of its 1873 issues refers to 'this age of scepticism and worldliness'.

Edmund was not afraid of the world. He wanted to go out and meet people, converted and unconverted, the saved and the sinners. He saw that separation from the world led to spiritual pride as well as lonely evenings. He had been brought up to believe that he must not relax in the company of the unconverted, that he must only consort with them in order to teach them and bring them to the true Christ. When he first discovered that he sympathized with and enjoyed people for themselves, without any impulse to save them, he was staggered. That is his own word.

In Marychurch, Edmund had never felt he could visit the parish church, let alone the Puginesque cathedral with its allegiance to Rome. In London he was braver; his father reacted like this: 'I see you are captivated with the liturgy of the Church of England. Beautiful it confessedly is . . . and if the object of the assembling of the Church of God were the gratification of a refined taste this "beautiful liturgy" would be a complete success.' He goes on and on: 'O my Willy! Read the Epistle to the Ephesians; and then re-read the Liturgy and say whether *both* can truly give the status of the same body. You profess to love *truth* and I believe you do. What is beauty of phrases, devoid of truth?' In the same letter the father suggests that Edmund might join them at Poole that summer and continues 'I am glad you have a Spenser. Is it his Opera Omnia? Or only *The Faerie Queene?*'

Spenser was in fact the subject of Edmund's earliest appearance in print. On 10th October 1868, the *Athenaeum* in its Miscellanea column carried 'a few lines on an interesting point in the literary life of Ed. Spenser', by E. W. Gosse, who had just had his nineteenth birthday. Written in measured, learned tones, it discussed the question of the dating of a sonnet which casts light on whether Spenser ever finished *The Faerie Queene*. It shows a tendency Gosse was often to show: to use poems as direct and reliable biographical statements – though as a poet he would discourage his readers from doing the same. In old age, he was to call this *Athenaeum* note 'precocious and absurd' and to say it was the only piece accepted out of dozens sent out. 'I sent contributions to every periodical of any respectability and invariably they were returned.'

A very large proportion of the words between father and son dealt in fact not with religion but with literature, and in particular with poetry. At times, Edmund saw poetry as part of the path away from his father. His assertion of himself as a poet, with his own ideas and his own individuality, was certainly an important part of his growing up and his growing away from Marychurch and the Brethren. But, in fact, Philip shared his passion for poetry. It was 'the one art by which he was vividly affected'. Wordsworth, Gray, Cowper and Southey were at his finger tips; he never tired of quoting certain favourite passages. He liked Southey because he thought him 'the best naturalist among the English poets'. He loved Milton too, though with some theological reservations. Surprisingly perhaps, in later life, he admired

Swinburne and Rossetti more than Tennyson and Browning. Sometimes he would show himself to be a more astute and sensitive critic than his son.

P. H. Gosse maintained he was glad that Edmund had decided for literature rather than science. 'I joyfully admit the blamelessness and freedom from danger of poetic literature in comparison with science – the science of *this* age. I have repeatedly thanked God . . . that He had not allowed you to follow your father's line of natural science but had led your tastes in another direction.' He recalled that Edmund had told him that he got his poetic power in direct answer to prayer. 'Did not you tell me that at school you had asked in prayer for the power to make verse and immediately after you found the power and used it! Surely you told me that as a fact?' The father admitted that 'the prevalent tendency of poetry is certainly not towards scepticism. Where it *is* evil, it is rather to sensuousness and lasciviousness. These are the rocks for a young Christian poet to avoid. Another, yet more dangerous, is the mawkish sentimentalism which idolizes man and nature.'

Philip Gosse was as worried about Edmund's *taste* as about his beliefs. (He always maintained that he never worried about Edmund's morals – 'I do not imagine you are doing anything morally wrong, that be far from you, and far from me to suspect.') Father and son disagreed fundamentally about F. W. Myers, a young Cambridge don whose poem *St Paul* was published that year, 1867. Edmund read George Meredith's review in the *Fortnightly* and rushed out to buy it 'with one of the half-crowns that were then scarce with me'. He read it with avidity, relieved to find poetry he admired on a subject he felt his father would approve. He read it to Miss Baker and she was intensely moved by the poem 'and gave away a great many copies, but in every case, with a brush of black paint, she turned the Puseyite cross into a star before she distributed the books'.

P. H. Gosse was disturbed by more than the Papish cross. He wrote to Edmund on 1st February 1868: 'We value the love which prompted your sending [*St Paul*]; but was it also sent to indicate to us the standard of poetic excellence to which you aspire? I hope not indeed . . . the noblest poetry is ever the simplest.' He wonders how on earth Edmund can admire such stuff, such 'turgid rant'. 'Would Gray or Cowper or Shelley ever have thrown together such words as these?' Myers is nothing but a poor ass. 'I am afraid lest you take up this hollow, sickly, fashionable tone of mere human sentiment and mistake it for godliness.' He continues through twenty closely-written pages.

Philip was particularly concerned at this point about poetry because

Edmund had raised the question of publishing a book of his own poems and had asked his father if he would pay for it. Philip said: 'You *know* that I do not grudge you the money, but I am very anxious that you should make no mistake, at the very hinge and pivot of your life. To make your debut before the world in authorship would be a very momentous step indeed for you. However much you might regret it afterwards, it could never be recalled.' He spoke of the raw experience of eighteen. Moreover Edmund was talking about a subscription list of friends and Philip was scornful: 'I have never asked a single friend to buy a book of mine and I never would . . . If a man's works cannot command purchasers, they are not worth the pushing . . . If a publisher refuses to risk a work in his own line, the work is not worth the *author's* risk . . . Wait a while.'

His father was far too inclined to accept the judgment of one of Edmund's young colleagues whom Edmund had foolishly quoted. He was working on a series of poems on the legends of Devon, and indeed had written to his father for some background material. ('I thought you might like to aid your ambitious boy in his attempt – I want to drag my beloved county up Parnassus with me if I can.') But when he showed his legends to a friend at the Museum, 'he gave me no encouragement'. He 'honestly, yet severely, almost cruelly criticized me'. When his father agreed with his friend, Edmund responded with some spirit: 'You seem rather to take for granted that I have not the least chance of success simply from the authority of a young critic of whom you know nothing . . . You tell me you are praying to God to give me a new object of attention, so that it evidently appeared to you lost labour to pray for more skill in the present object.' But he would not turn his hand to anything else. 'Never! Poetry or nothing. At least I will not give up hope because perfection [has not been] gained at eighteen . . . – I constantly ask you for real analytical criticism and you *never* give it. I feel sick and stupid. I should feel better if I could talk to you.'

He was reading the Pre-Raphaelites – not Rossetti until the following year (he was to be enormously excited when the *House of Life* appeared in the *Fortnightly Review* in 1869) but William Morris and Swinburne. Late in 1867 he had bought a *Pall Mall Gazette* on Taunton Station with a review of Morris's *Jason* and the same year spent six shillings on *The Defence of Guinevere* and had to defend it against his father's abuse of it as 'rubbishy minor verse'. Swinburne, who was to play a major rôle in his life, had early dazzled him with *Atalanta in Calydon. Poems and Ballads*, published in Edmund's last year at school, had 'roused a scandal unparalleled since Byron left England exactly half a century before'. Swinburne was, as Edmund himself put it years later, 'a flaming creature, instinct with genius whose vagaries were the wonder and terror of Society' – that Society with its 'intense respect for Mrs Grundy in her Sunday satin'.

It was to this flaming creature that the young Christian poet wrote for advice in September 1867, a week or two before his eighteenth birthday. And Swinburne, although, as he said, he had not much time for correspondence, returned a non-committal kindly letter, a sort of model for all established poets approached by aspirants.

I certainly do not urge you to resign the habit of writing if it gives you pleasure without interfering with other things; I have no right to give such counsel. What prospect of growth and advance in the art you may have is impossible to say. Less promising verses than yours have perhaps been the forerunners of success, and more promising ones of ultimate failure. A man's first attempts can never possibly afford reasonable ground for pronouncing decisively whether he is qualified or disqualified for the attainment of his hope. One thing, while sympathising with your wishes, I do advise you against; too much thinking and working in one channel. Neither you nor I can tell what kind of work you will in the long run be able to accomplish; but it is certain that good or ill success in this matter of poetry need neither make nor mar a man's work in life. I understand the impulse to write of which you speak, and the pain of checking or suppressing it; nor do I tell you to suppress or check it; only not to build upon it overmuch. To fret yourself in the meantime with alternations of hope and fear is useless if you are to succeed, and more than useless if you are not. I always thought so for myself, before I had sent anything to press. One wishes of course for success as for other pleasant things; but the readier we hold ourselves to dispense with it, if necessary, the better. I am not old enough to preach, but I am old enough to tell you how I thought at your age of this matter, which of course was to me as serious an aspiration as to you now. To encourage or discourage another is a responsibility I cannot undertake, especially as I think one ought to need or heed neither encouragement or discouragement.
With good wishes, Yours truly A. C. Swinburne.

Philip Gosse was incensed that Edmund had written to Swinburne. Had he not recently been described as 'the libidinous laureate of a pack of satyrs?' Had not he been addressed as 'Algernon Swinburne, Pagan, suffering persecution from the Christians . . .'? Of course, Edmund need not have told his father about the letter, but he did, and to Philip's criticism replied, 'Why do you ask me: "How could you, as a Christian, seek his acquaintance?" I did not. Merely as one gentleman to another, I asked his judgment on a purely literary matter i.e. his opinion of my verse. Surely you do not think I was so mad as to suppose that such a demand would lead to any further introduction?'

They did not meet for another three years; but in the summer of 1868 the young admirer saw the famous poet in dramatic circumstances. Gosse later wrote two accounts of that first sight of someone he was to know so well. Typically the dates he gives differ. It was either July 9th or 10th, either in the late afternoon or the evening, 'that I first cast eyes on the poet who was at that time the divinity, the object of feverish worship to every budding artist and faltering singer in England. The reason was accidental, the circumstances painful; it is enough to say that the idol was revealed to the juvenile worshipper at a startling moment of physical suffering and distress, and that the impression was one of curious terror, never . . . to be wholly removed. I shall not lose that earliest and entirely unanticipated image of a languishing and pain-stricken Swinburne, like some odd conception of Aubrey Beardsley, a *Cupido crucifixus* on a chair of anguish'.

What had happened was that Swinburne had fallen in a faint while working in the Reading Room of the British Museum, and had cut his forehead superficially against the iron staple of the desk. Edmund was walking along a corridor when he was passed by a couple of silent attendants carrying along in a chair what seemed to be a dead man. 'I recognised him instantly from his photographs which now filled the shop windows. His hanging hands, closed eyelids and red hair dabbled in blood presented an appearance of the utmost horror.'

Swinburne's own account is very low-key: 'I am none the worse for a fainting fit brought on by the damnable unventilated air of the Museum . . . I went early to the Brit. Mus. to look up certain references . . . fainted right out and in falling cut my forehead slightly.' The reason for the faint was not just that heavy air (which Edmund also used to complain about) but the fact that he was waiting to have lunch with someone who was late. It was not the late afternoon or evening. It is extraordinary how often Edmund's memory betrays him in trivial details. Compare his two published accounts (1912 and 1917), and Swinburne's letter, with the journal Edmund kept at the time but obviously couldn't put his hands on at the right moment years later:

Friday, July 10. 1868. This afternoon about two o'clock I was walking through the Reading Room when I saw a crowd of people in the passage by which readers enter. I heard someone had had a fit and on coming near recognised from the published portraits, the poet A. C. Swinburne. His great forehead, though bandaged, was bubbling with blood, and all his hair matted and gory. It was a great shock to me because unexpected and also happening to one whose works I know well and from whom I had had a letter . . . He had struck his forehead so violently against the staple of an iron ring as to make a gash 1½ inches long and penetrating to the bone.

So much for the slight cut and the truth of the eyewitness.

The British Museum was not short of poets at this period. Coventry Patmore had just resigned. (Gosse was to list Patmore and Swinburne as two of the three most influential friends of his early years – the third was John Leicester Warren, later Lord de Tabley.) As well as Marzials, there was Arthur O'Shaughnessy, whose first book in 1870 was praised by both Rossetti and Swinburne. In print Gosse was to call him 'the most blameless of gentle spirits', in a letter, 'that poor idiot'. O'Shaughnessy worked in the Natural History section of the Museum and Edmund remembered his amazement at finding that 'our official ichthyologist was writing poetry'. O'Shaughnessy worked in the very bowels of the building preserving fishes 'as graceful and pallid as himself'. Edmund used to tell a story that the poet didn't really know what he was doing and that, soon after his appointment, he let fall a number of fossilized fish skeletons, and fitted the parts together as they came to hand – the head of one fish with the tail of another, thus creating an entirely new species, which may well be in the Natural History Museum to this day. O'Shaughnessy used to go to Paris for his holidays before the 1870 war. He had been presented to Victor Hugo and brought Edmund 'authentic news of the Parnassians'.

Richard Garnett was at the Museum too. Later he and Edmund were to work closely on various projects. He had begun, like Edmund, as a copier of titles but was now a placer, which involved classifying and shelving new acquisitions. 'Those were the days,' Edmund wrote, 'when his activities were subterranean and before he emerged to public sight in the conning-tower of the Reading Room . . . He was always on his legs, moving from shelf to shelf . . . , weighing, placing, fitting in another tessera of the curious intellectual mosaic of his memory.' Knowing Garnett was part of Edmund's education. 'He would discourse with propriety of the sonnets of Shakespeare, and then, with no alteration in his voice, of those of some Portuguese of the sixteenth century, or some Pole of the nineteenth. He was among the earliest of those who admired Walt Whitman with moderation, Baudelaire with discretion, Heine with enthusiasm . . .'

Heady stuff for the provincial boy, and it was no wonder that, in comparison, the worthy Brethren of Tottenham seemed rather dull. But Edmund persisted with his suburban Christian life. He spent some evenings with Dr Barnardo. 'He was young then and like a flame . . . I worked with him in the East End. I did not make a success of it: the people intimidated me, which was fatal.' He continued to teach in Sunday School for years. He cared about children and was good with them, though at Marychurch on one visit he was bothered by the children's fidgeting and not much cheered when one of the 'saints' remarked 'Well, Mr Edmund, if you'd a took the trouble to be more interestinger, the children would a got quiet.'

He had taught small Brethren for years before coming to London and continued the work at Brook Street, Tottenham. Early on, his father had written: 'I am thankful that you increasingly love your labour for the Lord and your dear children. He will, I trust, give you as cherished a place in their hearts as he has in those of the little ones here.' He found it hard in Tottenham trying to attract a few unconverted boys to the Young Men's Meetings; they soon gave up going. 'I cannot blame them,' Edmund wrote in his journal, 'the meeting is as dull as dull can be for those who have no vital interest in its exercises.' Six years later, in March 1873, he would still be in charge of the Brook Street Sunday School.

At times, he overdid things. Philip had been brisk earlier about the seven miles of walking he had to do every day – from White Hart Lane to Wood Green station, from King's Cross to the Museum – and back again in the evening. His father thought it should be no hardship with his long legs; but at one stage he did enquire tenderly, 'Are you doing too much?'

I think you are right and that I have over-wearied myself. I think going to too many meetings has been the principal error. When I come home tired with my seven miles of dreary drudge, I eat on Mondays, Thursdays, and alternate Wednesdays a hasty tea and then rush out again to the chapel, a mile and a half away, on Fridays my [German] class drags me in a like manner, though only as far as Lordship Lane. Of course if the meeting be an interesting and practical one, it excites me prodigiously and all this is fearfully exhaustive. I think I must give up all meetings save the Thursday YMPM, to me the most vital of all, until at all events I am stronger. 'The Spirit, truly, is willing, but the flesh is weak.' Visiting being a more thorough change of scene and not so ingrossingly important is less wearing.

Specious reasoning, perhaps, but Edmund convinced himself: 'It is my good fortune to be so circumstanced that I can do what is right, and what is my work, without the two clashing.' In fact, there were, there always were, strains and conflicts. He described his meetings with the Brethren as 'a little haven in the tempestuous ocean'. But 'it is very hard indeed to walk with Christ,' he had to confess, and that time his father found his honesty cheering: 'Do not be discouraged; if you were not earnestly trying to walk with Christ, you would not be aware of any great difficulty in the matter.'

'I have prided myself on writing nothing that should ever hinder anyone a hand's breadth on his journey heavenward,' he wrote to his father in another letter at this period. Philip had been beseeching him, as usual, to walk and work always 'under your Master's eye'. Edmund responded: 'A position in which I was conscious of the Master's eye averted would be a strange one. I have known what it was to walk with such a cloud of my own making around my head that I could not see the eye that saw me. But I am truly thankful it is not so now.' He had parted from many of his father's tenets – he no longer, for instance, believed in an elect, or in 'the inerrancy of Scripture'. But he still had faith in Christ and in the power of Christ's sacrifice to save him and bring him to God. The belief that he would always cling to was that 'a human being who has a conscience is generally most happy when obeying it'. It was the evangelical call to witness that he found the real stumbling block and which finally – but not yet – would alienate him from any form of professed religion. In self-defence, under the usual spiritual cross-examination, he once quoted Clough to his father:

> O let me love my love unto myself alone,
> And know my knowledge to the world unknown;
> No witness to the vision call,
> Beholding, unbeheld of all;
> And worship thee, with thee withdrawn, apart,
> Whoe'er, whate'er thou art,
> Within the closest veil of mine own inmost heart.

And Philip of course replied: 'Mellifluous lines, enough! But that is not what God asks of a converted man. It is not the luxury of meditation and the cloister, but the unwelcome effort to spread a knowledge of the truth.'

In 1869 Edmund was able to keep a lot of Philip's usual interrogation at bay by sending him reports of his newly-formed 'Tottenham Actinological Society' and filling much of his letters with comments on the activity in the aquarium Philip had supplied. He asked lots of questions so Philip would have to fill his letters with equally uncontroversial subject matter. Things did not go smoothly in spite of all P. H. Gosse's expert advice. Edmund sent lists of the 'thriving' and the 'precarious'. 'We begin to despair; our little community is dwindling more seriously.' His father suggests they should 'aerate the water, pouring it from a jug held at a height. And do not leave this to be done by the ladies; but take *your* share of it, doing it every evening till the whole tank boils and froths.'

Edmund went to his first dinner party that May. He was invited by Jean Ingelow, 'the excellent and then highly-praised poetess'. She was herself an amateur naturalist and had had some aquarium correspondence with P. H. Gosse. In February 1869, she wrote to him, 'I felt much interested in your son: he has evidently a highly poetic temperament, – and I hope to see more of him.' This was Edmund's fortune – nearly everyone throughout his life hoped to see more of him. Of course the father was full of advice for that first dinner party. 'The honour of the Lord Christ is in your keeping.' He says Edmund should stand up for Christ as he would for his own father. 'Wine will probably be abundant; drink very cautiously. Go with prayer beforehand; be on your guard and work circumspectly.'

Edmund reported it had been a quiet affair and that really he didn't much enjoy 'drawing-room small talk' (later he would), that he had felt a 'horridly awkward self-consciousness'. Philip responded warmly, 'I had all the gaucheries of which you speak . . . I see more and more and wonder as I see, in how many things your idiosyncracy is moulded after mine; while in others you have quite a groove of your own.'

The grooves were, in fact, diverging month by month. The first real clash came in the summer of 1869, the same summer Charley Walker paid a brief visit to Sandhurst. Edmund had arrived alone at 12.50 am on a Sunday, leaving 'the world and the flesh and the Devil' behind, as he joked to John Blaikie, of whom we will hear much more. Edmund had plunged straight into the realities of life at Marychurch, going to chapel and hearing a Mr Harrison elucidate the exact manner in which the priest wrung off the fowl's neck 'and squeezed out the blood'. Edmund was always critical of preaching even in his most religious phases. He and Thomas Barnardo had listened to William Booth in the summer of 1868 – not long after he started the Salvation Army – and Edmund didn't think much of his preaching either. He was particularly scornful of snobs, including 'the most grievous twaddler Mr Saffery, who sickened us by telling us, as he paced with folded hands to and fro before the communion table, of the blessed experience of a lady of very high rank, with whom he had had much intercourse of late'.

Mr Harrison was not quite as bad as Mr Saffery but bad enough. 'After more lively and bloody talk, we came home to the frugal necessary meal.' Edmund was feeling rebellious, romantic, pagan.

He scribbled a verse to John Blaikie about the Brethren:

> Whose heads and hearts are fully crammed
> With that strange Calvinistic creed,
> Which leaves the courtesy of d——d,
> And tells you plainly you'll be damned.

He changed after lunch into 'eccentric' clothes and walked over the downs to Anstey's Cove, 'down the cliff with wild and maniac frenzy . . . where I stripped, heroically Leanderlike and swam through the tangle and whipcord into the quiet sea, came in, wrenched my shoulder blades in slipping down a gully, climbed up again, sank on the turf with quick faint pulse . . . wrote verses on a slab of white stone, sighed out a passionate ballad for my love, thought of tea and returned'.

He continued in that mood. His father saw 'horrid, insidious infidelity', working in his mind and heart with terrible energy. One morning in the hothouse, among the gorgeous waxed orchids, the enervated air soaked with the intoxicating perfumes of all those voluptuous flowers, Philip began to question him yet again: 'Are you walking closely with God? Is your sense of the efficacy of the Atonement clear and sound? Have the Holy Scriptures still their full authority with you?' Then Edmund's forbearance for once gave way. His replies were violent and hysterical. He begged to be left alone and demanded the right to live his own life.

The letters afterwards make painful reading. On 4th August 1869 Philip wrote:

> I can quite understand how my anxiety for you may be irksome; especially as I see how defective I am in tact and in the art of making things pleasant. The baby in Wordsworth is 'fretted with sallies of his Mother's kisses;' they tease him and he does not like them: yet they are the inevitable expressions of an unutterable unfathomable love. If I saw symptoms of typhus or of consumption in your body, should I not be anxious? How much more when I discern what I cannot but regard as alarming symptoms of spiritual disease? It is not that I have 'hard thoughts' of you. It is not a matter of blame, but of deep anxiety and sorrow. I know you love *me*; but do you love

God? I think of your dying Mother's prayers; of your early promise; of my joy and thankfulness when you avouched the Lord to be your Saviour; and I want to know what of this remains. You take your place still with the people of God; but is your faith 'the faith of God's elect'? This is what I am most anxious to know, and oh! how willing to believe.

Later, there was the long letter quoted at the end of *Father and Son*, which was actually dated 21st January 1870, months after he had returned to London. Edmund's account of the struggle between two temperaments suggests that this was the end of it – that at twenty (his birthday was in September 1869), the boy chose his own path and threw off once and for all the yoke of his 'dedication'. But in fact, as we have already seen, the struggle went on for years, and the young man continued to work for his heavenly father (those long years still to come in the Brook Street Sunday School, for instance) and to try to please his earthly one.

Part of Philip Gosse's trouble was that, though he seemed so encased in armour, so sure in all his ways, he had his own doubts. He actually needed Edmund's support and reassurance. There had been one extraordinary moment in 1868 when he admitted it: 'Your letter has revived and quickened my own drooping affection towards the Lord.'

The postal interrogation continued. 'Forgive the nuisance, for the sake of love,' P. H. Gosse once pleaded, sending pressed violets. And mostly it seemed Edmund could understand and forgive, but he no longer wrote as he had once done 'your letters are like angel-visits to me'. He would write of their 'threatening whiteness', which at breakfast destroyed the taste of his bacon, the flavour of his tea. But his long, reasoned answers continued for another three or four years, even when the warnings must have chilled his soul. In fact, he was never cowed or frightened in his responses. Exasperated, perhaps, even angry, but always brave and usually tolerant. He had learnt not to care, as he read words like these throughout 1870:

The awful future into which you are plunging, is midnight darkness. O Willy! my loved and cherished child! Is it indeed come to this? . . . The blinding tears fill my eyes as I write . . . You will say that you have a right to think for yourself . . . Of course . . . but have I not the right to counsel, to suggest, to entreat if I see you choosing fatal error . . . Have I not the right to *grieve*? . . .

Why will you consider my warnings and entreaties unkind? I see my child merrily pulling flowers in a wood and an assassin aiming at his life from behind a tree. I interrupt his sport with a loud cry of warning, and I am harsh and selfish for doing so?

Long afterwards, when his own son was leaving boyhood, Edmund would write: 'What a difference it would have made to me if my father would have allowed me to be his friend.' In *Father and Son* he would write 'I was his only friend', but in fact P. H. Gosse always felt the overwhelming responsibility, the lack of equality of fatherhood. They could not be friends; they could only always be father and son – but with all the tenderness that that can imply. I like to think of Philip Gosse, not thundering out his catechism, but helping Eliza with Edmund's birthday present – a pair of embroidered slippers to be sent to him in London: 'To save time I myself put in a few stitches.' I think of him, too, watching the bright green tree frogs in his fern house and taking his cat into his warm bed in the morning. There was much that was lovable about him – enough for Edmund to continue to try to be what he so much wanted over long, long years: 'my darling son, my pride, my joy, my crown'.

The father kept testing the son, remembering those plants growing near Tenby on that happy holiday so long before: 'As aromatic plants, when bruised, give forth their fragrance, so do you, under the wounded feelings produced by my jealous anxieties, yield most sweet and solacing evidences of grace and obedience and filial love.'

Money was another source of conflict. All that walking caused Edmund's boots to wear out rapidly. He had to order a new coat. His 'flannel drawers' were quite in rags when he finally bought some new ones for 11s 6d. Money 'oozes with fatal rapidity' through his fingers. His father considered 'a youth ought to save out of £100 a year, with so many perquisites as you have from me'. 'I wish I could understand money matters,' Edmund sighed in December 1868. At the end of each year, his 'stupid muddled accounts' would drive him half-wild. But he established good habits. All through his life he kept accounts. One can see exactly what he earned in any year and how much every holiday cost him. His father had very little reason to complain of Edmund's spending. 'I do not think I know a young man who spends so little on himself as I do,' Edmund claimed. Surely he was entitled to a few indulgences.

On 19th January 1870, he wrote a long letter of varied protest to Marychurch – the response to that last letter printed in *Father and Son*:

Your letter agitated me excessively and at night kept me quite sleepless till the grey of the morning. It is a terrible thing to any son when the father adopts towards him the tone which you increasingly affect; it must make him consider and weigh all his own conduct to see what can have justified so extraordinary a harshness. Much have I wondered and puzzled over it, but my conscience accuses me of no sin against your authority which can account for this behaviour.

When I first came to London, a child as inexperienced as it was possible to be, it was most natural and wise that you should chain me round with limitations and supervisions, warning here and forbidding there. But seeing now that for three years I have been more or less alone in the world, obliged in many ways to act for myself and use much painful vigilance, so that I have perforce gained the knowledge of the value of money and the needfulness of constant self-denial, I cannot tell why you should still with more bitter restrictions than ever, shut me up from those little indulgences, not, I make bold to say, frivolous or useless, which are the chief pleasure of my life. You are rich, that is you have a fairly large income and live in a quiet way, so that your allowances to me, were they as lavish as they are confined, would in no wise straiten you in any comfort. You have no other children to educate or provide for. I think I can most truly say that if you were poor or wanting money, it would be the greatest joy and pride to me to pinch and narrow myself in every way, that I might be no burden to you but a help. But when I know you have more money than you know how to do with (you have told me that you do not live up to your income) what reason or stimulus have I for this pinching and saving? Forgive me if I seem to speak strongly; I cannot understand the reason and motive of your letters and they pain me extremely.

His financial position was crucial to Edmund at this point. In March 1870 he informed his father that he wished to marry Mary Jane Johnson, the daughter of George and Martha Johnson of Cedar House, Tottenham High Road. He was still only twenty. Rather surprisingly, Edmund noted that P. H. Gosse was 'entirely favourable'.

But before we look at Mary Jane and the possibility of marriage, we must consider the progress of Edmund's poetry and of his friendship with J. A. Blaikie, with which his poetry was inextricably bound.

It will be remembered that, as early as the beginning of 1868, when he was just eighteen, Edmund had proposed that his father should help to pay for publication of a book of poems. Philip had encouraged him to wait a while. Edmund was burning for recognition as a poet. Poetry was what really mattered. He spoke later of 'his implacable fanaticism for verse' at this time – a time when, he said, 'a man might trudge forth from his house at the morning hour and meet angels in the street'. Certainly he might see Swinburne threading his way through the traffic unseeingly but unharmed – or Walter Pater at the Royal Academy, seeming more poet than critic, in a silk tie of brilliant apple green.

Edmund once said he started to write verse in 1857, the year he was eight, the year of his mother Emily's death. By 1870 he had had very little published – one poem on Anstey's Cove (which Philip had proudly sent to Kingsley) had appeared in the Torquay Directory. But he had tried most of the magazines and been rejected. 'I am weary; I desire to be in print.' Only a book, he felt, would establish his claim to belong to the company of his heroes. His first book was to be a shared volume with J. A. Blaikie. *Madrigals, Songs and Sonnets* (150 copies) was finally published at the end of 1870 by Longmans, Green and Co. but not at the publisher's expense. Edmund was just twenty-one; John Blaikie was twenty-two.

Their friendship began with letters. Mrs Curtis (she in whose house Eliza Brightwen had been lodging when she first met Philip Gosse) had brought them together. She wrote to John Blaikie, 'I think your critical mind would do him good by contact and interchange. I think you would do each other good.' She commended Edmund to John as 'so lively, so frank and open, yet very gentle. Like you, he finds very few who *really care* for poetry.' Both young men loved Mrs Curtis. She soothed and comforted them through the problems of putting the book together – problems largely to do with P. H. Gosse's concern – and it was eventually dedicated to her. Edmund paid tribute to John in 1918 when, on Blaikie's death, his brother returned Edmund's letters.

My correspondence with J.A.B. began in January, 1868. The stimulus was enormous. I read more than ever before or perhaps since. The B.M. being open to me, I browsed without restraint. The year 1868 – when I was 18–19 – was the time when my intelligence developed with the greatest rapidity and Blaikie had the principal share in this awakening. We wrote to one another incessantly.

John Blaikie was the son of a wine merchant in the City. He went to Torquay for his health just at the time Edmund was leaving school and there met Mrs Curtis. He was a sufferer all his life from a particularly debilitating form of asthma, which reduced his energy and interfered with all his plans. He published only one further book of poems and made no reputation, but the Book of Gosse, Edmund's lifelong record of visitors, bears witness to the fact that they continued friends all through their lives. And a number of letters show Edmund trying to secure him a sort of situation (1883), publication (1893), a small pension from the Civil List, and finally a refuge for his old age (1915).

Their first meeting was not particularly successful. 'We hardly agree at all,' Edmund commented. 'He is a very rank Tory . . . and thinks meanly of Dissenters from Milton downwards. He is queer and rather uncouth in appearance.' Before they had even met, they were frank critics of each other's poetry. Gosse decided, with adolescent frankness, that Blaikie's master-vice was 'crudity of thought and expression' and he expected the same treatment back: 'Here is a little madrigal of mine for you to slash.' Gosse was keen to establish that he was no prudish, conventional puritan, throwing in a remark about Keats irritating his palate with cayenne pepper before enjoying wine. 'Delightful sensualist!' But he early on found one of Blaikie's poems too erotic for publication ('in these days one could not write so of a girl one really *loved*').

By their second meeting, when Edmund visited Blaikie's parents' home at Lewisham, he had decided John was a great treasure – 'he has found a niche sooner than usual in the temple of my heart'. 'We do not agreed much with regard to our poets, save on such standards as Shakspere, Shelley, Keats, Byron.' Particularly they disagreed on Longfellow: drivelling poetaster, said Edmund; splendid poet, said John.

The letters they exchanged are the sort of letters one very young poet would like to get from another – full of self-conscious wit, puns, quotations, allusions. (Hermaphrodite for Middlesex; Beery Musey for British Museum.) Writing from Devon, Edmund tells John he swam in a sea 'ruffled with dark ridges and voiceful as a hexameter from *Andromeda*'. They compare notes on what they are reading: Webster, Wordsworth, each other. They criticize and encourage in great detail both the poems themselves and each other's criticisms. John is particularly impressed by Edmund's poems, though they seem to us to be too full of 'melodious caverns of the deep', a 'drowsy sense', pondering on the ways of God and the inevitable nightingale. But his technical skill is at times remarkable, and there is plenty of real feeling and real observation among the conventionally poetic conceits and the pathetic fallacies. Edmund's long poem 'The Tomb in the Garden', in spite of or because of his father's interference, is an impressive achievement for a boy of twenty.

John tells Edmund very early on 'It is likely enough that in more senses than one I shall be a Hallam to you.' Edmund was to write that

Tennyson's hold was 'like that of an octopus upon us in our salad days'. But at this point they don't really seem to have much time for Tennyson. In fact, they are not at all impressed with the current poetry scene. Edmund scribbles a verse for John in October, 1869:

The Poetry of the Period

The few great names that linger are grown old,
    And, though one young voice rings out true and clear,
    The fields of verse are desolate and drear,
    And the fine heart of Poetry beats cold.
Some chant their creeds, audaciously secure;
    One whines diffusely of his London woes;
    One powerful singer swells the band of those
    Who sneer at all things wise and fair and pure;
Some maunder feebly of babe-innocence;
    One Western maniac *'yawps'* a turbid song;
    A dozen ladies warble soft and long;
    But none of these are bards in the true sense.
But we, dear friend, are born for nobler lays,
And yet may win sun-haired Apollo's praise.

The lines are neatly annotated: Tennyson, Browning by the first line; William Morris by the second. Swinburne is there, of course, and Walt Whitman. Certainly, though the verse hardly justifies his ambition, Edmund felt there was room on the mount.

John Blaikie sings Edmund's praise in rather more attractive doggerel:

    . . . and thou art favour'd
    By charioteering, bright-haired young Apollo!
    Or how could Dames approve or Blaikie follow
    With words of constant praise thy muse aspiring?
    Then go, sweet Youth! a blessing on thy lyreing!
    O rise above, and with my holy benison,
    The mangled mawkish strains of Alfred Tennyson!
    Nor let bright Swinburne in thy verse infuse
    The vice of one sick mind and twenty stews . . .

There is a great deal more in the same vein and in others, including a nice glimpse of a rustic Gosse:

Eyes! turn not round
Heart! echo no sound
At the strange sight which stays my flight,
As I go homeward bound!
Gosse on a gate sits munching!
On a white gate
At a pitiful rate
'Tis a noble swede he's crunching
Which a neighbouring field doth sweetly yield
For his poetic lunching!

They dream of fame together. Edmund writes to John on his twenty-first birthday 'What a vista opens before us, full of desire and danger . . . How shall we succeed? It seems to me very much in our own hands.' He thinks the clue to success lies in 'systematic self-training' and 'personal abnegation'. 'It has laid much on my mind . . . to strive after the creation of a new school of religious poetry' which would express not a narrow creed but 'the peculiar joyousness of the revived religion of our day.' He says how hopeless he had felt a year before but now he feels able to look 'past Christians to Christ himself'. With Philip watching his every word, it was difficult for him to imagine himself as anything else but a religious poet. And yet the religious poems, of course, were scrutinized even more thoroughly than the others. If there were no metrical objections, there were bound to be theological ones.

As early as August 1869 John had suggested they did a book together and Edmund was very taken with the idea – but they would need Philip Gosse's financial support (Blaikie was going to borrow his share without telling his father, much to Philip's disapproval). Philip still said, as he had said to Edmund two years earlier, 'Wait.' But he was coming round to the idea. Eliza surprisingly seemed more of an opponent. Philip was most concerned about how the boys would be able to cope with either fame or disappointment. If it were successful, 'the tendency will certainly be to make you more than ever in love with this evil world'. In June 1870 Edmund went to see Macmillan.

I left him feeling that I really was a very frumpery item in intellectual London. Certainly I never experienced so fully what I have always held, that Poetry, like Christianity, means the taking up of a cross and bearing much scorn from the world. In short, for the moment, I, even I, am depressed, but shall soon, I doubt not, recover good spirits. One repulse does not mean a defeat for life. Macmillan was very scornful at the idea of *joint* authorship; it would never do, he opined, even if we were as great as Clough and Fairford! (Who is this last poetical potentate?)

Philip finally agreed to back them but took over the whole thing. He negotiated with Longmans for them. Having pared down his first grand idea (based on his old natural history books) of a thousand copies to the more realistic 150, he subjected the enterprise to a typical minute scrutiny. John Blaikie is at first amazed. Is he really going to go 'through our poetics pronouncing what are and what are not publishable?' As usual, P. H. Gosse pulled no punches. In general he would accuse Blaikie of obscurity, uncouthness of language and ruggedness of expression. But Edmund came off even worse. Edmund's annotated copy of the book shows some instances of changes the father insisted on and the son could not accept. But he that pays the piper calls most of the tunes. Edmund to John, 6th May 1870:

The Critic of the West has raised his oracular voice and great is the fluttering among the doves. I send you your share of whipping, you get off better than I do, though poor Cecilia certainly deserves and needs a Women's Rights' Committee . . . He says we both use 'most' too often and that is true . . . He says 'Don't be frightened, you nor John, if the criticisms seem just a little trenchant. One does not do this sort of thing with gloves on. I want to anticipate and disarm adverse criticism by and by.'
He concedes to both of us beauty and power . . . Write him a graceful answer. I know it will delight him. He is a man that thinks much of appreciative expression.

Philip sent pages of detailed criticism: 'Falling leaves don't *moan*.' 'Cowper at Mundesley', a poem he rather admired, was marred for instance by one line. Can apple blossom time ever be correctly described as 'golden' in hue? Edmund wrote to John, 1st October 1870:

. . . Shameful indignation at the knowledge that such pain is done you by my flesh and blood, has kept me silent . . . I am in hopes that my effort . . . has at least drawn the electric wrath upon me instead of you, upon me who can better endure it and who do not care . . . How I wish we were free to print and spread abroad what we please. I have suffered far worse than you have. My 'Garden' [The Tomb in the Garden] . . . has been monstrously transformed into a treatise on dogmatic Calvinism and would have had that hideous gangrene, the creed of Eternal Punishment, in it had I not in gasping despair

84

strenuously resisted that. In that effort I was victor but, all strength gone, I sank into a marish of dulness, a sort of walking swoon, through which I still welter.

'The slowness of the printing process is unparalleled,' Edmund wrote to John later the same month. 'Fancy this epitaph on us:
> Here lie two who died of exasperation
> Clay killed them and they are turned to clay.
I could turn to Clay, and beat him for his slowness.' But at last Clays had the proofs ready.

Philip advised the boys to look in an old number of the *Penny Magazine* – 'I think 1839 or '40' – where 'there was an article on correcting for the press, giving all the marks and modes used by authors and recognised by printers . . . I should like you to study it well and become master of its detail.' Another useful exercise. Philip also corrected these proofs himself. Edmund wrote to John on 4th November 1870: 'My father's acumen had wasted itself on one wee comma.'

Longmans sent some bindings for them to choose from. Philip worried about the lettering on the cover: 'Avoid any approach to the fantastic or "fal-la".' On November 26th (how quickly, we think), Edmund was able to write, 'I have at last seen the dear little volume. Everything about it pleases me' – apart from one terrible misprint, which makes nonsense of the relationship between a nightingale and a star.

The immediate reaction to the book was silence. In his Christmas letter, Edmund wrote to John:

The reviews	And, grown wise
Still refuse	Recognise
Even to look	In ourselves
At our book;	Merry elves
Do you think	Who some day
That they shrink	In horse-play
From a sense	May give back
Of their own omnipotence	Whack for whack?
	Ha! Ha!

Edmund did not say at the time, but he admitted in an interview in 1901, that of this first book, *Madrigals, Songs and Sonnets*, only twelve copies were actually sold. Obviously both father and son sent lots of free copies around. The Longmans' bill shows that Blaikie ordered only twelve copies of the book but Gosse paid for thirty-nine. 'Time will win us a hearing without fail,' Edmund wrote to John, early in January 1871. 'If we can manage to make ourselves expect nothing but neglect, every snatch of approbation will be an unexpected pleasure. Consider how things went with Shelley, Keats, Coleridge . . .'

Four years later he wrote: 'The form of the volume – its double authorship – was unfavourable, and the verses were very young, yet it had some slight success and brought me several friends of importance, especially the two eminent poets, Mr Rossetti and Mr Swinburne.' But before we look at young Edmund's first encounters with this 'powerful clique', we must go back to Tottenham and the anguish of his first love.

It is difficult to find out very much about Mary Jane Johnson. There is a note in Edmund's hand: 'In March 1870 I informed my Father that I wished to marry May Jane Johnson; he was entirely favourable.' In fact, it was in February, for Philip's reaction to the news is in a letter of 22nd February, 1870:

> Nothing could exceed the filial love, duty and deference that you have shown in communicating to me this most important matter of your youthful love . . . A pure and honourable affection set upon a worthy object is of very great value to a young man . . . specially assuming that both he and his love be earnest believers.

Philip approved his son's choice but cautioned him not to be hasty in committing himself. 'You will say you have already waited eighteen months' but

> You are choosing a daily, hourly companion for *life* . . . Is she truly converted to God? Is she passed from death into life? Are her tastes ritualistic? or 'Broad' or 'evangelical'?

He suggests Edmund should ask for Miss Buckham's help in judging 'as to the Lady's vital godliness'.

> What are her tastes and habits? Is she musical? Does she care for art? Is she given to reading? Is she well-informed? Quiet or dressy? Retiring or forward? Self-possessed in company or shy and timid? Plain or comely? Tall or short?
> What is her position? Is her father in business? or retired? or a gentleman of private fortune? What is his style of living? What family has he in all?
> Let us have categorical, and full, replies to these queries, so far as

you are able to give them – *before* you take any decisive steps. We do not ask any long delay: a day or two in addition to the eighteen months will not make very much difference.

Edmund must of course tell Mary Johnson's father he has only his official salary to count on. 'As you sometimes call me a rich man' (how Philip must have hated that – thinking of camels and the eyes of needles) 'and I think you hold some exaggerated notions about it' he decides to give details of his financial position.

When I left London, I had about £1000 or £1500, the wreck of what was left by your own Mother's Aunt, much of which we lost in an unfortunate investment. With this remainder, I purchased Sandhurst and lived mainly by my pen. The rest of what I live on is capital which was the property of your present Mamma, which, though I have the *legal* control of it, *morally* and *honourably*, I always consider *hers*. Then, of this, £400 a year, left by Mr John Brightwen, is hers *only for life*, so that if Mamma were taken from me £400 of my annual income would cease at once and I could not maintain my present establishment or manner of living.

Certainly Edmund should depend on nothing but his own earnings. (His salary from the BM this year was £105.) 'Of course actual marriage would be madness yet a good while. After a year or two possibly you may begin to think of it . . . You would have to look out for a very small and cheap house – the common standard is that Rent should not exceed one-eighth of the income.'

The first reference to Mary in a surviving letter is in February 1869 and shows that P. H. Gosse had already accepted her as part of Edmund's life. An acute pain in one of Edmund's hands in December 1868 had caused great concern. 'Go immediately to the most skilful surgeon in London . . . let it be absolutely a first rate man. When your own dear Mother was first conscious of her cancer, Mr. Paget was considered the first for such cases . . . Let not money be any question; of course I will gladly pay for the very best skill . . . I will come up to be with you if you wish; but my poor heart quails and trembles already, so that I fear I should but weaken you.' Later there are practical instructions. 'Let the operation be as early as the operator can make it, that it may be all over in time for me to bring you home hither the same evening.' P. H. Gosse must have met May (as they called her) on that day. When in February there was some 'thickening re-formed in the angle of the hand', he was relieved to hear 'that May thinks light of it'.

Mary Jane Johnson was the youngest daughter of George and Martha Johnson who lived just round the corner from Edmund's lodgings in White Hart Lane. George Johnson was an assayer with a firm in the City and was for many years churchwarden of St Paul's, Park Lane, Tottenham. It seems likely that St Paul's was the church Edmund was going to occasionally when he dared to tell his father how much he liked the liturgy of the Church of England.

Edmund had been ill a lot in 1868 – with vague neuralgic pains, with lumbago and rheumatism, which would recur later in life. In November 1869 he became desperately ill with scarlet fever. There were many sleepless nights 'on the border of delirium'. In January 1870 he convalesced at St Leonard's at his father's expense. Isabel Becker, his old German teacher, helped to make his winter solitude tolerable. But he could never bear to be much alone and his state was not helped by the fact that Mary was also ill. As he recovered, she grew worse. Edmund destroyed all his own letters home at this time, probably when he went through his father's papers on his death.

There are also no mentions of Mary in Edmund's letters to John Blaikie beyond two references. On 16th March 1870 he wrote 'I am in too deep a pit of sorrow and fear' and on June 8, 'I have been in strange and bitter trouble . . . and feel already as if years were added to my life.' We know something of this sorrow and fear from Philip's letters to Edmund. On the 25th March he wrote, 'We hope to hear good tidings of your loved Mary, for whom we constantly pray. It is good for you to have something that drives you to the throne of Grace.' On the 18th May he wrote, 'I pray that the beloved sufferer may feel that the tender arms of Jesus are around her. I am thankful you say she is calm. But it is you, my darling, that are the real sufferer. Should your Mary be removed to the presence of the Lord, it is you who will be left to mourn alone, with a heart broken and tender affections blighted.' Obviously Philip was reliving the terrible agony of 1857. And even in the midst of Edmund's anguish he cannot leave him alone.

God has said 'One shall be taken and another left' . . . The terrible thought constantly obtrudes 'What if I be taken and my child left!' He was thinking not of Mary but only of the father and the son. 'Watch ye therefore and pray always that ye may be accounted worthy to escape.' For a time will come when the Lord will take up to Heaven those who are watching for Him, leaving behind a mass of careless, worldly (though *real*) Christians to endure 'all the horrors that then will be poured on the earth'. 'I deeply feel your sorrow, but I desire to turn it to account . . . It is not for His pleasure that He inflicts this sharp and deep wound on your heart, but for your profit . . . *This is your first great sorrow.* May it have a mighty influence in shaping your whole manhood for eternity.'

Two days later there seemed some chance that Mary's life would be saved. 'Do I rightly understand that Mary's leg has been amputated? If so, below or above the knee?' But the operation was not successful. On 31st May 1870 Mary Jane Johnson, aged 21 years, died in Paddington. The certificate gives the cause of death as 'Osteoid Cancer of the knee joint 8 months. Pyaemia after amputation 8 days.' Philip wrote to his son:

> Resurrection is the only brightness in this Valley of the Shadow of Death, through which we are walking. You have early entered into the gloom of that ever-brooding shadow. O that you could see the brightness as near as I see it!

In a note among his papers Edmund wrote, 'In May (31st?) 1870, M.J.J. died. This was an event of extreme importance in my life. My Father was extremely tender with me about M.J.J.'s death but he did not understand.'

4

Our Youngest Poet

MISS BUCKHAM WANTED to go with Edmund to Switzerland, that summer of 1870. He had taken dear Mary Johnson's death so much to heart, she wrote to P. H. Gosse, and he was looking very poorly. He needed a bracing change. A journey abroad would also 'greatly enlarge his mind; his knowledge of books is much more extensive than of persons'. But by the end of July France and Prussia were at war and there was no question of Edmund's visiting the continent. He was intensely disappointed. Philip inevitably saw the European war, 'at the very moment that the Papacy crowns its arrogant blasphemy', as a warning to Christendom.

A Scottish tour was proposed instead, and Mansel Dames had time to spare, before he left for India, to go with Edmund. Philip sent Mansel £5 and Edmund £20 and said that he would do anything that needed doing as far as *Madrigals, Songs and Sonnets* was concerned. He dispatched them with only one stipulation, that Edmund should keep 'a copious journal for our use'. Of course he hoped there would be a chance for Edmund to lead 'dear Mansel to Jesus in the long solitary hours that you will be cast alone together'.

There is no evidence that Edmund made use of the opportunity. The journal was kept meticulously and with regard, of course, to what would interest and please his father. They went by boat to Edinburgh where they stayed at the Waverley Temperance Hotel and Edmund showed by his comments on the National Gallery how wide his knowledge of art was becoming. Most of his knowledge had been picked up by reading Ruskin and by 'going pretty often after office hours to lounge about the National Gallery' in London. Philip had once encouraged him with the words 'You may admire what is beautiful, so long as you do not become indifferent to what is wrong.' Now Edmund reported disapprovingly one chamber 'almost dedicated to some monstrous cartoons by Etty'. He also had the right reactions to Holyrood and 'the rooms redolent of that unpleasant personage, Mary Queen of Scots'. He had lots to report about his fellow passengers on the boat round the islands – one elderly lady turned out to be an admirer of 'that most popular of living naturalists, P. H. Gosse', another, by an amazing chance, was 'a church-member at Brook Street', and yet another the daughter of 'the celebrated Sir John Sinclair'. He admired the scenery extremely ('I found my cheeks flushed and my heart beating fast') and apparently knew Philip would not disapprove that he enjoyed 'a draught of good whisky, real mountain-dew . . . vastly refreshing'. He felt the memories of these lochs and peaks would similarly refresh his spirit when he returned to the monotonous Museum.

On his return Philip appreciated the journal. 'We have followed you with a good map all through the tortuous sounds and lochs, from point to point, from islet to islet.' He complained only of the lack of dates. 'This is the *only* fault our ingenuity of hole-picking has succeeded in discovering.' Edmund breathed a sigh of relief. What he had not told his father was of his encounter with a less conventional fellow passenger than the amateur naturalist, the fellow worshipper and the baronet's daughter. One night on board the *Clansman* Edmund found himself watching a youth of about his own age who had boarded the boat at Portree. 'His appearance,' Edmund wrote long afterwards, 'for some mysterious reason, instantly attracted me. He was tall, preternaturally lean, with longish hair, and as restless and questing as a spaniel . . . We stayed on deck till the latest possible moment and I occasionally watched the lean youth . . . with some of the little tricks with which we were later on to grow familiar – the advance with hand on hip, the sidewise bending of the head to listen . . .' Late at night they steamed up Loch Nevis – 'in a gorge of blackness, with only a strip of the blue moonlit sky overhead'. And the young man explained to Edmund, as they leant on the rail, that they had come up the loch to take off a large party of emigrants who had been driven from their homes in the interests of a deer-forest. Long afterwards the two men used to remember the sound of the wild keening they had shared that night, not knowing they would one day become close friends. The pale, lean youth was Robert Louis Stevenson.

Gosse's friendship with Stevenson ('the most fascinating human being that I have known') did not begin until 1874 when they met at the dinner table of Andrew Lang. On his return from Scotland in the autumn of 1870, Gosse felt 'bored with the present and melancholy at the future', as he wrote to Blaikie. His work at the Museum seemed, after Scotland, even more tedious. He hated the claustrophobic atmosphere, his confinement day after day. Moreover, he apparently had to spend long hours sitting opposite one particular clergyman, the bane of his life, presumably the dreaded Rev. Frederick Laughlin. He wrote to Blaikie:

> One ought to hate nobody; my Christianity revolts against the idea; but I do feel if an angel would take him painlessly into paradise, I would bless that angel . . . Lend me some fine blasphemy that, whispered softly in his ear, will blast him. Doubtless such a blasphemy would blast *me* too. Never mind! So long as I see him shrivel first. If I shrivel, edit my remains. One comfort is *he* will have no remains to edit.

But the main comfort was love.

Writing to a dying colleague at the Museum, he affirmed his faith in the power of love. 'I speak who know; death cannot divide love or destroy it.' He was obviously thinking of sweet Mary Johnson. But one cannot love only the dead. His feeling for his friends increased. He wrote to John Blaikie in words one might more usually use to a lover:

> How I long to know all about you! You are seldom from my thoughts. I think the time has already come, of which you spoke, when you said that one day our love would be so magnified that it would seem as though we had not loved at all.

Edmund used the word love as most of us are too inhibited to use it; he wrote in a language which soon becomes familiar in a series of intense friendships, with both men and women, throughout his life. He was ambitious, very ambitious, but the love of friends was the ruling passion of his life. He became impatient of solitude and afraid of it. Friendship was as necessary to him as sunlight and as sleep.

In a letter to his own son, he once said 'You must go on making useful friends . . .' and there is no doubt that, as a young man, Edmund had a knack of making friends with the right people – the poets naturally included future poets laureate, the novelists the best novelists on both sides of the Atlantic, the schoolmasters would turn into masters of Cambridge colleges, the soldiers into commanders-in-chief, the politicians became cabinet ministers, and even the few clergymen had bishop's mitres in their pockets.

But there were outsiders as well – the friends he named as the three most formative influences on his intellectual life in these early years were all men who stood alone: Swinburne, Leicester Warren, Coventry Patmore. In an undated 'Song for the New Year', which has some biographical interest, for all its conventional and sentimental expression, Gosse rejects the idea of a New Year wish for either peace or fame and asks instead

> For love, and love alone;
> More hands to hold out joy to me,
> More hearts for me to own;
> And if the gain
> In part be pain
> Since time but gives to take again
> Yet more than gold a thousand-fold
> Is love that's neither bought nor sold.

Time would certainly take friends away, sometimes through his own fault and sometimes not. Now Mary was dead; John Blaikie was in Devon, and Mansel Dames about to disappear to India. But other friendships were beginning, other doors were opening.

On 24th March 1870 Edmund Gosse had written to William Bell Scott, painter and poet, admiring Scott's *Albert Dürer; his Life and Works*, which had been recently published. A month earlier he had invited Blaikie to the Museum to see some treasures. He had special permission 'to see the Dürer sketches etc'. Now he wrote learnedly to Scott about the Patinirs in the National Gallery, adding, 'they have always somewhat attracted me'. He asked Scott some questions. The letter, Scott wrote in his *Autobiographical Notes*, had 'all the aplomb of an amateur of long standing, intimate with obscure early masters'. Scott invited the writer to call and talk over old German art. He must have been a little surprised at the bright-eyed, fair-haired youth who soon knocked on the door of Bellevue House, Cheyne Walk, Chelsea. Gosse had great charm, there is no doubt about that, and the visit was the beginning of a friendship which was to introduce him to many of the leading writers and painters of the day, to what twenty-five years later he would call a blaze of colour and a blare of trumpets.

Scott had known Swinburne for many years – they had first met in Northumberland in 1853 when Scott had been painting frescoes for the Trevelyans. There were times when everybody found Scott tedious. He said himself: 'I have all my life suffered under an incubus of seriousness, an old man of the sea in funeral attire, howling out a lugubrious chant about his bottle being empty.' Gosse, like most other people in his life, was to lose favour, but in the early seventies when Scott was 'aiding and coaching' the young man ('before he fell on his feet in Whitehall'), the relationship was warm and Gosse was always conscious of the debt he owed him for early introductions, particularly to the Madox Browns, and other kindnesses. He wrote on 30th September 1870: 'The fact that you have allowed me to love you as a friend can never make me cease to revere you as a Master.'

In spite of that slightly sycophantic tone, Edmund, in fact, early acquired a reputation for plain speaking. He found it suited the circles he was beginning to move in, which cared nothing for toadies. He wrote to his father: 'I am in the habit of expressing my views quite straightforwardly, for I have a very large circle of acquaintances and enough friends, and if people find me distasteful they may go away.' But another day, he admitted he was working rather hard to establish himself in the circle he admired. He told his father that even if he considered transferring to the Natural History section of the Museum (where the work might actually be more congenial), he would never give up 'belles lettres'. 'Having begun under such good auspices and having just pushed myself with so much difficulty into a powerful clique, it would be stupid to throw literature over.' It is interesting that he thought his acceptance by the Pre-Raphaelites had only been achieved with difficulty and determination. It looks to us as if his boyish charm, his talk and obvious talents, won him golden opinions from all sorts of people without excessive effort. Indeed, at the time of his humiliation and shame fifteen years later he admitted that he had 'been too easily successful, I suppose'.

Certainly William Bell Scott took Gosse up with enthusiasm in the winter of 1870–71. He was impressed with his poems and considered they showed 'good promise of your adding worthy work to the already long list of splendid English poetry'. Gosse wrote to Blaikie soon after the rhyme about the lack of reviews of their book: 'My good friends, the W. B. Scotts, are enthusiastic themselves, and have not been idle in pushing the book. Mrs Scott tells me they lent it to Swinburne, that he read it at once and "proceeded to admire". They are lending it now to Gabriel Rossetti and are trying to get it reviewed in the *Academy*.' A few nights before, he had been introduced to Swinburne at the house of Ford Madox Brown, where he was becoming a frequent visitor. He had had that sober letter of encouragement years before, of course, and had seen Swinburne on that extraordinary occasion in the Museum, two and a half years earlier, but this was the first time they had met. Swinburne talked in a beguiling fashion of the old dramatists and Landor and Leigh Hunt. He recited Cyril Tourneur, whose lurid tragedies had succeeded in making Edmund's flesh creep as he stood reading them secretly in the galleries of the British Museum. Swinburne also complained amusingly about the Poet Laureate, 'Alfred Tennyson DCL': 'We hardworking people pay him his £100 a year on purpose for him to write little odes and positively he forgets his duty!' Edmund regretted to Blaikie, 'I can't of course give you the slightest idea of the sparkling fun and delightful exaggeration of his talk.' But Edmund can't have seemed too much the dazzled provincial youth. He had been in London for four years; he had made good use of his time. Mrs Madox Brown sent him a note next day: 'Algernon took to you at once, as is seldom the case with him.'

37 Fitzroy Square, the home of Ford Madox Brown and his family, was a large stone-staircased house, described by his grandson, who became Ford Madox Ford, as 'one of the chief resorts of men of genius and talent who, like himself, were mostly officially unrecognised'. Ford Madox Brown, though quick-tempered and intemperate in his judgments (he had automatic abuse for all Academicians), was a good man to know if one had even the possibility of genius. His policy was 'Beggar yourself rather than refuse assistance to anyone whose genius you think shows promise of being greater than your own.' He was said, improbably, to pin labels on his friends' clothing so that, if they got into any sort of trouble, they would be brought to his house. Certainly Swinburne, on one notable occasion, had to be revived in the bath at 37 Fitzroy Square.

Swinburne's excesses were already more than just gossip to his young admirer. Edmund had been talking with Scott one day at a window on the first floor of his house in Cheyne Walk, when a hansom cab drew up below them. Walter Pater alighted elegantly in lemon-yellow kid gloves, followed by a plunging Swinburne, who landed on the pavement on all fours, his top-hat rolling into the gutter. 'Presently Pater appeared in our upper room, talking with dreamy detachment on indifferent subjects', but of Swinburne they saw no more and assumed he had been taken into another part of the house to be cleaned and sobered.

One wall of Ford Madox Brown's studio in Fitzroy Square was almost entirely covered with the splendidly intricate painting of Chaucer at the court of Edward III, which hung there for years until it was finally sold – his first picture to be sold to a public gallery – to Sydney in 1876. He was not, indeed, at this period, at all successful. It was years since he had painted *The Last of England*, but there were few commissions. In February, 1869, he was welcoming anything 'which might hold out a hope of hard cash'. It must have been at this point that he took as pupils a couple of promising young artists, Ellen Epps and Theresa Thornycroft, to work alongside his own talented children: Lucy, who would marry William Rossetti, Catherine, who was to marry Franz Hueffer, *The Times*'s music critic, and become the mother of Ford Madox Ford, and Oliver ('a perfect genius' before he was ten), the beloved Nolly who was soon to die. Madox Brown had been much praised as a teacher years earlier when he succeeded Gabriel Rossetti at the Working Men's College.

It was at 37 Fitzroy Square that Edmund Gosse eventually got to know Ellen Epps, who became his wife, and Theresa Thornycroft, whose brother would be more than a friend and whose son would be the poet Siegfried Sassoon. We know the almost-elderly Madox Brown must have been impressed by the very young Edmund Gosse. In December 1872, when Edmund was still only twenty-three, the painter asked the young man to use his influence for him at the Museum with one of the men who had a vote for the Slade Professorship of Art at Cambridge, for which Madox Brown was applying.

Edmund described the evening at Fitzroy Square when he first met Swinburne:

Mrs William Morris, in her ripest beauty, and dressed in a long unfashionable gown of ivory velvet, occupied the painting-throne, and Dante Gabriel Rossetti, who, though still almost young, was yet too stout for elegance, squatted – for some part of the evening at least – on a hassock at her feet. The 'marvellous boy, that perished in his prime,' Oliver Madox Brown, carrying on his arms and shoulders tame white rats, shattered the nerves of the ladies. Spontaneity of behaviour in society was at that time encouraged by the Pre-Raphaelites. But among so much that was wonderful, I continued riveted to the aspect of Swinburne, who indulged me with quite a long conversation. His kindness, at once, became like the kindness of an elder brother. In some ways he fulfilled, and more than fulfilled, the promise of my hero-worship.

At the same time, I have to confess that there was something in his appearance and in his gestures which I found disconcerting, and which I have a difficulty in defining without a suspicion of caricature. He was not quite like a human being. Moreover, the dead pallor of his face and his floating balloon of red hair, had already, although he was but in his thirty-third year, a faded look. As he talked to me, he stood, perfectly rigid, with his arms shivering at his sides, and his little feet tight against each other, close to a low settee in the middle of the studio. Every now and then, without breaking off talking or bending his body, he hopped onto this sofa, and presently hopped down again, so that I was reminded of some orange-crested bird – a hoopoe, perhaps – hopping from perch to perch in a cage. The contrast between these sudden movements and the enthusiasm of his rich and flute-like voice was very strange. In course of a little time, Swinburne's oddities ceased to affect me in the slightest degree, but on this first occasion my impression of them was rather startling than pleasant.

Swinburne, as we have already seen, was at the height of his notorious fame in these years. Gabriel Rossetti was equally in the public eye. His poems, so long immured in Lizzie's grave in Highgate Cemetery, had at last been published the year before. They created a sensation, and the painter took his place at once as one of the leading poets of the day. The first printing of a thousand copies had sold out within a week. In May an issue of the *Fortnightly* carried Swinburne's enormous article on 'The Poems of Dante Gabriel Rossetti'; it ran to no fewer than thirty-nine pages.

Robert Buchanan was lying in wait for them, but in the meantime Rossetti was on an even keel, in spite of Janey Morris. The trouble with his eyes seemed cured; he was painting again. There is a note in Edmund's hand that records that he was first presented to Rossetti on 23rd March 1871, though he had been in the same room before, as we have seen. Edmund was enormously impressed with him. After Rossetti's death, Edmund wrote to Edward Marsh: 'You could have carved twenty noticeable human beings out of Rossetti. Morris seems to me to make up rather less than one.' William Rossetti, in his dull discreet memoir of his brother, quotes Edmund: 'He was the most prompt in suggestion, the most regal in giving, the most sympathetic in response, of the men I have known or seen; and this without a single touch of the prophetic manner.' His voice reading his poems was so melodious that Edmund found it difficult to judge the poems rationally. He wrote to Scott on Rossetti's death: 'One chiefly thinks of what a wonderful man he was, and how different all one's view of life would have been without him; of how generous and noble he was in those days when he was really worthy of himself', before the persecution mania, the sleeplessness, the chloral.

Rossetti came to admire Gosse too. When Hall Caine was preparing his *Recollections of D. G. Rossetti* in 1882, he told Gosse how 'though Rossetti constantly talked of you', he regretted that there were no significant mentions of him in the letters. Rossetti certainly spoke highly, in a note to Scott, of Gosse's next book of poems and, as early as 1874, considered Gosse was already establishing himself as a critic to be taken seriously. Part of Edmund's 'systematic self-training' at this time was to read Sainte-Beuve. 'Other writers may be postponed, but at the threshold of a serious literary life, Sainte-Beuve *must* be read. It is the Sainte-Beuve of the *Causeries* and of the *Nouveau Lundis* that counts.' 'My little dream is to be the Gautier where you are the Sainte-

Beuve,' Marzials was to write in 1876 but, even long after this, Gosse hoped to be remembered as a poet and not a critic.

'I was affected, of course, by coming into personal contact with the Pre-Raphaelites, but particularly with Dante Gabriel Rossetti,' Gosse wrote years later. Though he joked about the phrase 'art for art's sake', he really never moved far from the position that art is a sufficient end in itself. 'They lived intensely in a sharply outlined circle of their own, and cared nothing about social opinion outside it. They were, in the aesthetic sphere, peaceful revolutionaries.' Though Gosse was to revert to a position where social opinion meant a great deal to him, the freedom of these evenings and the company of these people, with their essentially amoral attitude to art and life, provided a marvellous relaxation for his soul.

If Gosse was too late on the scene actually to watch Rossetti's wombat eating the cigars, he saw a great deal else to entertain him. And if Christina Rossetti, whom he says he saw much of in the winter of 1870–71, could survive with her saintliness untarnished (as she certainly could), well then, perhaps, so could he. Edmund has left a vivid description of Christina Rossetti. Our images of her are probably from her brother's portrait of 1866 – what Edmund called 'the singularly beautiful chalk drawing in profile' – and from his version of her as Mary Virgin in the year that Edmund was born. In real life, Edmund says, she dressed with an absence of style which was really distressing.

> Her dark hair was streaked across her olive forehead, and turned up in a chignon; the high stiff dress ended in a hard collar and plain brooch, the extraordinarily ordinary skirt sank over a belated crinoline, and these were inflictions hard to bear from the high-priestess of Pre-Raphaelitism. When it is added that her manner, from shyness, was of a portentous solemnity, that she had no small talk whatever, and that the common topics of the day appeared to be entirely unknown to her, it will be understood that she was considered highly formidable by the young and the flighty. I have seen her sitting alone, in the midst of a noisy drawing-room, like a pillar of cloud, a Sibyl whom no-one had the audacity to approach.

But Edmund, though young, was certainly not flighty, and he would summon up the audacity and be richly rewarded. He would realize the uselessness of conventional chatter and 'venture on real subjects', and then 'her heart seemed to open like an unsealed fountain'. The heavy lids of her weary-looking, Italian eyes would lift and display her ardour as she talked of the mysteries of poetry and religion.

These were certainly conversations he could report back to Tottenham, but Miss Baker still worried about the effect of the expeditions to the Scotts and the Madox Browns. On 13th July 1871, when Edmund was in Norway, she wrote anxiously to Marychurch, making an apparent distinction between 'meetings' and parties. There is no doubt, and who could blame him, that Edmund had not been telling Miss Baker and Miss Buckham exactly what was going on.

The great excitement of the last few months has been too much for him. The fortnightly meetings at the houses of these celebrities greatly exhausted him. Naturally, he was delighted, and it was most flattering to have such men as Dante Rossetti and others patting him on the shoulders and introducing him to one another as 'Our youngest Poet' – invitations to visit them are frequent, but hitherto he has not accepted them, and those for *Sunday* he has had the courage not only to decline but to add, that he never visited on *that* day. Association with such characters may be valuable to him in a literary sense, but alas! it sadly lowers the spiritual tone, which is a great grief to us – and when we speak to him on the subject, he admits the force of it, but says it is *needful*; that he gains instruction by intercourse with them. How true it is, that 'a gift blinds the eyes'. Our only hope is, that God will keep him from falling – for this we anxiously 'watch and pray' – the Lord alone must deal with him. We are glad to think there will be no more of these meetings – until next winter – the Lord in His grace may teach him many lessons before that time. I ought to add for your comfort that he always reads the scriptures with us of an evg (when at home) using his Greek Testament and often he very nicely enters into the subjects of the portion read. The night before he left us – it was very late when all was packed and ready and the dear boy full of excitement – I said go to bed at once and quiet down – he said Oh! No! What, won't you both commend me to God before I go to rest? Of course we did. I have again given you a peep behind the scenes that you may know how to pray for him.

Madrigals, Songs and Sonnets may have made no mark in the world; but it had earned Edmund, among the Pre-Raphaelites, that desirable accolade – 'Our youngest Poet'. In Marychurch, P. H. Gosse was worried rather than impressed. He had earlier been fuelling his own anxiety by reading Ritchie's *The Nightside of London* – 'a remarkable, nay a frightful exhibition of the pitfalls and snares which surround on every hand the thoughtless giddy youth of London. Women and wine, whoredom and drunkenness seem to be the Devil's most successful baits'. Ritchie's phrases were in his ears: 'We are standing in the very temple of vice . . . A few years hence the gay fast fellows around you now . . . may be walking the streets in rags or, it may be, dying in London hospitals of lingering disease, or . . . living on year after year with all that is divine in man utterly blotted out and destroyed. The path that leads to life is strait and narrow, and few there be who find it.'

The father did not want his son actually to read the book: 'To a young man, the very description of such scenes is inflammatory and defiling. Both Mamma and I have heartily thanked God that your home lies so far away from dissipated London, that you are thrown out of the range of the fowler's net; that you escape the temptation of walking the treacherously-baited streets at night unless you wilfully choose it (Proverbs 2, 10–16).' Now, he realized, sinners seemed as likely to entice Edmund in drawing-rooms as on the streets. Philip Gosse wrote calmly enough at just this time to his brother-in-law, James Green, who had published some devout poems, saying how much he rejoiced that all those nearest and dearest to him were indeed saved, but Edmund's soul continued to worry him.

The Pre-Raphaelites were enough to worry any devoted parent. He remembered John Morley railing on the publication of Swinburne's *Poems and Ballads*: 'The bottomless pit encompasses us on one side and stews and bagnios on the other.' Attacks on the group had been regular, but came to a head with the notorious article 'The Fleshly School of Poetry' by Robert Buchanan (under a pseudonym) in the *Contemporary Review* for October 1871. Whatever the father thought, back in Marychurch, there was no question which side the son was on. In 1919 he would write: 'In early youth we fight for the new forms of art, for the new aesthetic shibboleths.' He would speak of 'the happy ardour of battle,' forgetting the agony of the casualties.

The controversy raged and Rossetti wrote a reply in the *Athenaeum*, just as Gosse was to do, after a different attack, fifteen years later. Rossetti was 'mortally wounded' just as Gosse was almost to be. But before Rossetti drowned in chloral and whisky, he joked and so did his young admirer. The puritans organized a public dinner for their champion, Buchanan. The evening was varied by music and singing. By a strange chance, a song by Rossetti was sung by Malcolm Lawson. On this the young Gosse wrote the earliest of his triolets:

> 'Who wrote that song?' Buchanan said.
> They answered with one voice, 'Rossetti.'
> Embarrassed, shuffling, pale and red,
> 'Who wrote that song?' Buchanan said.

> They laughed till they were nearly dead,
>   This affectation seemed so petty.
> 'Who wrote that song?' Buchanan said.
>   They answered with one voice, 'Rossetti.'

Scott tells the story of Rossetti arriving late at a dinner party, bursting into the room and shouting out the name of his enemy. He read aloud the reply he had composed 'till the lives of his friends became too heavy to bear'. It was a pattern for Gosse's later behaviour. He never lost his contempt for Buchanan, though he would have reason to be grateful to him.

Tennyson was, of course, another matter altogether: 'In the world at large Tennyson was the English Living Poet par excellence, great by land and great by sea, the one survivor of the heroic chain of Masters.'

It was perhaps in the early summer of 1871, within a few months of meeting the Pre-Raphaelites, that Edmund Gosse had his first sight of Tennyson. He was working away in the horrible underground Den at the British Museum on some squalid task in what someone else described as an atmosphere 'scented with rotten morocco and an indescribable odour familiar in foreign barracks' when a Senior Assistant, W. R. S. Ralston, came down the curling steel staircase.

> Over me he bent, and in a whisper (we were forbidden to speak out loud in the Den) he said, 'Come upstairs at once and be presented to Mr Tennyson!' . . .
>
> As we climbed those steep and spiral staircases towards light and day, my heart pounded in my chest with agitation. The feeling of excitement was almost overwhelming; it was not peculiar to myself; such ardours were common in those years. Some day a philosopher must analyse it – that enthusiasm of the seventies, that intoxicating belief in 'the might of poesy.' Tennyson was scarcely a human being to us, he was the God of the Golden Bow; I approached him now like a blank idiot about to be slain . . . It is not merely that no person living now calls forth that kind of devotion, but the sentiment of mystery has disappeared. Not genius itself could survive the Kodak snapshots and the halfpenny newspapers . . .
>
> We found Tennyson with a single companion, in what was then the long First Sculpture Gallery. His friend was James Spedding, at whom in other conditions I should have gazed with interest, but in the Delphic presence he was not visible to my dazzled eyes . . . Ralston, for all his six feet six, seemed to dwindle before this

magnificent presence, while Tennyson stood, bare-headed among the Roman Emperors, every inch as imperial-looking as the best of them. He stood there as we approached him, very still, with slightly drooping eyelids, and made no movement, no gesture of approach. When I had been presented, and had shaken his hand, he continued to consider me in a silence which would have been deeply disconcerting if it had not, somehow, seemed kindly, and even, absurd as it sounds, rather shy.

The stillness was broken by Ralston's irrelevantly mentioning that I was presently to start for Norway. The Bard then began to talk about that country, which I was surprised to find he had visited some dozen years before. Ralston kindly engaged Spedding in conversation, and Tennyson now applied himself to me; with infinite goodness he even 'made conversation,' for I was hopelessly tongue-tied, and must, in fact, have cut a very poor figure. Tennyson, it miraculously appeared, had read some of my stammering verses, and was vaguely gracious about them. He seemed to accept me as a sheep in the fold of which he was, so magnificently, the Shepherd. This completed my undoing, but he did not demand from me speech. He returned to the subject of Norway, and said it was not the country for him to travel in, since you could only travel in it in funny little round carts, called *karjols*, which you must drive yourself, and that he was far too nearsighted for that . . .

Then somebody suggested that we should examine the works of art . . . Tennyson led us, and we stopped at any sculpture which attracted his notice. But the only remark which my memory has retained was made before the famous black bust of Antinous. Tennyson bent forward a little, and said, in his deep slow voice, 'Ah! this is the inscrutable Bithynian!' There was a pause, and then he added, gazing into the eyes of the bust: 'If we knew what he knew, we should understand the ancient world.' If I live to be a hundred years old, I shall still hear his rich tones as he said this, without emphasis, without affectation, as though he were speaking to himself. And soon after, the gates of heaven were closed, and I went down three flights to my hell of rotten morocco.

It was just at this time Edmund was offered regular work for the *Athenaeum*. His father responded warmly, on 12th May 1871: 'It seems to me a considerable honour to be on the regular staff of the *Athenaeum*. Are you wholly dependent, however, on the chief editor's requesting you to review certain books of his choosing? Or may you write a review "on your own hook" and submit it to him?' P. H.

Gosse suggests exactly the procedure which his son was often to follow throughout his life, right up to the last years as chief reviewer on the *Sunday Times*: 'Select some book or books recently published, *as a peg to hang your article on*, and then make it what you like.' There was no question that the father was now helping the son to the worldly success he at times despised. He was still, of course, more concerned with his spiritual welfare.

On Edmund's twenty-first birthday, his father had sent him yet another edition, with yet more annotations, of the Greek New Testament, on which he had been dutifully labouring every evening. Moreover the parcel arrived late. P. H. Gosse was extremely vexed and sorry about his mistake and tried to compensate by describing his son, at this important point in his life, as 'a man in whom I joy and glory'. Edmund was twenty-one, but he still seemed a mere boy. As late as 1874, when he was nearly twenty-five, he was having to beg his father to restrain 'your natural instinct to mould and fashion the character of your own child'. His youthful appearance didn't help his father to accept that he was now grown up. Throughout his life, over and over again, people commented on how young Gosse looked. There is a hint in an unpublished autobiographical fragment of this period (annotated by Gosse 'written in 1872, I think'), that Edmund was not very happy about his own appearance.

In a note to the fragment, added thirty years later, Gosse wrote that the pages marked 'the sudden expansion of feeling and observation that I experienced' (a different sort of observation from his P. H. Gosse training) 'after first coming into the company of the Pre-Raphaelites. I, of course am Tristram Jones', and he describes the youth as 'vexed at the weakness of his own face' and wearing 'a small moustache, so small it constantly eludes his grasp'. Edmund, according to his diary, finally 'shaved his lip' on 27th January 1874. But Emma, the girl in the story, speaks of 'this good-looking, clever, absurd boy' and from his photographs it would seem that Edmund had little need to worry about his looks. He was more than average height, with a thick crest of fair hair above a broad and finely-shaped forehead, and bright blue eyes. Even in old age, people would still speak of his trim figure and his dashing, attractive stance. Again and again, we hear of his 'wonderful fairness' and the brightness of his eyes behind his glasses. He always seemed to be on the tips of his toes, ready and eager for whatever might turn up.

The autobiographical fragment shows young Tristram Jones trapped in the conventions of Norton, the fictional version of Tottenham, nearly allowing himself to marry Emma Fields (in real life her name was Beddow), a suburban beauty with the dangerous possibility that she might grow to resemble her mother. She wants him to sing, imagine it, 'The Last Rose of Summer'. Truly, it would require a good deal of aesthetic training; 'would she bear it and was she worth it?' Tristram priggishly muses. Edmund asks us to agree that his hero, himself, is 'most unheroical', and we surely have a glimpse of a real-life social dilemma when Tristram is asked if he 'subscribes to the counterblast of our Royal James'. The boy does not know 'what that magnate had blasted or counter-blasted' and could not answer until his host eventually held up a slender cigar. No, Tristram Jones did not smoke.

But, innocent that he was and 'extremely weak and undeveloped', he assures us he belonged 'in the innermost soul of him, to the highest, most etherial class of existences'. Married to Emma Fields, he would probably simply have been respectable and clever. Without her, what might he not achieve? 'Neither Tristram nor Emma doubted the heat of the other's devotion. It was their own that was so rapidly falling towards zero.' Just in time, he walks out of the pretty cage, just as he had earlier left that more constraining one in Marychurch.

Thirty years later Edmund Gosse 'shuddered to recollect' how very nearly he became engaged to the Beddows' daughter. He blessed Miss Buckham and Miss Baker for their strenuous objections to the match. Just in time, he had begun to meet girls like Ellen Epps and Cathy Madox Brown and Theresa Thornycroft. It would be a long time before he would persuade Ellen to marry him but he would make no more mistakes. In spite of Tristram's assurances that 'I think people deserve great credit who rise from the ranks', it would seem that the real problem was not only an intellectual snobbery but a more ordinary kind of snobbery as well. 'In a sense one does marry one's mother-in-law. Could he polish his Emma's relations, even if she herself became the tenth muse, a wonder to her age?' It was hardly likely – and it was quite clear that Edmund already had in mind for himself a very different home background from 'the bright suburban upholstery' which made such a poor accompaniment to the 'old Italian music' in fiction ('the music being added as a blind') or the old volumes of poetry in real life. He didn't have to worry too much about his own relations. P. H. Gosse would occasionally enquire whether he had seen Uncle Edmund Bowes or Uncle William Gosse and he would occasionally go to see them – frail elderly bachelors, apparently grateful for rare attention. The others were either dead or far away. Some were in Australia; others would go to New Zealand.

The one family connection he was to cultivate was not, in fact, a blood tie. He began to see a great deal of his stepmother's brother, George Brightwen, and his wife who bore the same name as her sister-in-law, Eliza, but was a very different character. George Bright-wen was a great-grandson of the eighteenth-century Gurney who had founded Gurney's Bank in Norfolk. In June 1873, the Brightwens moved to the Grove, Stanmore—a splendid Victorian pile, just outside London, with vast conservatories, and grounds which included a substantial lake. Uncle George had had some initial reservations about young Edmund's manners, but the boy quickly endeared himself. He described his first visit to 'the new ancestral residence', obviously impressed with the cypresses, stone steps, stucco statues and urns 'in the approved taste of Louis Quinze'. There was a splendid view 'down infinite glades into the heart of Hertfordshire' and it was a naturalist's paradise – 'swans and herons on the lake and the woods thick with squirrels and martens, nuthatches and woodpeckers, wrynecks and goatsuckers.'

Eliza Brightwen was 'a very sweet and very intelligent woman full of all sorts of ingenious cleverness, and with a great sense of humour'. She was herself a naturalist and a writer, much encouraged by the man she called her nephew. Her investigations appeared under such titles as *Quiet Hours with Nature* and *Inmates of my house and garden*, but they were not vague, cosy ramblings; they were based entirely on original observation. Eliza would rise at five, the better to see what was going on. Nothing was alien to her – animal, vegetable or mineral. She would herself dissect and examine minutely any dead creatures that she found, but most of her work was from life. She had both a museum and a menagerie, and of course aquaria as designed by P. H. Gosse.

In Eliza Brightwen's wealthy widowhood, she was to become extremely adept at rebuffing what Edmund described as 'the righteous and the wanting, . . . from a gentleman, who threatened to drown himself if she did not send him £5000, down to a widow who was told by the Lord in a vision to go to Mrs Brightwen for 3s 6d a week'. Her advantages as a relative were marred by an occasional excess of evangelical zeal and also by ill-health. When Edmund wrote to Marychurch about poor Aunt Lizzie's health, P. H. Gosse wrote back: 'What a change to her will it be when "the Lord Jesus shall change her vile body that it be fashioned like his own glorious body".' Edmund's comment was, 'No, no! that's too hard! She has rather a nice figure when she's pretty well.' Eliza herself compared her health 'with the constitution of Austria or a cup in a picture, always falling yet never fallen'. But her endless curiosity and her humour made her good company, and the beauty and interest of the Grove were a necessary relaxation for Edmund, though her grounds were apt to be swarming with large parties of 'tired workers'.

Edmund wrote to Scott on one of his early visits: 'I have spend my days rowing over the lake, basking in the sun half-naked, and reading *Consuelo* among the bull-rushes. Consequently I am in buoyant spirits, brown and strong.' His health was not often so good in these years and he often felt weighed down and depressed. Like Tristram Jones, 'he wanted a strong new current to flood his stagnant life'. Tottenham was stagnant. Everything that was strong and new seemed to be centred in Soho or Chelsea or abroad. He was very ambitious; he saw life as a race and realized the runner needed particularly good starting-blocks if he had not been to university. In a few years, Fanny Stevenson would say shrewdly: 'I believe he will make a career for himself. He tries, which is what none other of the small poets do. They are all playing and they know they are.' Gosse appeared to play a good deal. He always knew how to enjoy himself. He certainly talked and laughed, walked and swam and played with cats. But he rarely lost sight of his goal. And he was never confident of securing it. His childhood was, we must suppose, the clue to his doubts. Was it perhaps true, after all, that nothing mattered but the grace of God? Under his bright façade, there was always insecurity. He reminded his father in 1872 that he was not 'of a naturally sanguine temperament'. Long afterwards, Cyril Davenport, one of his fellow clerks at the Museum, looked at the Gosse of these early years and commented: 'Gosse was one of the greatest workers that I ever knew – he realized how much headway he had to make up and I consider he worked nobly to make up for his early want of position and education.'

'It is my life's ambition to spend all my powers in the service of English verse,' he would write in 1879, not adding but meaning 'and to make my name in the process'. In fact he would widen the field to include all literature and not just English literature. Tottenham was not the right place for such ambition. But he could not leave Tottenham yet – that was too difficult. At least he could travel abroad; his father would see the point and not the danger of that.

Edmund was not quite sure why he chose Norway in the summer of 1871. Certainly Tennyson sent the young poet a letter of introduction to Professor Ludwig Kristensen Daa of Christiania after they talked in the Museum, but that seems to have been an effect rather than a cause, and indeed Edmund apparently did not use the introduction until his second visit the following year. The Scottish exploration of 1870 suggested the possible beauty of other northern landscapes. He seems to have had no particular literary plan in mind but he already had an interest in the Scandinavian languages. We remember the Swedish grammar about which P. H. Gosse wrote to Edmund's schoolmaster in 1865, and the contact with Elise Otté. In his journal Edmund wrote later that 'like the nun in Chaucer',

> I spoke the Norsk of Ollendorff and Co
> For Norsk of Throndhjem was to me unknowe.

And he refers learnedly in an article he wrote on the Lofoten Islands to Carl Vogt in his interesting *Nordfahrt* and to the *Reise durch Norwegen* of Herr C. F. Lessing.

He set off in high spirits. He would travel abroad regularly for the rest of his life, often more than once a year, and never lost his zeal for travel. And he never lost the habits of careful planning, observation and careful spending suggested by his father. His accounts survive for dozens of journeys, filled in with every detail, so that we know not only the cost of his hotels, increasing in splendour as his career prospered, but also just how much he tipped his porters.

He used no porters, of course, on that first Norwegian journey when he was twenty-one. He teamed up on the boat with a group of young Irishmen in training for holy orders. 'Each was a man whom to know was an advantage,' he noted in his journal. He ate bear's legs for breakfast and saw cod fishermen 'steeped to the eyes in blood and scales and entrails' and marvelled at the midnight sun: 'that cold yellow lustre, deepening to amber and gold behind the great blue mountains.' He was interested in everything, even boldly walking into a house, when there was no answer to his knock, to find a young woman nursing a baby. She did not rise or move save to respond to his 'Göd Aften' in a low sad voice. He developed a passion for a red fisherman's cap and went round all the shops asking 'Har De en röd Kappe? en Kappe for Fiskeman?' He certainly had a dictionary with him but when he went into a bookseller's in Trondheim for something to read – the day was too hot for any exertion – he was really looking for a Tauchnitz novel in English. It was only as idle conversation that he asked if there were any Norwegian poets. There were indeed, he was told, and a new book by the best of them had arrived in the shops that day. The bookseller was H. L. Braekstad, later the Norwegian vice-consul in London. The book was *Digte*, poems, by Henrik Ibsen. It was a lucky break.

Gosse brought the little green volume back to England and put it aside. Then, in talk with R. H. Hutton, literary editor of *The Spectator* – or it may have been with Ralston at the Museum – it was suggested that, if he wanted to make a name for himself, he should choose an unfamiliar field, which he could make his own. 'For three months, I worked incessantly,' he wrote in an article for *Ny Illustrerte Tidende* in

1875. 'In the Spring [of 1872] I wrote my first review of a Scandinavian book; it was printed in *The Spectator* and the book was Ibsen's *Digte*. It was the first time Ibsen's name had been written in English.'

In a poem 'To Henrik Ibsen in Dresden', Gosse wrote:

> That link between your land and mine,
> My English and your Norse denies;
> Your verses lie like gems that hide
> In coffers sealed from English eyes;
> Behind the veil we dimly know
> A solemn figure stands complete,
> But know not how the draperies flow,
> How poised the hands and feet.

Just how important that veiled figure was, Gosse could only guess. He says he was deeply moved: 'It seemed to me that this was a new planet.' He can hardly have imagined into what paths this poet would lead him, but he had an instinct about Ibsen's importance and poured enormous amounts of time and energy into his efforts to introduce Ibsen to England. The poetry was certainly not in the same class as the plays, and it was only luck, really, that those early *Digte* put Gosse on to a great writer. But nothing can diminish his determination and zeal in promoting his new discovery.

He managed very early on to convince Ibsen himself of his suitability as promoter. On 11th April 1872 (less than a year after Gosse had picked up *Digte* in Trondheim) Ibsen wrote to Michael Birkeland: 'A large edition of my works is being prepared by Mr Edmund Gosse, who has a wide familiarity with our literature.' Could Birkeland tell the newspapers? Apparently Edmund had suggested he would try to organize a team of translators. A fortnight later, Ibsen corrected the wrong impression he had had. Obviously Mr Gosse, 'although he is the man mainly behind the enterprise', was hardly at this stage a name to boast about and it would perhaps be best not to mention him. A few days later (April 30th), he wrote a very friendly letter to Gosse, encouraging him in their joint aim, but suggesting he should not begin any translations without some definite promise from a publisher, 'a reasonable compensation for the time and trouble'. Gosse disregarded the warning, worked hard on *Love's Comedy*, only to find that it had been a 'mere waste of labour; no one would publish, or so much as read it'.

He had similar difficulties with articles – one can imagine it would be even worse today. Who wants articles about a foreign writer no one can read because he has not yet been translated? An article on *Peer Gynt* was turned down by the editor of the *Saturday Review* because Gosse had used 'terms of so warm a eulogy that he could not publish, without some confirmation of Ibsen's merit. No sponsor of Ibsen's poetic respectability was forthcoming and the review did not appear.' But this must be the article which appeared in *The Spectator* on 20th July 1872, under the title 'A Norwegian Drama'. In January, 1873, the first long consideration of Ibsen appeared under Gosse's name in the *Fortnightly Review*: 'Ibsen: The Norwegian Satirist'. Edmund said he danced for joy when he received a letter from Ibsen just after this, saying he would send Gosse early copies of all his books, 'since you of all my friends in other countries, possess the deepest, truest, most poetical insight into what I mean by my work.'

Gosse published four articles on Ibsen in 1872 and the amount he earned from them – £19 7s 6d – was the total of his literary earnings that year. He had a long task ahead of him. It was not until 1889 that Ibsen gained any real fame in England. In one of his 1872 articles, Gosse described Ibsen as 'second to none of his contemporaries', prevented from enjoying an international reputation only by 'the remoteness of his mother-tongue'. Between March 1872 and March 1878, Gosse wrote twenty essays or reviews on Ibsen.

Ibsen was never an easy man, but the enthusiasm of his young English disciple naturally touched him. They continued to exchange friendly letters. 'English causes me some difficulty,' Ibsen wrote to Gosse on 4th July 1878, 'but when we leave tomorrow [for Amalfi] your book will be about the only one I shall take with me.' The book was *Studies in the Literature of Northern Europe*.

In a later edition of the book, the editor, Ernest Rhys, paid tribute to the importance of William Morris in the revival of interest in northern history and literature. And on 24th October 1871, a few months after his return from that first visit to Norway, Edmund wrote a long letter to his father, which included the news that Madox Brown had said that he thought Morris would like to meet young Gosse. 'Morris, the greatest gun of all!' In the same letter he reported he had just had the proofs of his article on the Lofoten Islands, which eventually appeared in *Fraser's Magazine* the following month. 'You can imagine how delighted I was, all the more so because I had begun to despair. I had even been consulting with Miss Ingelow what should be done with the MS when I got it back.'

A few days later, he was dining with the Scotts when William Allingham was a fellow-guest. 'It appears that he is sub-editor of *Fraser*. So Mr Scott asked him, in an offhand way, if he had seen anything of an article on the Lofoten. "Oh yes," said Mr Allingham, "It's going in; it's very interesting. Do you know anything of the man?'' which created a good deal of fun, of course.' Mr Appleton, editor of the *Academy*, was also there and Dr Hueffer and the Rossettis, Christina and Dante Gabriel. 'It was very kind of Mr Scott, I think, to ask me to a little party of people who were all sure to be useful to me.'

Madox Brown remembered his promise to introduce Gosse to William Morris. By the time they met, Gosse had already got to know Gudbrand Vigfusson, who was working on an Icelandic/English dictionary for the Clarendon Press. 'I saw him whenever it was possible. Under his encouragement, I had been struggling with the classic Icelandic and was making some little progress.' It was no wonder that he considered Morris 'the biggest lion'. 'Early in January, 1872,' he remembered, 'I spent five hours in the evening at Madox Brown's with W. Morris, who read to me his Journal in Iceland.' Gosse wrote to his father at the time:

> He was good enough to say he had heard all about me and would read the journal because he knew that I was interested in Northern matters. As this journal, in spite of the statements which have appeared in the papers, is not to be published, it was a great privilege to listen to it. It was very vivid and amusing . . . He was announced in one paper at Reykjavik as William Morris, Scald. Was it not funny to see the word in that modern connection? He is one of the most unassuming, homely people I have ever met. It seems to me very beautiful when great and sudden fame leaves the recipients of it modest and natural.

Morris was almost too modest and homely. Gosse has left a glimpse of him on another occasion when the young man had gone to a lecture on Iceland by Eirikr Magnusson at the Society of Arts in Adelphi Terrace. Morris had agreed to take the chair:

> . . . round and burly, with a shock of hair, and encompassed with many rough garments, [he] was with difficulty persuaded to ascend the platform. Once seated in front of the assembly, he was over-come with bashfulness. When he rose to speak, we trembled. He just barely managed to proceed so far as to say that 'Mr Magnusson is sure to give you, to give us, a – a – very interesting – a – lecture' and then he sat down and buried his face in his hands. He was very uncomfortable and restless during the lecture, in the middle of which he suddenly rose to interrupt the lecture with a joke inaudible to us, over which he chuckled a great deal. He yawned several times, but towards the end he discovered that, by judicious wrig-gling, his chair might be made to swing half round, and this little

exercise entertained him nearly all the rest of the lecture. At one time he disappeared altogether, for, having dropped his pocket-handkerchief, he quietly dived off his chair and under the table for it.

So 'the biggest lion' he had yet been introduced to certainly didn't have any teeth, and Gosse's youthful enthusiasm for his charm declined. A. C. Benson long afterwards would write 'William Morris is the real heroic figure' but Gosse, after Morris's death, could only lament, insensitively perhaps, the incoherency of his life:

> With his picturesqueness and his violent temper and his art and all, he had no real touch with humanity, at least not with mine. And while I like inconsistency, I don't like incoherency. Morris was incoherent – the romantic poetry and the carpets and the Socialism and the collecting of missals don't hold together . . . He was a strongish kind of man and we owe him a great revival of beauty, but I didn't like him.

Swinburne was different. It was Swinburne, it seems, who eventually gave Edmund the courage to break with Marychurch – not overtly, not violently. But intellectually and emotionally it was his love for Swinburne that released Edmund at last – probably not until 1875 – from any vivid relationship with Christ. Their friendship is a puzzling one. There was in it for the younger man so much anguish and confusion, and an alternating excitement and tedium, which were equally exhausting. There was no question that Gosse loved Swinburne, and that it was love – not a mere desire to observe the famous poet, the man he considered 'our greatest living poet' – that drove him to see so much of him at whatever cost. It was a time when Rossetti, who had also loved Swinburne, could write to Madox Brown: 'I now view him as the crowning nuisance of the whole world and have no longer the slightest toleration for his abominable ways.' Rossetti, at this period after Buchanan's attack, had continuous delusions of a conspiracy against him. But his comment on Swinburne was a rational one. Friendship with that 'flaming creature' was bound to be a liability, one would think, and calculated to ruin the reputation of a young man on the threshold of his career.

In his own words, Swinburne had a 'touch of Byronic ambition to be thought an eminent and terrible enemy to the decorous life and respectable fashion of the world'. One phrase, as Hardy pointed out – 'the supreme evil, God' in *Atalanta in Calydon* – had been enough to damn him in many people's eyes. Over and over again, in writing about Swinburne, Gosse was to stress his revolt against conventionality. By identifying so closely with him, Gosse shows his own sympathy for such a revolt. Gosse and Swinburne would both later settle into different kinds of respectability (the Pines and the House of Lords shared that quality, if nothing else) but it is important to remember Gosse's wilder ambitions in the early eighteen-seventies. Poetry and fame did not mean slim volumes of verse in virginal hands up and down the country. They meant something much more controversial and more radical.

Gosse described himself as the 'faithful henchman' of the most defiant poet of the period. 'He was not merely a poet, but a flag; and not merely a flag but the Red Flag incarnate.' He would always love the Swinburne of the seventies even when he came to consider that he was 'born without a heart', that his poetry had become 'so flatulent and uninteresting' and even when eventually, going through Swinburne's papers after the poet's death, Gosse had to admit 'I confess that Swinburne occasionally makes me physically sick.'

The young man certainly had a stronger stomach than the old one, but it is difficult to say just how much he knew of his hero's tastes and weaknesses in the early days. In the end he knew it all and left the evidence sealed at the British Museum; it was not published until 1962. Osbert Sitwell says that some of the letters Gosse read after Swinburne's death came as a tremendous shock, but a letter to Georg Brandes in 1874 rather suggests otherwise: 'At this moment there is no living person that possesses the materials for a biography of Swinburne that I possess. But these are in a great measure so impossibly confidential that they can scarcely be printed even long after his death.' This would seem to suggest not just drink and Adah Menken but flagellation brothels as well.

But Gosse said quite definitely in the essay he left in the Museum that Swinburne 'was a perfectly safe companion for youth'; and there is every reason to suppose, indeed Swinburne's letters bear it out, that he protected his young disciple from the seamier sides of his imagination. Gosse received nearly a hundred letters from Swinburne, in that neurotic handwriting. Gosse described them as 'splendid with wit and penetration'. A. C. Benson noticed, on reading in 1911 a privately printed pamphlet of some of them, their 'poignancy and obscenity'. But there was no talk, as there was in Swinburne's letters to other friends, of 'Whitman's bedfellows, the cleaners of privies' or of the flogging-block at Eton and cartloads of birch being insufficient.

In October 1871, there was Swinburne being denounced at a Church Congress in Nottingham as one who 'insulted Him as He hung on the bitter cross' and there was Edmund Gosse, the young

Sunday School superintendent, cultivating, with amazement perhaps at his own daring, his relationship with this extraordinary man. Certainly Gosse believed passionately that poets were not as other men were. Even if he himself secretly preferred a cup of tea to a glass of absinthe, he always had Bohemian longings in him. He once wrote with enormous admiration of the way of life of the Norwegian poet, Henrik Wergeland, who had died young just before Edmund's own birth. He had had rooms filled with snakes, and birds not caged but flying about the room. Gosse himself might prefer a William Morris wallpaper to Wergeland's negro murals, but he had the romantic notion that that was how poets should live, showing themselves at every turn as different from the common herd. The theme and tendency of his novel, *The Secret of Narcisse*, was to be the artist's natural rebellion 'against the restrictions of civic manners'.

Swinburne could be extremely courteous and civil, but his behaviour in these last London years, just before his incarceration at the Pines, was totally unpredictable. Edmund was naturally flattered by the famous poet's pleasure in his company. It was exciting to walk with Swinburne along the very streets where, a few years before, Gosse had chanted *Dolores* aloud (that 'marvellous and repulsive poem') on his way to the Museum from King's Cross. He told Arthur Waugh that he had done this. It doesn't matter whether he really did or not – in his biography of Swinburne it is the young men of Cambridge who join hands and shout the poem. The important thing is that *Dolores*, and Swinburne himself, stood for 'passion and flame and révolt', and young Gosse was full of them.

Swinburne was, in fact, often lonely and needed Edmund. At one stage, they were meeting almost daily. Swinburne would leave his lodgings in Great James Street at the same moment – four o'clock – that Gosse was released from the British Museum, and they would meet by arrangement on the northern pavement of Coram Street. If Swinburne was coming, he would be there at the precise moment Gosse reached the usual meeting place. 'But although the meeting was of his own making and the person to be met a friend seen every day, if I stood a couple of yards before him silent, he would endeavour to escape on one side and then on the other, giving a great shout of satisfaction when at length his eyes focused on my face.'

Swinburne seemed to lead a charmed life. Gosse would notice him cross a road totally unaware of the cabs and carriages bearing down on him. 'His vast brain seemed to weigh down and give solidity to a frame otherwise as light as thistledown . . . In the streets he had the movement of a somnambulist and often I have seen him passing like a ghost across the traffic of Holborn or threading the pressure of carts eastward in Gray's Inn Road, without glancing to the left or to the right, like something blown before a wind.'

Gosse thought Swinburne was perhaps the most learned of all the major poets, apart from Milton, and Gosse was stimulated by the atmosphere of 'intensely intellectual excitement' he seemed to live in. Their friendship was itself an extension of Gosse's education. They shared a passion for Marlowe, Webster, Ford and Massinger. They talked endlessly about books. 'Can I hope to see you in a day or so?' Swinburne wrote to Gosse on 21st February 1874, 'I have a dozen things to talk to you about.'

As Gosse commented years later: 'It was above all Swinburne's unflagging sense of the superhuman power and value of poetry which made his conversation so stimulating, especially to a very young man whom he honoured with the untrammelled expression of his opinions.' In 1894, when they scarcely ever saw each other, Gosse wrote to Swinburne that it was twenty-four years since he had first taken his hand and 'no second light has arisen during all that time that has been to me what the lamp of your great passion for poetry has been'.

Ordinary life – especially money – puzzled and confused Swinburne as much as alcohol. There is an undated note in Edmund's hand: 'In the autumn of 1871 there was a report that Swinburne had gone off his head, and was in confinement at Capheaton.' But Edmund certainly knew he was an alcoholic, even if he yet knew nothing of whipping-blocks. Swinburne himself, Gosse was quite sure, 'really did not know he was a drunkard'. He would be 'sober one moment, and quite drunk the next – quite drunk yet still able to talk, recite and alas! to shout. But I have often observed that his recollection ceased at a moment before the sudden inebriation, and his memory would be of having been very happy and gay, perhaps a little too gay, and then of waking up with a headache or an indigestion, which he attributed to the lobster or the cucumber.'

At meals, it was important, Gosse said, to keep the wine or beer or spirits out of Swinburne's reach, but it was difficult, and if he got the chance he would 'fill a tumbler in a moment . . . drain it to the last drop, sucking in the liquid with a sort of fiery gluttony, tilting the glass into his shaking lips and violently opening and shutting his eyelids. It was an extraordinary sight and one which never failed to fill me with alarm, for after that the Bacchic transition might come at any moment.' There was no heavy drinking. One tumbler would do it. He could not take any alcohol at all.

Morris used to tell a story of Swinburne taking a companion to a doctor in great alarm. 'He'll be better soon,' said the doctor. 'He's only drunk.' 'Is *that* what you call being drunk?!' exclaimed the horrified

Swinburne. Morris said, 'Having always been the first to get drunk he had never seen anyone drunk before.'

One of Edmund's main functions in Swinburne's life was as a listener. It was Swinburne's passion to read his poems aloud. He would read 'with ever-increasing emphasis and lilt, as though he must finally be lifted from his chair by his own chanting cadence.' Sometimes the manner made it almost difficult to concentrate on the matter. The flow of language swept over his young listener. The great Benjamin Jowett had commented on the undergraduate Swinburne's Oxford essays: 'It was all language. I never perceived that he was following a train of thought.' And so it was sometimes with the poems. But there was always a sense of occasion.

I shall never forget the successive evenings on which he read *Bothwell* aloud in his lodgings, in particular one on which Edward Burne-Jones, Arthur O'Shaughnessy, P. B. Marston and I sat with him at his round marble-topped table – lighted only by candles in two giant candlesticks of serpentine he had brought from the Lizard – and heard him read the magnificent second act of that tragedy. He surpassed himself in vigour and melody of utterance that night. But sometimes, in reading, he lost control of his emotions, the sound became a scream, and he would dance about the room, the paper fluttering from his fingertips, like a pennon in a gale of wind . . .

Sometimes, after an evening of such energy, Swinburne would 'sit back in the deep sofa in his sitting-room, his little feet close together, his arms against his side, folded in his frockcoat like a grasshopper in its wing-covers', and would have fallen asleep, apparently for the night, before Gosse could blow out the candles and silently leave the room.

Early in 1875 Dr Georg Brandes of Copenhagen, who had started a magazine called *Det Nittende Aarhundrede* (The Nineteenth Century), asked Edmund Gosse to write about Swinburne. He found it difficult to write. 'He seems to stand too near me,' he wrote to Brandes on 3rd July 1875. It was eventually translated into Swedish, Danish, German and Dutch and was by far the most comprehensive study of Swinburne that had yet appeared. It was not published in English until 1925, when a limited edition appeared. Gosse analyses not only Swinburne's poetry but that of the whole mid-Victorian period, in a provocative, readable style remarkably similar to that of the more familiar essays of thirty and forty years later. He comes down firmly on the side of freedom of expression. One hears the same tones as in the *Lady Chatterley's Lover* trial eighty-five years later – the continuing dispute about censorship and Mrs Grundyism and books not having to be suitable for gamekeeper's daughters. One must remember (as Gosse reminds us) that 'there were Victorian accounts of the English Novel from which the name of Fielding was excluded in the service of virtue.' Gosse waged a continuous war throughout his life (and should be given due credit which the young of his old age failed to do) against 'clergymen's wives who write up from the Vicarage, Little Pedlington' complaining that he was making 'young hearts acquainted with vice'. Once at a lecture he praised *Tom Jones* and a lady rose in the audience protesting against praise being given to books 'the very names of which should be unknown to a young Christian'. Not merely could a spade never be called a spade but its very existence was denied, he once said. On the whole he stuck consistently to the view that 'the weak and the immature must look after themselves' and that booksellers — and indeed publishers — should not boycott books. In 1911 he would write to Marsh about Sturge Moore's new Vigilance Society 'I count on you to have no truck with such prudery.'

So he started in 1875 as he meant to go on. At least he could be fairly sure that neither his father, nor indeed Tennyson, would read his Danish article on Swinburne.

> There has never been a generation so childishly timid, so delicately mealy mouthed, so respectable and so refined . . . In an atmosphere so moral in profession, so immoral in the highest reality, poetry was like a greenhouse plant, sickly, tame and pale. The one poet of that epoch was Tennyson, whose idyllic pictures of the amours of cottage-girls and curates were the strongest intellectual food the nation could digest. Robert Browning delivered his powerful and esoteric utterances unmarked by more than a few. Elizabeth Browning died in 1861, just as with her *Casa Guidi Windows*, and still more her stupendous epic-satire of *Aurora Leigh*, she was beginning to make the nation acknowledge a broader and robuster spirit possible in poetry. All was again sliding back into the most vapid condition possible; the only poets whom the press accepted were those whose works could be put without hesitation into the hands of the youngest girl.

Then came Swinburne, and Gosse saw him 'challenging and defying every prejudice of the British Philistine, drowning the mild voices of the idyllists in thundering melodies of lust and cruelty and blasphemy'. 'In the ranks of the Extreme Left' (surely an early use of that familiar phrase) 'none were more eager than he to unfurl the red flag in its most startling redness. But English poets have been republican in their youth and conservative in their old age.' (So would it be with Gosse.) 'Would not Swinburne also desert the good cause for a laurel or a ribbon?' He could not imagine the Pines. In the meantime – and this was the part which would have shaken his father – he describes pantheism as 'at least as comprehensive and reasonable a creed as any other now presented to the human faculty of faith'. It is perhaps no coincidence that Edmund wrote those words at the very time when, after eight long years, he at last left Tottenham and his charge of the Brook Street Sunday School.

Gosse also praised Swinburne's critical work – for what it had done to save poetry from being considered 'a thing for boys and girls, a mere back-water of sluggish sentiment with lyric lilies here and there.' People were no longer quite so sure that the art would die with Tennyson, even if they could not believe Swinburne's assessment of Rossetti as a 'superhuman combination of Shakespeare, Dante and Goethe in one'.

But what of the young critic's own poetry? It was certainly as a poet he wanted to be assessed. And how did he come in 1875 to be writing a critical article for a Danish journal? We must go back to 1872.

5
Northern Studies

It was Scandinavia, in fact, not Swinburne, that actually dominated Gosse's spare time in 1872. His own poems, heavily influenced by Swinburne, were, many of them, equally influenced by his northern travels. At the time he was publishing his first articles on Ibsen, he had also written his first piece of fiction: *A Norwegian Ghost Story*. But nobody seemed to want it.

P. H. Gosse, in Marychurch, welcomed his new studies: 'What you tell me of your increasing interest in the Scanian tongues is particularly agreeable to me . . . It does seem that this new path, of the Northern literature, has been opened for you by our gracious Lord, in answer to prayer.' He saw the special interest as particularly valuable as 'a preservative against frivolity and the grosser forms of temptation'. But then he would have second thoughts: 'The writings which you criticize and translate and commend and so help to publish are essentially "of the world".' Ibsen might be estimable in many respects but he certainly didn't love the Lord Jesus. The father's criticism became more detailed. He borrowed the *Fortnightly* with Edmund's Ibsen article from Torquay library.

> The reference to Ezekiel was objectionable . . . to bring the words of the Holy Ghost into mere literary comparison with those of modern satirists or those of such as Juvenal, was profane and shocking to a reverent spirit . . .
>
> As for *Brand*, it appears from the description to be a coarse caricature of godliness . . . It is easy to reply, 'No it was hypocrisy not godliness that sat for these portraits'. But the ribald world always calls aggressive godliness hypocrisy.

Such portraits, he realized, could be drawn of the father – and should be of the son, were he to continue faithful.

Certainly Edmund was, for the most part, eschewing frivolity and temptation and spending longer hours than ever at his desk, studying the languages. 'I persevered fanatically,' he noted, with some pride. His father was amazed and impressed at the progress he made, but worried also because Francis Palgrave, Eliza Gosse's relation, had been saying: 'I hope he won't give himself up to criticism; it is a poor thing for a man's life to be spent in turning over other people's thoughts. Let him produce something original.' This is ironical from the man who is remembered only for his *Golden Treasury* of other people's poems. P. H. Gosse was anxious that, though Edmund's critical articles were full of praise and written *con amore*, he might soon become a snarler and a carper like the rest of them. In fact, the book of poems Edmund was now working on would give his father more cause for worry than any snarling and carping possibly could. Meanwhile the father was worried by the son's use of the indicative for the subjunctive ('Don't you fall into this slipshod mode of writing') and fantasized that he might spread the sweet name of Jesus in northern lands afar. The good news was that the wife of the wooden-legged vegetable-seller in Marychurch had become 'deeply convinced of sin' and seemed in fact to have been saved.

This was more, he felt sure, than could be said of most of the people with whom Edmund mixed in London – the adulterous and sinful generation. The Duke of Somerset had just confirmed P. H. Gosse's own conviction that 'society' quite rejects the Bible. 'The literary, the scientific, the artistic, the polite, the fashionable circles of London are utterly alien from Christ. Now it is in this "society" that you are obtaining success; and it greatly excites my fears. O My Willy! You are walking in slippery places! Do you not feel there is the sorest temptation to be ashamed of Christ in these circles? You confess Him at Tottenham. Yes, but there is no cross in the confession there. Do you confess him in London? Do the people at the Museum – do those you meet at Mr Madox Brown's – know you are a Christian?' He had asked the questions before but Edmund *would* evade a direct answer. 'As you make your bed, so must you lie. Do not think of making the most of both worlds; there is no such thing. It is Satan's lie . . . I must leave it with your own soul and God,' P. H. Gosse ended the twelve-page letter. But he never could leave it. In a week or two the interrogation would begin again. 'I have no pleasure in wounding you,' he wrote on 1st March 1872, 'save as a kind and skilful surgeon wounds.' He asks his son, in sudden remorse, 'to pass by all that has given you pain, except as you may "suck honey out of the flinty rock"'.

Edmund, rallying his strength yet again to take on his formidable adversary, accuses his father of waiting for his beloved Lord, as a servant sits at a window, letting the work of the house go quite unheeded. The father is indignant at the suggestion: 'For what have I given up the paths of science and turned from the praise of man, but that I might labour in my Master's house?' Edmund simply cannot win, but in 1872 he had by no means given up the struggle to define a Christianity he could believe in.

At least he had plenty of absorbing work to take his mind off the question of belief. It was not easy work. There was no Grammar or Reader of the Dano-Norwegian language then available in English, and Gosse taught himself the elements of the language by comparing the original version of Henrik Scharling's novel *Nøddebo Praestsgaard* with an English translation *Nøddebo Parsonage*. To test himself and his increasing knowledge, he claims eventually to have read it aloud in English from the Danish copy, evening by evening, to entertain his admiring old ladies, Miss Baker and Miss Buckham. One day, when Gosse was enthusing as usual about his 'discovery', Henrik Ibsen, one of them told him kindly she was afraid he would weary people if he continued to talk so much about Henry Gibson, 'for so they had conceived the unfamiliar name'. But there was no stopping him. He had undertaken to become, in his own words, 'Ibsen's prophet to English readers'.

The task was not without hazards, as well as the problem of getting published at all. In his review of *Digte* in *The Spectator*, Gosse apparently misrepresented Ibsen's position on the language question, suggesting that he had rejected Copenhagen Danish when in fact he had not. Gosse claimed that he discovered his own blunder, before it was pointed out to him. Certainly at this time he was constantly increasing his knowledge of the complicated literary and linguistic scene he had taken on. Inevitably, he would make more mistakes. In fact, his knowledge of the languages was never as good as he hoped it was. He would often encourage his correspondents to write in their own languages, not in English, as he understood them 'perfectly', but there would be howlers.

Gosse was fortunate enough in the spring of 1872 to meet in London two men, one Danish and one Norwegian, who, charmed by his enthusiasm, were to open for him more doors in their own countries than he could possibly have hoped. The Dane was Dr Bruun Julius Fog, then Dean of Holmen's Church in Copenhagen, who would one day be Primate of Denmark. Gosse was introduced to him as someone greatly interested in Danish literature, 'who might be useful to him in his stay in London'. Sensibly, of course, Edmund Gosse laid himself out with zeal to serve him well and was rewarded by an invitation to visit his house in Copenhagen. Fog was one of the most influential men in Denmark. He inclined 'to the staid, traditional and official order of things, while cultivating a secret sympathy for the revolutionary . . . He was always a safe man, but so eminently safe that he could be daring'. He was endlessly helpful and informative and sympathetic to Edmund, as we shall see.

Jacob Løkke, the Norwegian, head of the Cathedral School in Christiania, was a very different character. He was a close friend of Ibsen and it was Ibsen who had put him in touch with his young English disciple. Løkke saw a useful relationship: Gosse would help him with his English text-books and in return Løkke would tell him anything he might want to know about contemporary Norwegian affairs. Gosse found Løkke 'a Tory of the most grimly despairing species' and 'quite a type of everything wooden, bigoted and pig-headed'. But of course, never willing to let slip an opportunity, he accepted with alacrity Løkke's invitation to visit Norway again.

So it was that the young poet, with Swinburne's revolutionary talk in his ears, found himself firmly in the hands of the Establishment when, in the summer of 1872, having been given two weeks' extra leave from the Museum, he visited Denmark and Norway 'for the purpose of reporting on the state of current literature in these countries'. He travelled via Hamburg to Flensburg, where the German waiter detected his sympathies were Danish (Schleswig-Holstein had only recently been annexed by Bismarck). The waiter told him he was only the second Englishman to visit Flensburg that year. He felt youthful and insignificant. Arriving at Dean Fog's house in Copenhagen, he found the Dean's sister spoke no English. 'That night not one word of Danish would come to my lips, so prospects seemed bad.' But soon he was able to make the most of all his opportunities. 'The necessity of talking was so useful to me that I could only compare it with the rough and ready way of learning swimming, by being thrown head-foremost out of a boat.'

'Hardly anybody anywhere I went talked English, so more and more I was forced into Danish proficiency.' By the time he visited the Dean's church, he was so confident that he showed off 'at the tombs of the fighting admirals' by reciting an ode in Danish about them. Everyone was amazed to find him so well-acquainted with their literature, and people began to tell him he spoke 'som en Svensker' – 'like a Swede, that is not correctly, but very prettily'. He learnt a great deal from the Dean, sitting up late at night after guests had departed and his sister had gone to bed.

Gosse went to hear Bishop Grundtvig preach, a famous ecclesiastic (a poet too) now in his ninetieth year. 'He began his exhortation in a slow dull voice, like a person talking in a cellar. I was intensely excited;

my heart beat fast. Rows of fanatic women, swinging themselves backwards and forwards as they sang, and singing, it seemed to me, rather to the poet than to the God the poet directed them to.' By September the old bishop was dead. Gosse found Tivoli democratic and surprising – working people and the fashionable world mixing happily together. In Tivoli there were busts of all the great poets of the north. 'With what a thrill did I see Ibsen's name under one head! It was the first glimpse I had of my great friend's outward seeming.'

The highlights of this first Danish visit were calls, in that summer of 1872, on two of the most important writers in Denmark.

The first was Hans Christian Andersen, the most famous man in Denmark and indeed one of the most famous men in the whole of Europe. He was old and in ill health and shielded by a bodyguard of friends 'against the incursions of the Philistine'. At that time he was staying at Rolighed, not far from Copenhagen, in the house of friends, the Melchiors, where three or four rooms had been set aside for his use. Dr Fog had secured an invitation for Edmund. The Melchiors welcomed him; no word was said of the object of his visit. Then, as they sat in the living-room,

There appeared in the doorway a very tall, elderly gentleman, dressed in a complete suit of brown, and in a curly wig of the same shade of snuff-colour. I was almost painfully struck, at the first moment, by the grotesque ugliness of his face and hands, and by his enormously long and swinging arms, but this impression passed away as soon as he began to speak . . .

The face of Hans Andersen was a peasant's face, and a long lifetime of sensibility and culture had not removed from it the stamp of the soil. But it was astonishing how quickly this first impression subsided, while a sense of his great inward distinction took its place. He had but to speak, almost but to smile, and the man of genius stood revealed. I experienced the feeling which I have been told that many children felt in his company. All sense of shyness and reserve fell away, and I was painfully and eagerly, but with almost unprecedented success, endeavouring to express my feelings to him in Danish. Andersen had at one time possessed considerable knowledge of English, and understood how to read it still, but had ceased to speak it with any ease. The rest of the company tactfully left us alone, and Andersen conversed about the many happy memories he had of England, his two bright visits to Charles Dickens, the shock of grief he had felt at Dickens' death, and his hope to come again some day to London.

He then conducted me over the house, showing off its magnificence with a childlike enthusiasm, and finally he stopped in his own bright, high room open to the east. He took me out into the balcony and bade me notice the long caravan of ships going by in the Sound below – "they are like a flock of wild swans," he said – with the white towns of Malmö and Landskrona sparkling on the Swedish coast, and the sunlight falling on Tycho Brahe's island. Then he proposed to read to me a new fairy-tale he had just written. He read in a low voice, which presently sank almost to a hoarse whisper; he read slowly, out of mercy to my imperfect apprehension, and as he read he sat beside me, with his amazingly long and bony hand – a great brown hand, almost like that of a man of the woods – grasping my shoulder. As he read, the colour of everything, the twinkling sails, the sea, the opposing Swedish coast, the burnished sky above, kindled with sunset.

When he had finished reading, he talked to Edmund about 'The Cripple', the story he had been reading, which he thought might be his last. And as he was talking, Andersen's voice abruptly faded away, to Edmund's alarm. He rang a bell. Servants came and summoned the family who looked at the visitor as if he had dropped one of their most splendid vases, but eventually calmed down enough to decide that the great man had lost his voice by the imprudence of reading aloud in the evening air. He was hurried away to bed.

This account comes from *Two Visits to Denmark* (published in 1911), based on the journal Gosse kept at the time. But there is another, less attractive view of Andersen, not mentioned in *Two Visits*. In an article in *Chambers's Magazine* in 1899, Gosse describes in great detail the writer telling one of his famous fairy stories to a group of children. The occasion was perfectly charming, but Gosse could not help feeling that the story-teller kept half an eye all the time on the adults, and that there were asides and allusions in the story which the children could not have understood. After Andersen had gone, Gosse discovered from his hostess that he 'would never tell stories to little children unless there was a background of adults'. In fact, Andersen was rather like the comedian who wants to play Hamlet. He told Gosse in 1874 how much he hoped that it would be his dramas and novels which would be remembered, not the fairy stories. He had no idea where his own strength lay. But he also had no modesty. He told Gosse, 'When I die *everyone* will come and put flowers on my coffin.' Gosse seemed charmed, rather than repelled, by his enormous vanity.

The second memorable visit was to the writer Frederik Paludan-Müller. We may not know his name but a visit to this Danish poet – a legend in his lifetime – was even more difficult than bearding Tennyson. He was a recluse, lodged by the King in grace and favour rooms in Fredensborg Palace, and guarded by a fearsome wife. Dr Fog, who had known Paludan-Müller long ago, had mentioned to the King himself that he had a young English poet who wanted to assay the impossible. The King said he thought a little excitement would do the elderly poet good. But both monarch and prelate thought it unlikely that Gosse would get very far. All the same, the young man sat up half the night re-reading the great poet's work.

When they arrived, they were told the poet and his wife were walking in the palace gardens. They must wait. So they went and walked themselves in the beech woods, which would suddenly reveal a marble nymph or faun. They were hot and thirsty and nervous. Dr Fog had not seen his friend for many years. It was said that no one save servants, wife and doctor had seen him for three years. It was not without cause that they were anxious.

When they returned, the door opened and Paludan-Müller himself appeared:

He was tall, and taller than he looked, for he was slightly bowed. He stood there, in the strong light, quivering with agitation, and hestitating – or so it seemed – as to whether he should not fly back into the house . . .

As we approached, I stole behind the Dean, concealed by him. Paludan-Müller came forward, trembling excessively, but greeted Dr Fog, who then moved aside to present me in my turn. Before he could speak, however, the poet had made a gesture as though to repel me, and, burying his face in his hands, turned to go back into the house. I was more shocked and confounded than I can express, but before Dr Fog could say a word, I had stepped two paces forward, and – I know not by what desperate deity inspired – had managed to say in high-piping Danish that I was a young English author, who adored Paludan-Müller's poems, and that in leaving England my greatest hope had been that I might see him whom I revered so greatly . . . I cannot conceive how I had the impudence to do it, but it was successful. No poet, it appeared, in those days of sentiment, could resist so ardent an admirer. Paludan-Müller wavered and turned back; he fixed his azure eyes upon me – Dr Fog all the time having the consummate tact to say no word – then slowly took my hands in both of his. Slowly he murmured, '*Ak, De er for smigrende! Men, Tak skal De ha!*' – 'You flatter me too much, but thank you!'

Mrs Paludan-Müller then arrived. If she had come a few minutes earlier she would undoubtedly have said that the poet was not at home. She was well known to be a bully and a Tartar. Dr Fog drew her aside and the young poet was left alone with the old one. 'He was like a person just saved from drowning, and still faint from looking into the face of death. He had swum up to life out of the deep waters of melancholia' and he looked at Edmund as if he were his rescuer. He regretted his ignorance of English and asked how Edmund came to know Danish. He laid his hand upon his hair and said, 'Why, you are a Scandinavian yourself! I believe you are a born Dane! You are as blond as we are, and not black like your countrymen.' He had the idea that all English people are swarthy. He spoke of his poems and of his hopes for the future.

The Dean and the poet's wife were astonished on their return to hear the old man exclaim 'I am going to London; I am going to visit our young friend.' He invited Edmund to walks in the woods and to eat with him. Mrs Paludan-Müller looked at the intruder and said very slowly in English, 'You are a very young man' – an indisputable fact, which didn't seem to offer any matter for discussion. So they said goodbye, and Edmund never walked in the woods with the old poet because it was his last day in Denmark.

But we know the old poet did not sink back into lethargy again. Certainly he never visited England, but on Edmund's next visit to Denmark, hearing of his arrival, Paludan-Müller actually called at Dr Fog's house. Edmund Gosse had by then endeared himself even further, as he was so often to do with writers he admired. He had discovered that what mattered to the poet himself was the memory of his father, and he had begun an essay on the poet's work with something about the bishop father. 'If I had been crafty, I had my reward,' Gosse wrote. He was often to be crafty as well as charming, and there were to be many rewards.

But Scandinavian politics were complicated, and Gosse, by coming out so strongly in praise of Ibsen, had alienated that other great Norwegian writer, Bjørnson. It is difficult for us now to realize that at this period Ibsen was one of a group regarded by their radical opponents as fanatically reactionary. Ibsen hated the liberals of Norway. His Danish champion, Georg Brandes, was to write that year: 'The political liberals are almost illiberal in intellectual matters, and he says it is better to be under the rule of one big tyrant than several little ones.' Gosse's own interpretation of the situation was that Ibsen's friends would in any other country at this time have been considered advanced liberals. They desired to introduce broad reforms within the Constitution whereas their opponents wanted to sweep away the

Constitution itself, and all remotely aristocratic institutions (including pensions for poets).

It was a time of great upheaval. Everything was being re-examined. Gosse tried not to get involved in the politics. He would write to Brandes in 1877:

I wish you would come out of the ranks of the politicians. Here in England there is scarcely a man of genius, of liberal views about religion, aesthetics and philosophy, who is not conservative in politics. Carlyle, Herbert Spencer, Huxley, Tyndall, Browning, all the best names are conservative. Swinburne is the only eminent exception and he only desires an ideal Republic. The commune and socialism have no intellectual supporters in England, and that, I think, is why we are progressing so rapidly in the emancipation of the intellect and the conscience.

It was certainly a view that appealed to Ibsen. Bjørnson saw Gosse as a danger. He was to write to Brandes in 1879, 'He means mischief, that man. I smelled a rat as soon as he came to see me, many years ago. I was also pretty distant. Since then he couldn't have done better if he had actually been in the pay of the party which he pretends not to belong to.' Brandes, who had been corresponding amiably for years with Gosse (they had been very useful to each other), replied placatingly: 'I am not quite clear about Gosse. I've only spoken a couple of times to him altogether. He seems to have come under the reactionary influence of certain Norwegians, with whom he must correspond. But who they are I do not know.' Strange words from 'Ibsen's Danish champion'. Brandes went on to say of Gosse, 'He is very vacillating in his political opinions; amusingly enough, he calls himself a supporter of an *ideal* Republic.' Obviously Brandes was half-remembering Gosse's description of Swinburne.

No one would believe Gosse was interested only in literature, not in politics. He had an introduction to Bjørnson from Hans Christian Andersen when he went on to Denmark from Norway in 1872. This was the visit Bjørnson mentions in the letter to Brandes I quoted. Gosse, recalling the visit long afterwards, remembered Bjørnson as not 'pretty distant' but rather as 'truculently cordial'. Gosse took an instant dislike to him. 'He sat there on his sofa in something like royal state, as though the homage of the world were his due.'

Like everyone else, Bjørnson hoped his work might become better known in England. He promised to send Gosse a copy of his next play when it was published. And he did. Obviously his hostility to Gosse in 1879 was not only because of his work for Ibsen but also because Gosse had criticized Bjørnson from time to time. In 1874 Gosse said he hated to see a gifted poet sink into a 'vulgar stump orator' and in 1877 he wrote of Bjørnson's 'deplorable decadence in style'. 'You seem to me to judge Runeberg well, Ibsen rather high, Bjørnson rather low,' Brandes would write to him. He had certainly taken on more than he bargained for when he sat up night after night teaching himself the language. Sometimes he must have wished he had never started, and it is no wonder that eventually he tired of his strenuous efforts to keep up with Scandinavian literature. But before that he would, in 1884, in an anonymous review, publicly criticize himself on the question of Bjørnson's merits: 'The most detailed English account of his career, that published by Mr Gosse in his *Northern Studies*, shows that the critic had entirely failed to comprehend the meaning of Bjørnson's new departure and the reader would do well to turn to the far sounder . . . judgment' of Dr Brandes. Gosse sent the review to Brandes with a note, 'You see that I do penance.' He would eventually edit the standard English edition of Bjørnson's novels.

The situation in Scandinavia was certainly very complex. In Copenhagen in 1874 Brandes' visit to Gosse at Dean Fog's house would even shock the servants. In Christiania in 1872, Gosse's visit to Bjørnson was much deplored by the friends of Ibsen, with whom he was spending much of his time. Ibsen was himself at this time in exile in Germany, where Brandes was soon to join him. Gosse's introduction to Ibsen's friends came, as we have seen, through Jakob Løkke, who had been in London the previous May. He also had the recommendation of Tennyson to Professor Ludwig Kristensen Daa.

The young man was fêted and entertained by a great crowd of respectable clerics and academics, all united in their opposition to the ruling radicals and in support of the absent Ibsen. It was flattering, but Gosse admitted in his biography of Ibsen that he found the society of Christiania 'boringly solemn, unsmiling, essentially provincial', after the 'grace and sweetness, the delicate, cultivated warmth of Copenhagen'. On one occasion, Michael Birkeland, the Master of the Rolls, stood up and said, 'English men often come to us that they may climb our mountains or fish in our lakes, but it is rare indeed for a young man of letters to visit us that he may investigate what is most dear to us, our native literature.'

On his travels in Norway this time everyone seemed pleased with his Norsk. One girl thought from his accent that he was a Dane, which pleased Edmund enormously. 'In Norway,' he found, 'one does everything for oneself and classes are not divided as with us.' In one hotel he was shown to his room, and found a youth in the other bed, who invited the girl, who had brought Edmund up, to share a cup of tea with them. 'I never find any difficulty in being a Thracian when in Thrace,' he commented smugly.

Gosse's description of this visit to Norway was not published until more than forty-five years later. Gosse said it was based on a full journal he kept at the time. It is accurate in most particulars though gently self-censored. The oddest thing is that, although he must have had the journal in front of him, the endings of the journeys are quite different. In fact, Gosse, having bought a little bust of Ibsen, left Norway on August 13th and crossed to Scotland. Forty-five years later he wrote, 'I returned to Hull towards the end of August.' It is as if he wearies of accuracy.

Edmund soon settled back into the familiar routine of life at Tottenham. In September, he told his father that at seven o'clock each morning (except on Sunday when he could sleep in until eight-thirty), the servant Mary would let his great white cat in to his bedroom. 'He jumps on the bed to caress me and that wakes me. I play with him for a few seconds.' Then after a quick bath and breakfast, at 7.45 he would walk to Wood Green Station, along White Hart Lane, which was just as 'lovely and countrified' as it had been when he arrived in Tottenham nearly six years before. 'I always read in the train but no longer while I walk, for my eyes could not bear it.' At 8.45 he would reach King's Cross, walk to the Museum, arriving there at 9.05. He would sign his name, take down his key, wash his hands and be ready for work. The first thing he had to do each morning was 'to alter the chief copies of the catalogue, correcting any mistakes that may have been discovered on the previous day'. He would also alter 'in the different copies of the catalogue the press marks of books whose shelves have been changed' and 'a variety of little work of this kind'. Monotonous work for someone who had just been the toast of the literary establishment of Christiania and who was 'the dear young friend' of Hans Christian Andersen. But Edmund, at this point, assured his father he found it agreeable 'because I am always moving about, because I am not under constant supervision' (from that dreaded clergyman or anyone else) and 'chiefly because the work is desultory and not, what wears me mad, methodical. At 12.30 I go out with Charlie Walker to dine. Here also we eschew method; we never decide where we shall go till we are in the street.' The end of this letter is missing, but his father's reply, welcoming 'the description of your well-filled and most diligent day', comments on the fact that he is writing poetry in the evenings. 'Are you then preparing another volume of your own poems for the press?' P. H. Gosse also hoped the baths he mentioned were *cold* ones, and taken in both winter and summer. He had himself taken a cold bath each morning, on jumping out of bed, for nearly twenty years: 'I am sure it is greatly conducive to health.' But all is not rigorous and spartan at Marychurch. Their 'favourite pussy' also wakes them in the mornings. Mamma has 'treated herself to a new seal skin jacket' ready for the winter, Philip Henry has reorganised the fernery in a more aesthetic manner and has been lying on the downs by the hour 'watching the yachts in the Regatta'.

The father approved highly of the way the son was still spending his Sundays: Household worship at 9.30; the Meeting at Brook Street from 11 till 12.45. Then either Mrs Robert Howard (whose husband had married his parents at Brook Street twenty-four years before) or Miss Stacey or some other kind friend was sure to ask Edmund to dinner. At 2.30 the Sunday School opened. He had 'the most important class'; about twelve boys, aged thirteen to fifteen or more. On Sunday evenings he would translate 'one of Dean Fog's sermons into English and sing hymns and read some scripture with Miss Baker and Miss Buckham'.

The only thing his father could find to criticize about one of these letters was that, although sometimes Edmund would divide 'words into syllables at the end of a line,' sometimes he would not. 'I recommend you to do so habitually. Here is a little matter in which I can *test* your value of my criticism. I shall judge your estimate of it *in other matters* by the result of it in *this*.'

The father was still nervous about the literary paths Edmund was treading. Dr Finch, in Marychurch, had given a visible start when, with a father's pride, P. H. Gosse had told him Edmund was writing in the *Academy*. 'The *Academy*?' he exclaimed, 'that's rather a heretical paper, isn't it?' Certainly Thomas Huxley wrote in it. The father made 'some light reply, about one correspondent being not liable for his fellows' sentiments', but his doctor's remark had hurt him, 'especially coming from one who is himself in no wise straight-laced'. Earlier that year, Edmund had assured his father that the *Academy*, 'if you could waive the department called theology, . . . is very scholarly and thorough'. In 1874 he would say it was now perhaps 'the very best literary paper published in England'.

But he wrote regularly for many periodicals. *The Spectator* and *Fraser's Magazine* (the one weekly and the other monthly) were both open to him and, as time went on, he was 'able to introduce English readers to as much observation of Scandinavian literature, art and even politics' as he had time 'to digest and reproduce'. In 1873 he told Brandes that 'whatever Scandinavian books are sent to the *Athenaeum* are forwarded to me for review'. In 1877 Scott advised Gosse that the *Athenaeum* was probably better than the *Academy*, as Appleton 'has taken up with every chance imbecile respectability', but he thought Appleton might be justifiably annoyed if his contributors sent their best things to the rival paper. Gosse throughout most of his life (until his late contract with the *Sunday Times*) managed to write for a very varied group of papers.

In the eighteen-seventies he was closely involved with the *Examiner*. William Minto asked him 'to cater for good poetry'. He was always encouraging his poet friends to send to it and, in the autumn and winter of 1874, he wrote a series of weekly studies of English poets of the sixteenth and seventeenth centuries for it. John Morley's *Fortnightly Review*, in which Gosse's first big article on Ibsen appeared, was considered an 'unrivalled platform for the advanced thought of the period' and Leslie Stephen's *Cornhill*, which 'pays splendidly', was another regular employer in these early years.

Gosse's first article for the *Cornhill*, on 'Danish theatre', appeared in September 1874. By 1878 he was in so much demand as a contributor that Stephen sent him 'a funny little note to say that the Editor of the *Cornhill* would be grateful if E. W. G. would remember his existence'. Stephen once regretted to Gosse that he was 'bound to think a little about the collective stupidity of the public', but he had an attractive faith that, though he 'could not count on the existence of any keen appetite for Icelandic poetry', for instance, in his readers, yet 'the appetite may grow by what it feeds on'. In fact, like many editors, he gave Gosse an increasingly free hand to write on whatever pleased him.

We have seen something of Edmund's friendships at this time – the midday meals with Charlie Walker, the walks with Swinburne, the evenings at the Scotts and the Madox Browns. He was moving in a secular society, and walking in slippery places. There is a tantalizing letter at this time, which refers fleetingly to Gosse's 'stormy passions' and 'garish life'. But his basic position, at the beginning of 1873, was that he was still a believer, a Christian, that he had moved through clouds, so he said, but had come out into the light with new strength in his own beliefs. He considered, however much P. H. Gosse's books may belie this, that he had been brought up to believe that 'what is pleasant must be wrong'; he had gradually been able to accept that, in abandoning the attitudes of the puritanical Brethren and their fear of the world, he did not have to abandon Christ as well. His long talks with Dean Fog in Copenhagen had helped. That eminent Christian saw no harm in secular music, in nudity in painting and sculpture, in dancing, in drama, in all those pleasures of the world which P. H. Gosse felt would distract his son from Christ.

It was hard enough when his father criticized his friends and the way he spent his leisure. When he also – alarmed, for instance, by the proximity of Huxley in the *Academy* – began increasingly to question Edmund's literary work and the very expressions that he used, the son wearily resumed the battle of words. Early in 1873, the father wrote: 'I will ask you if there are not several things – lines of thought, expressions and allusions – in both your last papers, which you would hardly like to be examined at the Judgement Seat of Christ.' Edmund pleaded innocent. He had no idea to what his father referred. He had read both the papers aloud in the evenings at Tottenham to Miss Baker and Miss Buckham. *They* saw nothing wrong. 'I have prided myself', Edmund wrote, 'on writing nothing that should ever hinder anyone on his journey heavenward. I have striven to do honest work in the world . . . to carry it out in an upright, honest and manly way.'

This declaration of innocence meant nothing, of course, to P. H. Gosse. It was not enough not to hinder anyone on that journey heavenward – repenting souls must be helped and the unrepentant shunned. Edmund must walk unashamed, bearing the banner of Christ, strengthened by the new life that was given him in baptism. This was the real cross. Edmund knew that he could not be a witness, that he could not devote his life to Christ, that evangelism sickened him.

But was he even convinced of the truth himself? The father began to doubt Edmund's faith, as he had so often doubted before. In the spring of 1873, he asked Edmund for 'a clear exegesis of his convictions'. And Edmund decided that the moment had come. He must be totally honest. It was now more than six years since he had left home. He was twenty-three. When his father asked him outright whether he believed, as he had been brought up to believe, in the plenary inspiration of scripture – the divine source of every word in the Bible – Edmund gave him a long, reasoned reply. He wrote with humility but with confidence. 'It is well known between us,' he said, 'that I am young and ignorant and you are learned with the accumulation of years.' But he had a right to his own views – views reached through painful self-examination and prayer and hours of studying the New Testament:

This question is of deep interest and more than a year ago I went through the New Testament to study it for myself. If any words might be supposed to be of paramount interest to us, they would be those words spoken by our Lord himself in the ordinance of His Supper. Yet these, given four times, are nowhere the same . . . It is obvious to me that the inspiration of the Scriptures is one of tenour and matter, not of word . . . No book has been so much in my hands during the last year as the Bible. Especially have I read with deep thought the books of the New Testament . . . seeking to discover its bearing on the Christian life . . . I have . . . sought to arrive at the real drift myself.

Boldly at last Edmund admitted that he could no longer believe in the necessity of the Christian's separation from the world or that his own object should be the proclamation of the Gospel.

In his increasing vigilance over Edmund's soul in its slippery places, P. H. Gosse had even betrayed his own real sympathies. He had foolishly called the study of poetry 'frivolous and profane'. Edmund sighed and wrote, as he might have written many times before: 'I think you are the most difficult Father to satisfy in all the world . . .'

Literature is my business as much as carpentering is a carpenter's business . . . Because a carpenter might . . . be tempted to carve wooden idols, there is in that no reason to give up carpentering, but rather determine against the carving of idols . . . As to your saying, that I live one life in Tottenham and one in town, it is a mistake. Everybody who cares to know, in London, knows that I am Superintendent of a little Dissenting Sunday-school, and everybody who cares to know at Brook Street knows I am a poet, critic and *littérateur*. You only have found these things inconsistent.

But he really knew himself of the deep inconsistencies and conflicts in his life.

In the same letter, Edmund declared his belief in the saving power of Christ for all good men, not for a small body of the elect. He believed in Christ, who gave His blood to take away the sins of the world. That was perhaps, now, when it really came down to it, all he did believe. At times in his life, he would believe in rather less, though he would rarely admit to it. The main impression is that, after this huge letter – it runs to nearly five thousand words – Edmund grew more and more tired of theological debate. There would be further exchanges between father and son. The long letters from Marychurch continued. ('A letter to you is not a matter to be jerked off at the tail-end of a morning'; 'You do not know how a parent's heart yearns over his only child' etc etc.) Edmund would put his own point of view, over and over again, courteously and at length. But the gulf was widening. The swimmer was definitely tiring of the stormy sea. Yet he never falters in his expressed love for his father. (Ernest Pontifex, in *The Way of all Flesh*, broke off relations with his father for far less reason.)

A year after this, when Gosse, at the mercy of a runaway horse, was faced with possible death, he told Blaikie that 'the Christian revealed religion had never seemed so little worthy of belief'. But he never spoke out as an agnostic, not even after his father's death. Through the years, he would talk endlessly on practically everything else, but very rarely about religion. He had had enough.

The following month, April 1873, Edmund was attacked by a fever which left him so weak that his doctor insisted on his taking leave from the Museum, going to convalesce in Devon and giving up for a while all literary work. The Museum had, in any case, been protesting about the amount of outside work he was taking on: 'What horrid news this is you have from the Museum,' Alice Boyd, William Bell Scott's painter friend, wrote to him in Marychurch in May. 'How is it possible that such tyrannical rules can be thought of as to prevent people doing what they please with their time in the evenings at home!' It shattered her illusions about the Museum as the one place in London where the troubled spirit might be at rest.

Edmund forgot such problems in exploring, as he had always loved to explore, the coves and caves of south Devon. On his return to London in June he was shaken by the suicide of a fourteen-year-old boy in Tottenham, not one of his own pupils but 'a Sunday School teacher at the Baptist chapel'. 'It is oddly characteristic of what the vulgar opinion of holiness is,' Edmund wrote to his father, 'that the parents said, "He was always such a good boy; he never played at ball or marbles in his life!" What a morbid child he must have been.'

On 28th June there were happier matters to report: the wedding of Mr Westland Marston's daughter to Mr Arthur O'Shaughnessy. 'I must tell you about an intensely pretty wedding I went to on Thursday,' Edmund wrote to his stepmother. 'It was quite a wedding in our set, you understand . . .' Most of the prominent Pre-Raphaelites, as they were still occasionally called, were there. 'Nettleship (but clothed and in his right mind!) was the best man. Marzials and I and five other people were groom's men.' There were eight bridesmaids, four in blue and four in red. In the church Malcolm Lawson, the composer with whom Marzials lived, played the loveliest things out of Wagner's *Lohengrin*.

Altogether it was a very poetical wedding indeed. A long table was set out with wine and sandwiches and cake etc and everybody helped themselves from 12.15 to 3.15. I enjoyed myself immensely. Robert Browning stood there, serenely smiling, looking so sweet with his grave white head. He made a very pretty little speech. The only jar on the feelings was a rather vulgar speech by Hepworth

Dixon, but then Dixon is always dreadful. Almost all the minor poets now living, that are recognised, were there . . . The nicest touch of all was the entrance of R. H. Horne. He is a funny little man with white hair in corkscrew ringlets and whiskers curled into one ringlet on each side. He brought his guitar with him and sang some pathetic Spanish songs to it, extremely prettily.

This account makes an interesting contrast with the published account in his *Portraits and Sketches* (1912) where 'the tiny old gentleman', all uninvited, sang to his guitar and Robert Browning saved the day by stepping up and saying in his loud, cheerful voice (just when everyone was getting really embarrassed by the unwanted concert) 'That was charming, Horne! It quite took us to "the warm south" again' and cleverly diverted the aged guitarist from continuing.

This was the first time Edmund had met Richard Hengist Horne; he was to see a great deal more of him. He was, as Edmund noted, a rewarding study for anyone who could be patient with his peculiarities. As a boy he had been a schoolfellow of Tom Keats at Enfield and would tell the story of how he once saw the chaise of Mr Hammond, the surgeon, standing at the school gate and, holding the head of the horse, Mr Hammond's apprentice, John Keats. There was snow on the ground and Tom dared young Horne to throw a snowball at his pugnacious brother. 'It used to be very thrilling,' Gosse said, 'to hear the old gentleman tell how he had actually snowballed Keats; almost as though one should arise and say that he had sold Shakespeare a cheese-cake.' After various American adventures Horne brought out his most famous poem, *Orion*, at the price of a farthing – to show 'the contempt into which epic poetry has fallen'. It was an excellent publicity trick. Horne became known as 'the farthing poet' and his poems sold in vast quantities. But his talent abandoned him.

At the time of the Marston-O'Shaughnessy wedding, he had just returned from Australia and was in great poverty. He was merry, vain and tactless to a remarkable degree. He had a strong resemblance to a curly white poodle and 'would throw his fat little person on a sofa and roll about'. In his eightieth year he challenged Swinburne to a swimming match in the Westminster Aquarium. He called his guitar his daughter and would ceremoniously introduce her as 'Miss Horne'. He would bend the drawing-room poker (when Edmund had a drawing-room). Amusing foibles, perhaps, but Edmund must have grown tired of them as, over the years, he helped Horne to keep his head above water, advising him about poems and placings, calming his anxieties. In 1878 Gosse agreed to become his literary executor. He would put up with a good deal for stories of Wordsworth and Leigh

Hunt – and Hazlitt on his deathbed with his hair 'like bunches of grey snakes'.

It may also have been at O'Shaughnessy's wedding that Gosse first saw Robert Browning. The relationship was to be very important to him, as we shall see. Browning was the only rival, in Gosse's mind, to Swinburne's pre-eminence. He was 'the source of some of the highest intellectual pleasure I have enjoyed', Gosse would tell him. He would write: 'You know my unfeigned reverence for you; other people may have other gods, you have been to me – ever since I came to years of discretion – the greatest English poet of the age, and I see less reason for changing my view every year I live.' Browning was a man much easier to love than Swinburne; no allowances had to be made. 'Of his beauty of character hardly too much could, I think, be said,' Gosse would write in 1911. But Hugh Walpole would report, long after even that, Gosse's imitation of the elderly widower 'dining out thirty nights running and proposing to any girl who happened to be around'.

Gosse had hoped to go to Denmark again in 1873, but Dean Fog announced that he was coming to England. He had to visit the Bishop of Bath and Wells and proposed that Edmund should afterwards accompany him on a tour of the British Isles. Edmund could hardly refuse after the Dean's hospitality the year before. He suggested the tour should start at Marychurch, contemplating with some curiosity a meeting between the two theologians. P. H. Gosse greeted Dean Fog cordially but things rapidly became heated. Neither man was accustomed to contradiction and they could find little common ground. Edmund and the Dean left for Wales rather earlier than had been intended. Edmund found the Dean, off his home territory, rather a burden. He 'has been like a child in my hands', he wrote to his stepmother. 'I have been valet, courier and walking Bradshaw, all in one.' By the time they got to Lancaster, he was sick of sight-seeing and Murray's guides, and both he and the Dean were sleeping badly.

> Some circumstances too trivial to mention upset our nerves at Lancaster and we both became very queer. The Dean's nervous organisation closely resembles mine, strangely resembles it indeed, in certain peculiar phenomena. We confessed to one another, long ago, some hallucinations, I may call them, which attack each of us at similar times, which I am sure I, at least, had never known to exist in anyone but myself. That evening at Lancaster we were very miserable . . . I was agitated and nervous to the last degree.

When they parted – the Dean was to return to Denmark via Edinburgh – Edmund ate with relief some fruit and a pennyworth of bread, instead of the sumptuous dinners they had been having. But the travelling had not been a waste of time for him. 'At least half of our conversation turned upon Danish subjects, about which my curiosity was insatiable.'

On leaving the Dean, he took up an invitation to stay with Alice Boyd and the Scotts at Penkill Castle in Ayrshire. This old grey castle with battlements, drawbridge, portcullis, mullioned windows – all the right romantic properties – was Alice Boyd's home. She took a keen interest in Scott's young protégé. Gosse has left no record of his own impression of the triangular relationship that existed between Alice Boyd and the Scotts. There was certainly nothing conventional about it, but Edmund may have been as ignorant as Christina Rossetti had been when she stayed at Penkill in the summer of 1866. The three were always together, at this stage, in London in the winter, at Penkill in the summer. But Edmund would surely not have mentioned Penkill to his father if he had been aware of the situation.

In London in the autumn of 1873, Edmund's main concern was with his first proper book of poems. He had, as young poets usually do, rejected the juvenilia of the book he had published with Blaikie. Introducing himself to Brandes, in a letter from the British Museum before they had met, Gosse had described himself as a poet.

> Poetry does not pay one's bread, of course, so I am also a journalist and assistant-librarian in this place . . . Three years ago I published a small volume of poems, which gave me some slight position here, but I will not send them to you, for they are very boyish and unformed, and I am wholly ashamed of them. But I am now preparing for the press a new book of verse . . . which will explain my aims to you better than any letter can.

As early as February, he had written to Scott, 'My book occupies all my thoughts. It seems absolutely necessary for me to publish and I am writing constantly.' He was a slow worker, spending a long time on one poem, polishing and altering constantly. He had already decided on the title *On Viol and Flute*, which sounds unfortunate enough to us, perhaps, but a little better than *On Fiddle and Flute*, which he rejected as 'too pot-housey'. By 30th September the sheets were ready to go to press. Henry S. King was going to publish the book. He had just signed a contract with Tennyson, guaranteeing him £5000 a year. 'That he is most liberal there can be no doubt,' Emily Tennyson had commented. But King was not taking any risks with young Gosse. The moment was, as Edmund observed, 'highly unpropitious for indulgence to young and unknown writers'. (It always is.) King required an advance payment from the young poet of £35 5s for printing five hundred copies. This was a great deal of money for Edmund, whose salary at the British Museum was still only £150 a year, even if that was beginning to be supplemented considerably by his literary earnings. One suspects P. H. Gosse came to the rescue again, though Edmund must have been well aware how little the book would please him.

Early in December 1873 *On Viol and Flute* appeared, in buff-coloured boards, decorated with a rather feeble Arcadian frieze by William Bell Scott. It was dedicated to Scott but also 'til Alle Mine Venner I Norden', and, 'as it was prettily got up, I did not hesitate to send it here and there, as a kind of visiting card'. Gosse was always a keen sender-out of inscribed copies of his books. Indeed his friends would consider it an indication of how they stood in his favour, whether they received the new book in the post or not.

Walt Whitman was one of the people to whom Gosse posted *On Viol and Flute*. He had told Scott in February that he was relishing Whitman and sharing his 'frank delight in life and the pleasure in men and women for their mere humanity'. He would write later of Whitman's 'amazing inequalities' and the fact that there can be no consistency in the readers' attitude. They are thrilled by him today and disgusted by him tomorrow. 'It depends not so much on him as on themselves.' But in 1873 he did not seem to realize how controversial his admiration was and sent with *On Viol and Flute* a letter of frank hero-worship: 'There is no one living by whom I am more desirous to be known than by you . . . I draw only closer and closer to you.' He thanked Whitman for giving him the power to express his own feelings, ending the letter, 'Accept the homage and love, and forgive the importunity of your sincere disciple.' Gosse also sent a copy of the book to Browning, who praised it gently, to the young man's enormous pleasure. 'A young poet can receive no tribute so delicious as the praise of the poet of the generation before him whom he has most revered.'

Gosse produced nearly fifty books, apart from the even more numerous pamphlets and editions with introductions and assorted papers which delight the hearts of bibliographers. It is obviously impossible to go into detail about each one and its critical reception; but it is interesting to look at his early books and to see how he gradually built up his reputation. Until the reviews of *On Viol and Flute* started coming in, he was very nervous. 'I am trembling with anxiety over my own little flame,' he once wrote to Scott. 'I wonder if it will go out at once into extreme darkness.' Gosse always wanted to be known as a poet. It would be a long time before he could accept that it was not his poetry that would bring him the fame he always longed for. He had a strong inborn conviction that poetry was superior to prose – he regretted, just at this time, that Ibsen had chosen prose, not verse, for the play that became *Emperor and Galilean*. The whole basis of his relationship with the Pre-Raphaelites, and indeed with Browning, was that he was a poet, one of them. They seem to have thought he was a good poet, or at least that he had it in him to become one. Swinburne, particularly, did a great deal to establish Gosse with some sort of reputation. He thought it ridiculous that Gosse should have to pay to have his poems published and he urged Chatto to take him on. 'Of course I told him – what was the simple truth – how well I thought of your work, and that it would be a distinction to him to become your publisher – but there was no need of that, as far as I could see.' His next book would be published by Chatto.

The press, on the whole, were as kind as Swinburne about *On Viol and Flute*, though the *Athenaeum* chaffed him about the fact that 'even in the robust air of the north, he cannot get rid of "clinging hands".' O'Shaughnessy was, loyally, 'deeply disgusted' by this review. There were other strictures, from different quarters, about the 'fleshly' element, about the lack of any forceful ideas, about a certain amount of imitation and affectation; but the general impression was that Edmund Gosse was someone worth watching, that readers should enjoy the present volume and 'look forward with hope to Mr Gosse's maturer work'. Walter Pater in the *Guardian* wrote a particularly perceptive review, and Andrew Lang also welcomed the book.

Some of the praise was calculated to go to Edmund's head: 'Since Rossetti's poems we have seen none so full of colour and melody . . . He has by this one book alone won a high place among English poets' (*Westminster Review*). 'It would be scarcely possible to surpass this blending of the triumphant passion of music with the colour and quiet of painting' (the *Academy*). 'The poems possess all the sweetness and rhythmic beauty of what has been called the "passionate school"' (*Graphic*). The *Academy* traced the influences Gosse acknowledged of Walt Whitman and Gautier (not to mention Goethe and Marcus Aurelius); lots of the papers drew attention to his connection with the Pre-Raphaelites. But what sort of book was it? The poem which got most attention, and which was constantly reprinted in Victorian anthologies, was 'Lying in the Grass'. Later – they had not yet met – Gosse dedicated it to Hardy, and one can see why. But, as Gosse wrote long afterwards, this poem, like many others, owed its 'ethical movement' to Walt Whitman. It has superficial echoes of Wordsworth's 'Solitary Reaper', but Gosse is far more sensuous. His mowers whistle as Wordsworth's reaper sings, but the music does not make the poet think of old unhappy far-off things or of anything else. He can only watch and feel, in the throbbing afternoon, heavy with heat and scents. He watches a girl in a red gown move along a white path through a dark green beech wood. One of the mowers greets her:

> But though they pass, and vanish, I am there.
> I watch his rough hands meet beneath her hair.

He feels part of their love, at one with a loving, glowing world. The last thing he wants is a 'well-stored mind'.

Over and over again this comes out in the poems: the bookish boy exulting in his senses: in the sea, the sun, in warm blood, the scent of wine, the songs we sing, the kisses that we kiss. Augusta Webster, thanking him for a copy, admits she is prejudiced 'by my British Matron morality'. Explaining the sensuality of the book to Cosmo Monkhouse, Edmund wrote: 'I was a very weakly invalid child and remained frail and delicate in health till I was about 22, when, suddenly, I don't know why, I became quite robust and strong. The ecstasy of the new-found enjoyment of all forms of existence' led to the poems in *On Viol and Flute*.

The poems are indeed very physical, full of clasping and embracing, of ecstasy and yearning, of sweet glimpses of young love. There are over-blown images inevitably, and a good deal of empty romanticism (the roses and the nightingales). It is always dangerous to interpret poems biographically (Gosse himself would make that mistake with Donne) but they do seem to add up to an attractive picture of a young man who knows what love really means. They are secular poems, nearly all of them, and it might be wondered what P. H. Gosse felt when he first read them. I found, in an American library, a couple of unsigned pages in a familiar script, dated 4th April 1874. They were headed 'Impromptu on reading some lines in *On Viol and Flute*.' There can be no question about the biographical interpretation of these lines by P. H. Gosse:

> My inmost spirit quails.
> I love the writer for his Mother's
> Sake who lives in glory,
> Whose last hours were spent
> In praying for her child,
> And who "fell asleep" expecting

To receive him in the land
Where robes washed white
In Jesus' precious blood, would
Be their mutual glory
Their only beauteous dress!
And can that precious son
Be satisfied with any
Flimsier clothing? Can he
Give his powers, his talents,
The true genius of his noble mind
To any lower objects? Will he
Aim at greatness here below
And lose the lustre of the
Heavenly crown, the crown of glory?
Forbid it gracious Lord!
Forbid it loving Saviour!
Reveal thyself afresh to his
Affections! By thy Blessed Spirit
Win them back, to find
His holiest, happiest, brightest
Joys in thee.

But it was too late for such heartfelt prayers. Edmund had tasted the joys of worldly success. He was more ambitious than ever for the paper flower high on the wall, marked out for him by his mother – 'the stars beyond his reach'.

There was one quite untypical poem in *On Viol and Flute* which, though praised by some, was singled out for particular castigation in an article on the modern ballad in the *Contemporary Review*. The critic was lamenting a tendency to give poetry 'the factitious look of antiquity'.

Its *reductio ad absurdum* has been achieved by one of the newest members of the brotherhood of young poets who look up to Mr Swinburne and Mr Rossetti as their masters . . . Mr Gosse has allowed himself to perpetrate such a *bêtise* as the following:

When the autumn nights were hot,
(*Peach and apple and apricot,*)
Under the shade of a twining rose,
Deep in the high-walled garden-close,
Guenevere, red as a sunset glows,
Plighted her love to Lancelot.

> Overhead, at a window unseen,
> (*Apple and filbert and nectarine*)
> Gawaine lounged in the hot gold air,
> Fingered a lute, and at last aware
> Of an eager face and the Queen's bright hair,
> Laughed a little in bitter spleen.

The critic, Henry Hewlett, fortunately left aside the picture of a bright red perspiring Guenevere, but he had great fun with the fruit. 'A lady to whom these stanzas were read, naively inquired whether their burden were intended to imitate the cry of an itinerant fruit-seller, or the *sotto voce* of a waiter handing round the dessert at a *table d'hôte*.' Hewlett saw Gosse as gifted with imagination, feeling, rhythm, scholarship but needing to beware of affectation and of what he had himself criticized in Poe: 'mere splendour of sound, irrespective of meaning or emphasis'.

But before these remarks had appeared, Edmund was to form a friendship which would last for nearly forty-eight years and encourage the very sort of poem Hewlett was condemning. In April 1874 Edmund attended for the second time a meeting of the Pen and Pencil Club at Aubrey House, Campden Hill, the home of a radical MP, Mr Peter Taylor and his wife. Writers and artists were invited to illustrate a particular theme. At one point on this April evening 'a slim young man, with dark eyes beneath a fine Horatian forehead, rose and read a short piece, in a voice attractive in its modesty and distinction'. This, a whisper told Gosse, was Mr Austin Dobson, whose *Vignettes in Rhyme* had just been published and were supposed to have been given an approving nod by Tennyson himself. 'As it happily chanced,' Gosse wrote years later, 'I had just read that volume with juvenile enthusiasm. But what greatly moved me was that I recognised (I alone, no doubt!) that the piece just read was a *rondeau* in the French form elaborately defined by Théodore de Banville in the 1874 reprint of his *Petit Traité de la poésie française*, a book which – as we ultimately discovered – was exercising a remarkable influence over several young English poets.' As the meeting broke up, Gosse approached Dobson with the remark that he had noticed he had kept to the rules of de Banville. Dobson was both surprised and pleased at the comment. They wandered out into the night together and 'late as it was, paced the streets in a kind of dream for hours, absorbed in metrical discussion'. From that night on, the two young poets – Dobson was nine years older than Gosse, so still then in his early thirties – exchanged their poems and subjected each other's work to rigorous comment and criticism. 'Remember,' Dobson once wrote to Gosse, 'I depend on you to drive the harvest mice out of my standing corn!' Dobson was a clever versifier, a skilled lyricist who loved the discipline and challenge of the French forms: the *rondeau*, the *chant royal*, the *villanelle*. He was the author of much amusing light verse. He was also a good friend, but the association with him was surely detrimental to Gosse's development and reputation as a poet. Gosse described the world of Dobson's poems as 'rose-coloured . . . suffused with a transparent radiance of ideality and founded, no doubt, more on an illusion as to what things should be, than an observation of what they were'. If Gosse's wild roses were romantic, at least they were alive. It was Dobson who loved the smell of pot-pourri.

He was a kindly, gentle man of whom no one ever spoke an ill word. He led a life of amazing respectability and dullness in Ealing. There was in his life, Gosse said, 'no glimmer of adventure or faintest tincture of romance'. His only real activity was mental; his favourite activity was revising his own poems. From that night in Campden Hill, Dobson would influence Gosse away from the incautious, the Bohemian, the passionate and the squalid, towards the solid bourgeois virtues. He would remind Gosse constantly that poets could be obedient husbands, commuters and quiet scholars. A. C. Benson, years later, would describe Dobson as 'like a funny little sea lion or a good little boy with a heavy moustache'. Edward Marsh, later still, thought him 'rather like a large, intelligent and kindly guinea pig', but the experiments were purely in verse forms. In life, he took no chances.

On Viol and Flute had contained some versions from the Italian of sonnets by Francesco Redi ('It is easy to translate what thoroughly delights me') and also a couple of extracts from Ibsen's *Love's Comedy*, the translation Gosse had not been able to sell to anyone. He was not deterred and continued to give priority to his Scandinavian studies. In February 1874 he published a rather ill-advised article in *Fraser's Magazine* on Norwegian affairs. It was rash of him to enter the political arena; earlier he had been trying to prove that it was *literature* he was interested in, but of course it is difficult to separate literature from ideas. This article suggested that Gosse had accepted Løkke's conservative ideas uncritically, but we know from his letters to Brandes that this was not so. Whichever side it was on, the article was full of errors; Løkke wrote to Gosse pointing out some factual mistakes. Gosse did not visit Norway again until 1898.

On 20th April, Gosse gave his first public lecture. It was on the 'Ethical Condition of the Scandinavian Peoples' and it was given to the Philosophical Society at the Victoria Institute. It was a learned body which included P. H. Gosse as one of its vice-presidents. The father was certainly looking, in spirit, over the son's shoulder, as he gave this impeccably Christian address to a body which admitted to its membership 'only such as are professedly Christians'. Edmund knew his father would read the paper when it was printed in the Transactions of the Society. In Marychurch, that very day, his father was writing 'You will I am sure meet with another example of your unvarying success; and I shall be proud and happy. My only fear is lest all this *couleur de rose* should make you forget the voice of God.'

It seems likely that Edmund had his father's feelings, not his own, in mind when he put forward the idea that the Northern races had higher moral ideas than the Greek and the Latin. Throughout his life, there would be this clash in Gosse's heart between the high, pure Northern and the sensual tempting Southern values. He was also thinking of his father, it seems, when he said, 'No part of a heathen life is so dreary as its close; never do the consolations of revealed religion appeal so strongly to the natural reason' as at the moment of death. For it was only four weeks since he had told John Blaikie, who was in North Africa for his health, how, at the mercy of a bolting horse, he had imagined death and realized how little he believed in eternal life.

In this same letter to Blaikie, he enumerated the work he had on hand, apart from the public lecture: reviews for the *Academy*, *The Spectator* and the *Athenaeum*, and a long article for *Fraser's* on Webster. 'All this amounts almost to an oppression. I have no time for poetry, for letters or for visiting.' But after the lecture, Edmund wrote cheerfully to his father. 'Monday was a great success. My friends are unanimous in assuring me that I read the paper clearly and quietly and emphatically and that my voice had a full pleasant sound . . . The discussion that followed was excessively absurd . . . I wish you had been there . . . to curb useless desultory twaddle.' P. H. Gosse, in his reply, was in a genial mood, sharing with Edmund 'the very best pun I *ever* met with . . . I daresay you have seen it but natheless I will give it to you. Why is a chrysalis like hot rolls? Because it is the grub that makes the butter fly. I can't even write it down without a burst of delighted laughter. Is it not wonderfully clever? The play on the word "grub"; on "butter fly"; on "makes", the undercurrent of slang; all are exquisite. How utterly incomprehensible to a foreigner – how untranslateable would be this specimen of paronomasia!' The cat had had four kittens, of which only one survived; all the forms in the Chapel at Marychurch had been varnished, and he was glad to send Edmund a cheque for £25 ('a gift of fatherly confidence and affection') to enable him to visit Denmark again, only advising him to buy the portmanteau he needed in a second-hand shop in Tottenham Court Road.

Edmund arrived in Denmark on 10th May 1874. He had learnt a great deal since his last visit, two years before. Many of his acquaintances from that visit had become friends, had been charmed into sending him letters, newspaper cuttings and books, which had brought his 'London lodgings into as close relations with the Danish world of letters as was possible'. Gosse would write of his 'greatly increased ease and fluency in speaking Danish' but in his talks with Georg Brandes, to Gosse the central figure of this visit, Gosse used English and Brandes Danish, and they understood each other perfectly. They had corresponded and now they met and, however much Brandes might suggest later to Bjørnson that they hardly knew each other, their relationship flourished. It was a measure of Gosse's increased confidence, in spite of the unfortunate Norwegian article, that he was able to see so much of Brandes, the reviled Jewish revolutionary critic, while staying as before with Dean Fog. 'It was difficult to account for the repulsion and even terror of Georg Brandes, which I heard expressed around me, whenever his name came up.' It was painful having to explain to Brandes that he could not call at the Dean's home. To Gosse, his opinions seemed without scandal. 'Indeed I remember thinking that he was even narrow in some of his judgements.' But his message of intellectual emancipation was an unwelcome one in Denmark.

It was another marvellous visit. Gosse was fêted wherever he went. The university students made him a member of their Union, but he found them 'bloodless, effeminate' compared with the 'vigorous manly work people'. The University Council invited him to a special supper where he was formally thanked for what he was doing for Danish literature. On Ascension Day he heard his host preach for three quarters of an hour to an audience including the Royal Family. Hans Andersen, though he was ill and seeing few people, sent a message round asking his English friend to call. He could hardly speak but he broke off a spray of beech leaves from a vase and gave it to the young man with his poet's blessing. Gosse kept the leaves until they turned to dust, long after Andersen's own death.

Gosse visited Sweden briefly, curious to see if it were possible for him to understand the language. He was complimented on talking such good Swedish, which amused him as he was trying to talk as good Danish as possible. 'But really one may do both at the same time, the languages being so closely related.' He saw Paludan-Müller again, and his wife, even nastier than she was two years before and doing her best to keep her husband under lock and key. On Whit Sunday there was a big family party at the Dean's and Edmund Gosse was complimented on all sides. 'The lady in pink flowers says she likes you *so* much!' someone would say, and another: 'The elderly lady in blue thinks you talk such *pretty* Danish.' He made friends with Holger Drachmann, for whom many years later he would arrange a banquet at the Carlton Hotel. Gosse praised him as a writer, 'so individual, so manly and so generously revolutionary'. Løkke would have been amazed to see that Gosse had written in his journal: 'I fancy the future of Denmark and Norway lies with the peasant farmers and, now that I have seen something of the class they will expel, I am hardly prepared to regret it.'

At a large farewell party in Gosse's honour, the Dean served a special delicacy that Edmund had brought with him from England. It was a plum pudding, a present from the Misses Buckham and Baker; describing to his father its serving Edmund makes no allusion of course to an earlier experience with plum pudding, when in his childhood it had seemed to his father the flesh of idols. He had brought the present, an uncooked cannon-ball, tied in a cloth, but had unfortunately forgotten to explain it should be cooked in its cloth. 'So it was served in a kind of moist, gravelly condition' – a sort of purée in a saucer, between the fish and the joint. Dean Fog made a little speech, referring to Dickens and the famous, the almost sacred, Plum Pudding of the English. Edmund said nothing, looking at the brown sludge in the saucers. Fortunately nobody appeared to know *A Christmas Carol* very well; no one was surprised that the sludge was not a speckled cannon-ball, blazing in brandy. They all ate cautiously and pronounced it delicious. The lady opposite Edmund said it 'brought the dear English nation so near' to her, disregarding mutters from the old Norwegian Andreas Munch. Gosse had criticized Munch for his extreme sentimentality in his article in *Fraser's* in October, 1872, and Munch seemed correspondingly aware of the shortcomings of the English. 'Heed him not!' Dr Fog declared. 'He grows silly now he is stricken in years.'

There was one more farewell celebration – speeches and toasts on Edmund's final evening. Edmund himself proposed the toast to Denmark. He left the city musing on the fact that 'there are four rival groups in the philosophical and aesthetic world of Copenhagen', and 'What is so very funny is that I was on particularly good terms with all four!' A great crowd saw him off at the station and, as he hated travelling alone, he had soon made acquaintance with some travelling Mormons.

From Denmark, Edmund had written to P. H. Gosse: 'Why do you do your better nature such a wrong? Why do you insist on stretching everyone on your own self-measured bed and cutting off feet and ankles because they push out further than yours do? Why . . . narrow the channels of God's grace to the mere streamlets that can run through your own garden?

'You permit the enjoyment of Nature in the fields and by the shore; you forbid the exactly kindred pleasure found in the society of one's friends . . . I feel that it is time that these mutual reproaches, which have embittered in past days our correspondence, should cease, that you also should consent to treat me, as everyone else does, no longer as a child to be whipped and put in the corner, but as an adult human being for whom the serious questions of life have as intense an importance as they can have for you.' If only, he thought, they could *enjoy* each other's letters. He longed to be free – 'as the *Melicerta*, after the security of its extreme youth, must envy the free and unattached rotifers'.

It was hardly surprising that, when late in July he found he had a week's holiday due to him, he kept away from Marychurch. On an impulse, he invited Elise Otté to be his guest on a flying visit to the Lizard in Cornwall. Elise Otté, who was probably the first person to interest him in Scandinavia, had remained in Torquay until the death of Professor Day in 1872. She had then moved to London and had been seeing a good deal of Edmund and writing cheerful letters about him to Marychurch. He said she had shown him so much disinterested kindness, he longed to do something to thank her. Fortunately, she was as unconventional as he was. She was fifty-two: surely no one would suspect any impropriety. The sudden idea startled her but she consented and rapidly packed a bag in order that they might be by the sea at full moon. The Lizard delighted them. The collectors who had plundered Devon had apparently not travelled so far. All the names that had not been on his lips for years came flooding back. The pools were paved with a mosaic of *Bellis*; other pools were starred with *Miniata*. In the roots of the *Laminaria* were little specimens of *Ornata*. He saw an unfamiliar anemone, 'clear pale green, like a *Safarta* in habit, but with obtuse tentacles, slightly knobby, the tentacles banded, the body uniform'.

On the last day, they went to Polpeor Cove. It was low tide. The collecting mania seized them. Edmund rushed to the inn, borrowed a hammer and chisel, begged a pickle-bottle and raced back. He found Elise Otté already on her knees, working away with a hairpin and her fingers. The serpentine rock was so hard that he broke the chisel and was reduced to using the hairpin and his fingers. They stuffed the pickle jar with scarlet crabs and all the 'slimy doubtful creatures' that gladdened Edmund's heart. There was an *Anthea*, swollen to an enormous size by a half-digested launce. A pipe-fish joined their treasures. Eventually they returned exhausted to the inn for dinner and tipped everything out in a basin. 'The pipefish was very brisk and merry.' The moment the meal was over, Edmund rushed back to the basin, only to find the poor pipefish stiff and dead, 'drawn taut between a *Mesemb.* and a *Gemmacea*', the one had swallowed its head, the other its tail. They returned to town by the night train from Penryn, leaving the Lizard at 1.15 in the afternoon and reaching London at 4.30 next morning. 'The whole visit seems like a dream; it was so sudden, so exhilarating, so brief.'

It was hard to return to the routine of life in Tottenham and at the Museum. On August 28th, he groaned to W. B. Scott about his lack of time: 'I am writing like mad every spare hour I have, and I will give a round sum to anyone who will show me how to get thirty hours into the twenty-four, or how to do without sleep.' There was a new long dramatic poem in his mind, but commissions too from half a dozen periodicals, which were providing more and more of his income. Editors were not always interested in Scandinavian matters, but there was much else he could write about.

On 11th September 1874 he wrote to his father:

Nothing has happened to me in the least out of the common. I have seen nobody, heard nothing and, sitting hard at work, evening after evening, I forget how time goes by . . . How much there is to know and to work out, and how useless it seems even to attempt to do either! You, who have never had an official life, can scarcely realize how dreary it seems sometimes to have to give up the best hours of every day to someone else's routine.

It was a low point after the early summer's fêting and exhilaration. But soon there would be other joys.

6

Love and Friendship

Miss Otté had been marvellous company. Edmund had revelled in 'the extraordinary wealth of her intellect, the prodigious equipment of her memory'. But he was looking for someone to marry. In the four years since Mary Johnson's death, he had loved briefly, hopelessly, unsuitably a number of times. There was his narrow escape from the Beddows' girl in Tottenham. There was the beautiful sister of one of his colleagues, at whose 'dangerous altar-flame' he said in 1873 that he went on burning his wings. There was perhaps (if we are to believe a poem) a girl in Norway. Certainly there had been one in Denmark. Most mysteriously, there was someone called L.A.V., whose initials pepper his diary in 1874. It seems to have been of her he was thinking when he wrote in the letter to John Blaikie about the runaway horse: 'I even thought of a certain person to whom no one would tell of my death, and wondered what construction would be put on my silence and non-appearance in that quarter.'

Obviously this was someone not in 'our set', as he had called it at O'Shaughnessy's wedding. Ellen Epps *was* in his set. He saw her frequently at the Madox Browns' and at the Scotts'. Her sister, Laura, was married to the painter, Lawrence Alma-Tadema, whom he had known for years. At the time of the marriage in 1871, Gosse had written to Tadema: 'You could not have chosen a lovelier creature'; the sisters were very alike. They had all been at the marriage of Lucy Madox Brown to William Rossetti on 31st March 1874. It was Ellen Epps whom Edmund began to court seriously in the following autumn.

There was never any suggestion that Edmund would want to marry an intellectual equal. We have seen how much he admired clever women: Isabel Becker, Elise Otté, Aunt Lizzie Brightwen at Stanmore, Christina Rossetti, the memory of Elizabeth Barrett Browning. He had been a fascinated listener at a dinner party earlier this year when Browning and Frances Power Cobbe had an animated discussion about good and evil. Miss Cobbe, who was the same age as Elise Otté, was a powerful advocate of the Rights of Women. They met at the table of Anna Swanwick, another clever woman, whose translations of Aeschylus had been said by *The Spectator* to hold their own with Mrs Browning's.

Ellen Epps – always known as Nellie – was born at 79 South Audley Street, Mayfair, on 23rd March 1850, the daughter of Dr George Napoleon Epps. He had worked for some years as pupil and assistant to his half-brother, Dr John Epps, the well-known homeopathic doctor and radical, who, after the ravages of the American's experiments, had finally treated Edmund's dying mother. Five years before Nellie was born, Dr George Epps had been appointed surgeon to the Homeopathic Hospital in Hanover Square. He was particularly successful in treating spinal curvatures and deformities, and had published in 1849 a book on the subject. He had been born into yet another of those families which had suffered 'a reversal of fortune' and had made his own way in the world, earning his own living while studying medicine. He became an extremely successful Mayfair doctor, being so devoted to his practice that he was said never to have slept away from home in twenty years.

His wife, born Charlotte Bacon, seems to have been something of a nonentity, or at least an invalid. She did not die until December 1890 but she is hardly mentioned and, when she is, unfavourably: 'I knew Mamma would be a burden and not a help . . .' There were six children – two boys and four girls. Nellie was the youngest. Dr Epps had died this very year, 1874, but Nellie had not been living with her parents for some time. She lived in Devonshire Street, London W1, with an aunt, her brother Washington Epps (also a homeopathic doctor) and her widowed sister, Emily Williams. The other sisters were Amy, who had married Charles Pratt, Laura, who married Alma-Tadema and became a mother to his two daughters, and Louisa, married to Rowland Hill and the only one of the sisters who did not paint. The other brother, called after his father's hero, Hahnemann, was always known as Tim and was also a doctor. They were, all things considered, the right sort of relations for Edmund to acquire.

Nellie was certainly a 'new woman'. She had had some further education, after the governess in the Mayfair schoolroom, having attended lectures at Queen's College, Harley Street. She certainly had intellectual tastes. Her holiday reading one year included 'Carlyle, Blake, the old *Spectator*, translations of Heine, early Meredith and Ruskin'. She was a feminist of the most attractive sort, totally aware of her own equality with men, but not strident in making them aware of it. She had serious ambitions as a painter and, after studying with Ford

Madox Brown, as we have seen, she became for a time a pupil and assistant to Alma-Tadema. She had travelled on the continent in 1873, painting and visiting the art galleries in France and Italy. By 1874, she had her own studio in Devonshire Street, was painting regularly and had begun to exhibit. Surviving paintings and drawings show her considerable talent. Edmund wrote proudly to Denmark that year that Nellie had 'no small reputation as a painter, for a young girl, that is to say'. In a few years, Robert Browning would praise her 'two jewel-like pictures' at the Grosvenor Gallery, and Andrew Lang would talk of flowers 'worthy of the pencil of Mrs Gosse'.

But, at this point, she was not yet Mrs Gosse and not apparently indeed very inclined to be. Edmund had gradually become convinced that she was the one woman he wanted to be his wife, and at a party in Devonshire Street on 22nd October 1874 he had been carried away and had told her so. He asked her to marry him; she said 'No'. He had been very precipitate and unconventional. Next day he wrote to the aunt and apologized and asked if he might call. Over a cup of tea, the aunt commended his choice ('She is about the best and truest girl in this world') but told him frankly the difficulties, which were:

1) That Nellie had a strong will and had determined never to marry but to pursue her art with all her might and make her own fortune, as she wished to be indebted to no one for a livelihood.

2) That she had never considered Edmund as a possible suitor and had no idea that he felt as he did.

3) That she was devoted to her family and had no wish to leave Devonshire Street.

They were formidable difficulties, but at least Edmund managed to persuade Nellie to admit that there was no other man she preferred. The aunt thought Edmund would do very well for Nellie, if only she could be brought to realize his virtues, but she was the sort of girl who would not be easily persuaded. Edmund worried that she had some idea of an ideal man in her mind and that he was far from approaching it. But he managed to get her permission to continue to call.

'I mean to fight it out to the last,' he wrote to his father, 'and perhaps a strong heart may win the fair lady. At all events I am certain that my happiness depends on it . . . Perhaps in the end [she] may learn to love me.' Edmund managed to persuade himself that Nellie had shown 'extraordinary sense and self control' in not accepting his proposal immediately, 'in managing to evade any distinct reply' until she knew him better. But it was a difficult time for him. Every time he went to Devonshire Street – she allowed him to call just once a week – Nellie seemed a little kinder, and almost as though she were struggling against a tendency to like him. They seemed to have a great deal in common. 'Our views are singularly alike,' he reported to Marychurch. It was needing both tact and patience to win her, but she had by the end of November completely dropped her rather defiant manner. On December 2nd, he wrote to tell them Nellie had 'suddenly capitulated, and without terms'. She was sure she loved him and that they could be happy together. She was, Edmund exulted, entirely prepared to give up all the luxuries of life for comparative poverty. 'I long to bring her to you; you will love her at once. She is so gentle, so tender, so womanly, and yet not in the least a fool, as sharp and bright as can be, with a coolness and clearness of judgment that surprises me often.'

The same day he wrote to Scott that he did not know whether he was walking on his head or his hands, that he and Nellie would be the happiest couple that had ever lived since the beginning of the world. The only cloud on the horizon was their limited means, but fortunately Nellie had 'the most frugal tastes and quiet ways, does not care for any society but that of near friends and makes her own dresses'. Edmund himself had rather more sumptuous tastes even if he didn't gratify them, and was beginning to care for entertaining and being entertained on a rather grander scale than his income justified.

Now he decided to leave Tottenham, after eight years of living with Miss Baker and Miss Buckham. It was too far from Nellie in Devonshire Street. He was losing too much time in travelling to and fro, 'and still more it is altogether too expensive living there'. Elise Otté had come to the rescue with the suggestion that he should have the little spare bedroom at the top of her house in Alfred Place, ideally situated, only a few minutes walk both from Nellie's home and from the Museum. Tottenham was, in any case, not really the place he wanted to be. That tedious walk from Wood Green station late at night had become almost intolerable since he had been attacked by what he called a highwayman, but fortunately only with a fist and not with 'any more sure and deadly weapon'. Scott had often thought his late walks were rash, 'the environs of London being exactly the most dangerous localities in the world'. And of course leaving Tottenham meant that he could, without embarrassment, give up his job as Sunday School superintendent and indeed abandon his regular attendance at the Brook Street chapel.

P. H. Gosse and his wife Eliza were both happy Edmund was to marry, but concerned of course about the state of Nellie's soul. When young George Fewings had married – the George whom Philip had chosen as Edmund's boyhood companion – Philip had lamented that his bride, though a girl of whom he had not heard any actual evil, was yet 'flaunty and dressy' and 'little calculated to help him to run the heavenly race'. He could hardly bear to ask whether Nellie was 'saved'. Eliza wrote a very warm, friendly letter congratulating Nellie on Edmund's move to Alfred Place, 'a locality that gives him so much greater facility of communion with your dear self. The more one can become familiar with the habits, sentiments, and character of one with whom he is to be so closely united, the happier is the union likely to be', she wrote truly but a little awkwardly. She enquired as a fellow artist about Nellie's work. Does she paint chiefly in water colour, in oil or in both? Where does she exhibit? 'Willie has told me that Mrs Alma-Tadema is your sister; he of course is so well known as an artist of high repute, that is quite a point of interest.' Eliza went on to say that it was their greatest anxiety that Edmund and Nellie should lead one another in the ways of God, assuring them that those ways are not morose and melancholy ways. We do not know how Nellie replied.

But there is no doubt that Edmund's approaching marriage had a soothing effect on his father. 'What you say of your darling appeals to our own hearts; I am sure we shall not fail to love her. We long to embrace her as a beloved Daughter.' The letters were never again so full of interrogation and theological parrying. Some would be regretful, sad, suggesting that when Christ comes again they might be shut outside, weeping and wailing. In others, God was hardly mentioned and priority was given to questions of exploring secondhand furniture warehouses in Tottenham Court Road. ('You and Nellie might do it together and it would be as good exercise as a three mile walk in the country.') P. H. Gosse even ventured a joke about Nellie's painting. 'I can quite imagine that lately her art has not occupied the whole of her thought; another image, far dearer, will come between. And perhaps she will not be sorry when she can say to her Picture, "There, you, go and be *hanged*!" ' He sent her orchids from his hothouse and she was appropriately rapturous. But she must have been rather relieved that he was far away in Devon.

The eight months of the engagement were difficult enough anyway. Edmund was working extremely hard at both journalism and poetry. The journalism included a note in the *Academy* about the first meeting of the British Scandinavian Society, notices of Ibsen's 'silver jubilee', reviews and articles on Swinburne, Chapman, Herrick. He had started a verse play, a tragedy, and it was possessing him as no work had done before. He wrote to Scott: 'I see it constantly; the characters move before me; they are more intimately real to me than the men and women I meet. I cannot express the extraordinary distinctiveness of vision I have about it; if only I can write down what I hear and see.'

More than a year later, Gosse told Austin Dobson, 'I am writing a

most ambitious poem, which keeps me on the tenterhooks of excitement – at one moment, the whole scheme seems so impossible, at
another rhymes flowed like the River of God.' The tragedy was called
King Erik. It was founded on the part of the Knythinga Saga which
deals with the Danish king's journey to Jerusalem to expiate a sin. The
subject was remote, but he aimed at realism: no long speeches, no
rhetoric, no soliloquies. He plucked up courage and asked Browning
if he might dedicate it to him, 'that I might be allowed to write on the
first leaf the name which I reverence as the highest of living names'.
Browning could hardly refuse.

It was difficult to apportion his time but Gosse, as he said, was not
afraid of hard work. After a day at the Museum, he would sometimes
work at his desk, without any break except for eating, from directly
after four in the afternoon till two next morning. 'A long engagement
is a heart-breaking thing,' he wrote in December when it had only just
begun. Years later he would urge those two middle-aged lovers,
Sidney Colvin and Mrs Sitwell, 'I am all against useless waiting.'

On February 13th, he wrote to Nellie at 9 o'clock in the evening
from Alfred Place:

> My darling, All today I have been in a state of the most abject
> depression – that is why I did not write. I could not. These fits come
> upon me sometimes, more rarely now than ever before, – they are
> moods when my intellect seems all commonplace and my thoughts
> borrowed, when my body seems a collapsed and abject thing . . . I
> have not had a day like this since the day before that first party, *the*
> Thursday and I never was so long without one as that. Minto came
> to the B.M. at 4, and we trudged through the mist and slush to the
> West End about some shopping of his. He was white and tired and
> had a bad cough. At 5 we came back to tea, and do what we would,
> we were savagely miserable. I do not know why I should be so; I am
> sure I ought not to be with your love and all the future before us.
> Minto went at 6, after we had stabbed and caressed one another in
> the oddest, angriest way. I tried to write at my tragedy. Goodness,
> how powerless my brain was! I lay on my back for 2 hours with my
> eyes shut. Now your dear notelet has come and made me a little
> happier.

On June 24th, his mood was still restless and unhappy:

> My precious darling, I wish we were down by the sea – a glistering
> cool sea somewhere, and pottering about in the little rock pools
> with our fingers! . . . Or I wish we were up on Dartmoor, lying in

the sun ('our heads crushing freshness out of little plots of thyme'). I bask like a salamander in the flame of it and you, close by, make a dark oasis with your parasol. Or in a boat, at sea 'and I not the least unwell' or 'on the peak of Teneriffe', in the Azores, at Fiesole among the nightingales or 'far north among the ice-bergs . . .' or any of the places I most long to be in, or anywhere out of this sultry horrible London, so full of labour and pain, and disappointment and delay, that makes me work so hard and keeps me from you and gives you pains in the back and makes our life that might be golden, so stupid.

Grumbling away, as usual, and teaching you to grumble. I had better stop.

Your true love,
Edmund.

In fact, things were beginning to work out very well for them. The date of the wedding had been fixed. It was to be on August 13th and the Alma-Tademas were organizing everything. Moreover the question of where they were to live afterwards had been settled, and in a way that was to allay Edmund's immediate worries about money. The Alma-Tademas were planning to winter in Italy and suggested that Edmund and Nellie should enjoy the splendours of Townshend House while they were away.

Townshend House, North Gate, Regent's Park, though not quite so magnificent as the Alma-Tademas' later house a few minutes walk away at 17 Grove End Road, was yet an extraordinary setting for a young clerk at the British Museum. Laurens (as then he was) Alma-Tadema had come to England with his two small daughters in 1870 after the death of his first wife. Born in Friesland in 1836, he had established his reputation in Brussels and Paris, and had first shown at the Royal Academy in London in 1869. In an article of 1883, Edmund described Townshend House as 'one of the most famous private dwellings of our time'. Every room was filled with strange and beautiful things: 'treasures of ancient glass, rare blue and white china' (a collecting passion Tadema shared with Rossetti), Japanese screens and curios. In 1874, the house had been shattered by an explosion in the early hours of the morning, when a barge laden with gunpowder and benzoline had blown up on the Regent's Park Canal. 'Of this barge, nothing more was ever seen, except a fragment with a piece of rope attached, which was found on the roof of Tadema's house.' In 1875 the first stage of the restoration had been completed. Eventually there would be 'a gorgeous succession of furnished chambers – of Roman, Oriental or Renaissance splendour'. Already there were painted ceilings, columns, leopard skins, stained glass, carved wood and trailing foliage.

Alma-Tadema was already extremely well-known. We have seen that his fame had spread to Marychurch. His enormous paintings sold for thousands of pounds. He was rich, generous, and absolutely devoted to his family. Nellie, who had worked with him, loved and admired him. She called him 'the dear warm-hearted man', though she knew he was 'restive and difficult with strangers'. He would exasperate Edmund from time to time. He had an unpredictable temper. His English was extraordinary – but so were his French and German. His family thought he spoke beautiful Dutch, until, 'in an evil hour, he took them to Holland for a holiday, went into a shop to make a purchase in Dutch and was answered by the shopman in English'.

Years later Alma-Tadema's daughter Laurence (confusingly named after her father) described her first meeting with Edmund Gosse. It was in the column drawing-room at Townshend House. Two small girls were sitting by the window, full of expectancy. Their father had some years before married again, giving them a new set of aunts, and now the most beloved of these was engaged to be married. 'He arrives, tall, spare, very neat, not gay at all, with rather a tip-toe tread, a delicate, nervous face and fine long hands.' The small girl decided he was suitable. She liked 'his fine features, his eager eyes, his whole sensitive presence' and was glad he had no beard. 'I should not mind marrying him myself!' Anna, the eight-year-old sister, declared. This was reported to Edmund and he wrote a poem for Anna, which ended:

> But if Aunt Nelly should elope
> To Germany with Mr Pope
> Then would I take you, on my life,
> To be my little pussy wife.

The stanza was made deliciously funny by the fact that Mr Pope, a frequent guest at the Alma-Tademas' Tuesday evenings, was bald and middle-aged and quite outside the pale of possible husbands.

Edmund further endeared himself to the girls that spring by composing for the family a splendid masque. The date – April 16th – in his notebook is recorded in Nellie's diary as a day when they dined at Townshend. 'E.W.G. and I walked home in the moonlight.' So one imagines Edmund late at night in his little room in Alfred Place scribbling away at the Masque of the Lady Laura, set in Temple Townshend, with parts for the small girls ('robed very sweetly in saffron'), the Lady Nellie, the Lord Tadema and for the poet himself 'with golden sandals winged at the ankle'. Edmund had found the family he had never had, a rich, extravagant, artistic background, fit for a poet.

Edmund continued to see something of his friends that first half of 1875, when he could tear himself away from his desk. In January he had pointed out to Swinburne that they had missed commemorating the centenary of the birth of Walter Savage Landor. But it was Charles Lamb's centenary on February 10th, and Swinburne determined to organize a joint-celebration of 'the two great men who loved and admired each other in life'. Edmund thought it was the only time in Swinburne's life he ever organized anything. 'Leave it to me!' he said, in his grandest manner. 'It was a rough entertainment,' Gosse recalled, 'and the guests were few, but it did come off.' There were only 'our dear and ever-cheerful William Minto . . . a rather trying journalist called Thomas Purnell,' Theodore Watts, Swinburne and Gosse. They met in a Soho tavern and ate some sort of dinner (either 'mediocre' or 'succulent'; Gosse's memory varied). Swinburne insisted on speeches and ceremony, suggesting that 'the little banquet was, symbolically, a large public affair'. He sat low in a huge arm-chair, 'his white face, with its great aureole of red hair, beaming over the table like a rising sun . . . Our shock was the bill – portentous! Swinburne, in "organizing", had made no arrangement as to price, and when we trooped out into the frosty midnight, there were five long faces of impecunious men of letters.' Swinburne was always glad to see Gosse, he said, when he was not working or 'engaged among the Philistines'.

There were several meetings that spring at Theodore Watts's place, with the usual crowd: Swinburne, William Rossetti, Madox Brown, Hueffer. Watts would become Watts-Dunton and eventually, over Swinburne, Gosse's enemy, but they were good friends at this period. Gabriel Rossetti and Swinburne, despite a brief meeting at Oliver Madox Brown's funeral, were still alienated, though Gosse saw them both. Rossetti read 'Rose Mary' to him. There is a first mention too, this year, of Churton Collins, who would be Gosse's scourge. Gosse read *King Erik* to Watts, who remembered his enthusiasm was 'as exhilarating as a draught of good champagne'. He read it too to Marzials. He dined with Holman Hunt at Jean Ingelow's table. He took Nellie a couple of times to Stanmore to meet the Brightwens. They also went together to visit the O'Shaughnessys and dined with the Scotts.

Sometime in this spring of 1875 Gosse met Robert Louis Stevenson for the first time since their chance encounter five years before on the

Scottish boat. Now they had both just started writing for Leslie
Stephen, the editor of the *Cornhill*, who would become another friend,
as well as the father of Virginia Woolf. Gosse had never met Stephen
when he and Stevenson were invited to dine. Somehow they had both
imagined a large dinner party. They met each other outside the house
in Onslow Gardens, South Kensington, hanging around – both too
early in their eagerness – waiting for other people to arrive. Finally
they went in. Leslie Stephen sat at one end of the table, his wife at the
other end, and her sister, Thackeray's other daughter, Annie, sat
opposite the two young men.

I shall always remember the surprise Leslie Stephen's appearance
gave me; the long, thin, bright-red beard, radiating in a fan-shape;
the wrinkled forehead; the curious flatness of the top of the head,
accentuated by the fulness of the auburn hair on either side; the long
cold hands, the distraught and melancholy eyes. The dinner was
extremely quiet. Scarcely a word fell from either of the Stephens,
and we two guests, although chatterboxes engrained, were subdued
to silence by shyness. Only Miss Thackeray, in her hospitable
goodness, did her best to talk for us all, and in the twilight – for the
room and table were meagrely illuminated by two or three candles –
her voice was heard, holding a sort of dialogue with itself.
It is characteristic, perhaps, of the impression which he always
produced, that this almost unbroken silence of our host – who for a
considerable part of the time lay far back in his chair, motionless,
with his beard on his bosom – though it greatly disconcerted, did
not offend or wound either of us at all. There was something so
genuine about Leslie Stephen, something essentially so kind and
good, that, although it was disappointing not to be talked to, it was
not humiliating. We (R. L. S. and I) were taken, I recollect,
half-way through the meal, with a terrible simultaneous temptation
to giggle, which we withstood; and then for the rest of the evening
we waited patiently for the heavenly spark to fall. But it only fell
upon kind Miss Thackeray.

It was also this year that Edmund Gosse saw Stéphane Mallarmé
wandering around London, a 'little brown gentle person, with an
elephant folio under his arm, trying to find Mr Swinburne by the
unassisted light of instinct'. In the folder were Manet's illustrations to
Mallarmé's version of *The Raven* by Edgar Allan Poe. 'I have read it
over and over,' Gosse was to say of 'Le Tombeau d'Edgard Poe', 'but I
cannot tell what it *says*.' He thought Mallarmé was wilfully obscure. 'I
used to notice that if I came upon him suddenly, or if he had to write a

telegram or order something from a shop, he could write the same sort of French as other people.' Gosse found it hard to come to terms with the Mallarméan principle that poetry should suggest and not express, but came to welcome Mallarmé's reputation as 'the only Frenchman of his day who possessed the gift of style'. Manet was equally puzzling; a far cry from Alma-Tadema.

Edmund called constantly on Devonshire Street. Nellie's diary records him arriving 'lily-laden', 'very tired', 'with roses'. 'E.W.G. could not possibly come in but yet somehow did'. He brought buttons to be sewn on, but also made himself useful. On July 24th, Nellie and her sister, Emily, 'brought blankets and socks. E.W.G. and Tim marked them in the evening'. Preparations for the marriage were now well-advanced. Nellie had spent £8 9s 6½d on filling her linen cupboard: unbleached Turkish towels, doyleys with red borders, two pairs of blankets, and a red and white quilt for fifteen shillings and ninepence. Every time Edmund called she seemed to be stitching away. People were asking about presents.

In a letter to Nellie, William Bell Scott suggested one of his pictures plus, perhaps, a silver teaset, if they hadn't one already or already been promised one. 'I write in this way because both you and Gosse are dear and intimate enough to allow me to take so free a step . . . I gave on a late occasion some candlesticks and no light but gas has ever been seen in the household!' They accepted the silver (George II) in spite of the fact that Amy and Charles Pratt (Amy was another one of Nellie's sisters) had given them a complete dinner and tea service. Charles had also given Nellie a couple of dozen 1863 port and Amy had given her a yellow silk dress and some creamy lace. There were silver teaspoons from Nellie's mother, £20 from Tadema, £10 from Tim, another £10 from the Devonshire Street aunt, a breakfast service from Washington Epps and glass from Emily Williams. Philip Gosse contributed no less than £153 to their income in 1875, John Epps £100 and George Brightwen another £50. Aunt Lizzie gave Nellie a handsome gold bracelet.

But even with all this family support, it seemed rash to marry on a regular salary from the Museum of still only £160 a year. Edmund had been trying to change his job for a long time. He had tried for promotion to Senior Assistant in the Reading Room, but even with letters to the Archbishop from Charles Kingsley and other supporters, he did not get the promotion. It was not yet his turn. Scott made some attempt to get him into the Department of Prints and Drawings. And Gosse had toyed with the idea of accepting an editorial job on one of the periodicals, but caution had prevailed. It seemed he was stuck in the dull hive with the catalogues and the red tape and the smell of decaying morocco. He longed to get away. 'I am permanently asphyxiated by breathing Bloomsbury air morning, noon and night,' he wrote to his father in July. 'Nellie is getting as thin as a scarecrow with trouble and worry, excitement and anxiety.'

Then on 4th August 1875, nine days before the wedding, he was able to write to Marychurch to tell them that a startling offer had been made to him. A man had called on him at the Museum, saying he had come from the Board of Trade to offer Gosse the post of Translator to the Board – at £400 a year, fixed, for life, with superannuation, hours eleven till five, and a room of his own where he should be his own master. 'No exception will be taken to my literary work, which indeed is what has brought this fish to my net.' It was almost too good to be true. Gosse protested half-heartedly that he did not know Spanish or Portuguese; but it was suggested he would have no trouble in acquiring them. He had French, German, Italian and, above all, the Scandinavian languages which 'were very difficult to secure'. Everything was arranged. He would start on the 24th September, having been allowed to take a month of his six weeks' annual leave at the beginning. 'I shall pocket my first month's salary of £33 for doing nothing!' he wrote to Marychurch in amazement the night before his wedding, in 'my last letter to you before you have not one child but two . . . I wish you could know how quiet, how content, how confident I feel. Nellie's nature is one that soothes, sustains and perfects mine in a manner indescribable.' He wrote of her unselfishness and her sterling good sense and devotion, and said he did not speak the foolish language of lovers when he believed he had found a wife in a million.

They were married on August 13th at the Register Office in the district of Marylebone. The reception afterwards was at Townshend House, and Tadema's love of hospitality and strong instincts of family solidarity were given full play. At the last moment Laura had written to try to urge Edmund's father to travel up from Devon, but he replied, as they had guessed he would, that he doubted whether he would ever see London again. He had warned his son that his beard was 'more decidedly white', yet Edmund would find them, when he and Nellie came, quite unchanged: 'We are just as cheerful, even merry and jocular; just as bright, just as keen in enjoying God's good gifts as ever.' He had sent melons and grapes from his own hothouses for the wedding feast.

Miss Buckham came to the wedding but not Miss Baker; Uncle George Brightwen but not Aunt Lizzie. Most of the guests were from Nellie's side – a great array of siblings and their spouses, and some small nieces and nephews too. William Minto was best man. The very first entry in the Book of Gosse, which was to chronicle the Gosses' guests for the next fifty-three years, is headed Wedding Reception Calls. Of the forty-eight names in the list, many are familiar: Mrs Garnett, Mrs Lynn Linton, Mrs W. B. Scott, Dean Fog, Mr Watts, Dr and Mrs Hueffer, Mr Blaikie, Mr Marzials, Miss Otté, Miss Helen and Miss Theresa Thornycroft, Mrs Austin Dobson.

Laurence Alma-Tadema carried in her mind a picture of Nellie in 'a soft creamy gown of striped oriental material, unusual in those days of substantial silks, and a veil of Honiton lace over her bright abundant hair. I suppose it was a gay wedding, that there was laughter and merrymaking. But I have forgotten that part of it. The bride and bridegroom, seated side by side at the head of the table, filled me with reverential awe, and I see them pale and solemn in my memory. The wedding-cake was flat, covered with sugar-crystals and a baby niece was held up to make believe at cutting the first slice: the last picture of the wedding that remains with me is the cutting up of the cake by the glowing-haired bride with a large ivory paper-knife.'

Edmund noted in his diary that day simply: 'Married. Slept at Salisbury.' Their honeymoon journey was a grand tour of the west country. Near the beginning there was an incident which sounds like something out of a Hardy novel. They had visited Stonehenge, and Bideford. Leaving Clovelly on the morning of the 16th August, a wild morning of storm, they turned a little aside at Hartland on their way to Bude, intending to pay their respects to the old poet, Robert Stephen Hawker, who had the living at Morwenstow. As they reached the village, they heard through the storms the sound of the passing-bell and, stopping to enquire, were told it tolled for the Vicar himself. In the midst of life, they were in death. Fifty years later Edmund wrote to John Drinkwater how great had been the impression this had made on them as they started on their journey through life together.

They visited Bude, Boscastle, Tintagel, Bodmin and Falmouth, bathing and painting. By the time they got to the Lizard, Edmund could write to Marychurch: 'We find ourselves a little weary of sleeping at a new hotel each night and propose to linger in this strange, beautiful place.' How much had happened since he had been here the year before with Elise Otté! 'That we are happy is not saying much, but that it is true in its widest, deeper sense is much; for my part I could not be happier, nor dream myself with one who more thoroughly, uniformly and completely delights me. We are one in sympathy, in tone; in our very weaknesses and prejudices we are one.' He suggests they stay at Marychurch from the 6th to the 17th of September. He is impatient to bring 'your new child to your embrace'. Nellie is painting hard, but Edmund is feeling lazy. 'The load of Italian books I brought down with me in purpose to study . . . ah me! ah me!'

So after Penzance and the Scilly Isles, Mousehole and Land's End, they finally came to Marychurch. All went well. Philip Henry Gosse and Eliza both became devoted to Nellie. She was all tact and sweetness. There were no storms or arguments. They gathered samphire at Anstey's Cove. Edmund wrote poems and tore them up. Awkward questions seemed to be avoided. People came to call and congratulate. On the 16th September they left for Weston-super-Mare to stay with Isabel Becker. And on the 22nd they arrived back at Townshend House.

They returned, sunburnt and restored, to find a wedding present from Edmund's friends in Norway, including Ibsen. It was a metal horn, made according to the pattern of old Viking drinking horns. 'It passes praise,' Edmund wrote in his letter of thanks, 'and seems so strangely lovely in form, colour, and character that we do nothing but contemplate it with astonishment and delight.' There were letters waiting too. Browning wrote warmly from Dinant, with pleasure at the news of their wedding. 'I seem as if I knew the lady – so lately have I been admiring a picture by her. Now the great thing will be for both of you to work hard and show the power of the double twist, the silver in the gold thread – the painter's power along with the poet's.'

Swinburne wrote from Henley wishing them 'all the joy and good fortune that can be wished, and without admixture of envy of that particular form of happiness which I am now never likely to share. I suppose it must be the best thing that can befall a man to win and keep the woman that he loves while yet young; at any rate I can congratulate my friend on his good hap without any too jealous afterthought of the reverse experience which left my own young manhood, "a barren stock," if I may cite that phrase without seeming to liken myself to a male Queen Elizabeth.' Poor Swinburne. Was he thinking of Adah Menken, who had told him in 1867 that biting was not enough, and had died the following year?

There was a letter from another 'barren stock' – strange Theo Marzials: 'Are you happy, and were you just as happy? I often think of you. I picture you young and very beautiful – the expression of your eyes grown as it were many miles beyond our sphere and your poet's brow lit with the ineffable light of fulfilled love, gazing into the glaucous eyes of your glad-coloured lady as her flexible hand portrays the accidents of hill, valley, flood or sunset, or sweeter yet the ever-varying light and shade of your own expressive features . . .' He went on and on. Certainly he loved Edmund. There is an extraordinary letter a little later which is full of jealousy and anguish, but also of affection and resignation.

It seemed everything was set fair. They were spoilt children of fortune, Edmund suggested to Scott, to whom something uncanny should happen to teach them a lesson. And on arriving at the Board of Trade to report for work on 24th September 1875 Edmund was faced with an extraordinary case of bureaucratic bungling. His appointment had been pronounced null and void, owing to some technicality. He would have to sit an examination and go through the proper channels, it seemed. All was smoothed over by a lucky chance. When he went to see the Civil Service Commissioners, he fell into the hands of a Dr Dasent whom he had lately had the opportunity to review, 'and deservedly very favourably', in the *Academy*. 'Needless to say, he did not refer to that fact but he ratified my appointment without further trouble.'

Gosse's situation was certainly very different from the one he had been in at the British Museum. He had a comfortable room to himself, looking over Scotland Yard to Charing Cross station and St Paul's. He could lounge back in an armchair. There was a fireplace, bookshelves, everything to make a study comfortable. After 'the unpleasant severity, the official discourtesy, the irritating surveillance of the BM', the change was astonishing. He was even supplied with enough Board of Trade stationery for his private use 'to satisfy a popular MP'. For the next twenty-nine years most of Gosse's letters would carry the crowned badge of the Board of Trade. Arthur Waugh described Gosse's job like this:

> There were hectic mornings, when a sheaf of dispatches had arrived from the Continent and a translation was required by afternoon; upon these occasions a tactful visitor did no more than put his head around the corner of Gosse's door before beating a silent retreat. But there were many more days when the official translator was free of official translating and found time for talk and confidences before he settled down to write an article for the *Saturday Review* or the *St James's Gazette*.

Edmund wrote to Marychurch: 'I shall be in clover indeed.' But there were some nettles. The work, when he did have to work, was almost as tedious as the work at the Museum, and much more demanding. Even his Danish was hardly equal to the technicalities of Charter-parties and Bills of Lading. 'You will guess,' he once wrote, 'what shockingly dull stuff I had to deal with . . . I have always held that one of the chief uses of the Civil Service is to provide a steady income for literary men.' At the Board of Trade, Gosse was joining Austin Dobson and Cosmo Monkhouse, 'dear old Monkey', another poet, who was to make more of a name for himself as an art critic. Dobson had described his job to a young sister: 'I sit all day in a large room with a great ink bottle and many pens and write in a great book.' When Edmund was still at the Museum Dobson had envied him the literary atmosphere. He had been at the Board for nineteen years, when Gosse arrived, and was to sit there for twenty-six more.

The Permanent Secretary, Thomas Farrer, had apparently wanted the translator job for his family governess, no longer needed by the family and an excellent linguist. Whenever Gosse got things wrong, floundering among the tariffs and commercial statistics, his fellows would gibe, 'Ah now, if only Mr Farrer's governess had been here, how different it would have been!' Mr Farrer never liked Gosse, and once declared there were two names that should be spelt with a small G – God and Gosse. But he seemed to have a general grudge against writers, using the public's time and stationery for the production of unreadable poetry. He once referred in a speech to the London County Council to 'certain civil servants who would have been excellent administrators, if they had not been indifferent poets'. Alfred Bateman, Gosse's immediate superior, was another matter altogether – a constant support. 'What a pearl is le bon Bateman!' Gosse would exclaim after years of working under him.

The verses and criticisms winged back and forth between Gosse's office and Dobson's. They tried every technical experiment they could think of. It was great fun, but hardly poetry. One typical piece of Gosse cleverness that first winter at the Board of Trade was called Pantoum, which is a Malayan verse-form and it seemed to be a sort of epitaph for such foolishness. It included these stanzas:

> Let two mandarins unscrew
> China beauties, fit for us.
> I'm a dusty bard like you;
> Let us both be buried thus.
>
> China beauties, fit for us,
> Porcelain let our tomb-store be;
> Let us both be buried thus
> In a grave of pot pourri . . .

'How do you manage to be so clever?' Dobson would ask; but the admiration was mutual. Gosse was sad that Swinburne had no time for

Dobson's poems. The highest praise he would give them was that some of them were 'charming bits of workmanship'. Gosse thought Swinburne had little understanding of light verse. 'All must be serious and passionate for him.' Gosse enjoyed Frederick Locker's dedicatory verse when he gave him a copy of *London Lyrics*:

> Our poets, write they ill or well,
> Complain their poems do not sell;
> And yet how often we are told
> The Poet does not rhyme for Gold.
> I'm satisfied that gold is dross,
> And so I *give* my rhymes to Gosse.

Once, having criticized Monkhouse very thoroughly, Gosse said, 'I shall not dare to come in for lunch for days . . . But I think one should say frankly what one feels.' Certainly Dobson would occasionally be aware of the effect he was having on Gosse's verse: 'Are not twine, bind and girdle rather too much of a good thing in one stanza?'

Laurence Alma-Tadema remembered the few weeks between the return of her aunt and new uncle and the family's departure for Italy. They had the front spare bedroom and the children gave up their nursery, which became the Gosses' private sitting-room. In the evening, as the small girls lay in bed, waiting for sleep, they could hear Edmund Gosse in the room below reading poetry to his bride. It was a good sound: Laurence thought she owed her life-long love of poetry to those cadences, and to the excitement and novelty of having a poet in the house.

On 18th October 1875 Nellie wrote in her diary: 'Our first breakfast at home and alone.' Obviously Townshend House, now that the Tademas had gone, could seem more like their own home. They made the most of the marvellous house: Mrs Edmund Gosse was At Home on October 21st, 22nd and 23rd, and there were big parties on November 17th, December 7th and December 20th. Edmund might have told his father that Nellie was a quiet girl with no taste for society, but she was obviously prepared to entertain for Edmund. He loved it. He had never been able to give parties in all the years at Tottenham; nor, indeed, in the months at Alfred Place. He discovered he enjoyed being a host even more than being a guest.

In December, *King Erik*, Edmund's tragedy with no whiff of pot-pourri about it, was published by Chatto. Edmund confessed to his father that each new publication date seemed rather less momentous. 'As a somewhat prolific author,' P. H. Gosse replied, 'I can very well sympathise with you. However the feeling with the public is perhaps the reverse: and so we may venture to hope that this coming one may bring you more profit and more reputation.' But verse tragedy, as someone remarked, is the most perilous of poetic paths. It was a failure. There was some praise. Swinburne thought optimistically that it would raise Gosse's name at once 'into a higher and clearer celebrity'. He wished he could have prefixed a line or two to it, in the old fashion of commendatory verses, but what would New Grub Street have said to that?

Browning was pleased with the dedication, though *Scribner's* reviewer in America thought it 'pretentious in its humility'. Browning wrote: 'I will say that the dramatic power and understanding management of character were something of a surprise, even to me, whose recognition of your faculty was from the first complete and immediate.' Theodore Watts, in the *Examiner*, wrote: 'It is a long time since anything so tender, so pathetic and so true has been given to us in dramatic poetry; and whatever may be Mr Gosse's shortcomings as a playwright, we now know the kind of beautiful work we have to expect from him.' No doubt Watts remembered Gosse's champagne-like enthusiasm; but even Swinburne had not succeeded in galvanizing the Elizabethan dramatic convention. No one ever acted *King Erik*. But a few years later, the boy William Butler Yeats read it and was enthralled. Years afterwards he told Gosse (who came to think Yeats 'our greatest poet') that reading it again he found the old charm and remembered how the 'learned princess sitting among the tropical flowers' had haunted him. 'I remember even, in a way I then had, trying to symbolise the impression of the scene and writing some lines of bad verse about a dead lizard covered with the pollen of flowers.'

1876 was a rather domestic year. The Gosses had been house-hunting all winter, determined to find a place of their own before the Tademas returned from Italy. The house they finally rented was 29 Delamere Terrace, overlooking the Regent's Park Canal, with barges through the poplar trees. Over the years, visitors standing on the balconies, seeing the reflections of lighted windows in the glittering water, would endlessly liken it to Venice. It was a continuation of Warwick Crescent, where Robert Browning lived at No. 19, and within easy walking distance of the Tademas. The relationship with Browning would flourish with the proximity. Gosse would often call in and spend half an hour when Browning was at home. Gosse had a passion to know the great writers – the fact that they were 'great', or that they might be, was obviously one of the attractions of such friendships; but the fact that he had so little difficulty in establishing these relationships is an indication of just what good company he was.

He was already establishing a reputation as an excellent talker. Arthur Benson said his genius was 'for recording a scene or a conversation not quite accurately but in a manner that was more truthful (and not just more entertaining) than the truth itself, adding a sprinkle of distilled criticism, which brought out the underlying savour of the original, as a touch of pepper is alleged to bring out the flavour of strawberries.' He was in fact a gossip: nearly all his talk was about people – people and their ideas, certainly, but never just ideas. As he got older, he added more and more stories to his repertoire, about the people he had known in the long years gone by. Now in the eighteen-seventies, of course, he was in the midst of those very friendships which would supply him with so much gossip in the future.

Unlike most people who talk extremely entertainingly, over and over again the people who knew him stress how little he seemed to want to monopolize the conversation. As a young man, he had learnt how to be a good listener, and he never forgot. He would make a brilliant catch, but instead of retaining the ball he would immediately throw it lightly away to some other player. At his best, he was always far more than a teller of anecdotes. Under the dancing words, he could 'convey a profound sense of reality and truth, to be the glorified showman of experiences, lending art to reminiscence'.

'Your talk's a feast,' John Leicester Warren wrote to him in 1877. Warren, who became Lord de Tabley, is now forgotten. There are just two of his poems in Quiller-Couch's *Oxford Book of English Verse*. But it is worth pausing to look at his friendship with Gosse, before moving on to more familiar names. For Gosse named him as one of the three most influential friends of his youth – 'the most formative friends on his intellectual life'. They shared three particular interests – poetry, book collecting, and natural history. (Warren was 'the greatest living authority on brambles'.) Gosse recorded that one week in the winter of 1875 he had never heard of him, the next he had become an essential part of his existence.

It seems that for both of them the forming of new friendships was a very conscious business. Gosse would constantly mark down people he wanted to know better. He loved the 'long and exciting confidences' of friendship, the feeling of being in close relationship, of knowing more than the world knew (unless he told them). Talk with friends was the most rewarding thing in life.

Warren had marked Gosse down as someone he wanted to know. 'I must have some new man, get some fresh blood,' he apparently said, as he walked across Hyde Park after a visit to F. T. Palgrave, who had been more cynical than usual. He decided on Gosse. Whether he thought that the young man might replace his long-lost George Fortescue, we do not know. Fortescue, the love of his youth, had slipped while climbing a mast on board a yacht in the Mediterranean, had crashed to the deck and been killed. He haunted Warren as Hallam haunted Tennyson. His life was full of distracting griefs and perplexities, and only those who knew him best, Gosse said, 'could divine what the foxes were that gnawed the breast under the cloak'. He perhaps had more reason than most writers for gloom, telling Gosse, with only slight exaggeration, that not a single copy had yet been sold of his tragedy *The Soldier of Fortune*, published that year without a murmur of recognition. He saw only too clearly that a democracy had more need of bacon than minor poetry, or indeed of a knowledge of brambles.

It was obviously a difficult friendship for Gosse. His own life at this time was so full of hope and promise and the love of his wife, now pregnant with their first child in that summer of 1876. P. H. Gosse observed from Marychurch: 'You can face all the storms of the world outside; for each has an inviolable refuge in the heart of the other.'

The worst storm brought them even closer together. In the first week of October, Nellie gave birth to a dead child. Edmund never referred to it later, but among his papers there is a fragment of a poem annotated: 'Written the morning after our first child was born dead.' It begins:

> When you were lying in my arms last night
> Death came and bowed over the shrouded bed,
> But we, though hearkening, knew not what he said
> Who called what should have been our hearts' delight
> Out of strange darkness into stranger light;
> Through pain as through a veil, the dawn broke red
> And we who waited knew not what had fled
> Nor whither the unknown spirit winged its flight;
> Rest, rest, dear heart, the rose of whose sweet face
> Not pain itself can mar with withering breath . . .

That winter, perhaps deliberately, thinking of the empty nursery, the Alma-Tademas went abroad again, but this time leaving the two girls – now aged nine and eleven – to stay at Delamere Terrace with the Gosses. Edmund had given the older one, Laurence, Palgrave's *Golden Treasury* for Christmas, and now he taught her, each day before he went to the Board of Trade, about poetry. 'He opened the *Golden*

Treasury, read a verse to me, made me – ridiculously selfconscious – read to him, taught me how to scan, how to dissect; I learned from him day by day the laws of prosody; and to this day', Laurence wrote in 1921, 'I can recall his fine voice,' reading Gray's 'Elegy' and Wordsworth's 'Ode on the Intimations of Immortality'. That sacrifice of twenty minutes of ease on a few weeks' winter mornings threw open a new world for a painter's daughter. Then in the evenings the girls would listen for his key and the sound of 'Nellie! Nellie!' as he came in the front door. They would play hide and seek, not allowed at Townshend House because of the 'destructible treasures'. The Delamere Terrace house, hardly furnished yet, was ideal. The little bare gas-jets 'shed but a dim light on the stairs. It was a fearsome hour of delight. Uncle Edmund threw himself heart and soul into the game, tearing back to Nellie's base in the dining-room' when the girls came across him in some dark upstairs room, crouched behind a William Morris curtain.

Most games did not interest him. He never played dominoes, draughts or chess. But pencil and paper games were another matter. Occasionally after supper they would play birds, beasts and fishes (what we now call 'Categories'), word-making (how many words from one word) or the poetry game (making verses from given pairs of rhymes). Edmund Gosse would always win; no one else had a chance. But usually, after the evening meal, he went straight to work at his desk in the book-lined back drawing-room, separated from the bright yellow front room by a double book-case and a curtain, which would be drawn back when they entertained.

Early the following summer, Swinburne came back to London. He had spent the winter with his parents in Henley, claiming to have been poisoned by the perfume of lilies in a closed bedroom. That spring his father had died and he seemed lonelier than ever on his return to Great James Street. He spent more and more time at Delamere Terrace. Sometimes he would call quite unexpectedly and stay the whole evening. He would come – with his pockets bulging with manuscripts – and dance about the room as he recited his verses to the entranced Edmund and the patient Nellie. Edmund described one particular occasion when 'he spent a long day at my house and read nearly half of what now forms the [1878] collection to my wife and myself . . . These performances were entrancing to some persons, of whom I was one, but annoying and even alarming to others. Watts-Dunton did not permit them after the exodus to the Pines, when Swinburne, although he read aloud more than ever, was not allowed to be corybantic.'

Nellie may well have been alarmed, but she was getting used to it.

She was pregnant again and spent a great deal of time reading novels in the drawing-room, at Edmund's insistence. He wrote nervously from Holland in August 1877, when he took ten days' holiday (with introductions from Alma-Tadema), leaving Nellie at home as it was too near her time for travel. He wrote every day to 'the sweetest of Nells'. He saw a great deal, 'inwardly conversing' with her all the time. She was busy 'settling the basement in order etc' and he implored her not to drag things about. 'I am quite anxious for I know how imprudent you are.' He had an appointment with a professor with whom he 'read early Dutch literature for two hours . . . My Dutch is very queer but I get along with it quite successfully.' It was some relaxation to go to the zoo, though 'a curious bird from Australia *would* show me its feet; they were not at all pretty, so very large for the size of the bird . . . How I long to be home! I quite count the hours.'

Swinburne was almost as glad as Nellie to have him back again. There were several extraordinary evenings at Delamere Terrace. Gosse describes in detail one such evening:

September 10, 1877
He was dining alone with my wife and myself at a time when his habits were a matter of scandal to the public and embarrassment to his friends. I perceived at dinner that Algernon was reaching the danger-point. I had taken the precaution of putting the decanter away, and when, after several disregarded hints, the poet asked for more wine, I grossly lied and said there was no more in the house, going out of the room in a pretended search. This was clumsily done and even Swinburne saw through the pretence of it. When I came back to announce my inability to find another drop, my wife was half-weeping with mingled obligations of hospitality and duty, for Swinburne had sidled along the table towards her and had said, slowly and in a low voice, 'Does Edmund really think it *possible* that I could ever be so little of a gentleman as to drink more than was good for me?' We were, however, firm and my wife, for whom Swinburne had a great affection and a great respect, managed to divert his thoughts, so that the craving passed away . . .

Four days later, Emily Teresa Gosse was born. This first living baby was of course received with particular joy. Her grandfather wrote from Marychurch, recalling that it was exactly twenty years since the child's father had arrived in Marychurch, as a child himself. 'Accept your precious gift from the hand of God, who thus once more says to you, "My son, give me thy heart!" ' He hoped that Nellie would have 'constant joy in her beloved babe!' Swinburne took the colour of the baby's hair as a personal compliment – 'as you say, it is my colour'. He loved babies and would kiss Tessa, as she was always known, and dance her on his knee for as long as he was allowed. The Gosses pandered to his feelings, sending white roses from Tessa as a birthday present the following April. 'My best love and thanks to the sweetest and kindest of babies for its birthday attention,' Swinburne wrote.

But he was becoming more and more an object of pathos, rather than admiration. Gosse would have to make sure he got back to his lodgings safely. There was one occasion when they looked for a cab and the streets of London rang embarrassingly with 'crescendo praises of the glorious beauty of Sark delivered at the top of his voice in a very shrill key'. Gosse had to placate a policeman. Then there was the time when Swinburne invited Gosse to hear him read a new essay on Charlotte Brontë ('How absurd of A.C.S.,' commented W. B. Scott). There were chairs and glasses set out. A crowd was expected, but no one but Gosse turned up. Swinburne had forgotten to ask them.

His bright hair was fading. He was physically frail, though he was only forty. He was 'glad to accept a hand to help him up and downstairs'. They rarely saw him in violent mood. One night when Nellie was out of the room, he shrieked, 'Damn God! Damn Jesus Christ!' in his most maniacal way – but stopped when she returned, and talked charmingly about Villon, managing to leave out everything improper when he read his own translations. On good days his conversation – usually about literature – could still delight and impress them, but he was now likely to visit the Gosses during the exhaustion and depression that followed a drinking bout, when he was tired of his loneliness at Great James Street and seemed 'to crave the comfort of home life and the petting that we lavish on him'. The two friends, the baby and the cat offered a picture of domestic bliss which would attract many lonely people. Swinburne would sit close to the fire, his great head bowed, his knees tight together and his finger-tips pressed to his chest. The cat purred at his feet.

This cat was Atossa, the first of many cats which stalked through the long years of the Gosses' life together, sketched, studied – even writing letters and poems with remarkable facility. There had always been cats at Marychurch – indeed Philip Henry had recently written a long and touching tribute on the death of one of his own favourites. There had been cats at Tottenham. Atossa, in Delamere Terrace, was apparently hard-hearted (Edmund's berth from Harwich to the Hook had been as 'hard as Atossa's heart'), but much loved. She had come from Walter Pater, who kept her sister, Pansie, in Oxford. The two cats would exchange verses. In one of these Atossa confided her aversion ('as I'm a Persian') for Swinburne and his excessive affection.

The two Tadema girls, who spent a lot of time at Delamere Terrace, helped Edmund baptize Atossa's kitten in a ceremony which would presumably have appalled P. H. Gosse, cat lover as he was. 'Dost thou renounce the forbidden delights – of stealing the fish, lapping the cream in the larder, upsetting the gravy boat to get at the melted butter, and all such dreadful things?' Edmund asked the godparent girls, who replied 'We do renounce them,' promising, on the kitten's behalf, that it would keep itself at home at night, and keep itself clean and unspotted in the burning question of fleas. ('Nothing drives the fleas away, unharmed the little darlings play,' as Edmund had written for Atossa in a verse letter to Pater's cat.)

Edmund would walk to Whitehall from Delamere Terrace and home again in the evenings. It was a good walk, one he enjoyed for twenty-five years. Most of it was through the Parks: Hyde Park, Green Park, St James's Park. On this walk, he saw on several occasions at this period, 'a victoria which contained a strange pair', in whose appearance, Edmund said, he took 'a violent interest'.

The man, prematurely ageing, was hirsute, rugged, satyr-like, gazing vivaciously to left and right; this was George Henry Lewes. His companion was a large, thickset sybil, dreamy and immobile, whose massive features, somewhat grim when seen in profile, were incongruously bordered by a hat, always in the height of the Paris fashion, which in those days commonly included an immense ostrich feather; this was George Eliot. The contrast between the solemnity of the face and the frivolity of the headgear had something pathetic and provincial about it.

Gosse never spoke to George Eliot and he always had mixed feelings about her. He certainly saw her, at this period, just after Dickens's death, as our 'premier novelist'. A portrait of her always hung in his study. *Middlemarch* engaged his attention again and again ('Look narrowly at it and you will see Lydgate is herself'), though oddly he would manage not to mention it in his survey of *Modern English Literature* in 1897. He always regretted he had not taken up an invitation from a mutual friend to go to Witley one Sunday – George Eliot was said to have read some pages of his 'with indulgence'. In December 1880 he sat behind her at a concert in the Langham Hall. 'It was chilly in the concert-room and I watched George Eliot, in manifest discomfort, drawing up and tightening around her shoulders a white wool shawl.' He mused on her marriage to Mr Cross, the strange wish for a return to respectability in a woman who 'had utterly flouted social position'. Four days later she was dead.

In October, 1877, Gosse tried to bring Swinburne and Leicester Warren together. Warren recollected dimly the brilliant boy at Eton, two years his junior, and Swinburne's influence on Warren's imagination had been great. Warren's article in the *Fortnightly* on *Atalanta in Calydon* had been one of the first to draw attention to Swinburne's genius. But the editor, G. H. Lewes, although Warren's article was signed, had toned down the ardour of it and introduced one or two slighting phrases which 'poor Warren carried about with him like open wounds', shuddering to think what Swinburne thought he thought.

Whether the *Atalanta* review was referred to when they met in Gosse's house we do not know. But the dinner was a disaster. George Saintsbury was there as well and remembered the occasion fondly enough. But Warren hardly opened his mouth and next day wrote to Gosse to say he felt they would have all got on much better without him. Gosse replied that that was absurd, but recorded afterwards: 'Our correspondence, which had been almost daily, fell absolutely through.' They had been in the habit of dining once a week alternately at each other's houses. When Tennyson entertained Gosse at Aldworth in 1888, he recalled that it was at Leicester Warren's house they had first met, forgetting Ralston's introduction at the Museum. But after the night with Swinburne, it was many years before Warren invited Gosse to his house again, or visited Delamere Terrace.

'On the 2nd of June, 1878, I determined, if possible, to bring about a reconciliation.' Gosse told Warren that he did not wish to force himself upon him, but he would still find the same warm welcome at Delamere Terrace. 'I expected a conciliatory, an apologetic answer; but on the next morning, as I sauntered up to my office in Whitehall, Leicester Warren was waiting at the door, and instantly strode over to me, his face as white as cream cheese with rage, his eyes rolling.' He brandished a large stick and threatened more than once to strike the young man. He was almost inarticulate with anger, but then started raving that Gosse was a rascal and he was a gentleman still, in spite of his torn coat and shattered fortune. A crowd gathered, interested in the row, and Gosse, keeping quite cool, begged Warren to come into his office. His coat was in fact an excellent one, Gosse noted, but he was unshaven and wild and 'looked more like a drunken rough than a gentleman'. He would not go into the Board of Trade; he would not say what Gosse had done to offend him. At last Gosse managed to get a cab-driver to take Warren home. At the bottom of the sheet of paper, dated 1878, which records this quarrel, Gosse eventually wrote: 'Quarrel made up today, April 25, 1893.'

So Warren was off the scene, at least for fifteen years. And Swinburne was very soon to be removed by Theodore Watts-Dunton to the long captivity in the Pines at Putney – to Gosse's permanent regret. Gosse continued to see Swinburne from time to time, but only under Watts-Dunton's aegis. There would be letters, but 1879 marked the end of their real friendship. In October 1879 Gosse wrote to Watts-Dunton from holiday in Devon: 'I am sure that you deserve the thanks of the lovers of literature for your devoted and unfailing kindness to A.C.S.. Myself I have long mourned that it was not possible for me, in my circumstances, to volunteer to take charge of him; nor could I do so with half the patience or the wisdom that you show. But for you I am sure he would be dead ere now. I shall keep the secret absolutely, as long as it is a secret –' that was, of course, that Swinburne was an alcoholic. 'I shall be most anxious to hear from you how the experiment works. You will not get so phenomenal a creature into working order without many slips and heart-breaking adventures.' Gosse was not always to feel so kindly disposed towards Watts-Dunton. But it must have been a relief at this point to have all responsibility for Swinburne taken from him. Swinburne was, however, anxious that he should not misunderstand the position. 'You need not put Watts' name on my address any more than mine on his, as we have both moved in together.'

What other friends were there? There were many. The Gosses had already established the habit which they were to maintain, off and on, for fifty years, of Sunday afternoons At Home, when a few of the afternoon's guests were encouraged to stay on for a cold informal supper in the dining-room downstairs. The Book of Gosse shows visits in these early years from Mr Blaikie, the Scotts, the Rossettis, Miss Otté, Arthur O'Shaughnessy, Marzials, Miss Buckham, as well, of course, as lots of Nellie's family. The Tademas were particularly regular visitors. There were some new names who were to be important; for instance, Robert Bridges, the Waterhouses and Churton Collins.

On 13th January 1878 (the day that Tessa, aged four months, made her first appearance at a party) both Bridges and the Waterhouses were at Delamere Terrace. Gosse admired Bridges. As early as 1874, he had written to Scott: 'The best thing in verse this year has been Robert Bridges.' It was 'a little modest volume . . . of which no one seems to have taken the least notice'. Warren once said you could only get on with Bridges if you were 'as humble as a black beetle', which made it difficult for Gosse; but Gosse always thought him a very great man and was glad when, long after this, he became Poet Laureate. As time went on, Bridges grew more and more averse to parties and crowds, and came to have something of the reputation of a recluse.

The Waterhouses were very different. At this time Alfred was working on his design for the Natural History Museum in South Kensington. The Waterhouses were another family – like the Tademas – who seemed to provide for Edmund something he wished he had had himself as a child. They too were keen on family theatricals. Gosse wrote for the four children 'a drama for private acting': *The Unknown Lover,* which was published by Chatto in 1878 and dedicated to Mrs Waterhouse.

Perhaps as a sort of thankyou for the play, the Waterhouses lent the Manor House at Yattendon in Berkshire to the Gosses that summer. At one stage, the Tadema girls were there and Laurence remembered, as they walked across a field of ripening wheat under a hot sun, asking her uncle Edmund who was the most celebrated man in the whole world. He replied 'Jesus Christ'. She did not think it a fair answer, but she did not question it. He was never wilfully unkind, she said, but sometimes he had a biting tongue that made one wince. We know very little about Edmund's attitude to Christianity at this time. It seemed that he really did not want to think about it, after all that he had been through. Certainly he still went regularly to church and made no issue of it. Certainly he never shouted 'Damn God! Damn Jesus Christ!' as Swinburne did. But Laurence remembered his writing verse in church on a small piece of paper inside his prayer-book. The only religious feeling she recalled was on an occasion, a few years later, when they stopped singing hymns one day when he came into his children's nursery, and he begged them to continue and to sing, if they could, some of his own childhood favourites. Together they sang (he, it seems, with sonorous fervour):

> I wish that His hand had been placed on my head,
> That His arms had been thrown about me,
> And that I might have seen His kind look when he said
> 'Let the little ones come unto me.'

At Yattendon they were joined for a while by Churton Collins. Collins – who would become the 'Old Enemy' – had gone down from Oxford with a disappointing third and, giving up his intention of going into the church, had been disinherited by a rich uncle and had gone to London to make his living with his brain and his pen. At the beginning he had been reduced to addressing envelopes at half a crown a thousand, but by 1874 he had found work coaching boys in classics and English literature at a crammer's. He stayed with this establishment for fourteen years, while he built up a reputation as a literary journalist and editor. He was a fanatical worker, often doing thirteen or fourteen hours a day. Like Gosse, he would write appreciative letters to people he wanted to know; Swinburne became such a friend.

Gosse reviewed Collins's edition of Dryden favourably in the *Saturday Review* and his Tourneur in the *Academy*. They were friends; but there was always something a little worrying about Collins, something fanatical. Laurence Alma-Tadema remembered long literary talks at Yattendon between the two men, which was like 'listening to a conversation in an unknown tongue'. One evening, as they sat out after dark, bats flitting and shrieking faintly, Churton Collins told ghost stories.

A series of letters from Churton Collins to Gosse at this time shows more than anything Collins published what sort of a man he was and on what a narrow edge he balanced. The tone is always extreme. Later in 1878 he wrote from Wales, on holiday in 'the very dullest and most intolerable hole it was ever my lot to be induced to take lodgings in'.

> Don't I wish you were down here. In my hunger for companionship . . . I have struck up an acquaintance with 1) an ignorant country dispenser of Foreign Languages 2) a non-descript sort of person who has softening of the brain 3) an itinerant lecturer in spiritualness . . . When I come back to London I come back to graceless and unbroken grind, but we must manage, if such at least be your pleasure, to meet, talk and walk and be happy when we can. Your poem about Orpheus and Eurydice has been ringing in my ears ever since last night when I was alone in a thick wood I was thinking of it and wishing I could remember more; also that other beautiful poem you read me at Yattendon. You *must* get them printed *must, must, must, must, must, must* . . .

In October, he encouraged Gosse to avoid, in capital letters, 'SELF-CONSCIOUSNESS IN ART':

> Fly it like a pest. Not only I . . . but others too . . . prophesy much good concerning you and look for good work from you. It is all nonsense about your poems lacking thought. If you go in for this sort of self-analysis, you will *maim* and *paralyse* your genius . . . You are all right. Never fear you will be among the right sort when the earth covers you, if you are true to yourself . . . I thoroughly believe in your haven, and your genius and your ultimate success – success I mean in the highest sense of the word, though I know from biography that those who have the privilege of being friends of men of genius may do something by their encouragement and honest advice to buoy them up in times of depression: and times of

depression are as unsuitable to the temperament of genius, as the
ecstacies and elation which are the springs of its being.

The message was quite clear. John Churton Collins thought Edmund
Gosse was a genius and his friend.

On the 4th November 1878 Collins wrote:

I think it is very kind and generous of you to bring my Dryden into
notice by giving it an article in the *Saturday*. Also with reference to
the other friendly part of your letter – let me say: as I think my
conduct requires explanation, and I do not wish to lose the regard of
those with whom I have so much intellectual sympathy. It is of
course impossible for me to go into society without my wife: it is
equally impossible for her and for myself, living as we do in this
unusual way, to be *of* society and therefore we have resolved not to
go out, except to one or two of her relations. I cannot go out to meet
ladies. Consequently you mustn't ask me. Don't let us quarrel for
you are one of the few men I know whom I care to be with and
who worship at the same shrines having the same Gods and the
same Heaven. I hope when my holidays come we may meet. I want
to take you to the opium dens with which I have become acquainted
since we saw each other.

The following June there was a letter which shows a touchiness in
Gosse which was to become characteristic. He appears to think Collins
snubbed him in the British Museum one day. Andrew Lang had
reported it to Collins, who wrote:

It is exceedingly painful to me to think that you could even suppose
that I could have acted in such a way to one from whom I have
received nothing but kindness and for whom I entertain so much
respect. *I never saw* you so far as I *know in my life* at the Museum. Of
course we must have been near for you to think I had behaved so
rudely, but I am very blind and very absent and have even been hit
by a stick and not known it . . . I hope . . . you will come to see me
and take our long promised walk to Elstree. I lead the life of a galley
slave . . . I would with all my soul apologize but as you will see
there is nothing I have *really* done.

Gosse's side of the correspondence seems to have been destroyed.
Presumably he never went to an opium den with Collins or even on a
walk to Elstree. If he never replied to that humble letter of apology for
an imagined slight, I suppose he deserved a little of what was coming
to him. It would be no less painful for that.

Then there was Robert Louis Stevenson. After their renewed acquaintance at Leslie Stephen's dinner table, Stevenson and Gosse began to see a great deal of each other. By 1877 they were both members of the Savile Club. Sometimes they would see Thomas Hardy there. When Louis was in town, Edmund wrote, 'I must have lunched with him on an average four or five times a week.' Edmund would walk across to Savile Row from the Board of Trade; Louis would turn up invariably at 1.15. Stevenson loved the Savile. 'Louis pervaded the club; he was its most affable and chatty member; and he lifted it, by the ingenuity of his incessant dialectic, to the level of a sort of humorous Academe.' Gosse once defined Stevenson's facination as that of his dual disposition: 'He grafted on a very sedate Presbyterian upbringing an insatiable passion for the laughing wandering adventures of a gypsy.' At one moment he could be 'a rather stern moralising disciplinarian', at the next 'an artist capable of the wildest indulgence'.

Gosse remembered their first lunch together at the club – Sidney Colvin had been with Stevenson but had gone off and left them to their own devices. Gosse did not get back to the Board of Trade that afternoon. As twilight came, they tore themselves away from the smoking-room at the Savile, and Stevenson walked with Gosse across Hyde Park, up Westbourne Terrace, nearly to his house. 'He had an engagement, and so had I, but I walked a mile or two back with him. The fountains of talk had been unsealed and they drowned the conventions.' Gosse went home dazzled by his new friend, loving him already and his 'rapidity in the sympathetic interchange of ideas'. Stevenson 'seemed to skip upon the hills of life. He was simply bubbling with quips and jests . . . When he had built one of his intellectual castles in the sand, a wave of humour was certain to sweep in and destroy it'. At this stage – before increasing ill-health, responsibility, worry of all sorts – he had 'the silliness of an inspired schoolboy'. He was never strong and this added to the magic of his presence. 'He was so bright and keen and witty, and any week he might die.'

Stevenson would visit London unexpectedly, making 'sudden piratical descents, staying a few days or weeks and melting into air again'. He came a lot to Delamere Terrace, envying Edmund his wife, his home, his child, his cat. He liked the large, bare drawing-room on the first floor, appreciating its lack of furniture, saying he always preferred to sit on cushions on the floor. But as, eventually, the Gosses acquired armchairs and settees, he would use them in his own particular way – with his long legs thrown sideways over the arms of them or using the back of a sofa as a perch. 'In particular, a certain shelf, with cupboards below, attached to a bookcase, is worn with the person of Stevenson, who would spend half an evening while passionately discussing some great question of morality or literature, leaping side-wise in a seated posture to the length of this shelf, and then back again.' (Swinburne used to sit on this shelf too, drumming his heels on the cupboard below; after he had gone to the Pines and was rarely seen, Gosse used to point out to visitors the marks of his drumming heels.)

There was nothing conventional about Stevenson – least of all his clothes. Later, like Edmund, he would take to a velvet jacket, but at this stage he would very often wear 'a suit of blue sea-cloth, a black shirt and a wisp of yellow carpet that did duty for a neck-tie'. Henry James, who had recently met Stevenson and Gosse at lunch with Andrew Lang, called Stevenson 'a shirt-collarless Bohemian'. (Gosse said James was 'absolutely charming' and quite the rage that season; we will hear much more of him later.) Gosse said that Stevenson's outfit caused some anguish to his more conventional acquaintances; but the use of the word 'acquaintance' seems specifically to exclude Gosse himself – civil servant as he was, in his inevitable top hat. Gosse was his friend. The question of Stevenson's hat did become rather urgent at one stage – the thing upon his head having lost any semblance it ever had to a human article of dress. Gosse and Andrew Lang went with him to choose a new one. 'Aided by a very civil shopman, we suggested several hats and caps and Louis at first seemed interested; but having presently hit upon one which appeared to us pleasing and decorous, we turned for a moment to inquire the price. We turned back, and found that Louis had fled, the idea of parting with the shapeless object having proved too painful to be entertained', and the idea of *paying* to be parted from it even more painful.

Money was always a problem. Stevenson was having a hard time getting published. He suggested to Edmund that they recited a commination for publishers: 'I think I hear the stage direction – "Here shall a fair white publisher's body be laid upon the altar," or "In choirs and places where they sing, here shall a publisher be shot out of a gun." ' That very evening, after the abortive hat-buying, trying to get back to Scotland and not having quite enough money for the London to Edinburgh third-class ticket, Louis offered to throw in a copy of Swinburne's *The Queen-Mother; Rosamond*. The railway-clerk foolishly refused, 'although the book was of the first edition and even then worth more than the cost of the whole ticket'.

In Louis's last letter to Edmund, the very last letter he wrote, he would remember how generous Edmund had been to him at this time:

I mentioned to you in my usual autobiographical and inconsiderate manner that I was hard up. You said promptly that you had a balance at your banker's, and could make it convenient to let me have a cheque, and I accepted and got the money – how much was it? Twenty or perhaps thirty pounds? . . . The same evening, or the next day, I fell in conversation . . . with a denizen of the Savile Club . . . To him I mentioned that you had given me a loan, remarking easily that of course it didn't matter to you. Whereupon he read me a lecture, corrected the legends as to your wife's enormous fortune, and told me how it really stood with you financially . . .

This was just before Stevenson went off to California, hoping to marry Mrs Osborne, if her divorce came through. Gosse was one of the few people who knew about the break with his father and how hard it was for him to raise the cost of his passage to America. Andrew Lang thought he was off to Russia; most of Stevenson's friends were in the dark. Edmund and Louis spent his last Sunday in London together, and Edmund would 'never forget his feverish unrest, the evidence of the frail condition of his health and his marvellous lack of all preparation for the huge, uncomfortable journey'. In October 1879, when *Travels with a Donkey in the Cevennes* was in all the bookshops, Gosse wrote to Stevenson in California, 'Many times, in a blue spot, I have lived over again the dismal clammy evening when we bid one another farewell at the corner of Berkeley Square, and have betted sixpence with my soul that I should never see your face again . . . I have found out your existence is very important to me . . .'

Stevenson had obviously imagined the young Gosses had Epps Cocoa money behind them. Nellie had an extremely rich uncle, James Epps, but she had no money of her own, beyond what she earned from selling a few pictures. It would be thirty years before she would see any of the cocoa money. The Household Accounts book for 1878 has survived and it shows a stringent economy. They hired extra china for one shilling for their Sunday afternoons At Home. They spent eightpence on rivets for the milk jug and one shilling on doing up E.W.'s waistcoat. The young maids' wages were eighteen shillings and sixpence a month and the charwoman cost another ten shillings. Atossa was very cheap to feed; her bloaters cost a mere penny. There were occasional extravagances: a cask of ale for eight shillings and sixpence, one shilling entrance for the Grosvenor Gallery and two shillings for a cab home from the Thorneycrofts. The birthday roses the baby sent Swinburne cost two shillings and 'extra photos of Baby' were an expensive item at seven shillings and sixpence.
    Occasionally the charwoman's husband, Mr Gaston, would come

in and do a little gardening for one and a penny. The garden was something of a problem.

> Soots conglomerate and harden.
> Nothing grows in our front garden,

Edmund had rhymed when they had first moved in in March, 1876, and it was a continual battle, Atossa not always keeping out the neighbourhood cats in a way to justify the expenditure on bloaters.

'Cut your coat according to your cloth,' P. H. Gosse wrote from Marychurch, expecting Edmund by now to stand on his own feet. 'With your professional salary augmented by literature, you two ought to live *au prince*.' But they were always careful about money in these early years. There is much mention of third-class railway travel, even when Alma-Tadema was travelling first on the same train. Edmund had his old office coat done up by a tailor who was prepared to do it for five shillings, rather than the first one Nellie tried, who would have charged eight. Edmund kept meticulous accounts of his earnings and outgoings; Nellie's household accounts were rather more chaotic. He was earning satisfactorily more each year from 'Literature', as he called it in his accounts. In 1877 he obviously thought they were in a comfortable enough position for him to start serious book-collecting, if only in a very small way.

In a talk, Gosse once used a passage from the Emperor Julian, which he freely translated like this: 'Some men have loved hounds, and the turf and covert-shooting, but, as for me, ever since I was a little chap, I have had a wonderful passion for books.' It was a sudden haul of Drydens, Donnes and Otways, in the spring of 1877, which determined him to begin collecting in earnest. Later the same year, John Addington Symonds, breaking up his home at Clifton to move for his health to Davos Platz, gave Gosse 'a thick volume containing eight first editions of Massinger'. It was in the dramatic literature of the age which followed Shakespeare's that Gosse began to specialize.

When his library was broken up after his death, in several large sales at Sotheby's, it raised no less than £26,000, at a time when that sum would have bought a street of houses in a desirable part of London. It included thirty-nine first editions of Dryden and the Westmoreland Manuscript of Donne. Yet Gosse very rarely spent more than a few pounds; there were such bargains to be had. As late as 1897, he was ordering a Pope folio dated 1737 for one guinea. He was never a real fanatic. He always valued books more for what was in them, not for the way they looked. 'After all, with every respect paid to "states" and editions and bindings and tall copies, the inside of the book is the really essential part of it.' And he could be refreshingly sensible about some of his minor dramatists. He once wrote about Heywood, 'Most providentially, about two hundred of these dramas have been lost, and I earnestly hope that they may never be found, not because those that remain are not interesting, but because we may have too much of a good thing.'

As a critic, Gosse was always motivated by a desire to share with others the infinite pleasures which literature had afforded him. Books were not merely a means to success in life, to reputation and position. They were the main business of life. It was the love of books – reading, writing and acquiring them – that really ruled him: that, and the love of friends. But friends were often temperamental and unpredictable. Books, in their sensible deal bookshelves, were endlessly handled and endlessly enjoyed. 'A folio Beaumont and Fletcher tilted against the stomach is a great solace at times.' Booksellers' catalogues were like windows opening on to promised lands, some corner of which he might hope to possess. It was through his book-collecting, of course, that Gosse became involved with the notorious Thomas J. Wise; but that was much later, and Gosse never knew how notorious Wise would become.

A present of a volume of Massinger from John Addington Symonds was, as we have seen, one of the things that started Gosse on his great library. Symonds (that 'strange, poignant, pathetic, brilliant creature' as Stevenson called him to Gosse) had first written to Gosse in August 1875, the month that Edmund and Nellie were married. Years later, in the revealing sexual memoir which Gosse would see lodged, unpublished, in the London Library, Symonds wrote, 'It requires all the romance and passion of a Romeo and Juliet to make a double bedroom in an English town hotel appear poetical. Marriage begins ill which begins with a prosaic tour of inns.' Gosse must have paused when he read these words after Symonds' death in 1893. Symonds had no idea, in August 1875, what Gosse's situation was. He had read some articles by him in the periodicals and he had put out a hand to a stranger, hoping he might find the sympathy he was always seeking. We know, as Gosse did not know for several years, that John Addington Symonds was a questing homosexual. It was not yet common gossip. (Later Gosse was to condemn his beloved Swinburne as a 'spiteful guttersnipe' for the designation 'Mr Soddington Symonds'.) At this time he was only suspect. He was canvassing for the Chair of Poetry at Oxford, and realized the clerics had 'found out that I am a pagan of frail moralities'.

Symonds believed that sooner or later we shall surely meet some sort of God and need to keep 'our souls inviolate' for that event. But his ideas of preserving the soul – or indeed of God – had nothing to do with conventional morality. Ancient Greece stood for him as the place, the time when Man 'was at unity with himself, with his physical nature, with the outward world'. The Greeks helped him to come to terms with his own homosexual nature, when a Victorian father and a Victorian doctor had sought to cure him through marriage. 'The great crime of my life was my marriage,' he wrote in his memoirs.

Symonds detected in Gosse's *King Erik* a 'strong and tender sympathy with the beauty of men as well as with women', and tested Gosse out by sending him a privately printed pamphlet of poems on the theme of Greek love. 'Of course,' Symonds wrote, 'this Greek love is different in quality from what can be expected to flourish in the modern world, and to attempt to replant it would be anachronistic. Yet I do not see, having the root of Calamus within our souls, why we should not make the Hellenic passion of friendship a motive in art.' Gosse was tentative in reply, but Symonds would not be dissuaded from the conviction that they had much in common. He would write in 1884: 'You who have the divine fire, the sacred thirst of what is beautiful and great in literature . . .' He hastened to assure Gosse in 1876 that he must not be alarmed: 'I fear lest I should have exposed myself to misconstruction . . . by poems which have no didactically ethical intention.' He agreed that this Greek love 'finds no place in modern life and has never found one. It is a special Greek compound of chivalrous enthusiasm and perverted sexual passion – the second of its two factors finding ample realization in Renaissance literature . . . As you care for me at all,' he ended, 'do not, by all that is sacred, dream that I want to preach its ethics to the present or a future generation.' But of course he did, if only people would listen and not revile him for the preaching. In time, he and Gosse would exchange more letters on this theme, though not for many years.

Meanwhile, in 1877, Symonds tried to get Gosse to write a long piece on his three-volume study of the *Renaissance in Italy*. He wrote on 12th February that he would like to approach the editor of the *Quarterly Review* and suggest that Gosse might do a good piece for him. 'There is no-one I should like to be reviewed by better than you; and when I say this, I know you will understand that I am far from wishing to escape censure when I need it. I only mean that I have great confidence in your critical judgement, combined with a pleasant sense of much intellectual sympathy . . . It is literally the first time I have ever done anything of the sort about a book of mine. I have always cast my bread upon the waters: and I should do so still, were it not that a work in several volumes like my *Renaissance in Italy* is more ponderous and wants a little pushing.'

Gosse had never written for the *Quarterly* and liked the idea (he had no reason yet to shudder at the very name), but he naturally did not want to go to all the trouble of writing a long article if he were not sure that it would be published. Symonds hastened to reassure him: 'I have such confidence in your literary powers that I feel sure you would send [the editor, Dr Smith] what he would think it a bonne fortune to print.' He reminded him of the *Quarterly*'s arch-conservative viewpoint and left him to it. In the end, the article – an enormous one of Symonds's suggested length – was rejected, and Symonds attempted to cheer Gosse by suggesting that the reason was not the article's merits but the fact that 'Smith must have made enquiries about you and found that you are in the "opposite camp". His mistrust of your article is therefore a compliment.' This was small consolation for Gosse. Nor was the eventual publication in October of his long essay in the *Westminster Review*, for this was both anonymous and unpaid. Symonds did rather well out of the whole business: the *Quarterly*, the following January, devoted a leading article of no fewer than thirty-four pages to his book. The Massinger volume he gave Gosse was presumably the consolation prize.

7

'Something better than a brother'

AT THE END of the year, looking back, Gosse characterized 1879 as the happiest year of his life. Everything was going well. He had two books published – his first prose book, *Studies in the Literature of Northern Europe*, and a collection of *New Poems*. He celebrated his fifth wedding anniversary with the birth of his son – Philip Henry George Gosse, called after both his grandfathers. But it was of neither literature nor child Edmund was thinking when he spoke of the peculiar happiness of that year. It was of his friendship with the sculptor, Hamo Thornycroft.

He sat writing to him on New Year's Eve, thinking that at the same moment Hamo might be writing to him.

Above all things I put the fact that *you* have come up out of the rank of a common friend into the first place of all, as something better than a brother. You are the inestimable treasure for which I was waiting nearly thirty years, and which, God knows, I long ago thought would never come at all . . . I do not think there is any peak or alp of the sculptor's art that you may not reach if you husband your powers and are true to the strong simplicity with which you have begun. Don't be too social and don't work too late a-nights, these are the only warnings I presume to give you.

You see I venture to watch over you. Do the same good office to me, in another way. I am sadly conscious of my faults, dear Hamo! Beside your serenity and seriousness, my ugly temper and frivolity show off in colours that are anything but pretty. I speak of this for once only, because I am often deeply ashamed, and shall feel happier if it is understood between us that I perfectly well know my own ugly ways. By and by, I hope to conquer my faults and grow more like you and worthy of you. Help me to do this, like a true friend.

Will you dine here at 6 next Monday? Do. If you positively cannot, tell me a day soon that I may come and spend an evening with you, when *you have no company* . . . If I write any longer, it will be 1880. My last thoughts in this year and my first thoughts in next year will be of you.

Hamo Thornycroft was certainly the Ideal Friend, handsome, talented, loving. Gosse had known him for years; they had met at the Epps's house in Devonshire Street before the Gosses' marriage. William Hamo Thornycroft – always known as Hamo – was six months younger than Edmund William Gosse; on that New Year's Eve Edmund was indeed just thirty and Hamo was soon to be. Both Hamo's parents practised as sculptors and had been much in favour with the Royal Family, but the son had been sent as a child to live on an uncle's farm and it was a love of nature, as much as of art, that he shared with Edmund.

Hamo had studied with his father and at the Royal Academy schools, exhibiting for the first time at the Academy when he was twenty-one – at just the time when his sister, Theresa, and her great friend, Ellen Epps, were studying painting together with Madox Brown in Fitzroy Square. Hamo had spent some time in Italy, particularly in a study of Michelangelo, but now he was permanently in London, with a studio in Melbury Road, Kensington, just behind Sir Frederick Leighton's house, which rivalled Alma-Tadema's in splendour. Unlike Robert Louis Stevenson, Thornycroft never 'melted into air again'. He was usually available and eager to join Gosse on any expedition he proposed. Gosse wrote in July 1879, 'We are so near now to one another by train, that you need never mind my finding you out if I casually call. I wander about a good deal, and I may as well wander towards Kensington as elsewhere.'

How Gosse was finding time to 'wander about' is not clear. He had so much work on hand, he said he had to make a strict time-table and not allow himself any time off unless he was up to date with his deadlines. There were tedious things to be done: 'an analysis of an Icelandic saga for the *Cornhill*', 'a long survey of Dutch literature for the *Encyclopaedia Britannica*'. It was much pleasanter to write poetry or to wander about west London. He was feeling restless and anxious that July. Both Nellie and Tessa, their daughter, had been unwell. Gosse was taking great pleasure in the small girl: she 'shows a lively sensibility, and, for so young a child, a tenderness and affectionateness that I hope augur well for the future'. Now she was sent away to stay with her aunt, Emily Williams, at Bexley, for Nellie was expecting another child the following month.

One day in May Gosse had been standing on Richmond Bridge for no particular reason, feeling very much bored with his own company, when suddenly he saw Hamo skimming under his feet in his father's boat, *Waterlily*. 'It was the queerest sensation and, if the battlements of the bridge had been lower, I don't know but what I might have thrown myself into the river and committed suicide out of sheer companionableness.' The river became a major theme in their relationship.

The following month they went on holiday together; Nellie obviously wasn't fit enough to go away. They cruised up the Thames in the *Waterlily* (five of them, including Hamo's father), bathing naked on warm summer evenings. To Nellie he wrote about the practical details: 'I am of course no use in navigating, so I am steward. I arrange the meals, make the tea, lay the table, and, which is much the most serious, wash up, a long process rendered exceedingly critical by bacon-fat, marmalade and mustard. I never felt better, rarely so well, in my life.' He wore his red Norwegian fisherman's cap, rolled-up trousers and shirt sleeves, and swabbed the decks. He hung out sheets and blankets to air on a line between trees on the river bank. He wrote every day and they walked along the tow-path from Goring to Oxford to collect letters from Walter Pater's.

On June 19th he told Nellie: 'We are lying now in a delicious quiet creek full of the scented rush – the calamus.' (No reference, of course, to its mythic connotation.)

We shall have a bathe soon, I suppose. This life is really superior in some respects to everything I know. The sense of quiet, the absence of responsibility, the perfect security from interruption . . . If you were also here, I should never wish to move or change: life would contain everything enjoyable. I feel quite sad to be enjoying this alone. I want to share every glow with you; and when the leaves are greener than usual or the Mays deeper in perfume, I long to emphasise it on your lips with a kiss.

He was full of desire for her. She was not there. She was pregnant, untouchable. But he was not alone, as he had suggested in the letter. Hamo Thornycroft was there. It was this day, this nineteenth of June in the quiet creek, which he was to remember all his life. He remembered lying on the deck, seeing sorrel and meadowsweet silhouetted against the sky. When he returned home, when it was all over, the feelings of longing and regret turned into a poem. He sent it apologetically to Thornycroft. 'You will be able to read between the lines, and to understand how the regret at such a beautiful time being over got translated into this exaggerated key. I hope you will be able to recognise the creek at Goring and the morning when I was seized with the absurd desire to draw your head, as I saw it in relief against the reeds. The horrid caricature I made was a good instance of the vanity of human wishes.'

> Already that flushed moment grows
> So dark, so distant; through the ranks
> Of scented reed the river flows
> Still murmuring to its willowy banks
> But we can never hope to share
> Again that rapture fond and rare,
> Unless you turn immortal there . . .
> Some for tomorrow rashly pray,
> And some desire to hold today,
> But I am sick for yesterday . . .

He said he was exaggerating but, several years later, he referred to the creek at Goring: he was 'so much haunted all the time . . . with a memory of that sedgey creek at the back of Goring, with the silence and the sunshine, and that mood of unbelief, the Pilgrim at the very gates of Happiness, turning back with tears to renounce Hope for ever'. Can we help seeing that as a moment of significant denial? Again, in January 1885 in America, Gosse wrote lightly, 'My dear Hamo, by the banks of the Susquehanna and the waters of the Squittersquash, I love you as much as I ever did by the sedged brooks of Thames's tributaries.' It was a love that would last until his life's end.

Gosse had already, through Nellie and Tadema, become concerned with art as well as literature. Now, through Thornycroft, he was becoming an authority on contemporary sculpture. 'So glad you liked the Art article,' he wrote to Robert Louis Stevenson in July this year, 'though the subject lies out of my path.' It was becoming more and more in his path. For one thing, he was scheming to have Hamo elected to the Royal Academy. ('I think it would be as well to go around to Townshend House on Tuesday night next.' The Tademas were always At Home on Tuesday evenings. 'Speak to Tadema yourself; he likes to be fussed.') The scheming and Thornycroft's talent paid off eventually. His *Artemis* was a great success at the 1880 Academy and in 1881 Thornycroft was elected ARA. 'Nobody can now accuse the Academy of not appreciating deserving youth!' Waterhouse wrote to Gosse.

Gosse took an extremely close interest in Thornycroft's work, as Thornycroft did in his. But Gosse's interest in art extended far beyond that. By 1882 he would be the regular art critic of John Morley's

Saturday Review. In sculpture, he had what he called 'a poet's prejudice against the Pretty', and a strong preference for realism. 'Is it not possible to give poetic treatment and poetic selection to real forms? It is, of course, the most difficult thing in the world, but it is the mode in which art can secure itself against the changes of time and fashion.' How much Thornycroft himself succeeded in surviving changes of time and fashion can be judged by any visitor to London gazing at Oliver Cromwell at Westminster, Dean Colet at St Paul's School or General Gordon in Embankment Gardens.

In August, 1879, Gosse's son was born. He reported to Thornycroft: 'We have a big ugly boy with an immense width of forehead. All doing well.' To Stevenson in California the report was of 'such a nice little bright-eyed boy'. Louis had written when he heard news of the expected arrival:

> Another Gosse, another dear,
> Another sixty pounds a year!

A first child is a rival; but the second is only a rival to the first; and the husband stands his ground and may keep married all his life: a consummation heartily to be desired for both you and me.

Writing to W. B. Scott, perhaps thinking of his own childhood, Gosse wrote: 'I am really glad to have a son . . . but I feel that a boy is a difficult thing to bring up well, harder than a girl, I think. I hope we shall have the grace to do it firmly and effectively.' He said the new boy was not as vigorous as Tessa was; 'his attractions belong to the pleasures of hope'.

Philip Henry in Marychurch felt 'very tenderly the filial love which has prompted your calling the dear child by my name', and hoped fervently, of course, that 'the dear babe may be the blessed key wherewith He will unlock the fortress of your heart, so long held shut against Him, and bring back to you the happy days of your child-hood's faith and obedience'.

Nine days after Philip's birth, Gosse was writing to Thornycroft about his new book of poems. It 'consists of a selection of all the best shorter pieces I have written since 1873 . . . I pin high hopes to this book: if it succeeds, I take a place at once that will have no dangerous rival among younger men than Swinburne. If it fails, I shall leave off writing verse most likely. Unless this is good, I cannot do anything good, – that is just the position. You see it is critical, and I am desperately ambitious.' He asked if he might dedicate the book to

Hamo as there was 'no one whose sympathy will be so certain if it fails, no one whose pleasure will be so genuine if it succeeds'.

It was poetry, not prose, that really mattered. And there had been so much prose recently. Gosse used to tell the story of Gautier calling on a poet to ask him to write for his paper. The poet was so poor he was in bed, for his clothes were pawned. But he was rude to Gautier, asking him if he supposed he would degrade himself by writing prose. 'What a delightful person!' Gosse would say. But his *Studies in the Literature of Northern Europe*, which had come out earlier in the year, had been treated with great respect, and that gave him considerable satisfaction. No reviewer was sufficiently familiar with the subject of Scandinavian literature to be able to evaluate Gosse's book. The *Saturday Review*, for instance, could only say, 'It is not given to everyone to know Frisian, Dutch, Danish, Swedish, Icelandic and to be intimately acquainted with the literature that exists in these tongues. It is probably safe to rely on Mr Gosse's accuracy . . .' – a statement which would rarely be heard again. The *Athenaeum* was a little sceptical of Gosse's claim that Ibsen was a great dramatist. Andrew Lang thought the book deserved to be a success and told Gosse to take no notice of the reviewers who 'will give you the skimmed milk of yourself, diluted with the water of tasteless and careless incompetence'.

From Marychurch, his father wrote lovingly to congratulate his dear Willy. 'Of course I must take your facts on trust.' He liked particularly his style and the 'total absence of that abominable sneering cynicism which too often nowadays pretends to be criticism'. He praised the way Edmund had roused his interest in a subject which did not promise much interest. He saw that his son had won his way to 'the upper walks of literature' – but if only God would lead him to lay all his talents at the Cross of Christ! 'I have long abstained from obtruding "religion" upon you,' but the result of that seemed to be 'this wide dark chasm between your heart and mine, while we talk lightly of trifles'. He went on to talk of trifles: their cats, the darling Baby's progress.

It was Stevenson, in a letter, who picked out the most promising characteristic of Gosse's first prose book: 'The book is good reading. Your personal notes of those you saw struck me as perhaps most sharp and "best-held". See as many people as you can, and make a book of them before you die. That will be a living book, upon my word. You have the touch required.' Gosse was to make many books of just such material, and the best book of all used that same talent.

New Poems was greeted with rather muted enthusiasm in the press – though, on publication, Gosse had been able to boast to Thornycroft, 'Gabriel Rossetti heads the tide of congratulation with a most generous and ardent letter.' Swinburne called the sonnet 'Alcyone' 'among the noblest in this or in any (even in Dante's) language'. P. H. Gosse was, of course, much less enthusiastic, acknowledging the skill but lamenting the poor aspirations of these verses, 'which will not look beyond the grave'.

'A few feet more and I must reach the light,' Gosse wrote in a poem called 'The Prodigal'. If he had not taken his place as Swinburne's heir, at least he was still on the ladder. The *Spectator* critic put it like this: 'Art indeed is never lacking but we miss the spontaneity of the poet who writes because he cannot help writing. Mr Gosse can rarely be said to fail, but, on the other hand, he never attains supreme excellence.'

A more recent critic suggests that 'from 1879 until the end of his life, this proleptic judgment was to become more generally accepted as Gosse's reputation as a prose writer grew more firmly established. In 1879 he was already at the peak of his poetic career, but the prevailing opinion was that he had yet to fulfil the expectation that had been encouraged by his earlier volumes. He never quite got out of the category of the "promising young poet".' William Minto, his old friend, suggested in the *Academy* that Gosse lacked any faith that poetry has a place in the modern world. There is too much antiquity, too little of the language of men. The *Saturday Review* said that 'even his own friends cannot refrain from using the word *frigid* in reference to this book'. The word 'pagan' was also tossed about. Yet there was no doubt the general message was that Gosse had confirmed his place as one of the leading poets of his generation. There was a long piece in *Fraser's Magazine* which gave Gosse great pleasure: 'It is so very pleasant to have a man survey your work, not piecemeal, but in its entirety.' Altogether, he felt justified in writing to Richard Watson Gilder: 'My *New Poems* had really a great success, which made me happy.'

Gilder was one of several American correspondents Gosse was fostering at this time. As early as December 1875, he had written to E. C. Stedman, poet, critic and New York banker: 'To myself the hope of recognition in America has always seemed one of the highest objects of ambition.' He had been unlucky to arrive just too late to be included in Stedman's influential study, *Victorian Poets*. Dobson had sent Stedman a copy of *On Viol and Flute*, but Stedman's critical book had appeared in both America and England only a fortnight after he had received it. Stedman wrote to Gosse to say how sorry he was: 'I think no other of equal importance is omitted from the survey.' Gosse then got Chatto to send Stedman *King Erik*, which he eventually persuaded Gilder to have reviewed in *Scribner's* along with *On Viol and*

Flute. The reviews seem to have made little impact, but in March 1880 a long and generous review of *New Poems* in *Scribner's* marked the real beginning of Gosse's American reputation, which will be explored further in the next chapter.

At the end of August Gosse was getting 'thoroughly knocked up with overwork' and took a few days' holiday with the Waterhouses at Yattendon. They were building a new house for themselves. This was Yattendon Court; Robert Bridges had taken the nearby Manor House, where Gosses and Tademas had listened to Churton Collins's ghost stories the year before. In 1879 Gosse wrote, 'We stayed out in the moonlight till quarter to twelve. The tower is already forty-five feet high; we climbed up it by the workmen's ladders . . . We felt like people getting into a beleaguered city at dead of night, the silence was so absolute. The moon shone so brightly that our shadows as we ascended and descended the ladders were shown black against the front of the house.' There were long walks – twenty-four miles one day. One night they sat, again in moonlight, listening to 'a young brick-maker playing the accordion in the village'. It was a good time.

As soon as Nellie and the baby, Philip, were strong enough, the small family (two-year-old Tessa happily re-united with them) took a long holiday at Torcross, near Kingsbridge, in Devon – 'a delicious place'. Nellie painted; Tessa played on the beach; Philip slept. Edmund had hoped that Hamo Thornycroft and his sister, Theresa, might join them, but they couldn't. He wrote to Hamo: 'The morning I got your letter saying you could not manage to come, I set off for a tearing walk and walked off my vexation after a few hours. I covered 27 miles, taking a round of the coast which astonished these lazy Devonshire people, who never walk if they can help it, and who take a donkey to go to a village two miles off.' But it was 'pleasant to be in a place so unsophisticated. We have made friends with all the simple folk of the hamlet and there are no ladies and gentlemen to interfere with our quiet . . . I have found some of the coastguards very good company; they get to be familiar with nature at unusual moments and see her when she thinks she is alone . . . I never felt so strong, I think, before; every muscle and nerve alive and balanced.'

Edmund had just come back from a brief visit to Marychurch, where Eliza's sister Lucy was also visiting. He had written to Nellie:

Everything is bright and pretty here but of course I am pining for Torcross. I hope to come tomorrow . . . I shall be so happy to see you all again. It is almost impossible to breathe here, and both Aunt Lucy and I are pale and speechless. Father is extremely hearty and in high spirits, talking away most volubly, but his whole heart and time are given up to the butterflies. It is quite curious: I think I never saw him so absorbed in anything. He can only spare us an hour this morning, and another hour this afternoon. Although he is exceedingly affectionate and kind, the air of the house is more than usually oppressive; not religious at all, – it seems as if the butterflies a little cast out the religion. Aunt Lucy has been as mum as a mouse ever since we arrived, and keeps close to me, as if she were a shy little girl out with her papa. I had no idea she was so afraid of Father. He is full of affectionate questions about you and the children and seems very fond.

Edmund signed the letter 'Your loving and longing Husband.' To Thornycroft, he wrote rather differently about his visit to Marychurch:

I have been over to see my father, who is not very well. He is only 70, but of late he finds himself much less able than of old to take exertion. It is strange and pathetic that the approach of old age and weakness have softened his temperament. He was, as I think you know, rather severe and unbending to me when I was a child and I went about the empty house in some dread of him. But now he is clingingly affectionate, and apologetic for trouble that he gives. I parted from him yesterday with tears in my eyes; there is something overwhelmingly painful in seeing the peculiar expression of weakness asking for forbearance, in the eyes of a man that has been very high-handed and stubborn. I hope my fears about his health may be unfounded: but I realized yesterday, with terror and for the first time, that his vehement eager life would not last for ever. I wish you could see him once: he has a magnificent head. He is in no feature like me, except the mouth.

He was seeing everything through a sculptor's eyes. And as he looked at Hamo's work, every muscle, every curve, he was becoming more and more aware of his own physical being and that of his friend. He described Thornycroft at work in a significant letter to John Addington Symonds:

He is very fine looking, extremely powerful in frame, a massive ruddy face, surrounded with tight curly golden-red hair; he was dressed in his white embroidered blouse, hard at work with the chisel on a mass of marble, the top-light in his studio isolating his red and gold head among all the white things, marble, plaster, blouse and so on. You would have thought him very picturesque, and his face, with all its unusual bright colour, has an extraordinary elevation that generally goes only with pallor. I give you this little water-colour sketch because you live at Davos, as one is excused for describing common things to blind people . . . He had both your *Greek Poets* there in the studio . . .

Gosse wrote to Thornycroft:

How your friendship has reawakened me, made me young again . . . Nature, the clouds, the grass, everything takes on new freshness and brightness now I have you to share the world with. You have swept all my cobwebs away, the sort of clubbishness that was coming over me; and now I have only one desire, to keep your love and fellowship all my life. After all my dreary, weary youth, I have a right, I think, to be happy now . . .

This was the least sociable, the least cerebral period of Gosse's life. Some of the time, anyway, he wanted nothing really but the quiet security of the home (the beloved wife and children in the background), and the excitement and passions of friendship and art. 'Why can't fortune let us alone,' he wrote to Thornycroft in January 1880, 'when we want so little, just a nest of domestic quietude in which to brood over our two blue eggs, Friendship and Art, till they hatch two fledgling immortalities.'

'Were you not happy on Monday?' he asked. '*I* was never so happy before.' They were skating together that winter. One day Gosse wearied before Thornycroft and, after he had taken off his skates, Gosse stood high above the lake watching his friend. It was too dark for him to distinguish anyone else. But there was 'a splendid bar of crimson in the west, behind the trees' and he watched Thornycroft until the light had entirely gone, then turned for home, aching in every bone. Gosse was a rash and reckless skater and liable to fall. Another day, after one such accident at Barn Elms, they rested together on a bench in the winter sun, recalling the summer before. Gosse wrote to Thornycroft afterwards:

Few people know how moving a sunshiny day in midwinter is; it sets all the summer veins pulsing, welling up blood from the heart in the great throb of the arteries, till the whole body is in a sort of melting ravishment, ready to take in every hint of colour and perfume and bodily touch. I could say many curious things about that bask we had in the sun on Thursday; but I saw in your eyes that you were thinking them too. I suspect few people live quite so much at their own finger-tips as we do . . . I could not help thinking as we skated about what a poor thing all the matters I used to boast myself of, – I mean mere acquirement of knowledge and book-learning – are in comparison with living one's life while one is young. It seems to me much more worth doing to be able to ride a colt across a rough piece of country than to be able to read a page of Thucydides. Ten years ago it would have seemed blank idiocy to me to have said that, but now the long months and months I have spent in stuffing the inside of my sheet of brown paper seem to me almost wasted. I think I could be quite happy to go with you to some place in the Back Woods, where we could make a clearing, build ourselves a hut, grow our own food and go off with our rifles into the forest when we wanted a change of employment. Do you know that you are a great wizard? I am very oddly bewitched; I scarcely know myself.

This is lover's talk, of course. There is no doubt that Edmund behaved constantly as lovers do – taking every excuse to mention the beloved name (an article on 'Sculpture Today' was – he admitted it – peppered with the name of Thornycroft), looking at the moon and wondering whether the beloved sees it too, quoting Shakespeare's sonnets, hoarding trifles of holiday heather, scheming to snatch an extra hour or two ('I hope that you will consent to come by the early train . . .'), making periodic efforts to get things into proportion. Gosse decided he would have to stop skating, to stop seeing so much of Thornycroft: 'Absent, you make me work. Present, there seems nothing worth working for.' At one stage, he rationed himself to one evening a week – but with letters in between to bridge the awful gaps. Then there was always the chance of running into him on Tuesdays at the Tademas.

When someone once asked Lytton Strachey whether Gosse was a homosexual, Strachey replied, 'No, but he's Hamo-sexual.' Siegfried Sassoon, talking to Rupert Hart-Davis, long after Gosse's death, confirmed this. Hart-Davis reported: 'Gosse, though perfectly normal in every other way, had what can only be described as a passion for Siegfried Sassoon's uncle, Hamo Thornycroft, the sculptor.' It was certainly of the aftermath of days such as the one by the sedgey summer creek, and the one by the winter pond, that Gosse was thinking when ultimately, in 1890, he confessed to John Addington Symonds in an extraordinary exchange of letters:

I know of all you speak of – the solitude, the rebellion, the despair. Years ago I wanted to write to you about all this, and withdrew through cowardice. I have had a very fortunate life, but there has been this obstinate twist in it! I have reached a quieter time – some beginnings of that Sophoclean period when the wild beast dies. He is not dead, but tamer; I understand him and the trick of his claws . . . And the curious thing is that it is precisely to this volcanic force, ever on the verge of destructive ebullition, that one owes the most beautiful episodes of existence, exquisite in all respects.

What a pity there should exist that martyrdom you speak of. It comes from ignorance and want of balance . . .

Gosse thought that anguish came from a confused conscience. He would come through himself, he said, 'without the shadow of a doubt as to right and wrong'; feeling sure that the right path is acceptance and not repression of feeling. 'To refine and cultivate – not to repress and destroy.'

Symonds in his memoirs uses the wolf or the wild beast as a metaphor for sexual desire. It was the wild beast, certainly, and not just 'some tiresome misunderstanding with the *Saturday Review*', which kept Edmund awake night after night in January, 1880. 'I write on because I am too tired to leave off and because the only thing that would really quiet me would be to drop my head into the paws of some feline creature – a Jaguar, for instance – and sleep a dreamless sleep . . . About four in the morning it begins to be so dreadful.' In later letters, Hamo himself becomes the 'golden Animal' capable of banishing all terrors.

It is no coincidence that the wild beast was most active at a time when Nellie was burdened and pre-occupied with babies. Babies took over women's lives, in spite of servants, in a way that they are not allowed to now. There were those long Victorian lyings-in; it was five weeks after the birth of their third child, Sylvia, on St Valentine's Day in 1881, that Nellie at last came downstairs again: 'It is very comfortable for me to have her about the house again, looking so bright and young and full of spirits,' Edmund wrote to Hamo on March 21st. Nellie was always loved, indeed adored. Edmund could not manage without contact with her for a single day. When he was away, he wrote to her every day, sometimes twice. In Birmingham, briefly, in April 1879, he wrote 'It was very dull and stupid to go to bed without you yesterday night.' The letters are full of intimate, loving private references to 'plump little partridges' and the like. Even when he was with Thornycroft, in Scotland, in Paris, in Switzerland, on holiday, he would haunt post-offices looking for her letters, and agonize if they were late. She was the centre of his existence for fifty-four years. If she had been a Catherine Symonds, unable to share his life, the wild beast would certainly have had a chance to destroy him. As it was, it was kept in check, and Thornycroft seems hardly to have been disturbed by the extent of Gosse's feeling for him. As for Gosse himself, the very depth of the love that he and Nellie shared seemed to make it possible for him to explore other, more dangerous feelings. She seems to have understood and to have tolerated his passion, sure of his devotion to her.

Gosse presumably destroyed the letters that Thornycroft wrote to him at this period—just as he did the more intimate of Blaikie's letters—but Thornycroft apparently had no such worries of misinterpretation and scandal. The passionate, revealing letters in Gosse's neat, legible hand have been carefully preserved. 'It would have been very nice to rest my rather throbbing head in your hands tonight,' he wrote after an exhausting lecture at Birmingham in the spring of 1880, which testified to his growing reputation. 'I had a crammed audience of 800 people, very attentive and sympathetic . . . People stood at the doors all through, without going away; and my stories were met with rounds of applause. But it took a great deal out of me.'

In June 1880 they hired canoes from Mr Salter at Oxford and picked them up at Lechlade, which they could reach by rail. They slept in riverside inns. They reached Cricklade, close to the source of the Thames, dragging the canoes the last mile or so up the dividing stream. Gosse had not been well and his doctor had advised exercise and open air. The doctor's advice echoed his own feelings, which he would always, however much work pressed, find possible to put into practice: 'Let us never persuade ourselves,' he wrote to Thornycroft, 'that we are too busy to take our frequent wanderings. I am deeply impressed with the belief that the greatest and most frequent mistake men make in life is to let their business absorb their leisure entirely. They have no time to eat their cake through all the morning and midday of their life, and at last when afternoon comes they have waited too long, and have no longer any appetite. And then comes the night, when nobody can eat or play again . . .' So it seemed at thirty. 'If life would only not hurry away so fast,' he wrote in 1882. But Gosse never lost his zests and appetites, until the night fell finally in his great old age.

These four years – 1879 to 1883 – Gosse called 'the summer of my life'. It was the only time in his life when he was totally free of those depressions he had written about to Nellie in the February of their engagement. At other times in life, there would always be patches, worst of all in 1910 and 1911, when he was a prey to deep depression, as he put it himself, 'scarcely fit for human society'. 'Neuralgic moods', Nellie called them, tolerantly. But looking back at this time, there seemed to be endless sunny days, at all seasons of the year, skating, canoeing, swimming, walking through beech woods –

> Ah, tell me, when we both are old, –
> On dismal evenings bleak and cold, . . .
> Ah! tell me then, how once we stood
> Transfigured in the gleaming wood.

In the summer of 1880, Edmund proposed that three-year-old Tessa and her nurse might stay with her grandparents in Marychurch. P. H. Gosse was naturally exercised about the visit. He wrote to Edmund on August 20th:

In the matter of your sweet child's coming to us, we cannot fail to be delighted with *her* presence and it will be our joy to take every care of her. But her tender age will require constant special attention night and day; and you spoke of a nurse attending upon her. Here arises a source of some anxiety. You have told us nothing of *her* character. You will at once see how much of our comfort depends on this. If the maid is well-behaved, discreet, submissive to our authority, all will be well. If, on the other hand, her example and conversation are such as to be injurious to our young maids (whom we greatly value); or if she is lawless, self-willed, likely to refuse my rule (on the ground that she is *your* servant, – not *mine*) – you know enough of me to be aware that I could not bear this in my house . . .

Your mother has some inquiries to make concerning the treatment of our dear grandchild; but the details I leave her to embody in a letter which she is contemplating to dearest Nellie . . .

Edmund was of course able to reassure his anxious parent that he would hardly be likely to employ a nurse of *bad* character. He also pleased his father by saying, 'We shall be very glad if you can find occasion to teach her any little texts or verses. She is old enough to begin to learn orally. And I should be grateful if you would frame a little simple prayer, for her to say at night, and would train her to say it. She should keep it up after she came home.'

The visit was a great success. Tessa charmed her grandparents and came home pleased with the little prayer, which she had repeated every night at her grandfather's knee.

This summer of Gosse's life, the years 1879–1883, included the years when the two younger children were born, joining the beloved

Tessa. The one agonizing time in these years, one of the worst times in Gosse's life, was his small son's acute illness in the summer of 1882. The family was staying at a farm at Gomshall, near Guildford in Surrey. It was 'deliciously peaceful' when Gosse went down at May and June weekends to join them. There were nightingales and marvellous sunsets. Thornycroft often went down with him. Andrew Lang was also invited one weekend and Edmund arranged for him to fish, and then was very irritated when he cried off the expedition at the last moment. Gosse wrote to Mrs Lang one of the letters that were to get him a reputation for touchiness: 'I can hardly believe that you can have put us to the trouble of taking a room for your husband and preventing us from inviting any other guest for so extremely frivolous an excuse as the one he gives.'

Austin Dobson, another weekend, was a perfect guest. Dobson neither offended nor took offence, even when he sent Gosse a couple of poems, asking which he liked and what he thought (RSVP) and Gosse simply sent the poems back with a scrawled 'Neither. E. W. G.' on the bottom of the letter. At Gomshall, Dobson went to church with Nellie's sister, Emily, while Edmund and Nellie, with Tessa fluttering around like a pale pink butterfly, strolled down a lane and up into the woods, using Nellie's new Claude glass, an ingenious device, which composed the landscape for a painter. 'One can lie on a hillside for an hour, not wishing to do anything but watch the landscape in the Claude.'

Edmund reported happily to Thornycroft that Philip – not yet three – was much admired by the locals, who say he is 'a little farmer born'. But in July the child was desperately ill with dysentery. 'He lies just hovering between life and death. We have been watching him all night. The family has behaved with splendid kindness as always. The Tademas are close beside us, at the inn, and Washington and Emily are nursing him with us . . . You can conceive our distracted state. We have scarcely any hope now.' A specialist was summoned. 'His life must now depend on his constitutional capital: if he exhausts it before he can take food, he must die. He is vividly flushed and his eyes are dilated; he looks more beautiful than ever.'

Philip was 'sweetly good and patient', but, hour after hour, his little voice would wail: 'Mamma, take hurt away.' It was very hard to bear. The child spent thirty hours in their loving arms. At last the crisis was past; Philip had survived. Letters of joy and congratulation flowed in. Swinburne, that well-known child-lover, wrote: 'I could hardly (I think) feel more sympathy if I had ever myself passed through the ordeal of such a time. But I know parents can hardly be expected to believe that "a barren stock" ', to borrow Queen Elizabeth's phrase, as he had at the time of their marriage, 'can be capable in imagination of entering into their emotions.'

Gosse loved all his children deeply and not just, as some Victorian fathers seem to have done, in theory and at a distance. His sonnet, 'To Teresa', celebrates her unquestioning love ('for love alone I care'), her red hair (that Swinburne-coloured hair), hanging, a little strangely, 'like ripe clusters of the apricot', and a conventional 'white innocence'; but the letters show a constant concern and engagement in their real activities. Although he worked so hard and was easily irritated, Gosse always knew how to enjoy himself and how to enjoy his children. He was determined, with memories of his own bleak, lonely infancy, that theirs should be full of warmth and pleasures. His son remembered him as 'the most indulgent' of fathers.

Their London winters were always followed by joyous summers by the seaside or on farms, often near enough London for their father to join them at the weekend, after his work at the Board of Trade. In the middle of the week, Nellie would keep him in touch. 'Your notes about the chicks are most delightful to me,' he had written in June 1881, when Nellie was at a farm near Haslemere with Tessa, nearly four, Philip, nearly two, and four-month-old Sylvia. 'It is fearfully difficult to resist the temptation of throwing up everything and coming straight away down to you.' On holiday with Thornycroft in Scotland that September, while the family were at Marychurch, he wrote, 'I find myself constantly wondering how you and the chicks are getting on. It is sad that Father takes no notice of Philip, but I hope Mother does. I have bought Tessa a birthday present of a pair of soft Shetland socks and I have another pair for Sylvia. For Philip I have bought a Fair Island bonnet, quite a curiosity and very barbaric and charming.' He was always begging Nellie for details of their activities, and, as they got older, he would admire their own letters and paintings – 'I knew at once what it was meant for, even upside down.'

Gosse wrote to Stevenson early in 1884, when he had just seen the proofs of *A Child's Garden of Verses*:

The young gentleman who hunts upon the forest-track is a tender memory of ME. I used to do that – and I daresay lots of other I's, for I see that to this hour my own children never eat their porridge nor paint their prints nor even play with their bricks, without pretending they are doing something else. They live in an unbroken vision, through which they prosecute the most ardent adventures, in which their mother and I are sometimes allowed to take part, but always on sufferance – merely because we are useful as Dramatis Personae. When we have played our part we are coolly dismissed.

And it greatly amuses me to see how mutely indignant they are when the happy illusion has to be broken by a constitutional walk or a washing of face and hands or any of those tiresome things which only grown-up idiots would think of wanting done. The other day, in a fit of annoyance at some trick or other, I called my son 'a pig'. A glow of gratified vanity swam across his face, instead of the shame I expected to find there. We found, after a good deal of cross-examination, that to become a pig (in reality) had long been his young heart's dream.

There were no pigs at Delamere Terrace yet, though there would be. There were, at one time or another, most possible pets. Cats, of course, always cats; but also guinea pigs, rabbits, mice and birds. Tessa's sixth birthday cake was decorated with mice and birds. On that same sixth birthday, Edmund told Tessa of his own sixth birthday in September thirty-four years before, when his mother was ill in bed and the scripture-reader took him out for a walk.

I can remember just where it was, under the railway-bridge and by the railing where there were swans and down the Caledonia Road to the poulterer's shop; and the scripture-reader stayed so long looking at the fat fowls and the Michaelmas geese that I got tired, so I slipped round the corner and ran home as fast as my legs would carry me, for I knew the way quite well. But the poor man thought someone had stolen me and when he got back to our house, he hardly had the courage to ring the bell. That was very naughty of me and came of my not thinking about other people.

Gosse suggested that Tessa would never be so thoughtless. Students of *Father and Son* will be interested to compare this version of the story with the one Gosse tells there, forgetting the Michaelmas geese and transposing it to a time sixteen months later.

Philip's earliest pet was a toad. On one occasion, when Nellie went into the night nursery before going to bed herself, she found Philip lying fast asleep in his cot with a large toad tightly clasped in his arms. She had some difficulty in disengaging the toad without waking the child up, or injuring the unfortunate creature. Another early pet was a Plymouth Rock pullet, which Nellie saw in a cage in a pet shop at Shepherd's Bush Green. It looked lonely and unhappy, so, out of pity, she brought it home to Delamere Terrace in a brown carrier bag.

Nellie was always fond of living creatures, even flies. There was a tragic family story of how Nellie as a child had made a pet of a blue-bottle fly, which she fed daily in its little cage on best Demerara sugar. But the day came when the family were going on holiday and Nellie was told she was on no account to take the fly with her. She piled sugar into the cage to keep her pet going until her return (fearing to trust the servants to feed it), only to find, of course, when she got back, the blue-bottle quite dead on its back from a surfeit of sugar. So the Gosse children's pets had always to go with them on holiday, in Sussex or Devon, wherever it was. Rabbits and guinea pigs would travel in hutches with them. One rabbit was Tessa's. When she was only three, Gosse wrote to F. W. Myers, just before Rossetti's death, that the child would chant her own version of Rossetti's lines:

> The honeycomb has a heart of honey
> And the bee's as heavy as bunny –

believing them to refer to her own pet rabbit. They would always read poems together.

The children's regime in Delamere Terrace was relaxed and convivial. They made early appearances at the Sunday afternoon At Homes, and when other appropriate visitors were in the house. Swinburne occasionally came all the way from Putney. Gosse would write in his biography: 'I shall never lose from my memory the picture of the poet seated stiffly on the sofa (his favourite station) in our house, with one of my small girls perched on each of his little knees, while my son, just advanced to knicker-bockers, having climbed up behind him, with open palm was softly stroking his bald cranium, as though it had been the warm and delicious egg of some enormous bird.' Swinburne remembered, on this visit, two-year-old Sylvia making valiant attempts to open the balcony door unassisted. He recalled her 'perpetually frustrated perseverance and renascent hope'. He wrote to the child's father: 'I never saw anything (or anybody) more memorably pretty.'

Swinburne enjoyed kissing their sweet toes, but Robert Louis Stevenson, who also took a close interest in the children from their beginnings ('I have just given my little rosy girl the kiss you sent her,' Gosse wrote), was not so good at close quarters. 'I do not think R.L.S. ever "held a baby",' Gosse wrote, years later. But he came into his own as they got older. Philip was to remember:

> It happened years ago when I was a child that there used to call upon us a certain romantic-looking gentleman, an old friend of my parents. I remember now little about him, except that he came to see us on warm summer evenings and that he used to wear over his shoulders a red silk shawl borrowed from my mother, as he sat on

our balcony, and that we children eagerly leant up against him while he told us wonderful stories. Such stories! All of the sea, wrecks, mutinies and pirates. Tales of blood-curdling adventures . . . It was on these occasions that our nurse would say, with a vexatious sigh, 'Whenever that there Mr Stevenson comes here, I never can get you children to sleep.'

Gosse, remembering the murder stories from the papers he had shared with his father as a child in Marychurch, never minded how blood-curdling Stevenson was. At one stage they planned to collaborate on 'a re-telling, in choice literary form, of the most picturesque murder cases of the last hundred years', but nothing came of that. 'You seem to me the personification of life,' Gosse once wrote to Stevenson. He loved to see his children respond and quicken to Louis's stories. He once defined that particular pleasure: 'the delight of seeing one's children delighted'.

Henry James, too, coming into their father's life at this time, much approved of the children. English children might be called 'the most completely satisfactory thing the country produces. The people are but the children magnified . . . and it is the children who are just of the right size. The elders strike one so often as too big for what they are.' Edmund Gosse certainly would strike James like that at times, insistent, persistent as he could be. But Philip (especially Philip) and Tessa and Sylvia were always just right. Philip early on admired James extremely. There is a glimpse of the boy in a green velvet costume, made by his mother, longing to have his curls cut off, so he could look like Henry James. James, as Gosse recorded, had at this time 'his dark brown hair cut short in the Paris fashion'.

The children used to call on Robert Browning, along the road in Warwick Crescent, with a bouquet for his birthday. Browning would ply them with chocolates. His sister, Sarianna, would sometimes send a cake round to Delamere Terrace for the children – 'a home-made cake with Miss Browning's love'. Browning was particularly fond of Tessa and brought her porcelain lambs from Italy; all her life they joined her crib at Christmas. He also drew pigs for her – the most unpiglike pigs one could possibly imagine. Tessa carried them happily back to Delamere Terrace and they now survive among much weightier material in the Ashley collection at the British Library.

Edmund Gosse was seeing a good deal of Robert Browning in 1881. They had been near neighbours for almost five years when Browning agreed to let Gosse write some sort of brief biography for the pages of the American magazine *The Century*, for which Gosse was now working. Very little about Browning was public knowledge at that time. For many years he had been thought of as 'the poet's husband', but *The Ring and the Book* in 1868 had brought him real fame. In 1881 he was recognized as a great poet but had 'not yet excited that degree of personal curiosity which soon afterwards began to be awakened'. Gosse had several times pointed out to Browning how valuable it would be to have some authentic account of his life, but Browning had always brushed aside the idea until, one morning in February 1881, Browning sent round a note to Gosse, saying simply, 'Come; and I will do what you wish.' Apparently the morning post had brought him an account of his life, mainly fabulous, which had considerably annoyed him.

Gosse recorded the sort of reception an expected visitor received at 19 Warwick Crescent from a Browning very different from the commonplace, hearty Browning who disappointed both Henry James and Arthur Benson at dinner parties. Gosse wrote:

> To a single listener, with whom he was on familiar terms, the Browning of his own study was to the Browning of a dinner party as a tiger is to a domestic cat. In such conversation his natural strength came out. His talk assumed the volume and the tumult of a cascade. His voice rose to a shout, sank to a whisper, ran up and down the gamut of conversational melody. Those whom he was expecting will never forget his welcome, the loud trumpet-note from the other end of the passage, the talk already in full flood at a distance of twenty feet. Then in his own study, what he loved was to capture the visitor in a low armchair's 'sofa-lap of leather' and from a most unfair vantage of height to tyrannize, to walk around the victim, in front, behind, on this side, on that, weaving magic circles, now with gesticulating arms thrown high, now grovelling on the floor to find some reference in a folio, talking all the while, . . . thoughts, fancies and reminiscences flowing from those generous lips. To think of it is to conjure up an image of intellectual vigour, armed at every point, but overflowing, none the less, with the geniality of strength.

On that February day, when Gosse arrived, Browning said, 'If you still wish to take down some notes of my life, I am willing to give you all the help I can; I am tired of this tangle of facts and fancies.' Gosse kept his wits and a notebook about him. And, for several hours one morning a week for several weeks, he sat at Browning's desk while Browning walked about and Gosse rapidly jotted down notes on the conversation. The Board of Trade must certainly have been a flexible employer. In a letter making arrangements, Gosse says, 'After Tuesday next, I have no engagements and would come in exactly at whatever hour of any day would suit you.' At Browning's suggestion, Gosse came each time with a list of questions. 'Frankly say that you will not answer, if my questions are indiscreet.' He would put one and Browning would talk until, at last, the flow dried up and another question needed to be put. When Gosse had collected a great mass of facts, gossip and opinion, he put it all into some sort of rough order and submitted it to Browning, who crossed out everything his maturer judgment did not wish to preserve. The rest Gosse turned into an article which duly appeared in the *Century Magazine* in December 1881. In 1890, after Browning's death, it was reprinted with additions as a small book, both in America and in England.

When Browning read the article, he took round to Delamere Terrace a note, thanking Gosse for 'all this partiality and praise . . . I wish yourself, when the years come, may find such an appreciator. You will at least deserve such an one – I hope and fear – better than does Your affectionate Friend, Robert Browning'. Browning was always kindly disposed towards Gosse – not just as an admirer of his own work but also particularly of Elizabeth Barrett Browning's. Certainly Gosse always admired her *Sonnets from the Portuguese* (an edition of which became a crucial plank in the case against Wise the forger); but after Browning's death he admitted he placed Mrs Browning lower than he would have done, because of her 'hysterical violence, the Pythian vagueness and the Pythian shriek'. Her contemporaries had placed her beside Tennyson, he said, but the succeeding generation, Gosse's own, could not forgive her turbidity, her carelessness; only the *Sonnets from the Portuguese* escaped this censure.

Gosse was to wonder later (possibly, as he sometimes did, suiting his words to the attitude of his correspondent) whether he had over-valued Browning. 'Perhaps,' he wrote to Professor Lounsbury of Yale in 1911, 'my personal affection has sometimes led me into an over-indulgent view of the poetry.' Certainly Gosse had no time for Furnivall and the trumpeting of the Browning Society. Working on the Browning article for the *Dictionary of National Biography* in 1902, he objected strongly to the idea that Furnivall had a right to speak for Browning. 'Browning once said to me, "Furnivall is certainly cracked". Browning would assent to anything for the sake of getting the terrible fellow out of the house.' But, of course, the Browning Society was useful in some ways to Browning. And probably Gosse's main objection to it was that he liked his geniuses as friends, not as remote heroes. Gosse would show visitors Talfourd's portrait of

Browning, which always hung in his study. 'Whenever Browning came here,' Gosse would tell people, 'he would pause before this portrait of himself with peculiar satisfaction.' The latter part of the inscription runs: 'I rejoice that it now belongs to my friend Gosse. Robert Browning. 10 April, 1883.'

After Browning's death, Gosse and Thomas Hardy would speculate endlessly about him. 'How could smug Christian optimism, worthy of a dissenting grocer, find a place inside a man who was so vast a seer and feeler when on neutral ground?' Hardy would ask, expecting Gosse to know the answer from his intimacy with Browning, 'if any living man can'.

There were no easy answers. Browning himself had answered no questions on anything obscure in his poems. Henry James said it was rather a relief, on hearing Browning read aloud, to find that 'at least, if *you* don't understand, then he himself understands even less'. His poems might be difficult, but the man himself, Gosse thought, was 'charming, courteous and interesting, as always'. His volubility was matched by his sister's. There is an account, in a letter to Nellie, of a call Edmund made in the summer of 1883: 'They both were most voluble and affectionate.' Browning could hardly get a word in edgeways, 'till at last Browning drowned his sister's voice in thunder: "Now I want to say something quite different, Sarianna," but Sarianna warbled on all the same.'

In 1883 Gosse again had a particular reason to be in regular contact with Browning. T. F. Kelsall, the biographer of Thomas Lovell Beddoes (the poet who had died in 1849, the year Gosse was born), had left all Beddoes' manuscripts and papers to Robert Browning. Kelsall had died in 1872 and, for eleven years, the box containing the Beddoes papers remained locked up and unexamined. In July 1883 Browning sent a note round to Delamere Terrace: 'Will you look in here next Sunday morning after your "early" wont? I mean to make a thorough examination of the contents of that dismal Box, and to see how much I can give you with a free conscience; all I can give – for there is a particular fact which is painful enough, – and I fear that it must remain a secret – at least for some time longer – but the other matters shall be at your disposal, and with all my heart.'

On July 15th Browning took the box to Gosse's house and gave Gosse the key, telling him to go through it. Gosse begged him to stay with him while he opened it, but Browning refused; he seemed to have an unaccountable horror of what would be discovered. However, a few hours later, curiosity got the better of him and he returned to Delamere Terrace. Together that afternoon they went through the papers. The result of that afternoon and of many subsequent days was

Gosse's *DNB* article of 1885, his edition of the *Poetical Works* of Beddoes (1890) and his edition of Beddoes' letters in 1894.

The following day, July 16th, Gosse wrote to Browning saying, 'I have been reading the Beddoes MSS with indescribable emotion. Various biographical details of some importance reward my search, but there will never be material for a new life of Beddoes. Kelsall's work is as complete and worthy as possible. I see that he was abominably treated by the Beddoes family.' He would think of that when he himself came to work on Swinburne. Browning's reticence in July 1883 was presumably about Beddoes' suicide, which Kelsall had suppressed. After Browning's death and Leicester Warren's reconciliation with Gosse, Warren wrote: 'Browning hinted Beddoes was always trying various necromantic experiments and had an idea he could get behind the veil and an insatiable curiosity to do so. Have you kept back any allusions or records of experiments in that direction?'

Beddoes was an anatomist and absorbed by death, but Gosse had no revelations to make about black magic. What he did suggest was that Beddoes was a lover of boys. Lytton Strachey refers to this in a letter to Duncan Grant in 1907, when he was working on his essay on Beddoes, 'The Last Elizabethan'. But according to Michael Holroyd, Strachey's biographer, Strachey's awareness of Beddoes' possible homosexuality was confirmed by a typical Gosse carelessness: Gosse had transcribed *Liebhaber von Knaben*, a lover of boys, instead of (as in another place) *Liebhaber von Knocken* – a lover of bones.

8

Playthings

IN SEPTEMBER 1880 Edmund and Nellie went to France, leaving Tessa at Marychurch, as we have seen, and Philip at Delamere Terrace (Sylvia was not yet born). It was Edmund's first experience of France, the country which was to mean more to him than any other but England. Gosse had already, with Swinburne's encouragement, made pilgrimages in spirit to the shrine of Baudelaire (though, much later, he would describe *Les Fleurs du mal* as 'satanic dandyism'). But this first visit was in no sense purely a literary pilgrimage. Edmund was the ideal tourist, as we saw him on his first visit to Norway in 1871. Everything interested him; he would read out endless information from the guide-book in his hand, with unfailing enthusiasm. A holiday was never a time to sit comfortably in a chair with a book; he did that the rest of the year. Holidays were a time for exploration and diversion, for attempting to discover exactly what it was that was special about the place he was in.

By the end of his life, there were many areas of France where he would know every village and small town, their legends, buildings and the peculiarities of the people. It would be his 'adored and adorable France'. He prided himself on getting off the beaten track. Nearly every year he would make an extensive tour of the 'other side of nowhere', often with Nellie. And for ten years he also made a regular short trip in the spring with a group of men friends. He believed there was nothing more important in the chaotic modern world than that the French and the English should know and understand each other, and he found great pleasure in self-education. 'To know a nation, one must know its literature.' His involvement with France would increase year by year; it would largely replace, though not yet, his concern with Scandinavia. When he was still a clerk at the British Museum, he had sent a letter of admiration to Théodore de Banville; he had been reading Montaigne, Racine, Sainte-Beuve, Zola, as well as Baudelaire. Now he started reading *Figaro* regularly and soon also the *Journal des débats*.

Gosse was always nervous about speaking French. In 1877, using it in Amsterdam, he had vowed: 'I never will leave England again without being able to speak French fluently and elegantly. It is extremely disgraceful not to do better,' though, in fact, he surprised himself by his 'temerity and eloquence'. Much later it was said that no one could have imagined him a French scholar who had heard him pronounce ten words of the language. Right at the end of his life, William Bellows recorded: 'His French was rather that of the Academy. I was to do the shopping, he said, because mine was a more useful kind of French.'

On this occasion, in Besançon in 1880, it was Nellie who did the talking in the market. She had, as we have seen, spent some time in France before her marriage. Now Gosse wrote to Richard Gilder in America that he had sampled 'the delights of garlic and frogs and snails', but he confessed to Thornycroft that snails were the one thing he could not learn to like, though Nellie took to them 'quite kindly'. They bought peaches and grapes, drank *vin de Jura*, 'full of blood and sunshine, at the price of a small beer in London', and Edmund naturally assessed the town's statues by a talented local sculptor. They were staying with French people they had met in London.

Half the fun was being 'in a strange land' and Gosse was a little disappointed that the Jura scenery reminded him so much of Scotland. On a three-day walking tour alone in the mountains (leaving Nellie, who was in early pregnancy, with their friends), he plucked a sprig of fern at Consolation to send to Hamo Thornycroft. He was tormented by his absence. Wearing the same clothes he had worn on the Thames earlier in the year (and the year before), carrying the same little white sketchbook with Thornycroft's drawings in it, he found it scarcely possible to enjoy himself. 'All the while there would sing in my brain "but oh! for the touch of a vanished hand!"'

He felt better on his return to Nellie and their friends at Besançon. There were picnics and expeditions. Edmund rowed to the Château of Montferraud and they had to take cover from a sudden storm in a rustic shrine hewn out of the rock. They disturbed a crowd of bats, which flapped around their heads as they sheltered. Then there was a wild drive home in a covered waggon, crossing the Doubs by ferry, the sheet lightning every now and again illuminating the strong silhouette of the mountains.

It was the sort of small adventure Gosse loved. There was a larger adventure on the way to Paris the following May. Gosse was commissioned by John Morley, who had recently moved from the editorship of the *Fortnightly* to the daily *Pall Mall Gazette*, to write about the Paris Salon. He and Thornycroft crossed a foggy Channel on the 7th May. 'We were standing on the quarter deck,' Edmund wrote to Nellie from Dieppe, 'when Hamo said to me, "If he does not turn her head more out, he is sure to run on the rocks".' Within a minute, a violent shock showed Thornycroft had been right. The captain ordered the boats out. 'Hamo and I went in the last boat that left the ship.'

It was a very curious spectacle, the sunshine thro the mist, the frightened people crowding into the boats, the vast white cliffs and deserted shore. We found that we were stranded at a point between the villages of Biville-sur-Mer and Toqueville-sur-Eu about thirteen miles NE of Dieppe. It was very trying for the women. The only way to get up from the shore, was to climb the cliff by a fisherman's path, almost vertical steps cut in the chalk, and here and there no path or steps, but a rope by which to swarm up. It was a fearful grind to drag our gladstones, shawls and umbrellas with us up this place, but we contrived to do it and at the village of Biville we rested a little and had some milk and cider. All the hamlets were crowded with the shipwrecked people, some lamenting their fate, some very loud and jaunty. Hamo and I made a great effort and walked on in the boiling heat to the village of S. Martin, where we were passed by a cart with some nice cordial French people in it, going to Dieppe. We laid our forlorn condition before them and they most hospitably insisted we should get in the cart . . . After some five or six miles suddenly the horse fell, the driver was precipitated to the ground, Hamo and I almost fell over the shafts, the French lady inside screamed for her life, and we generally felt that our last hour had come. Finally, about 2.30 p.m., we got safe and sound into Dieppe, the first to bring news of the steamer, whose non-appearance had given rise to great speculation . . .

This is a real adventure, is it not, but on the whole we have enjoyed it thoroughly. Our exercise in the open air has done worlds for us both, and if we have lost one day in Paris, we have gained a story which we shall tell to the end of our days.

The Salon turned out to be a few good works, 'isolated oases in a desert of incompetence and affectation'. It was the same the next year, when they repeated the visit. 'What acres and acres of bad pictures with here and there a jewel!' It would always be the same. 'Hamo meets many people who fly up and salute him, but we escape them all.' Thornycroft was becoming very well known. His *Teucer* had made a stir at the Royal Academy in 1881, the year of his election when he became the youngest Academician of his day. He and Gosse spent a great deal more time in Paris at the theatre than at the Salon, and lunched day after day on *sole au vin blanc* in a room looking over the misty river.

Gosse's interest in the theatre fluctuated. As he said in a letter to a Danish playwright, 'Literature and the drama are two distinct professions in England; a chasm lies between them . . . The literary classes do not go to the theatre.' But with his instinct for the tops of trees, Gosse was already acquainted with Irving. He had addressed a sonnet to him in 1878, sent it to him, and been invited in return ('How can I thank you? Hardly in words . . .') to see *Hamlet* and to go round to Irving's dressing-room afterwards. Gosse had joked to Dobson: 'I shall wear simple white, with a rose in my hair. Or do you think my amber satin will be more in tune with tragedy?'

Gosse's acquaintance with Irving would not stop him being extremely cruel, with a young man's cruelty, about his *Romeo and Juliet* in a letter to Stevenson the following March:

> Irving made a beautiful Romeo, 55 at least, with wrinkles painted in his neck and altogether a wonderfully careful presentment of amorous old age. In the noblest art of the actor, however, something is wanting and it seemed to me that a more shaky hand and more weakness of the hams would have emphasised his conception of the part. And a few white hairs carelessly stealing from under the black wig would have given a fine touch. Yet he did old wrinkled Romeo finely. He and the nurse seemed formed to make one another happy: yet nothing came of it.

In Copenhagen in 1874 Gosse had gone constantly to the Royal Theatre – 'a useful school to my mind'. In Paris, whenever he was there, he went night after night. He was disgusted at Sardou in 1881, delighted with Molière in 1882. Coppel's new piece at the Odéon 'is in verse and very stately and declamatory, but on that account all the easier to follow'. If only the performances did not go on so long. Victor Hugo's *Lucrezia Borgia* was wonderful but 'we did not get out of the house till ¼ to 12'. At heart, Gosse remained not very keen on the theatre. When he wrote to Oscar Wilde in 1893 to thank him for a copy of *Lady Windermere's Fan*, he said how much he had enjoyed *reading* it, in a way that can hardly have pleased Wilde: 'The brilliant merit . . . is only enhanced by the absence of stage disturbance . . . We might still have a drama if they would only close the playhouses.' And this was *before* the anguish of Henry James's humiliation over *Guy Domville*.

Gosse first met Wilde in 1881 at the Tademas at Townshend House. It was a masked party – a change from their usual Tuesday At Homes. Gosse wrote to Thornycroft to say he was having a grey satin mask made for himself. It was two weeks after Sylvia's birth and Nellie was still in bed. 'The only person who refuses to come masked is Oscar Wilde! The Tademas think this most conceited of him and beg that everyone will tease him as much as possible. At 12 o'clock every mask is to be taken off at the supper-table. Only 50 guests are invited: they want to make it very select. I have seen the list and they are almost all people we like – no Germans or musicians to speak of.' Whether Gosse dared tease Wilde we do not know. It seems unlikely. Introduced to him, Wilde murmured how glad he was to meet him. 'I was afraid you would be disappointed,' Gosse said. 'Oh no,' Wilde replied, 'I am never disappointed in literary men, I think they are perfectly charming. It is their works I find so disappointing.'

Gosse was to have very mixed feelings about Wilde. To give him credit, he liked him least when he knew least about him. And at this stage, it was the poems which caused him more disquiet than the man himself. There is a fierce letter to the American, E. C. Stedman, written this very summer, just before Wilde's American tour.

A curious toadstool, a malodorous parasitic growth, has been put forth in our poetic world in the shape of a volume of *Poems* by Mr Oscar Wilde, the fat young gentleman in the long hair, whose portrait appears in *Punch*. His aristocratic friends have clustered round him, and his atrocious book, which has no merit but its impudence, is in its 3rd edition. It is an amusing phase. People at a distance might think it something serious.

By 1892, Gosse was in a different mood. He publicly chided William Watson for gibing at Oscar Wilde. 'To peck at one another,' Gosse wrote in the *New Review*, 'is not the business of humming-birds and nightingales. Daws do it best, and are kept for that very purpose, in large numbers in the aviaries of Grub Street. Mr Oscar Wilde (with whom I seldom find myself in agreement) is an artist, and claims from his fellow-artists courteous consideration.' Robbie Ross sent the *New Review* to Wilde, who thought Gosse had been 'most charming and courteous. Pray tell him from me what pleasure it gave me to receive so graceful a recognition from so accomplished a man of letters'. It was obviously this reference that made Wilde send Gosse *Salome* the following February: 'Accept it as a slight tribute of my admiration for your own delicate use of English . . . I know that you have a welcome always for things that aim at beauty . . .'

Gosse was to become involved in Wilde's tragedy, through his friendship with Robbie Ross. But he could never like the man. 'What I principally hated about him, poor creature,' he would write to Ross in 1908, 'was not at all his vices, but his unreality. He was like Punch on a stick, squeaking.' But less and less could he bear 'the idea of punishing a man – who is not cruel – because he is unlike other men'. Gosse fought hard, or at least argued hard, for Wilde to be included in Ward's English Poets series. As in so many cases, Gosse's comments on Wilde depended not only on his mood but very much on whom he was writing to. To André Gide, in 1910, he wrote, 'The man was consistent, extraordinary, vital even to excess and his strange tragedy will always attract the consideration of the wise'.

To get back to 1881. The music and the Germans at the Tademas' At Homes were a constant problem. Nellie and Edmund loved Laura – and Alma-Tadema too, most of the time. But they did not take to their friends or their passion for music. In February this year, Theresa Thornycroft apparently spoke up on Edmund's behalf; Edmund called her intervention 'kind and chivalrous'. It was successful too: 'we had no music last night'. Edmund was well known to have no time for music. He was said to sympathize with a man who could not tell the difference between *Pop Goes the Queen* and *God Save the Weasel*. Swinburne was similarly afflicted 'and did not recognize *Three Blind Mice* when it was presented as an ancient Florentine ritornello'. As a young man, Edmund disguised what he came to see as 'one of the misfortunes of my life', and used to go to concerts and operas 'in the hope of training my ear' – but he soon found he had no ear to train. Long afterwards he wrote to his granddaughter, who was similarly unmusical: 'It is a privation to be unable to appreciate music, but fortunately there are other channels of pleasure.'

When Nellie, busy painting, and the children were away in the summer, Gosse would spend a good deal of time at Townshend House. The girls had become rather dull and quiet in their adolescence. 'I notice they never speak, except in reply, to their parents, – never, never. I do hope Tessa and Sylvia will be a little more expressive in the year 1893.' He need not have worried; they certainly would be. On Tuesday evenings, if he were unlucky, he would hear one of the 'three greatest living pianists of the world' – German, of course. 'The house shook with the bravoes of the assembled guests, but the performances were so long, and so often repeated, that I nearly died of fatigue and distress . . . There was Mrs George Lewis in yellow, Mrs Comyns Carr in deep red . . . Miss Bertha in scarcely anything at all (un peu scraggy); lots of hideous German musicians, odious Mr Schlosse and Mr Lowenstam and Mr Pope and all the other horrors.' Mr Pope was that same Mr Pope he had put in a verse in 1874 to make Tadema's daughters laugh. Mr Pope had not improved with keeping.

There was one rather absurd Tuesday when nobody dined and nobody came afterwards but Nellie's and Laura's sister, Louisa Hill. 'We were singing duets, Louie and I,' Edmund wrote to Nellie, 'while Tadema played on the floor with a toy steam-engine, and altogether there happened to be such a noise about 10.30 that we did not hear Mr Pope and young Mr Schlesinger enter. This rapidly cooled the party down. No one else came and those weary wretches stayed till one. But Tadema and Laura kindly let me go to bed at twelve.'

Another night, Tadema took him to *Wilhelm Tell* in German at Drury Lane. It sounds like a special form of torture for Gosse, but he bore up bravely. After the opera, they went back with the principal singer to his lodgings and Edmund did not get home until 3 am. It was already broad daylight, but he reported to Nelly that the inexorable Betsey had him up again at 8 am. The servants were an endless source of entertainment over the years. This one, Betsey Bacon, was a particular joy. Edmund, gratefully, gave her a ticket to hear Walter Pollock lecture at the Royal Institute. 'Betsey and I get on like a house on fire; she is in the most lively spirits,' he wrote to Nellie, 'and her tongue goes like a mill-wheel. I have nothing to do but listen and very entertaining I find it.' A couple of weeks later, things were not so good. 'Last night Betsey thought she was going to die: she had a heavy pain in the region of her chest, and thought there must have been a dead rat in some water she drank at the green-grocer's.' She also had terrible things to report about the dreadful life of her friend at Warlingham. 'The friend sobbed so much this time when Betsey left that Betsey was that flurried with her that she said "Oh you'd better have one of your gentlemen cousins up to comfort you. You can put him into my bed!" I assure you,' Edmund continued to Nellie, 'the whole performance was so racy (with jumpings up and theatrical rushings hither and thither), and she was so led on by my laughing, that I was quite alarmed for her sanity at last!'

Life at the Board of Trade was often more trying. Gosse was very vulnerable in his room, and unwelcome visitors could be a problem. He described to Nellie one such visit. A Hungarian actor called on him, someone called Moritz Neville, whom they hadn't seen for six years:

He has married a rich American lady, has settled at Washington, has broken down in health, has a 'moost lofely babe of seventeen months' from whom he cannot be separated without pain for more than thirty minutes and is altogether very agitating and curious.

He spoke of you in the handsomest terms: I was very glad you were out of town. He has entirely left the stage and wears an enormous moustache, curled and waxed at the ends. He is going to call on me again and again and again, he is so dreadfully fond of me; he has loved me all these years. He is going back to America in about ten days, so that there is a little silver lining to the cloud.

Nellie's letters amused Edmund as much as his amused her. He was always commenting that she 'would certainly write a good novel one of these days'. She *would* write – children's stories, art criticism, magazine articles on all sorts of subjects, but never the 'great comic novel' Edmund thought she was capable of. She really preferred painting – she was exhibiting regularly at the Grosvenor Gallery; and there always seemed so many other things to attend to – many of them for him. She kept everything going. When she was away, he missed her more and more, both practically and emotionally. He would write:

Please let me know by return of post:–
1. Where are my white flannel trousers and shirts?
2. Have I a decent pair of tennis shoes?

And on other occasions: 'Whenever you are away, I become immediately conscious of my utter helplessness without you, and how essential to my daily comfort your strength and knowledge and experience are. But do not imagine anything is going particularly wrong. It is only the crumpled rose-leaf.' 'I cannot sleep in that huge bed alone. I toss from Lapland to Patagonia in it and get into a state of fever indescribable.' 'It is so dreadfully fatiguing to have you away. You are so terribly indispensable, hands and brains and everything to your poor E.' It would always be so.

The weekends seemed to take a long time to come round. The cats were some consolation, though Selina broke things in the kitchen when concentrating on the catching of flies, and came to a sad end. Once, when Nellie was away, Delamere Terrace was temporarily without a cat as well, and the mice were riotous in the drawing-room when Edmund and Hamo Thornycroft sat quietly together in the dusk. 'Cats! cats is what we want. Or a heron. Herons are supposed to be excellent mousers. How would you like to have a heron?' Edmund asked Nellie. He was anxious for her to return, but she was keener to finish the landscape she was working on. He hoped she was thinking of Constable.

Sometimes Helen Zimmern (unmarried, thirty-five, scholar and translator of Nietzsche) came round to dinner: 'We had our coffee on the balcony and were smoking our cigarettes quite in the bachelor style,' Edmund wrote to Nellie, 'when Mrs Crosse came by and faltered and evidently could not tell what to make of it.' Mrs Crosse was a neighbour; they often played whist together. She, her son Ormonde and her sister Theresa sometimes came in for a game when Edmund had finished his evening's work. 'Mrs Crosse, Theresa and I swore a good deal. Ormonde made puns, which I think on the whole is worse.' One night Edmund sat on the leads above Hamo's new studio until nearly eleven. The moonlight was so delicious. It fell with a ghostly effect on Watts's colossal horse in the next garden – its head far away, by itself on a grassy bank. It was fifteen years since he had sat out on a similarly hot evening on Mansel Dames's roof in Clapham.

It was lovely still to be able to be so unconventional and to tell one's wife about it and know that she understood. Everyone thought Nellie was splendid. Before they had met, Fanny Stevenson, Louis's new wife, wrote perhaps a little mockingly, 'I understand from all authorities that you are the pattern wife and woman.' Others were to say the same. George Saintsbury said, 'I don't think I ever knew a woman more universally liked.' Lord Haldane would call her 'the perfect wife'. Siegfried Sassoon, fifty years later, talked of her 'greatness of heart'. 'When I hear of such grim women as Mrs Cecil Lawson,' Edmund wrote at the time, 'I thank God for giving me such a jewel – such a Koh-i-noor diamond – of a wife as you are . . . How dull the house is without you. I want you dreadfully.'

In the summer of 1881, Robert Louis Stevenson sent an invitation to Edmund Gosse to spend a summer holiday with him and his family at Braemar in Scotland. 'Mrs Gosse, my wife tells me, will have other fish to fry; and to be plain, I should not like to ask her till I had seen the house. But a lone man I know we shall be equal to. Qu'en dis-tu? Viens.' Much as he loved Stevenson, Gosse could write without mentioning his name to Thornycroft: 'I have just received an invitation to stay a week or ten days with some friends at Braemar. Whether I accept or not depends on your movements.' He would only go to Braemar if, afterwards, 'you and I could go by ourselves for a little tour in some out-of-the-way part of the Highlands, say into Sutherlandshire.' This is strange, this lack of eagerness to take up Stevenson's invitation. Edmund had met Fanny for the first time in London the previous October, on their way to Switzerland, but he must have been curious to meet Stevenson's parents and to see her with them. Fanny and Louis had married in May 1880, four years after they had begun to love each other and soon after her divorce from her first husband, Sam Osborne. Stevenson's parents had deeply disapproved of his match with a divorced American, ten years older than he was. But the breach had been healed; Fanny had won them over. They had spent the winter for the sake of Louis' health, in Davos, had gone armed with a letter of introduction from Edmund to Symonds – and now surely Edmund must have been wanting to see how things were working out.

But his thoughts that July, when Stevenson's letter arrived, were all of Thornycroft. A party in Melbury Road one evening had been agonizing. Some dim sort of drama (a 'family' drama, he supposed) was being enacted, but what it was and why he was punished for it, he did not know. Thornycroft had 'not one smile for anything or anybody all evening'. He spoke no word to Nellie or her sister Emily. Everyone but Hamo appeared to be bright enough, but Edmund considered 'that nobody seemed to be enjoying themselves'. He reached home too tired to go to bed. Was he thinking again of that jaguar of fantasy, in whose paws he might find a dreamless sleep? He felt he needed to spend some time alone with Thornycroft, away from London.

They agreed to meet on September 5th in Aberdeen, after Gosse's holiday at Braemar. From Braemar, Gosse wrote to Thornycroft still without mentioning any names, though he had c/o R. L. Stevenson in the address. It was as if he wanted to keep them apart, these two men he loved. 'I am very happy with my friends,' he wrote, without going into any detail, 'but my holiday will really begin when I start with you, for my friends here are invalids and I get little exercise and see little of the scenery . . . ; the weather could hardly be more lamentable.'

But Edmund was well prepared for the lamentable weather. Stevenson had warned him before he left London: 'If you had an uncle who was a sea captain and went to the North Pole, you had better bring his outfit.' He had then worried about his possible suggestion that Edmund's portmanteau should include nothing but sealskin. Bring whatever you like, he said. 'If you come in camel's hair you would still, although conspicuous, be welcome. Do not come in locusts and wild honey, however. I am sure you would be cold.' Edmund's luggage was full of warm and suitable clothing, and he was able to get out and about, whatever impression he might want to give Thornycroft.

Edmund wrote in much more detail to Nellie. ('How much I have been thinking of you today, and how dearly I love you.') He had had a

Riverside Scene. Algernon Swinburne taking his great new friend Gosse
to see Gabriel Rossetti. 1916

Henrik Ibsen, with his inscription

Andrew Lang

Hamo Thornycroft

Robert Louis Stevenson

Photographs given to Gosse by the sitters

'Scene: The Board of Trade. Time: Office Hours in the early eighties. Mr Austin Dobson and Mr Edmund Gosse, composing a ballade, are taken unawares by their President, Mr Jos. Chamberlain'. Cartoon by Beerbohm.

Sargent's portraits of Henry James and Coventry Patmore (above)

John Addington Symonds

Churton Collins

Sylvia, Philip and Tessa Gosse

Watts–Dunton and Swinburne at
the Pines (above left)

T. J. Wise (above right)

Robert Browning by R. Lehmann,
1884 (below right)

Edmund Gosse by Sargent, 1885

The wedding of Hamo Thornycroft and Agatha Cox. Nellie Gosse is at the extreme left, Tessa second bridesmaid from the left and Edmund, as best man, is between the two fathers, Thomas Thornycroft and Judge Cox.

bad journey north by sea. It had started off well; at the first meal he had met a Miss Kate Potter, who worked in the East End with Octavia Hill and knew the Huxleys. 'All the afternoon and evening we flirted together, or rather had a very interesting and sensible conversation.' But then he was seasick and eventually reached Braemar (after a coach ride of 2½ hours) 'apparently more dead than alive'. Revived by a glass of whisky and water, and a shave, he surveyed the family. There were five of them: Thomas and Margaret Stevenson, Louis and Fanny and Fanny's thirteen-year-old son, Lloyd. 'This is a most entertaining household,' he considered. 'All the persons in it are full of character and force: they use fearful language towards one another and no quarrel ensues.'

Stevenson, writing to Colvin, had been seeing things rather differently before Gosse came. 'If you know all that I have had on my hands, what with being ill myself, having other people most *painfully* ill, living in an atmosphere of personal quarrel, apologies and (God save the mark – what has become of all my themes) imminent duelling . . .' But there were no quarrels with Edmund. Stevenson would always turn the other cheek if Edmund seemed to be getting excited about something. 'I do most earnestly desire to have no more quarrels, except with the police,' he once wrote to Edmund. 'Don't you ever believe half the bad you hear about me; and I'll never believe any of the bad I hear about you.' After Edmund had gone, Stevenson wrote happily to W. E. Henley about his visit. Henley was to become, in Robbie Ross's words, the most severe of all Gosse's critics (only excepting Churton Collins), hating him, Fanny Stevenson considered, even more than he did her. Stevenson wrote to Henley: 'The poet was very gay and pleasant. He told me much. He is simply the most active young man in England and one of the most intelligent.'

It was amazing how everyone managed to be so gay and pleasant with the fearful language and the fearful weather and so much illness in the house. At one point, while Edmund was staying, Louis was spitting blood and his wife and mother were both confined to their beds. Edmund went on long walks with Thomas Stevenson and drives in the mountains and a visit to the Highland Games at Mar – in spite of whatever impression he wanted to give Hamo Thornycroft. Interestingly, Edmund considered Louis' father rather like his own and only slightly less delightful a companion than Louis himself. 'I have not had such excellent sound talk for a long time,' he told Nellie.

Alison Cunningham, Stevenson's old nurse, to whom he had dedicated *A Child's Garden*, was at Braemar too. She had been a pillar of the household ever since she came into the family in 1852. Now she cast a cold eye on Edmund, as one of Louis' questionable English friends. With extreme kindliness she combined a faint jealousy of outside influences acting on her lamb, whom she longed to protect from all the shocks of life, even from his own loving, fidgety parents. Long afterwards Gosse would suggest that 'the tattle-mongers who now talk Freudian nonsense about Stevenson's early "sins"' would never have done so if they could have met Cummy. Gosse himself would always leap to Stevenson's defence and love him too tenderly to analyse him. He would blush to remember how he had won Cummy over by the way he read the Bible at family prayers. She 'turned fiercely on R.L.S. and said "He's the only one of your fine friends who can do justice to the Word of God,"' a tribute which made the best, it seemed to Edmund, of 'a rather stagey manner of reading aloud'.

Before Edmund had arrived, Louis had started a story at Braemar, tentatively entitled *The Sea Cook*. It had begun, it seems, with a map showing hidden treasure. Lloyd claimed to have drawn it himself and given Stevenson the idea. Certainly it started as a boys' story, a story Lloyd would enjoy. Edmund said he heard the first three chapters on his very first evening at Braemar. Colvin had just left and had heard them too with enthusiasm. Fanny, who never quite approved of the book, wrote later: '*Treasure Island* which, before the advent of our visitors, had been thought of simply as an amusement for a small boy condemned to the inaction of an indoor life by inclement weather, now, under the stimulus of men like Mr Colvin and Mr Gosse, began to be regarded seriously as a possible novel.'

Stevenson was 'sadly weak, incapable of exertion, easily tired, excitable and feeble'. He and Edmund would play chess each morning after breakfast, the board on the counterpane on Louis' bed. They played silently; talking was forbidden until the evening, to save Louis' strength. After the game, Edmund would not see him again until the evening when there would be good talk over dinner and, after the meal, Stevenson would read by the fire what he had written during the day – with the storm howling beyond the closed shutters. The vivacity and sustained power of the invalid's voice were very surprising. It was a resonant and penetrating voice, tending to be shrill in moments of excitement. Long after Stevenson's death, Gosse said he sometimes recovered that voice in his dreams.

It seemed abundantly clear to Edmund that the older Stevensons had accepted their daughter-in-law and that it was true, what Louis had suggested to Edmund in a letter from San Francisco the year before: 'I do not think many wives are better loved than mine will be.' W. E. Henley was to say that marriage tamed Stevenson, killed the spark of defiance and unconventionality that had lit his life. Certainly Louis seemed tame that August, and Edmund even described Fanny to

Nellie as 'very sweet and quiet' – but he was soon to realize she was far more than that. 'She was one of the strangest people who have lived in our time, a sort of savage nature, in some ways, but very lovable – extraordinarily passionate and unlike everyone else in her violent feelings and unrestrained ways of expressing things picturesquely, but not literary.' Fanny meanwhile was weighing Edmund up. Fanny did not like English men. She seemed to exclude only George Meredith and Sidney Colvin, whom she saw as men of courage, from her aspersions on Englishmen – 'a pitifully craven lot'. And Symonds she liked, for his 'immense personal charm', though she found him, perhaps without appreciating the irony of her words, 'as full of fancies and extraordinary ways as a hysterical girl'.

Some of Stevenson's biographers have seen Gosse as the only one of his London friends who regarded the marriage without rancour: 'Only Gosse seemed to be able to retain balance and generosity.' But Fanny was to report in late 1884 to her friend Mrs Virgil Williams:

> He and I had a quarrel once and he bears malice, so I don't like him; but I believe he is, or thinks he is, honestly fond of Louis. He is a poet, and like most of his walk in literature, very good at business, smooth, silken, like a purring cat, very witty, rather maliciously so, but vain beyond belief. That is why he cannot forgive me. I was the unintentional cause of his acting in a way that he was bitterly ashamed of afterwards. He is very good company indeed and very pleasant to talk to.

Fanny Stevenson was a shrewd judge. Over the years many other people were to echo some of her words, though they had not read them. Other people found it easier to forgive him, because he was such good company, so witty, so pleasant to talk to. And Fanny was to feel more kindly towards Gosse after Stevenson's death. She would write to Graham Balfour, 'He was the only one of Louis' friends who was nice to me – I mean specially nice. He and Mrs Sitwell. Mr Gosse seemed to me more truly interested in hearing about Louis than any of them. We had long talks and he asked a thousand questions which showed his deep affection.' Gosse was never aware of Fanny's mixed feelings about him, or at least never admitted them. After her death, he wrote to Graham Balfour, 'I believe I was almost the only one of Louis' friends who never had any friction with her.'

Fanny had remarked on how pleasant Edmund was to talk to. Stevenson himself published his own version of Edmund's talk at this time, disguising him as Purcel in an article he wrote for the *Cornhill* on talk and talkers:

He is no debater, but appears in conversation, as occasion rises, in two distinct characters, one of which I admire and fear, and the other love. In the first, he is radiantly civil and rather silent, sits on a high courtly hilltop and from that vantage-ground drops you his remarks like favours. He seems not to share in our sublunary contentions; he wears no sign of interest; when on a sudden there falls in a crystal of wit, so polished that the dull do not perceive it, but so right that the sensitive are silenced. True talk should have more body and blood, should be louder, vainer and more declaratory of the man. The true talker should not hold so steady an advantage over whom he speaks with; and that is one reason out of a score why I prefer my Purcel in his second character, when he unbends into a strain of graceful gossip, singing like the fireside kettle. In these moods he has an elegant homeliness that rings of the true Queen Anne . . .

'It is all a dead secret,' Stevenson wrote the following year, 'known to the usual number; but I will not deny that Purcel was intended for yourself. If you don't like it, I'll make believe it was somebody else . . . you did recognise yourself, didn't you? or where was the point on't? I hoped you, I thought you would . . . – I only chose the men I loved to talk with . . .'

Thornycroft and Gosse spent a couple of days in the Orkneys. It was here that Edmund bought the presents for the children earlier described; he also bought white Shetland shawls for Nellie and Laura Alma-Tadema. Then they spent a week in Sutherlandshire. The weather had miraculously changed. Thirty-five years later, someone mentioned Aultnagalagach, and the name brought back to Gosse that marvellous autumn when the two of them climbed 'Suilven and Canisp, swimming in the black lakes, wherein we believed that the sword Excalibur might at any moment be brandished, dreaming all our dreams of poetry and art. The spirit of youth was dancing in our veins.' On Tessa's fourth birthday, they rested by a burn of clear primrose-coloured water leaping down a staircase of quartz on the giant side of Canisp and drank a health to her from their whisky flask. 'Hamo's health was: "May she long live to be a comfort and joy to you!" Mine was –' Edmund wrote to Nellie, ' "May she everyday grow to be more like her mother!" I made her a little fragrant posy of mountain-perfumes, – bog-myrtle, juniper, cranberry and thyme, and presented it to her in imagination.' He was feeling unrecognizably brown and strong, and certainly fatherly. But there is a poem 'A Wasted Afternoon in Sutherland' which has a different feeling.

The sky was brilliant blue, the mountain granite grey above them. They had tried all afternoon to fish but it was not fishing weather.

> Better the storm that fills
> The thunder-coloured rills,
> Better the shrouded hills
> And drifts of rain.

So Thornycroft felt, more or less. But Edmund knew he would remember that glorious afternoon, though nothing had been caught, 'when nerves forget to thrill, When hands have lost the skill, To play and slay.' Still Thornycroft watched the sky. Noon fell to afternoon; eventually the moon appeared. And still they lay there in the heather –

> So through that sleepy weather,
> Our rods and we together
> Lay on the springing heather,
>   Assuaged at last,
> And now, through memory's haze
> Best of our fishing days
> Seems just that cloudless blaze,
>   With never a cast.

There would be other holidays with Thornycroft: in Paris the two following springs, in Northumberland in the late summer of 1882, and most lengthily in Switzerland in the summer of 1883 when they stayed at a hotel in a large party with the Waterhouses and the Humphry Wards. But by then things had changed. For years, Edmund would think that 'the pleasantest dinner party in the world' was as nothing compared to an evening alone with Thornycroft, but there would be few such evenings. They would no longer sit in the studio together, in lamplight and firelight, in touch, talking. They would no longer swim naked in rivers and lochs.

Hamo Thornycroft had become engaged to Agatha Cox of Tonbridge. 'We are blind creatures,' Edmund wrote to Hamo on 2nd July 1883, 'and although I have often teazed you about Tonbridge, I had no notion that it was serious.'

I pray God with all my heart to bless you both, to teach her to love you as you deserve to be loved . . . I feel so serious and agitated about it that I cannot indulge in any of the gentle chaff which is proper to these occasions . . . At this crisis of our lives my one great thought is of gratitude to you for these four wonderful years, the summer of my life, which I have spent in a sort of morning-glory walking by your side. You will not think about this at first, and I should be sorry if you did. But as time goes on and we grow older still, it will all come back to you.

I can say nothing but what is stupid. God bless you and be good to you. When you find a spare moment you must try and prepare your future wife to like me. I am so very anxious to like her.

He had not met her; he was evidently stunned. He did not mention Nellie or the joys of marriage, though later, on reflection, he would say that he and Nellie had been thinking how much Hamo would enjoy having a fireside and babies of his own. Agatha, who was extremely young – just eighteen (Hamo was thirty-three) and meeting some opposition from the Thornycroft family – wrote correctly and sweetly to Edmund, hoping that they would soon meet. Edmund replied:

It was impossible that my wife and I should regard the betrothal of our dearest friend without an anxiety lest his future wife should be unwilling to accept us as his friends and make us hers. Your kind and generous words put an end to this anxiety . . . I am afraid that Hamo has been characteristically generous if he has told you that I have been much to him. I cannot tell what he has been to me; you will perhaps be incredulous when I tell you that, intimately as you know him already, you cannot yet have found out how great and good he is. He has one of the finest talents of our age, and yet I sometimes think his genius is the least part of him.

It was as well that there were other very important friendships developing: with Thomas Hardy and Henry James, his contemporaries, and with Coventry Patmore. Gosse seems to have first met Hardy in the late winter of 1874. Gosse, as we have seen, was often shaky on dates, even dates in his own experience. But in 1912 he wrote very specifically to Hardy: 'If we live two years more (and we *will*) our friendship will have lasted forty years.' In fact, they both lived until 1928 and their friendship lasted fifty-three years. On Gosse's golden wedding in 1925, Hardy sent the message: CONTINUED HAPPINESS FOR BOTH FROM ONE WHO THINKS HE HAS KNOWN YOU THE WHOLE TIME. They met at a time when Hardy, marrying Emma, was particularly aware how much he was moving away from his own Dorset beginnings. With Gosse he did not have to conceal anything.

Gosse too had unsuitable relatives lurking in the background – his uncle Tom, a particularly ungentlemanly black sheep, and poor old uncle William, as unsuccessful as his father, whom Edmund and *his* father were supporting at Ealing. Edmund's grandmother had been a domestic servant (of considerable strength of character) as Hardy's mother had been. Edmund's father had been born in lodgings over a shoemaker's shop in Worcester, in circumstances no grander than those of Hardy's stonemason father. If these things were not much discussed, they were known, and the two young writers certainly compared notes on their west country background – on Philip Henry's memories of school at Wimborne, for instance.

Then there was the thought that they might so easily have brushed against each other in the streets of Weymouth in 1853 or 1855. They would visit Weymouth together in 1890 and take photographs to commemorate the occasion and the connective possibility. Hardy and Gosse were always easy with each other when they were together, though their relationship, like nearly all Gosse's friendships, had its fluctuations and misunderstandings.

When Hardy had been so extremely ill in London in the cold winter of 1880–81, Gosse's visits to the bleak house in Arundel Terrace had cheered him as much as anything could. After the return to Dorset, Hardy visited the Gosses at Delamere Terrace whenever he was in London, and they also met regularly at the Savile Club. On 25th June 1883 Hardy was one of Gosse's guests at the sort of dinner party at the Club which Gosse was to give many times in the future. He had himself brought up fifty or sixty splendid roses from the Waterhouses' garden in Yattendon, had supervised the menu with some anxiety, and been relieved that everyone had seemed to enjoy themselves. Perhaps Du Maurier was a little surly, and Austin Dobson 'had to go to Mrs D. rather early'. But Woolner was loquacious, and Thornycroft and Hardy 'had a nice talk about country folk'. William Dean Howells, the American novelist, talked of it as 'banqueting with you immortals' and told stories about Twain and Emerson, which Hardy recorded in his diary. Only Browning had been unable to come.

Gosse loved to see Hardy. Already in 1886, when *The Mayor of Casterbridge* came out, he was calling him 'our greatest novelist'. When they were together in company, Gosse did most of the talking. Years later Edward Marsh would see Hardy 'content to bask in Gosse's beams'. When they were apart, they wrote to each other, and many of Hardy's letters to Gosse show a warmth and humour not often evident in his correspondence; it was only when writing to Gosse that he ever gave his address not as Max Gate but as 'Porta Maxima'. But Hardy had not yet built Max Gate when Gosse paid his first visit to him in July, 1883. He had taken a queer, rambling house in Dorchester, which was loud with the military 'bugling and marching' when Gosse arrived for the weekend.

Mrs Hardy, Gosse commented, 'means to be very kind'. Henry Moule came in for high tea, 'the local antiquary . . . son of the celebrated inventor of the Earth Closet'. In the evening, the three men walked around the town, which was thronged with soldiers and with farmers and labourers doing their Saturday night's shopping. Then they strolled round the old walls under the chestnuts by the light of the moon. On the Sunday afternoon, Gosse and Hardy walked through fields of head-high rye to the church at Winterborne Came, where William Barnes, the poet, was rector. Hardy knew of Gosse's admiration for Barnes, and Barnes was expecting them and had invited them to 'high tea' after the afternoon service. Hardy's diary entry records: 'Barnes, knowing we should be on the watch for a prepared sermon, addressed it entirely to his own flock, almost pointedly excluding us.'

Gosse was in no mood to be critical. 'Barnes is a wonderful figure;' he wrote to Thornycroft, 'he is in his 83rd year. He has long thin silky white hair flowing down and mingling with a full beard and moustache also as white as milk, a grand dome of forehead over a long thin pendulous nose, not at all a handsome face, but full of intelligence and the beauty of vigour and extreme old age.' He was certainly vigorous. After taking the entire service himself and preaching a rather long sermon, he stayed behind to hear the school-children's hymn practice and then walked to the rectory, as he had walked from it, rather over a mile. He wore black knee-breeches and silk stockings and buckled shoes – the last person in Dorset, Gosse understood, to keep up such dress. They stayed four hours with him at the rectory, and all the time he hurried about, showing them his treasures and talking about British antiquities and philology. It was difficult to get him to talk much about his poems.

Three years later Gosse saw him 'dying as picturesquely as he had lived' lying in a white bed, wearing a scarlet bedgown, with a kind of soft biretta of dark red wool on his white head – bright in the dark room, among the rows of brown books, the light from the window filtered through flowering plants.

Gosse found it hard to pin down the moment of his first meeting with Henry James:

It is often curiously difficult for intimate friends, who have the impression in later years that they must always have known one another, to recall the occasion when they first met. That was the case with Henry James and me. Several times we languidly tried to recover those particulars but without success. I think however it was at some dinner party that we first met, and as the incident is dubiously connected with the publication of the *Hawthorne* in 1879 . . . I am pretty sure that the event took place early in 1880.

In fact, it was in the late summer of 1879, when Nellie was recovering from Philip's birth, in that 'happiest year' of his life, that Gosse had lunch at the Savile with Andrew Lang and Robert Louis Stevenson and the sociable American, Henry James, who admitted to having dined out in London the previous winter no fewer than 107 times. James's *Hawthorne* preceded Gosse's *Gray* in John Morley's English Men of Letters series. It had been written with equal ease, without even any attempt to use primary sources. Americans were to grumble that James was already becoming too English; they hated the way he used the word 'provincial'.

Even W. D. Howells thought James might be accused of high treason. The abusive press reception in America for this book would help James to sympathize with Gosse when his turn came. In the meantime they had lunch together. James was not very taken with Andrew Lang. (Meeting him in Paris that autumn, he would find it ridiculously provincial that Lang assumed you could post letters there with English stamps on them.) In his reviews, Lang had demanded 'more claymores, less psychology', and here were claymores and psychology at the same luncheon table. James would maintain an uneasy friendship with Lang and so would Gosse. He saw him with 'the bright armour of Oxford burnished on his body to such a brilliance that humdrum eyes could hardly bear the radiance of it', but his house, Gosse thought, was built upon a rainbow. He could not bear the rocks of real life: Ibsen, Hardy, Dostoievsky. Stevenson called him 'garrulous as a brook'. We shall see him later, at Delamere Terrace, described by Max Beerbohm.

It was one of so many meals eaten in talkative company that it is perhaps no wonder that James and Gosse could not recall this particular occasion; but, if William Morris had been Gosse's largest literary lion in 1872, Henry James was even more lion-like in 1879. It was this year which saw the real establishment of his fame on both sides of the Atlantic. His work was translated into French and German and appeared all over the continent in Tauchnitz editions. The novels which had already appeared in America now came out in England, so it appeared that he was incredibly prolific. 'In the history of authorship,' Leon Edel said, 'few novelists have seen through the press so many books in a single year.' 'My reputation in England,' James wrote to his brother that year, 'seems ludicrously larger than any cash payment that I have yet received for it.'

It is in the summer of 1882 that Gosse gives his first word picture of his new friend. He had called on him in his lodgings in Bolton Street, off Piccadilly:

Stretched on the sofa and apologizing for not rising to greet me, his appearance gave me a little shock, for I had not thought of him as an invalid. He hurriedly and rather evasively declared that he was not that, but that a muscular weakness of his spine obliged him, as he said, 'to assume the horizontal posture' during some hours of every day in order to bear the almost unbroken routine of evening engagements. I think that this weakness gradually passed away, but certainly for many years it handicapped his activity. I recall his appearance, seen then for the first time by daylight; there was something shadowy about it, the face framed in dark brown hair cut short in the Paris fashion, and in equally dark beard, rather loose and 'fluffy'. He was in deep mourning, his mother having died five or six months earlier, and he himself having but recently returned from a melancholy visit to America, where he had unwillingly left his father, who seemed far from well. His manner was grave, extremely courteous, but a little formal and frightened, which seemed strange in a man living in constant communication with the world. Our business regarding Du Maurier was soon concluded, and James talked with increasing ease, but always with a punctilious hesitancy, about Paris, where he seemed, to my dazzlement, to know even a larger number of persons of distinction than he did in London. He promised, before I left, to return my visit, but news of the alarming illness of his father called him suddenly to America.

It was on James's return and permanent settlement in England, in the autumn of 1883, that their friendship really began to flourish. On Boxing Day that year, James wrote to thank Gosse for a Christmas Day letter:

My dear Gosse,
Your note of yesterday – or rather, I should say your copious letter – gives me real pleasure. It is very good of you to say to me all those ingenious and appreciative things. I appreciate them, in my turn, heartily, and am your debtor for that sort of sympathy that does one good, and which, in fact, when one meets it, is one of the best things in life . . .

It was one of the first of more than four hundred letters Henry James was to write to Edmund Gosse, who provided him for another thirty-three years with an endless supply, not only of the sort of sympathy that does one good, but also with the kind of literary gossip which particularly delighted James.

Gosse named Coventry Patmore, as we have already seen, as one of the three most formative friendships of these early years. Patmore was becoming elderly. He was twenty-six years older than Gosse. 'His familiars talk pityingly of "the crazy old pagan polygamist",' James Fitzmaurice Kelly wrote to Gosse years later. But this was the same poet to whom Gerard Manley Hopkins would write: 'Your poems are a good deed done for the Catholic church and another for England, for the British Empire.' If there was one attitude which had survived in Gosse since his childhood, it was his attitude to the Roman Catholic church. If he did not actually call it the Whore of Babylon, as his father had done, he certainly had little time for it.

Coventry Patmore had been converted to it in 1864. Gosse's relationship with Patmore and the way he deals with religion in his biography of him (as well as in his books on Sir Thomas Browne, Donne and Jeremy Taylor) show clearly how little Gosse took to rationalism, that opium of the mid-Victorian intellectual, as it has been called. If he could not entirely sympathize with Patmore's 'supernaturalism', Gosse was never an overt rationalist; he understood man's hungering for God. But there was little to suggest on their first meeting that Patmore would come to mean so much to Gosse. They first met at the Savile Club in 1879. 'He made a highly disagreeable impression on me,' Gosse wrote. 'I thought him harsh and sardonic, he said little and what he said was bitter.' He was in a dark period – nobody was paying him much attention. He needed Gosse's brand of devoted discipleship. They started by corresponding about odes; Gosse was preparing a collection which was published in 1881 by Kegan Paul. The only living poets in it were Tennyson, Patmore and Swinburne.

In January 1881 Patmore invited Gosse down to Hastings, for the first of many visits. Gosse would return from such visits 'dazzled with glimpses of a stronger light than common day'. Patmore 'was mischievously contradictory, paradoxical and arbitrary'. He was also a great exaggerator. 'If he heard a blackcap singing, it became at once a nightingale and, a few hours later, a chorus of five or six nightingales.' He would tell Gosse stories, stories Gosse would love to hear and would later tell himself. Behind Patmore stood the ghosts of Leigh Hunt, Lamb and Hazlitt, and of their associate, his father Peter

Patmore, who had fled the country after killing a man in a duel. Robert Browning told Gosse that when he wanted to introduce young Coventry Patmore to Thackeray, the novelist's immediate reaction had been, 'I won't touch the hand of a son of that bloody murderer.' Thackeray repented and acknowledged the young poet was hardly responsible for his father's sins, but the story shows what Patmore had to put up with in his youth.

Behind him stood, also, the two dead wives. The beautiful Emily was painted by Millais, commemorated on a medallion by Thomas Woolner, and celebrated in verse by Robert Browning. The second, Marianne, shone with Catholic sanctity and devotion, and was extremely rich, as Patmore had discovered rather to his embarrassment after he had proposed.

As a young man, Patmore had worked in the British Museum library, just as Gosse had done years later, and had seen a great deal of the Pre-Raphaelite Brotherhood. Indeed it was Patmore who, in 1857, induced Ruskin to take up the cudgels for the Pre-Raphaelites and write his famous letter about Millais' pictures to *The Times*. After abuse for Patmore's early volumes, of such venom as would hardly be possible today (*Blackwood's* compared some of his work to slime and 'the spawn of frogs' and called it 'the ultimate terminus of poetical degradation'), his book *The Angel in the House*, published in 1858, began to sell in hundreds, then in thousands, until it became the most popular poem of the day.

Gosse characterizes vividly the misjudged ardour of the readers of that book. Curates and old maids, he said, bought the poems of Patmore as 'the sweetest, safest sugar-plums of the sheltered intellectual life . . . They imagined the grim and rather sinister author to be a kind of sportive lambkin, with his tail tied in bows of blue riband. But Patmore was a man of the highest seriousness: he aimed at nothing less than an exposition of the divine mystery of wedlock . . .'

In the early 1880s, when Gosse became a regular visitor at Patmore's house, the success of *The Angel in the House* was long over. 'It was my privilege,' Gosse wrote, 'to be a thrilled pilgrim at the shrine. There were hardly any other worshippers; that was the dark hour of the public neglect of Patmore.' Gosse would sit in Patmore's study on one side of the fire. On the other, the older poet would stretch out, immobile but for his marvellous head (not yet quite so much that of an emaciated prophet as in the Sargent version in the National Portrait Gallery), 'moving sharply and frequently, almost as if on a pivot, the eyes darkening and twinkling, the Protean lips reflecting in their curves every shade of feeling that passed over the poet's mind. Out of this attitude, he would have only to pounce, with extraordinary suddenness, on one of the cigarettes which lay strewn about, like leaves in Vallombrosa, lighting it and then resuming his shrouded and pinioned pose. And so sitting, sloped to the fire, he would talk for hours of the highest things, of thoughts and passions above a mortal guise, descending every now and then in some fierce eccentric jest, always to be punctuated by a loud, crackling laugh, ending in a dry cough . . . a sort of bark at the close of each sentence.'

After hours of such talk, at night his pulse would begin to beat 'and would rise into an excitement which nothing but a long, wild stroll in the darkness would allay'. Gosse would walk with him, along the top of the sea wall, drenched by the flying spray, with Patmore in ecstasy, his loose, grey curls streaming in the wind. To Gosse he seemed a magician in charge of the storm who could quell it if he wished; but did not wish.

Gosse set out, just as he had with Ibsen, on a planned campaign to establish a reputation; but in this case, it was a re-establishment. He sprinkled the periodicals with articles on Patmore's work. Not that he thought *The Angel in the House* was the height of Patmore's achievement. It was *The Unknown Eros* Gosse most admired, that sequence which includes 'The Toys', perhaps the one poem of Patmore's which is still comparatively well-known. It is easy to see why Gosse found it particularly moving. What he calls Patmore's 'ceaseless oscillation of spirit between severity and tenderness' must have reminded him strongly of Philip Gosse. And we can see the influence of Patmore on Gosse's own poem 'The Wallpaper', written at a time when he was seeing a great deal of Patmore. I referred to this poem when writing about the early childhood incident it recalls. It would now seem worth looking at in full, at a time when Gosse was still regarded principally as a poet, but when that title, which he considered the most splendid any writer could earn, would soon be replaced generally by critic, biographer, 'man of letters'.

When Gosse finished his poem 'Firdausi in Exile', in October 1881, he wrote to Thornycroft: 'Perhaps what I have written tonight will be read after my death! I never felt more inclined to think so of anything of mine.' He dreamed of fame and immortality, saw himself, as he was soon to write to his new American friend, W. D. Howells, 'still hanging by my eyelids to the outer cliff of fame'. When he was a boy of eighteen, his father had warned him of the 'treacherous, insinuating temptation' of the desire of fame. He had ignored the warning. He did not often hear his father's voice in his ears these days, though the letters from Marychurch would still sometimes make him despair. ('Father's was so stiff and foolish that I tore it up,' he once told Nellie.) The cliff of fame seemed worth clinging to: already, in the early 1880s, he could attract large audiences at lectures, in Birmingham, in New-castle, in London.

His real fame would come from prose: it would be *Father and Son* that would be read after his death. (There would come a time, now, when one of our leading poets, a man of great literary erudition, could say to me: 'Did Gosse write poetry? I didn't know.') Gosse wrote his own poem on toys, human beings as toys. It was called 'Playthings', and the last verse was simply this:

> The toys are played with till they fall,
>   Worn out and thrown away.
> Why were they ever made at all?
>   Who sits to watch the play?

But 'The Wallpaper' is much more original: I think it his main claim to be considered as a poet. It skates near to sentimentality but avoids it: the ice does not crack. It is perhaps a reflection of how much taste has changed that Gosse left 'The Wallpaper' out of his *Collected Poems*.

> When I was only five years old,
>   My mother, who was soon to die,
> Raised me with fingers soft and cold,
>   On high;
>
> Until, against the parlour wall,
>   I reached a golden paper flower.
> How proud was I, and ah! how tall,
>   That hour!
>
> 'This shining tulip shall be yours,
>   Your own, your very own,' she said;
> The mark that made it mine endures
>   In red.
>
> I scarce could see it from the floor;
>   I craned to touch the scarlet sign;
> No gift so precious had before
>   Been mine.
>
> A paper tulip on a wall!
>   A boon that ownership defied!
> Yet this was dearer far than all
>   Beside.

Real toys, real flowers that lavish love
    Had strewn before me, all and each
Grew pale beside this gift above
        My reach.

Ah! now that time has worked its will,
    And fooled my heart, and dazed my eyes,
Delusive tulips prove me still
        Unwise.

Still, still the eluding flower that glows
    Above the hands that yearn and clasp
Seems brighter than the genuine rose
        I grasp.

So has it been since I was born;
    So will it be until I die;
Stars, the best flowers of all, adorn
        The sky.

Gosse's next book of poems, *Firdausi in Exile*, was not published until 1885, but the list of his published prose was steadily growing. His bibliography lists some diverse items between 1879 and 1883: there were several memoirs or studies in strictly limited editions – Samuel Rowlands, Thomas Lodge, Cecil Lawson, George Tinworth. Oddest was a short Stationery Office publication (of which several pages are signed E.W.G.) called *Résumé of a Pamphlet on the Industry and Trade of Germany, during the first year of the new Protective Policy*. Gosse's own comment on this was, 'Copies were sent to Germany, and one fell into the hands of no less a person than Bismarck. He read it and was furious; and he sent a request to the Foreign Office, through the German Embassy, that the author of the *Résumé* should be reprimanded. This was thought a great joke, and, so far from being blamed, I was commended.'

Much the most important work of this period went into Gosse's first long biographical study: *Gray*, in the English Men of Letters series, and into *Seventeenth-Century Studies*, which was a collection of pieces he had written for the *Cornhill*. Sending it to the publishers in June 1883, Gosse called it his 'little magnum opus, my seventeenth century book that has taken eleven years to write'. The first essay had actually appeared in the *Cornhill* in 1875. Gosse had also contributed largely to Humphry Ward's *English Poets*; he wrote twenty-nine biographical sketches in that book. He had also contributed a large number of pieces to the *Encyclopaedia Britannica* (largely on Scandinavian subjects) and had begun to write for the *DNB*.

Much of Gosse's energy was going into ephemeral journalism. In a letter to Nellie in September, 1883, there is a vivid instance of how he could not turn down a commission, and how conscientious he was, in a superficial context:

> At 1.30 Harwood wrote to me by hand asking for an article for this Saturday on the Flemish novelist Conscience, who has just died. I had never read one of Conscience's books, and I felt very much inclined to say no, but I did not like to do so, and assented. At 4 I went up to the B.M. and took notes for an hour, then to Kolck-mann, from whom I borrowed four of Conscience's books and bought 2 more. I read in the omnibus, in the train, walking home, all through dinner and after dinner till 9, when I turned to and wrote my article, finishing it and posting it on the stroke of 12. I don't think it is a bad article either. You must not think I am any the worse for it, on the contrary the excitement gave me a pleasant fillip: I am better today than I have been for days.

With the two books, *Gray* and *Seventeenth-Century Studies*, Gosse was, for the first time, subjecting his work to the scrutiny of reviewers with an intimate knowledge of what he was writing about. Alexander Grosart, Herrick's editor, had criticized Gosse's Herrick essay soon after its first appearance in the *Cornhill*, but only after having called it a 'brilliant paper'. The two books, though they were, as we now know, loaded with errors and inaccuracies, emerged almost entirely un-scathed. Indeed, attractive reading as they were, they did a great deal to establish Gosse's growing reputation.

The most clear-cut warning of what might follow came, in fact, in a review by Edward Dowden in the *Academy* of Gosse's collection *Odes*. 'It is to be regretted,' he wrote, 'that some inaccuracies of statement in the notes, and some provoking errors in the text, detract from the worth of a book made for delight. Of such errors, the most unlucky are *land* for *lead* in Collins's 'Ode to Evening' (which professes to follow the 1748 text of Dodsley, but does not precisely do this) and the *naught* for *not* in Shelley's "Pine for what is not".' Gosse may well have recalled this a few years later and regretted that he did not heed the warning.

A letter to Humphry Ward of 23rd February 1881, which lists corrections to the proofs of *The English Poets*, shows just how aware Gosse was, in theory anyway, of the need for scrupulous accuracy. These are typical notes: 'On p. 442 Mr. A. W. Ward has committed a curious error in calling the line "thou leap'st" etc an Alexandrine. It has of course 14 and not 12 syllables. p. 434 date 1860 should be 1680. This is a misprint but it is also an error for the author expressly dates this poem 1679.'

The case of Gosse's life of Gray is a particularly interesting one. On 13th March 1882 Gosse wrote to Austin Dobson: 'I am in a great state of agitation. I have just written the death of Gray, with inexpressible excitement. I have been crying, so that my tears blinded the page – how ridiculous – tears for a little man who died more than a hundred years ago. How ridiculous!' Morley's original advice, when he commissioned the biography, had suggested a rather less emotional approach. 'Let the book tell the story as much as possible: with as much transcript as you can give from Gray's charming letters. I would warn you against assuming any knowledge in your readers – and therefore against anything oblique or allusive in style.' He wanted plain description and facts. When the manuscript was delivered, Morley was delighted with it. It seemed to him full of painstaking knowledge and literary charm.

But the manuscript, now at Texas, shows little evidence of pains being taken. Gosse gave this manuscript, at that time the only original manuscript he had not destroyed, to Emilie Marzials, Theo's sister. He said he had 'picked it out of the wastepaper basket' and had it bound for her at Christmas, 1883, because she had said she would like a manuscript. The extraordinary thing is that Gosse says it is a first draft throughout. 'I never copy my work, and you may notice by the comparative cleanness of the pages that my sentences are formed before I write them.'

Morley was impressed. Swinburne was impressed: 'I congratulate you on a successful and delightful piece of work. It must have been a labour of love and one which needed a love of labour for its accomplishment.' He thought it was 'one of the very few jewels' in a poor series. Thomas Hardy thought the book delightful. Robert Louis Stevenson wrote more interestingly:

I have read your *Gray* with care. A more difficult subject I can scarce fancy: it is crushing; yet I think you have managed to shadow forth a man, and a good man too; and honestly, I doubt if I could have done the same. This may seem egoistic; but you are not such a fool as to think so. It is the natural expression of real praise. The book as a whole is readable; your subject peeps here and there out of the crannies like a shy violet – he could do no more.

Leslie Stephen, while noticing one wrong inference, thought it was one of the most charming biographies he had ever read. Borrowing from Gosse for the *DNB* entry which Gosse for some reason didn't want to write, Stephen thanked him in these terms: 'I have had to follow your *Gray* so closely that I feel like a thief and can only ask you to accept my apology for stealing and my gratitude for the stolen goods.' But handling stolen goods is always a dangerous pastime. Error breeds error, and errors which Gosse had made attained the authority of the *DNB* and multiplied. For all Morley's talk of 'painstaking knowledge' and Swinburne's assessment of the labour that had gone into the book, Gosse had, in fact, taken less than four months – and four months when he was daily at the Board of Trade. He began on 8th December 1881 and finished on 28th March 1882. But it was true what Stevenson had said. Gray was there, shadowy but there, in a way that he might not have been in the hands of some more rigorous biographer. 'None but a poet could have written of a poet with such sympathy,' Thomas Woolner told Gosse.

And he was unaware of the errors. Morley had been right in assuming ignorant readers. The critics were as happy about the book as his friends. It was generally agreed, as the *Athenaeum* put it, that it was 'the best life of Gray that has appeared'. It sold well and went into several editions. Two years later, Gosse published the first complete edition of *The Works of Thomas Gray*, to almost unanimous approval. The *Athenaeum* sang particular praise:

> When an editor does his part as well as Mr Gosse has done, the reviewer, having no errors to discover or omissions to lament, can but thank him for a task which could never have been achieved so perfectly without the most exact and persistent labour. The reader will appreciate the result, but he is apt to forget how many distinguished qualities were necessary to produce it: the patient research, the intimate knowledge of the period, the sagacity needed to retain and the courage needed to reject.

The critics obviously had a confidence in Gosse which was never to be shown again; they felt secure in praising him. At thirty-five, Gosse had acquired an immense reputation for learning and for a deep acquaintance with the literature of England and of northern Europe. In the thirteen years since his first note on Spenser had appeared in the *Athenaeum*, there had been no real setback in his literary career. He had increased in reputation as he increased his acquaintance with the leading writers of the day. Editors, in periodicals and publishing houses, competed for his services. If he had been content to be a poet and a journalist, things would have been very different. But Gosse, in spite of, or perhaps because of, the fact that he had had to educate himself from the age of seventeen, longed to be considered a scholar. Writing to the Norwegian editor who had requested a biographical note in 1875, Gosse said 'You do not require to be warned that my life is not full of incidents; when one is simply a scholar, and not yet 26, that is not surprising.' He had many of the attributes of the scholar – but he lacked one essential: a concern for accuracy.

At Pembroke College, Cambridge, there exists an interleaved, annotated copy of Gosse's life of Gray. At the beginning, in particular, there is hardly a page without one or more factual corrections. It is the work of Leonard Whibley, a distinguished Gray scholar. A reviewer in the *Times Literary Supplement*, asking for a thorough revision of the nineteenth-century *DNB* in 1949, wrote 'the late Leonard Whibley used to say that the life of Gray was not susceptible of correction; every sentence in it was incorrect or inadequate or misleading'. This was the Leslie Stephen piece making use of Gosse's *Gray*. It would be tedious to go through Gosse's errors in detail, but their varied nature can easily be indicated. Gosse wrote 'Gray took no exercise whatever', which is contradicted by an array of evidence in the poet's letters, for instance: 'At present I am better and take long walks again'; 'Mrs Oliffe was his mother's not his father's sister'; Whibley says that Gosse's suggestion that Gray was 'invited to meet Rousseau' comes only from a statement 'I have seen no Rousseau nor anybody else.' In many cases, however, Whibley contents himself with such notes as 'This is an assumption based on ignorance', or 'This is a rash statement, contrary to fact'; and sometimes his annotations are merely pedantic. For instance, where Gosse has written: 'On the 18th November they passed on to Genoa,' Whibley notes 'They left Turin on the 18th of November and reached Genoa on the 20th.'

More serious was the evidence of carelessness in Gosse's edition of Gray's *Works*. After all, *Gray*, the life for Morley's series, was a book for the general reader, which made no great claims to scholarship. The edition of the *Works* was a very different matter. In his Preface, Gosse put forward a claim which turned out to be unjustified. 'As far, then, as regards the largest section of Gray's prose writings – the letters which he addressed to Thomas Wharton – I am relieved from the responsibility of reference to any previous text, for I have scrupulously printed these, as though they never had been published before, direct from the originals, which exist in a thick volume among the MSS in the Manuscript Department of the British Museum.' Unfortunately, Gosse had in fact employed a copyist (always a risky undertaking) to copy the letters in the Egerton MSS, and the copyist, finding the script hard going and discovering that the letters had been published by Mitford, soon began to copy from the printed word and not from the originals.

A few errors were discovered by the American reviewers: the *Nation* critic found eight letters misdated. And the *Literary World* pointed out, as no one else had, several errors even in the text of the 'Elegy written in a country churchyard'. In Gosse's reprint of the Pembroke manuscript, there should have been six marginal alterations, 'of which Gosse gives us only four'. Further, while Gosse had printed one of these alterations in two places, the wording in each case was different, and in neither instance did it agree with the published facsimile of the manuscript.

But the strictures were mild and made no impression on Gosse's general reputation. It was not until 1900 that the Reverend Duncan Tovey called attention to the errors in Gosse's edition. Then, in 1915, Paget Toynbee pointed out further inaccuracies, which showed Tovey was also not without fault. There is a letter from Gosse to Toynbee in 1927, which refers to his own edition as 'a production marred by much juvenile inexperience'. But this was all far ahead, and in 1883, working on his edition with the help of the lazy amanuensis, Gosse was confident and relaxed. He was also ambitious for future recognition of his standing as a scholar. There had been rumours in the papers in 1880 that he was trying for the Professorship of Poetry at Oxford. Gosse called that 'an absurd invention'. He was, he pointed out, not eligible, not being an MA of the university. He was not, of course, a graduate of any university. But there was no doubt that he relished the idea of a connection with the ancient universities. There was one job going for which, it seemed, his lack of a degree did not rule him out. This was the newly founded Clark Lectureship at Cambridge.

In March 1883 Gosse started rallying support for his candidature. He decided to ask Matthew Arnold, whom he knew only slightly but was to describe as 'the prophet whom we loved and almost worshipped'. They had met at dinner tables in London a few times. The previous year, Gosse had sent him, as was his wont with people he wanted to cultivate, a warm comment on an Arnold poem in one of the periodicals. Arnold had replied at length though 'buried under Examination papers'. He felt the public was in a mood for realism, for poems 'about the suicides of agnostic operatives or perhaps the Wimbledon poisoning case. But believe me, that one who tries to maintain in his work what Shakespeare calls a "reserved honesty" values deeply such a suffrage as yours and is truly helped by it.' A few months later, Arnold wrote again at length to thank Gosse for his life of Gray. And in 1883, he was happy to recommend Gosse to the

Master and Fellows of Trinity College as their first Clark Lecturer.

So was Tennyson. 'I know of no one,' he wrote, 'more likely to fulfil the duties of the office satisfactorily.' Robert Browning, who, as we have seen, knew Gosse much better, wrote enthusiastically to Gosse himself:

> May I be permitted to say, from a real knowledge of your various qualifications for the Post, that I believe you to be, in every respect, thoroughly competent to the discharge of its duties; and that I am anxious to testify my own gratitude to the University which, a year or two since, so deeply obliged me by the bestowment of a signal honour, when I attempt – never so humbly – to enlist among her servants one so efficient as yourself.
>   Believe, me, dear Mr Gosse
>   Yours very sincerely, Robert Browning.

The next month Browning wrote to the Rev. J. D. Williams: 'My friend Gosse is a candidate for this new Professorship of Literature at Cambridge. He is an exceedingly fit man for the post, I think – as men now go and are in evidence. Tennyson thinks the same. I hope he has a chance.'

Obviously he had a very good chance. In addition, Gosse enlisted the support of Sidney Colvin, Slade Professor of Fine Art and Fellow of Trinity. He had given some information to Gosse and had questioned whether he could fit in the number of lectures (twenty a year) with the claims of his work at the Board of Trade. Gosse assured him it could be arranged, and Colvin, who was in Rome for the vacation, wrote to the Master of Trinity bearing witness to Gosse's capabilities.

> He is not only himself a poet, but a remarkably learned and minute student of poetical literature and especially the English poetical literature of the seventeenth century. On that branch of the subject he is, I imagine, the best authority living . . . He is accustomed to oral exposition and has a vivacious manner and good delivery . . . I feel sure he would be a very fit and creditable person for the work. He would moreover bring to its performance a zealous and enthusiastic desire of success.

In April, Gosse was alarmed to read in the *Athenaeum* that Leslie Stephen was a rival candidate. He wrote immediately to Stephen, whom he knew well, both socially and through his regular contributions to the *Cornhill* in the years of Stephen's editorship. Stephen was indeed a strong candidate. In 1882 he had been appointed editor of that mammoth Victorian enterprise, the new *Dictionary of National Biography*, but it was now 'shaking down into a kind of routine' and he thought he would have time enough for some lectures in Cambridge and the pleasant renewal of old associations. For Stephen, apart from his standing as editor and critic, was himself a Cambridge man.

He had distinguished himself as an undergraduate at Trinity Hall, and had eventually secured a fellowship which necessitated his ordination. This had apparently caused no problems, but after eight years, in 1862, he had decided he could no longer take chapel services. He was asked to resign his tutorship but lingered on in Cambridge. 'He could not tear himself away,' his biographer records. In fact, he did not resign his fellowship until his marriage in 1867. It was natural for him to agree when some Cambridge friends suggested he applied for the new Clark Lectureship. But it vexed him, he wrote to Gosse, to think that his success would be at the expense of anyone so well qualified as Gosse was, 'and the more as you seem to desire the position more than I do myself . . . I should be very willing to speak of your claims, if it would not, perhaps, look a little absurd.' Edward Dowden, Professor of English at Dublin, had asked both Gosse and Stephen to support *his* application. Hearing Gosse was standing, Dowden wrote, 'This is a horrible position.' It was certainly becoming a little absurd. 'And today I have heard from a bigger person than any of us, who *may* be a rival.' Dowden had thought Gosse was perfectly happy in that inscrutable office at the Board of Trade, piping on viol and flute.

In fact, Gosse was far from happy at the Board of Trade. A great deal of the work was 'shockingly dull'. He was always too prudent (his own word) to go freelance, but he felt the burden of his official life dreadfully. Though his masters seem to us to have been quite understanding, he recorded how much he hated 'the absolute necessity to appear at a certain hour every day at Whitehall'. As the years went by, the work seemed to increase and the salary stayed the same. In 1884 he tried to get back to the British Museum Reading Room. 'The Board of Trade has no desire to part with Mr Gosse,' the official memo read, 'but they think it a pity that a gentleman of special literary ability and acquirements, such as Mr Gosse undoubtedly is, should not be employed in a position where these abilities and acquirements would be more valuable and important than they can be in the performance of such work as the Board of Trade is able to give him.' But in spite of this tortuous reasoning, and an intervention from Robert Browning to Lord Carnarvon, the British Museum apparently had no need of him.

Nor, in 1883, did Trinity College, Cambridge. On May 19th, the Master of Trinity, W. H. Thompson, wrote to say that Leslie Stephen had been appointed but that if Stephen had not offered himself, there was no doubt that Gosse would have been the successful candidate. He hoped there would be some future occasion on which they might again discuss his merits, 'which were felt by all to be great'. 'P.S. I send back by the same post your testimonials from the Laureate and Mr Browning, also letters from Mr Arnold and Prof. Colvin, which you may like to have.'

Gosse wrote to Browning to break the news: 'I was only beaten by one vote. A failure so very near a success seems to me to be a matter for congratulation when the opponent is so eminent as Leslie Stephen; and I have always the delight of remembering that I was your candidate.' He was certainly not down-hearted, and his admiration for Stephen was real. He would write much later: 'Of all the remarkable men whom it has been my privilege to know . . . , there is not one on whom I look back with more respect than I do on Leslie Stephen.' Of course he commented, as everyone did, on his formidable silences, 'Alpine in their desolation'. He could even reduce Gosse to silence, which few could. Like James, Gosse would record 'immense walks, of a wholly speechless character' near St Ives. They walked over to Redruth, to see the annual meeting of Cornish wrestlers. 'But the implacable long legs of my companion, like a pair of brass compasses, with the fierce sweep of red beard at my side, reduced me to a sad condition before we reached the arena.' Like Stephen's daughter, Virginia Woolf, he knew that Stephen would never get anywhere near the letter Z. But neither would Gosse himself, of course, and he found Stephen 'temperate in judgment, strenuous without ostentation, affectionate without sentimentality'. The Clark election did nothing to harm their relationship.

In the May of 1884, Hamo Thornycroft was married to Agatha Cox, with Edmund Gosse as best man and Tessa Gosse, aged six, as one of the bridesmaids. 'Beauty and Strength were met together,' Edmund said, quoting Shelley. Agatha was indeed beautiful. Thomas Hardy told Gosse she was the most beautiful woman in England and that he thought of her when imagining Tess. 'Her lips are roses full of snow,' he quoted in his diary.

Thornycroft's wedding was an occasion that Gosse faced with considerably mixed feelings. He had accepted the idea that Thorny-croft should marry. But the fact that he should marry Agatha was more difficult. 'I long for your happiness with mingled hopes and fears, the one as irrational as the other. The problem is so terrible to the onlooker . . .' he wrote in April, when the date had at last been fixed. Then, on the Thornycrofts' honeymoon, he wrote: 'It is truly delightful to me to feel from the tone of your notes that you are deeply happy. It is the birthday of your life, is it not? . . . And you who have made others' lives blossom like the rose, are now at last and for the first time tasting the extremity of bliss.'

The Thornycrofts were spending some time in the Valley of the Rocks, near Linton in Devon, an area which is the subject of one of the sections of *Seaside Pleasures*, published anonymously in 1853. The family copy I have in front of me as I write bears the pencilled words '"The Valley of the Rocks" is the sole composition of my mother. E.G.' He wrote to Hamo of his shadowy memory of Emily 'with her red hair and sorrowful white face . . . You know that I take little interest in Parents as a rule; I think them a mistake, but I make an exception in my unfortunate mother with her morbid intensity and her touch of genius. If you see her ghost in the Valley of the Rocks, you will know her, for I am her image in features.' He was working on another sculpture article and found Hamo's name 'a singularly pleasant one to write; I dare say Agatha will sympathise with this'.

Agatha was, not surprisingly, a little wary of Edmund, just as he was of her. But she thought Nellie, Hamo reported, was 'enchanting'. At Yattendon in September, Edmund wrote to Nellie: 'Dear old Hamo seemed quite happy and satisfied and forgot to look anxious. Agatha is so genuinely fond of you and quotes you so frankly as a kind of final authority on all matters of taste and propriety, that I cannot help being indulgent to her. But the truth is she is improving as fast as possible.'

There was apparently, in the memories of the years that had gone, nothing to spoil a life-long, uncomplicated and devoted family relationship. Thornycroft sent young Philip a cricket bat for his fifth birthday (with sketches showing how he should hold it). Edmund would shake his head over the infant Oliver Thornycroft: 'wonderfully, almost nobly disobedient', who could only be wheedled off to bed 'by three persons, on the promise of toffee in his bath'. Much later, the two fathers would go together to look at bicycles for Tessa's twenty-first birthday. They would dine together regularly and, when out of London, exchange casual affectionate letters, full of references to children's measles and holiday haymaking. If Hamo Thornycroft had died young, as Tennyson's Hallam had died, Gosse's feelings for him in the years ahead would of course have been quite different. The last warm letter from Thornycroft to Gosse was dated a week before he died as an old man in December 1925, from shock following the amputation of a leg, just as Mary Johnson had died fifty-five years before.

9

America and After: the outer cliff of fame

As EARLY AS December 1875, as we have seen, Gosse wrote to E. C. Stedman, American banker and man of letters: 'The hope of recognition in America has always seemed one of the highest objects of ambition.' Gosse owed a great deal of his American reputation to Stedman, who made sure his work was reviewed in American periodicals and put him in touch with Richard Watson Gilder, in January 1880. Gilder was himself a poet, and editor of the important *Scribner's*, which was soon to be transmuted into the *Century Illustrated Monthly Magazine*. Gosse with his customary energy and tact was able to write to Gilder who was in London: 'I think I must have been almost the first person in England to peruse and enjoy your *New Day*, which emboldens me to say, "Years have flown since I knew thee first,"' quoting from one of Gilder's own poems. It was an excellent start to a new relationship. Gilder was able to write to his sister that he had lunched with Gosse and Dobson, 'tea'd with Gosse', on one of the Sunday afternoons that were becoming famous, and had had four chats with Browning, probably through Gosse's introduction. Shortly after Gilder's return to America, he published a Gosse poem in *Scribner's*, and early the following year Gilder commissioned Gosse to organize a series on prominent Victorian writers. Gosse's own piece on Browning, the genesis of which we have already seen, was one of this series. Gosse got Andrew Lang to do Matthew Arnold and J. A. Symonds to do Tennyson.

As early as March 1881 Gilder was suggesting to Gosse that he should take on an American lecture tour. In June 1881, when Roswell Smith, chief proprietor of the *Century*, visited England (together, to Gosse's amazement, with his personal chaplain) arrangements were made for Gosse to become the *Century Magazine*'s first London agent, at £200 a year, a useful addition to his basic £400 from the Board of Trade. There was an English edition published in London (first by Warne, later by Fisher Unwin) but its contents were identical with the

American edition. It was Gosse's job to pass on his own and other people's ideas for contributions, to commission work the American office wanted from English writers, and to read manuscripts submitted to him, passing on to America those he thought might be possible. 'My functions,' as he wrote to Unwin in 1886, 'do not in any way include the acceptance of articles.' This would cause problems: animosity from 'persons who have supposed me capable and not desirous of getting their things accepted in the *Century*'.

The *Century* paid well; it had an extremely large circulation by English standards. Writing to Thomas Hughes (author of *Tom Brown's Schooldays*) in 1882, to commission an article on the present condition of the English working man, Gosse told him that the magazine had a circulation of 150,000, 'and I need not point out to you how very large a field of influence this represents'. The large circulation was in fact also a problem. Gosse was a little highbrow for them. 'Are you not interested in anything but art and literature?' Gilder was to ask Gosse in exasperation on one occasion, encouraging him to get James's friend, W. E. Norris, to write an article on golf. The *Century* might serialize Henry James but, as Gilder put it, he would rather have an article by General Grant on a battle won by him than twenty articles by Daudet or Mistral. When Alice Meynell wrote an article on Illustrators of Dickens, Gosse was told to tell Mrs Meynell that 'as it at present stands, the critical is greater than the personal novelty in it'. They were rather keen on personal novelty.

If Gosse sometimes seemed most concerned with establishing his own American reputation and with finding American markets for English material, that was certainly not the whole story. He was genuinely interested in American literature, for all its lack of a long and impressive past. He did not see it, as so many critics did, as alien in the way German or French literature seemed, nor did he fall in with Matthew Arnold's short-sighted view of considering that there was no such thing as American literature, only English literature which happened to be written by Americans. There was never anything insular in Gosse's literary interests. He was soon to become the editor of a series of translations into English of the best of foreign literature, for the new firm of William Heinemann. He was particularly convincing when he said: 'There can be no patriotism in matters of literature. A man writes good verse or bad verse whether he is a Bostonian or a dweller in the parts of Libya about Cyrene.' Gosse did a great deal to review and publicize American writers, and can be justly seen as some sort of a pioneer of American studies in England; but he worried more and more about American critical chauvinism. 'Five-sixths of the poets lauded in the *Century* have no more notion what *verse* is than a tom-cat.' There should be no protectionism in literature. An editor's job, he reminded Gilder, was to get the best things wherever they came from.

'When will we have a strong literature in this country, if we do not give a place to it?' Gilder wrote to Gosse, sometimes preferring George Washington Cable to Robert Louis Stevenson. By the end of the decade, Gilder's policy had rendered an English agent unnecessary, but he remained interested in exceptional material. Gosse had persuaded Christina Rossetti to write on Dante. 'I like my 20 guineas very much,' she wrote to Gosse, thinking he had been too generous as so much of the article consisted of quotation. Browning could not be persuaded to co-operate. He said he did not want his poems to be found like uninvited guests by someone casually turning over the pages of a periodical. Wild sums were offered him by the magazines (even £400 on one occasion), but nothing would make him change his mind. In 1891 Gosse had the chance to introduce Kipling's early work to *Century* readers, in an article which stands as a useful critical summary.

Gosse himself came in for some of the prevailing anti-English feeling. A review by R. H. Stoddard in *The Critic* (22nd April 1882) put contemporary English poetry firmly in its place:

Rossetti is the intellectual sire of Morris, Swinburne, Gosse, Lang – the whole band of living English warblers, of whom the best are merely mocking birds . . . It is severe, no doubt, to call all late English verse rubbish, but rubbish it is, and it is shot largely upon us here in America.

Even Gosse's relations with Stedman, his first admirer, were not always happy; nor was it easy for Gosse to find an American publisher for *On Viol and Flute*. Austin Dobson had had great success with a volume published by Henry Holt, and Gosse hoped to follow in his footsteps. Holt finally did bring out an edition in 1883 (in a selection made by Dobson and Cosmo Monkhouse) but in February 1881 Gosse was feeling sufficiently 'hipped' (his word) with the American scene to dash off these lines to Dobson:

> From far-off pseudo-bards and yankee dolts,
> From gushing Stedmans and your brazen Holts,
> I turn where fortune at my elbow lends
> One genuine poet and the best of friends.

When *On Viol and Flute* did appear in America, Gosse found himself being reviewed by George Parsons Lathrop in the *Atlantic Monthly* along with Browning's *Jocoseria*. Lathrop, Hawthorne's son-in-law, was lavish in his praise. He compared Gosse's insight with that of Emerson; he talked of Gosse's fullness, sweetness, naturalness and 'the polished grace of his exposition', ending by describing Browning as an oak and Gosse as the 'violet growing in a hollow at the foot of the oak. Every one knows that to ascertain the relative value of the oak and violet, aesthetically, is out of the question, and that we cannot dispense with either.' Gosse saw the review as 'one of those rare messages of sympathy and encouragement which make an artist's life worth living'.

The rush of American visitors in London in the summer of 1883 was 'though enchanting to the highest degree, a little overwhelming,' Gosse wrote to Gilder. Chief among them (James, after all, was not a visitor) was William Dean Howells, whom Gosse entertained at the rose-laden dinner party at the Savile that June. George Moore was to remark that while Henry James went abroad and read Turgenev, William Dean Howells stayed at home and read Henry James. There was some truth in it, though Howells had in fact started his career as Lincoln's consul in Venice. He was at this point much more successful as a novelist in America than was James. But now, having just given up editing the *Atlantic Monthly* after ten years, he was enjoying some time in Europe. He had first met Gosse the year before and had shown an early extravagance in friendship.

Howells's *A Modern Instance* was then being serialized in the *Century*, and Gosse considered it the greatest work of American fiction since Hawthorne. (Stevenson hated it for its seeming to be a tract against divorce; James compared it with *Romola*.) Gosse thought that Howells's extreme popularity in America and the instinctive dislike of him in England was because he, as a democratic writer, questioned, as James did not, the English romantic-aristocratic tradition in fiction. Gosse wrote to Howells before they had even met: 'Our friend Henry James tells me that you dislike, as I heartily do, society with a capital S.' James was coming round to thinking that gilded halls, after he had been in so many of them, were 'a simple nuisance'. There would be a time when Gosse would feel differently but, for the moment, he was very happy to supply Howells with society with a rather small s.

Howells was bowled over by it. In August 1882, soon after their first meeting, Howells had written, ridiculously, to Gosse: 'I had such a lovely time last night that I would now like to cut the ties of husband and father, and come to live with you. Is there not some law or privilege by which you could adopt an elderly foreigner of fading intellect? I would do chores about the house, run errands, tell Theresa stories and make myself generally useful. Think of it seriously: I mean business.'

But Howells could not be taken seriously, of course. He was well known as a giggler and Gosse replied in kind: 'You shall be welcomed, oh! how gladly into the House of the Gigglers. In that home there are no chores to be done, and no errands to be run. It is giggling and making giggle from morning to night.' In a subsequent letter, after a visit to Stoke Poges clutching Gosse's *Gray*, Howells refers amusingly to the sort of provincialism which was a current theme in nineteenth-century literary relations between England and America:

A Boston man returned a copy of Shakespeare once with the remark that he did not believe there were ten men in the State of Massachusetts who could have written that book; and for my part I remember few churches in Ohio at once so old and so picturesque as that of Stoke Poges. I admit as much as that.

There seemed some question of the Americans underrating Dickens and Thackeray; the newspapers were full of it. Gosse sent Howells his 'doggerel by a candid friend':

Motto for the American critic
Ho!   the old school!   Thackeray, Dickens!
Throw them out to feed the chickens. –
Ho!   the new school!   James and H——s!
Lay the flattery on with trowels.

Gosse suspected that the reason why the Americans disliked Dickens and Thackeray was that they flourished under a corrupt and pestilent royalty. Howells boasted of his own 'crimson opinions', but wondered what he had been supposed to have been saying. He declared no Englishman could rate the novelists higher than he did, and said he would still be friends with Gosse even if he were made a peer.

The friendship flourished. 'How kind you were to us in London! When I think over the mingled sweetness of Mrs Gosse and yourself it seems too precious ever to have been poured into such earthen cups as we are,' Howells wrote with typical enthusiasm. On the way home to America in July 1883 he posted a brief letter to James Russell Lowell, the American Minister in London: 'I gave Gosse a note of introduction to you, mindful of the kindly feeling you expressed for him, and of his advantage. In this I hope I did not presume too far, and that I am not wrong in asking you to remember him in connection with the Lowell Lectures.'

Howells was to work extremely hard to secure for Gosse the invitation to give a course of lectures at the Lowell Institute in Boston. In October 1883 Lowell invited Gosse 'to dine quietly with us on Sunday if not better engaged'. Gosse had paved the way by sending not only Howells's letter of introduction, but also No. 2 of a limited edition of a poem he had written in tribute on the 75th birthday of Oliver Wendell Holmes. No. 1 had pleased Dr Holmes himself. But when the invitation to dinner came, Gosse was just starting for Switzerland; and there was no second invitation. 'You will be disgusted to hear I never saw Lowell,' Gosse wrote to Howells.

It must have made Howells's task a little harder. But he was not dismayed. He went to see Dr Benjamin Cotting, Manager of the Lowell Lectures, three times. On the third visit Cotting made the eminent novelist wait so long ('while my heart was getting hot, and my dinner at home getting cold') that Howells got up to go away, caught a glimpse of Cotting in an ante-room and murmured that he would not bother him, that he had written all that was necessary in a letter and he would hope to hear from him. Eventually the favourable reply came. Howells was in a new house, 302 Beacon Street, and wrote to Gosse: 'We have a roof over us at last, and if we had you and Mrs Gosse under it with us, we should be perfectly happy . . . We talk habitually of "the Gosses' room", "the Gosses' closet", "the Gosses' wash-stand" etc.'

On 15th February 1884 Howells gave evidence in a letter to Mrs James Fields of further unselfish activity: 'I have written to Dr Gilman at Baltimore hoping to get Gosse the Johns Hopkins course also. I wish something might be done at Cornell! The six Lowell lectures only give him $750 and that would be too little to come so far on.' Howells was, in fact, as he put it to Gosse, 'diligently working up a boom for you'.

In April Gosse was able to write to Marychurch that the Lowell Institute had made a better offer. 'I asked for a little time to think about it, and . . . they have repeated their invitation, this time offering £200 . . . Johns Hopkins University have made a vague offer to me to repeat the same six lectures at Baltimore. They talk of £100. So that I believe myself justified in accepting.' The Board of Trade had granted special leave of absence. He would be away for ten weeks: the six weeks of his total annual holiday for 1884, three weeks' special leave and one week of the following year's holiday. Nellie would go with him, and there was the possibility of other lectures.

If I could pocket £400, I should spend a very pleasant holiday without expense, and yet have something to put by when I come back.

The subject of my lectures will be "From Shakespeare to Pope", an enquiry into the causes and character of the change from the Romantic to the so-called Classical School of Poetry in the 17th century. The subject is important in the history of criticism, and has scarcely been touched. I propose simply to write a book on this subject, which I shall read on six consecutive nights and print on returning to England.

It didn't sound a very beguiling prospect, but Gosse was full of enthusiasm. He wrote to Howells that he was already thinking of epigrams: 'I fancy I may promise that this shall be the best book I have ever written . . . It would fill a gap in English criticism and my reading for fifteen years has prepared me to fill it. It would be no rechauffé of other people's notions. I can promise original research . . .' To Stedman, he wrote, 'I am most anxious that I should not lay myself open to the charge of being jejune, slovenly or thin. I believe I have never written so well before, I have certainly never tried before so original and difficult a thesis.' The lectures would be a great success; it was the book of them that would prove a disaster.

Edmund Gosse spent a hard-working, almost holidayless year in 1884. Besides working on the basic course of lectures for America, he wanted to have some single ones to offer: more popular ones he could give extempore on Hans Christian Andersen, Gray and Dante Gabriel Rossetti. But there were some diversions. He spent Easter at Stanmore with Eliza Brightwen; there was the Thornycroft wedding; he took Tessa down to Marychurch. He saw a good deal of Henry James. In March, James wrote in his notebook:

Edmund Gosse mentioned to me the other day a fact which struck me as a possible *donnée*. He was speaking of J.A.S., the writer . . . of his extreme and somewhat hysterical aestheticism, etc; the sad conditions of his life, exiled to Davos by the state of his lungs, the illness of his daughter, etc. Then he said that, to crown his unhappiness, poor S's wife was in no sort of sympathy with what he wrote . . . 'I have never read any of John's works. I think them most undesirable.'

James was apparently unaware at this point that Symonds's homosexuality was the real issue. But he saw '*un drame intime*', the clash over a child. 'If it were not too gruesome, the mother might be supposed to sacrifice him, rather than let him fall under the influence of the father.' It was the story which turned immediately into 'The Author of "Beltraffio"', published that summer in the *English Illustrated Magazine*.

Fifteen years later, Gosse told James an anecdote about a lady he had seen in a railway carriage, a widow in full mourning, seen off by sympathetic relatives at one station and greeted further down the line by a handsome gentleman. James wrote it in his notebook with the annotation 'kindly intended for a possible tip' – but deliberate tips are rarely useful. Gosse was more often a source, not of stories, but of encouragement. On June 9th when Gosse had just read 'The Author of "Beltraffio"', James wrote, with characteristic over-emphasis: 'You obey a very humane inspiration whenever you murmur bravo! in the ear of the much-attempting, slowly-composing, easily-discouraged and constantly dissatisfied fictionist Your ever grateful Henry James.'

But before the story was published, Gosse had received unexpectedly in the post several offers. On 24th April Gilder wrote enclosing an offer from Professor Henry Beers of a chair at Yale University. Gilder thought that the $3,500 salary might not be adequate: 'I am going to suggest that they offer two chairs, if such a thing is possible, one of Literature and the other of Scandinavian Languages, or something of that sort . . . The great question as to whether you would wish to come to America for permanent residence, is one no one can decide for you.' Gosse was certainly not prepared to abandon at this stage everything he had been building up in London. He rejected the offer, with profound thanks, by return of post. Gosse apparently also rejected similar offers from both Harvard and Johns Hopkins at this period. He told his father the Baltimore chair had a salary of £1,000. 'It was a temptation no doubt but one which I put aside at once.'

The offer which delighted Gosse was in a letter from the Master of Trinity College, Cambridge. It read:

> Mr Leslie Stephen, at the end of his completed course of lectures last term, sent me a letter containing his resignation of the office of Clark lecturer, on the grounds of its incompatability with the performance of his literary work in London . . . At the first meeting of the Council this term . . . we agreed unanimously to give you the refusal of the office Mr Stephen resigns.

The appointment would be from 1st October 1884, initially for two years. Twenty lectures in the year were to be given at times to suit his convenience. The lecturer's salary was £300 a year.

On Christmas Day 1883 Leslie Stephen (with eight children around him, including the infant Virginia) had written to his Bostonian friend, Charles Eliot Norton:

> I was weak enough to add lecturing at Cambridge to my burden and shall go and tell the lads that Addison wrote the *Spectator* and had a quarrel with Pope and that the heroic couplet was popular in those days, and bestow other new and valuable information. Really, I feel ashamed of it. I begin to think enough has been said about all those things . . .

After a couple of terms talking 'twaddle', as he called it, 'to a number of young ladies from Girton and a few idle undergraduates and the youthful prince', he had had enough of it. As a Cambridge man, Stephen could afford to be so cool. Gosse was overjoyed, of course. Ten minutes after getting the Master's offer, he was writing to Robert Louis Stevenson: 'I am writing to you today because I have just – ten minutes ago – become Professor of English Literature in the University of Cambridge.' He had not, in fact. The Clark Lecturer was no such animal, but the inaccurate up-grading seemed to stick. Gosse also circulated the misleading impression, considering his ardent canvassing for the job the previous year, that 'the offer from Cambridge is all the more flattering because I made no sort of appeal for it, not indeed having the vaguest notion that it was open'.

Hearing the news, Howells wrote enthusiastically: 'I can imagine you there in that beautiful old town, in some college with a "back" as lovely as one of Watteau's women, and if I could envy you at all, I should envy you that fate. But I can't envy you; I shall love you the more the luckier you are.' With everything fixed for the American trip, Gosse was feeling equally fond of Howells. He wrote: 'I once helped an eminent French painter to three bananas at once, and he wreathed his arms suddenly about me, and said "O thou dear angel of the good God!" That is just what I say of you.'

Letters of congratulation poured in. Robert Bridges wrote: 'When at Oxford . . . I heard that you had been elected to the Professorship of English Literature at the sister university . . . I am sure that you will be not less glad than I am that your attention will now of necessity be turned to the great writers.' As opposed, presumably he means, to reviewing the new poetry of such as Bridges himself. Andrew Lang wrote, more fantastically, to say how much he wished he had concentrated on 'sound learning that might be professed'. He himself would be condemned to produce endless copy for ever 'till Death or Idiocy' relieved him.

Matthew Arnold, who had just returned from America himself, was 'delighted to see how good an appointment they had made at Cambridge'. Arnold's own lecture tour had not been a complete success, in spite of the splendid trappings of showmanship. He had apparently travelled on a special train with tickets bearing the words 'Matthew Arnold Troupe'. Gosse thought Arnold was better suited to the study or the dinner table than the lecturer's platform. In private talk 'he was perfect', but Gilder told Gosse that the Americans had sensed 'his endeavour to propitiate a people whom he does not respect'. Gosse was invited to dinner by Arnold in June – the Humphry Wards were there too. Arnold told Gosse 'they did not like my manner. The Chicago newspapers said that I resembled an elderly macaw pecking at a trellis of grapes. How lively journalistic fancy is among the Americans! But they were very kind.' Gosse realized Arnold's 'voice and elocution were hardly suited to large democratic audiences. His eye-glass, his Oxford intonation, a certain air which seemed supercilious, in combination with a weak voice and a see-saw utterance, were obstacles to complete enjoyment.' Gosse had certainly heard Arnold lecture. In the preface to his *Collected Poems*, written long after this, he characterizes himself, perhaps a little misleadingly:

If I am a poet at all, I belong to the age of the Franco-German War, of the introduction of Japanese art into Europe, of the discoveries of Huxley and Häckel, and of the Oxford lectures of Matthew Arnold. I smile at this list of names, as a buttercup might smile to find itself rooted on a battlefield; but this is the intellectual topography of these rhymes.

Gosse was not writing much poetry at this period, but he was never prolific. In 1884 most of his energies were going into preparing his lectures for America and for Cambridge. He had, as he had admitted so frankly in that letter home to Marychurch, decided for the main fare in America simply to write a book and read it out. His first Cambridge lecture on 'Poetry at the Death of Shakespeare' was on 25th October 1884 in front of 'a splendid audience of about 200' in the Hall of Trinity College. On his first visit, back in June to make arrangements, Edmund had written to Nellie: 'One feels a very small atom whirled round in the vortex of the university . . . I am to have a set of rooms lent me and to be invited to dine in hall whenever I come. I think everything will be done to make me comfortable except by one or two people . . .'

He was nervous when he gave that first lecture. Laurence Alma-Tadema, who had gone with her aunt Nellie, could see it. 'He had a way, when nervous and agitated, of looking pompous, of thickening somewhat at throat and chin. But as soon as he was well launched upon his lecture his ease returned, the charm of his diction and of his erudition captured his audience.' Writing to Thornycroft, Gosse recorded the Master, sitting 'aloof in a kind of remote silver grandeur', smiling benignly, and the luminous face of young Austen Chamberlain. 'He came this evening, in the dusk, like Nicodemus, and talked in the most engaging way. He seems the cleverest young fellow here, by what people say.' Chamberlain would go on to hold most of the great offices of state, including Chancellor of the Exchequer and Foreign Secretary. Gosse was surrounded by clever young men. He looked little older than they did. People were constantly commenting on his youthful appearance. He was now thirty-five, but Chamberlain would describe him as 'seeming a boy coming up to Cambridge at an unusually early age'.

In America it was undoubtedly part of his appeal. But even before people had seen him there was tremendous curiosity about his visit. The American papers were full of inaccurate comments. Already in June, Elinor Howells was able to send Nellie Gosse a pile of cuttings, showing her the 'Gosse boom' had already begun. The *New York Herald* reported: 'Mr Edmund Gosse, who is professor of literature at Cambridge, England, and enjoys a place in the Foreign Office is described as "a prosperous son of the Muses who talks with the velocity of an American and the elegant precision of an English scholar."' Mrs Howells suggested the reporters would soon be knocking at their door, and Nellie 'had better send word all about your children and your housekeeping and your affairs generally'. She recommended that they should sail on the *Parisian* of the Allan Line. 'Harry James will tell you all about it.' Edmund had four copies of his six lectures printed before leaving England and mailed a copy to Howells, in case they were 'shipwrecked, delayed by icebergs or eaten of polar bears'.

But they reached New York without major incident, though 'constantly afflicted with seasickness'. There was a rather dreadful Thanksgiving Day when 'an attempt was made to get up a little entertainment in the Saloon. I, willing to oblige, consented to tell a story and stood up with a terrible peri-cardiac heaving, to try and be entertaining. Alas! it was a melancholy attempt.' While Edmund was writing to Marychurch about the voyage, Eliza Gosse was writing to cheer the children left in London: 'I have got a new little bird, a goldfinch, and Grandpapa is kind enough to walk into the fields and gather him some thistledown' – an attractive glimpse of the awe-inspiring old man.

If, in July 1884, Gosse had seen himself as 'still hanging by my eyelids to the outer cliff of fame', by the end of the year he must have certainly felt that he had scaled it triumphantly. He and Nellie spent their first evening in America, feeling worn and ghastly after the steamer voyage, at the Gilders' house near their hotel. Interviewers from the various papers came over, 'not such people as we know of', Gosse wrote to Dobson, 'but reporters who stood on the doormat and wrote answers to questions in a little note book, with their billy-cocks under their arms'.

The *Boston Gazette* reported a scramble for tickets for Gosse's series, which sounds more like the preliminary to a cup final than to lectures about poetry from Shakespeare to Pope. 'Last Saturday at 10 o'clock was the time appointed for people to get their seats to hear the far-famed Londoner . . . That morning it rained not only cats and dogs but guns but when your correspondent, fearing a ticket would not be forthcoming from any other source, braved the storm,' he found a crowd already waiting, dripping umbrellas and all. 'By 9.30, the line extended round the hall . . . Several ladies had brought books to read, some found a camp chair to roost on, others entertained themselves by watching the people come in and fall into line, a line that grew longer and longer until it doubled, and at length trebled round the great hall.'

At the first lecture, on Tuesday, 2nd December 1884, all 850 seats were filled and 150 people were turned away. Admittedly the seats were free, according to the custom of the Lowell Institute, but it still seems an extraordinary audience. In the front row, at every single lecture, was the eager aged face of Oliver Wendell Holmes, 'the most eminent man of letters now surviving in America', as Gosse noted with satisfaction. 'Your face in the centre of the crowd is as good as a laurel wreath put publicly about my brows,' he told Holmes. 'We have experienced nothing but happiness,' he wrote to Marychurch after his last Boston lecture. 'My audience all through consisted of the most distinguished literary, scientific and professional people.' When he was not lecturing, he was meeting the cream of his audience at one house or another. Howells gave the first big party he had given since he had entertained Bret Harte in 1871. Many of the Boston surnames crowding the brief entries in Gosse's diary are familiar ones: Longfellow, Aldrich, Perry, Fields, Parkman, Norton, Lowell, Hawthorne, Houghton, Eliot, Peabody. 'Life was crowded with every species of excitement and entertainment.' Everyone wanted to meet the visiting lecturer.

We know of one embarrassing incident at Augustus Lowell's dinner-table, when Charles Eliot Norton, talking about the deterioration of London society, happened to refer to Alma-Tadema's wife as the 'daughter of a cocoa-vendor', not knowing she was Nellie Gosse's sister. Apparently Norton did not notice Gosse's face and continued, thinking of a famous advertisement for Epps cocoa: 'I really do not know which one he married, "Grateful" or "Comforting".' Before Howells could change the subject, Gosse said grimly, 'He married "Grateful"; I married "Comforting" myself.' Gosse 'took Charles's faux pas altogether too tragically', Henry James commented to Grace Norton, hearing the story. Nellie was, of course, completely un-ruffled.

This seems to have been the only slight stain on the Boston visit. 'We have enjoyed,' Gosse wrote to Thornycroft, 'but I must not be reported to have said so – the greatest social success that any English man of letters has enjoyed since Thackeray lectured in Boston.' Oliver Wendell Holmes said to Gosse, 'We are all a little in love with you.' Invitations to lecture poured in from all over the country, from California and Chicago which he would never see. 'It is quite a surprise to find how well known I am in this country, how much wider an audience my books have than in England. And it is less of a surprise, but no less of a pleasure to find how warmly *you* are admired here,' he wrote to his father.

In Boston with characteristic energy, among all the junketing, he found time to borrow an advance copy from Oliver Wendell Holmes of his *Emerson* in the American Men of Letters series, read it late at night, and wrote a piece on it for the *Pall Mall Gazette*. It was the earliest review of the book to appear and comments on his piece were in the New York papers long before he left the States. He suffered the typical author's frustration of finding the bookshops completely out of his own books just at the time when there was most demand for them. He walked late at night with Howells round the dingiest parts of Boston. At one point, the novelist murmured, 'How happy I should be if I could see everything that is done and hear everything that is said in such a house as that for a week.' Gosse made various realistic suggestions about what might be going on behind 'those dull win-dows' and Howells did not smile. 'Instead he lifted his hand, as if to ward off a blow and cried "Oh! don't say that! I couldn't bear it; I couldn't write a line if I thought such things were happening!"' Gosse seemed to need to remind his socialist friend that life was not all nightingales and applause.

There was a cloudless sky and temperatures well below zero. They had the coldest night there had been in New England for eight years. Gosse was amazed by the central heating: 'Every house is heated by one or more furnaces, so that you turn out of the terrible parching

Arctic horror of the streets into a delicate tropic climate at a step.' His enthusiasm and interest in everything was of course attractive. 'My mind was just like touchwood, ready to be fired . . . I have been asking questions all day long. I came to America, intending to enjoy myself, but I have done so to an extent absolutely beyond my hopes.'

Of course, everyone likes to be liked. There were a few predictable anti-English mumblings in the papers, or at any rate a determination not to be too impressed. One paper muttered, 'It seems at first sight like a work of supererogation for this bright student of English literature to come all the way from London to Boston to teach the Americans about a dozen writers of whom they can learn all they wish to know through Johnson's *Lives of the Poets*;' but it came round to high praise of 'Prof. Gosse'. 'He is perhaps as fine a specimen of the modern man of letters, poet, prose writer and critic, as England has ever sent over to America . . . None of the younger English writers has within the last ten years come forward more rapidly in reputation and influence.' The *Washington Post* declared him 'an intellectual-looking, fine specimen of the Anglo-Saxon race', with 'light blonde hair and moustache'.

When he was talking in New York (a series of 'parlor lectures' at 5 dollars a ticket), the reporter from the *New York Tribune* spoke of his clear, musical voice and said, 'From the first word to the last, Mr Gosse was listened to with breathless attention, in a silence broken only by the ripple of applause as his last words were uttered and the manuscript closed.' The *New York Times* was amazed at his success, considering he was speaking on a rather unpopular subject. It praised the fact that his delivery was free from the mannerisms and positive defects of utterance that marred the lectures of several distinguished Britons who lately came across the Atlantic. He was certainly a more attractive figure than the elderly macaw Matthew Arnold or the 'fatuous cad' Oscar Wilde (as James had described him in Washington two years before). 'Edmund is liked everywhere he goes,' Nellie wrote to Marychurch.

'I feel more thoroughly fêted than words can say,' Edmund wrote to Thornycroft. 'It is curious how easily one slips into taking all this as a matter of course – to march in first to the dining-room, to rise in response to a flattering toast, to make a humorous, and then a pathetic and then a complimentary allusion, and sink to my seat in a flutter of sympathetic applause, – it all seems so natural now that I quite miss it when I happen to escape it. It will be hard, I suppose, to come back into obscurity and England again, but yet quite refreshing to find myself once more in the close quiet circle of home-friends, no longer a public character.'

In another letter, a fortnight later, he wrote to Thornycroft:

I will confess to you that with all the brightness and variety and all the incense of flattery and publicity, I shall be glad enough to settle down again at home. It has been a splendid episode, but through it all I am homesick to see my children and to see you. One of the three anchors of my life is over here, but two are on the other side of the Atlantic. I will not ask you if you love me still, because I know you do . . . It has been nice to think that Tessa has been with you. I hope she has been no trouble and that her little profile reminds you of mine . . .

As for Nellie, she was looking lovely. At the Charity Ball in the Opera House in Baltimore, 'she made quite a sensation. Red hair is very unusual here. Nellie puffed hers out so as to make a great mass of it, and then fastened a wreath of asparagus-foliage (like fennel) around it, and adorned it further with three blossoms of a lilac orchid – it was most daring and most successful. Among all the flashing Baltimore beauties, she quite held her own, with an originality and an individuality. She has enjoyed the whole affair like a child; we have had the most delicious time together, it has been quite a honeymoon.'

Back in Boston, Howells was finding the city palpitating with praise of Gosse. The Perrys were talking him over, and 'they said, *he* mostly – "And isn't *Mrs* Gosse nice, too! I liked *her*."' Howells avoided the eye of Oliver Wendell Holmes when they passed in Beacon Street. 'I could not stand any more praise of Gosse from him.' The President of Harvard (where Gosse had given a lecture, unpaid, to six hundred people and thunderous applause) was encouraging Howells to urge Gosse to come to their Cambridge for a year. 'Mrs Eliot and he were full of your sickening praise. I threw in a little ridicule and detraction.'

Gosse lectured all over the place; his extempore lectures on Gray were particularly successful. He travelled backwards and forwards, fitting in one lecture in New York between two in Baltimore on successive days. He liked Baltimore best of all the cities. He had to lecture there in the Peabody Institute, there being no room in the university large enough for the 650 who wanted to hear him. Even in the Institute, it was so crowded that several people fainted. Gosse found Boston 'slightly priggish, New York vague, vast and bustling, Philadelphia solid but dull, Washington dazzling but too fatiguing. On the whole Baltimore would be the place to live at. It is a lovely, southern city, full of light . . . The society is brilliant, but easy and refined, full of grace and charm, lots of lovely women, balls, parties and receptions going on all the time, the very Paradise of young people, without any parade of wealth.'

At Wells College, a girl student met him with a sleigh at the station and supplied him with whisky after the lecture. He lectured at Smith, at Cornell, at Yale – any fee between nothing and one hundred dollars would satisfy him, he said. (Perhaps he did not know that Wilde had been paid a thousand dollars a lecture.) He had been to Concord and gazed at Emerson's grave. His driver said, 'Mr E. hain't got his stone up yet; he's been dead long enough, but he was very particular about the stone and his son hain't found the right sort yet.'

'What is Concord without Emerson?' John Greenleaf Whittier asked Gosse, when he visited that aged poet, with his black eyes and black eyebrows, snow-white beard and snow-white hair. He told Gosse stories of the Concord riots of 1835 which seemed the only vivid episode in his quiet Quaker life. Whittier is the author of a favourite hymn:

> Dear Lord and Father of mankind
> Forgive our foolish ways . . .

But few read him now; and it is Gosse's visit to Walt Whitman which has been the focus of much more attention. The account of his visit which he gives in his 1893 essay on Whitman in *Critical Kit-Kats* has often been quoted. It is curiously in opposition with the facts, but, considering how unreliable Gosse's memory was, this was not necessarily a deliberate re-writing of history. In the essay Gosse suggests that he was not in any sense a worshipping disciple as so many visitors to Camden were.

> The visitor whose experience – and it was a very delightful one – is now to be chronicled, started under what was, perhaps, the disadvantage of being very unwilling to go . . . When I was in Boston in the winter of 1884, I received a note from Whitman asking me not to leave America without coming to see him. My first instinct was promptly to decline the invitation. Camden, New Jersey, was a very long way off. But better counsels prevailed; curiosity and civility combined to draw me, and I wrote him that I would come. It would be fatuous to mention all this, if it were not that I particularly wish to bring out the peculiar magic of the old man, acting not on a disciple, but on a stiff-necked and froward unbeliever.

It is quite possible that Gosse had forgotten his own passionate discipleship as a very young man. He may even have forgotten the letter he wrote on 29th December 1884: 'I am very anxious not to leave this country without paying my respects to you, and bearing to you in person the messages which I bring from Mr Swinburne and other common friends. I propose therefore if it be not inconvenient to you, to call upon you in Camden next Saturday next, in the forenoon.'

Certainly there is no diary entry for this letter he wrote himself, but there is one for Whitman's reply on January 1st. Whitman wrote simply:

> Dear Mr Gosse,
> I shall be glad to see you – Call about 11 forenoon if convenient – I live less than half a mile from the ferry landing here, crossing from Philadelphia.
> Walt Whitman

There could even have been another earlier approach from Whitman, for the day before noting Whitman's letter in his diary, he had already written to Thornycroft: 'I have just had a note from Walt Whitman, asking me to come and see him at Camden in New Jersey. So I shall see another of the principal American curiosities.' Certainly he wanted to give Thornycroft the impression, whether it was true or not, that the invitation came from Whitman.

Logan Pearsall Smith, who with his sister Mary had been in Gosse's audience in Boston ('Oh, Logan, we are at the very heart of things!' she had murmured, her eyes brimming with emotion, when Gosse mentioned the sacred word Botticelli), tells a lively story of how Mary, meeting Gosse on his way to Whitman's house, had crawled with him through a window as the poet did not hear their knock on the door. This story was picked up and now has wide circulation, but Gosse years later angrily denied this informal entrance and certainly his diary suggests Mary Pearsall Smith had as inventive a memory as Gosse himself. It was presumably she and her friend who had crawled through a window.

The diary report for 3rd January 1885 reads barely thus:

> By the ferry over to Camden. Walt Whitman's modest little house. W. Whitman on the plate. Hobbled halfway downstairs. Uncarpeted room with bright outlook on to the street. Stove which he constantly attended to. Long white hair, open shirt, broad white hat lying around. Genial manner. 'My friend.' Spoke of Swinburne and Tennyson. Most kind. Head from behind like Darwin. Brought a book. He read me a new poem, intoning it, not very distinctly. Miss

Smith and her friend, Boston enthusiasts, came in. Whitman consulting us about a preface and a portrait. He talked of his 'barbaric yawp' smilingly. Great sense of 'the calm within, the light around, and that content, etc' the boys, lovely days when he was young, and about with 'the boys' in the sun. Bathes now, and lies in the sun, in a N.J. brooklet in summer. Love of the sun.

Gosse shared that love of the sun, and sympathized with the old poet in that wintry room, waiting for the light and air of summer. He saw him as a cat, a high compliment from Gosse: 'like a cat – a great old grey Angora Tom, alert in repose, serenely blinking under his combed waves of hair, with eyes inscrutably dreaming'. And in writing of Whitman, Gosse told with feeling an anecdote about General Condé, which perhaps says something about Gosse himself. Apparently Condé, at the opening of his last campaign, melancholy and mad with fatigue and heat, reached at last the cool meadows in front of the Abbey of St Antoine, leapt from his horse, flinging away his clothes and his weapons, and rolled stark-naked in the grass under the trees to the astonishment of his officers. Refreshed and relaxed, he then calmly dressed and armed himself and rode into battle with his usual resolution. 'The instinct which this anecdote illustrates,' Gosse wrote, 'lies deep down in human nature.' The more we are muffled up in social conventions, the more we occasionally long for a return to nakedness. He saw Whitman as a defender of 'bare human nature, stripped not merely of all its trappings and badges, but even of those garments which are universally held necessary to keep the cold away'. Certainly Whitman had some influence on him when eventually he came to write *Father and Son* and to look unconventionally at the relationship of those two complex characters.

But for the moment, the social whirl continued. The night before his visit to Camden he had seen, on the other side of the iceblocked Delaware River, a performance of Browning's *A Blot in the 'Scutcheon* at the Opera House in Philadelphia. The director and leading actor was Lawrence Barrett, with whose family Edmund and Nellie had spent Christmas in New York (they took a sleigh ride on Christmas Day through Central Park and along the Hudson). Gosse wrote to tell Browning that Barrett's delivery would have pleased him. He had declaimed the blank verse with swing and cadence. Moreover he had not lopped any of Browning's branches 'to make the action clearer to the vulgar'. Gosse actually makes the evening sound disastrous, quite apart from the 'mechanical accident, such as you know is incidental to first nights . . . The electric light went out and left the group in so much obscurity as confused the audience a little . . . No doubt it will all improve,' he wrote cheerfully to Browning. But what had really thrilled him had been nothing to do with the play; he had shared the best box with General Sherman, and it had seemed like sharing it with Alexander the Great himself. The old tiger, who had led the north in the Civil War, was now tamed to 'a grand mousy-coloured purring cat' (that high praise again). He sat well forward listening to Browning's poetry and turning back, every now and then, to explain the action in a very loud whisper. Edmund told Nellie that, though General Sherman was as kind as could be, 'I felt really shy, for the first time in this country . . . and disgustingly young.' After the play, they sat up until 2 am while Sherman told 'the thrilling and absorbing stories of his victories and losses'.

In Washington Gosse met General Sheridan, that other great Civil War leader, who impressed him more than the President himself. But the excitement certainly culminated with their visit to the White House. Gosse confided to Thornycroft that they were 'frightened almost out of their senses'. Nellie wrote to Marychurch that President Arthur was most kind and showed them over the White House himself. 'He remarked upon Edmund's very young appearance' with a smile but was, on the whole, very melancholy, pausing under the portrait of President Garfield, assassinated so recently, and muttering, 'What a tragedy!'

The pleasures continued in New York, but time was running out. There were many more invitations to give drawing-room lectures which he could not fulfil. He saw a good deal of the sculptor Saint-Gaudens. He met Frank Stockton and Frank Millet, Stanford White, Julian Hawthorne, Roswell Smith and J. R. Osgood (for whom he would later work), Stedman, of course, and Gilder. There were dozens more. Gosse reckoned he had shaken 800 hands. The total count of names mentioned in the Diary comes to 262. It had been one long ovation. 'Most Englishmen,' Robert Louis Stevenson wrote to Gosse, go to America 'with a confirmed design of patronage, . . . and patronage will not pay.' But Gosse had gone to America with his usual zest and had found it 'the most interesting country in the world'. In spite of this, he resisted its blandishments without difficulty. He could not do without London and Trinity College, Cambridge. 'As you have publicly taken the vow of London Poverty in preference to American Affluence,' Howells wrote to him on the eve of departure, 'we trust to see you over your dry crusts in your simple hut at Delamere Terrace.'

There must have been times in the next two years when Gosse wished he had opted for American Affluence and the repeated ovations, for

England in 1885 and 1886 was to produce more than a reasonable share of slings and arrows.

It seemed that, whereas Americans patted everyone on the back, Englishmen hit everyone in the stomach, as Gosse would write in 1887. Only a few weeks after their return, Gosse wrote, his puritan conscience in action, to tell Howells, 'Since I came back to England, I have been ill, tired, bothered and over-worked, the proper penalty for having enjoyed myself too much.' But much worse was to follow before the end of the year.

Gosse started lecturing again at Cambridge on 28th February 1885. There was a large audience by Cambridge standards – about three hundred people – at the first lecture, but Gosse was 'conscious of the curious difference between the University audience and the impulsive, sympathetic American ones . . . Not a spark of applause, only perfectly hushed attention. I suppose they have settled down to considering the thing as a university ordinance. I spoke without flagging, almost without glancing at my notes, and had more to say than I had planned,' he wrote to Nellie. He was always in 'abject terror' before he started, he told her, thinking he hadn't more than '10 minutes' worth of stuff to say'. But it was all right once he got started.

There was some pleasant social life in Cambridge. Gwen Raverat (Charles Darwin's granddaughter) records a delicious meal Gosse ate in her parents' house on April 1st; and W. W. Skeat, the philologist, was only one of the many Cambridge men who welcomed Gosse to call when he wished: 'I am generally at home in an evening . . . If anyone drops in to tea at 6, we are always ready for them.' (They always dined at '2 or 2½,' he said.) Gosse would often walk to Grantchester or Madingley with Aldis Wright, fellow of Trinity (known familiarly as Dr Always Right). He said he sat opposite Prince Edward of Wales in hall, 'a very nice friendly boy'. There were invitations to lunch at the Master's Lodge. He would get to know J. G. Frazer, who was already working on *The Golden Bough*, his vast study of comparative religion. (Later he would get help for Frazer from the Royal Literary Fund.)

Nellie was at Marychurch that February and March, as Eliza Gosse was rather ill. Edmund was able to write to her that he had invested £300 in Metropolitan District Railway stock. 'It is now bringing in 4% – that is to say £12 a year, but it may very likely rise to 5% or £15 a year. At all events that will be a solid little reminiscence of our trip to America.' He told Howells gratefully he had made £490 in America, far more than Howells had led him to hope. 'The New York drawing-room lectures were very lucrative.'

With Nellie away, Edmund was even more involved than usual in his children's vivid life. Tessa was now seven and a half and feeling very grown up and responsible in her mother's absence. 'Tessa thinks it a great mistake,' Edmund wrote to Nellie, 'having "the children" down so much, it makes her forget important things about the management of the household . . . So I generally round them up after a little while and she unbosoms herself. She is delicious company.' But she was not impeccable.

'This evening Philip is wounded on the brow and on my asking how this came about, I was told by him that Tessa did it "playing with the toasting fork". Tessa admitting this soft impeachment, I read her a tremendous lesson and called Marion to witness.' Marion was the nursemaid, and the worst of her was her extreme vanity. Gosse commented she would always discuss the children's ailments 'in the form of a defence of her own care and judgement'. Now she saw herself as being blamed for negligence and cried out, like a priestess of Baal: 'Oh no, indeed sir, it was quite an accident, *I* shouldn't think of allowing them to play with the toasting fork, I can assure you, sir, that of course I shouldn't *think* of it,' and so on, until Gosse had to say 'All right, all right' and 'that wicked Tessa flashed a cold eye of triumph over at Philip'.

Mrs Watson, the cook, well known for Watsonian cynicism, was looking for a girl to help her in the kitchen at this point, and Edmund reported to Nellie her assessment of the two candidates who had called: ' "Well, the first girl that called wasn't a girl at all, just a staid woman, with notions of twenty pounds and beer found, so I told her, there, she needn't trouble to call again; the other was a respectable girl, but there was the Fringe! That's what it was and I spoke to her of it and she said, yes, she wished the day she'd never had it cut, it had lost her place after place, that Fringe had, but there, she said, I s'pose the cap'll hide it, and a clean sort of girl she seemed. Well! I'm sure I don't know, I'm sure." ' Gosse told her he thought they might put up with the Fringe if everything else seemed satisfactory.

Mrs Watson kept a firm eye on what Gosse got up to in Nellie's absence. One night he was out till 1.30, after a 'very merry and scandalous' evening with their neighbours the Crosses. 'Mrs Watson was shocked, I think, for she provided tea for breakfast in a very marked manner.' Generally things were very quiet and Gosse commented on 'the monotony of my existence'. The Tademas had given up their Tuesdays and were refusing all invitations 'until the Academy pictures are in'. The rest of life, as he wrote to Howells, seemed very flat after their 'lovely time' in America. Pater sent a copy of *Marius the Epicurean*, 'which everyone is talking about. Emily Williams called in on her way to hear Waterhouse at the R.A.' But usually, after his day at the Board of Trade and a couple of hours with the children, he got on with his writing.

He had been working on a novel which he called *The Unequal Yoke*, though Lang protested 'they never *were* yoked'. Lang was the only person, it seems, whom Gosse confided in about the story. He wrote to Macmillans, in the summer of 1885, as if it was the work of an unnamed friend. The Macmillan report described it as a story 'about the jilting of a young Baptist Minister's daughter by a young Government clerk, aristocratically connected. [The writer] is evidently penetrated through and through with the bitterness of non-conformity, and loses consequently his artistic self-control when he comes to represent the fashionable and prelatical side of things. His solecisms are frequent and extreme . . .' Gosse interpreted this decidedly lukewarm report as encouraging and was pleased to accept, 'on behalf of his friend', the offer of £30 for its use in the *English Illustrated Magazine* where it eventually appeared anonymously from April to June 1886.

In June 1886 he writes to Macmillan ingenuously that Andrew Lang had 'guessed the authorship', whereas in fact he had been sent it by Gosse when it was first written. 'I have read your novel,' Lang had written. 'The rum thing about it is the parts about the women might have been written by a woman. I think very highly indeed of many scenes – but it is spoiled for me by your hero . . . I don't mean to say that he is unnatural or impossible, only I have the virtuous desire to throw things at him.' The interesting thing about these criticisms, very just ones, is that they seem to indicate how much, at this stage, Gosse's understanding and sympathy was still with the dissenters. The story never appeared as a book in Gosse's lifetime and Gosse never acknowledged it. The authorship only came to light in 1967 when Simon Nowell-Smith edited a collection of letters to Macmillan.

The first scene, as Lang said, is particularly strong. Jane, the Baptist Minister's daughter, has rescued a boy from drowning and walks home in a borrowed blouse: 'It would be rather a good way of testing one's friends to see how many of them would walk down Colville Road with one, if one were dressed in pink sateen and a sopping skirt.' Jane is tough and independent and does not care what anyone thinks, until she meets Frank and the values of Kensington. Young Frank Capulet (his name, of course, suggesting how far apart the two families are, how impossible their union) falls in love with Jane. Frank has sisters, 'cold and stylish fine ladies', dedicated to the 'brilliant pursuit of pleasure'. The dissenters are 'full of freshness and high spirits'. 'It seems to me,' Frank says, 'you all live much more useful lives than the people I have been accustomed to meet.' After the engagement has been broken off, Jane comments sadly, 'He made me worldly instead of my making him spiritually-minded.' It is as if Edmund realizes and resents the strength of the world. If only Macmillan would publish the anonymous story as a book, Edmund said, he would dedicate it to Henry James, 'which would add a touch of mystification'. But they could not be persuaded.

In May 1885 there was the excitement of the unveiling of the Gray Memorial at Pembroke College, Cambridge. Gosse had laboured long the previous year to raise subscriptions for this, partly for Gray, more perhaps for Thornycroft, who was commissioned to make the memorial. The amount raised was £291 5s 2d and the subscribers ranged from the Earl of Derby and the Duke of Devonshire to the ladies of Wells College, Aurora, USA. Henry James contributed £3 and Gosse himself 5 guineas, as well as a great deal of effort. £220 went to Thornycroft and £55 2s 10d was, incredibly, the price of the pedestal. James Russell Lowell, just relinquishing his post as Minister in London, spoke on behalf of the American subscribers, and the bust was unveiled by Lord Houghton. The whole proceedings were reported in the *Cambridge Review* by one of Gosse's 'pet undergraduates at Trinity', and Gosse had the report privately printed in pamphlet form and circulated to the subscribers.

In June Gosse and Thornycroft were together again in Paris. The pictures at the Salon were, as usual, perfectly lamentable but they enjoyed the circus ('Philip would have loved it') and Corneille at the Théâtre Français, and afterwards they spent a few days wandering round Normandy and Brittany. Gosse was back on the continent in July, as one of the English jurors at an international exhibition in Antwerp, which shows that he still had some standing as an art critic. 'The English jury are not well received here. They have done nothing for us but give us a very ugly badge, which enables us to enter the exhibition without paying.' The English section, Gosse thought, was contemptible. It was to be compared not with France or Russia, but with Monaco or Paraguay. In fact, it was better than Monaco but worse than Paraguay. The only exception was Thornycroft's *Teucer*, which was very well placed and much admired. There were endless public dinners. In time he would thrive on such feasts, but now he felt 'I was not made for this life. I would give up the whole thing with delight in exchange for a couple of hours at Bucklebury or Embleton' – country lodgings they would take from time to time.

The following month – August 1885 – Gosse started work on a life of Walter Raleigh for a series of English Worthies, edited by Andrew Lang for Longmans. He would use the same material for his next series of Clark lectures. He was also correcting proofs of his two books, 'the prose and the verse, which are running neck to neck for autumn publication'. These were *From Shakespeare to Pope*, the book of his lectures, which was to be the cause of so much agony, and his new book of poems: *Firdausi in Exile*. The same month he resigned from his regular work (he said he was 'on the staff') of reviewing for the *Pall Mall Gazette*. It was for the *Gazette* he had first written about the Paris Salon, but he had moved his art criticism to the *Fortnightly Review* when John Morley, the editor, moved. He had continued to review books for the *Pall Mall Gazette*.

By January 1886 he was writing to Stevenson: 'I have quite broken with the newspapers, and as long as I can struggle along this side of beggary without them, I shall not go back.' There was no question of beggary. In 1885 he had earned, on top of his Board of Trade salary, very nearly a thousand pounds. Of that, not much more than £60 had come from the *Gazette*, the *Saturday Review* and the *Athenaeum*. The rest had been made up mainly from lecture fees in America (he had put down in his accounts £292 10s, not the £490 he mentioned to Howells, presumably knocking off his expenses), at Cambridge and at the Midland Institute in Birmingham. There was his £200 salary as agent for the *Century Magazine*. The rest came from books. He was doing extremely well and could afford to make the gesture of resignation from the *Pall Mall Gazette*. 'My last bond was broken,' he wrote to Stevenson, 'when the *P.M.G.* burst into its Romance of the Brothel. I wrote on the first day of those spurious revelations and said I could write no more for the paper. They have since done their dirty best to punish me.' But that was later in the year.

In the summer he was still revelling in righteous indignation about 'the obscene and forged revelations', which, he said, he knew from within, being on the staff of the paper, were worthless as fact, and he hated, in any case, 'the infliction of such a tide of filth'. This all refers to W. T. Stead's exposure of what came to be known as the White Slave traffic. The *Gazette*'s revelations about prostitution in London began under the title 'The Maiden Tribute of Modern Babylon', on 6th July 1885, and continued for several issues of the paper. It turned out that Stead had actually bought a thirteen-year-old girl for £3 and had taken her to a brothel, in order to speak with a sort of authority about the crimes he was exposing. The article contained a quantity of detail, including interviews with brothel-keepers, prostitutes and pimps. Gosse thought there was a good deal of hypocrisy in the whole business – that the *Gazette* was enjoying the scandals as much as exposing them.

Gosse apparently tried to persuade people to follow his own example and refuse to write for the *Gazette*. On August 14th, Matthew Arnold's reaction was: 'I quite agree with you that the harm it has done and is doing exceeds immeasurably what good it may have effected. Stead is a fanatic . . . I doubt any good being done by volunteer protesters. Officialdom is ignobly weak both against vice itself and against these corrupting exposures of vice.'

In the same month, Edmund wrote to Nellie:

London is horrible, simply horrible, heavy dead air everywhere. The political world has gone mad. Sir Charles Dilke has been discovered in an intrigue with his sister-in-law, and all the social-purity people are screaming that he must retire from public life. There is very little doubt that he will have to do so . . . The fact is infinitely discouraging. It is hardly doubted that, but for this, Dilke would have been the next Liberal Prime Minister. The P.M.G. triumphs at this and everything and boasts that the sewage it has poured on us already is only 'the tenth part of the black book of London's crime which we have yet to unfold.' The Salvation Army marches through the streets with the mottoes on its banners, which are unfit to be repeated, and the whole world has, in fact, gone vulgar mad.

In the end there were various results of the revelations. One was the Criminal Law Amendment Act of 1885, which, among other things, made 'indecencies' between males, even in private, a criminal offence subject to two years' hard labour. It was the Act under which Wilde would be sentenced. W. T. Stead was, in fact, sentenced himself for the offence of procuring in connection with the revelations. J. A. Symonds wrote feelingly to Gosse from Davos: 'I will not tell you what I think about Stead's action beyond this, that I regard his present sentence as too easy and that I should like to see his instigatrix Mrs J. E. Butler in prison too.'

Fortunately in September there was a very different world to distract Gosse from horrible London. The family spent September 1885 on the first of a number of visits to Broadway in Worcestershire. They took lodgings in Cowley House. Imagine Broadway without today's cars – that long village street of stone houses with their mullioned windows, running down from the edge of the Cotswolds into the Vale of Evesham. It was at this time the summer home of a group of American artists, including Edwin Abbey (who presented Gosse with the design for his bookplate), Frank Millet and John Singer Sargent. It was all delightful: roses, geese on the green, stone archways, dormer windows in mossy roofs, the smocks of the farm workers.

'I should like,' Gosse wrote to Alfred Bateman, 'to have £600 a year and a tricycle. I should never bother about London again. I hate the notion of coming up to town; everything here seems so calm and cool and lazy.' Millet was restoring the ruined Priory, behind his house, as a studio. Sargent was painting his famous Tate Gallery picture, *Carnation, Lily, Lily, Rose*, using the daughters of Frederick Barnard, an English painter who had also taken a house in the village. Gosse described the proceedings as Sargent painted each evening at just the moment when the sun had set, but a flush of colour was still in the sky. Though the sky would be unseen in the picture, the light on the children's faces was not only from the Chinese lanterns they were lighting.

> Everything used to be placed in readiness, the easel, the canvas, the flowers [the carnations in the foreground, the pink roses, the tall lilies above the children], the demure little girls in their white dresses, before we began our daily afternoon lawn tennis, in which Sargent took his share. But at the exact moment, which, of course, came a moment or two earlier each evening, the game was stopped . . . Instantly, he took up his place at a distance from the canvas, and at a certain notation of the light, ran forward over the lawn with the action of a wagtail, planting at the same time rapid dabs of paint on the picture . . . All this occupied but two or three minutes, the light rapidly declining.

Then, leaving the children to remove the lanterns, the easel, the canvas and themselves, he returned to the tennis court to have a last game, so long as the twilight allowed.

Earlier in the day he had been working on a painting of Tessa, begun on her eighth birthday, the 14th of September. 'One day,' Tessa wrote long afterwards, 'when Sargent was painting, we children came in from a picnic with branches of autumn colchicum – meadow saffron. He was so pleased with the colour of the mauve flowers, my red hair, white dress, that he quickly painted a sketch on canvas over a landscape'. When the oil was finished, he gave it to Nellie, the solemn child looking a little tentatively out of the canvas, her pale face framed in the dark red hair. There are also two Sargent portraits of Gosse, both dating from this period, one at the National Portrait Gallery and one in the library at Leeds University – with the soft, slightly Bohemian appearance, in such marked contrast with the harder, more dapper look of later years.

It is perhaps difficult to realize now how controversial Sargent was at this period. *Carnation, Lily, Lily, Rose* (which was in the Academy in 1887 and his first real success) is a 'pretty' work by any standard; but his portraits are glancing, honest and casual, with free, rapid brush-work. It is on record that he called himself an impressionist. He had been born in Florence, had trained in Paris, and his work bore no resemblance to the prevailing standards of the Academy in London. In 1884 his portrait of Madame Gautreau aroused a storm of vituperation when it was shown at the Paris Salon. He settled in London this very year, 1885, taking Whistler's former studio in Tite Street, Chelsea. Painting Tessa and Edmund in Broadway that autumn, he was in no sense yet the fashionable portrait painter he was to become.

They would continue friends. In 1889, Nellie would supply Sargent with painting rags, 'just in time,' Sargent said, and told the story of the painter who, complaining of the want of rags, was asked what he did with his old shirts. 'I wear them,' he said. It was Gosse who would encourage Sargent to paint his splendid agèd-eagle portrait of Coventry Patmore. In December 1915 it would be Sargent who would break the news to Gosse of Henry James's stroke.

Early in September 1885 Henry James joined the group for a couple of days, staying at the Lygon Arms. There is a sketch of James by Sargent at this period too. But not a great deal of work was done. 'The painters smoke and pretend to paint,' Gosse wrote to Thornycroft. They all took tremendously long walks. One day Nellie and Edmund walked to Chipping Camden: '12¼ miles altogether, by steep roads, which was pretty good. We both feel we are getting too plump.' They took a launch on the Avon from Evesham to Pershore, with Abbey accompanying their singing on a banjo. 'Nothing we do scandalizes the villagers,' Gosse told Thornycroft. 'Fred Barnard, with an enormous stage-slouch-hat over his shoulders, chased one of the Americans down the village street, the man chased screaming all the time and trying to escape up lamp-posts and down wells. Not a villager smiled. Miss Millet, yesterday, in the middle of the village green, was reposing on a bench when the wood gave way and threw her into Fred Barnard's lap. Not a villager smiled. Whatever we do or say or wear or sing, they only say "them Americans is out again."'

Lucia Millet, the one who was thrown into Fred Barnard's lap, was recording her own impressions in letters home to Massachusetts. On the 14th September she wrote, 'The boys are all at work on their pictures save Mr Gosse who spends a greater part of his days on his coming lectures. I find him very amusing and a charming country companion, his conceit seems wholly to have vanished since he came down here. I have great fun with him.' They celebrated Edmund's thirty-sixth birthday with goose in the Gosses' lodgings, drawing lots who would be the guests, as there was only room for two extra. Sargent gave Gosse a tall hat, known he said as a 'goss', decorated with laurel and magenta ribbons. Later, this hot day seemed almost the last unsullied happiness.

Soon after his return from Broadway, Gosse visited his aunt at Stanmore. Aunt Lizzie, to Edmund's dismay, was becoming more and more religious. Edmund had to go and hear her speak evening after evening in her 'iron room', but managed to get out of going to church on the Sunday morning, on the grounds that it would spoil the effect of Aunt Lizzie's evening peroration. In fact Aunt Lizzie was relieved, as 'Mr Jackson preached such a cold, dead, dark, unscriptural kind of sermon.' Miss Varini, Aunt Lizzie's companion, had a great deal of sense, in spite of a dreadfully sweet and incredibly holy smile.

> The atmosphere of the house gets holier and holier. I really can hardly bear it. But Aunt is less troubled and fussy than usual. Cox is going off his head, I believe; he moves about like a shabby undertaker's man, with a long green smile. Some morning they will find him in the pond, you bet.
>
> The liveliest person in the house is a delightful starling. The Peruvian guinea-pigs are too stupid to be very entertaining and yet we laugh at them at meals, faute de mieux. They have boot buttons stuck on under their shaggy coats; the only way to know which end is towards is to search for the boot buttons . . . You should have heard me singing 'Beulah' and 'Trust in Jesus' at the Room last night. It has gone off today a little and I would prefer a hand at whiskey-poker . . . I am going now to call on Mr Fortnum. Mr Fortnum is Aunt's last ungodly friend.

Edmund makes it all sound pretty dreadful, but, next day, with his usual resilience and adaptation to life's circumstances, he was assuring Nellie, still in Broadway: 'My Stanmore visit, after all, was a great success.' Aunt Lizzie had actually spent an evening 'being very merry and worldly'. And he really liked Miss Varini very much. 'She *is* holy, but quite nice and honest.'

Gosse's first lecture of the new term at Cambridge was on October 31st, when he started with 'The Early Life of Raleigh'. In the book based on the lectures, he would say his was the first attempt to portray Raleigh's career 'disengaged from the general history of the period'. Cambridge decided the Clark Lecturer needed an honorary MA. On 6th November 1885 the tailor came to measure Gosse for his gown: eight guineas for the gown, two guineas for the hood and ten shillings and sixpence for the cap. 'I think I shall let Aunt Lizzie, if she proposes it again, pay £10 of this . . . What an amusing change in the routine of life this Cambridge business is!' Edmund wrote to Nellie lightly. In fact, it meant a great deal to him, this degree. But of course it could do little to cheer him when the attacks began.

For some time there had been a feeling in some quarters that Gosse had been too successful. The reverberations of his success in America, coming hard on his unqualified appointment to the Clark Lectureship, roused some resentment. Even some who thought he deserved to be successful had a feeling that success was spoiling him. He lacked Austin Dobson's modesty, people said. It was presumptuous of him in his dedication to his new book *Firdausi in Exile* to bracket himself with Dobson:

> Perchance when both are gone
> Neither may be named alone.

Dobson was at this time, at least according to Gosse, 'by far the most popular poet under sixty' in England. Bridges was coming up; Browning, Tennyson and Arnold were all over sixty; William Morris was silent and Swinburne had become 'so flatulent and uninteresting'. How Gosse longed to be considered still in the running. But the *Pall Mall Gazette* took up the theme: 'The difference between the two writers is simply this, that Mr Dobson's manner is his own, while Mr Gosse's is everyone else's. Mr Dobson has done little things incomparably, Mr Gosse has done greater things tolerably.'

Other reviewers were not even convinced he had done them tolerably. *Firdausi in Exile* was widely and generally attacked. In his dedicatory poem, Gosse had written: 'We have fronted evil weather, Nip of critic's frost together . . .' But no nipping criticism in the past could possibly have prepared him for the mauling that was now his lot. On 25th January 1886 Gosse wrote to Stedman:

> It is true that my course, which had of late been very smooth, has had a rough check this winter. My Poems, before serious criticism could express itself at all, were attacked in the brutal articles of the *Pall Mall Gazette* and the *World* [*The World* had referred to 'feeble echoes strained to the cracking pitch'] . . . this seems to have encouraged the many who have no voice of their own, and the book has been received – with the solitary instance of the *Athenaeum* – with scurrility.

The anonymous *Athenaeum* review was by Theodore Watts-Dunton, Swinburne's keeper at Putney. Gosse had not yet fallen out with him. Indeed, on the 2nd November, he had written hoping he would review the book, 'announced for this week', and on 23rd January, the date the review appeared, Gosse wrote thanking him for 'a most kind, as well as a most accomplished and graceful review of my poems'. It was the only brightness in the prevailing gloom, as far as Gosse's future as a poet was concerned.

At this point, Gosse was able to tell Stedman that, though he thought the book of his lectures *From Shakespeare to Pope* had been a great failure in America, 'over here it has been received extremely well'. The further attack was slow in coming, and Gosse had a sense of false security about that book as he tried to cope with the attacks on his poetry. 'Your lectures have been excellently received,' Andrew Lang wrote comfortingly 'and only one or two unimportant people have snarled at your verses. You have been rather too successful to please everybody.' It was much better to think that than to face the possibility that his poetry really was not very good. In any case, Lang was sure the Raleigh book would be 'the gem of the lot' in the English Worthies series. Lang added a postscript: 'Don't worry yourself about the critical hydrophobia; it *really* is not worth a moment's thought. I wouldn't read reviews, if I saw people were trying to rile me.'

Gosse wrote to Howells: 'I have come in for a veritable vendetta of criticism – the storm has long been brooding – and my new books this winter have caught it from the crawling things of criticism.' To Symonds he wrote: 'It has somehow shocked me to find that I have so many enemies. I am not popular at all.' Howells wrote to Gosse, without any real understanding of his hurt: 'The fact is that, ever since I opened my Study in *Harper's*, the small fry of critics swarm upon me and it was impossible not to be glad another fellow was getting it too.' But he sent a paragraph he was publishing in *Harper's* in March, full of praise of Gosse and all his works. Symonds wrote to Mary Robinson, 'How Gosse is catching it from the critics! He has succeeded at last in making himself well hated.' But to Gosse he wrote: 'Attacks of this sort . . . are sure to be made upon a man just at the point in his career which you have reached. They are signs of his taking an assured position; the efforts of some to drag him from his seat, the questioning of others who cannot quite submit to recognise him . . . Just to get through it calmly and without losing heart or sweetness of temper, seems to me the right way. Christian preachers tell sufferers on earth to remember Christ. It is surely not presumptuous for a man of letters to remember Shelley then.'

Gosse had told Symonds: 'If I ever want to write again, which at present seems incredible, I should print for only a few friends.' Symonds thought that cowardly. 'Woolner told me that Tennyson once took to his bed because of a spiteful review, and had the humiliation of finding it was written by a prig of 16 years. And we know how much Rossetti's sensitiveness to Buchanan's brutality is supposed to have lost the world. It were surely better to imitate the gentle persistency of Shelley than the irritability of Rossetti.'

In fact, a number of reviewers, notably George Cotterell in the *Academy*, had written perceptive and shrewd analyses of Gosse's poetic achievement. He had said there was no point in comparing Gosse with the great poets:

> He lacks their imagination, their power to project bold outlines and fill them, to invest dry bones with life, to sound the depths and reach the higher levels of human nature. He can produce polished verse, but he cannot 'build the lofty rhyme'. His powers of observation are wide, keen, and sympathetic; he has facility and grace of expression, undoubted cleverness, a refined taste, a cultivated and scholarly mind; but all these do not make up genius.

From his violent reaction to this sort of thing, it would seem that Gosse had still imagined he might fulfil his youthful ambition of being numbered among the great poets. But he would never be so ambitious again. He could not admit yet his different talents, and preferred to imagine the reviews inspired not by truth but by personal enmity. In the attack on his critical book, which was yet to come, there was undoubtedly an element of personal jealousy and hatred. Looking at these years from the distance of a century later, it would seem almost as if Gosse were being punished for his inability to accept criticism, his inability to understand that reviewing is not always a case of friends and enemies, but of honest appraisal.

Churton Collins had been a friend, as we have seen. If he now became an enemy, it was not entirely because of jealousy and spite and resentment, but also, certainly, because he felt he had some sort of duty to uphold standards. We would think perhaps that he should have refused to review *From Shakespeare to Pope*, remembering those pleasant evenings in Yattendon in 1878, drinking Gosse's wine. But we will leave that attack to the next chapter and look at the rest of 1886 – Gosse licking his wounds and recovering with his customary verve, though with a certain increased touchiness.

Cambridge was still Cambridge, caring little what the world thought of the Clark Lecturer's poetry. He just took his place 'as one of the circle'. The *Cambridge Review* described his new course of lectures, which began with Chaucer and Skelton, as 'curious rather than fascinating'. But Gosse was confident enough to stick up in his room in Trinity a drawing by Howells's young daughter, Pilla. Gosse had told Howells that he was likely to go down to Oblivion on the arm of Obloquy, and the notion had charmed Pilla, who had depicted her friend, Mr Gosse, doing just that. 'I keep her libellous drawing on the mantel always in sight,' Gosse wrote, 'to inflame my undying resentment, and also to blush at the pretty profile she has given me. Everybody recognises it, I am glad to say, and then says, "Who's that repulsive old female?" "O that's Obloquy," I answer, easy like, as you might say O that's Miss Cleveland or the Queen.' He was keeping his sense of humour.

It was good to be able to invite friends to Cambridge. Henry James came in February. In June Gosse had an even more distinguished American visitor (so it seemed then): Oliver Wendell Holmes. James had once satirized his Bostonian complacency; he was part of his past. For Gosse, he was part of that magical American winter. Holmes had made him feel particularly special. He had told Gosse he had 'never known a stranger make such a conquest'. Gosse needed to be reminded.

Gosse first entertained Holmes in London; James came, of course, and Thomas Hardy, and Austin Dobson. It was a larger than usual Sunday at home; there were sixty-seven guests, all eager to set eyes on the autocrat of the breakfast-table. Browning was otherwise engaged and regretted he had no chance of doing 'what I wish with all my heart I could do'. He hoped 'the admirable and beloved autocrat' would understand. Hardy wrote in his diary: 'His is a little figure, that of an aged boy. He said markedly that he did not read novels; I did not say I had never read his essays, though it would have been true, I am ashamed to think.' James remembered that his father used to say that Holmes 'was worth all the men in the Club put together'. He had been 'the intellectual king of Boston all his life', Gosse told Thornycroft. He was now very old, and his own account of this visit to Europe is 'a bland concoction of rosewater and sugar' . . . 'There should be a thorn or two in such a bed of roses,' Gosse wrote to George Armour, his new American friend. 'And I happen to know that there were.'

Holmes's journey was triumphal: he received honorary degrees from three universities: Cambridge, Oxford and Edinburgh. As they travelled up to Cambridge, 'there was a great crowd beaten from our gates at each station,' Gosse reported to Nellie. 'The dear little lion was in excellent spirits, sitting bolt upright, "not to miss anything." ' In Cambridge, Gosse found him 'the most charming guest, like inviting up a delightful elderly bird, that sings whenever you ask it to. He is rather fragile, but has the most delightful readiness to go to bed – has been there twice already today . . .'

Gosse was feeling particularly happy that June weekend. He had just been re-elected to the Clark Lectureship (now that Stephen's term had run out) for a further term of three years. It was a great relief. The London periodicals and their criticism seemed far away. There had been periods of depression earlier in the year. In April he had written to Nellie from France, 'It is wonderful what a refreshment it is to get far away from anything English.' Now England and especially Cambridge began to reassert their attraction. 'The sense of its beauty grows and grows the more intimate with it one becomes.' He would look out of his window, down into the Master's garden, and it seemed to him that 'grass was never so green, nor sky so blue, nor the line of St John's dormers so red . . . A nightingale is singing away as I write'.

Friends were particularly kind about his *Raleigh*. Henry James read it 'with breathless admiration and interest. It seems to me wondrous well done'. Stevenson considered it 'a thoroughly sound piece of narrative, and brilliant, not in patches, but by general effect . . . I never read anything more unaffected and effective'. And this was not praise just for Gosse's benefit. Stevenson wrote to Henry James: '*Read Gosse's Raleigh*. First Rate.' But there was a ridiculous misunderstanding with Stevenson. The trouble was that Stevenson had heard there was to be an article on him in the *Century*, and he told Gosse that he wanted Colvin to write it. In fact, Gosse had already written to Colvin a week before suggesting he should write on Louis; and Colvin thought Gosse should do it himself. So did Gosse, and he was terribly hurt that Stevenson wanted Colvin to do it. Stevenson apologized handsomely for having said anything that could possibly hurt or offend.

> My dear Gosse,
> I am terribly mortified and pained by the harm I have done; but if you will give me a chance and hear me favourably, I do not believe you will make so much of it. We have been so long friends that I am very anxious to avoid anything that might prove a cloud; I regard you with affection, I am grateful to you for things done, I admire your talent; and I cannot call to mind anything in the whole of our personal relations that has been otherwise than delightful to me . . . I trust that after all we may meet without change and with no less affection. On my side, there will always be some remorse for having wounded one who has never wounded me.

The breach was healed – though Gosse refused several of Stevenson's invitations to Bournemouth that summer.

There was a similarly trivial misunderstanding with Swinburne, but relations with him had already become strained, though as late as 1918 Gosse would still call Swinburne his favourite poet. Swinburne was not prepared to say anything to conciliate Gosse as Stevenson apparently was. He was 'sorry and astonished' that Gosse had detected a sneer in an article Swinburne had written in the *Nineteenth Century*. 'I can only say that I am not ingenious enough to discern any cause for offence on my part, and that I regret you should have been so keen-sighted as to discover such cause . . .' Gosse wrote to Watts-Dunton: 'He was born without a heart.'

Thomas Hardy also received *Raleigh* with great pleasure, addressing the envelope of his letter to Professor E. W. Gosse, MA. 'How indefatigable your pen is! My wife is going to read the book aloud to me, she says because "we ought to read something more improving than flimsy current literature." So you may see the good you are doing in households by your latest production.' A week or two later, he invited Gosse to stay at Max Gate: 'Can you come now? Our life here is lonely and cottage-like, as you know, but I think you would be interested in going to one or two curious places in the neighbourhood recently opened up by the railway.' Nellie was not invited because 'at present we have only a bachelor's room'.

But before he went to Dorchester, Gosse spent a day with Maupassant in London. Henry James had invited them to dine with him at Greenwich. James reminded him of the occasion twenty-eight years later. 'Have you any recollection of going down the River with me to Greenwich, long years ago? in company with Maupassant, Du Maurier and one or two others?' One of those others was Count Joseph Primoli, on whom Gosse apparently made an ineffaceable impression. He wrote to James in 1914 to ask Gosse's address – he had remembered him all those years . . . James wrote, 'He made on dear du Maurier, I remember, an impression that remained – though not on your sterner nature! He is a Bonaparte (exceedingly so in looks); that is, his mother was a Bonaparte Princess.' Gosse was, it seems, more interested in James and Maupassant; he had not yet acquired his taste for the aristocracy, English or foreign.

Gosse went to Max Gate late in August. It was on this visit that Hardy and Gosse went to see the dying William Barnes, described in an earlier chapter. And it was this visit, too, which gave Gosse the theme for his dedication to Thomas Hardy, ten years later, of his book of essays called *Critical Kit-Kats*. Looking for the road to the railway station in Bridport, they asked a grave young man the way. For some unknown reason, the youth gave them totally wrong directions, 'up terraced paths and between walls clustered with creepers', until they found themselves emerging on the opposite side of the town, miles away from the station. 'I asked you, bitterly, if this was the vaunted courtesy of your Wessex yokel?' As they kicked their heels at last, much too late for the train, in the blank waiting-room, they speculated on the psychology of the thing. Was the young man perhaps an outlaw, flying from justice and glad to revenge himself on the very prophet of his country? Or was it not rather, as Hardy's kind heart suggested, that he thought he was right, that, inconvenient as his advice proved, he knew no better.

Certainly Bridport, in the language of these two friends, came to symbolize unhelpful or misleading advice – criticism which was of no use, which hurt rather than helped the one to whom it was given. The excursion lingered in Hardy's mind as a failure that was somehow his fault. 'I feel quite a sinking in my inside when I think how sadly I neglected to plan a good excursion – that terrible kettle at the Bridport pot-house rising as an accusing spectre . . . Give me another chance, please,' he wrote to Gosse, by then in Broadway in the Cotswolds again, disporting himself with the American artists, and going on regular walks with Henry James.

Gosse replied happily to Hardy saying everything at Broadway was pleasing except the weather. That encouraged him to quote 'that beautiful passage in Shakespeare: "Enter Third Citizen. Third Citizen: O bloody day!"' This was September, and storms of a different sort were fast approaching. On 22nd October 1886 Gosse wrote: 'This has been the most terrible week of my life.'

The Scandal of the Year

As WE HAVE seen, Gosse had chosen the subject of the lectures which formed his inaugural course as Clark Lecturer at Cambridge *before* he had been appointed. The lectures were originally planned for his American trip – and he did give them in full in Boston and in Baltimore and individual ones also at Yale and in New York, immediately after his first term at Cambridge in the autumn of 1884. If anyone did rise up and dispute any of his facts or conclusions, presumably he made alterations before the book – which had been planned from the beginning – was actually published. He wrote in the Preface:

> It has been no small advantage to me that among the distinguished listeners to whom I have had the honour of reading these pages, there have been more than a few whose special studies have rendered them particularly acute in criticizing the links of my argument. In consequence of such criticism, I have been able profitably to revise the work, to add evidence where it seemed wanting, to remove rash sentences and to remould ambiguous sentences. Above all, I have given a great deal of care to the accumulation, in the form of notes and appendices, of historical and critical data of a kind too particular for the purposes of a lecture . . . In an enquiry of this nature, exact evidence, even of a minute kind, outweighs in importance any expression of mere critical opinion.

It sounds impressive. It sounds as if he had taken enormous care and had worked with particular attention to detail. As we saw, he was pleased with the lectures, even before they had been so rapturously received in America. 'I believe I have never written so well before,' he had confided to Howells, to whom the book was dedicated with a poem which was to get its own share of abuse. Certainly the reviews had not been markedly enthusiastic when the book was published by

Cambridge University Press in 1885. Indeed, the *Athenaeum*, while finding very few factual errors (Gosse's knowledge is 'so extensive . . . that his readers will rarely disagree with him without hesitation'), had disputed his inclination to explain the change from romantic to classical literature wholly in terms of literary form. It had pointed out flaws in Gosse's argument and exceptions to his thesis which he had preferred to overlook. The *Academy* had been equally critical, but even more polite. The reviewer merely drew attention to a few shortcomings, after acknowledging 'It is mature in its scholarship, delicate and judicious in its criticism, brilliant in its illustration, easy and pointed in its style . . . It embodies the research and judgement of a scholar, who knows his subject intimately.'

It had been Gosse's poems that had drawn most of the critics' fire the year before. But now, in the autumn of 1886, this book of lectures which had seemed to fall quietly into place as part of Gosse's respectable body of work (maintaining his reputation, if not exactly adding to it), was attacked as a tissue of errors and absurdities. Gosse was seen as a man 'ignorant of the very rudiments of the history of our prose literature' and almost equally ignorant of the history of poetry. How Gosse dealt with this extremely well-presented and convincing indictment, and kept at least some part of his reputation amazingly intact, is worth examining in some detail. The 'beastly business', as Henry James called it, is in fact the central episode of Edmund Gosse's literary career.

The attack by John Churton Collins was in the *Quarterly Review* for October 1886. 'Don't let us quarrel,' Collins had written, as we have seen, in 1878, 'for you are one of the few I know whom I care to be with and who worship at the same shrines, having the same Gods and the same Heaven.' But they had drifted apart during the eighties. Collins had turned down invitations to Delamere Terrace. He was a galley slave, cut off from society. So he saw himself. Then in 1885 he had applied, with some solid work behind him and the knowledge that he was a brilliant teacher, for the new Merton Chair of English Language and Literature at Oxford. He had been turned down, and a philologist appointed. There was Collins, with his 'scrupulous conscientiousness', his extraordinary memory, his fourteen-hour days – and where had they got him? To Mr Scoone's cramming establishment and lectures in bleak halls around the country for the University Extension Society. And there was Edmund Gosse, poet, dilettante, with no university degree, no years of solid teaching behind him, appointed Clark Lecturer at Cambridge. Collins had not actually applied for the Cambridge job. (He would have done so if he had known about it; 'he applies for everything', Gosse said.) But he certainly saw Gosse as his successful rival, no less than if he had been actually defeated by him. The Gods had rewarded the undeserving; and when he read *From Shakespeare to Pope* and realized, with a painful thrill, just how undeserving was his quondam friend, he could not resist assembling the terrible evidence of carelessness and error.

'Wielding the hatchet is one way to make your mark,' as John Gross said of John Morley's attack on Swinburne's *Poems and Ballads*. The *Quarterly Review* had a particular tradition of bludgeoning attack. Was it not the *Quarterly*, as Gosse would console himself, which had snuffed out John Keats, though that was long ago? Collins, too, was already known as an attacker. He had made his name, such as it was, with some curious articles on Tennyson's source material, which seemed to praise the Laureate, while suggesting that everything in his poetry came from somewhere else. He 'makes me borrow expressions from men I never heard of', Tennyson complained. Then he had moved on to John Addington Symonds. A year before the attack on Gosse, Collins published in the *Quarterly* a fifty-one-page article pulling to pieces Symonds's *Shakspere's Predecessors in the English Drama*. In the course of this article, he also attacked Swinburne (whom he was visiting at the Pines), declaring him to be 'guilty of greater absurdities than any writer of equal eminence who has ever lived'. We shall hear more of this later.

There is no question that Collins was a fanatic and a pedant. Later in life he would search the registers of forty-two Norwich churches, trying to pin down the elusive birth-date of Robert Greene for an edition he was editing. But, as far as Gosse's book was concerned, Collins happened to be right. In spite of that impressive preface I quoted, *From Shakespeare to Pope* is full of extraordinary mistakes: mostly they were mistakes which Gosse's lecture audiences would have been unlikely to notice. But it is curious that no one in Cambridge or in America (and there had been many distinguished listeners, as Gosse reminded us in the preface) had picked up some of the more glaring errors which laid the book wide open to attack.

As well as being right in detail, Collins had right on his side in his general thesis. For Collins was not bringing out his hatchets and sledgehammers just to destroy one small book and the reputation of one man. He was fighting for the cause of academic standards, particularly in the new study of English literature. To understand the situation, it is important to realize the position of English studies at Oxford and Cambridge at this period. Collins, teaching English literature, along with classics, to civil service candidates in London, had been disturbed for years by the fact that the ancient universities totally neglected the literature of their own language. He wrote article after article advocating the conjoint study of English literature and classics. The establishment of the Merton Chair was in some sense due to his efforts. There had always been the fear that English would be a soft option, that it would degenerate into 'mere chatter about Shelley'. There was the feeling, so widespread was the study of it in adult education classes, that it was a sort of poor man's classics, that the introduction of English in the ancient universities would lead to a lowering of academic standards. William Stubbs, Regius Professor of History at Oxford, had dissociated himself in 1877 from a move to have a Professor of English Literature attached to the Modern History School. 'I think that to have the History School hampered with dilettante teaching, such as the teaching of English literature, must necessarily do great harm to the school.' The only English Chair at Oxford before 1885 was the Rawlinson Chair of Anglo-Saxon.

Gosse was on Collins's side in the sense that he believed passionately in the importance of the proper study of English literature at school and university. In France 'the examination and constant re-examination of the classics of the nation takes an honoured and a vivid place in the education of the young'. Whereas at Eton and Harrow, if not at Mr Edgelow's school in Teignmouth, it was still possible to come and go without once hearing the names of Spenser or Words-worth. In the last months of 1886, as the 'beastly business' filled the papers, Collins was actually sending off questionnaires to almost every eminent person he could think of – prelates and politicians and scientists as well as literary men, even to the reviled Symonds in Davos. He asked them to state their opinions on various questions, the most central being: 'Is it desirable that the universities should provide systematic instruction in English literature?' Matthew Arnold was typical in wanting the standard English authors to be studied, but not in a separate faculty. 'The omission of the mother tongue and its literature in school and university instruction is peculiar, so far as I know, to England. You do a good work in urging us to repair that omission.' But Arnold did not want his name to be used 'in a question which is mixed up with the merits of Mr Gosse'.

The English honours school at Oxford was eventually established in 1893, but the Cambridge tripos not until 1917. As late as 1913, A. C. Benson was writing in his diary at Magdalene: 'I had a tiresome squabble with Dickins on Tuesday about my suggestion for an English school. It is what we want here – we are so afraid of interesting the boys. If they grow interested, we think they are not practising gymnastics . . .'

In the meantime, in 1886 they had Edmund Gosse as Clark Lecturer, an entertainment on the side, and the boys *were* interested; but Collins's attack, drawing attention, as it did so violently, to Gosse's lack of scholarship, probably helped to postpone the very thing they both wanted. At nearly four o'clock in the morning of 23rd September 1886, after labouring at it for about four months (a much shorter time than he usually devoted to a *Quarterly* article), John Churton Collins finished his essay on 'English Literature at the Universities'. 'I am very dissatisfied with it,' he wrote in his journal. 'It seems loose and feeble: perhaps it will look better in print. I hope it may direct attention to a serious question.' He seemed to have no idea what havoc he was about to cause. One newspaper said 'It excited more interest than any merely literary subject has aroused since the days of Macaulay.' As Collins's son, not mentioning Gosse, put it in his biography: 'And not only was the whole of the literary and scholastic world involved in the controversy, but the ecclesiastical and political world shared in it. When such men as W. E. Gladstone, John Bright, Dr Benson (then Archbishop of Canterbury), Cardinal Manning, Dr Fairbain, Lord Coleridge (the Lord Chief Justice), Prof. Huxley, Matthew Arnold and Lord Lytton (to mention but a few) gave their opinions on the subject, it will be seen how universal was the interest shown.'

But it was not, as L. C. Collins tries to suggest, his father's educational proposals that aroused such interest; it was much more the attack on Edmund Gosse. In America, *The Critic*'s London Letter put it like this:

> The Gosse–Collins affair is, so far, the scandal of the year. People – literary people – talk of nothing else. It has generated such rumors as are not to be stated; it has split the town into camps, and by many it is opined that it will cause the death of two men – the assailant and the assailed: the one for his animosity and the suspicion of *mala fides* which is discovered in his work; the other for the ingenuous poverty of his defense against so brilliant, so determined, so irresistible an attack. As matters stand, the victory is to some extent with Mr Gosse.

Amazingly it was so. Although truth was on Collins's side, fortunately for Gosse Collins had gone much too far. He had overstepped all sorts of marks, and had even exposed himself to ridicule as well as bad faith. Friends were able to write to Gosse: 'The obvious malice and exaggeration of the attacks are producing a reaction in your favour', 'The intemperance will defeat its own ends.' Gosse himself could write: 'The grossness of his attack happily overshoots itself.'

The article began quietly enough. Indeed, Collins did not mention Gosse's name for six pages, though the details at the top of the long article indicated that his book was under review, and Collins began:

Edmund and Sylvia at Stanmore, July 1889

(Above) Aunt Lizzie Brightwen entertaining the Gosses at Stanmore, July 1889. Gosse wrote: 'My Aunt . . . has her starling on her hand and is exercised in vainly trying to keep that invisible demon quiet'.

(Below) The Gosse children c. 1890. Josephine Balestier, whose sister married Kipling, is next to Tessa. Nellie is behind Philip.

(Above) Gosse took this photograph and inscribed it: 'Mr and Mrs Hardy and Nellie. Weymouth Pier. Sept. 9, 1890'.

(Below) Sir Lawrence Alma-Tadema, Gosse's brother-in-law, and his daughters.

Edmund Gosse with Mopsy, one of a long line of indulged cats, 1906.

Edward Marsh, 1900

Siegfried Sassoon, 1914

Richard Haldane, c. 1920

Maurice Baring, 1895

Hanover Terrace, including no. 17

The dining room

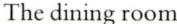

The drawing room and study

Edmund Gosse and Arthur Benson

'That such a book as this should have been permitted to go forth to the world with the imprimatur of the University of Cambridge, affords matter for very grave reflection.' Then followed that reflection, apparently disinterested, on the dangerous decline of standards in a world of mass-communication:

> It may sound paradoxical to say that the more widely education spreads . . . the greater is the danger to which Art and Letters are exposed . . . Scarcely a day passes in which some book is not hurried into the world, which owes its existence not to any desire on the part of its author to add to the stores of useful literature, or even to a hope of obtaining money, but simply to that paltry vanity which thrives on the sort of homage of which society of a certain kind is not grudging, and which knows no distinction between notoriety and fame.

Collins muttered about the 'spurious wares of literary charlatans'. 'It is shocking, it is disgusting, to contemplate the devices to which men of letters will stoop for the sake of exalting themselves with a factitious reputation.' With the aid of his log-rolling friends, Collins suggested, a mere literary journalist can palm himself off as a scholar. No one is interested in telling him the truth about his work. Reviewers 'know that what they mete out in their capacity of judges today, is what will in turn be meted out to them in their capacity of authors tomorrow'. This conspiracy theory, this accusation of mutual log-rolling and back-scratching, would also have its reverberations.

Collins saw the general decline into puffery and pandering to the multitude as too far gone to be reversed. What he insisted on fighting to retain, amid the 'general corruption', was the standards of true learning at the ancient universities. As Dr Johnson had put it of certain Methodists: 'They might be very good beings but they were not fit to be in the University of Oxford. A cow is a very good animal in the field but we turn her out of a garden.' If Gosse's lectures had been delivered only in America, if they had been published by Kegan Paul or Macmillan, Collins would not have bothered with them. But to have so worthless a book 'dated from Trinity College, Cambridge, and published by the University Press', that was more than he could bear; and Collins saw it as his 'bounden duty' to expose 'so evil a precedent'.

Collins took Gosse to task for many things. It would be tedious to go through all his objections in detail; they can be divided into five categories. Many of the errors were of negligible importance and so trivial that they actually weakened Collins's case. First, Collins said that Gosse had simulated familiarity with works which he had obviously not read. Two instances: that he had thought Sidney's *Arcadia* was a poem and had judged it as such, and that he had called Garth's *Claremont* a direct imitation of Denham's *Cooper's Hill*, with which it in fact has nothing whatsoever in common beyond having taken its name from a place. Second, Collins charged Gosse with 'habitual inaccuracy with respect to dates' and cites twelve examples. Third, as a prime example of 'the Dilettanti School', Collins quotes a particular piece of loose flowery writing:

> 'Late in the summer, one handsome and gallant young fellow' – Mr Gosse is speaking of the death of Sidney Godolphin – 'riding down the deep-leaved lanes that led from Dartmoor . . . , met a party of Roundheads, was cut down and killed'. Now Sidney Godolphin was killed at the end of January . . . when the lanes were, we apprehend, not deep-leaved; he was . . . not handsome, for Clarendon especially enlarges on the meanness of his person; he was not 'cut down and killed,' he was shot dead by a musket ball; he was not meeting a party of Roundheads in the lanes, he was pursuing them into Chagford.

Fourth, there was what Collins called 'officious egotism', where Gosse claimed to have made some discovery which in fact amounted to nothing. Fifth, more importantly, Collins charged Gosse with an 'ignorance of the simplest facts of Literature and History', and, in particular, criticized a ludicrous suggestion that it was Waller who had first written in distichs, and an even more absurd suggestion that for a hundred years only Milton and Roscommon employed blank verse. 'And this is a University Lecturer,' gasps Collins in righteous disbelief, in the midst of his criticisms.

Collins concluded his painful duty by pointing out how restrained he had been:

> We have even refrained from discussing matters of opinion. We have confined ourselves entirely to matters of fact – to gross and palpable blunders, to unfounded and reckless assertions, to such absurdities in criticism and such vices of style as will in the eyes of discerning readers carry with them their own condemnation. When we consider the circulation secured to this volume from the mere fact of its having issued from so famous a press . . . it is melancholy to think of the errors to which it will give currency . . . But whatever the faults of Mr Gosse's book, it will not, we hope, be without its use . . . it illustrates comprehensively the manner in which English literature should not be taught.

English literature, Collins concluded, is far too important to be left in the hands of dilettante teachers or philologists. So long as it is, so long will mediocrity, sciolism and ignorance prevail.

Gosse did not record his reactions as he read this indictment, but it is easy enough to imagine them, and there are plenty of references in his letters which indicate the degree of anguish and despair he felt. It was, indeed, the most terrible week of his life, that week in October 1886. 'No one will ever know what I have suffered,' he wrote. He reeled under 'the pure brutality of the thing, the shock, the disgust'. He felt as if he had been flayed alive with stinging nettles and subjected to 'a hail of vitriol'. It was appalling to have to face up to how over-confident he had been, and what stupid mistakes he had made. To a few people to whom he was particularly close, he admitted his culpability. 'I have grown cocky and careless,' he wrote to John Addington Symonds, who had also suffered and who found Gosse's admission 'manly'.

In public he put a brave face on things. It was the only way. Cambridge apparently stood solidly behind him. ('Everyone led by the strenuous and generous Aldis Wright is marshalled by my side,' Gosse wrote to Patmore.) There may have been subdued mutterings but Gosse did not hear them. Trinity had everything to lose if it admitted for a moment that it had chosen an ignoramus as Clark Lecturer, and he had nearly three more years of his appointment to run. Everybody (or nearly everybody) wanted to believe that Gosse had been appallingly wronged. He might have made a few minor errors, but somehow, he, the Poet, was, all the same, much more right than the Critic, who had attacked him in so ungentlemanly a spirit. (A broadsheet anonymous poem on the subject is called 'Critic versus Poet'.) Collins tended to be dismissed as an outsider, an envious pedant.

Arthur Sidgwick wrote a long letter to Symonds, who reported on it to Gosse: 'He asks whether I do not think it absurd to lay so much stress on a few slips here and there and none at all upon a man's power to stimulate the interest of his audience. He says he hears on good authority that Ch. Collins is himself a very inadequate and inaccurate Greek teacher at some Crammer's.' Many of Gosse's friends, who did not actually read the *Quarterly*, were similarly able to reduce the attack to the level of thinking that if he 'corrected a date or two' in the second edition, all would be well.

With his social cleverness, his charm, his marvellous talk, Gosse had somehow, for all his unorthodox background, succeeded in becoming part of the establishment, and now the establishment looked after its own. Churton Collins, for all his Oxford education and his well-born connections (his wife was a Strangways, kin of the Earl of Ilchester), was widely condemned as cruel, pettifogging, a blackguard, a jealous skunk, autocratic and vindictive.

Apart from the horror of having his errors and absurdities displayed for all to read, there is no doubt that Gosse found equally appalling the betrayal of friendship. Though he and Collins had hardly seen each other in the last five years, Gosse brooded on their old relationship. He sat at his desk and jotted down extracts of particular friendship and intimacy from those long-ago letters I quoted in an earlier chapter. He wrote out

To Stedman in America, Gosse wrote, 'I am not such a Christian as to be able to overlook entirely that Mr Churton Collins is a scoundrel. I befriended him when he was poor, I got his articles into magazines when he had no influence or connection, and his letters, which I possess, are full of eulogy of my writings.' He did not add that all Collins's enthusiasm had been for Gosse's poems, not for his criticism. Of the attack, he said to Stedman, as he said to many friends: 'It will be my own fault if it does not do me a great deal of good – it ought to make me more careful, more modest, more anxious to avoid offence, in short every way more human; and that I pray may be the result of it when all the sense of having stinging nettles applied to one's nerves has passed away.' To Howells, he wrote: 'I have been too easily success-ful, I suppose. I have glided on, and I can see that I have been negligent and have taken for granted that everything will come right. I think that, so long as one is not absolutely crushed out of competition, a blow of this kind is very useful . . . It may even turn out the best thing that ever happened to me.'

It was not. But he was determined not to be absolutely crushed. At first there were telegrams and anger, inevitably. Some decisions had to be made. Should he reply in some way to the attack? Could he bear to give his first lecture of the term as he was due to do? Should he indeed resign? Aldis Wright, Dr Always Right, urged him *not* to reply.

Trinity College, Cambridge. 17th October, 1886.

My dear Gosse,
There is a blessed passage of Scripture to which I always turn when I feel inclined to write in reply to Furnivall and the like. It is not to be found in the Authorised Version nor is its language strictly biblical, but for practical wisdom I say of it as David did of the sword of Goliath, There is none like it. You will find it among the English Proverbs at the end of Howell's Lexicon Tetraglotton where it stands thus:

He that wrastleth with a turd shall be beshit, fall he over or under.

Now think that over and don't reply to the *Quarterly Review*.

In all seriousness, you will consult your own dignity far more by taking no notice of the attack, the intemperance of which will defeat its own ends, while you could not afford the writer more complete gratification than by showing that you are wounded by his malig-nity.

When I received your telegram and letter I had not seen the quarterly article, nor have I now except in the extracts which the P.M.G. is glad to quote . . . We need not care much about the taste of a man who finds gratification in such carrion as Cyril Tourneur. Does he really mean that one cannot presume upon so much knowledge among English readers as to make it unnecessary to explain that *Paradise Lost* is not a prose work of theology or that the *Utopia* is not in verse? . . . This is all childish trifling and petty spite, unworthy of the name of criticism.

No, my dear Gosse, don't reply. Although you smart, seem senseless of the bob. Read my proverb (not aloud) and think better of it. Let the *Quarterly* bark as much as it will: it is a toothless old hound.

Yours ever,
W. Aldis Wright

In spite of this advice, on the 19th of October, Gosse wrote a letter to *The Times*, referring to the article in the *Quarterly Review*.

It will be my duty to deal in another place with the misrepresentations and errors which this article contains, but I will not attempt to fatigue you here with detail of a purely special and even pedantic interest.

There is, however, one point on which I ask your leave to speak from a platform broader than that of any literary journal. My antagonist in the *Quarterly* bases his attack on the fact that in noticing this particular book of mine 'Review has vied with review in fulsome and indiscriminating eulogy.' He says also that 'the men who write bad books are the men who criticize bad books,' and speaks, in connexion with me and my reviewers, of 'the relations which existed between Vinius and Tigellinus.'

Of late I have been accused from several anonymous quarters of these vile and secret arts of mutual puffery. No proof of the truth of these charges has ever been offered, because no such proof exists. I have hitherto disdained to take notice of such accusations, but now that the *Quarterly Review*, from its declamatory heights, repeats them, it is due to my official position that I should expose the myth.

Will you then, sir, allow me to state that of the articles to which the *Quarterly Review* refers, namely, I suppose, those notices of my lectures which appeared in the *Times*, the *Athenaeum*, the *Academy*, the *St James' Gazette*, the *Saturday Review* and the *Spectator*, I do not know, and I am unable to guess, who wrote any one except that in the *Academy*, which was signed by a gentleman whom I never saw, and with whom I never corresponded. The whole cry of 'cliques' and 'mutual admiration societies' proceeds, so far as I am convinced, from a disordered and malicious imagination, and I think that I may well be content to accept the judgment on me and my work of the reviews above quoted and of my colleagues and the electors of Cambridge, even though it be in opposition to the opinion of the *Quarterly Review*.

The other place, where he had decided to deal with the precise criticisms of his book, was the *Athenaeum*. The article duly appeared on 23rd October 1886. It sounded convincing: anyone reading it, as many did, without having read the weighty accusations in the *Quarterly Review*, might well have been convinced. Gosse dismissed entirely the accusation that he might have talked about books he had not read. 'My criticism may have every fault,' he admitted modestly, 'but it is certainly based on independent research and first-hand reading.' Again it would be tedious to go point by point through Gosse's defence, but very little of it actually holds. To give a very simple example, on the question of one date Collins had disputed, Gosse had said Roscommon's English edition of Horace's *Art of Poetry* was published in 1684. Collins had said it was 1680. Gosse now agreed that some authorities give 1680 but said that he had in front of him the first edition dated 1684. 'In matters of Restoration bibliography, the Quarterly Reviewer, if I may say so without immodesty, should be careful in attacking me. I believe I possess one of the fullest private collections of Restoration poetry and drama in the country; I have not neglected it and in this matter the reviewer's assumption of superiority is entirely out of place.' This was particularly foolish talk, for Roscommon's version of Horace's *Art of Poetry* dated 1680 was in the British Museum, whether 1684 was the first date in Gosse's library or not. Collins, in the guise of Oxoniensis, had some pleasure in pointing this out to Gosse two days later in the columns of the *Pall Mall Gazette*.

Gosse's defence ended on surer ground:

There are no stabs like those which are given by an estranged friend. My Quarterly Reviewer was once my intimate companion . . . When he devotes a page and a half to ingeniously persuading the reader that I am such an impostor as to describe Garth's poem *Claremont* without having read it, I marvel that even indignation should have so short a memory, and his used to be miraculous. Yet the first copy of Garth's *Claremont* which I ever possessed I bought in the Euston Road in 1878 for a few pence in company with my Quarterly reviewer. It was in the first volume of Cogan's quaint little 'Works of the Most Celebrated Minor Poets', he will remember. And I first read Garth's *Claremont* in the company of my

Quarterly reviewer that same summer, in the garden of a Berkshire house where he was staying as my guest.

It was a masterly ending to the counter-indictment. Few of Gosse's friends noticed – though Symonds did – how feeble had been the body of the defence. In fact, Gosse did not mention several points in which he was clearly in the right. 'My reply was not strong, I know; I am a wretched fighter,' Gosse agreed disarmingly with Symonds. 'My instinct is always to believe my opponent to be impregnable. I really wrote it for the sake of the last two paragraphs.' It must have been these that persuaded him to have offprints made of the piece in the *Athenaeum*; he posted them off to everyone he could think of. They did not all have quite the effect he intended. R. W. Dixon, receiving a copy in his remote Northumberland vicarage, rushed into Newcastle to seek out a copy of the *Quarterly*.

But letters of thanks and sympathy flooded in. Richard Garnett wrote to congratulate him on 'the remarkable temper and forbearance' he had shown in dealing with the unfair attack. Aldis Wright, finding the reply a little 'kid-glovey' if there had to be a reply at all, yet praised Gosse's 'Christian-like turning of the cheek to the smiter'. He found Oxford men a generation of prigs. Rider Haggard said he didn't know much about eighteenth-century literature, but 'I do know what conduct one gentleman has a right to expect from another.'

Among themselves, some of Gosse's friends agreed that he was indeed an inaccurate writer. Symonds cited examples he had noticed himself. Henry James wrote confidentially to W. D. Howells that Gosse had 'paid, fearfully, the penalty of a false position – for (between ourselves) I think he is in one in being at Trinity. But he stays there for the present and he is right'. To Gosse himself he wrote wonderfully sympathetic and sustaining letters, and sent invitations to dinner.

I heartily applaud your letter – it is perfect in tone and taste and temper, it is highly to the point as a vindication and the last few lines are a gem . . . It will do you great good . . . Calmez-vous, then soignez-vous, gird up your loins, do your work and do it better than ever; cease to count your bruises, and be conscious only of the life that is in you. All that will remain of the fray a short time hence will be a general impression that you were ponderously and maliciously attacked by an old friend and that it came out – by which I don't mean that it had been hidden before – that you were remarkably clever. Also, that all your old friends were not ponderous and malicious. I predict you an ovation at Cambridge.

But things were not allowed to die down. Aldis Wright was, as usual, right; Gosse should not have written his letter to *The Times* or his reply in the *Athenaeum* to the accusations. In years to come, Gosse would often give to young writers the advice he had himself ignored. He would tell them (for instance, Le Gallienne in 1893, John Drinkwater in 1913) to 'stand aside and be silent'. For now, in 1886, everyone knew of the attack, and letters on the subject crowded the papers and periodicals, day after day, week after week. 'One does not stand in the pillory of the press, for eight weeks, daily being pelted with rotten eggs, without beginning to be rather tired of it,' Gosse would write to his American friend, George Armour, in December. 'But I have had a great deal of sympathy from almost all the first literary men in the country . . . My own university is splendidly staunch . . . I mean to pull myself together and do work so sound and good, that the very fools and knaves that are hooting now, shall be forced to listen to me with respect.' Brave words from a heavy heart.

The 'first literary men' certainly helped. Colvin wrote that Tennyson, Browning and Meredith were all for Gosse and against his accuser. Henry James had written with more comfort on October 25th, suggesting that the brutality of the *Pall Mall Gazette* (where a great deal of the rotten egg pelting was going on) would do Gosse positive good because it would disgust people with his assailant and excite 'a tender interest' in Gosse himself. Next day, James wrote again:

I am infinitely distressed that you should continue to be overturned by this whole beastly business – & yet I understand it, for iteration will drive any man frantic. It is a matter of sensibility, & sensibility is much. All the same, sensibility apart, I really don't see what you have to consider except your own attitude – which I take to be simply that of continued and confirmed interest in your work, and ambition and purpose in regard to the literary life. Don't despair of that or of yourself – & the rest will be of course disagreeable, but still simple & superficial, like having been pushed without warning into a dirty pond, in which one splashes a moment & loses breath. The moment may seem long – especially if one is pushed again – but one scrambles out, as soon as one recovers one's surprise, without having left any vital part whatever behind. I repeat that the whole mass of the public d'élite feel the greatest sympathy for you at having been made to an almost unprecedented degree the subject of a peculiarly atrocious and vulgar form of modern torture – the assault of the newspaper – which all civilised and decent people are equally interested in resisting the blackguardism of . . . Avert your eyes – & your nose – & the rest will take care of itself. I shall come in & see you, if you have time, on Thursday evening (night) – being engaged to-night & to-morrow. Take my advice, & your nerves will bloom again like roses in June.

Thomas Hardy wrote perceptively and comfortingly too; he had turned up the *Quarterly* at the Dorchester Museum.

Do not, my dear Gosse, let it interfere with your digestion or your sleep for a single day. It seemed terrible at first – but after a while it seemed quite different. Virtuous indignation has an unhappy tendency to appear ludicrous in print, and the writer of the article does not seem to know this. Never did a man show himself more wildly in a rage, & with you personally. The literary points in dispute between you & your assailant are quite ousted from the reader's mind by wondering conjectures as to what you have done in private life to offend him so! . . . But I do seriously think that the article is a strong argument against anonymous journalism. I have suffered terribly at times from reviews – pecuniarily, & still more mentally, & the crown of my bitterness has been my sense of unfairness in such impersonal means of attack, wh. conveys to an unthinking public the idea of an immense weight of opinion behind, to which you can only oppose your own little solitary personality: when the truth is that there is only another little solitary personality against yours all the time. I repeat don't take it to heart . . .

Two weeks later, after reading Gosse in the *Athenaeum*, he wrote again:

We were immensely amused at the collapse of your assailant's attack. You might have hit back much harder if you had chosen to do so; but perhaps you were wise to be moderate. I cannot understand the *Quarterly* allowing itself to be the medium of anything so personal. Altogether (if I may so so) you have reason for self-congratulation – that is, if increased popularity be worth caring about at all.

It was very comforting. Colvin and Stevenson only restrained themselves from writing to the papers by reflecting on the fact that that would lead to further accusations of log-rolling. But, in fact, whatever Hardy thought down in Dorchester, the whole affair was still raging in London, and Gosse's sleep was still being disturbed.

Collins had replied to Gosse's reply in the *Athenaeum* on October

30th. In case after case, Collins upheld his attack and proved his points. Then he turned to the question of the betrayal of friendship. He recalled their distant friendly days – book-buying expeditions and visits to each other's homes. But for the last five or six years they had gone their separate ways. There was no quarrel. There was no personal element in his criticisms. Then he made a bad mistake – he mentioned Swinburne, as an example of a man who could accept criticism without letting it affect personal relations. He reminded *Athenaeum* readers that in reviewing Symonds's book on *Shakspere's Predecessors*, he had attacked Swinburne's disastrous influence on contemporary style. Now he reiterated his criticisms: 'As Mr Swinburne does not happen to be holding a professorial chair, I could not pronounce him to be totally unfitted for the post; but had Mr Swinburne been occupying such a chair, I should in the interests of education have protested against his election.' Collins was sure that Swinburne had not responded to his attack because it did not worry him. They had continued to be the best of friends, he boasted. 'I have yet to learn that Mr Swinburne considers me "no gentleman".'

Collins did not have to wait very long. The reason that Swinburne had continued to be friends was that he was totally unware of the references in the previous year's *Quarterly*. 'I did not even know that my name had had the honour to be insulted' he wrote to Gosse, on 27th October 1886. Now he made up for the time-lag by lambasting both the *Quarterly* and Collins in the *Athenaeum* of November 6th. 'May the God of letters preserve me from the deep disgrace of deserving his commendation!'

Less than two weeks before, acknowledging Gosse's *Athenaeum* offprint, Swinburne had written:

Thanks for your little pamphlet, which I have read with interest and sympathy tempered only with astonishment that any attack from such a quarter should be honoured by any notice from the person attacked . . . Macaulay, you may remember, admits that for one of Croker's blunders 'there is, we must acknowledge, some excuse; for it certainly seems almost incredible to a person living in our time, that any human being should ever have stooped to fight with a writer in the *Morning Post*.' And it certainly would have seemed to me, had I not this evidence to the contrary, not almost but quite incredible, that anyone living in our time should condescend to confute or to contradict a writer in the *Quarterly Review*.

The *Pall Mall Gazette* itself had said: 'Never since Macaulay annihilated Croker in the *Edinburgh* do we remember to have seen so cruel a castigation as that which Macaulay's disciple now administers in the *Quarterly* to Mr Edmund Gosse.'

But all Swinburne's tortuous reasoning counted for absolutely nothing when he was himself attacked; Swinburne renewed his abuse on November 20th. It was the end of the beautiful friendship poor Collins had boasted about. The Collins/Swinburne quarrel had diverted some attention away from the question of Gosse's errors and absurdities, but the papers seemed reluctant to let the business drop. The *Pall Mall Gazette* had attempted to close the correspondence on October 30th, but opened it again on November 17th, as the letters continued to pour in. In *Truth*, on November 18th, a columnist wrote: 'The amount of Gosse and Collins literature, in prose and verse, that I am receiving is enormous. My opinion of the matter is summed up in the following jingle of Dean Swift's rejingled:

"May I ask if it matters a halfpenny toss
Whether Gosse kicked C. Collins or Collins kicked Gosse?" '

But a lot of people obviously felt it *did* matter. The *Pall Mall Gazette* was still at Gosse 'like a hive of wasps, day after day'. Gosse said he was subjected to 'pails of journalistic slops', but in fact many of the letters were extremely learned.

The two main public defenders of Gosse's reputation were an unlikely pair: Robert Buchanan and William Archer. Buchanan was the same man who, long before, had attacked Rossetti and his 'fleshly school'. He admitted he had thrown many a random stone himself when young. Now he wrote: 'I have no particular reason to love this gentleman and perhaps some right to distrust the circle to which he belongs. I do love fair play, however, and when I see a man of letters coming under the ban of a literary vendetta, my sympathy is all for the victim . . .' He considered 'the poor purblind Quarterly Reviewer' to have 'about as much critical insight as Mr Wackford Squeers', a highly unfair crack at Mr Scoone's coaching establishment. He thought Collins belonged to the school of petty carping and fault-finding, and considered that 'in any book not written by a pedant for pedants, a schoolmaster may easily discover dozens of errors . . . Mr Gosse had proved himself a man who loves, honours and understands literature.' The men of the *Quarterly Review* had 'never said a kind word since the day they tried to kill John Keats'.

On October 26th William Archer (with whom Gosse would later translate Ibsen) sent an analysis of the twin perils in criticism of 'log-rolling' and 'log-rending' referring to an earlier letter he had written:

Literary log-rolling, I apprehend, means insincere, or at any rate ill-considered, eulogy, dictated by personal friendship and by a lively hope of reciprocal favours to come. This style of criticism is sufficiently prevalent and sufficiently despicable; far be it from me to defend it. To log-rolling I opposed a style of criticism which I called for the nonce "log-rending" – in other words, the evisceration and breaking-on-the-wheel of a literary work by a personal enemy (or an estranged friend) of the author. I then ventured to hint that log-rending is scarcely more honest and much less amiable than log-rolling – an opinion to which I must resolutely adhere.

Nowhere in Collins's article does Archer detect a pure enthusiasm for English literature; Collins is simply looking for offence. Archer sees Collins as guilty of log-rending because he always jumps to the most injurious hypothesis conceivable or inconceivable. Over and over again, Archer says, Collins brings in a charge of murder where manslaughter is the very worst interpretation the facts would reasonably bear. He has defeated his own ends by overstating his case.

Such letters made comparatively cheerful reading, though, as Gosse felt himself innocent of any real crime, even the reduced charge of manslaughter must have been unbearable. Gosse always knew the difference between fame and notoriety. 'I would give a large sum of money to be sure that my name would not appear in print for three months,' he wrote to Gilder on December 17th, and undoubtedly meant it. Even the servants had given notice because 'they said they had found from the newspapers that we were not a respectable family,' as Gosse wrote to Patmore. But presumably the notice was not accepted; Mrs Watson and her cynicism were still with the family in 1887.

There were other friendly letters: W. R. Ralston, his old colleague at the Museum, and an old Trinity man, declared comfortably that Trinity had no need of the opinion of the Quarterly Reviewer and could make up its own mind about the Clark Lecturer, fine Scandinavian scholar that he was. An undergraduate at Trinity wrote to confirm how Gosse had opened doors for them and lit candles that no Quarterly Reviewer could blow out. Some writers were prepared to admit that few of us 'in these busy pushing days are sufficiently without sin to throw a stone!'

But there was a rather general impression, fuelled largely by Collins's own interjections, under the guise of Oxoniensis, that Gosse was not worthy of the public's trust, that his reputation was in ashes and that, though Collins might indeed be an envious pedant, Gosse should retire defeated to the Board of Trade. An American correspondent had commented cruelly: 'At home we do not employ government clerks to teach literature.' 'Oh my asinine compatriot,' Henry James had groaned, reading the *Pall Mall Gazette*. The American friends were extremely loyal. 'You needed no defence with us,' Howells wrote. But at Oxford they said, if anyone made a howler, 'he has made a Gosse of himself'.

In the midst of all this, Gosse had given his first Cambridge lecture of the term, the first of six lectures on Shelley, a particular hero at such a time. Coming back to Trinity after the attack, Gosse found it was like 'coming back into a family of affectionate brothers – the smile a little brighter, the pressure of the hand a little longer and harder, that was all the difference'. 'Cambridge is *not* gushing, as Colvin said, but it is very just and has a hearty contempt for outside clamour.' The hall was packed for his lecture. W. R. S. Ralston made a point of being there and recorded his impressions:

> Cambridge was agog. Would he refer to what had happened? Twice in his lecture he began sentences which seemed to herald an approach to the subject. He said something had happened since he last addressed an audience at Trinity, which was of great interest to him and some interest to the College. A thrill ran through the hall: it was supposed that he was about to be incautious. He was only about to allude to his re-election as Clark Lecturer. Later he referred to something which had occurred recently that had given him personally great pain and had cast a shadow on the college. Once more curiosity sprang into life: once more it was doomed to disappointment. Mr Gosse was only alluding to the death of the late Master of Trinity . . .

Ralston continued, 'I have listened to many lectures: but I do not remember ever having heard any on a literary subject more intrinsically good, and delivered in a more excellent style.'

Edmund wrote to Nellie that evening, after spending it pleasantly 'in the Vice-Master's rooms'. 'No-one says one word about my lecture – that's the way of the place – it is taken as a matter of course.' The next day he was able to add:

> I am quite jolly, – the cloud seems to be rapidly dispersing. Cambridge is entirely enthusiastic and scornful of my assailants and has delightful little comfortable theories about the whole thing, excessively to my credit and such as I would not disturb for the world . . . . I feel more attached to this dear place than ever; there is something exquisitely soothing in the atmosphere of gentleman-

like sincerity and confidence after the vulgarity we have been suffering from . . . so – I suppose – this wretched incident closes, leaving me bleeding here and there, but, on the whole – already – with a more solid and prominent position than I had before.

It was not so, however much he wished to reassure Nellie. Collins's attack had made sure Gosse's position would never be the same again. The reputation for carelessness and inaccuracy would stay with him until his life's end. He was 'not sound'. Frank Swinnerton, nearly eighty years later, recorded two examples of how Gosse's reputation was permanently affected:

When I suggested in the early days of Everyman's Library that Gosse might contribute an introduction to some volume in that series, my employer, the late J. M. Dent, who was no scholar, replied, 'No; he's not quite sound, I'm sorry to say.' Two or three years later, R. B. McKerrow, the editor of Nashe's Works, in lending me a copy of *The Unfortunate Traveller*, in another edition, said 'Don't take any notice of the Introduction: it's only old Gosse.' Here then were two estimates: one derived from hearsay, the other representing a scholar's verdict upon an amateur who had ventured into his particular field.

Gosse would continue to be read and admired for his fluency, his wit, his wide-ranging acquaintance with so much literature. But in his continued attempts to establish himself as a serious scholar, he was now irrevocably handicapped. However much he 'pulled himself together', as he had promised he would do in that letter to Armour, however much sound work he produced, the contemptuous verdict of Churton Collins would never be forgotten.

There was another contemptuous verdict that would echo down the years, given wide circulation in biographies of Tennyson as well as in stories about Gosse. Osbert Sitwell in *Noble Essences* records:

That happy, never-to-be-forgotten afternoon, when, still smarting from the murderous attack made upon him in the *Quarterly* a day or two earlier by Churton Collins – one whom he had considered his friend – he had arrived, in fulfilment of a promise made long before to stay at Aldworth with Lord Tennyson. Tennyson was forty years older, and in the full blaze of his great fame, and involuntarily Gosse trembled before the ordeal. It was tea-time when he had arrived, and he found the poet at the head of a long table crowded with guests, and at the other end a place empty. He said, 'How do you do?' and sat down. The poet surveyed him, and then called down the table between the ranks of attentive ears,

"Gosse, shall I tell you what I think of Churton Collins?"

Gosse could not refuse the challenge, and had apprehensively assented, whereupon he heard the great man roll at him the following alliterative and assuaging sentence: 'He is a Louse upon the Locks of Literature.'

That this was Gosse's own story there is no doubt. Edward Marsh assured us he had it from Gosse's own lips. The celebrated phrase derives in fact from Smollett. In *Humphrey Clinker* occurs this passage: '. . . he damns all the other writers of the age with the utmost insolence and rancour. One is a blunderbuss . . . another a half-starved louse of literature . . .' Tennyson may well have used the phrase at some point, but the afternoon at Aldworth is fully documented, and very different from Sitwell's description.

In fact, the occasion was not a day or two after the *Quarterly* attack, but in August 1888, nearly two years later. Gosse had not seen Tennyson in the meantime. He was staying with the Pratts at Marley near Haslemere, only four miles from Aldworth. Amy Pratt was Nellie's sister. Gosse had told Tennyson he would be in the neighbourhood and had asked permission to call. He walked across from Marley and saw as he approached the house 'a sort of butterfly dancing about in blue velvet, which was the poet's second grandson, Michael Tennyson'. He had been asked to arrive at five and was a few minutes late. Hallam Tennyson and his wife were looking out for him and on the lawn Lord Tennyson was pacing up and down, 'a queer figure on that August afternoon in black broadcloth, with a soft black sombrero, and black kid gloves, shuffling along without a stick, a book under his arm'. Gosse asked him how he was. 'Grown old and ugly, old and ugly,' Tennyson replied laughing. 'How do you come?' Gosse told him he had walked and was urged to have his tea at once. They went into the dining-room, and there, to Gosse's surprise and pleasure, he found Aldis Wright: there was no other visitor in the house. (How strange that later he had described a table crowded with guests.) They sat round a small table for tea. Tennyson, Gosse thought, 'has grown very queer and Rembrandtish, the skin like parchment, all the hair gone from the dome of the head, and scanty grey tufts over the ears, a thin long grizzled goatee on the chin: he looks like a very old Yankee preacher of the conventional *Punch* type. Otherwise just the same, only not formidable at all, but very kind and genial.' He startled Gosse at tea by saying, 'How's Churton Collins?' and then 'Would you like to know what I think of him?' Of course Gosse said he would.

'Well! he's a jackass. That's what he is. But don't say I said so.'

Gosse wrote all this next day to Nellie at Marychurch. 'Jackass' has hardly the same ring as 'louse upon the locks of literature', and it was typical of Gosse to improve on stories with time. But it was assuaging all the same, this companionable tea party with Tennyson at Aldworth, and the contemptuous verdict on his assailant. For the wounds had still not healed.

The Death of the Father

In February 1889 Coventry Patmore, who had paid Gosse a sympathetic visit in Cambridge at the height of the beastly business nearly two and a half years before, wrote: 'I am glad you are lecturing at the Royal Institute. It is a sign that the storm has blown over and left you unscathed.' Gosse was certainly not unscathed but the dust had indeed settled. As early as 24th April 1887 Henry James had written: 'I am delighted the air of your life is clear again – I *did* foresee it would be. One has only to hold fast and it always is.' But those two years, 1887 and 1888, were hard years for Gosse. Very few people had come out against him, perhaps only Frank Harris and W. E. Henley. But Gosse sensed 'a gang of malefactors' at work against him and half of England hunting him with a tin-kettle tied to his tail. 'For many a long day to come I shall find it impossible to secure anything like justice for anything I do,' he wrote to Gilder.

In 1887 and 1888 there was rather less from Gosse in the periodicals. He was asked to write the introduction to a volume of Shirley's Plays in the Mermaid Series for Unwin. But English editors were certainly wary. His American reputation was never seriously impaired and indeed, in the middle of the storm, he had had a request from the *Independent* in New York to contribute a regular series of gossipy articles on the books in his own library. These eventually, together with some similar articles which appeared first in England, formed his collection *Gossip in a Library* (1891). It was a good idea, even if now we tend to shudder at the title. At least there are no pretensions to scholarship; it is just casual, pleasant talk for friends and people of similar interests. Gosse could display his erudition, his knowledge of particular books in his own library, without running into danger.

In one essay, Gosse refers to an attack on Camden's *Britannia* by a man called Ralph Brooke, 'who would otherwise be forgotten'. The parallel, nearly three hundred years before, with Gosse's own case is apparent. 'Suddenly, about twelve years after its unchallenged appearance, there was issued, like a bolt out of the blue, a very nasty pamphlet, called *Discovery of certain Errors Published in the much-commended Britannia*, which created a fine storm . . . Brooke had formerly been an admirer of Camden's, his "humble friend", he called himself; but when Camden was promoted over his head to be Clarenceux King of Arms, it seemed to Ralph Brooke that it became his duty to denounce the too-successful antiquary as a charlatan . . . He was able to convict Camden of a startling number of negligences . . . It can hardly be doubted that Camden had sailed too long in fair weather, or that he needed a squall to recall him to the duties of the helm,' Gosse wrote.

Gosse took his duties very seriously, and he knew if he was ever to retrieve his position he must produce a more important work, solid and accurate, as well as these charming gossipy essays. In a letter in his old age he wrote:

In 1887 I was very down on my luck and could get no work. A Mr Erik Robertson, who I think must be dead now, was very kind to me, and said that he thought he could induce Messrs Walter Scott to publish the book about Congreve which I had written. They did so and ultimately gave me a very small sum of money, but I don't think there was any agreement and I never heard any more about it from that day (1888) to this (1923).

'Professor Eric S. Robertson, MA' was, in fact, the editor of a series called *Great Writers*. The book was published with a minimum of critical attention. Very little was known about Congreve; very little would be disputed. His life appears to have been almost entirely uneventful. Working on it, Gosse commented to Armour: 'There is so little material that I am dismayed.' It was the first proper attempt at a life of Congreve. Gosse said that 'in this kingdom of the blind, however one-eyed', he was king. Indeed, it was not until the nineteen-twenties that further work made Gosse's biography no longer the sole authority. *The Spectator* described the book, gratifyingly, as 'a master-piece of fine prose and of sound comprehensive and conscientious criticism'. Gosse handled with particular tact the question of changing taste and Victorian Grundyism. He warned any lamb-like readers that, in the menagerie of the Restoration dramatists, he must expect to find lions. The book made Colvin re-read Congreve, but he was glad 'to get the taste of it out of my mouth with half-a-dozen Waverleys'.

Next, Gosse tackled a far more dangerous assignment. In fact, he took a deliberate decision to cross a sort of minefield. He started work on a *History of Eighteenth-Century Literature*; Macmillan had apparently retained some faith in his abilities and commissioned it as part of a series on the history of English literature. Gosse got very nervous about it. On 22nd October 1888 he thanked Dobson for going through the proofs and wrote, 'I hate the book. There is not a sheet of it that could not be improved; it is dull and incomplete and nobody will like it. But it must go now and it will fortunately soon be forgotten.' In fact, it wasn't. It was a considerable success, at least commercially. The book remained in print for the rest of Gosse's life, going into twelve reprintings by 1930. He was criticized in *The Spectator* for his praise of *Tom Jones*. ('It would almost seem that he regards the novel as fitted for what is called "family reading".') The *Athenaeum*, inevitably, considered that Gosse's theories 'must not always be taken too seriously', but was able to find few factual errors. The overwhelming impression was that Gosse had learnt his lesson and had written an attractive and useful book.

This would be consoling; but Gosse was finding life difficult. He had been touchy before; now he was even touchier. He had had patches of depression before; now they were certainly more frequent. Mary Robinson, poet and frequent visitor to Delamere Terrace on Sunday afternoons, said she liked him particularly because he was unjust, quick-tempered, sensitive. She thought it the poetic temperament. 'All this time of suppressed and most bravely controlled nervous excitement and suffering, has so worn your nerves one feels that things are all to you of torment or delight, which should be mere pleasant indifference . . . Do not over-feel,' she begged him in February 1887. 'You ought to go to sleep for three weeks at a stretch.'

Gosse kept as calm and worked as hard as he could, sustained, he said, by a knowledge of his own powers and character. He was still ambitious – for acclaim and for money – but was ashamed, at least some of the time, of the pursuit of them. 'Fame and money,' he wrote, 'these are the two chief spurs which drive the author on. The statement may sound ignoble, and the writers of every generation persist in avowing that they write only to amuse themselves and to do good to their generation.' The author who wishes to succeed, he knew, 'must be wide-awake and he must take a vast deal of trouble'. He had not taken enough trouble; the memory was always with him.

In a letter to Hardy, offering to do some 'arrant log-rolling' for *The Woodlanders*, he regretted that his 'influence for good is almost gone . . . I am as downcast about the future as possible,' he wrote, but 'I have persuaded the *Saturday Review* to let me notice *The Woodlanders* and I have stirred up Coventry Patmore to make the same attempt with *St James's Gazette*.' He recalled how many details of *The Wood-*

landers he had already heard from Hardy's own lips. They were in close contact. Hardy would come to Delamere Terrace on Sundays whenever he was in London. From Rome, in the spring of 1887, Hardy sent Gosse two pressed violets from Keats's grave.

Robert Louis Stevenson was setting off for America, persuaded to try a complete change for the sake of his health. The only book he seemed to be taking, Gosse told Hardy, was *The Woodlanders*; but he also took, among his household chattels, a barometer from Gosse. Gosse was already regretting he had never made the effort to visit Stevenson in Bournemouth, in spite of telegrams and a publication day copy of *Kidnapped*, which Gosse loved. He had seen him only on his rare visits to London. Stevenson was very ill when he and Fanny finally made the decision to leave England in August 1887. They were lodged in a small hotel in Finsbury Circus, ready to catch the steamer at the Albert Dock on the following day. It was doubtful whether Stevenson would be fit enough to receive visitors.

Gosse went to Finsbury Circus early on Sunday, 21st August. He waited half an hour, and suddenly Stevenson came into the room, very pale and dressed entirely in black, for he was in mourning for his father. The clothes were new and rather stylish – black velvet coat, black silk neck-tie, so that instead of looking 'like a lascar out of employment, as he generally does, he looked extremely elegant', his hair over his shoulders, but shiny from brushing. He prowled about the room, in his usual noiseless panther fashion, talking all the time. There was some talk of Gosse witnessing Stevenson's will but no other reputable witness could be found. The entire staff of the hotel had apparently gone to church. This started Stevenson on a notion that any suitably piratical fellow, defying the spirit of Sabbatarianism, could make a handsome revenue by sacking deserted hotels between the hours of ten and twelve. A mask might perhaps be worn for the spirit of the thing, but all that was really needed was a brave heart and a study of the City Postal Directory. Gosse blushed for the youth of England and its lack of manly enterprise.

This was how Gosse recalled his last visit to Stevenson in *Critical Kit-Kats*, years later, after Stevenson's death. It was a good story, but in real life we know that Gosse and 'the housekeeper of the hotel' did indeed witness the will in the Sunday quiet of the small hotel. Stevenson and Gosse would keep closely in touch during the Samoan years, though letters would go astray and Stevenson sometimes felt he was writing 'to feed the maw' of Sydney Post Office. It amused Gosse to see Stevenson strangely anxious to make the South Seas seem like the Hebrides, in spite of 'the photographs of wild seductive groups, all brown flesh and hibiscus blossoms'. The newspapers 'pullulated with gossip' about him, Gosse told him. It was very confusing. He made up a few examples:

> All our readers will rejoice to learn that the aged fictionist L.R. Stevenson has ascended the throne of Tahiti, of which island he is now a native.

or

> The vineyards which are cultivated in the island of Samoa by Mr Stevenson, have been visited by desolating storms; the gifted romance-writer fears that he will, this season, expect none but elderberry wine.

or

> Mr R.L. Stevenson, who is thirty-one years of age, is still partial to periwinkles, which he eats with a silver pin, presented to him by the German population of Samoa.

'We are quite disappointed,' Gosse wrote, 'if the newspapers pass a single day without a paragraph of this kind, and I am sorry I do not know how your future biography is to be compiled from the enormous mass of conflicting materials.'

Stevenson, of all Gosse's friends, was one of the few who dared to bring up the subject of Churton Collins. Gosse might call him Shirt'n Collars himself; most people were wise not to mention him. But Stevenson told Gosse there were two barometers at Vailima, one, Gosse's own present, known as Gosse, and another one on the verandah, which registered only unpleasant weather and was known as the Quarterly Reviewer.

On 1st December 1894, two days before his death, Stevenson wrote to thank Gosse for the dedication 'To Tusitala' in *In Russet and Silver*, the book of poems Gosse had just published. It recalled the distant day when the two young strangers had stood together on that Scottish boat, and it regretted Stevenson's exile. Stevenson's letter was a moving one, as if he knew, though he certainly did not, that it was the last letter he would ever write. He recalled Gosse's loan to him in the hard-up early days in London, and went on to contrast their paths in life.

> I was not born for age . . . Come to think of it, Gosse, I believe the main distinction is that you have a family growing up around you, and I am a childless, rather bitter, very clear-eyed blighted youth. I have, in fact, lost the path that makes it easy and natural for you to descend the hill. I am going at it straight. And where I have to go down is a precipice.

Well, my dear Gosse, here's wishing you all health and prosperity, as well as to the mistress and the bairns. May you live long, since it seems as if you would continue to enjoy life. May you write many more books as good as this one – only there's one thing impossible, you can never write another dedication that can give the same pleasure to the vanished
　　Tusitala.

Long before the letter arrived Stevenson had indeed vanished; his body had been borne on the shoulders of his Samoan friends to its last resting place on the narrow ledge high on Mount Vaea. Of the letter, Gosse wrote to his daughter, Tessa: 'I feel as if it was almost the very most precious thing I possess, this good bye from the great genius that I loved so much.'

As Stevenson had realized, it was the children, growing up around him, who restored Gosse's enjoyment of life after the literary strife of 1886. In the summer of 1887 Sylvia was six, Philip eight, and Tessa had her tenth birthday. Their father wrote to Thornycroft from Paignton on September 22nd.

I have had one or two long walks, but otherwise our time has been spent on the beach in indolent play with the children. I never had so much of the company of my family before and I find that with middle life (I was thirty-eight yesterday!) a new pleasure comes that I had never thought of, the delight of seeing one's children delighted. We have had such excitements as collecting cockles, catching prawns in pools, bathing on the sands and climbing over the strange crimson promontories; and Philip has been my companion in longer excursions along the coast.
　　My mother is our guest here, and we go over frequently to St Marychurch to see my Father. The latter is very sweet and gentle, wonderfully mellowed at last by the softening hand of age; and I have felt an affection for him and a pleasure in his company, this visit, that I am afraid I never really felt before. And so, in the evening there is light.

In his life of his father, Edmund described a day the whole family spent together on the rocks in the centre of Goodrington Sands, the last of so many expeditions over the years, with young Philip much the age Edmund himself had been on those early explorations after his mother's death. 'No-one on that brilliant afternoon would have guessed that the portly man with a grizzled beard, who stood ankle-deep in the salt pools, bending over the treasuries of the folded seaweeds, lustily shouting for a chisel or a jar as he needed it, and striding resolutely over the slippery rocks, was in his seventy-eighth year, and still less that his vitality was so soon to decline.'

Writing next day from Marychurch to Paignton, the father thanked the son for making the day such a happy one for him. 'It was delightful to see around me your dear selves and the sweet eager children engaged in diligent and successful search for my gratification. When you all come over again, you will think the tank a busy scene worth looking at . . .' They would see sea-horses, crabs, pipe-fish, the little black and white *Cottus*, a scarlet and blue Galathea lobster. 'The children will be interested in these details,' their grandfather wrote.

No letters survive between father and son from the months in the previous year when Edmund had been under attack. Some news of the conflict must certainly have percolated to Marychurch: Edmund records sending his *Athenaeum* defence to 'Mother' as well as Aunt Lizzie. It would be interesting to know how Philip Henry Gosse reacted. One might imagine he received in sorrow this further evidence of the instability of earthly joys and reputation. The criticisms would have been particularly hard to take, for he thought he had trained his son in the importance of absolute accuracy, as well as in observation and exact grammar. On the publication of *Gray* in 1881, he had written 'You know what a Dragon I am for correctness!' But as Edmund recorded in that letter to Thornycroft, his father was in mellow mood in the summer of 1887. It was a last calm before the anguish of the final months.

There are several glimpses of the Paignton holiday in other letters. With a mouthful of butterscotch, Gosse wrote to thank the Armours for sending such delicious stuff to his children, the 'thankless infants' themselves being on the shore from morning to night and unable to be cajoled to the writing-table. He rhymed to Mrs Armour that the children

> How and wherever they may be
> Make noise enough for thirty-three

and he described Nellie

> Upon her lap of watchet-blue,
> Unfurling the *Saturday Review*.

She was still painting too and exhibiting at the Grosvenor Gallery. One day in 1887 she recorded painting for seven hours on end, and then taking a run to get rid of her headache.

Gosse had gone down to Devon 'in a feverish and agitated mood', but family pleasures and reading Dostoievsky restored him entirely. He thought *Crime et Châtiment*, reading the long Russian novel in French, 'the most powerful, the most daringly successful novel I have ever read'. Thirteen years later he was still admiring the book intensely: it opened a door for the reader, he told A. C. Benson, and you went into another life. It was your own life that became unreal and you thrilled with the tragedy of the book. But in his old age, he would write to André Gide: 'We have all in our time been subjected to the magic of this epileptic monster. But his genius has only led us astray and I should say to any young writer of merit who appealed to me – Read what you like, only don't waste your time reading Dostoievsky. He is the cocaine and morphine of modern literature.'

Paignton had not been Gosse's only holiday in 1887; he had his usual spring visit to France, and also a visit to Germany with George Armour in July. He admired Armour's organizing ability ('I would trust him with a lark's egg through a field of battle'), but he longed for Thornycroft's company, particularly when looking at sculpture in Nuremberg.

Cambridge was as congenial as ever. Passing through the great gate of Trinity, 'looking up at the line of the battlements against a deep purple sky and the Hall with its coloured festal lights, I felt that indescribable feeling of joy that I have felt so often'. Arriving from London on his regular visits, he would find a great fire, his gown put out to warm, the tea laid and the kettle singing. The feeling of belonging and acceptance was infinitely soothing. The new Master at Trinity, Montagu Butler, was particularly friendly, though he disconcerted Gosse a little by writing down notes on one lecture in the palm of his hand, 'with a balmy air of sanctity. I can't think why', Gosse wrote to Nellie. He was talking about Matthew Arnold and the hall was packed. Someone guessed there were three hundred people.

Watching the tennis on the backs in Trinity Term, Edmund wrote to Nellie: 'Such a mass of handsome ruddy strong-backed youth all in flannels – in the clear green fields under a soft blue sky – how beautiful and really how Greek it is! . . . I wish you were here; it is all so lovely.' There was certainly a note of regret that his own youth had not been like that, but shut up in that frowsty cage in the British Museum. This letter surely suggests that Nellie knew his feelings about male beauty and male friendship. He could persuade himself that his pleasure in the Cambridge boys was as much aesthetic as sexual, though he knew, and admitted (unusually for the period) in his biography of Patmore, 'the enormous part that sex takes in the whole comity of man'.

An American student, Clinton Scollard, wrote letters home which give a further sight of Gosse at Cambridge the following winter, entertaining the young man to lunch in his rooms at Trinity, after a lecture on Thompson and Blair.

It was exceedingly jolly, – the open fire, the cozy little dining-room and then the great chairs before the fire in the book-lined sitting-room afterwards, not to mention the lunch, which came piping hot from the college kitchen – chops with a thick gravy, crisp fried potatoes and then jam and bread and butter, a very fashionable Cambridge luxury. We drank claret and Mr Gosse said to me, noticing I did not partake very freely – 'Come, you must do better; I have a poor opinion of a man who does not like a good wine.' Imagine such a speech from a man of Mr Gosse's position at home!

One morning, Gosse's bedmaker was surprised to find a bottle of brandy in his bed, but there was no real cause for alarm. He had acute toothache in the night, and had rinsed his mouth with brandy – taking the bottle to bed in case the pain returned, but falling asleep and forgetting all about it in the morning.

Nellie, meanwhile, was at Marychurch, helping Eliza to nurse Philip Henry Gosse. He had contracted bronchitis while studying the stars through the telescope at his open bedroom window that winter. He had, at this last stage of his life, become addicted to a study of the heavens. His belief persisted that at any moment he might be taken up into the sky to join his Lord. Seeing his wife's distress when he was ill, he said 'Oh darling, do not trouble. It is not too late; even now the Blessed Lord may come and take us both up together.'

For months Philip Henry Gosse clung to life 'in the same melancholy and precarious condition'. He refused to die in the way that ordinary people died and fought to stay alive. For years he had prayed that he might be 'one of the favoured saints who shall never taste of death, but be alive and remain until the coming of the Lord'. He was convinced that he had been promised 'translation', not death, and brooded for hours on what particular honour the Lord would do him when he reached heaven. Would he send an archangel to the gate, or might not the Lord Himself step down from his throne and come to the gate to meet His faithful servant?

Edmund himself was at Marychurch in March, while Nellie was at Marley with the children. His father had had a good night and was very cheerful, but Sandhurst was 'at odds and sixes. There is a very awful parlour maid, six feet high and as impudent a hussey as ever you saw.' She would refuse to answer the bell and poor old Mrs Gosse would run into the kitchen to fetch a knife that Laura had forgotten, rather than try to summon her and be cowed by her tongue. In the morning, Edmund would find the drawing-room ashes cold in the grate and the chairs all topsy-turvy, to punish them for sitting there last night, he thought. 'Poor dear little Mother is horribly weak and irresolute: Father retains all his brain-power and strength of will', though confined to bed. He had them running round in circles, knocking on the floor with his stick.

> Rap, rap! Edmund flies up.
> Father: I want to see your mother.
> Son: Can't I do anything for you?
> Father: No! thank you, I won't trouble you. I'm chilly.
> Edmund flies down.
> Son: Mother, what does he have on when he is chilly?
> Mother: Oh, the rug in the drawing-room.
> Edmund flies up with the rug.
> Father: Hasn't your mother come?
> Son: She's so tired. May I wrap your shoulders in this?
> Father: No, I want to see your mother.
> Edmund goes down very slowly. Mother ascends. This goes on four times an hour. The doctor calls and pronounces the father strikingly better.

This doctor was a new one, and something of a worry. There was talk in the village that he was not only a Papist, but the lessee of a theatre as well. If Philip Henry discovered such facts, no one could bear to contemplate the consequences. The doctor was also insisting that they should employ a night nurse, but old Mrs Gosse thought of a thousand objections. It really needed Nellie to set things straight. 'Everything here is very uncomfortable and incompetent.'

So Nellie went to Sandhurst in May. George Meredith wrote to Gosse from Box Hill on May 17th. He had been hoping Gosse might visit him there, might 'join the rush of good things' in the spring.

> I must write to join hands with you under this affliction. I have looked through the black door of recent years . . . It is only the senses which are hurt by a facing of death or the wrestler with him for our beloved . . . I remember reading a sonnet of yours, on a Dream of the Loss. It spoke this anguish well. But our final thought shall be that we have souls to master pain and fear: Death, the visible feeder of life, should be our familiar. I have him on my left hand and

am, not irreverently, at home with him. To feel this is to be near upon touch of the key of wisdom – but, for the wisest of reasons, it is only good in the white heat of our trial to have it in the grasp. For us, who are not at present being tried, there is danger of its leading to cold philosophy. Not so in your case. I trust to the best that may be wished for you.

But it was Henry James who wrote the most sustaining letters, just as he had throughout the Churton Collins business. Not surprisingly, Gosse called James 'the best of men'. In the winter of 1887/88, they were both seeing their dying friend, James Cotter Morison, author of *The Service of Man*, 'the most powerful attack on Christianity that has been produced in England during this generation', as the *Athenaeum* put it. 'He is on my mind all the time', Gosse wrote in January, visiting him every second day. Morison finally died on February 26th.

Henry James seemed to need Gosse's talk more than ever at this time. 'You are right in supposing that my talk with you the other night made me feel better. It quite set me up, as if I had received a cheque for £1000.' He would be 'famished for a little literary conversation'; and Gosse, he told Howells in America, was the only man of letters not 'quite dense and puerile'. James *cared* about Gosse, too, worrying that he concerned himself too much with the 'odd jobs' of literature, too little with the 'finer opportunities', knowing he needed to do something really important as an answer to his assailant. James would be glad, he told Howells, when Gosse had finished at Cambridge, 'as I think he will then be in a much freer, sounder position'. The term as Clark Lecturer would finish in the summer of 1889 and Gosse would not stand again, giving up reluctantly 'the ever-glittering prestige and excitement'.

James understood entirely Gosse's situation that spring and summer of 1888. He had not actually seen his own father dying. Crossing the Atlantic on news of his father's decline, James had entered the harbour at New York just as his father's body had been buried in Boston. Henry James senior had not fought death, indeed his last words had been 'I am going with great joy.' But his son could of course imagine the special tension of his friend's situation, 'so long as the terrible *process* of your poor father's extinction goes on. It's not death that's bad – it's dying. Why can't we be dead – or even be living without it? I rejoice with you in the change of your father's feeling – or manner; it must make the thing very different. I wish him and you equally the End – and I wish you and your wife nerves and spirit and resistance till it comes . . .'

Gosse had told James that his father was affectionate and gentle and liked to hold his hand, but now he sadly reported that his father's loving sweetness had not lasted; and James replied:

> Greatly do I commiserate your situation and that of your poor wife. There is nothing to do with our great hard natural debts but to pay them to the last penny – and economise afterwards. But hold on – it always pays afterwards, to have held on – and simplifications *do* arrive – suddenly – and everything stops and there is relief and a retroactive feeling which makes us glad for everything we didn't fail to do. Your father appears to be a veritable Ravager of Life – a sort of domestic Attila or Devonshire Hun! But though he makes a desolation where he passes, the flowers will grow again, quickly on the blighted spots – and he will do little hurt if you don't let him really kill patience – much as he may bruise and bleed it.

In May and June Edmund was mostly in London with the children while Nellie was in Marychurch. Edmund worried about her sitting up at night. Apparently Philip Gosse's breathing was so difficult that he could not lie down in his bed. He had thought she had engaged a nurse. 'I think you have avoided telling me distinctly about this, to conceal the fact that you do most of the nursing yourself . . . I have been very unhappy about you all day . . . I want you so thoroughly to understand that I could come at once, any day, without inconvenience, if you summoned me. I am carefully making no engagements.' And Bateman, his chief at the Board of Trade, was being very understanding. As Edmund would write at the beginning of *Father and Son*, above all the 'ties of close family relationship must be honoured and sustained'.

The children, though apparently very kind to their father, were missing their mother. At breakfast Philip, aged eight, announced one day 'a developed scheme of action for the Gosse family'. 'It's a pity that Mother should leave off nursing Grandpapa. Why should not we three and Miss Danger', that appropriate governess, 'go down to lodgings in Marychurch and see Mother when she can get away and we might do lessons just the same?'

Edmund wrote to Nellie: 'Such is the proposal of this Wise Child. What do you think of it? I think it has much in its favour. If a fatal occurrence should come, it will be very desirable to have all of us on the spot immediately afterwards . . . The children would enjoy the summer. You would feel more at ease. I would come when I could.' And the decorating could be done at Delamere Terrace. They were always white-washing and painting at Delamere Terrace. Each summer it seemed they would have an onslaught of workmen. 'That marvellous yellow paper has cleaned better than ever!' Edmund would exclaim. Mrs Watson would lash the workmen on. 'She is the best and fiercest domestic watchdog I ever knew.' Her only disadvantage was that she would maintain, 'Cats is all very well in their place, which ain't in my kitchen.'

The children went to Marychurch. Edmund went each day to the Board of Trade, suffering it seemed beyond the call of duty on one occasion when he was asked to sample some English-grown tobacco, which had been sent to the Board of Trade journal for review. 'It was simply horrid and we are all feeling a little unwell.' There was also this year the Sugar Bounties Congress, which had provided some social diversion but also a great deal of tedium. There were long hours pretending to listen to the Dutch delegate wrangling with the Belgian delegate. But dining and sleeping at Hatfield House, he felt close to affairs. Lord Onslow was closeted with Lord Salisbury. A party given by the Countess of Onslow, for the Sugar Delegates, was the most fashionable gathering Gosse had ever attended. It was the first of many such. 'Most of her Majesty's Ministers were there, three of the Royal Family and lots of people whose photographs one sees in the papers,' he wrote to Marychurch.

Gosse would go down to Devon for a long weekend and then return to London to work. Some evenings he would lose money at whist with the neighbours in Delamere Terrace. (Someone reading through the family letters has crossed out the words 'lost my money' at whist and substituted 'played'.) But grander invitations were becoming more frequent. Gosse was moving more and more in society with a capital S (the sort he had, only five years before, told Howells he could not stand). Somehow he had got to know Sir Redvers Buller and Lady Audrey; at their house he met Lady Dorothy Nevill, who was to become one of his closest friends. 'It seems to me that I was lifted, without preliminaries, into her intimacy.' She was already near sixty, 'but she possessed a curious static quality, a perennial youthfulness'. She prided herself on her eccentricity, cooking (and eating?) guinea pig and horse, encouraging Gosse to send her vulgar postcards. She hated bores, and Gosse was never boring. How boring, she thought it, for the poor wolves in the zoo to have to live opposite a cow. 'I do hate a ruminant,' she murmured when Gosse and she went to the zoo together.

In 1892 Gosse would dedicate his novel *The Secret of Narcisse* to Lady Dorothy Nevill. This was a medieval romance, set in France, that did little to add to his reputation, beyond confirming his extraordinary versatility; though Beardsley tried to get Heinemann to let him illustrate a large quarto edition, Hardy wondered 'how you could get to know a foreign town so exhaustively', and Mallarmé praised it. Rebecca West, much later, would assert that it 'seemed head and shoulders above what was being written at the time'. Gosse wrote to Watts-Dunton about it: 'You and Swinburne are very kind to have been reading my little novel. I am afraid the donnée of it was not transparent enough for less intelligent readers. What I meant to depict was the failure of sympathy between a girl of slight intelligence but very strong instincts and a man of comparatively feeble sexual powers, easily distracted by art. Her robust and fiery temper finds him cold, and she cannot understand it. So in a vague tumult of anger she brings the charge of witchcraft against him.' The world saw it as a simple case of the artist suffering at the hands of a philistine society; the sexual element Gosse indicates in this letter was totally ignored. That Gosse makes his artist a sculptor adds to a suggestion that Thornycroft was similarly consumed by art, not instinct.

At Her Majesty's Jubilee, in 1887, Gosse had had a seat in a stand at the Board of Trade, with cold luncheon available at two shillings and sixpence a head. Now he seemed to be moving much closer to the seats of power. Lord Lytton invited him to dine. He was soon to be Ambassador in Paris, and told Gosse, 'You will not forget that you have a friend at the Embassy whenever you come that way.' At Andrew Lang's dinner table, Gosse met Lord Wolseley. Wolseley was the Adjutant-General of the Forces. Soon he would be Commander-in-Chief in Ireland and Gosse would stay with him in Dublin. Wolseley would appeal to Gosse, 'the highest living authority', to find out if 'z' had been entirely superseded by 's'. It was civilization he was worrying about.

Late in May 1888 Gosse reported to Nellie in Marychurch that 'Lady Audrey Buller and the Countess of Carnarvon have sent Colvin to ask me to give a course of five lectures to fifty ladies of fashion in Lady Carnarvon's drawing-room. I to choose my own subject and be paid £50 . . . Fancy my suddenly bursting into "la vie élégante" in this way! I am quite sure that the good Colvin has used his offices in the matter, but he declares that I was the Ladies' own choice and they are set on me. It will be a delightfully easy way of earning a little money and one may make useful acquaintances. What do you say to it?'

The series was a tremendous success, but it was a step in a direction it was perhaps unwise to take. Gosse would never say, as D. H. Lawrence was to write to Lady Ottoline Morrell: 'I would give a great deal to have been born an aristocrat.' But the fascination with titles, with coronets and white waistcoats, would undoubtedly distort the rest of his life. It would make him enemies as well as friends and disturb many of the friends he already had. Gosse thought they were dear things, the Ladies of Quality, listing some of them proudly for Nellie's and Eliza's 'amusement'. Lady Egerton of Tatton, Lady Wantage, Lady Romilly, Lady Shrewsbury, Lady Londonderry, the Countess of Stanhope, the Marchioness of Stafford – and last of all, arriving when there seemed to be no seat left in the room, imperious Lady Stanley of Alderley, over eighty. She was a florid, fierce old thing, with wisps of rebellious white hair struggling out of her bonnet – wonderfully vigorous, witty and coarse, Gosse thought. He sat at her feet and flattered her.

Lady Stanley was duly impressed with Gosse. A few weeks later, he was able to report that James had just heard from Jules Jusserand (the French Chargé d'Affaires in London, later Ambassador in Washington) that her Ladyship was holding forth at her dinner-table on the merits of Edmund Gosse as a lecturer. The Earl of Pembroke, James also reported, had been defending Gosse to Oscar Wilde. 'So you see,' Edmund wrote to Nellie, 'I am assured of the sympathies of the Upper Classes.'

But there were still the old circles. A party at the Alma-Tademas at their marvellous new house, Grove End, included the Burne-Joneses, the Madox Browns, the Hueffers, and Henry James, with superb music, Gosse admitted, from Sir Charles Hallé. On a Sunday at Grove End, Gosse distinguished himself by cleaning out the garden pond. Tadema was fidgeting about the weeds choking the water lilies. Gosse knew the only way was to wade in and pull the weed out with his hands. 'I cleaned all the lilies carefully; I stayed in about half-an-hour; the temperature of the water was exquisite. Roll my trousers as high as I could, they got wet, but I had some brandy (of 1842, a dream!) and afterwards raced about the lawn . . . I am feeling vastly better for my delicious day at Grove End,' he told Nellie. 'They were all so very brotherly and sisterly.'

The papers too were being kinder. They all reported a speech by Sir Arthur Blackwood, the permanent head of the Post Office, who said there had been a long list of illustrious civil servants – 'from Geoffrey Chaucer to Edmund Gosse'. ('And I don't know him from Adam,' Gosse said.) The disreputable *Star* was so flattering in that summer of 1888 that Gosse was a little worried. 'If it goes on comparing me with everybody, to everybody's disadvantage, 'twill do more harm than good.' At the Pope Commemoration celebrations at Twickenham (a water pageant in dismal weather two hundred years after Pope's birth in May 1688), Dobson and Gosse were both on the platform; but a dull lecture was given by Professor Henry Morley. 'It suggested indeed a contrast with a lecture which Mr Edmund Gosse has more than once delivered on the same subject. During its delivery, Mr Gosse appeared to sleep . . . ,' which was hardly tactful of him, but the *Star* certainly didn't hold it against him.

In July there was a big Society of Authors dinner. Gosse spoke, proposing the toast to 'American authors and authoresses'. One of the 'authoresses' was Frances Hodgson Burnett (half-English, half-American), much in the news for her fight over the copyright of *Little Lord Fauntleroy*. Gosse and she would become good friends, and Gosse too would become more and more involved in the copyright question. Oscar Wilde was less than pleased with the arrangements for the dinner. He wrote to J. S. Little: 'I know you were not in the slightest degree responsible for the gross mismanagement and can only hope that if the Society gives another banquet the arrangements will not be left to a person like Gosse.' Gosse was certainly on the committee, but seems to have had little to do with the seating arrangements. Wilde had been irritated to find that he was sitting next to Lady Colin Campbell, with whom he had not been on speaking terms since she had called him 'The Great White Slug'. One of the problems was that all the American authors had to sit on the top table together, 'in order that the waiters may not make unpleasant mistakes regarding the wine etc'.

Then in August there was the famous visit to Aldworth, already referred to in the last chapter. It was important to Gosse to be so accepted by the Laureate. Looking at contemporary literature at this time, he listed the names he admired: Tennyson, Ruskin, Browning, Pater, Lang, Herbert Spencer, Matthew Arnold, George Meredith, Swinburne, William Stubbs, Robert Louis Stevenson, Thomas Hardy. He knew nearly all of them, and loved the fact that he did. It is only 'disappointed journalists, who have themselves failed to climb Parnassus, . . . who bring back a false report that those upper glens are empty. It is not a sign of intellectual vitality, but of intellectual sterility, to say that all the wit and wisdom was with our fathers.'

Tennyson was of course a legend in his own lifetime. There seemed something immortal about him; but he was pleasantly human that day in August 1888. Grumbling about Churton Collins over tea, he said he had been charged with having imitated the last two lines of an unpublished Chinese poem of the twelfth century. Gosse said, 'So much the better for the Chinese poem.' 'That's very good,' said Tennyson. 'So it is, all the better for the Chinese poem. I don't believe there is any such Chinese poem . . . The dunces fancy it is the thought that makes poetry live; it isn't, it's the expression, the form, but we mustn't tell them so – they wouldn't know what we meant.' He spoke to Gosse as a fellow-poet and a friend. He took him in to see Lady Tennyson for a few moments. Gosse saw her bright smile as she lay flat on her back, an 'old-martyr sort of lady'.

Then Tennyson showed Gosse round his grounds, asking him first solicitously whether it would not tire him, as he had already walked so far. It had been difficult, Tennyson said, to settle at Aldworth, the old Lord Egmont putting every possible obstruction in his way. Tennyson told Gosse that when the house was being built, Lord Egmont rode up to see how it was getting on; Tennyson's foreman had put up a notice reading *Tresspassers will be prosecuted*. Lord Egmont growled out, 'Call him a poet? He can't even spell.' Gosse admired one little lawn surrounded by conifers, murmuring that he thought it, 'like a vale in Tempe'. Tennyson corrected him instantly: 'Cliffs all round Tempe.'

Then he insisted on showing Gosse all over the house, right up to the top to see the view. Gosse was conscious of Tennyson's near-sight: 'He seems to infer the features of the landscape rather than see them.' He pressed Gosse to stay to dinner, said they would drive him to Marley afterwards. But Gosse felt the moment had come to leave. Tennyson walked with him to the end of the drive. 'Never come to Marley again without coming over to see us,' he said waving good-bye, 'the strange old piratical figure, tall, in black, with the flapping hat and the thick-rimmed spectacles, like a sort of vision of a super-annuated highwayman.' The next day was his birthday; he entered his 80th year.

Tennyson could hardly have been kinder, but Gosse's relations with him were not to end on so happy a note. The following year Gosse would call Tennyson 'the rude old Bear' and suggest he cared for nothing 'except flattery and a good glass of port wine'. Tennyson had some reason to be rude about Gosse. He wrote to Watts-Dunton: 'I fear Mr G. is a most inaccurate man. He had made three statements in his notice of me in the *St James's Gazette*, all more or less false.' And Hallam Tennyson wrote to Watts-Dunton: 'My father is naturally exceedingly annoyed by Gosse etc. Two mistakes in so small a thing.' The thing was Tennyson's poem 'The Throstle'; it appeared in the *New Review*, which Gosse was temporarily editing. He obviously kept the original manuscript himself and copied it out (inaccurately) for the printers, for it was among the treasures which were sold by Sotheby's at his death; it is now in the Huntington Library in California, with a note in Gosse's hand attached to it.

At the time of Gosse's visit to Aldworth, Philip Henry Gosse, the patient in Marychurch, was becoming more and more difficult. 'But his strength, how perfectly amazing that is!' Nellie was extraordin-arily patient as the long summer days passed and still he struggled to remain alive. At one stage in July, Edmund had to rush down from

London, for Nellie herself broke down, 'with the nursing in a hot room and all the nervous strain', and she had to take to her bed for a day or two, on doctor's orders. Edmund spent ten days, mostly in his father's room, but one afternoon, 'when the gloom of decay was creeping over his intellect, Philip Henry Gosse was carried out for a drive, the last he would ever take, on an afternoon of unusual beauty'. Edmund described it in his life of his father.

We passed through the bright street of Torquay, along the strand of Torbay, with its thin screen of tamarisks between the roadway and the bay, up through the lanes of Torre and Cockington. My father, with the pathetic look in his eyes, the mortal pallor on his cheeks, scarcely spoke, and seemed to observe nothing. But, as we turned to drive back down a steep lane of overhanging branches, the pale vista of the sea burst upon us, silvery blue in the yellow light of afternoon. Something in the beauty of the scene raised the sunken brain, and with a little of the old declamatory animation in head and hand, he began to recite the well-known passage in the fourth book of Paradise Lost:
> Now came still evening on, and twilight grey
> Had in her sober livery all things clad.

He pursued the quotation through three or four lines, and then, in the middle of a sentence, the music broke, his head fell once more upon his breast, and for him the splendid memory, the self-sustaining intellect which had guided the body so long, were to be its companions upon earth no more.

The father was still just alive when Henry James wrote to the son on 22nd August 1888: 'I am very sorry to learn that you are again *en pleine crise* and I take the liberty of devoutly praying, on your behalf, that it may be for the last time. How terrible to be such a trampled, ensanguined battleground (of life and death) as your poor father must be – the victim of so grim and interminable a tussle. His 96 hours' fast is like the doings of the "early Gods" and there is apparently something primitive and Titanic in his composition.' How Philip Gosse would have hated this pagan analogy. 'For a strictly human son, I can well imagine how discomfortable this may be. I hope before long to hear from you that he is at rest, and that you and your wife are too.'

There was not long to wait; but the final hours were the hardest of all. At the time Edmund and Nellie said nothing to anyone but in 1927, near his own death, Edmund told Harold Nicolson of the terrible last hours on earth of Philip Henry Gosse, as at the end he turned against his God, reviling Him for treachery. The son and his calm strong wife *knew* that the father had lived his life in false hope and a faith that could not be rewarded on earth. They knew, though he had amazingly denied the knowledge, that he must die like everyone else. And they wept with him as he shouted blasphemies and asked his God why He had forsaken him. Through the long dark hours, as August 22nd became the 23rd, they struggled to hold him down. At 1 am he died aged 78 years, 4 months and 17 days, as the son calculated. Nellie and Edmund went to their own rest, their muscles aching with exhaustion.

Henry James wrote with sympathy, sharing in their relief. 'How sensible must be the removal of so unmitigable a presence.' Thomas Hardy regretted that the father's death might mean the son would journey westward less frequently. He spoke of how much Emma had read the father's *Romance of Natural History* as a girl. Many people praised the naturalist. The official report of the Royal Society, recording his death, said that no man had ever done so much to popularize the study of natural history in England.

Hamo Thornycroft, now RA, hearing the news, seemed to have little idea what they had been through. He hoped the children would tend to cheer old Mrs Gosse. 'I suppose it is the first occasion they have realized a death.' He recalled his own sister's death when he was a child. He was becoming very child-centred. His son, Oliver, was more impossible and more adored than ever, 'a domestic thunder bolt', Gosse thought him, as his parents smiled indulgently. 'It seems so unfair that two such gentle people should be trodden underfoot by so tyrannical a child,' Gosse wrote to Nellie. There was another child expected very soon. Edmund was actually in the house when Hamo's first daughter was born. Perhaps, Gosse hoped, she would have a civilizing effect on her brother.

Eliza Gosse had not really been prepared for her husband's death – the house so empty without that 'unmitigable presence'. At one moment she had seemed to realize the situation, the next she had said 'You don't mean to say it will take Dr Cash a year to get your Father well?' And now he was dead and she herself a worry to them. The visits to Marychurch would continue for another twelve years. Very soon there would be 'ructions among the "saints" at the Room' and accusations that Eliza was 'under the corrupting influence of her worldly son'.

Philip Henry Gosse left a considerable estate: £16,196 8s 1d. The house, Sandhurst, was valued at £800 and the Room – 'the chapel and schoolhouse' which was apparently P. H. Gosse's own property – at another £400. He left everything to his beloved wife, Eliza, except for

£1000 to Edmund William Gosse. £5000 of the residue was for Eliza to dispose of as she wished; the rest was hers for life only and would descend to Edmund or his heirs. 'How thankful I am,' Edmund wrote to Nellie, 'that our entire future does not depend upon Mother's caprice, dear and nice as she is.' But the father's immediate legacy was certainly more than just a thousand pounds. It was a freedom at last from the need to justify, at least in theory, every divergence from the stern paths laid down for him in childhood. It was a removal of that too-anxious love, which had caused so much anguish, even though it was many years since Edmund had seen himself as a bird, 'fluttering in the network of my father's will'.

There was a marvellous feeling of relief and release; but there was also, inevitably, guilt and regret. The son's struggle for independence had been the most important thing that had ever happened to him. And now that, at last, he felt truly free, what more could he do with his freedom? The wider world he had escaped to had its own horrors and constrictions. Thinking of his father, he thought how far apart they had grown. 'Man was the creature he was least interested in,' Edmund would write in his life of his father. Nothing could have suggested more clearly how far apart were their sympathies: the father at times almost a recluse, the son, more and more, hating to be on his own.

Reading through his father's papers, Edmund came across a manuscript memoir of a cat, which reminded him strangely in its intimate, searing detail, of the memoir of the beloved Emily, his mother. Edmund himself must surely have wept as he read of his father's attempt to remove the dead kittens from the mother cat's vulva, trying to save her life, and then, when the attempt had failed, how 'having restrained my emotions before my servant' – the old gardener – he had come into the parlour and wept himself, surprised by the extent of his grief.

P. H. Gosse had thought of himself as 'cheerful, even merry and jocular . . . as keen on enjoying God's gifts as ever', as he wrote to Edmund in 1875. Certainly his 'joy in earthly things', sea anemones, orchids, butterflies, was unusually ardent for someone of his particular religious views; but it is hard for us not to think of him stern and weeping, at Emily's death, at Edmund's intransigence, at God's betrayal in the final hours, and at the death of that small female cat.

At the funeral service, one of the 'saints' fixed her eye upon the family. 'I fancy she thinks we are not sorry enough,' Edmund thought. A crowd followed the coffin from Marychurch to the grave in Torquay cemetery, which bears almost the last words in the Bible: *He which testifieth these things saith, Surely I come quickly. Amen. Even so, come, Lord Jesus.* Nellie's mourning bill was 'a marvel of cheapness'.

There was no formal mourning. Edmund was dining with the Thorny-crofts in London only a week after his father's death, and next day winning a shilling at bézique and two shillings at whist at the Crosses at No. 32 Delamere Terrace. Then he returned to Marychurch to sort through his father's papers. It was now he discovered his pure Massachusetts ancestry on his mother's side. How strange it was that he had not known it before. But some of his American friends said they had sensed it all along.

That was his own mother's late gift to him. Now, to assuage his guilt, he needed to look at his father's life and do justice to it. It was almost like paying another of what James had called our 'hard natural debts', but it was also a release. He had the chance to write a very good book, which would lead on to an even better one. Almost immediately he began work on *The Life of Philip Henry Gosse F.R.S.* He wrote to George Armour that it 'should be interesting, but it is very difficult. My chief hope of success is that I am thoroughly conscious of the difficulty.'

One of the difficulties was the widow. At Marychurch, in July 1890, the proofs were arriving, and Edmund wrote despairingly to Nellie:

> I am pretty well exhausted. I suppose I knew the height and depth of the Dweller in this abode. But oh! what a time I have been having of it – not unfriendly at all, you understand, but dense, suspicious, blunt, confusing and confused. Each sentence misunderstood, a thousand irrelevant questions asked about each turn of the Biography . . . I am alive, just alive. Even the heat seems treacherous, 'it brings out the damp so much'. Her wheels grind more slowly than ever and more independently of one another . . . Her cap has been coming on and off all the day and at last I had to twist up a long piece of dry grey hair and decently push it down behind her ear.

All the same, he concluded, 'She is very dear and quaint.' She would become even quainter. But at this time she wrote her own recollections of her husband, which were attached as an Appendix to Edmund's *Life*, and show that she cannot all the time have been as confused as he suggests in that letter. But Marychurch seemed 'so decadent and sordid, such an air of dry rot over everything, and everybody so old and infirm'.

The *Life* was extremely well received. There were even some suggestions that it was a masterpiece. Henry James admired it: 'Gosse has just published a singularly clever, skilful, vivid, well-done biography of his father, the fanatic and naturalist – very happy in proportion, tact and talent . . . He is altogether prosperous and productive . . .'

Reading the *Life*, John Addington Symonds wrote: 'I wish there were more of *you* in your Father's *Life*. You could write a fascinating autobiography if you chose; and I hope you will do this. Only how can we do veracious psychological self-portraiture? I have felt, all my life, like a man whose right hand was tied up and covered.' George Moore also saw an autobiography beyond the biography. He had settled down in London after his unconventional youth in Paris and had been seeing a good deal of Gosse. Long before, he had left a card one day when he had himself published nothing, but admired *On Viol and Flute*. His *Confessions of a Young Man* (1888) had set something of a fashion; no one earlier had thought of writing an autobiography before reaching the age of fifty.

Finishing Gosse's *Life* of his father, Moore glimpsed in that book the great unwritten story of the relationship between father and son. Should he wait until he was due at Delamere Terrace the following Sunday? He could not wait. He rushed to the National Club in Whitehall Gardens, where he knew Gosse would be having lunch. Gosse now only went to the Savile on Saturdays. 'One realizes the desperate and decayed sense of letters by lunching there among the fallen divinities', he wrote to Robbie Ross. The National was nearer his office, jollier but even more respectable, full of bookish civil servants who would be knighted before long: such as Alfred Bateman, his boss at the Board of Trade, and Thomas Elliot at the Board of Agriculture. (Dobson preferred a solitary table at the other end of the room, but would join Gosse after lunch for coffee and cigarettes.) This clubbishness (which Gosse had sensed as a threat to himself as early as 1879) was, in fact, one of the things Moore had against his dear friend, Edmund Gosse. In his *Confessions*, Moore had written: 'Literary Clubs have been founded and their arm-chairs have begotten Mr Gosse; but the Tavern gave the world Villon and Marlowe . . . You can't have a Club without a waiter in red plush and a silver salver in his hand.' It was all too respectable. Perhaps Moore's idea would shake Gosse out of his clubbishness, which was in the 1890s insidiously transforming him.

There was certainly nothing stuffy or respectable about George Moore, although he himself became a member of Boodle's and changed his tunes in several ways after Gladstone had approved of his controversial *Esther Waters* and his sales soared. He remained, how-ever, the sort of man who said he believed you must have rules in poetry, if it is only for the pleasure of breaking them, just as you must have women dressed, if only for the pleasure of undressing them. He often seemed to want to shock. Twenty-five years later, Siegfried Sassoon would record Moore describing 'The blisters he got on his behind while riding from Joppa to Jerusalem on a mule', and 'doing his best to be at his worst'. Gosse and Moore for forty years had a close 'slightly catty' relationship, Moore always aware of the claws in the velvet paws.

Fortunately, there was that day at the National Club a spare place beside Gosse. He said, 'Have you come to lunch?'

'No,' Moore replied, 'but I've come to tell you that all the morning I've been reading your *Life* of your father and I could not wait before letting you know how much I liked your book.' ('Gosse in his demure way was capable of much literary excitement, his face flushed and he trembled at hearing his book praised.') 'I admire your book,' Moore continued, 'for itself, and still more for the book it has revealed to me, but I missed the child, I missed your father's life and your life as you lived it together – a great psychological work waits to be written – your father's influence on you and your influence on him . . . and as a background you will have the Plymouth Brethren . . .'

Gosse was taken with the idea but saw all sorts of problems. 'No one will read it,' he thought. 'And a great many of the people of whom I could tell are alive.'

'Oh Gosse,' Moore said (so he tells us), 'your record will be full of sympathy. There will be no reproach . . .' Gosse seemed to lose consciousness of Moore's presence and of the bustle of the Club going on around them and started to talk about his childhood. He told of the night his mother came home from the doctor. 'I saw my mother standing in the doorway and as she saw my father, she said "Oh Philip, it is cancer . . ."'

It was many years before Gosse published the book that Moore had suggested that day. It was not, as Symonds had felt, that in writing his own autobiography Gosse would feel handicapped by having one hand tied and covered. There were no such problems if he were to look simply at his childhood. But the image is counterpointed in the vivid correspondence Gosse and Symonds had at this time, to which I referred in an earlier chapter. It is obvious that Gosse is still fascinated at this period by his own buried feelings for Thornycroft. He reads and re-reads Symonds's sonnets on the theme of *'l'amour de l'impossible'*, with more admiration and sympathy than he can express. He admits they bring tears to his eyes. He agrees entirely with what Symonds has said about the effect of the repression of one's instincts on one's health.

It is 'absolutely in accordance with my own experience. The position of a young person so tormented is really that of a man buried alive and conscious, but deprived of speech. He is doomed, by his own timidity and ignorance, to a repression which amounts to death, because, so far as he can see, it is final, as final as blindness or mutilation could make it. This corpse however is obliged to bustle around and make an appearance every time the feast of life is spread. Happy those who learn to break the cerecloths in time: it is less difficult than might be imagined, with luck and the grace of God. Then come in another set of dangers, and the need of other virtues, but what a change of light and aspect.'

Strong and confusing words; but Gosse is certainly looking back. It was the young man's predicament and passion – ten, eleven years before. And that side of his sensual nature was now, if not dead, at least quiet. The Wild Beast had been tamed. (Gosse always felt strongly about the dangers of lust, of mere physical infatuation, loathing the idea that it could ever excuse 'ingratitude, disloyalty, cruelty'.) Now, in 1890, Gosse told Symonds, he was nothing but a 'jaded old hack of letters', and his 'cheerful and trivial muse' took things in a very different way from Symonds's. Moreover, he said, he had 'come out of the fire absolutely clear in conscience and without the shadow of a doubt as to right and wrong. To refine and cultivate – not to repress and destroy, that is one's duty, as it appears to me.'

It is rather interesting to speculate that these letters survive by a deliberate act on Gosse's part. He was a biographer; he hoped his own biography would be written. After Symonds's death and the death of Horatio Brown, his literary executor, Gosse came into all the Symonds papers, to dispose of as he thought best. He and Hagbert Wright, the Librarian of the London Library (where Gosse was on the committee for many years) had a bonfire, sparing little but Symonds's manuscript memoirs, which were deposited in the London Library, not to be available for fifty years. Gosse confided all this to Janet Vaughan, Symonds's granddaughter, one Sunday afternoon, not long before his own death – and she was furious at his attempts to whitewash her grandfather. She walked out of his house and never went back.

But these crucial letters from Gosse to Symonds were not burnt, as Gosse would instruct Fred Benson to burn his letters to his brother, Arthur (knowing what could be made of that tempestuous relationship, and not knowing that Arthur's enormous diary would survive). It was as if Gosse really wanted some future world to know how much he had felt and suffered. In 1924, when *Corydon* was published, Gosse wrote to André Gide (to whom he never confessed his own early homosexual feelings, but only his sympathy): 'Perhaps you thought I should be "shocked". But that is not my way . . . There is nothing in the whole diversity of life which serious men cannot seriously discuss. No doubt, in fifty years, this particular subject will cease to surprise anyone, and how many people in the past might wish to have lived in 1974.' At the same time, Gosse would tell J. C. Squire that he believed 'conscious moral falsity' – in other words hypocrisy – a far graver failing than an 'instinctive abnormality'. But society forced men into falsity and furtiveness.

Writing to H. H. Furness in 1899, when Furness had sent from America at Gosse's request Whitman's newly published Letters (and used the word 'revolting' to describe them), Gosse suggests the reason he wanted the letters was to settle the doubt one had always had. 'One doubts no longer. But I cast no stone . . . The strange old creature, in his loneliness, getting this queer gratification for his impulses.' Gosse writes to Furness as an outsider, but then shows his sympathy: 'I wonder why we are so very anxious to have everybody cast in exactly the same mould? . . . When he rages at the "damned fool" that bullies his Peter, we are in the presence of Harmodius and Aristogeiton. Is it not so?' They were Athenian youths who loved each other.

Whitman's letters were of course not published until after his death in March 1892. Symonds had been an ardent disciple of Whitman's, just as Gosse had been, in those days when they had both first read *Leaves of Grass*; but Whitman, in 1890, had finally rejected Symonds's invitation to come out into the open about his sexuality, and the implications of *Calamus*. 'That the *Calamus* part has ever allowed the possibility of such construction as mentioned is terrible. I am fain to hope that the pages themselves are not to be even mentioned for such gratuitous and quite at the time undreamed and unwished possibility of morbid inferences – which are disavowed by me and seem damnable.' Symonds was bitterly disappointed. It was some consolation that it was just at this time that Gosse was moved to write so frankly and sympathetically years after he might have confided in Symonds. At last they had come 'so suddenly and clearly into sympathy'.

Symonds was in the habit of sending his friends photographs of himself. There was nothing very unusual about that. The Victorians were always sending each other photographs of themselves. Gosse's archives are full of the faces of his friends, relations and acquaintances, mounted on small rectangles of cardboard, often inscribed. What was more unusual was that Symonds sent his friends, as well as photos of himself, photos of Angelo, his favourite gondolier, and of other young men he knew. There was an excellent amateur photographer in Davos; Symonds often mentioned him in his letters. Symonds sent photographs not only to men, but also to his great friends Mary Robinson and Janet Ross. There is no suggestion, even in relation to one photograph he sent Miss Robinson of a naked young man with a sword between his legs, that anyone might consider them obscene or offensive. Symonds was working on his biography of Michelangelo, and would encourage models to pose in 'the impossible positions discovered by Michelangelo'.

The description of Gosse taking furtive looks at pornographic photographs during Robert Browning's funeral service in Westminster Abbey is based on the letter Gosse wrote to Symonds on the 31st December 1889. But the way Gosse expresses himself shows that the photograph was not an opportunity for sexual titillation or distraction, but rather bound up with his feelings at the death and decay of a genius, who was also his friend, and the fear that he himself might be nearer death than youth. He was thanking Symonds for the photograph and a book, and wrote:

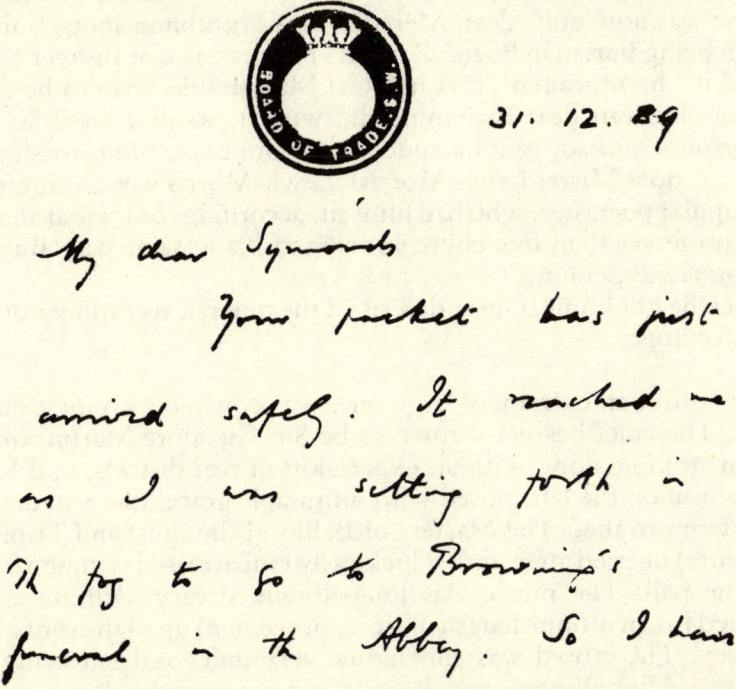

only yet been able to enjoy the beautiful photograph, which is full of poetry. As I sat in the Choir, with George Meredith at my side, I peeped at it again and again, and at last, while waiting in the deep silence for the ceremonial to begin, with many thoughts of love and life and genius and decay, moving in my mind, this sextain formed itself – I hardly know how – and I send it to you as the onlie begetter of all that sehnsucht:

Dark-stamen'd flower, across thy beauty
Sighing, I cast the veil.
In Youth's high spring-tide Love's a duty
And rose-crowned hopes prevail;
But autumn comes, and brings I see
Not rose, but rosemary for me.

There was plenty of time to look at the photograph before the service began – what was more natural than that he should look at his morning's mail during the long wait for the procession? The Abbey was crowded. There was Gosse sitting with George Meredith, Mrs Humphry Ward was behind them; Burne-Jones just opposite. It was more than an hour before the coffin arrived. Meredith was full of chat, but it was rather difficult, as Gosse had to answer to his further ear; the left one was now quite deaf. Meredith was grumbling about Bulwer-Lytton being buried in Poets' Corner: 'The presence of Bulwer . . . so defiled it,' he muttered, 'that no Real Man should wish to be there! Nevertheless our dear Browning did wish it, so all is well! So does Tennyson – and so,' with a sudden spit-fire expression, tossing his chin . . . 'does Mister Lewis Morris!' Lewis Morris was an ambitious and popular poetaster, who had himself, according to Gosse at another time, no fewer than five chins; his slogan, Lang said, was 'Buy *me*, nothing else is genuine!'

When he got home, Gosse described the funeral, recording nothing of his feelings:

The coffin, an extremely large one, was covered by a long purple pall. The chief bearers seemed to be Sir Theodore Martin, on the right, toiling along with an expression of real distress, and Sir F. Leighton on the left, posed with inimitable grace, like a statue of a modern prophet. The Masters of Balliol (I thought) and Trinity (I am sure) hurried after, rather lucklessly embarrassed with the fringe of the pall. The music was long-drawn, dreary, delicate and it floated for an infinite length of time, (it seemed) up to the roof of the Abbey. The crowd was enormous: very quiet and unusually decorous. After all was over, Poets' Corner was quite deserted for a while and, making for it –, I found the grave open, with the coffin exposed to view, a few flowers resting on the bare wood.

12

Sunday Talk

STAYING TO SUPPER, after the Sunday afternoons in Delamere Terrace, was regarded as a great honour, but it was not an honour reserved for smart people or famous names. Arthur Waugh, who came to London as a young man seeking his experienced relative's advice, recalled those Sundays in the 1890s. One obvious reason why Gosse always entertained on Sundays was a determination to transform the dreary Sundays of his childhood. (Even in 1898 he was writing to Nellie while with his stepmother in Marychurch: 'How trying Sundays are at Sandhurst.') Waugh wrote in the *Fortnightly Review*, after Gosse's death:

The party would begin between four and five o'clock; the relays of tea and cakes were continuous; the room hummed and bubbled with conversation. To the newcomer, who might perhaps know hardly anyone present, the first impression was apt to be over-powering. Where in all this crowd were his host and hostess? He stood irresolute at the door, and the maid's announcement of his name was audible only to those in her immediate neighbourhood. But out of the corner of his eye his host had marked the latest entry, and bore down upon him with out-stretched hands. In a moment he was whisked away and presented to his hostess, presiding over the tea-cups, and then carried off to be introduced to some other guest, with whom he had to find a topic of conversation without delay. By the time he had got well embarked upon a mutual interest, he was probably transferred to someone else, for the host had a chronic suspicion that his guests might get bored with one another. The flying ball of conversation passed from side to side; the stream of visitors came and went; towards seven o'clock it thinned out, and perhaps a dozen or so were left. These were the afternoon's chosen few, to whom Gosse had whispered, during his flittings to and fro, an invitation to stay to supper. When the number was made up, he would disappear to the dining-room below, to make sure that enough places were laid, and to bring up the wine from the cellar. He had settled in his quiet way where everyone was to sit, and he slid into his place at the head of the table, and set the talk going afresh with renewed and undiminished energy. He was now at his best, and the little party circled round his personality. He picked up stray remarks and turned them into entertaining channels; he told anecdotes, and evoked others; he was as good a listener as a talker, and he inspired the company by his example.

I read in a recent volume of reminiscences that the invitation to make one of this intimate circle was reserved by the host for the more distinguished of the afternoon's guests, and that it was to be regarded as something of a snub if one were allowed to go away with the early crowd. Nothing could be further from the truth. My own memory of the Gosses' Sundays goes back for much more than forty years, and began when I was myself the shyest and most provincial of intruders. But I was nearly always of the supper company; and among those I met there were many who, like myself, were living in lonely and rather shabby London lodgings, and looked forward to these entertainments for the best meal and the happiest evening in the week. Gosse loved to be a patron of the young, and he was a patron who did not patronise. It is true that he always liked to be the first to acclaim a new talent. If some other voice had been the first raised, he was disposed to challenge it. 'Who is this new poet', he would exclaim, 'that the *Chronicle* compares with Keats and Heine? Why not with Goethe and Shakespeare, while they are about it?' But the mood soon passed. After a day or two he had possessed himself of the new poet's book; and, if he found it good, he forgot all his doubts and hesitations. Next Sunday the young poet was of the company; and, as likely as not, remained to supper.

Waugh remembered Gosse fluttering round Patmore, who made Waugh think of the prophet Elijah, rugged and menacing. (Sargent used him, in fact, as a model for Ezekiel in his frieze at the Boston Library.) Gosse continued to visit Coventry Patmore from time to time. Patmore had now moved from Hastings to Lymington, to a rather strange house with thirty-five rooms. There had been one visit early in 1888 that Gosse could hardly bear to recall. Patmore said to him at breakfast one day, looking grimmer and greyer than ever: 'You won't have much to do as my literary executor, old boy!' It turned out that Patmore had just burned the entire manuscript of his *Sponsa Dei* on the advice of Gerard Manley Hopkins, who later wished he had spoken more guardedly. Gosse had read the book and lamented its loss. 'I hardly know any prose of our time more delicate or penetrated by a greater charm of style.' But Patmore had decided the world would misunderstand it, his interpretation of the love of the soul and God by analogy with the love of man and woman. It was a treatise on Divine desire seen through the veil of human desire. From the time of this destruction, Patmore seemed to grow old. He had never kept in touch with things that were going on. One day he asked Gosse, 'What is Ibsen?' He visited Gosse in Delamere Terrace on Sunday afternoons until his death. Not long before that, Nellie reported in a letter to Tessa: 'Mr and Mrs Coventry Patmore came – Mrs P. more silent than ever, Mr C. P. in an extra-bad temper – they did *not* stay to supper.'

Thomas Hardy often stayed to supper. Waugh remembered him 'never by word or look suggesting any consciousness of his own distinction'. He remembered Andrew Lang, arousing himself from a dream of boredom to murmur 'Norman Gale talks about a girl's knees being polished; they are nothing of the sort,' to which Gosse replied quietly, 'My dear Lang, what do you know about girls' knees? You haven't seen any for years.'

There was one Sunday – 12th April 1891 – when Waugh met at Delamere Terrace not only Thomas Hardy and Henry James but Lord and Lady Wolseley (later there would be many more lords and ladies), William Heinemann and young Arthur Symons. Symons, who would be such an influence on Yeats, came from a background very similar to Gosse's. He had spent his childhood in Devon and Cornwall; his father was a narrow Wesleyan preacher; he had left school at seventeen and had worked at the British Museum. It was not surprising that he was particularly welcome at Delamere Terrace and that Gosse was trying to use his influence to get Heinemann to publish Symons's poems. 'It seems more difficult than ever to sell verse', Gosse wrote to another aspirant, Ernest Rhys.

Writing of Lady Dorothy Nevill, Gosse once said: 'When we tell our grandchildren that [she] was the finest female wit of her age, they will ask for examples of her talent, and we shall have very few to give.' Witty talk is almost impossible to preserve and what Gosse himself actually said on these Sundays is hard to imagine. Later, in the new century, we will have the Sitwell and Sassoon versions of similar occasions; in the 1890s, Max Beerbohm gives us a glimpse of Gosse and Andrew Lang at Delamere Terrace. Lang was 'a very beautiful thing in the room'. It was as if he had been placed there as an ornament. 'From the buzzing human throng, he seemed to be quite as detached as any palm in a pot.' Eventually he did detach himself and moved out on to the balcony. To Beerbohm, his unanimated eyes looked so valuable that he wondered if Lang went about armed, or unarmed but very heavily insured. Gosse was used to those eyes. He took the young Beerbohm out to the balcony to introduce him to Lang, who was gazing into the dingy canal. 'The angler aroused,' murmured Gosse. And 'Yes' he said to Lang, in that mock-lyric tone which his friends knew so well, 'that is where I always go a-fishing, the first thing in the morning. Oh, you should breakfast with us! Trout, salmon, dace – I know not what!' He had a strong sense of the ludicrous and the unlikely.

Over and over again, people praise Gosse's talk. Kenneth Clark, much later, remembered the talk at a lunch Gosse gave was 'as brilliant as a page of Proust'. Sir George Trevelyan said it was 'as light and bright as the dialogue in a Restoration Comedy'. Somerset Maugham would call him 'on the whole, I think, the most interesting and consistently amusing talker I ever knew'. Maugham said he would talk about Swinburne, whom he had known intimately, 'in an entrancing fashion, but he could also talk of Shelley, whom after all he could not possibly have known . . . I am sure he made them more amusing than they really were.'

But it was not all set-pieces. Gosse would often come out casually with remarks which would make people smile – such as his remark when asked how he had enjoyed a Swinburne play: 'We were as nearly bored as enthusiasm would permit.' Seeing an advertisement in a newspaper, 'Messrs Gunter send their celebrated Invalid Turtle to all parts of the kingdom,' he remarked, 'I conceive of it travelling with a lack-lustre eye.'

But so much of his talk turned upon gesture, intonation, look, that it is impossible to reproduce. So Benson would write in his diary. Gosse was undoubtedly a marvellous mimic – not only of the famous but even ('in the most perfect and complete manner,' as Nellie wrote once to Tessa) of the baby crying next door: 'the sob, and the choke and the catch of breath'. In his voice, people said, you could catch the very echo of the other people speaking. 'He could grumble with the growl of Tennyson, giving to the voice the exact burr and mumble of the Lincolnshire Wold; he could flutter and shrill with the hands and tremolo of Swinburne; he could grin as Matthew Arnold grinned; or lower like Rossetti; and pat plump hands even as Browning patted in Trinity gardens or boom moralities like Huxley. "The poetry of Swinburne, my dear young man" (this is Huxley booming), "is the poetry of profligacy composed for profligates."'

There was a story about Morris and the Rossettis. Gosse used to say that when *Sigurd the Volsung* came out, Morris sent it to Gabriel Rossetti and called a few days afterwards to hear what he thought of it.

Rossetti said languidly he could not read it: 'I can't take any interest in a man whose father was a dragon.' Morris boiled over with wrath, 'I don't see that it is any worse than being a man whose *brother is a fool.*' Gosse particularly liked this story because he shared Morris's opinion of William Rossetti, especially as he went on to 'exploit every leaf and scribble' of his famous siblings.

There was also the story of Gosse meeting William Rossetti on an omnibus at the time of the Italian anarchist scares of the 1870s. It was so crowded that Gosse was standing when he noticed Rossetti, wearing his usual huge black coat and huge black hat, sitting with his daughter. Remembering a paragraph he had recently seen in the newspapers, Gosse greeted Rossetti down the length of the omnibus, 'Mr Rossetti! Mr Rossetti! Is it true that you have become an atheist?'

'No, Mr Gosse,' Rossetti replied, 'I must differentiate. My daughter, here, is an atheist; I am an ANARCHIST.' The bus quickly emptied and Gosse was able to travel home in comfort.

There were other omnibus stories. There was the Master of Trinity meeting the Master of Jesus on a London omnibus one day and enquiring solicitously 'And how is Jesus?' That perturbed their fellow passengers too. And there was the headmistress who saw a solicitor in the next seat – a man with a large family – and said loudly to him: 'I see you have no idea who I am but you might like to know that you are the father of one of my children.'

Then there was Browning's story which Gosse handed down with relish. Guests were assembled for a dinner party at one end of a room, most of which was occupied by an unusually large table. The butler threw open the door to announce Mr Alfred Austin. 'And I give you my word of honour,' said Browning, '*nothing whatever* came into the room . . .' Of course, this story only works if you know, as all Gosse's audience would know, that the future despised Poet Laureate was barely five feet tall.

There were lots of well-told anecdotes, but Gosse also had the ability, so it seems, 'under a dancing levity of words, to convey a profound sense of reality and truth, to be the glorified showman of experience, lending art to reminiscence and differentiating it from anecdote'. He talked to enjoy and share, his admirers said, and never just to show off. He had a genius for relaying a conversation or recalling a scene in a manner that made it seem more truthful, as well as more interesting than the truth itself. He was no egotist and had a game he played himself when confronted with egotists; he would sit back and count the number of times he heard the word 'I'. As he grew older, talk became increasingly Gosse's main recreation. (By 1913, he was saying that he hated writing and loved talk more and more.) As we shall see, there would be times when even one of his friends felt that he had heard it all before.

Arthur Waugh also described the occasion when he was invited to supper at Delamere Terrace to discuss his future. He was an ambitious literary young man, grandson of the cousin, Mrs Morgan, who had taken the small boy, Edmund, into her Bristol home immediately after the death of his mother. Eventually he would father Evelyn, who would take a crueller view of the distinguished relative in his old age. Arthur Waugh arrived in his evening suit, nervously, far too early. Gosse came to greet him with both hands outstretched, a gesture that was soon to be familiar. He was wearing a brown velvet jacket which filled the provincial youth with discomfort, afraid lest his host should think his shirt-front a vain display. But Gosse knew how to put a boy at ease, and so did Nellie. Soon young Arthur was sitting eating and drinking, with Gosse dazzling him with literary stories but also drawing him out to discover what he had read, what he cared about. Just as they were finishing the meal, the maid announced that Henry James had called – he often did around nine o'clock – and was upstairs in the drawing-room. 'Grasping at my last chance,' Waugh said, 'I ventured to ask my cousin what he thought I had better do to make a beginning in life.' He peered at me through his spectacles and said thoughtfully, 'Well, my friends tell me there are excellent openings for a young man nowadays in the wine merchants' business.'

But he was only testing him out. The following Sunday, Gosse introduced Waugh to Wolcott Balestier, 'a very brilliant young American publisher, whom it may be useful for you to know'. It was indeed. Soon Waugh was working for Balestier in his office at 2 Dean's Yard, Westminster, that 'picturesque' office which Henry James would blame for Balestier's early death. Two years earlier, in 1889, Gosse, fresh from an excited reading of *Soldiers Three*, had drawn Balestier's attention to the amazing new writer, Rudyard Kipling. 'Rudyard Kipling?' queried Balestier, languidly. 'Is it a man or a woman?' Gosse was nettled and retorted: 'You will find that you won't be allowed to go on asking questions like that. He is going to be one of the greatest writers of the day.'

It was Gosse's conviction that he introduced Kipling to Balestier, but it seems likely that they had already met at the home of Mrs Humphry Ward. Gosse had been bowled over by young Kipling, so recently arrived from India, by the man even more than by the work. Early on, he sent him the new edition of *On Viol and Flute*, though he must have realized his poetry was hardly to Kipling's taste. There is an apparently unpublished verse letter from Kipling to Gosse, amusing himself with the difference between their poetic steeds. It begins:

> Dear Misther Gosse,
> Your winged hoss
> That crops Parnashian grasses
> Was bred and bitted
> In climes unfitted
> For oriental asses!
>
> I thried to lead
> My own poor steed
> Up that same hillside, sorr
> But the rarey faction
> Disthurbed his action
> My garron nearly died, sorr . . .

Angus Wilson sees Kipling's life-style at this time presenting 'a brave and teasing puzzle to publishers, editors and critics determined to place him'. Gosse made a stab at it in a letter to Gilder in June 1891:

Kipling is one of the most extraordinary beings ever created, out of Naples or Malacca. He is like an infant might be that smoked manilla cigars all day and was none the worse; or a tarn among mountains with a volcano concealed underneath . . . What he really and soberly is most like, I suppose, is the child of god-fearing dissenting parents, who has run away and enlisted in a thoroughly blackguard cavalry regiment. Only that does not account for the Malay element and a suspicion of knives whipped into your vitals. Not a commonplace young gentleman, Mr R.K., nor do I suppose that any one has a sweeter and more deferential smile and a more awful use of language, both at the same time on tap.

His conversation and company fascinate me horribly, but they are in their effects like long potations of green chartreuse. They make one's hand tremble and one's eyes see visions. All this has nothing to do with his books, which are quite ordinary by the side of himself, because he is not allowed to talk in print of the things he has seen and known and grown bold in.

Gosse had an article on Kipling in the October 1891 issue of the *Century* magazine. In November, through Gosse's arrangement, the *Century* started serializing the novel *The Naulahka*, which Balestier and Kipling had written together in the excitement of the discovery of each other. In December Henry James was carrying to Dresden a 'pot of English flowers' from Nellie, which one of Balestier's sisters would throw into the grave of the 'poor yesterday-so-much-living boy', as James called him, writing to Gosse on the day of that German funeral. William Heinemann was there too at Balestier's graveside. They had recently set up together a new soft-cover publishing imprint to challenge Tauchnitz on the continent.

Heinemann was becoming an important figure in Gosse's life too. He was now editing for Heinemann a series called the International Library: novels from different countries, each one containing 'a specially-written introduction by the editor'. Heinemann would one day publish *Father and Son*. In 1912 Gosse said: 'Mr Heinemann has been my main publisher since 1891.'

Gosse seems to have been overwhelmed by Balestier's death – that was his own word at the time. Eliza Gosse, sending her sympathy from Marychurch, wrote: 'I knew when Nellie told me of it, it would be a great shock to you. You were bound up in him.' Gosse wrote to Gilder: 'I know not how to get on without him – without his sympathy, his energy, his encouragement.'

At the time of Balestier's death, Kipling was in India. Gosse would tell the story that Caroline Balestier, Wolcott's sister, sent Kipling a wire: 'WOLCOTT DEAD. COME BACK TO ME.' He came. On 18th January 1892 they were married in All Soul's, Langham Place, scarcely five weeks after Wolcott's funeral. Gosse wrote to Gilder that day: 'At 2.8 the cortège entered the church and at 2.20 left it, the sharpest thing of modern times. Henry James gave away the bride and I supported the bridegroom.' Heinemann was there and young Tessa and Philip Gosse, but hardly anyone else. Philip remembered the occasion because he wore his first Eton suit – he was now twelve – and was compelled to wear the stiff white collar outside and not inside the new jacket. He had a floral buttonhole bought at Whiteley's for the enormous sum of one shilling – and afterwards he treasured among his souvenirs a hairpin attached to a paper on which he wrote in childish scrawl 'Greatest sight on earth!!!!! Hairpin worn by Carrie Balestier at her wedding. Valued at £5,000,000.'

The Kiplings dined at Delamere Terrace, four days after the wedding, before they went off to America. Very unusually, their names are annotated in the Book of Gosse. The entry reads: '22nd January, 1892. Mr. and Mrs. Rudyard Kipling (recited B.R. Ballads).' *Barrack Room Ballads* was published soon after, and received no fewer than forty-nine reviews in three months.

In spite of his feelings in 1891, those strong overwhelming feelings, twenty years later Gosse could betray both Balestier and himself in a letter to George Douglas: 'You would have detested him. I should have detested him, but that he happened to like me very much. He was a queer, strained tight little type of strenuous Yankee: not important, not (perhaps) worthy of a place in the gallery, but curious and original in his common and imitative way!' Yet J. H. Shorthouse (author of the best-selling *John Inglesant*), with whom Gosse used to stay when he lectured in Birmingham, in his letter of sympathy to Gosse, commented particularly on the impression Balestier left, 'so refined and delicate in its charm'.

The revulsion is somehow tied up with Gosse's later feelings about Carrie Balestier's effect as a wife on the marvellous Kipling – the star of the East, the star of the hour, as James and Gosse described him. At the same time that he was writing so unsympathetically about Wolcott to Douglas, Gosse was telling Arthur Benson that Carrie had annexed and imprisoned Kipling. 'She will now hardly let him leave home and his powers are gone,' he told Benson in 1912. The intensity of Gosse's feeling for Kipling at one time is indicated in an undated note, written presumably in 1899 at the time when, with his child Josephine dead, Kipling himself was apparently dying. The note reads simply: 'I can think of nothing else than of Kipling. It is the most distressing thing that has happened in our time. E.G.' Carrie had been a close friend of the Gosse family before her marriage. She had written warmly from Vermont in 1893 to invite the Gosse girls for an American holiday. They had not gone. By the new century, the two families had drifted apart and Gosse certainly felt strongly that Carrie 'overplayed her guardianship', as Angus Wilson put it. Wilson says, in answering criticism of Carrie's régime, 'It is often necessary in a mature, busy life to miss meeting some charming people.' This was something Gosse could never understand. Meeting charming people generally came first, especially, as he got older, if they were powerful as well.

In the autumn of 1890, Nellie and Edmund Gosse paid four visits. They spent some days with the Hardys at Max Gate. 'The house here seems so quiet,' Nellie wrote to Tessa, 'with no little ones running about and shouting.' The days are commemorated by photographs taken with Edmund's new Kodak. (His previous one, 'after a world of troubles', had been lost at Vézelay on his usual Spring week in France.) There is a photo of Nellie, Emma and Hardy on Weymouth Pier, and one Nellie took of Hardy and Gosse together. Hardy wrote affectionately: 'The most interesting to me is where we are standing together – you and I.' Hardy was trying to persuade the Gosses to buy a country retreat in Dorset: 'I shall pester you with advertisements.'

At various times Gosse considered such a purchase but never made it.

They stayed with the Stephens at St Ives, the visit on which even the normally irrepressible talker, Edmund Gosse, found himself quietened by the 'silent Stephen, the almost speechless Leslie', as Henry James called him. Virginia was eight that year, a year younger than Sylvia; there is no record of what she and Gosse thought of each other at this stage. Gosse was still seeing a good deal of Leslie Stephen these days. As a contributor to the *Dictionary of National Biography*, he was trying to obey Stephen's instructions to all contributors: 'No flowers, by request.'

The Gosses also went to Marychurch to the widowed Eliza. And they spent a few days at Ditchingham in Norfolk, with the Rider Haggards. There are some rather bad photographs taken on the golf links at Bungay. One of Gosse himself is annotated by Philip: 'Unique photo of my father playing golf!' In 1900 Benson would record how much Gosse loathed the game and criticize him for sacrificing his principles so far as to spend all one Sunday walking round a links with A. J. Balfour, very soon to be Prime Minister. 'An otiose and brilliant chatterer is as much out of place on a links as a bird of Paradise in the House of Commons,' he noted disapprovingly.

Gosse admired Haggard. He thought *She* placed Haggard 'in the very front rank of imaginative creators. I am aware that these are strong words and I am not in the habit of flinging such things about.' He was 'thrilled and terrified' by *She*; *King Solomon's Mines* had hardly prepared him for such pleasure.

Haggard was now preparing for a visit the following January to Mexico, to gather background material for a book. The Gosses would do anything to help; it was agreed that Jock, the nine-year-old son, should come and stay at Delamere Terrace during his parents' absence. He was 'younger than Sylvia but taller than Philip,' Edmund reported. They would enjoy his company; and so they did. Jock Haggard's arrival was one reason why the Gosses did not go north to see the first night of Henry James's new play *The American* at Southport. He counted on them, he wrote, at any rate to spend the evening in 'fasting, silence and supplication'.

Tessa, now thirteen, was staying with aunts, first Amy at Marley and then Laura at Grove End, reading Scott and Dickens, and skating. 'From now dates the time of my hair being tied up,' she wrote in her journal for 1891, an extraordinarily scruffy document, full of doodles and blots and wild handwriting, quite unlike the neat copperplate of a correctly brought-up Victorian schoolgirl.

Nellie wrote to Tessa:

Jock has arrived and he is very popular with Philip and Sylvia. S. said that she found him much nicer than she had anticipated, for she found that he could giggle. They all went to the Holman Hunts' party on Saturday. Harriet took them and fetched them and she seems to have had a very lively time of it on the return journey when Launcelot Crane [Walter's boy] from one part of the train and our boys from the other part of it, descended at various stations to have a paper fight (whatever that may be!) during the short stoppages of the train.

Now they were just off to the Aquarium with Cousin Arthur Waugh. When they got back they found that Father had helped some visitors to eat up the little feast set out for the children's tea. 'I'm scribbling to you while I wait for Father to give me some copying that he wants to have done for him this evening.'

On the 16th of January at Marley, Tessa wrote in her journal that they had played bagatelle. 'We finished the game by 9.50, then Aunt Amy retired and we remaining four played vingt et un. After which Uncle Charles brought in a bottle of 40 year old Lunelle. We each had a glass of it and were altogether very merry, so merry in fact that Aunt Amy came down. She tasted Uncle Charles's, talked a little, then sent us off to bed at 10.55.' 'Sis came out in measles,' Tessa added later at the top of the page. Next day, she wrote 'Pip has got hold of the measles.'

On 31st January 1891 Edmund Gosse wrote to George Armour in America: 'The Rider Haggards leaving, as probably you know, for Mexico, we took in their son Jock, a very intelligent boy about the size of our Philip. He brought germs of the measles with him and he and our two youngest verily developed the disease – Teresa, being fortunately away at the Alma-Tademas, has missed it. So that has kept my wife busy, but we have got through it and are all fumigated now and out of this little state of quarantine.' A few days before, Nellie had told Tessa they were all going on very well with 'carbolic baths and different pleasant entertainments of a similar kind'.

On the 8th February, just over a week after Gosse's cheerful letter to Armour, nine-year-old Jock Haggard was dead. All the books about Rider Haggard – his letters, his journals, the biography – refer to the boy, Haggard's beloved only son, dying of measles while left in the care of Edmund Gosse and his wife. In Sylvia Gosse's old age one of her friends came across such a reference and asked Sylvia what she remembered about him. She remembered nothing: 'I just cannot believe it. It just is not possible. I never heard this mentioned by my parents . . .' It was not just that she could not remember the boy's death; she could not remember the boy himself, although she was nearly ten at the time, and she had giggled and played with him for nearly four weeks. Early in January, they had skated on the Round Pond and then, in quarantine, had knelt on the nursery window-sill and watched dangerous boys poling themselves about on rafts of canal-ice. They had nibbled together at the gingerbread men sent by Tessa with no bones broken. They had watched Tessa's baby mice turn into youths in her absence.

Memory is a strange thing, but it seems certain that Nellie and Edmund kept the news of Jock's death from their children and never mentioned him again. He died in Kensington of peritonitis following a 'perforating gastric ulcer', according to the death certificate. It is not a possible complication of measles and gastric ulcers are extremely rare in small boys. It is possible, a doctor has suggested, that he had swallowed some of that carbolic bath. Carbolic is a corrosive poison; the effect on the peritoneum would be similar. It is an appalling thought. One hopes it never occurred to Rider Haggard. He never recovered from the boy's death. After Kipling's son John was killed in 1915, Haggard wrote in his journal: 'He said today that I was lucky to have lost my son early when I still had youth to help me to bear up against the shock and time in which to recover from it . . . (which I never have done really).' And had Kipling himself ever recovered from his daughter Josephine's death when she was nearly seven? Haggard, in his grief, seems never to have blamed Gosse.

Their friendship continued. From 1908, when Haggard joined the National Club, they would see each other more regularly; Gosse would regretfully note Haggard's 'loud laugh and goggle eyes and the joke repeated two or three times for fear you have not perceived it'. Haggard would think how strange it was that Gosse had changed so little in the thirty-three years since their first meeting.

But he *was* changing, of course. In the 1890s, in his forties, Gosse was already beginning to take on the rôle of a sort of elder statesman, so early had he made his own reputation, so thoroughly had he managed to recover it after the Churton Collins episode. Gosse mixed a great deal with younger men – particularly with Arthur Symons, Yeats, Maurice Baring, Arthur Benson, Eddie Marsh, Richard Le Gallienne, Henry Harland, Beerbohm and Aubrey Beardsley.

Maurice Baring, recalling his first meeting with Gosse at Arthur Benson's in the summer of 1893 – when he was just about to go from Eton to Cambridge – spoke of how 'subtly flattering he was to the young by giving them to understand that they understood as much as he did, that they were in the secret . . .' Benson, proud schoolmaster as he was, thrust at Gosse an essay the boy had written on William Collins:

> Gosse took it in his hands and scanned it searchingly, all his critical feathers alert, as they always were whenever literature, and especially the literary efforts of beginners were in question, and he glanced through it . . . seeming to absorb what was going on at a glance . . . Turning to me, he said, 'I see you do not mention Collins' Ode on Greek Music.' This is the Ode which Collins is known to have written and which has disappeared. It was characteristic of Gosse that in so cursory a glance he should have been able to pick out at once a missing link. He was encouraging and highly flattering, using the most subtle form of flattery, not praising, but reading out a sentence here and there, as if conferring the matter and the manner.

Baring was intoxicated by Gosse's talk and by the feeling of contact with the almost legendary names of an earlier literary generation. By now they were all dead, the three great poets – Browning, Tennyson, Arnold – who had supported Gosse's application for the Cambridge job.

Gosse was delighted by the literary young. He wrote to Richard Le Gallienne this same year, 1893,

> The time will come, I am afraid, when you will blush to think you set my common clay so high. But may you when you reach my age, know the exquisite pleasure of finding one of the brightest and most vigorous of all the younger generation . . . as generously respond-ing to your advances as you have to mine. This younger generation knows nothing of that intense yearning for its sympathy that we older fogies have . . .

The time came for Le Gallienne to lose his wholehearted admiration for Gosse rather more quickly than Gosse might have expected. In 1900 in his *Sleeping Beauties and other prose fancies*, Le Gallienne gives what must be a devastating portrait of Gosse, described as Tabby for his mixture of velvet and claws (Benson and Sitwell would also use a feline image – the alternate hissing and purring).

> Whenever he sees a young reputation stepping gaily along the road of literary fame, he sidles up to it with charming manners and intoxicating praise. Then he sucks the blood of its young confidence . . . and draws the life from the poor young thing . . . He fears the young and yet it is only by killing and feeding on the young that he can keep up his semblance of life. The moment a young reputation escapes him his end is near.

This is the voice of a disappointed man, of course, someone who had not fulfilled Gosse's expectations and had felt the sting of his criticism. But most of this group of young men, though not sycophantic, had a continuing regard for Gosse as mentor and master. He enjoyed that rôle as much as he had enjoyed his Pre-Raphaelite days as 'the youngest poet'.

Most of all, perhaps, the young men enjoyed his hospitality and his talk, and what Baring, after his death, called 'the unflagging alertness, the undimmed keenness, the infinite humour, the fun'. They relished his inveterate curiosity, his zest for literature and for life. He would tell them to enjoy life, 'to suck at it as a wasp drains a peach'. And he had plenty of practical advice to offer after twenty-five years of the literary life. He also had considerable influence and power; that influence and power, which he had thought almost gone after Churton Collins's attack, now seemed amazingly restored, even if he did continue to make blunders himself.

In fact, there were other problems in the January of 1891. Henry James wrote to a friend:

Poor Gosse has just passed through one of his periodical episodes – a ferocious attack from William Archer, in the *P.M.G.*, on the subject of his translation of Ibsen's last (and queerest) play *Hedda Gabler*. Again he has been almost saved by the extravagant malevolence (as it seems to me) of his critic. But he *has* a genius for inaccuracy which makes it difficult to dress his wounds.

Before looking at this particular episode, it would be as well, perhaps, to see how far Gosse was still involving himself in the Scandinavian studies which had first established him as a critic twenty years before. During the eighteen-eighties and nineties he did not find time or energy to keep in touch with many of the new writers who were emerging, but he continued to write about Ibsen, Bjørnson, Brandes and Hans Christian Andersen, and also about the Icelandic Sagas. Many of the notices and articles he wrote on Scandinavian themes were, in fact, obituaries of the writers he had met and studied in the eighteen-seventies. But somehow he managed to preserve his reputation of being Britain's leading Scandinavian expert. There was not a great deal of competition. He was justifiably celebrated as the man who had introduced Ibsen to English readers and less justifiably as a great Scandinavian scholar. In the eighteen-nineties, he began to be asked by publishers on both sides of the Atlantic to act as an adviser, editor, the writer of introductions, whenever Scandinavian literature was being considered for translation. For instance, he edited the novels of Bjørnson for William Heinemann in no less than thirteen volumes, with a long introductory essay and bibliographical notes for individual novels.

As for Ibsen, Gosse had considered translating the play we now know as *A Doll's House* back in 1880, soon after it had first been published in Norwegian. He asked and received Ibsen's permission to do so, but he never completed it. On 15th December 1880 there was one performance of William Archer's translation of what he called *The Supports of Society*, but Ibsen's time had not yet come. No one could see him as a commercial proposition; the English translation of *The Pillars of Society*, as it became, was not even published until 1888.

Gosse claimed in an article in the *Sketch* in 1898, at the time of the celebrations for Ibsen's seventieth birthday, that it was his 1873 monograph on Ibsen in the *Fortnightly Review* that introduced Archer to the great Norwegian. In a graceful tribute to Archer's work in popularizing Ibsen, Gosse wrote: 'English readers know Ibsen mainly as they have had him revealed to them by Mr Archer, and they could hardly know him better if they read him in his own language. Mr Archer is the host, and his the guests and the dances; but it was I who swept the floor and who lighted the candles; from this humble pre-eminence in time no-one can depose me.'

Replying to this article, Archer wrote privately to Gosse. He did not deny that Gosse had first introduced Ibsen to English readers. It was of course true. But *he* had discovered Ibsen for himself as a boy of seventeen in Norway, in that very year 1873. Though a Scot, he had family connections in Norway, spent a great deal of his boyhood there and was bilingual. Years afterwards he was delighted to find, he told Gosse, that his 'boyhood admiration was shared by so eminent a critic as yourself'. The tone is friendly, even deferential; Archer had put well behind him the 'extravagant malevolence' James described in 1891.

On 2nd November 1889 the *Academy* observed that 'Ibsen's vogue seems spreading through all parts of the world.' It reported a rumour that a complete edition of Ibsen's works, under the joint supervision of Archer and Gosse, was being planned for publication in New York. But, in fact, Archer and Gosse were working separately, as Ibsen had himself realized when his publishers reported a request from Gosse for translation rights in his next play. Ibsen wrote to them: 'I must pay regard to Mr W. Archer, to whom I owe so much and from whom I can expect in time a similar approach to the one which has come via you from Edmund Gosse.'

The new play was *Hedda Gabler*, and Gosse's particular keenness to get hold of it may well have been because in June that year, 1889, Ibsen had had his first real breakthrough on the English stage with a translation by Archer of *A Doll's House*. Archer wrote, years later: 'The Ibsen controversy, indeed, did not break out in full virulence until 1891, when *Ghosts* and *Hedda Gabler* were produced in London but from this . . . production onwards, Ibsen was generally recognized as a potent factor in the intellectual and artistic life of the day.' It was natural that Gosse, who had spent years trying to establish Ibsen's reputation (remember those twenty articles in six years) should now want to share in the profit from this new interest in Ibsen.

Gosse had some misgivings about where Ibsen's genius was leading him. Neither he nor Archer really understood *The Wild Duck*, for instance. Indeed Archer would tell Gosse in 1898 that he doubted if the Old Man himself really understood his own plays (which 'makes it so much more interesting'). At the beginning of 1889, Gosse had written about *The Wild Duck* in the *Fortnightly* in an article called 'Ibsen's Social Dramas': 'There is no doubt that it is by far the most difficult of Ibsen's dramas to comprehend.' Years later in *Father and Son* Gosse would tell how this play recalled 'memories of the embarrassing household of my infancy' which helped him 'to realize Gregers Werle, with his determination to pull the veil away from every compromise that makes life bearable'.

In 1890 Gosse continued to help further Ibsen's reputation; he wrote an introduction to Eleanor Marx-Aveling's translation of *The Lady from the Sea*, and for the Heinemann edition of Henrik Jaeger's *Life of Henrik Ibsen* he had specially translated the numerous quotations from Ibsen. At Stanmore he wrote to Nellie: 'The hours slip away in a kind of dream.' There was a hammock slung in the tulip tree. 'I have been translating the bits of poetry in the Ibsen book.'

On 29th November, Ibsen wrote enthusiastically to Gosse about the handsome English edition of Jaeger's book and hoped he was now receiving regularly the proofs of *Hedda Gabler*. He ended the letter warmly: 'I feel impelled to express to you the sincere pleasure and satisfaction I feel when I see how my literary works increasingly gain entry to those extensive English-speaking territories where a foreign poet generally finds it so difficult to establish a foothold. Please be assured that I shall never forget what in this respect I owe above all to you.'

The problem with *Hedda Gabler* was that Heinemann thought he had bought for Gosse the sole right to translate it; Ibsen thought he had sold only the *first* right, and that later Archer would be able to translate it for his projected collected edition. Archer had already paid Ibsen a fee for this which Ibsen now returned with regret, sad to think that 'the great collected edition will thus remain incomplete'. Ibsen had every confidence in Gosse's version, he said, but in fact his English was not adequate to judge how accurate Gosse was.

Archer was obviously in a mood to find fault if fault was to be found. His article in the *Pall Mall Gazette* on 23rd January 1891 was grimly entitled 'A translator-traitor: Mr Edmund Gosse and Henrik Ibsen'. In it, he said that Gosse's translation was 'so inconceivably careless and so fantastically inaccurate as to constitute a cruel injustice to Henrik Ibsen.' He had known for a long time how imperfect Gosse's Norwegian was but had hesitated to criticize someone who had done so much to introduce Scandinavian literature to English readers. Now he condemned Gosse for asserting his sole right to translate the new play and felt he must point out 'that the version on which, if Mr Gosse has his way, the English-speaking world will have to depend exclusively for its knowledge of *Hedda Gabler*, is one of the very worst translations on record, and reproduces the terse and nervous original about as faithfully as a fourth-form schoolboy, translating at sight, might be expected to reproduce a page of Tacitus . . .'

From earlier translations, Archer now recalled some Gosse howlers:

a phrase meaning 'distinguished himself on the battlefield' Gosse translated as 'always voted right at elections' and 'holde en tale' he considered meant 'have a talk', not 'to make a speech', as it really does. After listing some similar howlers in the new play, Archer suggested that Gosse's offence was worse than Hedda's in the play. She only burned Løvborg's manuscript, whereas Gosse had defaced, stultified, published and then claimed sole copyright in Ibsen's play. Archer's view had strong support years later from James Joyce, who called Gosse's translation 'wretchedly bad'.

The misunderstanding about copyright seems to have been Heinemann's fault rather than Gosse's. It was amicably resolved; indeed the dispute served to bring Archer into contact with Heinemann, who eventually published the complete standard edition of Ibsen's works. Volume III contained Archer's translation of *Hedda Gabler*, not Gosse's. But, as if to emphasize publicly their complete reconciliation, the 1906–08 revised edition contained a version with both their names attached to it.

As usual, when Archer's ferocious attack came, early in 1891, Gosse had staunch friends who put their own construction on what he was supposed to have done. On January 25th, Andrew Lang wrote sympathetically, disregarding the howlers and his own lack of Norwegian; 'What a nuisance it is, all rows are, but, as to the translation, a cow could see you didn't invent the dialogue, nor pervert it, but let it take its chance.' Gosse himself semed to remain unbowed. In a letter to Dobson on January 31st, he wrote, 'Poor Heinemann gets so excited that I fear he will burst. The poet Young foresaw this scrimmage, and prophesied of it:

> 'Insatiate Archer! could not one suffice?
> Thy shaft flew thrice; and thrice my peace was slain . . .'

On February 24th, he told Nellie that Braekstad, his old friend, the bookseller turned Norwegian vice-consul, was 'helping me to revise *Hedda Gabler* . . . Peace with Archer seems to be the order of the day now.' Apparently Archer had told the actress Elizabeth Robins that he had not yet made a translation 'and they had better use mine', Gosse said. But Elizabeth Robins has described how she worked with both Archer and Gosse on a workable version for the stage, which finally appeared at the Vaudeville Theatre that April with Miss Robins as Hedda. Now it was the play itself that was abused. Ibsen might be 'a potent factor' in the life of the day but he was coming in for an extraordinary amount of execration. Yeats, seeing the 1889 production of *A Doll's House*, had left the theatre muttering 'Art is art because it is not natural.' But with *Rosmersholm, Ghosts* and *Hedda Gabler* – all of which had their first London productions in 1891 – the critics' mutters rose to screams. Phrases such as 'hideous nightmare', 'the foulest passions of humanity', 'mean and sordid philosophy', 'pretentious triviality' poured from their pens. Archer commented: 'Alas poor Ibsen! It is well that he does not read English.' But at least, by the end of 1891, Ibsen's name was known to every reader of a London newspaper, and Henry James was at last, after *Hedda*, able to find Ibsen interesting. Up till then he was sure Gosse made Ibsen out to be more interesting than he really was. He had been 'embarrassed by his lack of appreciation'. 'Must I find these things works of skill?' he asked Gosse.

Gosse and Archer were undeterred. With Ibsen's consent, they worked on a joint translation of *Bygmester Solness* (*The Master Builder*). Elizabeth Robins herself knew some Norwegian and was able to take the part of Hilde in the copyright reading at the Theatre Royal, Haymarket, on 7th December 1892, with Gosse reading Dr Herdal. It was the first performance in any country, five days before the play was published in Scandinavia. Gosse recorded: 'It marks my solitary appearance as an actor! It was odd to think that all this could go on in the very heart of London, where everybody thirsts for something new, and yet totally escape the newspapers.' Ibsen *was* news indeed. Arthur Waugh said that Ibsen and Kipling were the two names he heard most frequently in his early days in publishing.

Gosse came to agree with Ibsen that the prose dramas were the significant part of his work, but he remained convinced that *Brand* was 'one of the great poems of the world'. In his early work on Ibsen, Gosse had lamented that Ibsen had abandoned 'the language of the gods' for the real talk of human beings. There were times certainly in the 1890s when Gosse wondered where Ibsen was leading him, and some critics of his biography in 1907 suggested that Gosse no longer sympathized entirely with the writer he had done so much to introduce to the English-speaking world. Gosse's inclinations, as he grew older, were fundamentally conservative but his temperament remained optimistic. Ibsen could be described as both a 'grim old Tory' and a 'fiery old Radical'; at times he seemed a complete anarchist who wanted to 'blow the existing fabric into the air'.

Gosse could go no further than Yeats, who said he could not escape Ibsen because 'though we and he had not the same friends, we had the same enemies'. Convention, respectability, meaningless propriety, hypocrisy (what Gosse called 'conscious moral falsity'), the defeat of the individual – for all Virginia Woolf's gibes long after, these would always be Gosse's enemies. He also sympathized entirely with Ibsen's attitude to women – how could he not with Nellie for a wife? Ibsen,

Theatre Royal, Haymarket.

Sole Lessee . . . **Mr. H. BEERBOHM TREE.**

SPECIAL MÅTINÉE

FOR THE FIRST TIME

December 7th, 1892,

AT 10 A.M.

BYGMESTER SOLNESS

SKUESPIL I TRE AKTER AF HENRIK IBSEN.

PERSONERNE:

Bygmester Solness - -	Mr. R. L. Braekstad.
Fru Aline Solness -	Miss Amy Haldane
Dokter Herdal - - -	Mr. Edmund Gosse.
Knut Brovik - - -	Mr. Wm. Heinemann.
Ragnar Brovik - -	Mr. M. Sejaman.
Kaja Fosli - -	Mrs. R. L. Braekstad.
Froken Hilde Wangel - -	Miss Elizabeth Robins.

Handlingen foregaar hos Bygmester Solness.

Manager - - - Mr. Fred Harrison.

ADMITTANCE—ONE GUINEA.

after all, was the first great writer to see women as themselves, not in relation to man and his importance. In an amusing article at this time in the *Century*, Nellie quotes 'our great champion': '"We must look upon man's mistakes with some leniency because we are not blameless in the matter ourselves." Fancy that, Hedda! I am afraid that we are not indeed, and yet how desirable it is, at this magnificent moment, that we should be.' Nellie pleaded for tolerance and sensitivity as 'bloodily, bloodily falls the battle axe' and 'one by one the privileges of men are falling'. She had been sent from Chicago, 'as I happen to be a woman and was once a sort of artist', a splendid volume of *Art and Handicraft in the Woman's Building* and read in it with pleasure and without surprise that 'the World's Columbian Exposition has afforded woman an unprecedented opportunity to present to the world a justification of her claim to be placed on complete equality with man'. Turning the pages, she felt her cheeks flushing with pride to think that 'my sisters had, unaided, produced these pretty "designs for stools in leather-work". Oh, may they be enabled to take their noble triumph generously! May they be magnanimous in the hour of victory!' For every Rebecca who was refusing Rosmer, there were a hundred bowed over their leather-work stools and glad not to have to run the world. Like many women who know perfectly well that they are as strong and clever as their men (or stronger), Nellie Gosse saw the dangers and disadvantages as well as the justice of feminism. 'I entreat women,' she wrote, 'in this heyday of their success, to be moderate, and above all not to ride rough-shod over the susceptibilities of the fallen sex.'

Gosse never publicly repudiated Ibsen – how could he? He had put so much into his early conviction that Ibsen was a great writer and, now that the world was sitting up and taking notice of him, the last thing Gosse wanted to do was to disown him. But there are glancing references that suggest he began to weary of what H. A. Jones, a less demanding playwright, called 'those searching Scandinavian blasts'. In 1891 Gosse was encouraging Kipling to go to *Hedda Gabler* and Kipling was praising the music hall and its superiority to the 'new theatre'. But in 1899 Gosse wrote to Pinero urging him to stick to comedy – 'no more melodrama or farce or Ibsen'. In *French Profiles* he would remember the eighties, with all its 'searchings into theories and proclaiming of gospels, all the fuss and strain of Ibsen and Tolstoi and Zola'.

Gosse, of course, remained officially an Ibsen admirer. In 1898, he and William Archer jointly organized a subscription for the seventieth birthday. Shaw had some criticisms of their handling of the affair, but Archer wrote to Gosse: 'I quite agree with you that it doesn't matter a jot what Shaw or anyone else says – the Old Man has been gratified and England has played a creditable part in the celebrations,' – 'thanks mainly to you,' he had written in an earlier letter. Archer had met Ibsen long ago in Rome but it was not until 1899 that Gosse at last set eyes on him. It was twenty-seven years since that first review of Ibsen's *Digte*, 'a picture drawn in the dark', as Gosse described it.

In 1899 he wrote to Brandes: 'My wife and I were six weeks in Norway this summer . . . I saw a great deal of Ibsen, Bjørnson and Grieg.' We don't know much about these meetings, though years later Gosse recalled that Bjørnson called Ibsen a scoundrel but 'one doesn't print such memories', Gosse said.

They stayed at the Victoria Hotel, Christiania, and Nellie wrote to Tessa about the joys of a 'telephone terminus' in the bedroom. They could telephone for whatever they wanted: 'white gloves for F. to wear at the Palace and a choice spray of flowers for Mrs G's shoulder for the first night.' She said 'I have to be very careful, for he gets so over-nervous with all the excitements.' Packing and travelling had their own tensions. Nellie had sat down to write to Tessa the night before they left their rural hotel to come to the capital:

Dear F. is trying to do his own packing – but, oh! the anxious face! We are to leave here at 7 tomorrow, so all the packing was done before supper except the clothes F. had on, and our toilet articles. F. said, 'I think I'd better put together the things I mean to travel in tomorrow,' to which I replied that I thought he would find them all right on the chair in his room. I heard a good deal of moving about in there, and then F. appeared, with a very drawn face, and in his night-shirt, bearing in his hands the clothes he had taken off. 'Why,' I cried, 'surely you don't mean to go to bed so early as this! It's not 10 yet – and the bread and cheese supper we've just had!' 'No,' F. replied, 'it's only 9.30 and I don't at all want to go to bed yet, but what am I to do?' We both of us laughed very much about this, and I advised a book in bed. So that's what's happening . . .

Meeting Ibsen on September 1st was apparently comparatively straight-forward, though Gosse's personal observations on his visit to Ibsen's house have been revealed as typically inaccurate. He drew conclusions from the absence of books, for instance, but he had not been shown the library. That same evening the Gosses attended the opening performance of the Norwegian National Theatre. To avoid having to decide between Ibsen and Bjørnson, a Holberg play was performed, with Norway's two great living playwrights both sitting in the centre of the dress circle, but separated by a vast garland of red and white roses. Gosse was there the next night too when *An Enemy of the People* was on the stage and the audience shouted 'Long live Henrik Ibsen' over and over again.

In March 1902, Gosse wrote a poem for Ibsen 'on entering his 75th year.' 'Thine is a splendour never doomed to die,' he wrote, 'Long clouded by man's vapours, long delayed, But risen at last above all envious shade.' Gosse's work for Ibsen went on. There was a long article in the new edition of the *Encyclopaedia Britannica* in 1902 and a further one in the 1911 eleventh edition. When Ibsen died in 1906 the long obituary article which appeared in *The Times* was, of course, by Edmund Gosse. There was an even longer article in the *Atlantic Monthly* that July. In 1907 Gosse's biography of Ibsen was published. Even the most enthusiastic reviews suggested that Gosse, in order to avoid eulogy, had gone too far in the opposite direction. The critics seemed to resent the fact that Gosse was not wholeheartedly enthusiastic about everything Ibsen had written. (Arthur Symons in a letter took an opposite view, liking the book but disliking Gosse's admiration for *Brand*.) Michael Meyer, the author of the standard biography, rather strangely (considering the reaction at the time) says that Gosse 'admirably expresses the attitude of the Edwardian age towards Ibsen'.

However much his interest was privately flagging, Gosse kept up his Scandinavian reputation until the end of his life. He would write letters to *The Times* pleading for the preservation of Ibsen's birth-place and against the censorship of *Ghosts*. Towards the end of the war, he was appointed chairman of a newly-formed committee for the promotion of Scandinavian studies in the University of London, wrote more letters to *The Times* in an effort to raise money for the establishment of university lectureships, and was partly responsible for the first department of Scandinavian Studies set up at University College, London, in 1918. He co-edited the *Oxford Book of Scandinavian Verse*, an apparently rather unsatisfactory volume, in 1925. He was honoured by the governments of all three countries – Norway in 1901, Sweden in 1908, Denmark in 1912. Yet there is no doubt that after 1880 he was never so closely in touch with Scandinavian literary affairs as his reputation should have demanded. Kai Friis Møller would tell a story of how, in 1919, Gosse had enquired in the course of a fireside conversation about a paper called *Faedrelande* which had ceased to exist in 1882. When, as cautiously as possible, Møller told him so, Gosse took it bravely: 'Well, yes, of course – after all it was Ploug's newspaper,' adding, as if citing some long ago lesson learnt by heart – 'Carl Parmo Ploug.'

In March 1928 Gosse was invited to attend the Ibsen centenary celebrations by the Norwegian government but he was too old to go. He did, however, give a lecture on Ibsen in London to mark the centenary. It may have been his last public appearance.

In Max Beerbohm's marvellous parody of a Gosse Portrait or Sketch, one of the two Great Men in that section of *A Christmas Garland* is Henrik Ibsen. Beerbohm imagines Gosse bringing about a meeting which never happened between Ibsen and Robert Browning – with Gosse a minnow 'swimming to and fro between Leviathan on the one hand and Behemoth on the other'. Neither of the Great Men had heard of the other, but Browning consented to send his gondola for Ibsen, 'so large and lovable was his nature that, had he owned a thousand of those conveyances, he would not have hesitated to send out the whole fleet in honour of any friend of any friend of his.' Ibsen seemed to regret his acceptance of Browning's invitation, particularly when Gosse saw fit to translate into Norwegian 'God's in his Heaven, all's right with the world', but the dreadful meeting proceeded. It seems both funny and remarkably convincing, as all the best parodies do. Gosse himself would groan to Max: 'I shall never be able to draw another portrait without calling down upon me the sneer: "Not half so amusing as your dinner with Ibsen and Browning."'

One of Gosse's problems in facing up to the implications of his championship of Ibsen was basically that he preferred not to take sides. There was certainly a Vicar of Bray element in Gosse's character. He would tend, genuinely I think, such were his feelings of sympathy and friendship, to agree with the person he was with, the correspondent he was writing to. It was not hypocritical; he really did see that particular version of events, that particular side of the story. He was a feeler rather than a thinker. Gosse once suggested in a letter to Stevenson that there was 'a gift entirely denied to me, the gift of thought'.

If I can be said to think at all, it is flashingly, along the tip of the tongue or the pen; and when I hear people talk of a sustained exercise of thought, it is of a thing unknown to me. If I am strenuously honest, I should have to confess that when I am not working, my mind is absolutely idle. I have no anxiety about my soul – I am infinitely and sufficiently amused by the look of people, by the physical movement of things; out of doors I stare at the girls – one of the pleasures of life, which I had always expected to cease or change, but which shows no signs as yet; at home I think of my meals, of little personal ambitions, of what my children say and do, little palpable things that carry me over the pleasant blanks of non-

348

working time. I am not without terror, sometimes, at the idea of this sensual sufficiency in life coming to an end; I have no idea how the spiritual world would look to me, for I have never glanced at it since I was a child and was gorged with it.

This is not quite accurate, of course, as we remember the letters long after he had come to man's estate; but it was certainly true that he never agonized about religion now. Literature – 'this is quite as much as religion!' he wrote in that same letter to Stevenson. 'I grow a deeper idolator of this deity every day – the great books, the phrases of the great men, give me a more thrilling pleasure the older I live,' and seem to 'satisfy my nature more completely'.

This thinking 'flashingly, along the tip of the tongue or the pen' is one of the things that made Gosse such a good talker, of course, and so easy to read. It also inevitably lays him open to charges of superficiality and inconsistency. As for religion, he still, I think, in the 1890s adhered to the view that he had expressed to his father in 1873. 'I have prided myself on writing nothing that should ever hinder anyone a handsbreadth on his journey heavenward' – if there really were, by any chance, a heaven. At Stanmore, where the household had been joined by a marmot (spotted by Sylvia in Whiteleys), Gosse was faced on Easter Sunday, 1891, with 'the religious public in its gorging hundreds', and saw himself as 'a child of nature'; but staying in church-going households he would generally go to church. With Augustus Jessopp, the Donne scholar, in 1892, he wrote to Nellie: 'I am going to church this morning, fortunately, for the Dr has written a sermon expressly for me . . . I think it will have a quotation from Donne in it for my benefit.' Gosse's *Life and Letters of John Donne* was not published until 1899, but already in an essay in 1891 he had suggested that 'to chronicle the career of this extraordinary man . . . would be a fine piece of work for a writer of leisure and enthusiasm'. As early as 1887, A. H. Bullen had suggested to Gosse that 'in dealing with Donne's poems, we must be very wary indeed'. He should have been deterred, but he was not, and all through the nineties he was working towards one of his most considerable achievements.

But to return to church-going – staying with Archbishop Benson at Addington Park in 1896, Gosse apparently went to six different services. Travelling with Arthur Benson, as he would over the years, Gosse often accompanied him to church, occasionally sleeping during the sermon, but more often reading the Bible, with every appearance of holiness and devotion. Re-reading the book of Job on one of these occasions, he exclaimed at its merits – 'so modern, so rationalistic, so philosophical'. Writing to Thomas Hardy one birthday he would say:

'I would pray (if I knew any God to pray to) . . .' but to Lord Haldane, on another birthday, it came just as easily to fall into the language of religion: 'The Lord bless you and keep you. The Lord make his face to shine upon you, and give you peace . . .'

Is this hypocrisy, opportunism or is it, rather, just another example of a lack of thought and a need to be liked? Gosse really does not know what he thinks, so it is reasonable to say whatever pleases. It is the need to be liked that dictates so many of his words. Friendship is what matters. He once wrote to Tessa, 'We live, indeed, by the comfort which, as poor human beings, we are able to transmit to one another.' He saw friendship 'as one of the great elements in a happy life'.

There are countless examples of how he would say and do almost anything to bind to him the people he valued. He would wade through a three-volume novel by the young American Henry Harland and find time to 'write discriminatingly of it' to Harland's great pleasure. He would send swan quills to Lord Wolseley, who was complaining of abominable steel pens ('the Quills will, I know, improve not only my temper but my spelling'), and re-write Wolseley's letters to *The Times* (thinking a draft 'full of indiscreet matter, too angry to be wise'). He would send off inscribed copies of his books, congratulations, letters of sympathy and birthday greetings at every possible opportunity. On his book-collecting expeditions, he would find books other people had been looking for for years and have pleasure in passing them on. 'Of course I will do anything to please you,' he once wrote to Edward Marsh, not knowing how much Edward Marsh would one day displease him. Gosse's malice and touchiness are better known, but it should never be forgotten how kind he could be, what endless trouble he took to keep his friendships in good repair.

He could give time and energy to helping acquaintances and strangers too. Letters over and over again pay tribute to his solicited advice, for instance: 'You were so considerate as to send me a long reply that, in a sense, influenced my life,' wrote George Sampson, who would later as an editor on the *Encyclopaedia Britannica* cut Gosse's pieces with particular care. And C. S. Evans, of Heinemann, wrote even more enthusiastically: 'There is nothing I can do to repay you for all you have done for me, but I shall always be grateful and one day, perhaps, I may be able to pass it on – to someone who needs a friend as badly as I did.'

In the 1890s, Gosse was already becoming involved in the work of the Royal Literary Fund and in recommendations for Civil List Pensions. In 1893, he raised a private subscription for William Watson, the poet, whose brother feared 'that he may never be able to think or write again'. Sadly, the money in this particular case had 'clearly all been wasted', and Watson continued to 'scour the country in his old excited fashion', instead of sitting quietly in a hotel in Switzerland paid for by the fund. But Gosse was not deterred. Over the years he was involved in dozens of similar cases of writers in need and hardship, writing to publishers (checking up on allegations of malpractices), sponsors, the Prime Minister himself. He refused to believe, as Walter Besant declared in the *Author*, that 'those who now apply are unfortunate because they are failures'. Gosse knew that good work does not always bring financial reward. Where would Henry James be without family money behind him? And where would he himself be without the constricting Board of Trade?

Gosse was becoming a public man, a committee man. Indeed he had been on the committee of the London Library since 1884 and would serve on it for the rest of his life: from 1912 on he was generally chairman, from 1922 vice-president. He was on the committees of the Royal Literary Fund, the Royal Society of Literature and the Society of Authors. There were other aspects of his increasing public promin- ence: such as the request from Prague, asking advice on what Burns poems would translate best into Czech. ('I know well, dear Sir, that you have very little time to spare . . . but I know you as one of the few English men of letters who care for the poetic literature of foreign lands.') Few requests were made in vain. Robbie Ross would joke that it became necessary to form a Society for the Protection of Edmund Gosse, to intercept begging letters and consign to the flames presenta- tion copies of poems.

He was also in more and more demand as a lecturer and after-dinner speaker, proposing toasts to chairmen at the annual dinners of the Society of Authors, responding (for fifteen years on end) to the toast to 'literature' at the Royal Literary Fund annual dinner, speaking at a bibliophiles' society, the Sette of Odde Volumes, on 'the Poetry of William Barnes', speaking in Sunderland on 'Old English Ballads', In Lancaster and Dublin on 'Reading as a Recreation'. In Dublin he stayed with Lord Wolseley ('Commander of the Forces in Ireland') and reported 'Tickets for my lecture tomorrow can't be got for love or money,' though he advised his fellow house-guests to 'sneak out of it somehow'. He was still keeping some interest in art, lecturing on 'the Place of Sculpture in Modern Life' at Toynbee Hall, with his brother- in-law, Alma-Tadema, in the chair. In reports of his lectures, he tended to be called 'Professor Gosse', though he was not and never had been. He would tell Richard Le Gallienne that it *is* possible 'to remain true to literature . . . and yet be light and entertaining'. He took chairs himself too, all over the place, whenever he was asked, it seems – at a meeting to discuss the teaching of French in schools at Westminster

Town Hall, at the Irish Literary Society ('Mr Yeats was very eloquent'), at Sunday Popular Debates.

Then there were the memorial and centenary committees. There always seemed to be someone to commemorate; Lord de Tabley (his old once-estranged friend, Leicester Warren) considered Gosse had been specially sent into the world to manage such things. James Russell Lowell had now died and there was a ceremony in Westminster Abbey. Then Gosse spoke at the centenary of Shelley's birth in Horsham (muttering about 'the laziness of reporters in expecting to be supplied with copy before the speaker starts') and he went up to Oxford for the unveiling of Onslow Ford's Shelley at University College. He wrote an ode to celebrate the planting of a rose tree from Omar Khayyam's tomb on the Suffolk grave of Edward Fitzgerald. Then there was the unveiling of the Keats Memorial at Hampstead, a splendid present from his American admirers. Gosse gave an 'admirable oration, turning upon all the points in the life of the poet upon which one desired to be instructed', according to Aunt Lizzie Brightwen. When he had finished, Tessa hung a laurel wreath on the white marble bust.

It was three hundred years since Marlowe's death and that had to be commemorated too. The Marlowe Memorial gave Gosse a good story. It was to be at Canterbury, and Gosse invited Irving to unveil it.

We of the Marlowe Committee went down by train together to Canterbury, and on the way, Henry Irving expressed a fear that attendance at the ceremony might be meagre. 'I don't believe they care a rap about Marlowe at Canterbury,' he said. He was mistaken; the concourse was immense and the eminent actor much gratified. But pride was to have a fall.

We dispersed to meet at the hotel for luncheon. I was walking thither with Alfred Austin, who had come over from Ashford for the unveiling, when a man accosted us very politely with, 'Excuse my asking, gentlemen, but was the widow able to be present?' 'Widow?' we both exclaimed in stupefaction; 'The poet was a bachelor, and he died 300 years ago!' 'Oh!' said the man, 'then there's some rummy mistake, for all the crowd thought the monument was to the late public executioner, Mr. Marwood.' That remarkable man had passed away in 1883.

But it was of course not only the good people of Canterbury who could get names wrong. So could Gosse, with that 'genius for inaccuracy' Henry James talked about. Even on holiday it pursued him. Gosse was feeling the burden of the Board of Trade more than ever. It wasn't even secure – every year or two there were alarms that he might be made redundant. Now there were 'fresh and much more irksome restrictions'. Ernest Rhys described his office as having 'an unofficial leisurely character', full of flowers and new books, with a Japanese curtain hiding 'a tea equipage'. But however pleasant the surroundings, nothing could palliate the tedium of translating the new Portuguese customs law. Gosse had also taken on new work as first European editor and literary adviser to something called the Associated Literary Press. He was employed by S. S. McClure – 'the American newspaper-syndicate man', who seemed to be someone 'of extraordinary force and future'. It was this work that brought Gosse into close contact with Frances Hodgson Burnett, of similar force and future, now high on the tide of fame after the publication of *Little Lord Fauntleroy* and her fight over the copyright of the play of that book. She was often at Delamere Terrace in the eighteen-nineties. It was Gosse who had drawn her attention to the pirated French production. She found him 'delightfully clever', and took him to see Pinero's *The Notorious Mrs Ebbsmith*. (Mrs Patrick Campbell asked Gosse what he thought of the play and he replied 'I am afraid I was thinking only of you.')

Gosse was also temporarily editing the *New Review* ('Archibald Grove has gone off for some months and has left the *New Review* entirely in my hands'). He was altogether ridiculously overworked. It was at this time he got into trouble with Tennyson over his carelessness. Perhaps exhaustion contributed to a particularly vivid carelessness or confusion on a farmhouse holiday at Rodgate near Pulborough in Sussex. The farmer was called Smale and his dog was called Smart; Gosse was always muddling the names of master and dog. One day he protested to Mrs Smale: 'You really must not allow Smale to come into our part of the house, he has just been sick again on the carpet.' Nor were matters improved when, wishing to make amends for this regrettable error, which had been pointed out to him with glee by the children, Gosse greeted Mrs Smale, who was standing in her garden talking to some friends. He raised his hat with a polite bow and purposely laying stress on the name, he said 'What a lovely day it is, Mrs Smart.'

13
Enough of Nightingales

'YOU'RE UNWELL BECAUSE your life is insanely arranged,' Henry James wrote to Edmund Gosse in June 1894, 'but keep alive till I come back . . . The curse of our lives is indeed the huge incubus of "people". One is cursed by knowing so many *unoccupied* people – people who have nothing in life to do but conspire with a hideous amiability and an infamous good conscience against one's own concentration.' As I have already suggested, Gosse welcomed this curse, this distraction. He could not do what James did in cutting himself off for months on end, working on *The Spoils of Poynton*, and merely pressing Gosse's last letter to his bosom again and again (so he said), rather than taking time to reply to it.

Gosse was indeed unwell from time to time. 'You are evidently overworked yourself – which is the reason of your nervousness,' Lord de Tabley wrote sympathetically. Nellie would cosset him. She wrote to Tessa: 'Father is very well; he thought, yesterday, that he was going to be very ill with a cold. So we've insisted on treating him like an invalid today – beef tea and shawls on the balcony! – he was, of course, nervous about his throat too; but if you had heard his strong voice and hearty laugh at supper time, you would have giggled with us others about his alarming symptoms.' There was a suggestion that Gosse was something of a hypochondriac in Nellie's report to Tessa that the maid had broken 'Father's *favourite* bottle of medicine'. His cook, deploring his proneness to frequent bouts of illness, said, 'And it's no wonder, him sitting all day with his stomach pressed against a desk.' Soon he would take up bicycling, like everybody else.

'Hamo is a splendid teacher,' he told Tessa. It is curious how difficult they all thought it was, the art of riding a bicycle, even remembering how much heavier the early machines were. Gosse said he spent his first week 'under the sway of fear, the most rousing of the passions'. Hardy wrote that he had 'almost forgotten there is such a pursuit as literature in the arduous study of bicycling! – which my wife is making me learn to keep her company, she doing it rather well'. One day, while staying at Max Gate, Gosse broke his glasses in a fall – 'those sarcastic spectacles' Henry James dreamed about. 'I find that I have everything to learn,' Gosse wrote to Nellie. But the exercise would do his health the world of good.

Gosse must have been really unwell to miss the dinner to launch *The Yellow Book* in April, 1894. Nellie had to write to John Lane, the publisher, to apologize for his absence. Arthur Waugh went with W. B. Yeats. 'Have you met him?' he asked Gosse, who had indeed – 'a tall, sallow black-haired youth with the jaw of a monk and a sort of catch in his voice – rather an interesting personality, tho' he would talk about the theory of poetry inside a 'bus, which seriously alarmed two homely old ladies and scandalized a city man. It took a bit o' doing to discover the restaurant in a very Bohemian back street: it really seemed unnecessary to choose such a smelly, ill-favoured place!' Henry Harland was at the top table with John Lane, and Aubrey Beardsley, Walter Sickert, Garnett, Theo Marzials and Ernest Dowson. George Moore was in his element with Pearl Craigie (who wrote as John Oliver Hobbes) on one side of him and another 'lovely lady', Olivia Shakespear, on the other. When the 'dessert assorti' was brought in, 'Harland rose and read your verses,' Waugh told Gosse. They were 'received with great applause and then everybody drank everybody else's health. Lane . . . said Harland was a good fellow; Harland repeated the jest to Lane'. Henry Harland, the young American novelist, was the editor of this controversial publication. Someone called him 'a sort of lemonade Henry James'. James himself thought he had literary longings beyond his faculty. Harland was Stedman's godson and so had come via Paris to London in 1889 with an introduction to Gosse. He had been warned, apparently, of Gosse's 'mauvaise langue', but found him all kindness.

Gosse had spent a week in the spring of 1893 in Paris with the Harlands, plunging about 'like a porpoise in my shallow French'. Speaking French was never Gosse's strength, though reading and understanding he found easy – apart from Mallarmé. That spring, Gosse and the Harlands and a crowd of hangers-on went up to the Latin Quarter day after day seeking symbolists, 'each of whom has a favourite café, where he sits surrounded by disciples, who pay for his absinthes and grenadines in return for the poet's repeating his verses'. They wandered the streets of Paris, from café to café, 'under the yellow lamps and the blue moons', with Bobinette, 'as delicate and innocent-looking and playful as if no such thing as the marriage-bond existed' – and La Reine de Golconde, 'not painted or powdered in the least degree'.

They heard Verlaine was at the Café Soleil d'Or. 'Thither we proceeded,' Edmund wrote to Nellie, 'now having become a party of twelve (three ladies) and broke in upon an almost empty café:' There was no sign of Verlaine. They were told he was downstairs and a deputation went down to ask him to come up. The deputation returned dejected.

> Then Moréas collected us all round a table, and we ordered drinks. Suddenly, at the side door, something flopped up out of the darkness like a moth, – a timid, shambling figure, in a soft black hat, with jerking hands, and peeped with the intention to disappear again. But there were cries of 'Venez donc, Maître' and by and by Verlaine appeared and was induced to sit by me. He was very decently dressed; he explained that it was the suit he had been lecturing in in Belgium and he shot out real white shirt-cuffs with a strange pleasure. He would not, for an instant, take off his hat, so I could not see the Socratic dome of forehead which figures in all the caricatures of him. Recitations were called for and Verlaine repeated one of his lyrics, in a low voice, without gesticulation, very delicately. Then Moréas, in exactly the opposite manner, with roaring of a bull and modulated sawings of the air with his head . . . Imagine an English place of entertainment with poets outshouting one another with thundering verses . . .

Moréas shouted 'Il y a dans la poésie française cinq grands noms: Ronsard, Racine, André Chénier, Victor Hugo – et Moi!' Presumably Verlaine had disappeared again by now. 'Bobinette produced a huge bunch of narcissus poeticus and decorated us all with it.' It was *la vie de Bohème* indeed.

Another day, he told Thornycroft, he was giving a breakfast-party at Saint-Germain. 'My guests will be arriving – poets in straw hats and pink shirts.' He felt that with Thornycroft, visiting the Salon and eating their soles together, he had never really touched the life of Paris before. On Easter Sunday Gosse dined with the Harlands in the Forest of Saint-Cloud and danced on the bridge ('sur le pont, sur le pont'). 'It was glorious.' Even Henry James, the austere and melancholy James, was induced to stroll down the Boulevard Saint-Michel with Bobinette and the Queen of Golconde on either arm.

It was the right sort of thing for *Yellow Book* people to be doing, though *The Yellow Book* had not yet been thought of in the spring of 1893. It was in January 1894 that John Lane and Henry Harland lunched with Gosse at the National Club to tell him all about their new project. Arthur Waugh was there too and recorded that, far from it being, as was later made out, 'the organ of a sere and sallow deca-dence', Harland and Lane, so far at least as Lane could get a word in edgeways, were planning a magazine which was to be 'representative of the most cultured work which was then being done in England'. There was to be 'no hall-mark except that of excellence, and no prejudice against anything but dullness and incapacity'.

John Lane was enthusiastic. He was often enthusiastic. A. C. Ainger put his attitude in a nutshell when he sent Gosse an unfortunate misprint in one of the Bodley Head advertisements. It had announced 'The Letters of Thomas Lovell Beddoes, edited by Edmund Goose.' Ainger wrote:

> Heed not this last bétise
> Of John's:
> We know that all his geese
> Are swans.

Lane was in fact, though so enthusiastic, dreadfully afraid of offending anyone and extremely cautious. At this lunch at the Nation-al Club, the suggestion that Aubrey Beardsley was to be art editor was made tentatively. What would Gosse think of that? In fact, Gosse admired Beardsley enormously. He was often at Delamere Terrace; Gosse wrote of his 'wonderful, pure line'. It was Gosse who suggested Beardsley should illustrate *The Rape of the Lock* and his edition is dedicated to Gosse. Whistler had been prejudiced against Beardsley's work but when he saw the Pope illustrations, he changed his attitude: 'Aubrey, I have made a very great mistake – you are a very great artist,' he said solemnly.

There were lots of people who were prejudiced against Beardsley. *The Yellow Book* was greeted with storms of protest. The poems by Gosse, the Henry James story, the Arthur Waugh essay on 'Reticence in Literature', all were ignored, as the critics talked of Beardsley's 'repulsiveness and insolence' and 'audacious vulgarity'. Thornycroft's friends wrote to Thornycroft asking if he had 'any influence with Gosse' to urge him to use it 'for the future suppression of such nauseous and soulless beastliness as Beardsley's . . . and such waste-paper rubbish as Sickert's sketch.' Thornycroft sent a 'violent denun-ciation' to Gosse, who said he was 'amused' to realize the denunciation included Gosse's own poems. Even young Maurice Baring (whose hoax telegram telling Gosse of his own unexpected death was hardly conventional) was disconcerted. Finding Henry James and Gosse and Arthur Benson in *The Yellow Book*, he murmured, '*Que diable font-ils dans cette galère?*'

When Gosse returned from convalescing at Dunster in Somerset, at the Luttrell Arms, where the family spent many happy holidays, he found objections to Beardsley running high. William Watson refused to let his work be published by the Bodley Head so long as Beardsley was art editor of *The Yellow Book*. Sargent refused to let his portrait of Gosse be reproduced. Mrs Humphry Ward was full of indignation. In the end, Beardsley was sacked, though John Lane would always declare that Beardsley 'had no more sympathy with Oscar Wilde and the vices of the Nineties than Hogarth had with the vices of his period'. Oscar Wilde, one must remember, never actually appeared in *The Yellow Book*. It was an error of association. A newspaper headline read ARREST OF OSCAR WILDE. YELLOW BOOK UNDER HIS ARM. In fact, it was a novel in yellow paper covers.

Gosse was emotionally involved in Wilde's arrest, through his friendship with young Robbie Ross. Ross was a friend of the family. He was often at Delamere Terrace; they all loved him. He had been born in Canada, where his father became a provincial attorney-general, and had come to Cambridge as an undergraduate. As a boy of twenty, he was working for W. E. Henley, and his book reviews and his pieces on plays and art exhibitions began appearing in several papers. The same year – 1889 – he met Oscar Wilde and was captivated. Wilde was already a literary lion. By 1892 Ross, but not Wilde, was a regular visitor to the Gosses' on Sunday afternoons. Years later, Ross said Gosse was the first distinguished man of letters to express any appreciation of his work by word or deed. Obviously Wilde had not been interested in Robbie's work. It was for Gosse, Ross said, that he had laboured to give the best that was in him, to do the best work he was capable of. But Wilde was the focal point of his life.

As early as January 1894 Henry James was writing to Gosse about

poor tragic Bobby R., who has taken me (all earnestly sympathetic) into the confidence of his trouble, and whose nervous demoralization (which he must, and his friends must, absolutely stand up against in him) affects me as rending the heart. He tells me you have been extraordinarily and admirably kind and helpful to him – and indeed what a state of things when the 'authorities' are open to influence from a man with D's infamous history! It's like something of the ugly age of English legal or judicial history – the 17th-18th Century. But you will tell me more about it, occasion offering, and meanwhile B.R. haunts me. What a torture, truly, is the faculty of pity!

The events surrounding the Wilde trials are confusing; but it seems that Wilde accepted Ross's advice to instruct his solicitors to institute proceedings for criminal libel against the Marquess of Queensberry. It seems extraordinary that Ross could have believed Wilde would be able to clear his name; Ross and Wilde were to pay dearly for that miscalculation. Of course, Queensberry was cleared of the libel and a rider added that he had acted 'for the public benefit'. Ross drove from the court with Wilde and Douglas to the bank, then to the Cadogan Hotel, noticing they were being followed. At court on 6th April 1895, Wilde was remanded. It was while everything was coming out in court in May (and Harland reported to Gosse that six hundred gentlemen had crossed from Dover to Calais on a night when normally sixty would have travelled) that Gosse wrote Robert Ross the letter Virginia Woolf was to hold up to such scorn. 'If only his pagan and sensual joy had not been dashed by perpetual caution!' she wrote in an essay. 'Is that the voice of friendship, disinterested, fearless, sincere, or the voice of an uneasy man of letters, who is terribly afraid that dear Lady C. will not ask him to dine, or that divine being the Countess of D. will not invite him for the weekend if they suspect him of harbouring Robert Ross, the friend of Oscar Wilde?' To Vita Sackville-West she wrote, 'Lord what a letter to Robbie Ross. Did you read it? How cold, cautious and clammy, like the writhing of a fat worm, red, shiny – disgusting.' This was after Gosse's death when the letter had been published, but not the letters Ross would write to Gosse in 1914. If she had seen those, Virginia Woolf might have felt differently. This is the letter she hated so much:

My dear Robbie,   17.5.95

I am very glad indeed to hear from you, because I wanted to write to you and hate sending off letters to vague addresses. The recent intolerable events have vexed my soul – mainly (I confess) on your account, my regard for you turning what would else (perhaps) have been comedy, or satiric drama, into pure tragedy.

Now the great thing is to forget. Your action throughout, so far as I understand it, has been quixotic and silly but honourable. In this dark world no one can do more than walk by the light of his conscience. If it is any pleasure to you to know it, you preserve all our regard (my wife's and mine), and in future, calmer times we shall both rejoice to see you and give you any support we can, if ever you want support. I miss your charming company, in which I have always delighted, and we all miss it, for you are a favourite with every member of this family. I would say to you – be calm, be

reasonable, turn for consolation to the infinite resources of literature, which, to your great good fortune, are open to you more than
to most men. Write to me when you feel inclined, and however
busy I am I will write in reply, and in a more happy season you must
come back, to be truly welcomed in this house.

My wife unites with me in joy that you have written to us, and in
the expression of true and warm sympathy.

I am, my dear Robbie, now and always,

Sincerely yours,

Edmund Gosse.

The letter Ross had written to them Edmund sent to Nellie with the
words 'Read and tear up this melancholy note from poor frightened
little Robbie Ross.' She did.

However much Virginia Woolf was to despise Gosse's suggestion
that Ross should not visit Delamere Terrace until a happier season,
Ross was certainly not offended. Indeed he would call Gosse 'the best
and most loyal friend I ever had'. In 1911, in public, he would speak of
Gosse's 'personal friendship to me at a time when I most needed it . . .
I had already broken those promises made by my godfathers and
godmothers in baptism, but neither the world, nor the flesh, nor the
devil, nor failure, nor ostracism could mar the friendship of Edmund
Gosse when once it was accorded you.'

Gosse was to help Ross again when he had further trouble with Lord
Alfred Douglas in 1913. Douglas had brought an action for libel
against Arthur Ransome for allegations in his *Oscar Wilde*, which had
apparently originated with Ross. His biographer called Ross, 'next to
his father, the man whom Douglas most hated'. In 1914, he tried to
bring charges against Ross of having 'committed certain acts'. He
seemed determined to ruin him. In a letter to Gosse from the Reform
Club on 2nd January 1914, Ross described Lord Alfred's persecution –
how he had taken rooms 'in the same flats on the same floor as mine
last Monday and had cautioned the Porter *not* to let me know he was
there . . . Tonight I pass the night under the same roof as Douglas,
who has come with the avowed purpose of suborning the servants (I
have also purchased a German waiter, who was bribed to steal my
papers) . . . This is AD 1914 and you will not think me either
melodramatic or mock-heroic when I tell you I return to my rooms
tonight with firearms . . .' This was a far cry from the sort of verbal
violence which had given Gosse his own worst moments.

On 10th March 1914 Ross wrote to thank Gosse for his 'unparallel-
led loyalty and friendship, . . . but for your representation in a certain
high quarter I should have been arrested . . . I could never have

recovered any prestige even on an acquittal after a charge of the kind. It was both directly and indirectly due to you that I was protected. So I owe you, dear friend, all I have left of honour and God knows how much beside. Alex [his brother] tells me you will not even allow me to regard the cheque a debt'. But even Gosse's influence could not protect him from the course of the law. He did have to appear in court, though he was acquitted. On July 13th, Ross wrote 'the first letter I have been able to write since the disaster . . . – which was still a disaster, though it was an acquittal. It is largely due to you, dear Gosse, that I have kept up my health, let alone my failing courage, during the last year. Ever yours, Robbie.'

There are two more letters before we return to the eighteen-nineties. In September, Ross wrote to Nellie. Someone had apparently inflamed Gosse against him. 'I am terribly conscious of at least not being worthy of all that Edmund Gosse has done for me and been to me . . .' The letter ended: 'I asked for protection both from the law and from highly placed friends. I realize that neither could have done more for me than sympathise: the law did not even do that. Gosse was the one person who really tried to *act* for me by practical steps. That he could do nothing only makes my obligation to him greater. I am where I was five years ago at the mercy of two vindictive families, minus everything except my devotion to Gosse and his family, Yours always, Robert Ross.'

In October 1914 Lord Alfred Douglas returned to Britain from a continent at war and was promptly arrested for slander on a warrant issued on information from Ross. Now Gosse could do something. It was in this trial that he stood up in the witness box to be counted, giving evidence of Ross's character alongside H. G. Wells and Wilde's older son who would soon be killed. In fact, the prosecution entered a *nolle prosequi*; it could proceed no further for lack of evidence. Douglas was triumphant, but Ross emerged the victor as far as the public was concerned. Soon after the case was dropped, Gosse was instrumental in raising a public subscription for him. A gift of £700 and 350 signatures were presented to him. The signatures included those of the Prime Minister and the Bishop of Birmingham.

It might be assumed that Gosse's sacrifices for Ross (and there was certainly some sacrifice in standing up in the witness box) were part of some homosexual solidarity. Certainly there must have been a faint 'There but for the grace of God' feeling behind Gosse's actions. If Thornycroft had himself been a homosexual, who knows what might have happened? But a letter from Gosse in March 1908 shows quite clearly, I think, that Gosse never confided in the younger man more than a general sympathy. In fact, after Symonds's death in 1893, I doubt whether Gosse spoke again of the wild beast he had laid to rest. As Wilde's literary executor, Ross produced in 1908 a limited edition of the *Suppressed Portions of De Profundis*. There were just fifteen copies and he sent one to Edmund Gosse, who wrote to thank him:

> They are in themselves picturesque, and they aid us in estimating the character of Wilde. To that character I am afraid I shall always feel instinctively hostile. But the interest of it, and even the fascination of it, I feel more and more, and most after reading these additions.
>
> Moreover, the older I get the more individualistic I get. I detest nothing so much as the *cliché* in mankind. And more and more personal liberty becomes a passion, almost a fanaticism with me. Less and less can I endure the idea of punishing a man – who is not cruel – because he is unlike other men. Probably, if the hideous new religions of Science do not smother all liberty, we are in the darkness before the dawn of a humane and intelligent recognition of the right to differences. Perhaps poor Wilde (who alas! was in life so distasteful to me) may come to be honoured as a proto-martyr to freedom, now he is in his grave.
>
> The letters to the *Chronicle,* at the end, are astonishing. You did right, and you did wisely and cleverly, to publish them, for they put Wilde in a better, more human, less ridiculous light than anything else that he wrote. Here is, for once, a man speaking, with real pity, real indignation, real pain. What I principally hated about him, poor creature, was not at all his vices, but his unreality.

It must be remembered that Virginia Woolf, for all her marvellous virtues, was 'mentally, morally and physically a snob', as Leonard Woolf used to tell her, and there is nothing like one snob for criticizing another who, she feels, has less right to be one. Virginia Woolf said Gosse could be 'as touchy as a housemaid and as suspicious as a governess'. She also, more than once and for no particular reason, called him a 'grocer'. There was certainly some suggestion that he belonged below the salt. She patronized Gosse, for observing formalities punctiliously 'which are taken as a matter of course by those who have never lived in dread of the instant coming of the Lord, and have ordered their clothes for generations in Savile Row'. That Gosse was the first of his family to order his clothes in Savile Row (Virginia Woolf refers to this extraordinary fact twice in her clever essay) somehow makes it more understandable that he should care so much for the opinions of dear Lady C. and the Countess of D. But that Gosse cared for their opinions more than he cared for Robbie Ross's feelings is an unjustifiable slander. Gosse does writhe a bit in that 1895 letter. Certainly he was cautious and uncertain about how much he could risk – he was much more confident of his position in the world by 1914. He finds it embarrassing to say what he feels he must say in 1895, but it is not quite so disgusting a letter as Virginia Woolf, in the full flush of her animosity to eminent Victorians, suggests.

Gosse did indeed love a lord, as Osbert Sitwell would tell everyone, and he would love more and more of them, and their ladies, as the years went on. In the 1890s it was all just beginning. He could still find considerable pleasure in the friendship of the inn-keeper at Dunster, but he was becoming a welcome guest in a considerable number of more fashionable houses. He was giving another series of lectures – this time on Matthew Arnold – to 'some of the smartest ladies in London' in Bruton Street, while, oddly enough, his old enemy Churton Collins was lecturing not far away in St James's Square. 'The ladies were, all of them, charmed,' as Nellie wrote to Tessa. Gosse considered that each smart lady thought the presence of the next a guarantee of quality.

'The Duchess of Bedford is convinced that dear Lady Carnarvon would not come if it were a second-rate article,' he wrote to Henry James, 'and the presence of Mrs Asquith gives everybody security – "she's so clever". They are all ladies, except a bearded figure at the back, semi-recumbent on a sofa, like a water-god – Sir Wilfred Lawson. Unless Mrs Dugdale muffs it fearfully, I ought to get quite a nice lot of money, but the countesses come streaming up, and whether anyone takes their guineas is what is unknown to me and Lady Audrey Buller (my faithful familiar, who has really got up the whole thing). But this, you will justly say, is vulgar without being amusing.'

In the summer of 1893 Gosse stayed at New Haven Court, Cromer, with Frederick Locker-Lampson. Lord Houghton was a fellow-guest and they lunched with Lady Lothian at Blickling Hall. The following November, he was actually a member of 'the Marchioness of Lothian's house-party, where pheasants were shot by day and the fool was played at night'. He had mixed feelings about shooting. It was obviously one of the things gentlemen did but he could not quite accept it. He himself did not shoot and hated seeing the pheasants wounded. (If they were killed outright and fell 'like meteors out of the sky', it was apparently another matter.) The party at Blickling included 'one Minister, Sydney Buxton, and one Whip, Leveson-Gower, and a baronet and his wife and other miscellaneous people. The nice old butler looks after me, almost all (I think *all*) the other people having brought their own servants'. They played charades and walked over to Mannington Hall; it was the home of Lady Dorothy Nevill's brother, the Earl of Orford, which made Gosse feel less of an outsider. Lady Dorothy was more of a friend than ever. (She would tell him how much happier he had made her life – he and Lady Airlie and dearest Winifred Burghclere.)

Henry James, writing to Gosse in July 1895, lamenting that he had not seen him recently, said 'You are sure to be, at the present hour, the joy of some baronial hall,' but weekends in grand houses were still, in fact, few and far between. On the whole, in the eighteen-nineties, Gosse's pleasures were simpler ones. They could be very simple. Writing to Nellie on the train between Preston and Lancaster, he breathed contentment: 'It has been a most comfortable quiet journey. One man in the carriage as far as Rugby, since then all by myself. I have written an article for the *St James's Gazette*, had a good lunch, smoked four cigarettes, had two naps and altogether have thoroughly enjoyed myself.'

Gosse continued to have regular literary lunches at the Café Royal and the National Club. There were the usual annual trips to France. There were visits to his stepmother at Marychurch. These were more from duty than pleasure, of course, though there were incidental pleasures. Eliza told him on one occasion that she thought Dr Finch wanted to marry her, 'But I really could not think of such a thing. After your father, anyone would seem such a descent!' Her brown eyes flashed and the shell-pink came out in her 'pretty silly old cheeks' and she kissed Edmund with a melting tenderness and said, 'O, I am sure you need not be afraid of my taking any step of that kind.' Soon after this she said that if she *did* marry again, Henry James was more the sort of man she would choose. (She had met him on one of her infrequent visits to Delamere Terrace.) James was so amused by Edmund's report that he addressed a letter to him as his 'beloved step-son'.

Life at Marychurch was very luxurious these days, with boiling hot baths and lashings of clotted cream and champagne – though a bottle of Burgundy stood on the sideboard, half-full from one visit to the next, and gave Eliza the chance to say, when Nellie drank it with less than enthusiasm: 'That shows you don't know much about wine, dear; it's the very same one you said you enjoyed so much last time you were here.'

Eliza was becoming confused. One day she turned to Edmund and said, 'Let me see, dear, did your dear Father marry anyone else before he married me?' Edmund felt in a rather dubious position. She made him read aloud from a commentary on the Apocalypse – endless, tedious stuff, which took him back to those dark days in Pimlico when, as a seven-year-old boy, he had read to his dying mother. After an hour or more, when Edmund's brain was reeling, his stepmother said sweetly, 'I hope *you* like it, dear; it seems to *me* simply bewildering.'

He took the waters with Aunt Lizzie Brightwen at Woodhall Spa: 'They must be beneficial; they are so extremely nasty.' Then Gosse stayed with Hardy at Max Gate again, and they called on Bertha Newcombe at Corfe Castle. She turned out to be ill, but her sister entertained them. 'Other visitors (local ladies) came in and were asked to stay to tea, but the little servant-maid had gone out for the day. So Miss N. and I went into the kitchen leaving T. H. to amuse the ladies, and prepared tea. I carried in the tea-things and cut the bread and butter and Miss N. made the tea.' Emma had gone off to London to see a sick relative and Gosse stayed on at Max Gate rather longer than he had meant to, to keep Hardy company.

At home he could be found, before a party, helping to make fruit salad while Nellie decked out the salmon and the children blanched the almonds for the trifle. The Sunday entertaining continued. Sometimes there were problems: 'a Swedish bore' (Philip's description) came uninvited and 'stayed the whole afternoon and had, apparently, *three* teas! But several people managed as many as that. Mrs Armstead seems to have gone off with one of our antimacassars on her back, and neither the waiter nor our policeman had the courage to mention it to her.' Sometimes too many people turned up and tea had to be served in order of merit, and chairs made available only to the halt and the lame.

The children, who were hardly children at all, were now usually busy on Sundays handing things about. So the 'Sundays' continued even with Nellie away. Tessa, after being absolutely indispensable and delightful, went through a difficult phase at fifteen, and Arthur Waugh had to entice her downstairs again one afternoon after she stormed off in a temper. 'Her tongue is a fiery engine,' Gosse wrote to Nellie. 'As so many guests were present when she went to bed last night, I did not kiss her. I suppose it rankled.' When he hugged her in the morning, she said, with flashing eyes, 'I suppose that's last night's kiss.' But mostly she was 'as companionable and sweet as it is possible to be'. She and her father were reading a lot of poetry together – Rossetti and Browning and Pope. He would miss her dreadfully when she spent some time in France in 1896: 'Tell us the smallest things,' he wrote to her, 'every detail will be delightful.' In fact, their father told their mother that all three of the children were 'perfect darlings', though Charles Nathaniel the cat, without Nellie's eye upon him, was 'a Beast and scarcely speaks to us'.

There is one last vivid glimpse of the children as children in Gosse's poem 'The Wounded Gull'. The family is walking on a lonely beach and sees a multitude of gulls silent on a rock:

> The children could not choose but shout
> To see those lovely birds so near,
> Whereat they spread their pinions out,
> Yet rather in surprise than fear.
>
> They rose and wheeled around the cape,
> They shrieked and vanished in a flock;
> But lo! one solitary shape
> Still sentinelled the lonely rock.
>
> The children laughed and called it tame!
> But ah! one dark and shrivell'd wing
> Hung by its side; the gull was lame,
> A suffering and deserted thing.
>
> With painful care it downward crept;
> Its eye was on the rolling sea;
> Close to our very feet, it stept
> Upon the wave, and then – was free . . .
>
> We watched it till we saw it float
> Almost beyond our further view;
> It flickered like a paper boat,
> Then faded in the dazzling blue.

When critics think of nightingales – and pot-pourri and lutes – in connection with Gosse's verse, I think of the realism of that wounded gull, and the children who could not choose but shout. In fact, Gosse had had enough of nightingales. When he grumbled to Austin Dobson, that high priest of poesy, that he had been kept awake by nightingales one night in Cambridge, Dobson neatly responded:

> Of old the Poets gladly heard
> The nightingales a-weeping:
> Our modern minstrels curse the bird
> That hinders them from sleeping.

In 1892 Philip went to Haileybury to school. It was a disaster. He had had an unconventional Victorian childhood. Much loved at home, he was not sent away to prep school but attended Mr Wilkinson's school in Orme Square, where Max Beerbohm had been a few years earlier. On holiday he had always spent a great deal of time with village boys. Indeed at Dunster in Somerset, he had learnt to disembowel in the slaughter house, with the son of the village butcher. But he had no pleasure in killing for sport or anything else. Visitors to Delamere Terrace would recall him frowning over his Latin ablatives and stroking the cat, one of the cats, at the same time.

The house and back garden were full of the children's animals. Nellie would make journeys to the canal each spring distributing surplus tadpoles who threatened to take over the house. There were prolific families of white (or mottled) mice. There were grass snakes and a water vole called Moses, who was allowed a daily swim in the bath. A bird called Jacky Daw splashed about in all the liquids he could find – cups of tea, bottles of ink, Philip's dishes of photographical chemicals. Only once, it seems, did Edmund put his foot down, when Philip brought a badger up from Somerset. 'My father asserted his authority as head of the family by declaring the thing had gone far enough. A few more nights of such energetic excavation, he said, would cause the house to fall about our heads.'

Philip hated nearly everything at Haileybury (though fortunately there was one master who kept an armadillo). He hated the violence of both boys and masters which culminated in the public flogging of two sixth formers for something the Headmaster mysteriously referred to as 'Blackguardism'. When he was still fifteen, Philip was 'turned out as a dunce', to use his own words, but there was more to it than that. 'Feeling all the agitated helplessness of love,' Arthur Benson wrote from Eton, advising Gosse not to fight the Headmaster's decision. 'There is a certain independent type of boy, who, if he gets into conflict with the authorities, is much better away from a school, for his own sake . . . What is a careless independence in him, may be copied in insubordination by others.' Philip had written home: 'Raynesford always tries to get me not to work.' 'How little we can help him!' his father had sighed.

The Headmaster recommended farming. Philip went off to Wellingore Hall in Lincolnshire with his pockets stuffed with a pistol, catapult and cigarettes, which showed he had no intention of giving up that 'careless independence' Benson talked about. In fact, it stood him in good stead all his life. In 1896, at only seventeen, he went off to South America as naturalist to an expedition climbing Aconcagua in the Andes for the first time. Henry James had a good deal to do with it, happening to know the right people. On his return, when Philip presented him with a record of the trip, James wrote:

How good and glorious of you to go forth into far away frost and fever, the peril of the serpent's tooth, the buffalo's horn and all the rest, in order that I may sit in slippers by my fearsome fire and acknowledge, however affectionately, your Results . . . I talked of you lately with your father and then had my Results: which was an extreme regret that I haven't a possession that can give me the same sober and yet just enough richly-rosy satisfaction that you give *him*.

There would be anxieties; Edmund would agonize over his son almost as much as Philip Henry had agonized over him – but mostly secretly, privately, not pressing or distressing the boy. Visiting Bruges with Philip the year the boy was twenty-one, Edmund wrote to Nellie: 'We have no differences of any kind and (I am sure) are more like two friends than like father and son. What a difference it would have made to me at P.'s age if my father would have allowed me to be his friend!'

On Philip's return from South America, in 1897, there was the great question of what he was to do for a living. He seemed to have no ideas beyond being a keeper at the zoo, which did not suit his father. Gosse thought of the army as the sort of active, outdoor life that might suit Philip and packed him off to see his old friend, Lord Wolseley, Field-Marshal and Commander-in-Chief. Philip arrived early, too early, at Lord Wolseley's house and was asked to wait in the study. It was a blazing hot summer day already, and the boy was dressed in honour of the occasion in a new frock coat and a high stiff collar. He sat there waiting, sweating and, seeing a box of cigarettes on the table, remembered he had heard smoking was supposed to soothe the nerves. He lit a cigarette and threw the match into the fireplace, in which, it turned out, a fire had been laid in readiness for the autumn.

At last the Commander-in-Chief appeared, and at the same time Philip noticed the fire blazing in the grate. 'I am sorry to have kept you waiting,' Lord Wolseley said, smiling faintly, 'but I am glad to see you have made yourself at home.' Philip's army career had ended before it had begun. But Edmund lived long enough to see his son not only a qualified doctor and a practising naturalist (supplying the Natural History Museum with specimens and even new sub-species, just as his grandfather had before him), but also a successful writer and a Fellow of the Royal Society of Literature. 'He is terribly illiterate,' Gosse had written to Maurice Baring on Philip's return from the Andes with a cockatoo on his shoulder and a macaw on his wrist – though 'the very best of good company – and I am a doting idiot.'

Gosse doted equally on his daughters. Tessa was clever and talented, the most intellectual of the three children. At school she played the lead in Robert Bridges' *Achilles in Scyros* 'in a golden scaly garment which passes for a cuirass'. Henry James came on another day to see her in Sheridan's *Critic* and enjoyed it more than an Irving first night at the Lyceum. 'Tessa acted Mr Puff better than any of her blushing fellow-nymphs acted anything else,' James told W. E. Norris, which, of course, might not have been saying much; but her father wrote to Philip that she acted *splendidly* and 'it was the greatest possible fun'. Tessa went on to Cambridge, to Newnham, delighting her father by speaking in debates. ('That Newnham is in need of complete reform.' Proposer T. Gosse.) 'Father is very much interested and likes to have the minutest details,' Nellie wrote. Another day she told Tessa that it was 'not enough to be fond of Father, you must *tell* him you are'. Later Tessa went on to take a BSc in Psychology at Bedford College, London, and to please her father rather less by devoting her talents to the service of the suffragette movement. But it was probably Tessa to whom Gosse was always closest. In Arras in May 1893, he wrote to her: 'When I am in any very beautiful place, I always wish you were with me, or hope some day to see it with you.'

Sylvia became an artist, an extremely talented one, as good, some think, as Walter Sickert, who was her teacher and the love of her life, though she was not his. Her paintings and etchings are in numerous galleries. Siegfried Sassoon presented her portrait of Sickert to the Tate. Her father was in fear and trembling every time she exhibited, starting in panic and despair and ending in pride, she said. Both girls were spirited, hardworking, warm, independent, unconventional. Indeed Tessa became eccentric as she grew older, taking out a bathroom which had been installed in a country cottage she had bought and returning with pleasure to a Victorian washstand and an outside earth-closet. Lord Haldane wrote to Nellie after Gosse's death: 'Your children have been models in relation to their father.' But so was he, on the whole, in his relation to them. They humoured him and loved him. The one thing he could not understand about them was their lack of ambition. All three of them cared little for worldly honours. Philip always swore he was allergic to baronets. (He also hated weddings, and in old age said he had only been to four in his life – three of his own, and Rudyard Kipling's.) Tessa certainly preferred ducks to baronets, indeed to most people, though she was rather proud of the Order of the Serbian Red Cross, which she received after the First World War. Sylvia preferred painting simple people and simple things. She seemed uninterested in fame. She would not read notices of her exhibitions. There was an excellent one in *The Times* not long before her father's death. 'Sylvia did not wish even to see it. I can never get over my surprise at her detachment,' he wrote to Philip. 'From which of us does she inherit it? It seems so strange to me.'

In the November of 1893, Verlaine came to London. Gosse remembered him flopping out of the darkness like a moth the previous spring in Paris. In an essay, Gosse used the same image he had used in his letter to Nellie. He writes of haunting the neighbourhood with a butterfly net on the look out for that giant hawk-moth, Paul Verlaine. What a charming game it was, racing up and down the Boulevard Saint-Michel on the look out for live poets. At this stage no one but Arthur Symons, who was becoming a close friend of Gosse's, took very seriously the symbolist movement in France, but Verlaine would soon be established, as Yeats put it in his introduction to his Oxford Book, as the hero of the revolt against Victorianism, of those who wanted a return to pure poetry. Verlaine was less difficult, more accessible than Mallarmé. An American critic, writing about the introduction of French symbolism into England, uses an article Gosse wrote in 1893 on Mallarmé as an example of Gosse's 'flexibility of adaptation to the prevailing winds of thought'. This article in the *Academy*, the writer concedes, was one of Mallarmé's first and best notices in England – nearly a year earlier than Arthur Symons's initial study of the new movement. But in 1893 Gosse was not at all sure that the symbolists would make a permanent impression. His most enthusiastic defence of symbolism was not until 1913, when he looks back to the remarkable experiments of the nineties and says 'I cannot help believing that the immense importance of this idea is . . . perhaps the greatest discovery with regard to poetry which was made in the last generation.' By 1916, he had decided that Mallarmé's influence in England was disastrous.

In an article on 'Current French Literature' in the June 1896 issue of *Cosmopolis*, soon after Verlaine's death, Gosse said that he hoped not to mention Verlaine 'because I think that enough has been said in England about that lamentable genius to last till the year 1900'. But what of that lamentable genius's visit to London? It seems to have been William Rothenstein's idea that he should come. He had been drawing Verlaine in Paris (as he was later to draw Gosse) and had found him discouraged and almost destitute; 'his eyes had a half-candid, half-dissipated look, the effect of drink and white nights'. He needed money and told Rothenstein that he had recently read from his work in Belgium and Holland. Rothenstein thought the same sort of thing could be arranged in London. Verlaine decided to 'speak of French poetry at this moment of the century (1880–93) with plenty of quotations, several of them from myself'. Rothenstein, now back in

London, arranged that he should stay with Arthur Symons, and Symons arranged with an American friend in Paris to make sure Verlaine got on the right train, just as sixty years later the organizers of poetry readings would try to make sure that Dylan Thomas actually turned up. 'You may count on me,' the friend said. 'Cheques, directions, amulet to conquer the Evil one, I expect by return of post.'

A storm delayed Verlaine's crossing. He finally reached Symons's rooms in Fountain Court in the Temple at two o'clock in the morning of 21st November 1893. Verlaine reported that 'the very sympathetic journalist, M. Edmund Gosse, came to take us out to lunch in a sumptuous restaurant nearby, where my forces were sufficiently recuperated to enable me to put my finishing touches to the causerie for the evening . . .' Gosse had an item in *St James's Gazette* that day, encouraging everyone 'not to miss so singular an occasion. They will look at and will listen to one of the strangest men in Europe, and what they pay at the door will relieve a poverty which is neither disguised nor peevishly insisted on. They will see a physiognomy which is infinitely discussed in Paris and yet most rarely looked upon . . . the incurably unfortunate man of literary genius.' It was no wonder that Barnard's Inn at 8.45 that night was packed.

Symons reported that he lent Verlaine a copy of *Sagesse* for Verlaine to read from. Rothenstein grumbled that Verlaine 'spoke in a low, toneless voice; he had brought nothing with him, and he knew but few of his poems by heart'. Gosse was in the chair. It was a perfectly respectable occasion – Symons had rushed out and got hold of a suitable suit for Verlaine and a nice clean shirt. Some of the audience must have been rather disappointed. The aftermath of the talk was slightly less respectable, when they moved on to the Crown Inn in Charing Cross Road and Verlaine declined the offer of an ex-ballet girl (presumably one of Symons's friends, for that was the sort of company he kept). It was reported long afterwards that Gosse, overhearing the proposal, 'beat a shocked and precipitate retreat'. But this was the sort of thing people did say about Gosse with hindsight. He was probably just quite happy, that late in the evening, to get back to Delamere Terrace. And no doubt he *was* glad that he had dissuaded Lady Dorothy Nevill from coming with him, much as she had wanted to meet the author of *Parallèlement*. Gosse had felt obliged to tell her that 'neither Verlaine's clothes, nor his person, nor his habits admitted of his being presented in Mayfair'. Nor would he let her join them at a meal in Soho. Gosse liked to keep his two worlds apart.

There is a brief entry in Arthur Benson's diary for 22nd January 1893: 'An opening friendship with Edmund Gosse very delightful.' Benson had not yet begun the vast journal, which would run to four million words and would keep secret until 1975 more words about Edmund Gosse than anyone else wrote in his life-time. We shall read some of these words in the remaining pages of his book, and it is worth knowing something about the man who wrote them. We have already seen Benson introducing the young Maurice Baring to his new friend, and also his affectionate concern at the time Philip was asked to leave Haileybury.

Arthur Benson, remembered now perhaps only for the words of 'Land of Hope and Glory', was the son of Edward White Benson, who had become Archbishop of Canterbury in 1883. E. W. Benson had six children, none of whom married. In some sense, Arthur Benson belonged to both of Gosse's worlds. He was a writer, a schoolmaster; his father had risen from poverty (the grandfather having gone bankrupt). His mother was a Sidgwick – all her brothers were dons at either Oxford or Cambridge. Arthur Balfour was Benson's uncle-by-marriage. Benson once wrote: 'We have got a middle-class taint about us. We are none of us aristocrats in any way.' But the Bensons belonged to that intellectual aristocracy with which Gosse never felt entirely at ease, and touched at many points on the less-intellectual aristocracy, whose applause Gosse was beginning to relish. (Benson, criticizing Gosse's snobbishness, would talk of his 'ill-breeding'.)

Starting his enormous diary in 1897, Benson wrote, 'It is the answer to all people like myself who want to write but cannot.' It seems an odd remark from someone who had already published half a dozen books, was then working on a two-volume life of his father, and would end up with a list of more than fifty books to his name. But he was always modest, always conscious of the fact that 'I had a good start; I ought to have done better'. He hardly needed the sort of friend Gosse became who, perhaps with some inherited Puritan streak, seemed to see it as his duty to find fault with him and to try to make him raise his sights, to produce something worthier, more profound. Reviewing *Beside Still Waters* in 1907, Gosse would patronize it as being very thin and obvious and pleasantly written. 'I disappoint people in all directions,' Benson would write.

Benson recorded afterwards that 'Hugh Walpole and Gosse were the two people who made violent friends with me – laid violent hands on me – and it has been a failure in both cases.' It is a curious expression, and in fact there is little sign of this sort of strenuous petitioning for friendship on Gosse's side in the early letters. On 31st January 1894 Benson wrote to Gosse: 'I am much moved by your letter in every way – most of all by your expressions of friendship which are very precious to me. If it has been pleasant to you to have found a friend, what do you think it is likely to have been to me, especially when you have had all to give. Promise me never to doubt of my affection: I am often moody, but never unfaithful.' This moodiness (his mother wrote of his 'swift, furious, baseless' moods) was, in fact, a recurrent sign of a deep mental instability. Gosse would be at his best, his most loving and understanding, at the time of Benson's recovery from a complete mental breakdown, when he was still in severe depression.

Already, in 1895, Benson would talk of 'the torture-chamber which I call my life', and be haunted constantly by the expectation of dire calamities. Gosse also suffered, if not constantly, at least sometimes, from 'a sense of impending disaster' (Philip would call it a 'family disease'). But this was on a more trivial level. He would expect to miss a train, or the post with important proofs, to catch colds and leave his pen at home. Benson would expect to die alone. He found physical sex impossible to contemplate. 'I think . . . I have suffered,' he wrote in his journal, 'by being brought up to regard all sexual relations as being rather detestable in their very nature: a thing per se to be ashamed of.' He could only love the untouchable. In that same 1894 letter Benson told Gosse not to imagine that he was growing too old to make new friends: 'Your magnet will charm the hearts out of the bodies of those you meet, as long as sweetness has any power: you would always be as young as Sophocles.' Benson was thirty-two that year; Gosse would be forty-five. Benson was flattered that Gosse should seek his friendship. He readily assumed the rôle of devoted acolyte, a rôle he would come to resent.

But they would grow into a curious relationship. In 1907 Benson wrote, 'He is a real friend: the odd thing is that I see his faults clearly, but am very deeply attached to him, by a kind of insoluble tie, like relationship.' On another occasion, he wrote of Gosse, 'He was very gracious and brotherly.' Benson, of course, had brothers already. E. F. Benson was one, who seemed at one time unlikely to fulfil Gosse's prediction that he would 'set his mark on English fiction', but is now far more read than his older brother. Gosse perhaps needed a younger brother – someone he could love but also criticize with impunity. Benson thought Gosse could hardly understand an equal relationship – that Gosse himself *had* to be in the superior position, to be the one who was always right, always in control. But, in fact, Gosse was rather good at friendships where *he* was a rather realistic hero-worshipper. It had been so with Thornycroft. It had been so with Swinburne and Browning and Stevenson; so it was now with Hardy and Henry James. He would never behave with any of them the way he behaved with Arthur Benson. For Benson was no hero. Gosse would be with him demanding, pettish, exhortatory, irritable and, as Benson became the distinguished Master of Magdalene College, Cambridge, even jealous.

The thing that really mattered to Gosse in a chosen friend was a fair degree of devotion. It did not really matter what the person was, whether poet or peer – though he preferred his friends to be one or the other, or at least novelist or notability of some sort. There was that very revealing remark he made about young Wolcott Balestier; Gosse would not have cared for him at all, he said, if Balestier had not cared so much for Gosse. He collected devotion and admiration; that was what mattered. And certainly at the beginning Benson was devoted and impressed. 'It is such a pleasure to me to think that you are in the world and can be spoken with sometimes,' Benson wrote. 'I do not feel that I have deserved it, that you should be so ready to receive me.' With a present of his autobiographical first book *The Memoirs of Arthur Hamilton*, Benson sent Gosse a poem which included these stanzas:

> Edmund, the critical,
>> Edmund, the subtly wise,
>>> Take thou the gift I send,
>>> Gift of a humble friend; –
>> Veil, veil your kindly eyes; –
> Smile, enigmatical.

> Edmund, the tender heart,
>> Edmund, the friend of friends,
>>> This was myself, you know,
>>> Ah! but so long ago; –
>> Love to the meaning bends,
> Pitying the sins of art.

> Be analytical,
>> So thou art genial,
>>> As thou art tender:
> Only not critical
>> Here, of the menial
>>> Love of the sender.

It was the sort of thing to go straight to Edmund's heart. Devotion and admiration offered would enable Gosse to read dull manuscripts, lend his most precious first editions, write long, kind letters, raise funds for writers in distress, even stand up in court as he did for Robbie Ross. And Eddie Marsh, knowing the tricks, would one day write to Rupert Brooke: 'Be nice to him . . . A little kindness does wonders with him.'

'He loves me too well to suspect himself of jealousy,' Benson would write in 1904, by then not quite as devoted as he had been. Gosse was undoubtedly jealous, seeing Cambridge honours bestowed on someone whom he considered to be without '*marked* academical distinction'. Just as Gosse despised Benson's books, so Benson despised Gosse's, though he might confine his criticisms to his journal: 'Sciolist and amateur as I am, I am yet horrified at Gosse's work – its slender equipment, its rash generalisation . . . For Gosse to accuse me or anyone of being sloppy . . .' On another occasion, he wrote: 'He has written many graceful things but has never fed the heart.' This was in October 1905, before *Father and Son* (which Benson would greatly admire), and had some truth in it.

Lacking that fundamental sympathy with each other's work or any real appreciation of each other's talents, they seem to have had little to give each other, though they certainly shared an endless curiosity and interest in people. They often enjoyed each other's talk. Lunching together in 1900, in a party that included J. M. Barrie, Maurice Hewlett and Stephen Phillips, Benson commented in his journal: 'Gosse was, of course, the most brilliant, flitting about like a butterfly and talking beautifully.' Benson was, I suppose, a manic-depressive. In good times, he was charming and funny and perceptive. Edward Marsh, seeing Benson across a London drawing-room, found himself suddenly musing on 'how delightful it's at any rate *possible* to think him'.

In 1894 Gosse and Benson went to Dunster together in February. In the summer they went – with Tessa and Nellie as well – to Switzerland. Henry James was apprehensive about the purgatory they were all rushing off to – 'the high Swiss mountain inn, the crowd, the cold, the heat, the rain, the Germans, the scramble, the impossible rooms and still more impossible anything else – the hope deferred, the money misspent, the weather accurst . . . and meanwhile I sit here' (he was in St Ives, near the Stephens) 'in *my* nice bad stuffy insular inn, thanking God that I am not as Gosses and Bensons are. I am pretty bad, I recognise – but I am not so bad as you.'

It can't really have been too bad, for the following year they went again to the Hôtel Bel Alp in the Valais, with Arthur Benson's friend Herbert Tatham as well, another Eton master. Gosse wrote to Maurice Baring, 'Arthur and Tatham are very proud to go off on solitary expeditions. Tessa and I go with extravagant chains of clergymen and the like trapesing over the glaciers . . . Nellie has sprained her ankle, which is very tiresome, and delivers her up into the hands of the fussy matrons who bask around the hotel.' In fact, this one fully justified James's view of Swiss holidays. It was one disaster after another. Arthur's and Tatham's pride came before a fall: Arthur slipped down a crevasse which nearly resulted in the death of both of them. Another guest at the hotel was found horribly smashed on rocks near the hotel, which had the curious effect of making the surviving guests hardly dare to leave the premises. 'There are 88 English and 2 French in the house . . .' At night the French man would chase the French woman into their bedroom 'and you hear him beat her and then kill her'. In the midst of all this, Arthur wrote poetry, 'lots of sonnets on the Marmot, and the Mountain Goat, and the Gentian and the After Glow. Seriously, he is writing some exceedingly beautiful things, though his fluency and continuance are alarming to me whose tiny vein always, even in its voluminous days, oozed drop by drop.' Arthur, reading the letter over Gosse's shoulder, added a note by the word 'alarming': 'He means disgusting, A.C.B.' Gosse felt close enough to Benson this year to ask him to be his literary executor.

It was not of course only the small quantity of poetry that he himself was writing these days that worried Gosse; he was also concerned about the quality. Was he really, he asked himself yet again, a poet at all? Chatto weren't interested in his new collection of poems. De Tabley wrote sympathetically: 'Let me take the bundle round for you . . . A friend can do this better for a man than he can for himself . . . There is King. There is Macmillan . . . The verses are charming – so melodious. Hang Chatto.' In the end Heinemann accepted the manuscript but the difficulty in getting it published increased the feeling of melancholy that surrounded it already. This was the book *In Russet and Silver* that was dedicated to Robert Louis Stevenson, the book Stevenson received just two days before his death.

Gosse had already felt the chill of autumn, the fall of the year, at Browning's funeral, as we saw. There seemed to have been a lot of funerals – he had seen Tennyson and Walter Pater buried and his aged Uncle William, his father's indigent painter brother, whom he had helped to support. ('How the cost of funerals must weigh upon the poor,' Edmund wrote to Nellie, as he packed up his uncle's few pathetic belongings, 'all the little nothings poor old persons hoard.') Soon Coventry Patmore would die too; and now Gosse was writing obituaries of his friends, John Addington Symonds and Robert Louis Stevenson. Before long, he would review Horatio Brown's bowdlerized biography of Symonds. Later there would be difficult decisions, and that bonfire. Both deaths caused problems as well as grief.

There would be Charles Baxter, Stevenson's sole executor, 'bestially drunk', in Colvin's phrase, at the Savile Club, and rows about who was to edit the letters and who was to write the biography. There would be more when eventually the biography *was* written, not by Gosse (refusing on the grounds that he loved R.L.S. too tenderly to analyse him), and Henley produced his famous denunciation of the unrecognizable 'Seraph in chocolate, the barley-sugar effigy', who had been his good friend. Gosse would lecture on Stevenson again and again over the years, and go on to edit the enormous Pentland edition of his works. He would be caricatured, by Max Beerbohm, trotting around with Stevenson's ghost. He would be told by Isobel Strong (Fanny Stevenson's daughter) that Stevenson had loved Gosse 'the very best of all his friends', and would be denounced by Leonard Woolf, at the time of the great slump in Stevenson's reputation, as one of the creators of a Stevenson legend swallowed whole by the romantic nineties.

Symonds was only nine years older than Gosse; Stevenson a year younger. Throughout *In Russet and Silver*, particularly in the title poem, Gosse suggested his own day was past, that time was running out:

> This body, that was warm of old
> And supple, grows constrained and cold,
> These hands are drawn and dry, these eyes
> Less eager as they grow more wise.

The book is full of what his friend Mandell Creighton, now Bishop of Peterborough, called 'the subdued gloom of middle age'. He had not yet actually heard 'the first tap of the grave-digger's pick' (he would hear that on his fiftieth birthday) but for all his youthful appearance – he was only forty-five anyway – his poems had an autumnal melancholy. The *St James's Gazette* suggested that 'if Mr Gosse had done nothing else in this charming volume, he would at least have shown us how to take middle age gracefully'. In fact most of the reviews were cheering: 'So much is good and not a little of the very best.' 'Not many of his own particular generation have attained to equal distinction in the double rôle of poet and critic.' 'Mr Edmund Gosse does all things becomingly.' (This last was Arthur Quiller-Couch.)

De Tabley suggested the *Spectator* review was 'what Swinburne would call beetle-headed and grudging'; but it was the one in *The Times* that made Gosse say: 'I feel I shall never have the heart to write another sentence.' It was a brief review with a chilling lack of enthusiasm. 'There is no piece that strikes us as inevitable and supreme, none, on the other hand, which falls conspicuously below a worthy standard . . .' Gosse wrote to Dobson the same day asking for comfort – 'after thirty years of practically thinking or caring about nothing but poetry', which was something of an exaggeration. If he had really not risen above 'the commonest level of mediocrity', he felt it was better he should know it 'and make no more ridiculous attempts'. He was totally cast down, but he would recover sufficiently to save among his papers (with the annotation 'This parody of me was written by Maurice Baring in 1894. E.G.') a poem containing the following stanzas:

> The chiselled silver stars inlet
> In midnight's sapphire parapet,
> Glitter upon the fragile glade
> Like reefs of frozen marmalade.
>
> Ah me! the nervelets now take fright
> At topaz, jade and chrysolite;
> The doctors tell me to desist
> From eating melted amethyst.
>
> I stroll no longer down Pall-Mall
> Engarlanded with asphodel;
> No more (I did it every day)
> I knock at doors, and run away.
>
> No more, with hat and boots that shine,
> I leap into the Serpentine;
> If still I dare to do it, bold,
> Strange shivers seize me. I catch cold.

There would be one more book of poems – *The Autumn Garden* in 1909 – with no conspicuous absence of opal, eglantine, emerald, azure, halcyon gleams and 'shivering silver nights'. There was also a curiosity called *Hypolympia*, which Gosse called a 'fantastic sort of poem'. James and Pinero thought it a masterpiece but the 'Press generally is treating it,' Gosse reported to his American friend, George Armour, 'as absolute imbecility and rot unparalleled'. It was a sort of masque; the characters were the gods of Ancient Greece, but the time was the twentieth century. Whatever its virtues, and it has some good moments, it is certainly more prose than poetry.

There would be the *Collected Poems* in 1911 and, in the preface to that, Gosse admitted he had remained the poet of 1872. But in 1894, what he admitted to himself though not in print, was that he now knew he would not be among the English poets on his death, which had been, for thirty years, his dearest ambition.

14

Scribbling and Scribbling

GOSSE'S RELATIONSHIP WITH Henry James in the nineties was intermittent but intimate. Sometimes he would appear regularly every week at Delamere Terrace – nine o'clock at night was his time of arrival, and Tessa would recall knowing that a bell at nine o'clock was always Henry James. At other times he would disappear for months on end, abroad or in the country, working. James was still hoping that Gosse would write the 'really important thing which would answer his assailant'. He would have to wait until 1907. Early in 1895 Gosse was close in sympathy with James when he himself went through a 'cruel ordeal'. 'The night of 5th January 1895,' Gosse wrote, 'was the most tragical in Henry James's career.' It was the disastrous first night of his play *Guy Domville*.

Telling Edmund there would be tickets for the play ('they are not to be paid for'), James had written on December 27th that he had been reading Brown's memoir of Symonds and that 'the ghost of poor R.L.S. waves its dusky wings between me and all occupations'. Soon his own immediate humiliation would put aside even thoughts of those dead men. There was some talk of James spending the evening in a neighbouring pub, with Gosse reporting in the intervals how the performance was going, but in the end James decided to watch the Wilde play at the Haymarket to take his mind off his own. 'All thanks for the charitable intention I frustrate,' he wrote to Gosse. 'The second Act isn't over till 10.15 or 10.30, even, and it is to get to that period (at the pub, or at home) that would be the devil.' He asked Gosse to lunch the next day; he can hardly have imagined how he would be feeling.

The audience at *Guy Domville* on that first night included Arnold Bennett, Shaw and Wells, the rising young men, all of whom Gosse would come to know. He had yet met none of them, it seems, though Bennett had published a story in *The Yellow Book*, Shaw had attacked Gosse's 'bogus Shelleyism' in 1892, and James and Gosse would soon cycle across the Sussex marshes to call on H. G. Wells. 'I looked up to you enormously when I was a beginner,' Wells would tell him in 1926. They were all writing for the papers – Shaw for the *Saturday Review*, Wells for the *Pall Mall Gazette*, Bennett, under the name of Cécile, for a magazine called *Woman*. Gosse did not review plays. He was there to enjoy himself.

But there was no enjoyment for anyone that night, though the stalls, as Gosse told Tessa, were 'crammed with our friends. Close to us were the Burne-Joneses, the Humphry Wards, Norris, Sir Frederic Leighton, Sargent, Du Maurier, all sorts of people.' Everything went wrong. Early on, at Mrs Domville's ludicrous hat, the gallery began to titter. Soon they were hissing and booing, 'as they used to in old times, but such behaviour is very rare now'. When finally George Alexander declared 'I'm the *last*, my lord, of the Domvilles,' a voice shouted from the gallery, 'It's a bloody good thing you are!' Henry James arrived at the theatre with the applause for Oscar Wilde – it was six months before the trial – ringing in his ears. Alexander rashly took him on to the stage to respond to the 'Author!' cries of his friends. The gallery's hisses and jeers and cat-calls got louder and louder as the stalls and dress circle tried to suggest to James that it was not the disaster it was. 'It was very painful and exciting,' Gosse told Tessa. And just as he had decided, a few months before, never to write another poem, so James now decided never to write another play. Neither of them stuck to their despairing resolutions, but this exposure to a hostile mob was certainly comparable to Gosse's earlier trial by Churton Collins; and as James had supported and comforted him so nobly at that time, nine years before, now Gosse comforted James.

James's biographer disputes almost entirely the account of Gosse's visit to James the day after that dreadful first night. As so often happened, Gosse's memory had betrayed him. (He once said that his memory was like a colander, full of holes, and that the holes got bigger every year.) Twenty-five years afterwards, Gosse suggested that he had arrived at breakfast time and found James astonishingly calm. The fact was rather that he was a luncheon guest and that James's apparent calm was a state of shock and nervous exhaustion, in which he could hardly respond to Gosse's 'fine rich gossip'.

The long-term effects of that first night were good ones, Gosse surmised. 'His violent disillusion with regard to theatrical hopes and ambitions took the form of a distaste for London and a determination . . . to breathe for the future in a home of his own by the sea.' In 1896 James took a house at Playden near Rye and then the Vicarage in Rye itself before, eventually, in September 1897, he signed the lease for Lamb House. Gosse stayed with him in all three houses; over and over again at Lamb House, in what he called 'the almost cotton-wooly hush'. In the summer of 1896 Gosse wrote, 'I was much alone with him at Rye.' Nellie told Tessa 'they had all their meals out-of-doors, under the shade of the trees, on a terrace overlooking the broad salt marshes'.

James's biographer calls their relationship 'literary-gossipy'. We know that it was intimate as well as gossipy by a memory Gosse recalled of Rye one summer:

As twilight deepened we walked together in the garden. I forget by what meanders we approached the subject, but I suddenly found that in profuse and enigmatic language he was recounting to me an experience, something that had happened, not something repeated or imagined. He spoke of standing on the pavement of a city, in the dusk, and of gazing upwards across the misty street, watching, watching for the lighting of a lamp in a window on the third storey. And the lamp blazed out, and through bursting tears he strained to see what was behind it, the unapproachable face. And for hours he stood there, wet with the rain, brushed by the phantom hurrying figures of the scene, and never from behind the lamp was for one moment visible the face. The mysterious and poignant revelation closed, and one could make no comment, ask no question, being throttled oneself by an overpowering emotion. And for a long time Henry James shuffled beside me in the darkness, shaking the dew off the laurels, and still there was no sound at all in the garden but what our heels made crunching the gravel, nor was the silence broken when suddenly we entered the house and he disappeared for an hour.

James always enjoyed Gosse's visits when they happened, just as he enjoyed seeing the New Year in at Delamere Terrace, however much he might criticize the entertainment provided. ('An interesting example,' he muttered to Edward Marsh in 1897, of a marionette performance, 'An interesting example of Economy. Economy of Means – and – and Economy of Effect.' The conjuror in 1898 was far more effective.) There was always excellent champagne at midnight. The contemplation of further interruptions to his work at Lamb House was not always so welcome, though Henry's nephew William, aged nineteen, witnessed Gosse's healthy influence on his uncle: 'When Edmund Gosse, a very perceptive, but genial and at times almost playful personage, came down he came out of himself completely, was at times quite frolicsome and even descended to a pun.'

James wrote to Norris in September 1900 about a near-quarrel with Gosse. It shows how much James was just the sort of friend Gosse needed, refusing to be offended or irritated, though his right cheek had, he felt, been smitten:

> This is constituted the first moment of my being by myself for about four months. It may last none too long and is, already, to be tempered by the palpable presence of Gosse from Saturday to Monday next.
>
> Gosse . . . comes down here on Saturday as a sequel to a letter lately received from him in which (heaven forgive me to be plain) he quite – or all but – tried to quarrel with me for not, during months of impossibility, having asked him to do the same. It was such a letter as, had I been such another, would have, vulgarly speaking, put the fat on the fire. But I'm *not* such another! I answered in mildness, in meekness, and he arrives as I tell you, and I await him with the other cheek turned.

Three months later, James reported that he had seen Gosse in town: 'I saw of course Gosse, a few evenings ago, as light-hearted as a young duke first attaining his majority. He is flushed still with the pleasant social episode of his aged relative's demise. If he could only lose four or five a year, I think he would be kept in spirits. The spoils of "Sandhurst", moreover, if not quite those of Poynton, appear to have proved richer than he feared; so his Christmas is probably as merry a one as we know.'

Edmund's stepmother, Eliza Gosse, died at Sandhurst, Marychurch, on 14th October 1900, suddenly, as she sat in her chair. Edmund had certainly been fond of her and had realized his debt to her; but the visits had become an increasing burden and the money would be very welcome. 'Be ye also ready,' she had said to Edmund, not long before her death, 'for you know neither the day nor the hour when the time will arrive to carry *me* off.' 'Seven coaches of "saints" were at the cemetery,' Nellie wrote to Tessa. 'There are forty years' accumulation of letters etc. to be gone through. Father and I have worked like Trojans . . . The orchids *must* be disposed of while the weather remains fairly warm.' She found she was so fond of the house that she hardly liked to give it up, but the decision had been made. At night she read *Northanger Abbey* aloud to Edmund, hoping to soothe him.

On the 20th and 21st November 1900, almost the entire 'Furniture and Effects, Valuable Books and Orchids, belonging to P. H. Gosse, F.R.S.' (though he had been dead for twelve years) were put up for sale. Some things had been removed to Delamere Terrace and distributed among relatives (Nellie's sister Emily was given a 'mug-candlestick' and a 'patience board' and cards) but nearly everything else was sold, including three beetle traps, a cinder riddle, a glazed specimen case containing ten butterflies and moths, a 'game of parlour croquet with board and accessories complete', even P. H. Gosse's own watercolour drawings of Oddicombe and Babbacombe, and a 'medallion by Thornycroft of Edmund William Gosse'. Even 'the very fine and powerful microscope used by the late Mr P. H. Gosse, F.R.S. in his investigations, with extra binocular attachment, numerous lenses, stages and fittings, condenser, mahogany case, glass shade and stand'. There were fossils, homeopathic medicines, seaweeds, theological and scientific books, dozens of crayon drawings of shellfish, sea anemones, crayfish and butterflies, a pair of globes (celestial and terrestrial), and the contents of orchid houses, greenhouses, a vinery and a conservatory.

Edmund was not there for the sale. In his diary on November 5th he had written: 'Return from Sandhurst for the last time.' Henry James had written from Rye to urge them to keep the house, for the joy of a refuge out of London, but Edmund was glad to cut the last cord binding him to the place. He told Thornycroft, 'The little house which has been home for 43 years will pass out of my life.' It was sold for only £260, though it had been valued at £800 on P. H. Gosse's death, and the lease still had 55 years to run. Eliza's estate was valued at £16,256. A third of the residuary estate, after some legacies, went to her stepson, Edmund William Gosse.

In an article entitled 'The Greedy Author' in 1895, Gosse had deplored 'the way in which a mere grasping commercialism has been allowed to push into the domain of letters'. Gosse hated talking about money. Although he was extremely businesslike about contracts, he could never bring himself to bargain about amounts. Nellie once wrote to Tessa, 'I find, more than ever now, that it is I who must take interest in money affairs.' In 1899 she had written in a way familiar in the household of any freelance writer: 'About funds – no we're not bankrupt yet, but cheques being "so backward in coming forward", Father wasn't able comfortably to pay out all the moneys he was owing. But at last it's come all right, and Newnham, Scheverin and Barts are all three of them settled up with now. Still, we shall remain pretty quiet and "accumulate" now for a time.' But on the next page she was talking about Sunday entertaining as usual, so that obviously was not regarded as an extravagance.

That same year, the year before Eliza Gosse's death, Nellie was still being careful about money. 'Phil and I cabbed down, but frugally bussed back,' for instance. Edmund was always generous, if careful. He encouraged Nellie not to make false economies by telling her the

story of the English consul at Milan who saved the cost of three words
and caused endless confusion by telegraphing the Foreign Office the
news: KING ITALY MURDERED MONZA. 'Was Monza a man and why had
the king murdered him or had Monza killed the king and was the
Queen expected to express condolence with the Italian Embassy?'

After Eliza's death, there was no need for small economies. By
1905, Gosse's actual income was around £2000 a year, a very comfortable amount at that time. And two years later Nellie was to inherit,
unexpectedly and quite unfairly, more money than they had ever
dreamed of. Arthur Benson tells the story in his diary: it was, indeed,
just as he said. It happened like this:

James Epps, the maker of cocoa, was Mrs Gosse's uncle. He died
leaving £750,000. He had in his life made great gifts to his three
children, but it turns out that he did not marry their mother till after
their birth. His only son died and it was pointed out to the old man
that the grandchildren would not inherit under his will as not being
legitimate, unless he specifically left his property to them – but he
refused to alter his will. The result is that it seems clear that nearly
half a million of money will pass to the ten heirs-at-law, of whom
Mrs Gosse is one . . . The son's children have already nearly a ¼ of a
million by deed of gift. The thing that would make me squirm is
that by the will, the old man made it clear by leaving small sums to
the heirs-at-law that he did not mean them to inherit – and if the case
was fought, I think the court would award the money to the
children because Epps' wishes are so clear. This does not seem to
weigh with Gosse at all . . . It is a curious and exciting business. He
amused me by telling me that Mrs Gosse mused a long time, then
said "Then I shall be able to give you a dressing case."

In the end, Nellie Gosse, née Epps, inherited £46,000 of this cocoa
money. It was 'like a fairy tale', as Benson said. But how little would it
give Gosse that he had not got already, he added.

When *Tess of the D'Urbevilles* had been harshly criticized in the
Saturday Review on its publication in 1892, Hardy had written to ask
who Gosse thought was responsible. In his reply, Gosse revealed
both percipience and prejudice. 'There are certain traces I think I
recognise of a female hand that has done this sort of thing before . . .
Your letter helps me to see what I cannot see when one of these
vultures swoops down on myself and tears my liver, but what in your
case I can plainly see.' He said how little such ill-judged criticisms
mattered. 'Your book is simply magnificent and wherever I go I hear

its praises . . . You have strengthened your position tremendously, among your own confrères and the serious male public.' The review turned out to be by Mrs Andrew Lang, whose husband had also been a dissenting voice in the general praise, in the columns of the *New Review*.

Hardy doubted the review was by a woman ('my courage has done the whole sex a service'), and Gosse's anti-feminist remarks in that particular letter are surprising on several accounts. Gosse was, in fact, unusually emancipated in his attitude to women. Although he spent so much time in male clubs, in exclusively male company, he also relished the company of women, of his wife, his daughters and the many female visitors who came regularly to Delamere Terrace; many of them were unmarried, and even some of those who were came in their own right and not always with their husbands. There was Sarojini Naidu, the Indian writer who called Gosse her 'literary foster-father'. There was Mrs Robb, just returned 'from travelling *alone* through the length and breadth of Mexico'. There was Emma Lazarus, the American poet, who died young, whom Gosse found delightful and inspiring, breathing 'an atmosphere of moral distinction'.

Gosse consistently saw women as unjustly typecast. Reading Mary Shelley's letters, he said, 'I have a great feeling of sympathy and affection for Mary.' Writing about Catharine Trotter, the late seventeenth-century dramatist ('precursor of the blue stockings'), he spoke warmly of her 'real voice . . . raised to defend her sex and conscious of the many indignities and disabilities which they suffered'. When explaining his attitude to the suffragettes a few years later, Gosse would sound more anti-democratic than anti-woman.

But in 1897, writing to Hardy, Gosse went on to 'dread more than any other sign of the times, the prominence which women are getting in journalism' – an odd comment at a time when Nellie was writing more and more for the papers, with his approval and active support. He admired *her* writing enormously. She wrote 'delightful papers', in Austin Dobson's phrase, on many subjects. ('Ignorance' and 'Happiness' for a start, but also 'Mice'.) She wrote several children's stories for *St Nicholas* ('I shall have it typewritten and send it off to Mrs Dodge,' Gosse would say). She reviewed W. D. Howells in the *St James's Gazette*, wrote a long piece on Alma-Tadema for the *Century*, and numbers of anonymous pieces on modern art for the *Saturday Review* and the *Academy*. There were also travel pieces and nonsense verse.

By the nineties she was writing more than painting, though in Norway in 1899 she was recording the scene, as she had always done on holiday. Edmund described her in a long letter to Henry James as 'half-buried in whortleberry-bushes, with a comical expression of intense seriousness and one eye shut, trying to get the tone of the white birch-trunks against the blue of the fjord'. It was on this holiday that Gosse told Edward Marsh: 'I don't know when I have been so happy as I have been these three weeks.' So the World was, apparently, not as necessary to him as he sometimes thought it was. 'The weather has been glorious, the company (my wife's) that which suits me best in the long run, I have been inaccessible to posts and telegrams and I have been splendidly well. I have even been writing verses, the rarest expression of contentment with me nowadays, and I have spent immense spells of time thinking of nothing, stretched in the sun and bathing in the lake.'

Gosse nearly always loved holidays. The next year in Denmark – when they celebrated their silver wedding – he would write: 'I think I never enjoyed a holiday so much.'

Edmund Gosse reviewed Hardy's new novel, *Jude the Obscure*, not once but twice. The first one appeared in *St James's Gazette* in November 1895 and the second in the first number of a new periodical, called *Cosmopolis*, the following January. Gosse, though regretting the bleakness, the gloom and grime, thought the book 'irresistible . . . a splendid success' and saw to the heart of Hardy's intention with Sue, though Hardy naturally hesitated to endorse his phrase, 'a terrible study in pathology'. Gosse thought the '*vita sexualis*' of Sue was the central interest of the book, but it was this that caused an outcry. Among phrases such as 'shameful nightmare', 'Jude the Obscene', 'Hardy the Degenerate', Gosse's was one of the few sane voices. Hardy wrote to Gosse: 'Your review is the most discriminating that has yet appeared. It required an artist to see that the plot is almost geometrically constructed – I ought not to say *constructed* for, beyond a certain point, the characters necessitated it and I simply let it come . . .' It was of *Jude* that Gosse asked the much-quoted question: 'What has Providence done to Mr Hardy that he should rise up in the arable land of Wessex and shake his fist at the Creator?' It was not a question that Hardy cared to answer.

Many of Hardy's critics thought that Hardy had deliberately set out to horrify his readers. Why then should he complain when the readers were horrified and outraged? Hardy professed that his serenity had been, in the end, very little ruffled by the attacks. But he never wrote another novel. *The Well-Beloved*, which Gosse reviewed the following year, was merely a new version of a story that had been serialized years before. 'I never cared much about writing novels,' Hardy would say in 1920, when questioned about the *Jude* attacks. George Douglas, writing to Gosse, said that 'with all his modesty', Hardy is 'fortunately not without a proper portion of the great man's quality of belief in himself and is above the pampered sensitiveness of a Keats or a Rossetti'.

But Gosse himself one day, in the sort of showy, controversial talk that he enjoyed, offended the man he so admired. Hardy said nothing at the time, but in 1909 when Gosse challenged him on some mischievous rumour that was circulating in London ('I have never said anything of the sort'), Hardy admitted that there had been that one time when Gosse had made him really angry. It was 'when you said to my face at the lunch-table at the Savile that *Jude* was the most indecent novel ever written'. Hardy was no longer angry. 'That was long ago and I had nearly forgotten it.' Gosse did not have to justify that word *indecent*. (Is it decent, he might have said, to face us with those baby deaths, that boy's suicide? Isn't it *meant* to offend us?) Hardy's letter was totally friendly, ten years or so afterwards, offering Edmund and Nellie tickets for a tragic opera version of *Tess* at Covent Garden, with 'a Wessex dairymaid singing her woes in choice Italian'.

On 1st October 1899, Thomas Hardy wrote to turn down Gosse's suggestion that he should contribute an introduction to a Zola novel in a series of translations Gosse was editing for Heinemann under the general title 'A Century of French Romance'. Gosse's feelings about Zola were ambivalent. He certainly admired his 'active and forcible' talent. In 1892 he had written a long essay on his short stories as an introduction to *The Attack on the Mill and other Sketches of War*. He despised the priggish Oxford man who saw *La Bête humaine* on Lady Dorothy Nevill's table and said it was 'no book for a lady'. (Lady Dorothy, of course, said it was just the book for her.) But when Zola was tried for libel after the Dreyfus affair, and there was some question of a telegram of support from British writers, Gosse wrote: 'English people do not seem to realize in the least that the most thoughtful and upright Frenchmen, however willing they may be to acknowledge the purity of M. Zola's motives, are convinced that his method of action was totally indefensible.' It was a question of politics; writers should not get involved. It was a feeble attitude, some might think, but then politics always made Gosse nervous.

George Saintsbury in his obituary of Gosse in the *London Mercury* would say categorically: 'In politics he certainly had none at all.' 'I care nothing about politics,' Gosse had written in 1879, forgetting how much he had hated Blaikie's Tory views eleven years before. 'I judge merely as an artist. For all I care, the poet may be a republican or imperialist, a communist or the King himself—the art alone is all I care about.' And in an interview in the *Observer* forty years later he affirmed: 'politics, business, the affairs of the world have meant nothing to me'. But it is difficult not to have views, and to react to other people's. In public now, with his growing personal admiration for Asquith (who first appears in the Book of Gosse in 1901 and whom he would eventually call 'the greatest of living statesmen') and for Haldane (whom he would first dine with at the House of Commons in 1899 and who would be his closest friend towards the end of his life), Gosse would increasingly seem to take the Liberal side, but Benson's diary reveals him becoming more and more reactionary. He would irritate Benson, whom he seemed to like to irritate, with tirades against socialists and his fears that if the reformers had their way there would be no landed property in England in seven years' time. He would even, Benson grumbled, show a Tory attitude to bikes in Cambridge.

At the same time, he would report winningly to Thomas Hardy, whom he wanted to please, that 'Lady Londonderry writes to me very solemnly "things look bleak when power is put into hands without culture", but I should like to know how much "culture" the ordinary Tory M.P. possesses'. Gosse had told Hardy years before not to waste time writing about ladies and gentlemen – 'they are not worth the pains – one wants to have you telling one about real warm creatures that have worked in their clothes till they fit them'. Again, eager to please, and keeping up the feeling that they had both sprung from the people, and were somehow more real and warm than the average Tory MP, Gosse told Hardy in 1909 that he had been reading his new poems aloud, but feared that he did scant justice in his pronunciation to Hardy's Wessex speech. 'Yet I talked Wessex of the South Devonian sort when I was a child.' So he says, and so it may have been. By this stage he regarded Hardy, he said, as without any rival. 'The very first among the stimulating army of contemporaries.' 'The man whom of all my living contemporaries I admire and delight in the most.'

Hardy was impressed with Gosse's industry, with the amount of work he was turning out in these last years of the nineteenth century. One article which he eventually read was in the *Contemporary Review* in April 1898, about Ferdinand Fabre, the French novelist, who had just died. Hardy probably read it in fact when it was reissued in the volume *French Profiles* in 1905. In this essay, Gosse compares Fabre several times with Hardy and writes that Fabre's description of cattle being brought to the church door on Christmas night is 'described as Mr Thomas Hardy might have described them if Dorchester had been Bédarieux'. Hardy then reminded Gosse of the Dorset belief that cows kneel on Christmas morning – he had mentioned it in *Tess* – but it is tempting to believe that Gosse's essay put the story back into his mind and led to 'The Oxen', one of the best loved of all Hardy's poems.

Gosse contributed regularly to periodicals on both sides of the Atlantic and in France as well; his essays would be as regularly collected into volumes. *Questions at Issue* (1893) followed *Gossip in a Library*. This included a number of essays first written for publication in America – one on the controversial question 'Has America Produced a Poet?' The answer was No – though perhaps you could count Poe – hardly a popular answer, and worth remembering by anyone who thinks Gosse always wrote to please. Most Americans were indignant on behalf of Emerson. But Gosse said that people seemed to like this book 'better than anything I have published before. People like the contemporaneous; I am not sure that I do.'

The next collection was *Critical Kit-Kats* (1896). It started off with an article called 'The Sonnets from the Portuguese' which, with hindsight, we can find particularly interesting. This essay, a note tells us, was originally printed as a preface to an edition of the poems, and it is this which brings us face to face for the first time with the most notorious of all Gosse's friends, the forger Thomas J. Wise. The case for and against Gosse's involvement in his friend's highly skilled and remunerative crime has been argued at great length over the years. The whole subject is immensely complicated, and those interested in its minute particulars can refer to the new Scolar Press edition of *An Enquiry into the Nature of Certain Nineteenth-Century Pamphlets* by John Carter and Graham Pollard, whom Wise described as 'sewer rats'.

It was Fannie Ratchford, in 1944, in her edition of *The Letters of Thomas J. Wise to John Henry Wrenn*, the American book-collector, who first accused Gosse of complicity in creating forgeries. Her accusations have been well disputed, and clear evidence shows that Gosse could not have known what was going on; but the suspicions still linger. In 1958 Robert Pitman in the *Sunday Express* was stirring the story, under the banner headline: WAS SIR EDMUND IN THE RACKET? And in a letter in 1980, Christopher Dobson, grandson of Gosse's old friend Austin Dobson, told me that an American collector of his grandfather's work 'has little doubt that Gosse was a party to Wise's forgeries and active in selling copies of them'.

Gosse was not able to clear himself, as I am convinced he could easily have done, for Wise was not exposed until six years after Gosse's death. The knowledge that Wise had deceived him for thirty-five years would have dealt Gosse a blow almost more serious, I think, than the one Churton Collins dealt him. Though entirely innocent, Gosse had been extraordinarily credulous and misguided. He had been in fact a dupe, gulled by someone cleverer than he was, a sort of literary cuckold, one might say, taken advantage of at every turn. The revelations that Wise had been a thief and a vandal, pilfering leaves from British Museum volumes of the Jacobean plays to make up imperfect copies in his possession, mainly for sale to J. H. Wrenn, might well have shocked Gosse even more than the forgeries. Wrenn was worth a thousand pounds a year to him, Wise once boasted; but he would not have said so to Gosse.

Iris Murdoch has said that it would be difficult to overestimate the amount of illusion in any human life. We all deceive ourselves in dozens of different ways. Certainly one of the most powerful illusions in the last part of Gosse's life was his belief in T. J. Wise, his admiration for him as a bibliographer and book-collector and generous friend. 'Your goodness passes thanks,' Gosse wrote in 1906, when Wise as usual was seeking to lend authenticity to some forgery by placing it in Gosse's respectable library. Wise was a powerful illusionist; Gosse was only one of hundreds of people whom he deceived. As a very young man, a clerk in the City on a few pounds a week (producing on the side facsimiles for the Shelley Society, which probably put the idea of faking into his head), Wise managed already to convince people of his affluence and power and erudition. It is very mysterious how he did it. Hugh Walpole would call him 'a nice kind common little man', he who was so nasty, ruthless and extraordinary. J. C. Squire called him 'an uncultivated and boastful little plump vulgarian' and wondered how the fastidious Edmund Gosse could have been so closely associated with him. So might we all, except that we realize that, beyond the genuine shared pleasure in books, it was the old situation of Gosse lapping up praise and appreciation, from whatever source.

There is no denying the closeness of their association. There are hundreds of letters between Wise and Gosse, nearly all on bibliographical matters. For many years Wise produced more or less legally (if sometimes ridiculously) limited editions, in pamphlet form, of anything he could get hold of that collectors might collect – in the end, the contents of Swinburne's wastepaper basket, salvaged by Watts-Dunton, from whom Wise bought them, boasting that he had spent £3000 to save the material from getting into the wrong hands. Gosse was always Wise's adviser, his endlessly-knowledgeable colleague, his decipherer of manuscripts, writing prefaces, vetting proofs, occasionally putting his foot down and saying a particular poem or letter really shouldn't be printed.

There was no financial reward in all this for him. It was a labour of love. 'There must be no talk of payment,' Gosse said on several occasions when agreeing to write an introduction. And he had no idea, of course, what vast sums of unjustifiable profit Wise was salting away. He genuinely believed that Wise was performing a great service to literature, by preserving material which might otherwise have been lost. He believed so entirely in Wise's unselfishness and generosity that he could never have imagined his taking pecuniary advantage of anyone. 'I love to be associated with you in your beautiful and disinterested labours,' he wrote in 1913. He thought that he and Wise would 'go down to posterity, hand in hand, as two entirely conscientious bibliographers'. The catalogue of Gosse's library, which was published in 1924, is 'inscribed with admiration and respect to Thomas J. Wise'. In asking Wise to accept the dedication, he had been even more enthusiastic: 'To the friend who has taught me more about books than the rest of the world put together.'

But Gosse was not entirely under Wise's spell. He saw that there was something slightly ludicrous and certainly fanatical about Wise's approach. Philip Gosse remembered his father saying 'I am sure that on the Day of Judgement Wise will tell the good Lord that Genesis is not the true first edition' – a statement with its own ironical reverberations. There was in fact always some restraint between Wise and Gosse. Gosse never called Wise 'My dear Tommy Wise' or 'Dear Tommie' as John Drinkwater and E. V. Lucas did; he never sent *love* as Mrs Conrad did, and Wise's entries in the Book of Gosse are few and far between, considering how involved they were professionally. I suspect Nellie had no time at all for Wise. When, after Gosse's death, she offered him some books in return for his help in preparing the library for sale (for which he took a dealer's profit), his greed showed some bounds. He would take, he said (he had already taken some letters, he admitted), only something of trifling value, such as a volume inscribed to Gosse by Henry James.

Gosse would criticize Wise for his ignorance in rendering Spenser as Spencer (one might as well write Biron, Coalridge, Driden or Po, he said). He would chide him for not wanting to leave anything of Swinburne's alone, suggesting that he was not only in danger of rubbing the dust off the butterfly's wings but even of scrubbing them to a skeleton. And very shortly before his death, Gosse wrote one of many letters which could not have been written by someone aware of forgeries, bewailing the impudence of the dirty scoundrels who were pirating Conrad material and suggesting to Wise that if he had not, in his generous wish to put money in Conrad's pocket, 'started printing as pamphlets perfectly worthless fragments of his prose, all this would never have happened'.

Wise was not, of course, the first literary forger, but he was one of a new kind, one who could only have flourished in a time when 'modern first editions' had come to be much sought after, when immensely rich, particularly American, collectors were building up fine libraries for themselves, often for the eventual glory of their names in magnificent benefactions to university libraries. Wise early realized that imitations of books would always be discovered, that you have to *invent* an edition if you want to avoid the comparison with a genuine original. He created spurious editions for a collector's market, which were only discovered when tests of paper and type were made of a kind that could not have been imagined in the eighteen-nineties, the heyday of his crimes. Wise was undoubtedly inspired by greed for acclaim as much as for money. He was given much credit, not only for his bibliographies, but also for the generosity which he could well afford. Before he was exposed, he was given a degree and made an honorary fellow of Worcester College, Oxford, having showered 'munificent' gifts on both Balliol and Worcester. There is a smug photograph surviving of him in his master's cap and gown. His library, known as the Ashley Library, was bought for the British Museum after his death and has its own special press-mark.

Fannie Ratchford thought two things in particular pointed to Gosse's guilt. The first was his authentication of the spurious 1847 edition of *Sonnets from the Portuguese* in the preface to the 1894 edition. The second was the presence of a large number of Wise's forgeries – no fewer than twenty – among the books sold at Gosse's death. But, as I have already suggested, the gifts to Gosse were part of Wise's plan. Wise would also make sure copies of the forgeries were on the shelves of the British Museum, the Huntington Library in California and the University of Texas, who were equally free of complicity, of course. The presence of the spurious volumes in the published catalogues of these respectable institutions gave the forgeries their own respectability.

One letter gives a particular indication of Gosse's innocence. It is one of the earliest extant letters from Gosse to Wise, dated 21st June 1893, and relating to the preface to the *Sonnets from the Portuguese*. In this, while assuring Wise that he would be 'chronicling the existence of the Mitford volume', which was what Wise wanted, he mentions that he would not 'borrow it from Forman. I hate borrowing valuable books.' Now if Gosse had really been a party to the forgery, there would have been no question of borrowing it, he would certainly have had a copy of this most 'desirable' of all Wise's forgeries. The value of this created rarity was such that Wise could hardly have given it to Gosse, if Gosse was innocent, as he did so many others, without it seeming suspicious; much as he wanted Gosse's library to contain it for respectability's sake. Gosse certainly would not have bought it at the market price. By 1901 a copy was sold in New York for $440. In 1930, six years before Wise was unmasked, the 1847 *Sonnets* fetched no less than $1250.

Gosse had swallowed whole from Wise's lips the story of the origin of this 'Mitford volume', an edition of the 'Portuguese' sonnets, which was supposed to have been printed at Reading in 1847, under the supervision of Mary Russell Mitford, a close friend of Elizabeth Barrett Browning, three years before their earliest known printing in the 1850 *Poems*. In fact, it was surely Gosse telling him Browning's story of his first sight of the sonnets that gave Wise the idea of the spurious 1847 edition. Gosse got the date wrong; we know he was notoriously careless about dates. It was not in 1847 but in 1849, as letters show which Gosse would not have seen, that Elizabeth gave Robert the sonnets, and it was at Bagni di Lucca, not at Pisa; but otherwise that part of the story was true. Gosse said in letters that Browning had told him about it himself. It is also surely quite understandable for Gosse in the printed preface to describe himself as 'a friend'. He was, indeed, a friend. Wise's forged edition fitted in so beautifully with the facts that Gosse *thought* Browning had told him (of course it did, as it followed the story), that it is not surprising that Gosse was taken in by the forgery and told the world about the recently-discovered first edition, without making any particular investigation as to its credentials. He had no reason to be suspicious. Browning, of course, was dead by the time the spurious edition came to light.

Even if Gosse had been suspicious, Wise would have been ready for him. He presumably did tell him in some detail the story he told on many occasions and which eventually appeared in print in his introduction to *A Browning Library* in 1929. As I have already suggested, there is no evidence that Gosse ever had a copy of the spurious edition. Wise's statement, in this introduction, that Gosse had, is in itself an indication of Gosse's innocence. Wise told how he had come to acquire his copies from an old friend of Miss Mitford, now of course dead. For greater authenticity, Wise even recalled the 'high tea' he had eaten at the old gentleman's house, the sausages and the hot buttered toast. He bought two books, he said, and named a number of people who, at his suggestion, also acquired copies. By 1929 all the names on the list were conveniently dead. It included the name of Sir Edmund Gosse; but what is interesting is that Gosse's name was added on the proof – and the reason for this was that Gosse had died between the proofs and publication. So he could no longer deny the story of his acquisition of a book he never possessed. Wise's adding of Gosse's name was obviously to add more authenticity and respectability to his fabricated story of the discovery of the unknown edition. It is hardly conceivable that the name had been left out in the original manuscript of Wise's introduction by a mere oversight – for Gosse was quoted at length on the very next page with his story of Elizabeth showing the sonnets to Robert.

If we still need convincing of Gosse's innocence, there are several instances where Wise gives Gosse a faked provenance for a forgery in a way that he would certainly not have bothered to do, if Gosse had known what was going on. On 19th October 1896 Wise told Gosse a background story of John Ruskin's *Leoni* of 1868, later proved to be a forgery. In 1895, Wise wrote about a Tennyson forgery to Harry Buxton Forman, the Keats scholar (who did know what was going on): 'We print *Last Tournament* in 1896 and want "someone" to think it was printed in 1871,' but to Gosse he wrote: 'The other I bought for £30 from Dr George Macdonald, who also has a copy of the *Last Tournament* of 1871, given him by Strahan.' This different approach, as Graham Pollard wrote, 'makes no sense unless we recognise that Gosse was not in the plot to forge the pamphlets and that Wise intended that he should never know that any pamphlets had been forged'. And of course he never did.

Gosse once said to Wise 'I don't think anyone "collects" me yet except a few crazy Americans and half-a-dozen too-indulgent English friends.' But Gosse's reputation was beginning to stand very high indeed in many quarters and it was no wonder that Wise saw him as a perfect cover. Admittedly *Critical Kit-Kats* itself, with the Browning essay, came in for a certain amount of abuse, and Gosse received from Henry Harland, who was still editing *The Yellow Book*, one of those comforting letters he had so often needed in the past.

My dear Master,
Your letter simply wrings my heart. I have not seen either 'Blackwood' or 'The Academy', but I am surprised by no journalistic infamy in these days. Indeed, I am surprised at no infamy in our so-called literary world, where envy, hatred, malice, and all uncharitableness are the laws in constant force. But *you* – my dear splendid friend and master – you must not allow the mud flung by those envious wretches to affect or hurt you one little bit. You know that you have the enthusiastic respect and admiration of all men and women for whose respect or admiration you can possibly care one jot. You know that your literary work, your poetry, your criticism, your fiction, your biography, is among the very small amount of distinguished work that has been done in our generation; and you know that the men of your own rank, the Jameses, the men who count (not in England only, but in France as well) recognise your

work and recognise *you*. Then you must not allow the gutter writers and gutter prints to trouble you one little bit. Think of what James would say of you – of the high distinguished writer, and the noble generous – no, the *heroic* man; the true friend, the beautiful husband and father. Think of the opinion and the love of men of your own sort – and feel a righteous contempt for the envious pygmies who publish anonymous filth in the 'Blackwoods' and the 'Academies'.

My dear master, if I could only see you, and press your hand. It is awful, the grief and despondency you cannot help feeling, in spite of wiser counsels.

There was certainly, as Harland suggested, more praise than blame in the eighteen-nineties, if Gosse had been able to get things in proportion. He was gratified to be awarded his first honorary degree in 1899, an LLD from St Andrews. J. G. Frazer told Gosse in 1895 that 'You are the only great author I know.' Quiller-Couch told him he was one of the only five or six people in the country whose opinion he prized. Pinero said, 'There is no one from whom I would rather receive a pat on the back than yourself.' There was a lot of praise flying backwards and forwards, as well as the mud from the gutter prints. When Augustine Birrell praised Gosse's biography *Sir Thomas Browne*, he asked Gosse *not* to 'write back and say how much you like my *Andrew Marvell* for to do so would make us both bear the full brunt of Johnson's famous remark in *his* life of Browne "that the reciprocal civility of Authors is one of the most risible things in the farce of life"'.

Henry James, as Harland suggested, could indeed be extravagantly enthusiastic: 'How pleasantly you write, how well you *say* and, above all, how much you know! . . . You and I ought to write all the books ourselves,' he said. He had spent charmed hours with Gosse's *Jacobean Poets*. 'The book is without a dull sentence. Let nothing divert you from writing – and you will always divert *me*, at least, from everything.' As for that French reputation, James had reported Gosse 'gratified at a charming article (on his genius) in the *Débats*'. Gosse read the *Journal des débats* every day, and also the Norwegian paper *Verdens Gang*. It was a reasonable way for a translator at the Board of Trade to spend part of every morning; it kept him in touch. And was far more pleasant than 'translating hideous powers of attorney by the light of five wax candles' as he was forced to do on many foggy winter afternoons. But that word 'genius'? 'As somebody says, how hard it is to be a genius when one is middle-aged,' Gosse wrote lightly to young Gilbert Murray, who had begun work on a volume on Greek literature in a series of fifteen short histories of the literature of the world, which

Gosse was editing for Heinemann. Gosse himself had decided to write the volume on English literature from the fourteenth century.

The letters to Murray are interesting as an indication of the immense care Gosse took as an editor, a care which indeed many of the edited may have found over-enthusiastic. He was lavish with both criticism and praise: 'The beginning was rather stodgy and what was worse, rather lax and careless in expression' – but the passage on Pindar was 'one of the most beautiful pieces of didactic criticism that I ever read.' The Euripides section 'reads like a handful of notes for a lecture, scrappy, dry . . . Do break up the gigantic paragraphs.' He was full of detailed suggestions and criticisms and in constant touch with all his authors, chivvying them along. His involvement was such that, when he read in *The Times* on Christmas Eve 1896 'the news of the finding of Bacchylides', he rushed to the printers to stop Murray's '37th galley', knowing Murray would want to make some alteration to incorporate the new discovery.

Gosse's own *Short History of Modern English Literature* was published late in 1897. Correcting the proofs, he had felt 'sick with dissatisfaction'. It seemed to have turned to ashes. 'I am tired to death of it.' He was understandably nervous about the reviews. It was the first book since the reviled *From Shakespeare to Pope* which attempted some sort of overall theoretical framework. At first it seemed that the chorus of praise was such that his recovery from the Collins attack was complete. The general opinion was that it was an immensely readable and useful book and 'never degenerates into what Mr Gosse stigmatises as a gabble of facts'. There were a few minor grumbles; he had not, for instance, done justice to Marvell or George Eliot. *The Spectator* disliked his use of 'styptic' as an adjective applied to style. (Gosse defended it with graceful conviction.) A number of errors were inevitably found but accepted as unimportant. Gosse caught himself out in one carelessness. Thanking Richard Garnett for gently pointing out a few misprints, Gosse wrote on 4th November 1897:

> The misprints you point out are bad enough, but one more terrible has just met my own eye. What hepatic demon, trebly damned, made me write and read and revise '*Harold*' when all the time the inner word and pen were writing '*Rufus*', p. 375? I take you to witness, if any horrible reviewer charges me with hideous ignorance, that I pointed it out first myself!

It was his old 'genius for inaccuracy', as James had described it. But there was much more than such a slip for one particular 'horrible reviewer' to be concerned about. Churton Collins, his old enemy, was about to attack again. The year before, Gosse had written to Garnett with the apparent feeling that Collins could now do him no harm: 'I saw with much laughter on my own account, and some qualms on yours, that your unfortunate good nature to me had brought down Churton Collins upon you in the *Saturday Review*. What an inept and blundering pedant he is!'

Gosse was right in his confidence. Very little notice was taken by anyone of Collins's second attack, almost as condemnatory as the first, and often manifestly unfair. It was given permanence by its publication in Collins's volume *Ephemera Critica* (1901), but Gosse had learnt his lesson. He drew no one's attention to the attack; he made no defence. Once again, it was part of a general attack on the state of literature in the universities: 'They do not scruple to circulate works teeming with blunders and absurdities of the grossest kind.' Collins ignored the fact that Gosse now had no formal connections with any university. 'There is not a chapter in the book which does not teem with errors,' he said, and proceeded to go into detail, bemoaning 'the slushy dilettantism' and displaying his own enormous erudition, which would in 1905 – but far too late for Collins – be rewarded with the Chair of English Literature at Birmingham. In 1906 Collins's own edition of Robert Greene was savaged by W. W. Greg in the *Modern Language Review*. 'It is high time that it should be understood,' Greg wrote, 'that so long as we entrust our old authors to arm-chair editors who are content with second-hand knowledge of textual sources, so long will English scholarship in England afford undesirable amusement to the learned world.' Less than two years later Churton Collins was found drowned in a ditch near Lowestoft. Among the unpublished maxims he left behind were the words: 'Suicide is the worst form of murder, because it leaves no opportunity for repentance.' *The Times*'s obituary said: 'He was apt to let his own disappointments colour his estimate of those who were more fortunate than himself.'

Collins's attack on Gosse had no effect on the sales of *A Short History of Modern English Literature*. As Collins had feared, it became a standard text. There were ten new impressions by 1923. But the next book was the one Gosse had really staked his reputation on. He had been working for years on Donne; had first contemplated writing a biography as early as 1880. In 1891 he had said in print that a life of Donne would be 'a fine piece of work for a writer of leisure and enthusiasm'. In 1893 he published an article, 'The Poetry of John Donne', in the *New Review*. He had not much leisure, and his enthusiasm, as he worked, was sorely tried by the material.

It seems extraordinary that, at this stage of his career, Gosse was prepared to tackle so huge an enterprise (as he called it), a task that was so obviously full of pitfalls, even for the wary. The main material for a life of Donne consisted of a collection of letters printed in 1651 and in such confusion, Gosse said, 'that no biographer has hitherto ventured to unravel the knotted and twisted web'. The edition had been printed with a complete disregard for chronology. The letters were full of misprints and misreadings; there were wrong attributions and absent dates. It is no wonder that Gosse was often 'on the point of breaking down, not merely under the pressure of the obscure mass, but under the intense irritation caused by some features of Donne's character . . .' Human nature, in its lax modern moods, seemed unable to support the strain of all this crabbed and obsolete invective. As for the sermons, Gosse breathed a sigh of most unscholarly relief that so comparatively few of them had been preserved.

What kept him going was his admiration for Donne's poetry, an intense admiration which was unusual enough at the time. It was Gosse, a more recent critic has confirmed, who 'raised the torch to brighten the way to Donne's re-emergence as a reputable poet', though it was not until Herbert Grierson's masterly edition of the poems in 1912 and his *Metaphysical Lyrics* of 1921 that Donne finally emerged as the major poet we now recognize. In the nineteenth century the word metaphysical was a term of abuse: Dr Johnson's 'the most heterogeneous ideas are yoked by violence together' was accepted as a convincing impeachment, though it was Johnson who had brought back into literary discussion, as Helen Gardner points out, 'a body of poetry that had largely sunk into oblivion'. Interest in Donne grew in the nineteenth century, culminating in Gosse's *Life*, which prepared the way for Grierson.

When first starting on his life of Donne, Gosse had discovered that Augustus Jessopp was at work on the same task. They proposed to join forces but found collaboration impossible as Jessopp, like so many of his contemporaries, 'had never been able to feel much enthusiasm for Donne as a poet', and Gosse was interested above all in the poetry. After Jessopp had completed a study of Donne in the Leaders of Religion series in 1897, he turned over all his material to Gosse. It was Gosse's enthusiastic use of the poems as biographical evidence in reconstructing Donne's early life which caused more criticism of the book than the inevitable errors and carelessnesses. In his preface Gosse thanks Maurice Baring for 'suggestive ideas regarding the biographical value of the poems'. It was an unwise path to follow.

Herbert Grierson acknowledged Gosse's contribution to Donne's reputation. He said there was no higher authority than Gosse on the poet's 'character and mind', and that Gosse was the earliest writer to afford a view of Donne in correct perspective. After Gosse's death, he would tell Nellie he would never forget the spontaneous kindness which Gosse showed him 'when I first approached him about my work on Donne'. Helen Gardner has also paid tribute to the charm and grace of manner of Gosse's book and noted that its 'deceptive air of learning lightly carried gave it a wide influence'. But she regretted that Gosse had started criticism 'on the hopeless quest of deciding which of Donne's poems were written to his wife'.

At the time, there was a great deal of ungrudging praise, though the book is so weighed down with facts, and possible facts, and undigested letters that it is rather less readable than most of Gosse's books. The *Athenaeum* called it 'a brilliant portrait; it is also a laborious and exact work of literary history'. *The Times* found Gosse's scholarship impeccable. The *Academy* found his criticism brilliant. The *Times Literary Supplement* suggested that while A. B. Grosart had collected the seventeenth century's bones, 'Mr Gosse was the first to make them dance.' Andrew Lang wrote: '*Donne* seems to be universally applauded.' Dobson rhymed engagingly, imagining the talk of two of the regular civil servants at the National Club lunches, Alfred Bateman and T. H. W. Pelham.

B: Here at this noonday hour,
  let us mingle our voices together.

P: What shall we sing of? Boyle?
  or the Boers? or the change in the weather?

B: Nay, there is Gosse, his book,
  with its delicate scholarly phrasing;
 There is a theme, in truth –
  if you truly desire to be praising.

P: Many a cheek will tingle
  and many a rival will burn, Sir!
 Donne has been done of yore,
  but now he is done to a turn, Sir!

B: Think of the toil unheard,
  and the numberless facts to be spotted.

P: Think of the t's to be crossed,
  and the infinite i's to be dotted!

B: Surely a work per se,
  and as modest in tone as pretension.

P: Gosse should be made C.B.
  or at least have a government pension.

It would be thirteen years before Gosse got that CB and five before he achieved a position and salary far more desirable than a government pension. In the meantime, there was more criticism to face. It was *The Spectator*, almost a month after the earliest reviews, which first disputed Gosse's biographical use of the early poems, as many later critics have done. It also judged harshly Gosse's treatment of Donne's conversion. (Incidentally Gosse's account of the missing and probably non-existent 1614 edition of Donne's poems in the previous chapter would undoubtedly have aroused Fannie Ratchford's suspicions if Wise's skills had been inclined to forge seventeenth-century editions.) In December, the *Athenaeum* carried a letter which called attention to a serious error. Gosse had apparently confused Donne with a Daniel Donne in a case which Gosse had used to illustrate Donne's character. This may well again have been the result of relying too much on a research assistant, always a risky practice. Gosse thanks one Minnie Curran. The suggestion was that Donne 'did dirty work for Somerset in the miserable business of the Essex divorce', to use a phrase of one of his critics. It was unfortunate, but the public criticism seems to have caused Gosse less annoyance than a private letter from H. C. Beeching, literary Rector of Yattendon, whom Gosse had known for years, and who confessed he had written the review in *The Spectator*.

'Why o why,' Beeching wrote, 'have you smirched your charming book on Donne by so incredible a theory as to his taking orders before conversion? The church is in arms against you.' Beeching wrote lightly, but Gosse saw the word 'smirch' as an insult. Beeching could not remember using it but withdrew it, when challenged, and apologized; and then found himself saying that he would have wished to see a book he liked 'purged of what I thought a serious disadvantage to its usefulness'. He added a postscript: 'I see, on re-reading this, that I have used the word "purge" which you will say is also a covert insult. If you like you can.'

This trivial exchange of letters is a good instance of how touchy Gosse could be. Nellie would sometimes manage to intercept intemperate letters written without the thought that they might end pleasant friendships. Obviously she was not always successful.

But it was an American reviewer, in the *Nation* in February, 1900, who made the most devastating criticisms of Gosse's life of Donne. He took Gosse to task for 'a habitual mis-reading and misunderstanding of the poems before him', and summed up the book by quoting a sentence from one of Donne's letters: 'I will adventure to say to you, without inserting one unnecessary word, that the book is full of falsifications in word and sense, and of falsehoods in matter of fact, and of inconsequent and unscholarlike arguings . . . and of letting slip some enormous advantages.' A damning judgment; and eighty years later an American scholar confirmed the indictment, pointing out discrepancies between the holograph and Gosse's versions, and numerous cases where Gosse made wrong attributions of recipients of letters. Why Gosse so often preferred the reading of the 1651 edition rather than the holograph, even when it was available, is mysterious. Presumably, as one of his critics said, he was not very good at deciphering seventeenth-century handwriting. There was one good case when he retained 'preserud' ('preserved') from the holograph where 1651 had 'presented'. But this was an exception. Gosse modernized spelling and punctuation for greater legibility, which raises the question of what audience the book was intended for. In one important previously unpublished letter there are no fewer than 179 changes. Obviously Gosse was trying to make a book accessible to the general reader, or at least a book that Lang and Dobson and Lady Dorothy Nevill would enjoy, as well as the Cambridge people whom he still longed to impress. It was an aim incompatible with the demands of twentieth-century scholarship, even supposing he had not had that old genius for inaccuracy. The book is nonetheless a considerable achievement and cannot be denied a large influence on later attitudes to Donne. It was not until R. C. Bald's *John Donne. A Life* in 1970 that Gosse's *Life* was replaced by a more accurate and critically balanced biography. Bald saw Gosse's *Life* as 'peppered with errors', but said 'his services to the reputation of Donne were many and great . . . one is constantly impressed by the learning and acumen' Gosse brought to his task.

Gosse wrote to George Armour in America: 'I daresay you see my humdrum career punctuated with publications. I suppose I shall go on scribbling and scribbling until somebody says "Do look at old Mr Gosse; he does not seem to be making any marks on the paper," and they will find that I am dead. But that will be a long long time yet. I have pints of ink to spend before that time comes.' He was quite right that he would go on writing until just before he died, but there were increasingly times when he felt the world full of superfluous books, and more and more he seemed to be seeing the wrong writers rewarded.

As he rushed round collecting signatures for a tribute to George Meredith on his seventieth birthday, Gosse admitted to James and Hardy – who agreed with him – that the celebrated novelist was practically unreadable. He refused an invitation from Clement Shorter to write on him: 'I shrink from saying anything in public about Meredith. I could not so word my criticism as to fail to wound his excessive sensitiveness, if what I said should meet his eye; and I like him as a man so much more than I respect him as a writer that I would not hurt his feelings for the world.' Even as a man, Meredith was rather hard to take. He was so excessively cheerful. He told Gosse that Hardy's pessimism had grieved him, and Gosse wrote to Hardy: 'I wonder whether you were not saddened by his optimism? There is something to me almost flighty in his cheerfulness. You know he has broken his ankle? He appears to be quite cheerful about that too. What a curious thing temperament is – there seems no reason at all why Meredith should be so happy and in some irrational way one almost resents it.'

Gosse himself had times of deep depression. He was fifty as the century died, hearing that 'first tap of the gravedigger's pick'. It worried him that fame, like Madame Mantalini, hated 'elderly persons and frumps'. He was troubled by neuralgia. He was too busy, 'so busy in fact that it seems useless to begin anything,' as he wrote in a letter to Hardy's 'rare, fair woman', Florence Henniker. He was almost 'tired to death' from his work on Donne. There was the terrible anxiety over Kipling, and then anxiety on a larger scale. Friendships made him feel close to the heart of the Boer War though the fighting was so far away. On the night that war was declared the Gosses shared a box with the Wolseleys at a performance of *King John*. Like everyone else except Kitchener, the Commander-in-Chief was confident the war would be a short one. He was radiant and calm, whispering 'And "Victoria for Mr Kruger"' in Gosse's ear, as the words rolled out from the stage:

> Here have we war for war, and blood for blood,
> Controlment for controlment.

Gosse was also seeing a good deal of the Bullers. Soon Sir Redvers (who had won the VC in the Zulu Wars) would sail off to South Africa to command the British forces. Gosse went off to Aldershot to stay with them just before the embarkation. 'These little changes evidently suit F. very well,' Nellie wrote to Tessa in Cambridge. She was herself often happier sharing a tin of sardines with Mopsy, the current cat.

Gosse found himself arguing England's case in print, for there was a wave of anti-British feeling in many of the small countries of Europe. An article Gosse had written on 'Culture and the Small Nations' in Lady Randolph Spencer Churchill's *Anglo-Saxon Review* was reprinted in *Verdens Gang* in Norway. Ragna Neilsen, a leading suffragette, replied to his article. 'Edmund Gosse om Kulturen og de smaa Nationer' was in effect an attack on England's attitude in the Boer War. Writing to the Editor, Gosse said: 'Would Fru Neilsen have had us abandon our possessions and our loyal citizens in South Africa, and sail away, bag and baggage from Cape Town? *But this was our only alternative.* Ask her if she thinks that would have been honourable or just on the part of a great responsible government like ours?' Eighty-two years later people would ask similar questions about the Falkland Islands. 'England made no war on the Boers: she was, unprepared and greatly against her will, forced into a war prepared for and cunningly led up to by the Boers. England had to face a desperate conspiracy to drive her wholly out of Africa. Even you have to admit that a "large" nation (to be "large" seems in your eyes the unpardonable sin!) must struggle for its own life. Our life, our honour, all that makes us a nation, would have been lost if we had permitted the Boers to drive us, as they hoped to do, out of Africa.'

As for literature, the scene was hardly cheering. 'Never before, I am convinced,' he wrote to his Dutch friend Maarten Maartens, 'has literature, taste, intellectual probity of every kind been at so low an ebb in this country. God has lost patience with us at last and has smitten us with taste-blindness and style-deafness, so that we like nothing but what is false and vulgar.' The sales of Marie Corelli and Hall Caine appalled him – Caine, particularly, for years before he had thought Caine showed some promise. And now Caine wrote terrible books, thought himself Shakespeare and would eventually leave the largest fortune ever made by a pen. Gosse told the young men of the Oxford Union (invited as a 'distinguished stranger' by young John Buchan) that the large public is happiest with third-rate things. In an essay, he lamented that the money standard was becoming the standard of merit, though many of our most distinguished writers receive 'the barest pittance for their writings'.

Thomas Hardy, 'the greatest novelist now living', had abandoned the novel altogether. Gosse would go on regretting that he 'vegetated in Dorset and wrote nothing but verse', much as he admired the verse. Gosse would react fiercely when Sir Edward Clarke gave a gloomy lecture at the Working Men's College in Great Ormond Street, lamenting that there were no novelists or poets in the succeeding generation to match Thackeray and Dickens, Tennyson and Browning, except perhaps the Rossettis. Gosse countered with the names of Swinburne, Morris, Hardy and Stevenson, but he felt almost equally gloomy himself, much as he hated 'utterances of dismal hopelessness' and talk of 'literature all going to the dogs'. He knew there would be the 'inevitable recurrent Spring'.

All the same, he was depressed by the shelves of public libraries, weighed down by all the 'old shocking rubbish': 'the useless bad editions of the poets, the ancient handbooks of ignorant science and displaced legal information, the shelves of bad theology, all the musty stuff'. He would tell Mark Twain's story, how he replied to the toast of literature by regretting it was such a melancholy subject: 'Shakespeare is dead, Milton is dead – and I don't feel very well myself.'

The *Academy*'s round-up of the Favourite Books of 1899 named little fiction or poetry. The novel, the triumph of the Victorian period, did indeed seem to be dying. Gosse himself selected Stevenson's *Letters* as the book that had interested him most in the year, and so did Pinero and Thornycroft. Cheeringly, both Mrs Craigie (John Oliver Hobbes) and Maurice Hewlett chose Gosse's *Life and Letters of John Donne*. Hardy chose the Browning *Letters* but also Yeats's *Wind among the Reeds*.

Gosse saw Yeats as the main hope in poetry. They were seeing a good deal of him at Delamere Terrace these days. He would become wonderful after supper and tell of visions he had seen 'with his natural sight' of a woman shooting at the stars and a blue turkey on the hearth-rug and a horse with a man's head and shoulders. Nellie found it rather a problem when Yeats said he was only eating 'what is good for him *mentally*' – but Edmund felt it was the way poets should behave.

15

On the Fringe of the Real Thing

IN HIS LIFE of Donne, Gosse had written: 'Donne *lived*. His soul was thirsty with the consuming strain after experience, and it was in active movement and in personal contact with widely various types that he discovered that relief which gentler spirits find in meditation . . .' It is impossible to read this sentence without applying it to Gosse himself. He could not meditate. He could not spend *all* his time scribbling and scribbling. He was thirsty for the diversions of society, of contact with 'widely various types'. Nellie spoke of him being 'restless with energy' at this time. Gosse wrote of Donne moving 'among people of wealth and ostentatious expenditure'.

The morning post now included, along with the invitations to write articles and books, preside at meetings and dinners, to give lectures, advice and comfort, more and more invitations to just such houses of wealth and ostentation: to Belvoir, to Taplow, to Temple Newsam. There were invitations too to come and see a stained glass window designed by Helen, Countess of Radnor (on coroneted paper with 'Helen' floating in a silver cloud); to luncheon with Lord and Lady Brownlow ('he very red and sleepy'; she asking incessant questions and giving her own answers, 'just like Sisera's mother'); to dine with Richard Haldane at Westminster. Lord Burghclere so valued Gosse's opinion that he sent a new version of one passage of his translation of the *Georgics* with a telegram for reply 'Yes' or 'No'. Was it an improvement or not?

Gosse was an outsider, of course, and he was not always totally at ease. At Esher Place, with 'real Botticellis' hanging on the wall, he suspected that Lady Helen Vincent, his hostess ('a little caustic and unsympathetic') had not really wished him to come. 'Her husband did, I feel.' And he liked his hostess's sister, Lady Ulrika Duncombe, blue-stocking of the family, studying at Newnham and interested in Tessa. The other guests included Asquith and Balfour (both exceedingly pleasant), Lord Revelstoke (Maurice Baring's brother),

Lord Kenyon, the Willie Grenfells. One invitation led to another. He would visit the houses of all those fellow-guests.

'I ought to feel shy,' he wrote when staying at Panshanger with the Cowpers. 'But somehow these are not the sort of people who make me shy.' It was 'an extraordinarily gorgeous party': Lord Roberts, the Grenfells, the Duchesses of Portland and Marlborough, Austen Chamberlain, several Cabinet Ministers, Lady Poynder, Lord and Lady Arran, Lord Lytton. Balfour was also there. He always seemed to be there. At Wynyard Park one year when Gosse injured his leg, Balfour pushed him around in a wheel-chair; but Gosse was relieved when he got tired of it, for he *would* take the corners too abruptly. Still, it was pleasant to be on such terms with the Prime Minister. On 15th July 1900 there was the sort of telegram anyone might be interested to receive: CAN YOU DINE WEDNESDAY NEXT EIGHT THIRTY VERY SMALL PARTY DO COME ARTHUR BALFOUR 10 DOWNING STREET.

At Panshanger, in June 1901, there were twenty-eight to dinner, with Lord Cowper seeing human nature through rose-coloured spectacles, from a great distance. Gosse had a *tête à tête* breakfast with Lord Roberts, who talked all the time of South Africa and the war. 'If only I could remember what he said,' Edmund wrote to Nellie. Fleeting joys indeed. Arthur Benson looked at Gosse clearly when he gave a dinner party at the National Club in 1903, confidently mixing H. G. Wells and Alfred Bateman with Asquith and Haldane. Wells was full of nerves, without and within, talking about 'the governing class' in an embarrassing way. Gosse, on the other hand, though 'a little too fussy, is not afraid of these big men and holds his ground'. Asquith would be Prime Minister and Haldane Lord Chancellor; they were both becoming close friends. Benson detected the humour and tenderness in Haldane – and the affection for Gosse – 'behind the big white pig-like face'; they would win Gosse's entire devotion in the last part of his life.

Gosse kept on expecting to be over-awed, to be overwhelmed by the grandeur of his new friends and their surroundings. That same year, on the first of many regular Easter visits to Mountstewart, the Marquess of Londonderry's Irish estate, he wrote to Philip: 'It was funny that I should have dreaded being too "grand" here, for I have simply never been in a house where life went so easily. One lounges in and out as one pleases, and there is always company if you want it, or not if you don't.' Mountstewart remained his favourite of all the great country houses he visited. The house-party would sometimes include all the most important men in Ireland – the Chief Secretary, the Solicitor-General, the Lord Chief Justice. The most intimate secrets of Irish politics were discussed openly in the smoking-room and he could not help but be interested. But the best of it always, he told Philip, was the lough and the sailing. Lady Londonderry and he would often sail alone, watching the wild swans and the strings of barnacle-geese flying and the rows of cormorants with snaky heads standing on the rocks. There were days of great beauty with the Mountains of Mourne seeming cut out of lapis-lazuli against the further sky and, when the tide ran out, enormous flats of sepia and silver.

Lady Londonderry was at Crewe Hall on his first visit there and was a 'considerable solace' to him. 'She thinks the conversation kept too high a key and so do I,' he wrote to Nellie. But Lord Crewe was 'very chummy and merry and we laugh uninterruptedly for hours'. Society, as Osbert Sitwell would reiterate so mockingly in *Triple Fugue* (with Gosse appearing as Professor Criscross), was becoming 'exceptionally artistic'. But Gosse was, in fact, welcomed more as a sort of court jester than as an arbiter on the artistic or as a practising artist. He entertained them; he made them laugh. There is no doubt about that. His social successes were many and various: in Ireland once he entirely charmed a ferocious cockatoo belonging to Lady Dunleath. Everyone said 'Take care, take care', but the bird laid a hot, beady eye against Gosse's cheek and had violent hysterics when he realized Gosse was going away.

Lady Dorothy Nevill wrote from Eridge Castle to say how often she and Meresia, her daughter, had laughed at Gosse's 'impertinent remarks about our dearly beloved quadrupeds – you were too insolent about the dear things'. So she said, but she lapped it up, and only regretted that she felt Gosse was 'not much amused at our party'. 'You are very fastidious,' she said, remembering how, when going to Madresfield to the Beauchamps, he had written, 'I hope I shan't drop into a dull party.' She wondered what he thought of HRH and hoped he would deign to write and tell her.

We know what he thought of their Royal Highnesses, the Prince and Princess of Wales, when they were staying at Wynyard Park, another Londonderry house, near Stockton-on-Tees. The Prince (the future George V) fussed when there was no boiled egg for his tea, but of course it was soon brought. He was 'very much like an amiable and noisy schoolboy'. Excessively good-natured and easy, he seemed, like all these great people, to be 'fearfully indiscreet, talking about that low fellow, Lloyd George, and losing no opportunity of abusing the government'. (It was by then 1908.) Gosse quite liked this government; it was a great deal better than the last one. 'Most of the Liberals whom I know are as steady law-abiding people as any of the so-called Unionists,' he wrote to Hardy. 'I am sure there are fewer pure vulgarians and swine of sorts among them than among the money-grubbing conservatives.' But this was not the sort of thing one said at Wynyard Park to the Princess of Wales. She insisted on Gosse sharing her carriage – along with the Portuguese Minister and Lady Ilchester – when they went to visit the Scarbroughs at Lumley Castle. It was quite fun with crowds lining the way, waving flags and trying to get a glimpse of the Princess, but he found the conversation pretty heavy-going, while admiring the fact that the Princess seemed to have 'a certain wish to be on the serious and good side'.

There were flags for someone else, too, on an earlier occasion when he and Nellie were fellow guests with the Bullers at Crewe Hall, not long after the end of the South African War, and Sir Redvers received quite an ovation when they visited the railway works, with hundreds of boys and men singing 'For he's a jolly good fellow.' Nellie reported this particular visit to Tessa in great detail, but she did not often go with Edmund. She generally preferred to visit her old friend, Theresa Sassoon, to go to a hotel in Folkestone with a daughter, or to stay at home with the cat. Nellie continued in her own unconventional paths: on Mafeking Day she and Sylvia had sat on the steps of St Paul's to rest in the press of the dense rejoicing crowds.

At Crewe Hall she wrote: 'The much-talked-of clothes are, all of them, a great success. It really is a convenient plan to have plenty of changes; it gives one a lot to do, these "rapid changes". I've changed three times already today' – for breakfast, for the visit to the works, for lunch. And soon she would put on her tea-gown for tea and then her black evening dress for dinner. 'We have flunkies in beautiful pink stockings at dinner. And an Invisible Being arranges my room and puts fresh towels there several times a day – or at least so it seems to me.'

Henry James shook his head at all this gadding about, though he had done it himself in the past. He thought of Gosse 'doomed to draughty Dukeries', dressing and undressing. Inviting him to Lamb House for one of his regular visits, James stressed, '*No* dress clothes'; a simple tunic would do, with a few flowers in the hair. He wrote to W. E. Norris on 17th September 1903:

> The grand features of his career and character reproduce themselves from month to month in the most punctual and genial way. He is only rather more a child of the World and a presider at the Table, than hitherto, and his World and his Table and his relation to the same and his pursuit of society and conversation and of the Great and of the Small – and of everything – and everyone – remain the same bewildering and baffling enigma as ever to me (in respect of

their compatibility with the cultivation of Letters and with the interests of the Board of Trade).

If Henry James, that master of insight, found Gosse at this period an enigma, who are we to find him anything else? He was at a low ebb. He thought 1902 had been, perhaps, the worst year of his life: 'a tedious year for me – languid and dispiriting,' he wrote to Maurice Baring. The year before, they had moved house, which had caused considerable agitation. Staying at Lord Kenyon's house, Gredington in Shropshire, Gosse had written of longing to get back to his 'squalid little home' in Delamere Terrace. It had begun to seem, after twenty-five years, intolerably cramped, if not really squalid. After Eliza Gosse's death, it seemed reasonable to take on something a little grander. On 8th April 1901, Gosse wrote to George Armour, who was always urging him to cross the Atlantic again, 'I have bought a house! It is a good deal out of repair and Mr John Belcher A.R.A. is going to make some structural changes and put it fully into a modern state for us. The builders go in this week and we hope that by July at latest we may be settled in . . . There is no view more beautiful than from our upper windows . . . There is a vast balcony where we hope to live entirely in summer.'

It was certainly a beautiful house, and it still is. Number 17, Hanover Terrace is part of a splendid Nash terrace overlooking Regent's Park. It was 'so silent and calm, you might be in the depth of the country', Gosse wrote, yet it was also so convenient. Henry James declared the arcade, running the length of the Terrace, reminded him of Bologna. In Number 17 Mrs William Collins, an artist's widow, had lived from 1844 to 1859, with her sons Wilkie and Charles. Dickens had been a constant visitor; Holman Hunt and Millais had also visited the house. Part at least of *The Woman in White* was written there. Now, GLC blue plaques bear witness to the fact that H. G. Wells and Ralph Vaughan Williams later lived in the same terrace. It was the right sort of house – but Thomas Hardy wrote: 'A background to you which is not the old familiar one passes my powers of imagination to realize!'

Gosse wrote to Alice Meynell: 'Please note the present address, as it is my own property, and in it to all probability, I shall die.' He would indeed live there until his death, for another twenty-seven years, but the way he spoke of it was, typically, with slight exaggeration. Hanover Terrace is in fact Crown Property; he would have it on a series of seven-year leases. Arthur Benson, very early on, would describe tea on the balcony, 'looking across the shining water, the bird-haunted islands of the Park, brightly set with flowers to a line of woods – only the dashing cabs and the sullen roar behind recalled London'. In the dusk the view seemed to be of the park of a château – 'misty thickets and glimmering waters'. George Moore would describe 'the pink hawthorn in full bloom against the lake and the blue smokey distance'. Now the trees are so large and thick that in summer one can scarcely see the park at all, but just occasionally one can hear the roar of a lion in the zoological gardens, and always still that other steady roar of an unseen London.

Nellie hoped the new home, once the agitating business had been settled and they were at last straight, would rouse Edmund from a depression which was only temporarily alleviated by the grand country house weekends or interesting literary work. Queen Victoria's death had given him an agreeable employment. With Lady Ponsonby's help (she was Maurice Baring's aunt and a Lady of the Bedchamber), he had written an anonymous article on the Queen in the *Quarterly Review*, which had caused a tremendous stir. If today the article reads as a straightforward and rather uncontroversial attempt to estimate the Queen's personal qualities, at the time it hardly escaped the charges of treason and sacrilege. Gosse bravely criticized the current tendency to treat the Queen, both in her life and now in death, as a fetish and a myth rather than a human being.

The young Lytton Strachey was already, as all Bloomsbury would be, critical of Gosse. Hearing him lecture on Leigh Hunt at Newnham in 1900, Strachey wrote, 'Law! He *did* think himself clever.' And the undergraduate thought the lecturer abominably rude to complain of draughts, to send Virginia Stephen's cousin Katherine scurrying to alter ventilators, and then to say, 'Oh, it really doesn't matter.' Reviewing Strachey's *Queen Victoria* in 1921, Gosse would muse on what would have happened to Strachey if he had published his book twenty-five years before. He would have been pursued, Gosse surmised, to the Reading Room of the British Museum and there scraped to death with oyster shells. He must have felt he had barely escaped such an end himself. 'He is the earliest of the biographers,' Gosse wrote of Strachey, 'to insist that a cat, and still more a careful student of the whimsicalities of life, may look steadily at a queen.' In fact, Gosse does himself an injustice, for, in a short span, he had done just that himself and paved the way for Strachey. Gosse admired Strachey enormously; in 1922 he would call him 'the best writer living under fifty'. He thought he looked like Christ painted by El Greco. Virginia Woolf reported that Lytton meeting Gosse 'in ducal society, says he is very amusing', but she would never admit to finding him so herself. In 1926 she would tease Strachey with a rumour that he was 'getting up a subscription to give Edmund Gosse gold sleevelinks on his 100th birthday'.

But it is 1902 and Gosse is not yet fifty-three, though to the young it already seemed he had been around for a very long time. In March and April, he felt himself badly ill ('I was afraid I was going to break down altogether') and underwent a Swedish treatment, called 'positive massage'. In spite of the new house, he was finding life flat, stale and uninteresting. 'As life goes on,' he wrote to T. J. Wise, 'it seems more and more to run in a rut and the adventurous grows more difficult to grasp.' He had no idea, as we have seen, what dangerous adventures Wise had been indulging in. His own life seemed unrewarding, even with the temptations of a glittering society. (Sylvia would leave off any jewellery when he took her to parties, as she could not compete with the diamonds.)

At the end of the year, he was still seeing the doctor. The 'passing disorder' in the spring now seemed to be threatening his health, spirits and capability in a serious way. His doctor called it 'nerves' and cheered him with the thought that nerves can be got right more easily than, say, lungs. A friend, the Reverend William Hunt, said he had worked too hard and his 'naturally excitable and sensitive disposition', the very thing that made him 'so brilliant in society and in writing', now needed a complete rest. It was always difficult for Gosse to pause and rest, but it was even more difficult, as James saw, to reconcile his pursuit of society with the cultivation of Letters and the interests of the Board of Trade. He seemed constantly tired in the first years of the new century. He told Alfred Bateman at the Board that he was always grateful to him, but that he felt, nonetheless, undeservedly stranded in an official backwater. He had been a reluctant civil servant for more years than he cared to remember. The salary remained the same: £400 a year. Dobson, who was himself about to retire, rhymed an epitaph for Gosse:

> This person died of discontent.
> He never had an increment.

The work got increasingly heavy. On 1st January 1903, he gave his customary statement of his year's work: there had been 342 pieces of translation, compared with 311 the year before; and the 342 pieces had amounted to no fewer than 822 foolscap pages from nine different languages, the most frequent German, Dutch, Danish, Swedish and Italian.

As for Letters, his main work at this period was going into a fascinating book which would add nothing to his serious reputation. This is *English Literature: an illustrated record*, which he and Richard Garnett worked on industriously for several years. It is a sort of mammoth coffee-table book, but in four large volumes. The first volume was by Garnett; the second by both of them, the third and fourth by Gosse alone. It is a popular history of literature, illustrated at nearly every opening with pictures of writers and their houses, with facsimile letters and autographs and pages of manuscript. One almost expects to find a lock of hair and a bloodstained cloth as in those Denis Wheatley compendiums. Macmillan & Co. brought the volumes out in New York; Heinemann in England. The two last volumes by Gosse himself were particularly popular. First published in 1903, they were reprinted in 1906. They were his final attempt at any work of literary history.

Gosse was still editing the Short Histories of World Literature. The American volume took him back to his old worry about relative values. Should Wigglesworth (1631–1705) really be treated with as much gravity as Chaucer? Gosse continued to write regularly for American magazines, in particular for *Cosmopolitan*. But his old enthusiasm for all things American was wearing thin in the face of so much American rejection of all things English. He wrote to Gilder: 'All our English authors, except a few flashy novelists, have to complain that America is no longer a field for their ideas. You have cut yourselves off entirely, in your fantastic national pride, from sympathy with us. I believe this can only be a passing phase, and the happy relations which used to exist between our provinces of literature will be resumed.' In the meantime, there were irritations. Edwin Mead, editor of the *New England Magazine* (and a cousin of Mrs Howells, which made it worse), sent Gosse a pamphlet which attacked him in passing. Why should anyone care whether he thought America had produced a poet, or indeed whether he thought contemporary England had? Colonel Higginson's judgment, that of Emily Dickinson's dear Colonel, was of far more consequence. Gosse wrote to Higginson much more in sorrow than in anger: 'My conscience tells me I have never made the silly error of depreciating American culture or American intelligence. No one – I may surely boast – has made a closer study of American talent, no one has sympathized with gifted Americans, no one has striven to see the American standpoint more than I. I think that I deserve less than most English writers the contemptuous hostility of such patriots as Mr Mead.' Fortunately there were still warm and comforting letters from his old American friends – Armour and Gilder and H. H. Furness. And there were good American friends closer to home too: Henry James, of course, but also the Harlands, with whom he had stayed at Dieppe in the summer of 1901, reading them *Hypolympia* under the pine trees.

In these years, early in the new century, much of Gosse's working time at home was spent on his own and other people's contributions to the *Encyclopaedia Britannica*. He had, he said, 'been entrusted by the *Times* with the editorship of the section of Belles-lettres (English and Foreign) in the supplement which is projected'. The work caused endless problems and irritations; he was working in co-operation with Hugh Chisholm, who would sometimes treat him, Gosse considered, as if he were a fourth-form boy. The work continued until 1908, with his article on 'Style'. Chisholm wrote to thank him for his 'monumental' contributions, which made such a long list it was no wonder he felt some of the pangs of parting.

Gosse's editorship of Heinemann's Century of French Romance series gave him the chance to get Henry James to introduce *Madame Bovary* and Balzac's *The Two Young Brides*. James's biographer writes of the importance to him of the revaluation at this time of the writers who had meant most to him. Gosse himself translated *La Dame aux camélias* but Dumas had no particular significance for him. Unlike James, whose critical work was so closely related to his creative activity, Gosse's work seemed scattered, unrelated, lacking in pattern or point. Sometimes he wondered if he had any creative ability at all. He was, he supposed, above all a biographer and he believed in the importance of biography.

'There is no species of writing,' Gosse considered, 'which requires the exercise of a finer sense of proportion, of a keener appreciation of the relative values of things and men, or of a deeper sense of literary responsibility.' As early as 1882, asking Leslie Stephen for work on the *DNB*, Gosse had written 'Biography is my foible.' Twenty years later, it was much more than that. He wrote the article on it in the *Encyclopaedia Britannica*. It was one of his favourite lecture subjects.

Gosse would decry the old attitudes to biography, the writers who thought their job was to 'produce a grandiose moral effect', to celebrate virtue and dignity, to give lessons. He praised Boswell's *Life of Johnson* as the best biography in the language, that first biography which recognized the satisfaction of curiosity, and an observation of life unclouded by 'moral passion or social prejudice'. The temptation was always to sort things out too neatly, forgetting the incurable illogicalities of life. Gosse regretted the Victorian tendency to a 'certain false and timid excess of refinement' which made it 'more and more difficult to learn the truth about an eminent person, if that truth could be considered in any sense undignified'. 'How decent is English biography,' Carlyle had written. 'Bless its mealy mouth.'

Gosse regretted the bulky respectable tomes which flung together every letter without selection or arrangement and included a history of the times for good measure. He particularly regretted those edited by widows, lurking behind the 'apparently unprejudiced name of some docile author'. 'There is hardly a Life printed nowadays that does not offend by the publication of too much of everything – too many letters, too many extracts from diaries, too many "impressions" contributed by unobservant people, too much undigested material of every description.' Every three-volume biography would be better in two; every two-volume might be better in one.

But, in fact, Gosse loved the telling detail, and even the untelling one. Reviewing Festing Jones's biography of Samuel Butler, Gosse said that there might be readers who did not care how many times Butler brushed his hair every day: 'I am not one of them; these little things . . . are my delight.' He loved to know that Butler, travelling abroad, carried diarrhoea pills in the handle of his Gladstone bag.

His own *Donne* had been in two volumes but his other biographies of this period were slim affairs: *Jeremy Taylor* (1904), *Coventry Patmore* and *Sir Thomas Browne* (both 1905), and *Ibsen* (1907). In February 1903, Gosse wrote to Lady Dorothy Nevill: 'I have been absolutely absorbed in work, going nowhere and seeing nothing. I live all day in the company of Jeremy Taylor and dream of him at night.' On July 12th he showed Benson his 'neat, dapper MS'. It had to be brief, as he had explained to his research assistant, Louisa Guiney, asking her to keep a careful note of the time she spent and to allow him to settle with her on her own terms: 'It is to be no more than a volume of the English Men of Letters series, occupying 200pp. I shall therefore have no room to quote documents in detail. But the personal facts about Jeremy Taylor are very scanty.' He longed for her to find 'unprinted letters, anecdotes, records of movement'. But she did not have much luck. Arthur Symons found admirable the skill with which Gosse had extracted so much interest out of matter which is in itself 'decidedly dry'.

Gosse was often to write to the restricted length dictated by a series. His *Raleigh* had been an English Worthy, his *Congreve* a Great Writer, his *Gray* also an English Man of Letters. The lengths of *Coventry Patmore* and *Ibsen* were dictated by the fact that they were both in Hodder's series of Literary Lives, but in any case there had already been full-length biographies of them both: Basil Champneys on Patmore, and Henrik Jaeger on Ibsen. This gave Gosse the chance to write more glancingly, more personally. Arthur Benson objected, in his diary, to this personal element when reading the proofs of the Patmore:

They are delicate and subtle of course – full of colour and movement, but the book is not somehow satisfactory. Gosse *will* put
himself forward . . . The sticking of the autobiographical element
in, in patches, is not nice. It is the need of skipping and posturing
before the people, of bowing them in to the show, of wanting to get
a recognition of your own cleverness, that is so distressing.

Benson was always Gosse's severest critic, lamenting his 'feverish
and feminine desire to make an impression at all costs'. Benson little
realized at this point that in a very short time he would be encouraging
Gosse in the 'autobiographical element'; that in concentrating on
himself, Gosse would soon write the best book of his life.

Before he started work on *Father and Son*, when he was still in that
depressing flat period, when nothing seemed more than momentarily
exciting and life at the Board of Trade was more tedious than ever,
Gosse received an invitation to visit Paris as the guest of honour at a
banquet and to lecture at the Société des Conférences. It was February
1904. The initiative had come from Henry Davray, who for eight
years had been writing a column called 'Lettres anglaises' in the
Mercure de France. He had long been an admirer of Edmund Gosse and
had often written of him in his column. Now he had asked a group of
French writers to join him in honouring the man who had done so
much for the reputation of French writers in England, who had always
aimed to see literature 'with the eyes of a citizen of Europe, rather than
of Little Pedlington'. 'I believe I have read more French than English,'
Gosse had said in 1901. He had always tried to concentrate on a
cosmopolitan rather than an insular view. It was almost as unusual
then as it is now.

Gosse had continued to spend some part of nearly every year in
France. In the autumn of 1903 he and Nellie had spent nearly two
months among vines and chestnuts and meadows full of purple
crocuses, going further south as September changed into October.
Gosse would work from seven until eleven and have the rest of the day
free. He would often say, listening to some elderly keeper of a roadside
débit de vin discoursing about Rostand, or the patron of a small hotel
being wise about the architecture of the local church, how little he
wanted to return to England, where the innkeepers had barely heard of
Shakespeare. His anti-imperialism sprang from the same source. The
colonies were more interested in cricket than in Swinburne, he feared.
'They add absolutely nothing to that which makes life valuable to me.'
Benson would describe how well Gosse knew the French language –
reading aloud from a novel, for instance, translating easily and fluently

as he went – but the thought of writing a speech in French for an august audience intimidated him. 'Speak French correctly or with elegance, I never shall,' he wrote to Eddie Marsh from Isère after a fifteen-mile walk, 'but I get good practice in speaking it with ease.' Fortunately he was asked to give his speech, on the influence of France upon English poetry, in English. One of the distinguished audience, at the dinner certainly, and probably at the lecture, was André Gide. The occasion was the first remote contact between Gide and Gosse. Gide followed it by sending Gosse a copy of his latest book. Further contact would have a great deal to do with Gide's subsequent reputation in England.

Davray thought Gosse's lecture simply admirable. Gosse was continually interrupted, at every sentence, by applause. Marcel Schwob, at the dinner, had found him 'charming but pedantic'. The *Pall Mall Gazette* thought Charles Dickens the last Englishman to get such a reception in Paris. It was a fine hour.

Then came a finer. 'At fifty-four,' Gosse wrote, in his biography of Patmore, 'a man has usually tasted all the dishes which make up the banquet of life and has no great desire to begin the feast over again. He has formed his opinions and appeased his curiosity.' But Gosse, at just this age, was invited to a new series of banquets which would give him endless pleasure, and arouse and satisfy his perpetual curiosity. It was exactly what he needed.

William Heinemann was with him in Paris; they were staying at the Hôtel Romain and there arrived on 6th February 1904 a letter from Sir Harry Graham offering Gosse the job of Librarian of the House of Lords. Gosse wrote to Graham saying he knew nothing of the duties or the salary but would be returning to England in a few days and would call on him. But telegrams of congratulation began to arrive. The announcement of Gosse's appointment was in the papers on February 9th, the very day of the dinner in the Restaurant Durand in Paris.

Apparently the King had been keen to appoint a 'dependant' called Fortescue. This must have been George Knottesford Fortescue, who was Garnett's successor as Superintendent of the Reading Room at the British Museum and who had been Keeper of Printed Books since May 1899 and President of the Library Association in 1901. Why he was a nominee of the King and why Harry Graham was so opposed to him, we do not know. But the appointment was apparently Graham's prerogative and the only way he could see of refusing the royal candidate was to say that Gosse was already appointed. Graham wrote to Lady Desborough as early as February 7th saying he had been lucky enough to secure Mr Gosse. 'Nobody sent me a letter of recommendation except your own little notes – but from the list I have felt that he was the very man for the place . . . I assure you that I have had the very best Librarians and Literary men competing for the post.' Lord Revelstoke, at any rate, thought Gosse's friends had helped: 'You know I think that your friends were working for you.'

Looking back with satisfaction twenty-four years later Gosse would say: 'Where others have had to toil and wait, things have often come to me. The Librarianship of the House of Lords was a case of this. The post became vacant and it was offered to me. It came to me, in fact, and it was just the work I needed.'

It was in fact not nearly such an unexpected invitation as Gosse tries to suggest. In Benson's diary in January there is talk of 'a plot to get Gosse the Librarianship of the House of Lords'. On January 31st Benson had certainly discussed the possibility with Gosse and had written both to the Prime Minister and to Lord Northampton.

Writing to Gilder, Gosse called the House of Lords Library 'a very charming and stately retreat for the old age of an over-worked man of letters'. He had asked Harry Graham, 'Can I do any of my own work there?' Graham laughed and said, 'You will find there is very little else to do.' Everyone seemed to see it as a sinecure, a reward for a lifetime devoted to literature. J. M. Barrie was glad the Lords had got 'the very best man possible'. Eddie Marsh wrote, 'there has never been anything so suitable since the accession of Queen Victoria'. Frederic Harrison wrote of 'the round man in the round hole', and spoke of Gosse now having his 'whole life free to give us more books'. Andrew Lang hoped there would be 'little to do and plenty to get . . . The Peers are not a very bookish lot and you will be able to pursue your private studies.' There was certainly 'plenty to get', both financially and otherwise. The salary was a generous £1000 a year, a great improvement over the £400 Gosse was getting at the Board of Trade. And the holidays were long.

Two months after Gosse had begun his new job, Arthur Waugh thanked him for a gift of plover's eggs:

> But lo! a cousin's heart that beats
> With tender and harmonious chords
> Wafts to our poor suburban streets
> The menu of the House of Lords.

It would be nice to think of the infant Evelyn in Hillfield Road, London, NW, having his first taste of the lordly dish he would celebrate in *Brideshead Revisited*. It was not only the menu at the House of Lords which suited Gosse. In spite of his self-mocking remark in the letter to Gilder and the reactions of his unaristocratic friends, Gosse was determined to become fully involved in his new place of work. He was, after all, among friends. Now he could notch up many more lords among his acquaintance; after his first six months he reckoned he knew 'personally, more or less definitely', nearly one hundred peers. 'Everybody is extremely kind to me and I find the House absorbs all my interest.'

Gosse had no intention of spending a great deal more time writing. The attractions of the library were far too powerful for that. Benson reported he was in high spirits, spending all his time in talk. On 2nd March 1904, Gosse recorded, in the full diary he had begun to keep, an incident which emphasized the splendid satisfactions of his new position:

> Our quiet is disturbed from 2.30 to 3.30 by members of the House of Commons, who come to show the Library to their friends. They used to make themselves quite at home, but the Lord Chancellor has now enacted that they must get permission from the Librarian. Accordingly, my big policeman bars the way and makes them come and ask Worfell, who asks Hugh Butler, who asks me; by the time I am reached, the boldest M.P. is a little cowed. The other day a wild Irishman, with a train of ladies, would not be left outside. The policeman was looking for me, and the M.P. pushed in and found Lord Stanmore reading near the door. He said, airily, 'I suppose I may visit the Library?' Lord Stanmore put on his grandest manner and replied, over his long grey beard, 'I cannot do what you wish. I am not the Librarian. *I am only a Peer.*' The M.P. wilted away, and fled, followed by his flight of ladies.

The emphasis is Gosse's own.

Gosse kept a beady eye on the peers themselves, as well as the MPs. Those who accused him of loving a lord, and there were many, might not have realized that Lords, even more than Commoners, were in the line for pitiless criticism. Their weaknesses and foibles amused and roused him far more than their splendours impressed him. Gosse did not suffer fools or bores gladly, and there were many fools and bores in the House of Lords. Far from flattering them, he believed in putting them in their place, and not always only in his diary. Arthur Benson, in *his* diary, reported he had heard from Baring (who would have heard from Revelstoke, his brother, or Althorp, his brother-in-law) that Gosse was rather unpopular with his 'Venetian manner', but on another occasion Benson had heard Gosse was 'universally popular' – 'so obliging and amusing'. As always, he was different things to different men, and even to the same men on different days.

One by one, Gosse criticized the peers: the Duke of Devonshire showed 'extraordinary naïveté' when giving the causes which led to his leaving the Cabinet. He talked 'like a bass voice out of a stone mask'. 'The bore of the House is Lord Muskerry, who pops up on all occasions, waylays Peers hurrying to the lavatory, and tries to hold them till they promise to vote for him.' The Duke of Marlborough was pathetic: 'His physical appearance is that of a shrimp' and he 'never has the dread of death out of his mind'. Lord Dudley had debts in Dublin amounting to £100,000; Lord Crewe had speculated and was ruined: £600,000 was the figure mentioned. Lord Portsmouth, with his great empty smile, was extraordinarily exasperating. Lord Ellenborough, known as Lord Yellingbugger, Gosse fancied to be 'almost illiterate'; certainly 'his handwriting is like that of a servant'. Lord Tenterden turned up at a committee 'helplessly and noisily drunk'. Another peer, Lord Haldon, a bankrupt who had never actually taken his seat, had the obnoxious habit of coming in and stuffing his pockets with House of Lords stationery.

But worst of all was the Bishop of Hereford: 'His voice, like the bleat of sheep upon a hillside, throws everybody into a sort of distress.' 'The House simply hates the Bishop of Hereford. I heard a peer say last night in a loud whisper as the bishop stood talking "I should like, just once, to put a bullet through him," and the Lord Chancellor, quite audibly in a careless aside, remarked, "The Bishop of Hereford is very fond of saying 'I may be wrong' and *he always is*."' Two years later he was still just as much of a trial. Lord Rosebery, who appointed him, told Gosse, puffing out his purple cheeks, that 'Whenever the Bishop of Hereford rises every peer in the House looks at me with a look that says "I should like to stick a knife into your heart" and I cannot pretend to deny that the suggestion is a plausible one.'

Arthur Benson, seeing a handful of peers in the library on one of his visits, thought them 'very shady and dickey-looking', 'these brightest jewels in Britannia's crown, enshrined in all their lustre in their padded cases', the leather arm-chairs by the library fire. It should have been enough to turn anyone into a socialist, he thought. Gosse certainly believed that he would live to see the House of Lords abolished, but in the meantime he loved his dark private room with its mullioned windows and the gold portcullis on the red leather chairs; and he loved the feeling of being close to the men of power.

Gosse gradually came to recognize and know by name most of the peers, at least those who spoke in the Chamber and those who used the library. But every now and again an unfamiliar face would appear. One day he wrote in his diary:

I passed as a great wit this morning, by accident. An unknown peer strayed into the Library and, on my asking what I could do for him, expressed no wish but to know if there was a smoking-room here. I took him immediately to it, and he snuffed up the cigar-smell with rapture. Surprised at this insistency, I thought it safe to say 'I see your Lordship has no objection to tobacco!' At this he reacted with laughter, smote me on the shoulder, and declared that was 'the best thing he had ever heard'. My modesty was overwhelmed at this tribute, which absolutely mystified me. However, when he went, all was explained, for this was the new peer Lord Winterstoke, lately Wills, the Bristol tobacco-merchant.

At this stage, Balfour was Prime Minister, and Balfour, as we have seen, was already a friend. It gave Gosse enormous kudos one day when the Prime Minister, striding back to the Commons after listening, as he rarely did, to a speech in the Lords, caught sight of Gosse, paused, and forgetting the inexorable call of the Commons, accepted Gosse's offer of a cup of tea. As they walked to the tea-room, Lords kept pouncing on him. 'He kept hold of my arm, however, and presently I steered him to a table, where we were alone except when Lord Spencer came and hung over him, murmuring, or Lord Tweedmouth stood at attention and smiled. Lord James, with his harsh voice, cried out "What, come up to this House *already*?" But in spite of these interruptions we had a delightful intimate talk about literature.' Gosse told Balfour he had bought his books for the House of Lords Library. 'That's what it is to have a friend!' Balfour exclaimed. 'Now in the House of Commons library there is not a single copy of any book of mine.'

Gosse's involvement with the affairs of the nation became greater as the years went by and his intimacy with Richard Haldane increased. Haldane gave up £25,000 a year at the Bar, Gosse recorded, to take over the War Office on the Liberal victory in 1905; he had been MP for East Lothian since 1885. He would become a peer in 1911 and Lord Chancellor in 1912, eventually becoming a member of the first Labour government.

Gosse would lunch with him alone in his room at the War Office and find the sweep of his mind amazing and exhilarating. 'He seems like thought itself made flesh . . . The more I see of him, in delightful intimacy, the more he seems to me our one great intelligence in public life.' 'The play of Haldane's intellect is the most wonderful fact now in my daily life,' Gosse wrote in March 1905. He would meet Ramsay MacDonald at Haldane's dinner table and find him 'plausible without being sympathetic'. Haldane's attitudes would help to soften Gosse's increasingly reactionary views.

Gosse relished as onlooker and observer the daily comings and goings of our legislators. It was not always easy to know what was going on. At 6.45 on 21st April 1904, Gosse wrote in his diary: 'What is up? In the gathering twilight the Duke of Devonshire has been pacing up and down in front of my table, having sent off a letter. His messenger returned: "Mr Chamberlain will wait upon your Grace in a moment" and immediately enters Mr Joseph, eyeglass and orchid complete. They shook hands mysteriously, without effusion, and now have withdrawn, out of my ear-shot, into the Truro Room. What are they concocting?'

Sometimes Gosse was himself involved in a drama. The Archbishop of Canterbury came into the library one day asking for a volume of holograph marriage-licences of the Royal Family in the nineteenth century. Apparently he had given them to the previous librarian to take care of and now the King wanted to see them. Gosse told him he had never seen a sign of the book, whereupon the Archbishop, with a comical gesture of despair said, 'But the legitimacy of the Family depends upon it.' Gosse searched high and low in every possible safe and cupboard, looking for the volume described by the Archbishop as 'a large folio bound in old worn brown calf, with no lettering or tooling on the sides.' Eventually the Registers were discovered at the house of the former librarian and proved other people's memories could be as fallible as Gosse's. The missing volume was in fact a rather small quarto 'bound in pale purple velvet, and with an immense and very bright gold coat of arms . . .'

For royal visitors to the library a favourite exhibit was the death warrant of Charles I. It seemed 'extraordinarily attractive to royal personages', Gosse noted, bringing it out for the Queen of Saxony, various German princesses, and Prince George, the future king of Greece. The Princess of Wales paid a visit in March 1909 and was reported to have listened to Gosse with the rapt attention of a disciple. The library did not have a great many treasures, but it was not a mere repository for 'old Lillywhite's Guides', as Andrew Lang had supposed. It was certainly a better library by the time Gosse left. A printed catalogue in a limited edition bears some witness to the fact that he did not spend the entire time talking. He was very irritated one day to hear Lord Avebury say to some ladies, 'There are no nice books here . . . nothing but law books and acts of parliament.' Gosse hastened to correct him: 'We have a very remarkable historical collection, the lacunae in which I am incessantly filling up. No science, it is true, and scarcely any belles lettres, but a fine library of memoirs, French as well as English, an unusually good set of internal books of reference, capital sets of county histories and all the kinds of books a statesman's library should have.' Lord Avebury apologized in some embarrassment, muttering that his authority was Gosse's predecessor, Arthur Strong. Like many of his fellow peers, he had never actually looked at the books himself.

But there were a few peers who were of a different calibre altogether. The Duke of Rutland at Belvoir talked marvellously of Disraeli and allowed the public to come every day into every part of his gardens. Gosse asked him did he not find that irksome. 'No,' he replied, 'I like it. I like to see them there; I like to think they are enjoying what I enjoy. And I find them invariably civil.' Old Lord Knutsford pleased him too, sitting in the library day after day reading Lucian in Greek for his own amusement. Not finding Euripides for him, Gosse ordered a complete set of the Greek dramatists.

Gosse loved entertaining at the House of Lords – luncheons at the Lords become more and more frequent in the Book of Gosse. He would write to Max Beerbohm, for instance, telling him 'to show the enclosed paper to a constable and gently insist on being shown to the Library at once. There my people will be waiting for you with open arms.' Sometimes Gosse's literary friends would lounge around in the red leather arm-chairs, which their Lordships themselves might be wanting to use. In his velvet coat, he ruled his staff and the lords alike with a benevolent rod. Sometimes it was not so benevolent. There was the terrible day when Lord Camperdown extinguished one of the little lamps always kept burning for the melting of sealing wax, and would neither re-light it nor apologize.

But more of the lords became friends than enemies. There are surviving several hundred letters to Gosse from Lord Althorp, who became Lord Spencer in 1910. He was Maurice Baring's brother-in-law and great-grandfather of the present Princess of Wales. Bobby Spencer, as he was always known, became devoted to Edmund Gosse. In February 1905 his brother seemed about to become Prime Minister, though the King apparently said to Haldane, who told Gosse, 'Who told Spencer that I am going to call on him to form a government? I am sure *I* didn't.' Balfour said to Gosse, 'What an amazing example Spencer is of what can be done in this country by a noble presence, a great hereditary position, and a fine personal record, assisted by no intellectual parts of any kind! Such a sweet and even such a beautiful character, and no ability at all . . .' Gosse admitted 'his mind works very slowly'. Balfour said, 'It does not work at all. He has no mind. He has character but no mind.' His half-brother, Gosse's friend, was fortunately a different matter.

As it was with Lord Spencer, so with Lord Ribblesdale. Poor Lord Ribblesdale was fortunately too languid, Gosse considered, to commit suicide (like his father). One son had been killed in Somaliland; his young heir was a republican and a revolutionary. He seemed to need Gosse's company. So too did Lord Redesdale, Nancy Mitford's grandfather, who would write constantly to Gosse when they were apart, every few days towards the end of his life. Gosse would speak of the 'redundant vitality of his character. His nature swarmed with life, like a drop of pond-water under a microscope.' There would develop a new element in Gosse's social life: not the crowded glittering house-party (though those continued) but the quiet weekend alone with some noble lord who valued his talk and needed to be cheered. 'You come here and lift me out of the dolefullest of dumps,' Lord Redesdale would write.

Arthur Benson began to worry about Gosse more than ever in the summer of 1906. Eliza Brightwen at Stanmore was dying of cancer and it seemed, just as it had when Eliza Gosse was dying, a terrible repetition of those days in Pimlico so long ago when the boy had read aloud to his dying mother. Day after day, he visited Aunt Lizzie, with the book that was to be *Father and Son* already partly written. On the Sunday before she died, he read chapter after chapter of the Bible, as wild squirrels came in from the garden and a robin 'perched on the edge of a cup listening very steadily to the reading'. Gosse found very hard, he told Lady Dorothy Nevill, the loss of one he had loved for forty years.

At the National Club, Benson found him very tired and excited, but full of amusing, polished reminiscences of his father and the Plymouth Brethren. Gosse had first mentioned *Father and Son* to Benson the previous December. It was 'a little autobiographical book he meant to write – his early days with his calvinistic father – the contest of Paganism with rigid Faith. I asked him what he believed. "Nothing supernatural, thank God!" he said. I have never heard him speak of the subject before.' Gosse had certainly been writing the book in October 1905 when he and Nellie stayed at the Hotel Bellini in Florence, trying to escape 'chattering academical English people who wanted to be intense and talk about literature . . . If there is anything I hate on my travels, it is this sort of thing.' It was this Florentine visit that is the source of the reference, in chapter five of *Father and Son*, to the confluence of the Arno and the Mugnone, as an analogy with two hostile streams of belief.

Benson saw part of the manuscript the following year and worried that Gosse was not getting on with it. He stayed with Benson in his Cambridgeshire house the last weekend in June, 1906. 'Gosse came in a very pleasant mood,' Benson recorded, 'though confessing himself to be tired out; and he looked so. His parties, the great people he knows, his work, his writing, all take it out of him. Is it worth it?

'He is only on the fringe of the real thing, of course, but does not know it. He told me of a luncheon he gave, containing, I really think, all the most truly distinguished people in England: Arthur Balfour, the Desboroughs, Haldane, Thomas Hardy, the Londonderrys etc etc – but it is not quite *real* somehow. It does not come to him – he schemes for it. He is not even writing his book – the finest thing he has ever done.' The next year Benson would reiterate the theme: 'He feels, I think, that he has climbed the social ladder and is among the Upper Ten – but it is all a sham.'

Certainly it was a strain. To write *Father and Son*, to go through the early letters, to feel his father's faith and strength, undiminished by death, while toying with the worldly joys of the House of Lords – there is no question that it was a strain. The family letters of this period are almost entirely missing, and we know little of how Nellie regarded Edmund's intoxication with the House of Lords; but it was surely with a certain amount of affectionate exasperation. There is the one telling story, passed on by Osbert Sitwell. Edmund had a cold. 'I must have caught it in those draughty corridors of the House of Lords,' he complained to the assembled company. 'Edmund is so fortunate,' Nellie observed in her gentle voice. 'Edmund always catches *his* cold in the draughty corridors of the House of Lords, whereas I and my daughters catch ours on the tops of omnibuses or in tube stations.'

There were other family strains too. Philip was engaged to a remote Australian relative, Gertrude Hay. Her family seemed to approve of nothing but the fact that his name was Gosse. He could not afford to marry; he was not yet fully qualified, having failed far more exams in his life than his father had ever taken. On 20th March 1905 Gosse wrote to Gilder: 'My three children, though so long grown up, still live at home, although Philip is now betrothed, to our great satisfaction, to a charming girl, and will marry as soon as he can afford to do so.' It would not be for another three years.

Henry James continued to find the young Gosses delightful. They moved him over and over again to ruminate on what he had missed. After Sylvia had distinguished herself at the Royal Academy School, he wrote rejoicing in her triumph and saying he was weaving a garland to fling over her neck. 'I think I am *as* happy for you and her mother,' he wrote to Gosse, 'for these must indeed be the purest joys of parenthood. I often fancy I am gleeful at not having *bambini*, then I think how rich and mellow it must be to have them like yours, and I feel then that I have failed of the true life.'

Arthur Benson, on the other hand, wrote in his diary 'Gosse feels the weight of his two unmarried daughters.' Certainly there were problems. The Council of the Society of Painter-Etchers found Sylvia's naked old women extremely objectionable and would not elect her to membership. She would fall in love with an 'odious young man'. 'She gave him up and acquiesced but it has knocked her life to bits, poor thing,' Benson recorded. Philip did marry, and it would not be an easy marriage; but Gosse was never to know that Philip's child, Helen (born in 1909), grew up to be a member of the Communist Party. Tessa would go to her suffragette meetings; there would be 'rather fierce disputes about it'.

According to his mood, Benson would find the domestic atmosphere in Hanover Terrace either oppressive or soothing. Sometimes 'it would seem an intolerable burden and better to be an old bachelor'. At other times he would enjoy 'the easy talk, the ideas, the smiling faces'. At dinner parties, he would find the atmosphere subtly different from that of most of the houses he visited. In March 1905 he wrote: 'It was rather an *odd* party. We had a magnificent dinner, champagne etc, but there hung over the whole a sort of slight bohemianism, which was not unpleasant. The very chairs of the dining-room, the unconventional lighting etc were all unlike the social order.' Osbert Sitwell would recall how Gosse stuck happily to middle-class habits, always carving the roast birds himself, and Benson would resent having to do his own packing when he occasionally stayed the night, and being expected to help Gosse carry his luggage downstairs himself – 'the kind of job that nothing would make me do, I suppose surviving from their simpler days'.

Henry James's only grumble was that Hanover Terrace was not kept as warm as he would have liked. For the 'general orgy' on New Year's Eve 1905 he told W. E. Norris he would be donning 'augmented underwear'. He recalled Gosse's last Rye visit when he was quite at his best, 'all the more that we lunched, the Sunday, with my amiable neighbour Lady Maud Warrender "to meet the Connaughts". Gosse met them immensely – there were very few people, almost nobody else! and Gosse was the life and soul of the occasion. I think things are as well with him as they can ever be, with one to whom the freshness of joys (even of Connaughts) turns so easily to bitterness. However new joys always come!'

Gosse had certainly enjoyed his meeting with the Duke and Duchess of Connaught, particularly the chance to offer advice. 'I do wish, Ma'am, you would use your influence with Queen Maud to make her enter a little more into the interests of her Norwegian subjects; she disappoints them very much.' The Duchess seemed interested and not surprised at Gosse's words. 'Maud is so lethargic,' she said. As for the Crown Prince, all he cared about was games. 'If you could shut him up in a tennis court, he would never know if he was King or not, nor care.'

There was no question, James thought, that Gosse was enjoying 'the great period of his life'. At almost the same moment, Gosse was saying that Henry James had 'entered upon his period of real greatness', but Gosse was talking about literature; James was talking about life. He wrote to W. E. Norris: 'His love of society of the sort he originally seemed least dedicated to (which largely explains his appetite) has a chance to spread like a majestic river – or, in short, he is a case of realized (after a good deal of paying for it in advance) human felicity. Great for me would be the fatigue and intolerable the chatter of it (putting the intolerable only at that) but he has comparative youth and positive – well, what is it that he has positively?' James left Norris to finish the sentence and continued over the years to observe with amazement Gosse's appetite for 'dancing the tight-rope (and across Niagara)'.

James thought he kept his balance; Benson observed the falls from grace. But Benson, one must always remember, was himself unstable. His falls would land him in nursing homes, surround him with doctors. One must read his diary with that in mind. Still, his accounts of Gosse in these years make very disturbing reading. Gosse obviously behaved with Benson as he never behaved with men he admired, with Hardy, with James, with Haldane. But does that excuse it? It would be tedious to tell too many of the sad stories, of trivial misunderstandings and quarrels and reconciliations – and some sort of abiding affection – that fill Benson's diary in these years. But they cannot be ignored.

If Gosse could sometimes be called touchy, so could Benson. Take, for instance, a tiny incident at the Royal Academy in February 1906. (On one such occasion years before, Gosse had been delighted to find his sister-in-law, Laura Alma-Tadema, enraptured in front of one of her own paintings; she had never been allowed to forget it.) Now Benson recorded he met Gosse and Lord de Tabley –

G. with inflamed eyes, very jumpy. He told me about poor Mrs Brightwen, dying of cancer, whom he visits daily. Presently I wanted to go on. I don't come to the Academy to talk to other people. G. said a v. rude thing about my invariable and apparent delight in saying goodbye. I rather lost my temper and said 'You must not say things which make both the recipient and all those who hear it supremely uncomfortable.' He was not vexed, but laughed. Today however he writes to apologize and to say that he was really almost beside himself with irritation of eyes, business and harrowing visits to Mrs B. Moreover he had quarrelled with Sidney Colvin over Stevenson.

The quarrel was about the fact that the family had wanted Gosse, not Colvin, to edit the Pentland edition. Gosse comes quite well out of that trivial encounter, but Benson took some delight in recording that same month a conversation he had had with Lady Ponsonby. Gosse had called on her when she was under the influence of 'Indian hemp' which she had apparently been prescribed to help her bronchitis. She saw people double, she said, not side by side, but a shadowy one in front and a real one behind. She told Benson she was overcome by sudden irritation at Gosse's presence: 'One of you I can stand,' she declared, 'but two is really too much.'

Not long afterwards, Gosse visited Magdalene College, Cambridge, where Benson was now a Fellow. Gosse was 'in his most excited, childish, pettish mood, bent on fascinating and showing his power'. He insisted on Benson accompanying him to a Cambridge party, an invitation Benson had already refused. Gosse would not listen to Benson's protests. It was a terrible party with twenty people crammed into a little ugly hot room – 'No one was shifted or introduced . . . where we fell, there we lay.' Gosse made everything 'far worse by saying in shrill tones "I have captured him and dragged him here; and here he is: he screamed and protested all the way!"' Gosse then put kittens on people's bare shoulders, Benson reported. 'When he is like this, I think I almost hate him. I got away at 11.30 and walked wretchedly back, cursing audibly – my evening spoilt, nothing gained; feeling like a performing bear; and all just to please Gosse's sense of power.'

In July 1907 they were on holiday in Suffolk together, with Gosse writing a speech for the unveiling of the Whistler Memorial. There always seemed to be speeches and memorials. Benson went to the summer-house at the request of Gosse, who then stood up and declaimed what he had written. Benson had a pencil and paper in his hand to make notes of any criticisms he might have.

Gosse stopped declaiming and said, 'I can't bear to see you scribbling. What is it all about? You can't be attending. It fidgets me inexpressibly.'

'Some notes of small points to mention later,' Benson said and stopped writing.

'Why do you put nothing down?' Gosse asked, a few minutes later. 'You are not attending. I suppose it does not interest you?' Benson often had the feeling that whatever he did was wrong, yet it was only the day after this exchange that Benson wrote in his diary the passage quoted earlier: 'Well, he is a real friend. I see his faults clearly, but am very deeply attached to him, by a kind of insoluble tie, like relationship. I am very sure of his affection.' There was that cat-like element, Benson noticed, as so many others had done: the claws in the velvet paws. 'He every now and then wants to scratch.' Benson would feel himself treated as unsatisfactory younger brother, as disappointing son, even as wife. 'He uses me more and more as he uses his wife, as a litter-basket for his grumbles,' Benson would write in 1911. The long story of their relationship in Benson's diary does often suggest that of some bad marriages – not at all that of Gosse's own good marriage. They were devoted, but they irritated each other profoundly. There was endless sparring and bickering on top of a deep affection.

At the end of 1906 Gosse recorded in his diary Hardy's remark that 'it is only those who half know a thing who can write about it'. 'I now begin to know the House of Lords entirely and I can write no more.' As early as August 1904 he had foreseen he would find it difficult to keep it up: 'The life of the place has now so completely seized me that I can no longer make outside observations on it.' The last months of 1906 were 'full of overwhelming excitement. I have become, suddenly, acquainted with Lord Northcliffe and have joined his congeries of editors.' Gosse had been invited to edit a literary supplement to the *Daily Mail*. Northcliffe offered him £600 for six months, plus three guineas a thousand words for his own contributions. It was extremely generous pay by the standards of the time, but Gosse had scarcely realized what hard work would be involved. Benson thought it 'strange that a man will consent to such a burden'.

Caricature by Max Beerbohm whose caption read: 'Lord Northcliffe suggesting a head-line to Mr. Edmund Gosse.'

The idea behind *Books* was a purely commercial one, of course. Publishers had recently withdrawn advertising from *The Times* and its literary supplement (which had begun only four years before), in a protest at the foundation in 1905 of the Times Book Club, which not only lent books as soon as they were ordered but also sold recent books ('virtually as good as new') at a greatly reduced price. Northcliffe hoped to pick up a great deal of the advertising which would otherwise have gone to *The Times*. A letter shows how closely commercial considerations dictated what was reviewed, in spite of the fact that the first leader declared: 'Books will be noticed on their merits' and 'Only by avoiding the taint of commercialism can literary criticism speak with a certain voice.' But on the 20th October 1906 Gosse asked Dobson to turn out 'five hundred very graceful and pretty words' about Trollope. 'The fact is this. We have no book of Bell's this week, and he is a leading personage in the trade . . . All I can think of is a recommendation of the series of the Barchester Novels which Bell is now bringing out, very courageously, I think . . . The difficulty of meeting all these divided interests is extraordinary.'

Gosse gathered together an impressive list of contributors: Archer, Baring, Benson, Chesterton, Dobson, J. G. Frazer, Hardy, Lang, Newbolt, Robert Ross, Symons, etc. That would be one way of putting it. In fact, the first issue suggests how much the whole thing was designed 'to gratify his friends', as he himself would admit. Northcliffe wrote: 'Everyone seems to like it,' but Arthur Benson certainly didn't: 'It is very bad indeed, worse than I could have believed. It has a silly mannered poem by Dobson, smelling of the coterie most rankly, a long review of Gosse's Stevenson!! much too long, and careful reviews of reprints and compilations – so that it is like a publisher's circular – and the only two notable books . . . dismissed in five lines.' There was also a review of Lady Dorothy Nevill's surprisingly boring memoirs, which include the unmemorable sentence: 'By no means a recluse, Mr Gosse indeed combines the best attributes of a man of letters with great social charm.' Benson was particularly annoyed because Gosse had sent him three books for review without asking him first – 'heavy tiresome books'. 'I must do them, of course, or he will be furious.'

Soon Northcliffe was asking Gosse to make the Supplement 'a little lighter'. In March Gosse was writing to Baring: 'The labour of bringing out *Books* every week has been a very trying one, largely because I am an old dog to be set at a new trick. I don't know how long I shall be able to keep it up. The dilemma is one which I heard put by . . . an old woman . . . describing with horror the exposure of her person which some maiden had to make at a music-hall. "What an awful position for a chaste young girl! Of course – she is generously paid to do it." That is exactly my prostituted case.'

On the 5th April 1907 Gosse wrote to Dobson: 'The blow has fallen! Next Saturday's *Books* is my last. I got my dismissal this afternoon.' Dobson suggested cheeringly that 'Not to have succeeded in these days of *new* journalism, is rather a distinction than otherwise, for it means that you must have avoided all sorts of opportunism, clap-trap, superficiality and the like. I believe you will really be glad when you get over the first quite justifiable annoyance.'

Gosse certainly should have been glad. He had something much more significant on hand in 1907: the completion and publication of his most important book.

16

The Masterpiece

GOSSE, AS WE have seen, had begun to doubt his own creativity, his ability to be anything more than critic, biographer, literary consultant. Although his love of books still nourished his days, he had turned more and more to the consolations of the world, to the pleasures of talk and power. He was nervous about the new book he was writing, the book George Moore had suggested more than fifteen years before. He told William Archer: 'This particular book causes me more nervous anxiety than anything I ever published before.' He told Moore so, too, thanking him for his part in it. Moore replied modestly: 'All I did was to egg you on to write a subject which you related to me: you'll say, but that is a good deal – well, if you like, it was a good deal, and it is pleasanter that you should think it a good deal than that you should think it nothing at all . . . So you are nervous about your book; after thirty years of continuous publications you are still afraid. Strange human nature.'

Unlike most of Gosse's books, which were written with remarkable rapidity, *Father and Son* was a long time in the making. 'I put the whole passion of my mind into it,' he would tell André Gide, but he kept setting it aside. It was a difficult book to write, and there were no financial pressures to complete it. He was already writing it, as we have seen, in Florence in October 1905. In January 1906 Benson noted in his diary: 'The new book is to be in three stages. The child taking the Calvinistic teaching without frustration; then the stage when he begins to have his own ideas side by side with the others – but no struggle – and then the gradual victory of his own artistic ideas. It ought to be most interesting.' It did not turn out quite so neatly, but it was even more interesting than Benson had suspected. In April Benson was reading 'two more chapters of G.'s *beautiful* autobiographical book. Really perfect art; and for once true and tender emotion. I have the *greatest* hopes of this book.' In May 1906 Gosse was reading the chapters aloud to George Moore, who worried that Gosse was afraid of being sentimental. In December Moore seems to have read the whole book in draft and was suggesting Gosse should add several more chapters, to end 'when you have got into the British Museum and are beginning to make your own living'.

In February 1907 Benson thought the book ('the best thing he has ever done') finished – but said Gosse 'seemed averse to publish'. 'How dark you kept it,' Thornycroft would say. There are some interesting suggestions, in later letters, about what Gosse felt he was trying to do. To Sydney Holland, he wrote:

> The real central point which was in my own mind as I wrote it, [is] namely the exposure of the modern sentimentality which thinks it can parade all the prettiness of religion without really resigning its will and its thought to faith. You have most excellently said it is either my Father's creed 'or nothing'.
>
> To tell you the truth, what I should like to think my book might be – if the idea is not one of too great temerity – is a call to people to face the fact that the old faith is now impossible to sincere and intelligent minds, and that we must consequently face the difficulty of following entirely different ideals in moving towards the higher life. But what ideals, or (what is more important) what discipline can we substitute for the splendid metallic vigour of an earlier age? . . .
>
> There must be found some guiding power, influencing artists, financiers, the meditative and imaginative, the self-centred and the speculative, alike. The strength of Christianity was that it did not influence unselfish and lofty natures only, but the publican and the prostitute also . . .
>
> I am glad you were pleased with the form of the book, and that it did not leave upon your mind, as upon that of my reviewer in the *Revue des deux Mondes*, the impression of a bitter cry from a world without tenderness and without gaiety, 'a lamentable world of darkness'! The perfectly consistent Christian is not dark, and he is not lugubrious.

Two years later, in a letter to Frederic Harrison, who had asked Gosse to advise him on the problems of writing an autobiography, Gosse wrote: 'A very great difficulty is to select. My own view is that one ought to take certain vivid passages as samples or examples, elaborate them into living pictures, and entirely omit other passages of no less interest . . .' One fails if one 'tries to sow with the whole sack'.

Gosse eventually handed over the manuscript of *Father and Son* to William Heinemann in May 1907, but it was still 'far from ready for publication'. When Heinemann read the draft, like Moore he felt it ended too soon. He suggested Gosse added a final section, the epilogue. Gosse had intended to finish at the moment when, at the apex of his striving after holiness, he called on his Lord and, unanswered, turned from the schoolroom window muttering 'the Lord has not come, the Lord will never come'. But on 10th August 1907 he wrote:

> My dear Heinemann
> I send you the final chapter, at which I should like you to glance, before sending it to press. I cannot thank you enough for so very kindly urging me to write it. Had I not done so, the book would not merely have ended abruptly, but in quite the wrong key. I hope you will like this ending, and will think that the book is now brought to a worthy close.
> Ever yours
> Edmund Gosse

Two months later, on 25th October 1907, the book was published anonymously, though very little attempt was made to conceal the authorship. It seems to have been a ploy to arouse curiosity and increase comment. In a letter from Rome on October 5th, Gosse had listed a number of useful journalists who might be sent copies of the book, also 'Lady Northcliffe and other female bigwigs'. He then named some friends he wanted to receive the book 'with the author's regards', including Archer, Benson, Moore, Lang and the Right Reverend the Bishop of Birmingham. 'These are the only friends of mine I can think of who might probably be immediately useful if their curiosity were excited. I hope the secret of the authorship will be kept as long as possible.' But of course Benson and Moore, at any rate, knew perfectly well who was the author. Gosse wrote a postscript next day deciding there was no use in wasting a copy on Andrew Lang. 'I should like that to go to Arthur Symons instead.' On October 28th Gosse wrote to Benson: 'The reviews of *F & S* have been tremendous: on the other hand, it seems that there was hardly any "subscription" for it, and no sign yet of sales. It is amusingly my fate: the public will talk about my work, and even praise it, but buy it they never have and they never will.' In this case, his fears were a little premature.

Six days after publication, he told Thomas Hardy that he had asked for a copy of an anonymous book, called *Father and Son*, to be sent to him. 'I shall take it as a kind favour if you will try to read it.' There was no word of his own authorship, but most people seem to have known who had written the book, right from the beginning. The *New York*

Times Book Review on November 30th headed its notice: 'Edmund Gosse's *Father and Son*'. But Henry James in his annual Christmas letter to W. E. Norris, musing as usual on Gosse's character and position, only hinted that Gosse might really at last have written 'the important thing' James had wanted for so long. He suggested that Gosse was now 'quite the image of the middle-aged paunchy person who, having struggled up the hill of difficulty and found it very long, is at long last taking breath ever so comfortably and gratefully on the social summit and surveying all the Kingdoms of the earth. There is a very interesting fact about him . . . which I mayn't yet speak of . . .'

Even before the book's release in America, Heinemann's New York representative had written to Scribner's: 'Will you please remember that the book is to be published anonymously, although the name of the author is to leak out at once. Mr Heinemann thinks he will no doubt be recognized from the boyish picture.'

The book was an immediate success on both sides of the Atlantic, though Gosse did not seem to have much confidence in Heinemann. He bombarded him with letters about inadequate advertising, about people not being able to find the book in the shops, all the usual author's complaints. On November 10th, he wrote:

> In the bargain and partnership between us, I have fully done my part. Now it is your part, as the distributing agency for a knowledge of it. If you will take a real interest in spreading curiosity about it, it ought to sell in thousands. If you grow languid about it, because it does not sell at once, automatically, you will do me a great injustice.

In November, the publishers at any rate were calling it 'Literary Sensation of the Year'. In December two further impressions were called for, but on December 10th Gosse was still in agony: 'If you do not safeguard my interests, I am absolutely helpless.' In March 1908 a fourth impression appeared, with a new title-page carrying Gosse's name, and a note to the effect that: 'It is indicated to me that the slight veil of anonymity, which I originally drew over this narrative, was long ago torn to tatters, and to preserve it would now be affectation.'

The reviews had nearly all been excellent, although *The Times* 'dismissed my book in one contemptuous paragraph' Gosse said, and the *Times Literary Supplement* was also rather cool:

> The author of this book has no doubt settled it with his conscience how far in the interests of popular edification or amusement it is legitimate to expose the weaknesses and inconsistencies of a good man who is also one's father.

The *Academy* reviewer admired the book extremely, but also had some qualms about it: 'It is a great book, but for our part we scarcely like this close anatomisation by a son of a father.' The *Athenaeum* analysed the book's permanent importance:

> This book is unique. It is at once a profound and illuminating study in the concrete of the development of a child's mind, and also an historical document of great value . . . It is the clash not of two creeds only, not even of two temperaments, but of two whole universes of thought and feeling, which is presented in this work, and will make it deeply illuminating long after the echoes of its controversies . . . [are] silent and forgotten . . . That is why the book is so interesting. Its nominal material is detailed, particular, local. Its real subject is a difference as great as that between light and darkness, a conflict no less profound and eternal than that typified in the Oriental dualism as existing from the dawn of things.

The *Athenaeum* also touched on the question of accuracy. Gosse had made much in his preface of the book's scrupulous truth; it was offered as a document. He denies 'any tampering with precise fact' except in the changing of names. Reviewing Margot Asquith's autobiography in 1920, Gosse would stress: 'There must be no faintest suspicion that the facts have been tampered with (as may freely be done in a novel) in order to make their sequence more amusing or more probable.' But in 1887 he had admitted how remote already was his childhood: 'We shall find that our memories are like a breath upon the glass,' he had written, 'like the shape of a broken wave. Nothing is so hopelessly lost, so utterly volatile as the fancies of our childhood.' It was none the less true twenty years later. And in the course of the earlier chapters of this book we have seen some examples of how Gosse did, in fact, rearrange truth, probably unwittingly. He thought he was writing while his memory was 'still perfectly vivid', but we know how unreliable that memory could be. Gosse himself admitted that 'the end had been slightly arranged'. He told Harold Nicolson so, and Nicolson recorded it in his diary. As we have seen, there was no total break with his father at twenty-one, as the epilogue suggests.

As for the rest, the *Athenaeum* reviewer puts the case for the 'truth' of *Father and Son* extremely well:

> It is, of course, possible that the writer's literary skill has embellished some of the incidents, and that his feelings at the moment were not always of that elaborately self-conscious character which he now believes them to have been. But we must remember that an

event includes its consequences in the mind; that what we think of it in memory is as much a part of it as what we feel at the moment.

The book brought Gosse hundreds of letters. It aroused in particular a great chorus from people who said they had been through the same sort of thing themselves. Richard Gilder wrote: 'My own experience (how many must have told you that!) was somewhat similar.' Rudyard Kipling wrote:

It's *extraordinarily* interesting – more interesting than *David Copperfield* because it's true. I had a few years in my boyhood somewhat under the shadow of the same terrific doctrine, and curiously enough, the same idea of avoidance of my surroundings by 'natural magic' (in my own case by a charm. I used to make 'em out of old bones stuffed with wool and camphor-scented). It is a strange shadow to lay on a young mind, and they that do it must be more sure of themselves than most of us.

But the delicacy of the psychology, the inferential revelation of the milieu, and, above all, the wonderful realisation of your father, have given me very deep delight. I don't say pleasure because the thing is too near certain of my own experiences to only please.

The devil of it is that that life still persists – I could give you awful instances – and I have a notion that your book will undam some tides of revolt in some darklingly Christian homes. I only hope and pray it will be so.

As the reviews *won't* say – the book 'ought to be in the hands of all parents and teachers'.

'It must do good,' Sydney Holland suggested. 'It must widen the views of those whose views are nearly as narrow as your good father's were.' Others were astonished by its unfamiliarity. Frederic Harrison, whose own father had never suspected he was 'either an infidel or an author', wrote:

I never knew of such a world . . . To think of *you*, of all men, coming out of such an upbringing! If I had been asked to guess the author, I think I might have tried a hundred names but not yours . . . It was a difficult task to sustain so long a story of rank cruelty and almost insanity – as to us agnostics it must seem – . . . and yet avoiding any word of . . . unfilial ingratitude.

One of the virtues of the book is that the father is not less valued than the son; his strengths are given full due; his humanity confronts us as much as his fanaticism. Indeed, the book takes much of its power from what Edmund rejected. Henry Tonks, writing to Robbie Ross, who had given him a copy, saw 'that monstrous Father' as 'one of the most terrible people the world has produced'. More readers saw that this was not so, that his 'ruinous errors' were due to his creed and not to his character. Haldane wrote that he was filled with reverence for the father, 'so single-minded and distinguished in character'. Lady Londonderry could sympathize with a parent's feelings and the pain of finding out that the child would always think differently. It was in no ironic spirit that Edmund was able to talk of the book as a monument to his father, 'a good and even great man, whose character was too powerful not to have its disconcerting sides'.

Father and Son has been described with every shade of enthusiasm. Even Ezra Pound, who saw Gosse as the epitome of cant and fustiness, thought it excellent. Others have thought it 'one of the supreme masterpieces of the twentieth century', 'an imperishable book', 'an amazing book', 'a permanent addition to the interest and sadness of life – to the beauty too'. 'It is a glory all round – an immense triumph', subtle, rich, 'a signal victory for intellectual liberty', altogether remarkable for style, for humour and pathos, for tact and truth. It is perfection, a thing unique in literature, 'admirable and delightful, a most original and entertaining book'. It is 'a work of genius', Gosse's 'one great artistic achievement, soaring high above the level he generally achieved'. Gosse heard most of this praise, the repeated assertions that it was 'a book that will live'; but somehow he found it difficult to believe, least of all W. D. Howells' extravagant suggestion that 'the pathetic tale could not be better worded if a syndicate of masters rose from their graves to do it: say Milton, Dante and Shakespeare'. Haldane assured him more soberly that *Father and Son* was 'in itself enough to put you among the Immortals. Literature is a medium . . . more enduring than politics or even the battlefield.' His name would be remembered when Haldane himself, Buller and Wolseley meant nothing to the man in the street or at least in the bookshop. Maurice Baring described 'the whole literary world ringing with the praise of Mr Gosse's *Father and Son*, which has been instantly and universally recognized as one of the finest pieces of portraiture ever written, and as a book to which only one epithet is applicable . . . namely "classic".' In 1949, a hundred years after Gosse's birth, the book appeared as a Penguin Modern Classic.

In 1907 it seems indeed that the 'modern' period is beginning. *Father and Son* feels modern in tone, in a way that one of its few antecedents – Mark Rutherford's *Autobiography* – does not. 1907 was the year of the publication of *The Longest Journey* by Forster, of Synge's *Playboy of the*

Western World, Belloc's *Cautionary Tales* and James Joyce's first book, albeit a conventional one, *Chamber Music*. It was the year Auden and MacNeice were born. Accustomed as we are to the great variety of autobiographical confessional writing of the twentieth century, it is quite difficult to realize just how original *Father and Son* is. There had been a strong feeling in the nineteenth century that private life should be private. It was not only Tennyson who thanked Almighty God that the world knew nothing of Shakespeare but his writing, and that he knew nothing about Jane Austen.

Gosse himself said that 'the peculiar curiosity which legitimate biography satisfies, is essentially a modern thing and presupposes our observation of life not unduly clouded by moral passion or prejudice'. Harold Nicolson, quoting this in his *Development of English Biography*, found it strange that Gosse, who laid no particular stress on form, believing the form of a biography less important than its content, went on to produce the most 'literary' biography in the English language. Nicolson called *Father and Son* 'a masterpiece in which, by consummate power of selection, the author has been able to combine the maximum of scientific interest with the maximum of literary form'.

Gosse was depreciatory about the book from the beginning. He wrote to the anthropologist J. G. Frazer:

> If you come across an anonymous book called *Father and Son*, which is just published by Heinemann, let me tell you that it is I who have written it and that it contains some observations about the growth of moral (or savage) ideas in children such as I should not dare to lay before you, but such as I should be pleased if you thought of value. And with this squinting and trepidatious hint, I leave you to more important studies.

To William Watson, Gosse wrote: 'If you did not care for the subject, you might like the careful prose.' As well as the praise, there had been inevitably, considering the subject, some abuse. He once told Maurice Baring he had received 'the usual insulting letter about *Father and Son*, from a man who presumes a "mercenary motive" must be the only one which could induce me to write "so useless and destructive a work".' 'The practice of literature,' Gosse reflected, 'is not very rewarding: this is the sort of thing it brings, or else entire neglect.' In 1918, he would tell Moore that he thought *Father and Son* was 'already almost forgotten'.

Arthur Symons, whose own lot was far worse, tried to reassure him in April, 1908: 'You are entirely wrong in what you say about yourself. Your last book has been universally recognised for what it is, the best you have ever written. In France, which we both care for so much, you are more and more known and admired.' Gosse had been complaining that editors were no longer interested in him, seduced by the new school of 'Chesterton and Belloc Co. Ltd.', as Symons called it. He said to Gosse, 'the attention of editors is of course no sign of anything but their lack of judgement . . . It is very wrong and idle to speculate about the consequences of one's death, but one thing *you* are sure of: to live as one who has many friends, which is better than having the voice of an unreasoning crowd.'

The literary world seemed to be interested only in the new. Gosse felt himself taken for granted. He felt 'a jaded and despised old man'. H. G. Wells agreed in 1911: 'You're known and you're admired, but you really don't get a tithe of your right.' Wells loved *Father and Son*: 'It lives, it breathes, it is warm and kind like a friend, one turns it over and looks at it here and there and looks again and recounts little fragments to others who have read it and tells anecdotes about it.' In 1912 Gosse was cheered that the book was translated into French by his old acquaintance Henry Davray and honoured by the French Academy. But he reminded himself what Mrs Kenwigs said to her daughter Morleena. 'If when you are playing with the neighbours' children in the court, you tell them you are having French lessons, be sure you say "But I am not proud, for Mother says that's wrong."' On his second visit to Paul Desjardins' summer seminars at the Abbaye de Pontigny (where he had developed his friendship with André Gide the year before) he experienced the rather 'intoxicating phenomenon' of seeing 'twenty people of varied sex and charm all reading *Father and Son* in French at once'. But he was still sceptical. He wrote to Robbie Ross: 'Do you know that your poor friend has made quite what they call *un succès considérable*? Two copies of my book have been sold at Tarbes: and three (but one was returned to the publisher) at Brienon-sur-Armançon. God keep us humble.'

At Pontigny, in 1912, Gosse and Gide took daily walks together. One of the strongest threads in the last part of Gosse's life was his admiration for and friendship with Gide, who was little known in France and unknown in England when Gosse wrote an article on him in the *Contemporary Review* in September 1909. It was not always easy to champion Gide. An English critic once enquired: 'How could a man make himself more generally disliked than by believing in the Gospels, disbelieving in private property and practising pederasty?' Gosse saw *La Porte étroite* (which Gide had sent him – the only copy he sent to England) as some sort of Gallic counterpart to *Father and Son*; they both owed to literature their liberation from the constraints of Calvinism. 'Between you and me there exist some very close spiritual and intellectual ties,' Gosse had written before they had met. Gosse wrote little in the periodicals at this stage (though soon he would be writing regularly in the *Edinburgh Review*). He told Gide how eager he was to make Gide's writing known in England. Gide was grateful. He said he knew 'de quel poids est votre parole et de quel crédit jouit votre opinion'. He admired Gosse's perception: 'Vous parlez de mon oeuvre avec une rare compréhension et compétence – aux quelles mes compatriotes ne m'ont guère habitué.' Years later he said Gosse had believed in him 'alors que presque personne encore ne me considérait en France'; but he worried, in his journal, that Gosse seemed animated less by genuine feeling, than by 'une sorte de self-respect'.

At Christmas 1912 Gide unexpectedly turned up in England and shared the Gosses' Christmas dinner at Hanover Terrace, with Henry James. James commented to Norris: 'I did dine with him and with Mrs Nelly and with Tessa and Sylvia, and a single other guest, an interesting Frenchman, André Gide, rather than have a bowl of Benger in bed at my dim little hotel.' The friendship, between Gide and Gosse, though warm, remained a literary one. Almost all the surviving letters are concerned with books. It is only when the books themselves rouse more intimate questions that the tone becomes personal. It was on reading *Corydon* in 1924 that Gosse first raised the question of homosexuality, and in January 1927, reading *Si le grain ne meurt*, Gosse revealed that he had realized for twenty years, ever since he read *L'Immoraliste*, that Gide was a homosexual. But they had obviously never talked about it and even then, when Gosse questioned Gide's motives for his frankness in the novel, Gosse never revealed that he had himself known long before something of the feelings of which Gide writes.

> The facts here related offer me no surprise . . . This has not affected my feeling, personal or literary, since I have never allowed the idiosyncrasies of my friends to blind me to their qualities. I am not a critic of temperaments, nor so ignorant as to believe myself fitted to be a judge.
>
> But now you have gone much further, and I cannot help asking myself, in the face of this narrative – Was it wise? Was it necessary? Is it useful? I am incapable of answering these questions, which leaves me in a very painful perplexity.
>
> Heaven forbid that I should be such a prig as to put my instinct in the matter before yours. You have acted not without reflection, certainly not without a marvellous courage. You possess so unusual a genius that perhaps it may claim to be a law to itself. But why have you done it, and what advantages to anyone can accrue from it?

With Lord Spencer at Althorp, 1921

With William Heinemann, George Moore and Haddon Chambers at Ockham, 1919

A news agency photograph captioned: 'Mr Edmund Gosse (centre), the eminent litterateur, with the bust presented to him yesterday by Mr Balfour (left) on behalf of 250 admirers . . . On the right is Lord Crewe.' November 9, 1920

'The Birthday Surprise'. Presentation of the bust as seen by Max Beerbohm (*facing page*)

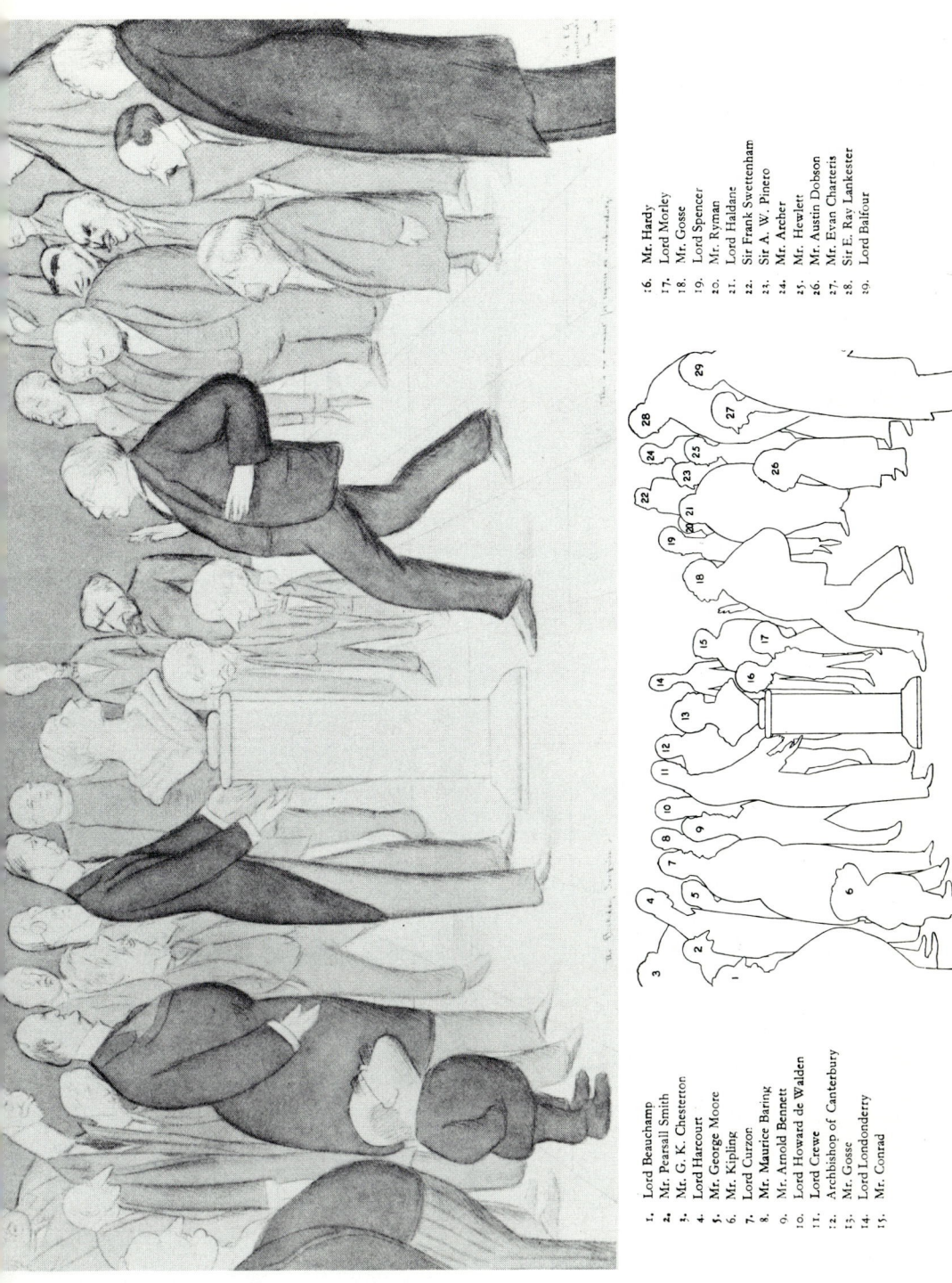

1. Lord Beauchamp
2. Mr. Pearsall Smith
3. Mr. G. K. Chesterton
4. Lord Harcourt
5. Mr. George Moore
6. Mr. Kipling
7. Lord Curzon
8. Mr. Maurice Baring
9. Mr. Arnold Bennett
10. Lord Howard de Walden
11. Lord Crewe
12. Archbishop of Canterbury
13. Mr. Gosse
14. Lord Londonderry
15. Mr. Conrad

16. Mr. Hardy
17. Lord Morley
18. Mr. Gosse
19. Lord Spencer
20. Mr. Ryman
21. Lord Haldane
22. Sir Frank Swettenham
23. Sir A. W. Pinero
24. Mr. Archer
25. Mr. Hewlett
26. Mr. Austin Dobson
27. Mr. Evan Charteris
28. Sir E. Ray Lankester
29. Lord Balfour

Sylvia Gosse's portraits of parents in old age

Edmund Gosse, towards the end of his life

With Thomas Hardy at Max Gate, June 29, 1927

With André Gide in Paris, May, 1928,
two weeks before Gosse's death

Nellie and Edmund Gosse picnicking in Dorset, June, 1927

'Are you saved?' from Max Beerbohm's 'The Old and the Young Self'

If you think that my old (and undiminished) affection gives me a right to ask you this question, I beg you to send me a full and clear reply. I do not ask it from curiosity, or in a priggish or dictatorial spirit; I ask it in deep sympathy and in an earnest wish to comprehend your position.

I am, my dear Gide, now as ever,

> Your attached friend
> *Edmund Gosse*

Mon cher Edmund Gosse

Quelle excellente lettre je reçois de vous, et combien profondément elle me touche!

Pourquoi j'ai écrit ce livre? – Parce que j'ai cru que je devais l'écrire.

Ce que j'en attends? – Rien que de très fâcheux pour moi (et pas seulement pour moi, hélas!). Et certes il a fallu que cette obligation morale fût bien impérative pour me faire passer outre; mais, vraiment, il m'eût paru lâche de me laisser arrêter par la considération de cette peine et du danger. Je sentais que je ne pourrais mourir satisfait si j'avais gardé tout cela sur le cœur.

Cher ami, j'ai mensonge en horreur. Je ne puis prendre mon parti de ce camouflage conventionnel qui travestit systématiquement l'œuvre de X, de Y, et de tant d'autres. J'ai écrit ce livre pour 'créer un précédent', donner un exemple de franchise, éclairer quelques uns, en rassurer d'autres, forcer l'opinion à tenir compte de ce que l'on ignore ou que l'on affecte d'ignorer – au grand dam de la psychologie, de la morale, de l'art . . . et de la société.

J'ai écrit ce livre parce que je préfère être haï, qu'aimé pour ce que je ne suis pas . . .

Je vous parle sans effort et sans crainte, et même je suis heureux de vous parler. Veuillez voir dans tout ce que je vous dis un témoignage de ma grande estime et de mon amitié profonde. Votre reconnaissant et dévoué

> *André Gide*

Gide would remain devoted and grateful until Gosse's death.

To set against this recognition of Gide's genius, there is Gosse's lack of recognition, at just the same time, of E. M. Forster. Virginia Woolf scorned his attitudes to both of them, seeing his Victorian decorum rocked both by Gide's revelations and the illegitimate baby in *Howards End*. Gosse's letter to Edward Marsh, who had sent him a copy of Forster's new book (learning he had admired earlier ones), shows him repelled by manslaughter and bastards, the more sensational elements of the book, and admiring Forster's talent for the 'delicate, ironic painting of straightforward natures' such as the excellent Aunt Juley. To Marsh he says the closing chapters of *Howards End* are full of 'lurid sentimentality, preposterous morals'. He went even further, on holiday in Clevedon in January 1911, when Professor Fitzmaurice Kelly joined Benson and Gosse for lunch. Benson recorded: 'Unfortunately *Howards End* was mentioned and Gosse flared up. He said it was a vile, obscene, decadent book . . . that Forster had prostituted charming gifts to a sickening lust for popularity, and so on. Of course it spoilt the whole meal. It is partly jealousy, I think, partly a touch of the old Calvinism, which crops up unexpectedly and grotesquely . . . What can one do with such a friend? One never knows when these tempests may not rise and it takes away all freedom of intercourse.' There may have been other reasons, less able to be expressed, even subconscious, for Gosse's extreme reaction to *Howards End*. In Leonard Bast, that unsatisfactory character, Gosse may have seen glimpses of his own young self, with his aspirations and cultural longings, reading Ruskin in a suburban sitting-room. He might also, in Helen Schlegel, have seen some glimpses of his own artistic unconventional daughter Sylvia and her unmentionable involvement with the odious young man, which was much in his mind.

Benson was often to ask that question, 'What can one do with such a friend?' They saw a great deal of each other in these years, far too much. They took no fewer than nine holidays together between 1908 and 1912, sometimes on their own, sometimes with other people, and there were constant irritations and arguments. There were so many that one wonders why they kept returning for more, until one realizes how trivial they really were, how much else there was, and how easy it is for Benson's recording of their differences to loom too large, simply because it is so unusual to have such detailed accounts of the minutiae of everyday contact.

Benson was extremely grateful for Gosse's friendship at a time when most of his friends were offering him advice but not their company. In July 1908 he had written warmly in his diary about a letter from Gosse suggesting they should take a holiday together in Yorkshire that August. 'There is something really beautiful about this, involving real self-sacrifice on Gosse's part and all to cheer a heavy and melancholy wretch, who is an utter nuisance to himself and his friends alike.' Benson had been close to suicide. Gosse's patience and affection were wonderful. 'I could not have a dearer companion.' 'He is invariably cheerful, goodhumoured and kind,' Benson wrote on August 18th. Two days later, he recorded Gosse at his most irresponsible, amusing himself at Benson's expense, simply to make a good story.

The Mayor of Richmond had offered to show them the town plate, and for some reason they had accepted. 'Gosse was seized with speechlessness,' a most unusual event. Benson, 'out of sheer desperation, had to admire every single piece of plate'. That night they dined with the Jameses – he a son of Lord Northbourne, she, Lady Evelyn, a daughter of the Duke of Wellington. Benson recorded:

> I overheard G. doing a thing which illustrates why people don't trust him. He gave a very humorous account to the James' of our seeing the plate – it was dangerous enough anyhow to make elaborate fun of these local people, who had after all been very kind to us – but to make his story more picturesque, he represented me as making ridiculous mistakes over every piece of plate. 'Now that is a fine old bit!' 'No, it was given us new last year.' 'This I suppose is modern?' 'No, it is the oldest bit we have, 1580!' and so on. Not a word of truth in it. I had only talked and asked questions because he had not said a word and I had been rather lucky in giving correct dates to the cups etc.

And yet, six days later, as Gosse returned to London, Benson wrote in his diary, 'The train puffed in and G. went off. I could not say how grateful I was. I love life, as it was and as it might be, better than ever.' And on the 28th August, 'A charming little tender note from G., who says he has *really* enjoyed himself.'

At Lyme Regis the following January, Gosse was 'a delightful companion, so sprightly and so good-humoured and Mrs G. a dear'. Benson thought her 'so utterly unselfish, always thinking about everyone else, never of herself for a moment – yet with a keen faculty for enjoyment'. Benson felt himself 'in *hell* before their very eyes'. They were 'very tender and sweet seeing the shadow' over him. Gosse continued to 'behave like a brick'. On holiday in Derbyshire that Easter, Benson was envying Gosse's 'busy zest, his glad mingling with men and affairs'. He 'has been the kindest and best of friends to me', 'so sweet-tempered and considerate'. At lunch with Lord and Lady Newton, Gosse was 'very amusing and easy'. Benson thought his manner had improved, that he was 'less effusive and more natural', but he seemed to be enjoying a little too much his rôle as Good Samaritan. 'Everything is fine as long as Gosse gets his own way or the way that he has decided to play.' On one occasion he loses his temper and says, 'How tiresome people are! Why can't they be made to do as one wants them to do!' It is the voice of a petulant child, a voice one hears more and more frequently in Benson's diary, alternating with the more agreeable tones of the cheering friend.

As Benson's depressive state improved, Gosse's own mental state in his company seemed to worsen. In Wales, in January 1910, Benson observed his lack of concentration, his lack of any serenity, his hungry desire for recognition and appreciation. A monk on Caldy Island, his long white habit blowing in the wind, recognized his name. 'Mr Edmund Gosse! Haven't I seen your name in the papers lately? You are a bit of an archaeologist, aren't you?' Gosse said rather stiffly: 'No, I am not an archaeologist – but no-one escapes the papers now.' His spirits had lifted and been dashed. On wet days he could not settle to anything. He maddened Benson with his grumblings, 'his tone of ultra-pessimistic feudalism (caught in the House of Lords), his interruptions. He read, he tried to sleep, he read again, he yawned. He read things aloud. He was incapable of silence for five minutes. His stories got longer'. Benson counted to 938 during one anecdote one evening.

In April 1910 Benson wrote: 'A very gloomy and depressed evening. Letter from G. from Lord Ilchester's. He says that he is sinking into helpless misery and portends an illness like mine. I *think* he is only ill and overtired – but the terrible way he spends his Sundays [it was actually often whole weekends], going down ill and tired to some big house, and then getting excited and talking all day long and coming home a wreck, is bad for him in every way.'

In May, he wrote to Edward Marsh: 'Gosse has written to me once or twice lately in a strain of deep melancholy. But everyone who has seen him, talks of him as if he were like Mercury on the fountain in Shaftesbury Circus – poised and riant.' To many people, Gosse did indeed seem poised and laughing; Benson in his diary would record more of the contradictions and ambiguities, the *voltes-face* from day to day.

When Gosse suggested they spent some time that summer together, Benson said he had to be in Cambridge in August. Gosse said, 'Ah, when you were ill and could get no-one to travel with you, you were glad enough to fall back on me – but now that you are well, you don't care for my company.' Benson wrote, 'The perversity, untruthfulness, nastiness, injustice of this little speech is inconceivable. Even if it were true – and it has not a word of truth in it – it ought not to be *said*. It can't be treated as a jest – it can *only* wound and vex. It makes me despair! . . . It is mostly, I think, ill-breeding, but also the desire to make a momentary sensation, at any price. It is like M. Baring emptying the mustard down the back of one's neck.' Benson saw him as a 'feminine' character, needing to impress, to make himself felt, at any cost. But Gosse was quite unaware that he had said anything that could hurt. They dined together at Hanover Terrace. 'The house very nice, the roof garden leafy and embowered. Mrs G. very comfortable and Tessa pleasant. We dined agreeably. Sylvia gave me two etchings of her own, very shyly – and I felt very much one of them.'

At times, Gosse would seem 'grateful for his good fortune' and contented with his lot. Benson listed his blessings: 'wealth, fame, honour, interesting friends and all this he has made for himself', forgetting for a moment the Epps cocoa money. But his spirits would 'jump up and down with marvellous celerity'. 'The more assured his position is, the more greedy he seems to be of honour and reputation.' He longed for some recognition from the monk at Caldy but the last thing he wanted was the status Frank Harris would accord him, as one of the people's gods – along with Hall Caine, Marie Corelli and Arnold Bennett.

There was an unforgettable confrontation between Benson and Gosse in September 1910, after which their relationship was never the same again. Benson records that dark day, which started off with a casual argument about retiring ages, the authorship of an article in the *Saturday Review*, and butterflies:

G. made some wild statements which I did not dispute . . . G. picked up a flint, which he said was an arrowhead – and pointed out some Sarsen stones. I suppose I answered carelessly. We strolled on. When he suddenly said 'I must protest against the extremely insolent way in which you have contradicted everything I have said today. You have to be always right, whether you know anything about the subject or not . . . It is insufferable. I have been bottling up my anger all day and now I shall speak out. It all comes from living with undergraduates and pulling them up with insolence – but you dare not show them the insolence which you show me. It is arrogance and incivility combined. You used to be so pleasant and sympathetic. That is all gone and is succeeded by this intolerable effrontery.' I looked at him – he was pale and wizened, black about the eyes and glaring at me. I said something about it being a sudden and unprovoked attack – but he said 'I mean it, every word.' It took me so aback I could hardly speak . . . I said – it was useless to argue – 'Very well, I can only say I am extremely sorry and shall try to avoid it in future.' Gosse said: 'You make it impossible for me to talk on any subject.' I said: 'Well, you have certainly made it impossible for me to speak.' We were climbing a fence. 'I really think that under the circumstances I had better go back tomorrow.' He said nothing for a minute and then broke out again in the most passionate exclamation of sorrow and abasement. 'It is not true, not a word of it,' he said. 'It grew as I spoke and I felt it was all untrue as I said it – it was simply monstrous of me. I am here as your guest and I value your friendship more than I value the friendship of anyone in the world. I would rather have cut my tongue out than speak as I did. I am ill and in pain and you must put it down to that. I am in a serious state of health and I don't know what I say. It is just like me to throw away my happiness like this. I am good for nothing. I must make haste to flee a world where I can be of no use or pleasure to anyone.' I tried to stop him but could not. He said 'When you were ill I tried my best to be kind and patient with you – you must try to be patient with me – you must think no more of it. If you will dictate me an apology in the most humiliating and abasing terms possible, I will repeat it.' I said, 'I don't want an apology – I don't want to increase or add to your distress in any way – that is no kind of satisfaction. The misery is that you should say it or think it. If it is true, it makes me out a damnably odious person and if it is *not* true – it is the intention of giving all the pain you could which is so horrible to me.' He said that I was not generous: 'If you will admit that you have been just a little contradictory, I will admit that I have been abominable.'

I said, 'Of course I admit it – You could not have said it, without there being *something* in your mind to cause it. I think it comes from my long illness – the return to life makes me ungracious and inconsiderate.'

'But I don't want you to think it,' he said 'because it is not true – everything must be just as before.'

I said 'No, that can't be. If you suddenly fell on me with a stick and beat me, your regret wouldn't take away the bruises. You must give me time.'

We were now at the road and he went on lamenting in a very pathetic way, till I said, 'I don't think this can be mended by argument – we had better never mention this matter again.'

We walked on talking affectedly about general matters, found the car and went back. It was a shocking evening. He did his very best, that I must say, to be nice. But I simply could not recover my spirits at all. We found the Master of Trinity Hall in the dining-room, very fuzzy and fat. We drank wine in a sign of amity and hurriedly agreed with every expression of opinion. But as things settled down, I had a horrid feeling that he felt he had on the whole done right and that I needed a lesson which he had been right to give me – I am not sure that he *did* really regret it. But what *ease* can there be about such a relation? The only result is that one simply can't say what one thinks.

When we first made acquaintance, I was a young schoolmaster of

28 and he a man of letters of 40. He has forgotten that our respective positions have altered, and expects a sort of amiable submissiveness. But it *is* a lesson too, of course. I think I am more fractious and argumentative. It is partly that my nerves are more highly strung, and partly the living with younger men, like G. L. Mallory etc with whom one argues very frankly without giving offence. I must try to be more courteous and more indifferent about the questions I argue. Heat never converts – and one may say what one likes if one is only deferential.

But the horror is that with all recollection of G's patience, kindness, tenderness and goodwill, one can't risk these shocking and frenzied scenes. Friendship, hopefulness, joy, interest burn up in them as in a swift fire. They are *wholly* horrible and devastating. Yet I think G. rather likes them, both at the time and afterwards. He feels he has put me in my place, made a dignified protest, asserted himself – and if the manner was a little heated, why that may pass. It is stupid, ugly, savage things like this that make life such a puzzle.

Benson did not break with Gosse there and then. As he said, 'it is all much too deep for that'; but it was hard to be friends with someone who believes 'he should say what he likes by way of criticism or reproof but receive neither himself'. 'Gosse understands no language but that of adulation,' Benson said, on another occasion. They trod warily, gingerly for the rest of the holiday, 'as a man might push among nettles'. The last few days were also overshadowed by the possibility of an NER strike affecting his holiday in France with Nellie. When they finally parted, Gosse said, 'When I get back, I shall fall into the deepest dejection.'

Benson said hesitantly, 'What about?'

'About the possibility of the NER strike affecting the French railways!'

What indeed could one do with such a friend? Benson also gives dreadful suggestions of Gosse's snobbery. At Clevedon in January 1911: 'G. is in very good spirits today, very kittenish and jumpy. He has changed his clothes thrice. All this because we are going to Clevedon Court to tea with a Baronet . . . It would be a different matter if it were tea with a clergyman or a doctor, I fear . . . He came back in high spirits, having given and received distinguished consideration. He was loud in praise of Lady E. and as loud in condemnation of Mrs D. Yet I could not help feeling that if Mrs D had been Lady E., he would have liked her kindliness, while if Lady E. had been Mrs D., he would have called her dowdy and shy.' But perhaps most of it was in Benson's mind. The next day he wrote: 'Gosse is difficult just now –

he lamented loud and long about the misery of having to go and stay with Curzon of Kedleston. How it would upset his digestion and his nerves and be expensive and boring . . .'

Benson thought Gosse 'obsessed with the wish to show himself a person of consequence – and to be afraid of being treated as if he were an ordinary man. But the difference of his behaviour when he is with people of consequence and when he is not is terrible. At the Ribblesdales, the Newtons, the Eltons he was all wreathed in smiles, jesting, on tiptoe, bowing. Yesterday he took offence at something at Lis Escop and stalked about pouting, looking gloomily at things, brooding. It is this awful *valuation* of people, thinking whether it is worthwhile being civil to them, demanding recognition from them, which sickens me: and when I feel rather responsible for him, it deprives me of all power of speech. What poor Mrs G. must have suffered – my feeling of her *heroism* goes up on days like these'. When Gosse talked of his wife, Benson liked him best. 'The thought that anything might happen to Nellie makes my heart like a stone. I can't say what she is and has been to me.' But Percy Lubbock thought much of Gosse's impossible behaviour was because he was used to being spoilt by his family, his every whim acceded to. Henry James saw Nellie as 'a poor brave-hearted kindly woman, whose one attitude to life must be of one responding to a litany and, at each new escapade of Gosse's, crying out "Again!" "Again!"' A few days later Lord Courtney turned up at the hotel to call on Gosse: a rather absurd old man in a chocolate overcoat and a scarlet tie, 'with a high belief in his own perfections, rather like the non-conformist idea of God'. 'It was amusing to watch Gosse,' Benson wrote. 'All the most captivating little wiggles and giggles came on: he tucked himself up at the other end of the sofa and his voice rippled out, silvery like a fond charmer. It was almost like a bar-maid in its flirtatiousness – he gave the impression of sitting on Lord C's knees and pulling his old ears like a petted child.' What a contrast from that morning when Gosse had been lying aimlessly on the sofa, staring with haggard eyes at the fire, an uncut Swedish novel in his listless hand.

In September 1912 Gosse and Benson together visited the Hardys at Max Gate. Both men left long descriptions of the visit and vividly describe Emma Hardy, who would be dead within ten weeks. Gosse saw her 'absurdly dressed, as a country lady without friends might dress herself on a vague recollection of some nymph in a picture by Botticelli'. Benson said Gosse 'took her by both hands and talked to her in a strain of exaggerated gallantry, which was deeply appreciated'. The cat was less appreciative when Gosse amused his hosts by nursing the reluctant animal swathed in his napkin, while Mrs Hardy carved the chickens as if engaged in some curious handicraft. She confided to her guests that she 'beat her husband', but 'only with the *Times* rolled up'. Gosse found Hardy brightened by their visit, talking of little incidents they had shared thirty years before, but remaining 'what he has always been, a sphinx-like little man, unrelated, unrevealed, displaying nothing that the most affectionate solicitude can make use of to explain the mystery of his magnificent genius'. Benson hated 'leaving him to his accustomed life inside the dark copse with the cat and the niece and Mrs Hardy with her flighty and peevish activity'.

On 12th December, Hardy wrote to Nellie: 'Probably nobody in London knew her better than you did . . . Innumerable times we have shared your hospitality. I have been full of regrets that I did not at all foresee the possibility of her passing away thus . . .' It was a time of deaths. The following July Gosse wrote to Wise: 'We have, indeed, had a great deal of trouble this year, but we must expect that as we get on in life. The deaths of so many of our relations – seven in four years, and this including my wife's four sisters – have given us a very hard shock: we can hardly expect ever to face life with quite the same courage again, if indeed much more life is left for us to face. But we have had a very happy time in the past and we only have to look forward now to what all the world experiences.' Speaking of Nellie's losses, he wrote to Philip: 'It sweeps her youth away.' The same month, he wrote to Hardy: 'My daughter-in-law has given birth to a dead child, which is very disappointing. I wanted a grandson.'

17

The Formidable Adventure

GOSSE'S SOCIAL LIFE was as glittering as ever: there were all those country house visits Benson thought so damaging. He stayed at the same great houses and at others as well – over and over again with the Londonderrys (his May 1912 visit to Mountstewart was his eleventh), with the Asquiths, the Charnwoods, with Lord Halifax at Hickleton, Lord Curzon at Hackwood, Lord Montagu at Beaulieu. The Duke of Marlborough invited him to Blenheim. At Melbury he talked with Lord Kitchener about gardening and old Eastern china, not subjects dear to Gosse's heart but the only subjects which seemed to interest Kitchener, apart from soldiering. Gosse found him 'hideous, with great expressionless eyes (like Sargent's), a crushed winged sort of nose and such curious confloptions in the cheeks and chin that I think they must be the effect of wounds'. Gosse found Lady Desborough's parties at Taplow too large: 'There are already 23 guests and more are coming . . . The Ribblesdales, Lord Grenfell, Winston Churchill, Lord Cobham and his daughter . . . Outside driving rain and inside nothing but vain and foolish talking.'

There were innumerable social engagements in London too. At one stage Gosse explained, turning down an invitation from the Dunedins, that he could not dine out every night. At his own dinner table, he still had more writers and painters than peers. One night in 1912 there were Yeats, Sickert, Robert Ross and the very young Freya Stark, who recorded her impression of Gosse: 'pale, and, as it were *bleached*, shoulders, hands, moustache, all gently drooping, guiding his team with a voice of silky suavity which disguised the cutting edge. Beyond Yeats's dark hair and heavy chin like that of some prelate not too ascetic, and Sickert's aquiline profile, the open windows showed the heavy garden laburnums pale in candlelight against the sombre leafage of the park'. She forgot what they talked about, but the pattern of the talk remained: 'Dancing to and fro across the table . . . easy and effortless . . . here was the real thing, the Art of Conversation.'

Gosse met Kitchener again in London, at Haldane's luncheon table, on 18th May 1911, with Curzon, General Sir John French and Ramsay MacDonald. His contacts with the world were such that one can hardly believe Benson's suggestion that he was over-excited by a baronet in Clevedon. Lord Redesdale invited him to dine with the King at the Marlborough Club. He saw a good deal of the new Prime Minister, Asquith, in and out of Westminster. They belonged to the same, very exclusive, dining club, Grillion's. Gosse negotiated with Macmillan for the publication of Asquith's speeches. Most important of all, they conferred about the granting of Civil List pensions. When Asquith fell in 1916 ('the fall of Phaeton-Asquith, dragging Maecenas-like Eddie with him') Gosse would lament: 'Never was there a P.M. who cared a third part as much about letters and the sorrows of scribbling men, as Asquith did.' But when Eddie Marsh included Asquith's son in *Georgian Poetry III*, Gosse was immediately critical. 'I read him forward and I read him backward and I see nothing,' Gosse wrote to Marsh with justice. 'If he were a Herbert Snooks . . . no-one would ever have looked at his verses. And people say that the "age of privilege" is passed!'

Marsh was used to being rebuked by Gosse. There was one occasion in 1910 when their long friendship ('one of the treasures of my life', Marsh called it) nearly foundered on Gosse's more than usually intemperate behaviour. 'Beast!' Gosse had snarled at Marsh. 'I watched you all dinner. You never spoke a word to my wife but talked the whole time to Lady A.' 'There can never have been a more absurd falling-out,' as Marsh wrote. He refused to apologize and admit his discourtesy, though his biographer feels sure 'his benefactor's grievance was not unfounded'. Benson wrote to Marsh: 'There is in Gosse a Puritan touch, the impulse to improve other people at all costs.' The whole thing was 'like a mist, which meant so little and yet hid so much'; eventually it cleared.

In 1910 Gosse was much involved in securing a Civil List pension for W. B. Yeats. 'We cannot neglect our greatest poet,' Gosse had said, as Yeats reported happily to Lady Gregory. Gosse had arranged a meeting between Yeats and the Prime Minister. He confided to Lady Gregory that the poet is 'as easy to help as a faery', but there were rather unfaerylike problems. Yeats had said no Irishman 'could accept anything from the government which limited his political freedom'. Gosse could assure him there were no strings. On 29th July 1910 Gosse was able to tell Yeats that his petition had gone in to Asquith 'with support of such a kind as few such appeals can ever have had'. Yeats was granted £150 a year. 'I thank you,' Yeats wrote to Gosse, 'for what will set me free from a continual anxiety and permit me to do only the work I am most fitted for. But for you I would never even have thought of such a thing . . . You have taken much trouble and given much thought for my freedom and my well-being and I am grateful and always shall be.'

This was only one of dozens of grants to writers – both Civil List pensions and sums from the Royal Literary Fund – in which Gosse was involved. The archives of the Fund, on the committee of which Gosse served from 1894 until his death, are full of letters from him and application forms filled in by him. Sometimes it was distressing work. On one occasion when Gosse succeeded in getting £100 for Lascelles Abercrombie, he said, 'We had 27 applicants and only about £600 to divide'. Some years earlier, he had been instrumental in securing a grant for Joseph Conrad, filling in as the 'cause of distress', 'slowness of composition and want of public appreciation' and copying out in his own hand a supporting letter he had solicited from Henry James. Conrad was also not easy to help, resenting some of the Fund's queries and the apparent suggestion that he needed 'saving from himself'. Gosse had also filled in the application for poor Arthur Symons ('now in an asylum at Crowborough'). He never forgot old friends. More than once he organized assistance for John Blaikie (in 1899 reduced to selling 'the last few books of value that remained in my library to keep myself from starving') and towards the end of her life he obtained £100 for Elise Otté ('one of the most learned women I have ever known').

In 1915, Yeats wrote at Ezra Pound's suggestion to Edmund Gosse about the plight of 'James Joyce, an Irish poet and novelist of whose fine talent I can easily satisfy you . . . I am sorry to trouble you but I know in a case of hardship you do not think anything is trouble.' Gosse agreed to read *Dubliners* and *Chamber Music* and reported them 'certainly up to our standard'. Later he would change his mind about Joyce. He came to think him a 'charlatan', one of his favourite terms of literary abuse. There is a letter which has been much held up to scorn in which, in 1924, Gosse wrote to Louis Gillet, the literary editor of the *Revue des deux mondes*:

I should very much regret your paying Mr James Joyce the compliment of an article . . . You could only expose the worthlessness and impudence of his writings, and surely it would be a mistake to give him this prominence. I have difficulty in describing to you, in *writing*, the character of Mr Joyce's notoriety . . . It is partly political; it is partly a perfectly cynical appeal to sheer indecency. He is of course not entirely without talent, but he is a literary charlatan of the extremest order . . . There are no English critics of weight or judgement who consider Mr Joyce an author of any importance.

Even Virginia Woolf, after all, was made to feel 'desperately lady-like' by Joyce's 'gratuitous and impudent coarseness'. And at least Gosse had read *Ulysses*, as he pointed out to John Drinkwater when chiding him for taking the chair at a dinner for Joyce in 1927, which was more than Drinkwater had. 'If *Ulysses* really is a work of distinction,' he would say, 'I have lived in vain, and all that I have honoured and striven to support for 60 years is rubbish.' It seems fair to add that Virginia Woolf thought it 'more and more unimportant'. Even Yeats never finished reading it. When Gosse said he was unable to help with a further grant to Joyce in 1917 (five years before *Ulysses*) he gave as his reason that his 'influence with the Privy Purse ceased when Mr Asquith ceased to be Prime Minister'. But long after this he was still concerned with the Royal Literary Fund. He once wrote to Edward Clodd: 'If you had as much as I have to do with the tricks of the begging-letter writer, you would have a hard heart. Mine has become leather.' But many had cause to thank him for showing that it was not really so.

1910 saw the establishment of one of Gosse's dreams. It bore the cumbersome title of 'An Academic Committee of English Letters'. It was to number no more than forty and to represent pure literature in the same way that the Royal Academy represents the fine arts, the Royal Society science and the British Academy learning. It was under the aegis of the Royal Society of Literature, in which Gosse had long been active. Its aims were those of the French Academy – 'to maintain the purity of the language', to reward distinction in literature and so on. 'I don't want an Academy but if there is one I should like to be in,' Benson wrote in his diary; and many writers felt the same.

The original list included, as well as Gosse (of course, that prime-mover), Binyon, Bridges, Conrad, Dobson, J. G. Frazer, Haldane, Hardy, James, Lang, Morley, Newbolt, Pinero and Yeats. Benson was elected that July, which gave him 'deep and real pleasure . . . Shaw and Kipling have refused but otherwise it is a body consisting of the foremost literary men in England'. Kipling thought it should be for critics – 'a judicial body that can maintain and impose standards'. In 1912 Wells wrote to tell Gosse he adored him and James 'but I am bitterly, incurably, destructively against Literary Academies'. There was considerable argument about who should be invited to join. Some who had been excluded did their best 'to damage it by saying that it is simply the friends of Gosse'.

Beerbohm observes arguments at the Academic Committee

It provided more committee meetings for him, along with those of the Royal Literary Fund, the Nobel Prize English Committee, the Trustees of the National Portrait Gallery, the Anglo-French Society, the London Library and so on. It focused literary opinion on some important topics. In 1912 Yeats wrote to Gosse urging him to head a deputation from the Academic Committee about the new Censorship Bill. 'I write to you first, before talking to anybody else on the Committee, because you have done more against the book-censorship than anyone else.' This seems to have been true, which makes his reaction to *Howards End* the more inexplicable. (Not that Gosse wanted that censored, of course.) Gosse was always writing to *The Times* against the activities of the Vigilance Society, the Circulating Libraries and all those in high places worrying about what writers write. 'If they have the power tyrannically to stop their opponents' pens today, how is it that they do not realize that their own may be snatched from their hands tomorrow?' he would write towards the end of his life.

It was certainly while Asquith was still Prime Minister that Gosse was at the height of his influence. Asquith was always turning to him for advice: on the appointment to the new Cambridge English Chair, on the new Lord Chamberlain, whether Meredith should be buried in the Abbey and who should be, in 1913, the new Poet Laureate. In this last case, Gosse approved of Bridges. Violet Asquith hoped that that was so, that he didn't support 'what Father calls "Eddie's spavined team"'.

On 6th March 1912 Gosse described lunch at 10 Downing Street in a letter to Nellie:

> I sat by Miss Violet Asquith and Mr Lloyd George, whom I was introduced to for the first time. I succumbed helplessly to his charm. We got on like a house on fire. I had a most interesting talk on oratory . . . He is an improvisator. He tells me he never says exactly what he started by meaning to say, his imagination works. He says that it was so in his too-famous Limehouse speech. He laughed and said, 'I confess I was carried away – the place! the faces!' Lady Dorothy Nevill was there, so scandalised at meeting so many radicals. Haldane told her that Lloyd George ought to be presented to her. 'Oh, no! no!' she said. But I at once urged Haldane to go and fetch him, which he did, leaving me with Lady D., who desired me to take her away. Of course, I wouldn't. Up came Haldane with the bland Lloyd George, who bowed very smilingly. Lady D. scarcely bowed and said in her most frog-like voice, 'You are a wicked man!' Lloyd George laughed and smiled and said 'I'm afraid I am! I'm afraid that's true!' Two minutes afterwards they were chatting together like old friends.

Gosse's friendship with Haldane developed as his friendship with Benson died. He demanded no adulation from Haldane, and ventured no rebukes. Gosse had always been conscious of his own inferiority to Haldane, and always behaved better when with people he considered his superiors. In 1904, trying to understand Haldane's abstract reasoning in one of his philosophical books, Gosse wrote with genuine humility: 'You are the one of my contemporaries who amazes me most – who alarms, who exhilarates, who fills me with most despair.' It was a despair he relished; it was an exhilaration he needed. As they grew closer, the deep affection of someone he could admire without reservation meant more and more to Gosse. There was also the compelling attraction of being so close to the seats of power.

If Haldane had to excuse himself from an engagement, the reason was likely to be impressive. On 11th August 1911 he wrote to Gosse, 'I am kept here by the strike. I have 30,000 troops under arms.' It was in these years that Haldane in the Commons was carrying through the legislation necessary to give effect to his schemes for the reform of the army. It was Haldane who established an Imperial General Staff, built up an Expeditionary Force and initiated the Territorial Army for military defence at home. He also improved arrangements for both the victualling of the army and for medical and nursing services. He established 'a scientific machine susceptible to expansion in time of war' and 'it was a sad irony', as Lord Islington wrote to Gosse that, when that war came, Kitchener 'refused to use this machinery ready to his hand'.

It was also at this period that Haldane was visiting Germany, learning from what he saw but incurring as a result, at the height of the war, accusations of pro-German sympathies. In 1912 Haldane left the War Office and became Lord Chancellor, but on the outbreak of war, Asquith would ask him to return.

Gosse kept a full diary in July and August 1914, which owes a great deal to his friendship with Haldane. He describes it as 'a record of scenes witnessed and words heard almost at the centre of affairs, by one of no authority or responsibility who was a careful observer'. But so little did Gosse appreciate the seriousness of things, even after a long talk with Haldane on Friday 31st July alone at his home over dinner (Grey, the Foreign Secretary, pausing to greet him before going on elsewhere), that he hoped that he and Haldane would take one of their usual walks in the country that Sunday. A note the next day told him the Cabinet was in almost permanent session. During the days of crisis, however, Haldane was never too busy or too tired to see Gosse for a few minutes. 'Your company does me good,' Haldane would say. 'It rests me to have a quiet talk with you.' The difficulty is, Haldane told Gosse, 'we are not united. There are four of us who see it is impossible to leave France in the lurch. Fancy, the German ships bombarding every French port in the Channel from Dunquerque to Brest, and we looking on with our hands in our lap! It is unthinkable, but our colleagues don't see it.' Gosse said 'Who are the four?' He answered, 'I think you know' – it was Asquith, Grey, Haldane 'and Winston, who is perfectly splendid, like a tiger'.

'We may see Winston develop great powers,' Gosse wrote to Spencer. He asked Haldane: 'Shall we be able to beat Germany?' Haldane said, 'Yes, at last, after dreadful sacrifices, we must win, we will win, we cannot possibly fail to win, even if it takes fifteen years to do it. It will be a war of exhaustion, of strangulation, and when

Germany is bled absolutely white, we shall have red blood still.' As Gosse left, the German Ambassador, Lichnowsky, was shown into the drawing-room. Gosse had met him several times at 10 Downing Street, at the Londonderrys', at Lord Charles Beresford's. His face was 'that of a violinist or a chiropodist but never of a Prussian Junker'. His talk was 'rapid, inconsequent, superficial'. Haldane was convinced he was not in the counsels of the War Lords in Berlin. The Ambassador wept when he said goodbye.

Asquith asked Haldane to give up the Woolsack and take over the War Office. Haldane said he would rather act in Asquith's name. 'Later on you may wish to . . . have a soldier at the War Office.' Gosse was in the Princes' Chamber on August 5th when he overheard Lord Newton say 'I saw Kitchener today and he is in a rage. He says that no attention is paid to what he thinks and no advice is asked for from him . . . and he is not going to stand it any longer. There is that fellow Haldane ensconced at the War Office . . .' Gosse moved quietly away from the group of peers discussing the neglect of Kitchener, and at the nearest table wrote a brief note of warning to the Lord Chancellor, who was sitting on the Woolsack. Almost directly a pencilled note came back: 'Please wait till the end of the sitting and be in my room when I come out of the House.'

Gosse was there; it was nearly eight o'clock. Haldane greeted him: 'What you have told me is of the greatest importance. I had not the least notion that Kitchener was in that mood. We have had two War Councils at which he was present and he was perfectly amiable. It is very awkward: I will go this minute and consult Asquith on the subject. I am sure he is as unconscious as I am that we have wounded K. of K.'s susceptibility. You will see, it will all come right; but I am glad you lost no time in telling me.'

On leaving Gosse, Haldane went to see the Prime Minister. He told Asquith what Gosse had told him and said he had come to the conclusion that it was absolutely necessary for Lord Kitchener to take over the War Office. There were problems. Grey wanted Kitchener for Egypt, but Haldane persuaded them it was more important for him to stay at home: 'The mere fact of K. being at the War Office' would unite the country more than anything else. Asquith agreed; Haldane saw Kitchener before midnight – and next day Kitchener settled down to his task 'with the utmost cheerfulness and vigour'.

Gosse then busied himself with sending copies of Grey's White Paper to friends in Holland, France and America. In America he included Woodrow Wilson, Taft and the Presidents of the principal universities. The White Paper contained the statement of why England was at war. On Sunday 9th August Gosse made the following entry in his diary:

> Lord Haldane paid us a surprise visit at 17 Hanover Terrace. He had walked, and he was with us from a quarter past four to a quarter to six. We got out a large map, and he explained what his views are about the probable development of the war. Haldane is a broad rather than a sound geographer, and I was shocked by his inability, without help from me, to find the Vistula. However, he knew exactly where to put his finger upon Berlin. He is very well pleased with the mobilisation, but he is not sure that Kitchener is well-advised in wanting so large an army. Haldane says that Kitchener mentions figures which seem to Haldane excessive; he will never get these hundreds of thousands to enlist. However, Kitchener is very determined, and he has the art of making himself obeyed.

Late in the afternoon of August 24th Gosse was in the library of the House of Lords, when he heard rumours that Namur had fallen. He wrote in his diary:

> When I went into the streets, the placards of the newspapers were already appearing with 'FALL OF NAMUR'. I was in the habit of taking that walk, from Westminster to Regent's Park, several times every week, and I very seldom saw a face I knew. But that afternoon, by a rather odd fatality I happened every few hundred yards to meet an acquaintance, and every one seemed to want to stop and talk. First of all, on the north side of Pall Mall, it was Lord Lansdowne, mouching along with his hatchet face, and his inevitable long frock coat, who stopped to say to me 'Have you any confirmation of this rumour about Namur? It is incredible! The strongest place in Europe.' Then, at the corner of St James' Palace, it was young Lady Arran, very lovely and fluttered and incoherent: a few yards further, opposite Rumpelmeyer's, it was Lady Crewe, with her enigmatic smile. At St James' Place, it was Evan Charteris, very anxious to proclaim his ultimate optimism, and immediate despair, prophesying the total bankruptcy of the professions, the end of social order, and his own intention of going to the front at once in the hope of killing one or two Germans before he died himself. Higher up St James' Street, it was Lord Grenfell, with flushed cheeks and angry eyes, declaring that it must have been treachery – 'nothing but treachery could have brought Namur down within four weeks. Why, if I had a piece of paper here I could show you how impossible it is to take a place like Namur in a moment.' 'Ah!' I answered, 'and I

would make fortifications for your Honour something like a tansy.' He caught at the quotation, for he is a good Shandean, and he smiled a little, relaxing, and said 'You remember Uncle Toby found it necessary to understand a little of projectiles.' And then I reminded him how, years ago, before he was a Field Marshal, he and I and Sir Edward Carson and Lady Londonderry were becalmed on Strangford Lough, and how he (Lord Grenfell) passed the tedious hours by pretending that we were watching the movements of an invading Japanese flotilla. And so I got him to smile again, all but his sad old eyes which never smile now. Other friends I met on this incredible afternoon, as I walked home, and all wished to talk, and all were moved to queer excitement by the blow which had fallen upon the Allies in the sudden collapse of Namur. In my experience, it was at this moment that the larger proportion of English people first woke up to the fact that the war was not a curious spectacle but a highly alarming condition of affairs with the progress of which we were intimately linked. The newspapers had been blowing trumpets and beating drums, but they had not carried their readers with them.

It is impossible to over-emphasize the closeness of the friendship between Haldane and Gosse. It was largely due to this friendship and to Gosse's work for the *Sunday Times* after the war that Haldane could describe Gosse in his old age as a happy man, something 'one could not say confidently of many people'. Haldane involved Gosse as an equal, as a treasured consultant and confidant, in the affairs of state. In 1915 he wrote: 'You are the most perfect of friends and you have been a tower of strength to me in these troubled times.' 'No man ever had a better friend than I have,' he reiterated in 1918. Over and over again, there are such phrases in the letters as 'You are a wonderful friend', 'It is a lasting comfort to have such a friend as yourself, so unselfish and helpful . . .', 'the truest and staunchest friend a man could have'. Gosse would say: 'I love you so much that I venture to send you this word of comfort.'

Haldane, unmarried, beset by great problems of national importance, needed Gosse in a way that perhaps none of his close friends had ever needed him before. He would send for Gosse to cheer him up between Cabinet meetings. He would often find talk – talk with Gosse – 'the only rest possible'. As early as 1905, as we saw, Gosse had called 'the play of Haldane's intellect . . . the most wonderful fact in my daily life'. By 1917, Gosse would describe him, with slight exaggeration, as 'the only human being in whose welfare I take an interest', outside his own family.

Nellie found her occasional visits to Cloan, Haldane's Scottish home, rather a strain. She would write to Tessa on one occasion: 'I do mean to get on well with our host and not to be panicky', but she felt that another day of 'high-living, high-voiced talking and general hospitality' might well do for her altogether, though she tried not to let the Scottish nobility interfere with the long walks she and Edmund liked to take together. Another year, she told Sylvia that Haldane himself was 'more *human* than his sister', whom she found terribly domineering. 'I am careful not to assert myself,' she wrote. Nellie was adept at avoiding clashes.

Elizabeth Haldane and Edmund Gosse seemed to enjoy a conspiracy to protect the Great Man, as they would call him in their letters. Some of Gosse's letters to her in Scotland show just how involved Gosse was in Haldane's career. At the height of the 'pro-German accusations', Gosse wrote to Haldane: 'I have many friends in Unionist circles and I hear a great deal of gossip. There is growing up and thriving by ignorant repetition, a thoroughly twisted and false legend about your negotiations in Berlin in 1912 . . .' To Elizabeth Haldane, Gosse wrote: 'I do not suppose my opinion weighs with Grey but I felt it my duty to let him know (in writing) that I thought the time had come when the Foreign Office ought to defend your Brother's credit . . . I am very angry indeed with the Lord Chancellor for putting his resignation into Asquith's hands ten days ago when the attacks were at their worst . . . I have made him give me a promise that he will not do this again, under any circumstances, without discussing it.' There is a hint here of the arrogance Benson had so often complained of, but Haldane needed it; he needed someone who cared and watched over his every action.

Haldane sent Gosse a cutting from the *Daily Express* in December, 1914 which suggested sending Haldane to Germany to his 'spiritual home'. This was too much for Gosse. He wrote a long letter which appeared in the *Morning Post* on 9th January 1915, showing the origin of the phrase. Apparently, at the Humphry Wards' dinner table in 1912, Haldane had said politely on meeting a German academic: 'Looking back over nearly forty years, he still regarded the Göttingen of Lotze as something like "a spiritual home . . ."' If one philosopher meeting an alien philosopher at a dinner table is to be taken to task for such a harmless courtesy, what is to become of social life?' Gosse said he wrote 'as a person who is not identified with politics and who until lately was constrained by official decorum . . .'

This referred to the fact that on 26th September 1914, Gosse's post as Librarian of the House of Lords had come to an end. He had reached the official retiring age. He was sixty-five. He had hoped his appointment might be renewed; he hated to be thought old. (Rider Haggard would say in 1920 that Gosse was 'an evergreen that the frosts of time never seem to touch'.) Many of his lordly friends commiserated. Lansdowne and Crewe pressed for Gosse's term to be extended by five years, but Sir Harry Graham, Clerk of the Parliaments, 'said that the age of retirement should only be broken when the department would suffer. This could not be pleaded in the case of a wholly otiose post' – a rather unkind adjective when one thinks of how many noble questions had been answered ('When I want a question of literary interest answered, I naturally appeal to headquarters,' Lord Cromer had written) and how much the House of Lords library had been improved in Gosse's ten and a half years as librarian. The committee vote was 11 votes to 8 against an extension. 'I thought we would win till the Clerk had gone three-quarters round the room. The House won't be the same without you,' Lord Monk Bretton wrote, 'but then the House won't be there at all much longer.' Many people had the same feeling, since Asquith's success in ending the absolute veto of the House of Lords. Henry James thought its 'knell, to my sense, would seem to have virtually rung' as early as 1906. In 1911 Gosse had written to him of 'an ancient order obstinately poised against public feeling'. But Gosse loved it, he would say, 'as though one should love a mangy old poodle . . . When it drove me forth without a word of regret, I felt hurt and I still feel hurt. I deserved better treatment from the mangy old poodle.'

In 1914, of course, there were other more important causes of anguish and regret. Gosse wrote a poem 'To Our Dead' which was printed in *The Times* on 20th October 1914. He did not often write poems these days; this one caught the awful patriotism of the hour. Here is the second stanza:

> Your ashes o'er the flats of France are scattered,
> > But hold a fire more hot than flesh of ours:
> The stainless flag that flutters, frayed and tattered,
> > Shall wave and wave, like Spring's immortal flowers.
> You die, but in your death life glows intenser;
> > You shall not know the shame of growing old;
> In endless joy you wave the holy censer,
> > And blow the trumpet tho' your lips are cold.

In Dorset Thomas Hardy was now married to Florence Dugdale. Earlier in the year Gosse had written to Wise: 'What distresses me is that he should so soon experience the misfortunes of an old man who marries a young and ambitious wife.' Hardy and Gosse were not in close contact. Hardy rarely came to London and Florence, at any rate, thought he worried that Gosse would gossip about him. She wrote to Rebekah Owen: 'I think my husband dislikes his affairs being discussed outside Dorchester even more than here, for things trickle through to editors, and friends like Mr Edmund Gosse.' But Hardy admired 'To Our Dead'. He told Mrs Henniker it was 'among the few good poems that have been brought out by the war'.

Lady Duff, whose husband's death was reported in that same issue of *The Times*, had the poem specially printed to send to her friends and told Gosse how much it meant to her. Lady Desborough, who would lose both her sons, Julian and Billy Grenfell, wrote to Gosse of the poem, 'How one's spirit leaps to meet it . . . What uplift underlies the anguish.' In France Gide read it 'avec l'émotion la plus vive'. He cut the poem out of the paper and carried it around with him.

Gosse wrote back to Gide with equal emotion: 'All the civilised world is launched upon the formidable adventure . . . For you French we feel an affection so close and so fraternal that there has been nothing like it before in our history.' Gosse's love of France and his involvement with its fortunes and its literature had increased with every year that passed. 'Hardly anybody else in England thinks of what is going on elsewhere,' Fitzmaurice Kelly commented in 1912, wanting to dedicate the French translation of one of his books to Gosse. In 1913 Gosse had been awarded the Légion d'Honneur for 'les services que vous avez rendus au Gouvernement Français'. He wrote to Henry James: 'No-one was more astonished than I, and I still think it must be a hoax or blunder. But if ever one goes to France again . . . I am told that the rosette ensures one an easy time in the Customs.'

Now, in 1914, he wrote to Lord Spencer, 'All must depend on France.' He told Hardy, 'Like you, I have felt incapable of any exercise but poring over newspapers and meditating, now hopefully, now dejectedly upon the situation.' Philip was in the Army, a doctor with an ambulance unit just behind the front. 'His mother and I are completely pleased, and if we had ten sons, we would give them all,' he wrote to Spencer early on in an outburst of patriotism. But then added 'Perhaps it is easier to give ten than one.' And as, day after day, the casualty lists came in, it was increasingly difficult to feel 'completely pleased'. By July 1916 he would write to Gide, 'Our son is at Béthune, at the front. Imagine what we go through! He has . . . had men killed on each side of him, but he lives still.' In 1917 'the Germans were shelling his hospital and killing his nurses'. Philip survived the war but his parents lived 'in the constant anguish of anxiety'. Already in November 1914 Gosse could tell Gide, 'The losses in our private world are terrible! I know at least twenty families where the son of the house was an officer, who has already died in France.'

Gosse took Rupert Brooke's death particularly hard; like everyone else, he had loved him. He wrote to John Drinkwater the day after he heard the news: 'I am very much agitated today, because I dreamed about him last night . . . He appeared to me in his usual guise, but with an expression insufferably sad. He seemed in an agony to say something, but no sound whatever came from him, and I woke – not once, but twice, in the agony of trying vainly to help him to speak. I rarely dream and the vividness of this vision has quite unmanned me.' Gosse told Eddie Marsh after reading his Memoir: 'You will be remembered with Rupert as Severn is with Keats.' He sent Brooke's poems and the Memoir to Gide hoping he would translate them.

Staying with Lord Ribblesdale at Gisburne Park in May 1917, Gosse and his host took tea at a little inn. 'The woman who waited on us said in answer to some question of Lord Ribblesdale's about a man, "Oh, he was the last to go." We said, "Do you mean to go out to France?" "Oh, no," she said, "the last to die. Now *all* the young men that went out from this village have been killed."' By the end of the war the deaths in Gosse's own world included Raymond Asquith, John Kipling, Lady Desborough's two sons, William Archer's son, Lord Redesdale's son, Hamo Sassoon (Thornycroft's nephew, Siegfried's younger brother); dozens more.

Siegfried Sassoon had interested Gosse for years. Sassoon had first seen Gosse in 1903 in Hampstead Town Hall when he was about seventeen: 'the occasion being a dance given by Mrs Gosse and my aunt Mrs Hamo Thornycroft. Mr Gosse had looked a little agitated, I thought, as though he wasn't addicted to giving dances – or even going to them. All the young people were in fancy dress . . . and his professorial evening clothes and gleaming spectacles suggested that he would be more authentically "at home" were he delivering a lecture on Congreve or someone like that.'

It was in 1907 that Thornycroft first wrote to Gosse about his sister's 'literary son'. The boy was not yet twenty-one; Thornycroft had become a trustee on his brother-in-law's death and Siegfried seemed likely to give up Cambridge without taking a degree. 'How the world tears us apart,' Gosse had written to Thornycroft in 1904, the year he had gone to the library of tne House of Lords. Now, from time to time, Thornycroft's literary nephew would bring them together. Gosse was continually asked for help and encouragement 'in the difficult path he has sworn to follow'. Thornycroft was worried that young Sassoon was spending too much time with 'inferior country intellects' (those fox-hunting men); he wanted Gosse to help him meet 'literary men'. Sassoon was determined to be a writer. Years before, Nellie, staying with his mother, had enjoyed what may well have been his first book, called *George the Berglerear*. The child had 'an index to his book, and a list of illustrations, and writes on one side of the paper only'. He intended to go far.

'I look for great things from you,' Gosse wrote to him as early as 1909. The year before, Sassoon had sent him an 'unactable one-act play' and a parody of Swinburne with the words 'My uncle Hamo has told me he thinks you might like to look at a thing which I have written . . .' Dreaded words, and it must have been a considerable relief to Gosse to find that his old friend's nephew did indeed have talent. By 1913 Gosse was encouraging Sassoon to send poems to Edward Marsh. In 1915 he introduced him to Robert Ross. Both were introductions of seminal importance. It was Ross, rather than Marsh or Gosse himself, who encouraged Sassoon's more satirical side, the poems most admired today. After Gosse's death, Sassoon would say how Gosse's letters to him are 'a splendid testimony of his eagerness to encourage young poets'. He said that Gosse did 'more to guide and encourage me in my poetry than anyone else I have ever known . . .' In 1933 he would write, 'I find E.G. altogether irreplaceable.'

In 1912 Gosse wrote to Sassoon: 'Yes, I am quite pleased. I see progress. But take a longer flight. Try your hand at some objective theme. You must not spend all your life among moon-beams and half-tones.' Two years later, the war gave Sassoon his powerful theme; and it is strange that in 1916 the young poet could see Gosse, at least according to Robert Graves, as a retarding influence, 'keeping me to my moons and nightingales and things'. Gosse kept in close touch with Sassoon during the war, admiring his 'fantastic deeds of Derring-do', as Graves called them, sending parcels to the front, visiting him when wounded, agonizing over his passionate outburst against the war, when everyone wanted to label him insane. ('The only trouble is you're too sane which is as great a crime as being dotty and much more difficult to deal with,' Graves wrote.)

Gosse would take Sassoon to task, but always with affection. There was only one occasion when a phrase of Sassoon's really riled Gosse. A reference to 'many a slender, sickly lord' seemed to Gosse 'a cruel and unworthy libel on the House of Lords'. Sassoon asked Thornycroft to intercede. 'Of course I meant my own preciosities of pre-war days. I wish you would tell him how sorry I am that he mistook my meaning. But it's thin ice for me, as I can't refer to his well-known liking for people in Debrett!'

Sassoon gave Robert Graves a letter of introduction to Gosse. 'They are ripping friends to have,' Graves wrote after tea at Hanover Terrace. 'We had a long and inspiring conversation,' Graves told Sassoon. 'He's an awfully nice old man.' But later Gosse would be partly the cause of a breach in the friendship between Graves and Sassoon. Graves would come to consider Gosse 'a vain snobbish old man'; 'I was polite to Gosse for too long,' he wrote in 1930. He had found Gosse 'backbiting me, to strangers, in his usual grotesque way'. He had been glad enough of Gosse's praise of *Goliath and David*, his second book, published when he was twenty-one. 'It is not often that one of the great ones of the senior generation,' he wrote, 'will stoop to pat so unclassical and irresponsible a junior on the head.'

Sassoon was always loyal to Gosse. In the bitter exchange of letters which marked the end of their friendship, Graves uses the ultimate gibe: 'Be a Sir Edmund Gosse, if you must; you'll be a good one.' Sassoon responds: 'I shall be glad to become a Gosse, if it means preserving vitality and enthusiasm and hatred of humbug until I am seventy-nine (with a little pardonable – self-defensive – vanity added).' Gosse always remained loyal to Sassoon, too, even when his protégé claimed to be the first to use 'syphilitic' in a poem and became literary editor of the *Daily Herald* in a bright red tie.

In 1917 Gosse wrote an article in the *Edinburgh Review* about 'Some Soldier Poets'. He started with a tribute to Edward Marsh and his *Georgian Poetry*, which had given coherence and organization to a revival of interest in the art of poetry in the two years before the war. Reviewing the first *Georgian Poetry* at the time, Gosse had observed 'a rawness in the approach to life itself'. He would later suggest the Georgians were 'so determined to be simple that they succeed in being silly'. He would wish them 'to quit addressing poetry to lambs and donkeys and badgers' and would complain to Blunden that they were 'satisfied to appear in public with their slippers on their feet and their braces hanging down their flanks'. But, in kindlier mood, he saw the best Georgians as jewellers whereas the great Victorians were sculptors. (Sculpture, Gosse often suggested, inspired by Thornycroft, was the noblest of all the arts.)

The 'Soldier Poets' were not jewellers, of course. They were writing about 'their actual experiences and their authentic emotions'. After warning against the current tendency, two years after his death, to turn Rupert Brooke into a plaster saint and praising him for what he really was, Gosse wrote of Julian Grenfell, Maurice Baring, Robert Nichols, Robert Graves, and then of Sassoon, and the 'note of bitter anger which differentiates him from his fellows'. Gosse evidently knew nothing of Sassoon's new friend Wilfred Owen. Of Sassoon he wrote: 'His temper is not altogether to be applauded, for such sentiments must tend to relax the effort of the struggle, yet they can hardly be reproved when conducted with so much honesty and courage.'

Graves wrote to Gosse: 'I have read your *Edinburgh Review* article with great delight, and found your judgements the soundest of any I have yet seen delivered on my friends' work. I am especially pleased at your recognition of Bob Nichols' genius . . . About my animal spirits: I am glad you have seen how anxious I am to be cheerful . . . "even in the cannon's mouth" . . . I suffer all that S.S. suffers, or nearly all, only I'm hiding it till after the war: now I have to laugh and make merry, however much it hurts.' To Sassoon, Graves wrote: 'Old Gosse has given us a good puff . . . but he's a bit sick with you evidently. *Georgian Poetry 1916–1917* is dedicated to him – he's very bucked about that.'

Gosse recorded that Robert Nichols also had no military enthusiasm, no aspiration after *gloire*. Gosse, for all the anxiety and the horror, could not avoid a strange enthusiasm for the excitements of the hour: the amazing air-raids, thirty-three airships in the sky at one time high over Hanover Terrace or a blazing Zeppelin 'descending like a huge crimson lamp'. The war had so affected their cat, Gosse told John Drinkwater, 'that he spends the whole day in a hay-lined box; he has trained the servants to bring all his meals to his bedside. What an ideal life!' But he did not mean it. Nothing would persuade Gosse himself to retreat into comfortable idleness.

Early on, his war work consisted mainly of his chairmanship of the Red Cross Committee to raise funds, in conjunction with Christie's, by the sale of books, manuscripts and autographs. Hardy was on the committee too, but admitted to going rarely to the scene of his supposed labours. He once wrote to Gosse saying that he pictured 'the unpacking of those 2400 packages by other hands than mine with comparative calm'. Gosse wrote that 'Mrs Hardy's gifts of your MSS are much admired'; but a great deal of the stuff they were sent seemed to be what ladies 'could not bribe the Dustmen to take away'.

There had also been a good deal of 'propaganda', articles encouraging the war effort in one way or another, some aimed at America. And like the Hardys, the Gosses were doing their bit. 'I hope you are economising,' Hardy wrote. 'We put on our coals as it were with sugar tongs, drink cider only in wine glasses and send out ancient shoes to be mended instead of buying new ones.' It was all very tedious. But in November 1915 Gosse was offered the chance of a closer participation. He was invited to France as a guest of the French government to record some observations which would encourage Anglo-French solidarity. Lord Redesdale saw the invitation as a supreme compliment: 'It was right that it should have been given to you who have had and shown so great a sympathy with French genius.' Gosse had been asked to 'paint a true portrait of the French army and its achievements'. He accepted with 'a good deal of hesitation on account of age and breath'. He really felt that to write 'that kind of thing requires the training of a military journalist'. But he wrote to Edward Marsh, 'I am embarking on a certain adventure, no doubt to be the latest in my faded career. It frightens and yet exhilarates me.' The adventure finally came off in September 1916. Lord Newton, writing to Gosse about a visit *he* had made, said: 'It rather reminds me of a race meeting. You have luncheon and then go out to see the fighting and talk about a "good" or a "bad" day, as if it were Ascot.' Certainly the war Gosse saw bore no resemblance to the war Sassoon was writing about.

On 21st September 1916, his sixty-seventh birthday, Gosse wrote to his wife:

> I have had one of the most wonderful days of my life . . . I was received by the Cardinal Archbishop of Reims (such a glorious old man!) . . . I saw *everything*. The Government had given orders that I was to be taken everywhere. After examining the noble and melancholy ruins – which surpass all imagination – we were driven to Cernay, the outpost of the army, and were taken walking along miles of trenches, and saw just below us the village, with the lines of the Germans *between the village and us*, not a third of a mile away. And while we were at the very outside of all, looking through the observation hole, the Germans suddenly began firing, and the French replied, and it went on for a little while. I have had the intoxicating pleasure of being under fire!
>
> I can write no more but I shall have an infinity to tell you. The kindness and hospitality of the French to me is incredible . . . On Saturday I lunch with the Prime Minister and dine with the French Academy. The dream of my life has come true at last.
>
> What a birthday this has been.

A yellowing cutting with this letter talks of dining with the French Academy being 'the rarest of honours . . . not known to have been offered before to an Englishman', and of Gosse's visit 'binding our two nations together'. He saw Gide twice in Paris; Gide recorded: 'Il commence à se retenir au moment où il commencerait à me plaire.' Gosse noted in his diary the 'indescribable exaltation of spirits' he had referred to in his letter to Nellie. This strange effect of being under fire must have been tied up with the usual feelings of guilt and impotence experienced by those too old to fight in what they feel is a just war, what Gosse described in his *Times* poem as 'the shame of growing old'. To be under fire, even for a moment, made him feel he was sharing in the danger and in the possibility of sacrifice.

But the race-meeting atmosphere was never far away. On arriving in Paris, he had found a card from the Prime Minister making him a member of the Automobile Club for the duration of his stay. Going home, he found the Duchess of Marlborough and Lady Harcourt were both in the train from Paris to Le Havre. At Le Havre they had a 'picnic lunch in a lighthouse'. There were 'wonderful views', Gosse commented.

Henry James, through these years, continued to make his occasional comments to W. E. Norris on his view of Gosse. In 1911 he was struck 'as ever with his having in these years the time of his life and of it going not a little to his head, but of his *meaning* well to all men too (as by the rosiness of his felicity) so far as the levity of that organ permit of straight sequences'. He wrote to Norris on Christmas Eve and again a few days later when he reported on his dinner that night at Hanover Terrace:

> It was very pleasant and peaceful. I came away without a scar from a perfectly bloodless field. He is the rarest person for 'being himself', striking punctually his own very hour, however, and the mixture in him of ability (that is activity) and levity is quite indescribable. The levity is as incurable as the activity is irrepressible and his very virtues are like tricks and pranks, though I'm not sure the latter are always like virtues. His great present prosperity goes much to his head, I am told, socially speaking – by which I mean goes exorbitantly to his tongue and yet there is something in him which keeps that apparently from doing him the last injury. May he come through – for his retirement is more or less within sight – without accident befalling. Your remarks about him are of a perfect justice – he dances the tight-rope (and across Niagara) under a special Providence. His levity, really, most *generally* saves him.

The following Christmas, the one where James met André Gide at the Gosses' dinner table, he regretted Gosse's putting an 'oh so quite tragically mistimed and irrelevant tissuepaper cap' upon his helpless head. 'But he is the inimitable and only –!'

Gosse had been keen to crown Henry James with more than a paper hat. In 1911 he told Edith Wharton that he had begun 'to think seriously about the Nobel Prize for Henry James'. Gosse had been on the English Committee of the Prize for years but had become disheartened by the way the Swedish Committee had never taken any notice of its recommendations. 'We were unanimous, year after year, for Swinburne but the prize was never given to him.' Gosse felt James would have most chance as an American candidate – America had not yet received the Nobel Prize for Literature. Gosse would bring his own efforts to bear privately as much as he could. He wrote to Per Hallström, a member of the Swedish Academy: 'With the sole exception of Thomas Hardy, he is doubtless the most eminent living writer of the English language.' The English Committee was 'foolishly pledged to Morley (who most certainly will not get it)'. Howells wrote to tell Gosse he was 'truly sweet' to take up James's cause so generously. 'It is such a good cause I feel it *must* fail.' And of course it *did* fail. The prize went to Maurice Maeterlinck.

In October 1912 James asked Gosse if he would guarantee his respectability to the landlords of the flat he had taken in Carlyle Mansions. Gosse replied:

> Let me say how flattered I am that you should have pointed me out to your blundering landlords as the very beacon of respectability . . . But what kind of asses must they be who ask *you* for any proof of quality. They shall go down to posterity with the bailiff who asked Miss Wordsworth whether it was true that her aged Father wrote verses? And with the young lady who exclaimed 'What *are* Keats?' They must be men of evil lives; and irresistibly the question surges up 'Can they themselves be respectable?'

On 15th April 1913 James celebrated his seventieth birthday and Gosse was one of his English friends who were determined to mark the occasion in some appropriate way. James was presented with a 'Golden Bowl' – a silver-gilt Charles II porringer; there was also to be a Sargent portrait and a bust by a young sculptor. The following day, Gosse wrote to Nellie that James 'was in a state of beatitude. You could almost see a purple light of love exuding from him.' It had been 'an exquisite incident . . . most beautiful and flawless,' James wrote to Gosse. The memory of it undoubtedly helped James, when war came, to feel that he wanted to be English. In June 1915 Gosse would be the first person, apart from his solicitor, to whom he told his intention. And yet, just two months before he had, apparently, betrayed Gosse to Arthur Benson over lunch at the Athenaeum. Benson was angry with Gosse that day. There had been a sad betrayal too by Father C. J. Martindale SJ, who had sent on to Benson a letter from Gosse declining to take part in a tribute to Hugh Benson, Arthur's younger brother, who had just died. It was not a letter meant for Arthur's eyes. Benson had the letter with him; he showed it to James, encouraging him to agree that the letter was loathsome. 'He ate a plentiful meal of veal and pudding but he spoke to me very gravely of his physical condition and his chronic angina.' Over the coffee James agreed, according to Benson, in lamenting 'G.'s grotesque theory of intimacy, his intolerable levity, his application of flippancy to all relations, his dreadful juvenility.' It soothed Benson to record James murmuring about feeling Gosse's 'soil to be incurably shallow', and his final exclamation: 'And yet the tragedy of it is that he cares – he cares – there is a strange, petulant claim for affection, for what he realizes as affection, running through it all.'

That James did feel that affection Gosse needed from him is surely shown by his letter to Gosse on 25th June 1915: 'The force of the public situation now at last determines me to testify to my attachment to this country, my fond domicile for nearly 40 years . . . by applying for naturalization here . . . You are the first person save my solicitor . . . to whom the fact has been imparted.' James had to obtain references from four honourable householders, again that he was respectable, that he spoke and wrote English decently, and so on. 'Will you give me the great pleasure of being one of them,' he asked Gosse, and did he think 'our admirable friend the Prime Minister would perhaps be approachable by me as another of the signatory four?' 'Don't hesitate to ask him,' Gosse said. He was delighted about the whole thing. Later he told James how 'romantically pleased' Asquith was 'to be in it'. And so of course was Gosse. But before the year's end, he had seen James for the last time. On 27th February 1916, after nearly three months of dying, James died. In *The Times*, a few days later, Gosse wrote of his 'noble and tender heart' and of his passionate love for England. It was a note that would cause some resentment in James's relations – his sister-in-law and his niece – who would gaze, so Gosse told Edith Wharton, with 'no warmth of feeling' on the box in which Gosse kept James's 'more than 400 precious letters'. Certainly there was some feeling that they did not want Gosse to edit the collected letters; that was something he had to accept. The death itself was perhaps easier to accept; the death in wartime of a man, full of years and achievement, is not so hard. 'I always adored him,' Gosse wrote to Marsh. 'But now that he is gone, he seems to me almost supernatural in the beauty of his sympathy and intelligence.' One must be glad he knew nothing of the remarks James made to Benson.

Gosse, though so fond of the famous, yet had longings for the approval of the young who still had their way to make in the world. He had told Benson how much he envied him, in his position as Master of Magdalene, his regular contact with the clever young. In the war years, he made a deliberate effort to encourage the young poets. Like Graves and perhaps for the same reasons, Gosse was bowled over by Robert Nichols. (Graves after reading Gosse's *Life of Swinburne* would say Swinburne was a 'curious cyclone of a man . . . exactly like Robert Nichols'.) Commenting on Gosse's piece in the *Edinburgh Review*, Nichols says with what discernment Gosse uses the phrase 'mournful passion' – 'the very words I should most have liked to find applied to my work! That was what I strove for.'

In a letter to Drinkwater at this time Gosse said it would not surprise him if Nichols went mad. Later he would describe him as 'distractingly violent, mercurial and excessive, but most attractive in his flaming zeal and pale vehemence'. But there seemed to be new poets springing up on every side. 'I shudder at the sight of the slender and elegant volumes of verses, all so clever and all so alike and all so empty,' he wrote to Drinkwater, and to Mrs Henniker: 'The bulk of it crushes one's judgement.' All the same, he had high hopes of Nichols. He behaved the way Gosse had always expected poets to behave. Graves encouraged Nichols to 'write to Gosse or call on him *very politely*' to try and get Gosse to help in arranging a lecture tour for him in America. 'He should be able to work it.' Osbert Sitwell said he had once heard Gosse mention Nichols in the same breath as Keats and Shelley. But in July 1919 he wrote to him: 'I am afraid that flattery and excitement and the silly criticism of an adoring circle of admirers have completely turned you, for the time being, out of the true path . . . Be very careful, for you are on the brink of poetical bankruptcy.'

But that was not the end of their relationship. Later Nichols went to teach in Japan and told Gosse about one result of the disastrous 1923 earthquake in Tokyo: damage to the Library of the Imperial University. Gosse made a large contribution to the restoration. Years later, Graves would say of Nichols: 'I like him but he is too much of an embarrassment to have about.' Aldous Huxley found him an embarrassment even then. He 'raved and screamed and hooted his filthy war poems like a Lyceum villain who hasn't learned how to act'. This was at the famous poetry reading in Sybil Colefax's drawing-room on 12th December 1917 – 'famous' because poetry readings were rare in those days, and this one has been much described.

Nichols wrote to Robert Ross on November 18th, discussing the arrangements: 'All this makes me nervous as we shall dish our applecart as well as upsetting Mrs Colefax's star-climbing wagon, and Gosse into the bargain, if we ain't well organised . . . I don't think we ought to take very long each . . . besides Edmund the Ever Ready is to hold forth, isn't he? He does us a power of good – he ought to get a gallop.'

On November 20th, Gosse wrote to Marsh:

I have been dragged into promising to preside at a reading of poets
got up by Mrs Coalbox and Madam Fan-the-Devil, who would talk
any human being into anything. I don't know what I have let myself
in for, but at all events some sound 'Georgians' will be represented –
Nichols, Graves, Sassoon. But the protagonists are Edith and
Osbert Sitwell, of whom I know nothing. I pray Apollo that they be
not pacifists. I told the two fiery ladies that I would leave the house,
not to say the chair, if the names of Alfred Douglas or Ezra Pound
are mentioned, but they swear their poets are perfectly respectable.
(I nearly wrote 'respectful'; I am sure they are not that!)

'What shoals of poets there are!' Gosse wrote to Drinkwater on
November 27th. He had just met the Sitwells for the first time. 'Have
you ever heard of the Sitwells? There are three of them, a sister, and
two brothers. Impossible to think of a greater contrast than with
Nichols; the Sitwells are alert, rather elegant, with beautiful manners
and a formidable reserve of humour. But whether really gifted or not,
I do not know. Of Nichols' gifts no doubt is possible.' He worried
where poetry was going: 'The simple, poignant things seemed all to
have been said', as he had put it in an address to the English Association, of which he would become President in 1921. Sassoon recorded
in his Diary in 1922 that Gosse came to think the Sitwells 'an excellent
joke', while admiring 'Edith's originality and distinction'.

In the event neither Sassoon nor Graves was able to turn up and
Gosse was lucky if the name of Pound was not mentioned, for Eliot
was one of the number who had been invited to read. Osbert Sitwell
records that Eliot turned up a little late. The starting hour was five and
Gosse was brooking no delays, for he had a dinner engagement at
eight and intended 'to decamp at 6.15 whatever is happening at the
moment'. Eliot had come straight from Lloyds Bank and found himself publicly rebuked by the Chairman, but he 'showed no trace of
annoyance at being reproved', certainly nothing to justify Gosse's
later attitude to Eliot which Sassoon would record in his diary; he
thought him in 1922 a 'conceited literary humbug'. Aldous Huxley,
who also read, thought that he and Eliot 'were the only people who
had any dignity'. 'The Shufflebottoms [i.e. the Sitwells] were respectable but terribly nervous.' Osbert himself thought Gosse was nervous, for 'though an excellent chairman, he would glance with plain
exasperation if anything went wrong'. Huxley thought Gosse 'the
bloodiest little old man I have ever seen' and resented Nichols

'thrusting himself to the fore as the leader of us young bards – (*bards* was the sort of thing Gosse called us)'.

Nichols, whose ranting went down better with the fashionable audience than it did with Huxley, further endeared himself to Gosse by reciting one of Gosse's own poems. Gosse himself read for the absent Graves, who was tied up as 'commander of a detachment of five hundred Fusiliers'. But four days later, he told Gosse eventually, 'I never confessed that on December 16, 1917, I came to call on you with Nancy; but becoming engaged almost on your doorstep we lost our heads and drifted past till we awoke with a start somewhere in Holborn. Nancy sends a belated apology for leading me astray.' They invited Gosse to their wedding but he did not go.

Gosse continued to publish books regularly, as he would do for the rest of his life: the great majority of them were collections of essays which had first appeared in periodicals or newspapers. His account of his long-ago *Two Visits to Denmark* was particularly well received when it appeared in 1911. Moore said that Gosse had always written about books until he had pointed out that his strength lay in people. 'Mr Gosse's interest is in humanity . . .' *The Times* said. 'A dairymaid is more to him than a dairy, a socialist more than socialism.' His awareness of the weaknesses and frailties of his subjects as well as their strengths makes *Portraits and Sketches* (1912) seem curiously modern.

During the war he was preoccupied with France. The *Boston Transcript*, reviewing *Inter Arma*, said the book emphasizes 'the practical service that may be given to his country and to the world in time of war by a man of letters'. *Inter Arma* sold out in June 1916 and there was no paper for a second edition. Haldane wrote enthusiastically about *Three French Moralists* (1918): 'You are really contributing greatly to bringing the two nations into mutual understanding. It is a fine bit of public work.' The *New Statesman* on 6th July 1918 confirmed Haldane's opinion, and also confirmed Gosse's generally high standing at this period in many people's minds:

Mr Gosse is a figure almost unique in English literature. He is the nearest approach we have ever made to a writer comparable with the great French succession of accomplished and scholarly essayists and critics, Sainte-Beuve, Lemaître, Brunetière, and the Anatole France of *La Vie littéraire* . . . He has not only expounded French literature to the English and so, in a quite perceptible degree, prepared and strengthened the relations between the two peoples. He has also helped to naturalise and establish in England the tradition of ease, charm and urbanity in the criticism of letters which is peculiarly French.

In pursuing this amiable mission he has achieved a standing in which it is really almost impossible for him any longer to do anything wrong. He has written so large a number of books, presenting so many agreeable qualities, that their virtues accumulate in the mind while their faults disappear; and one turns to a new volume with a full expectation of being charmed once again.

But before Gosse published these essays in volume form, his last major book appeared – *The Life of Algernon Charles Swinburne*, which he had been working on in some sense since before Swinburne's death in 1909. Gosse's innocent association with the forger, T. J. Wise, examined in Chapter 14, had continued through these years. Wise had been printing a steady stream of pamphlets of previously unpublished bits and pieces likely to appeal to collectors, for which Gosse often wrote introductions. 'For my trouble in editing and deciphering these MSS, I am paid one copy of each pamphlet.'. He re-affirmed over the years: 'I assure you there must be no suggestion of payment. The whole point of these little introductions is that they are voluntary.'

With Swinburne's death, an enormous amount of material became available. The situation is described by Nicolas Barker:

Theodore Watts-Dunton (aged seventy-seven) had been left almost the entire estate, including the contents of the house, and a great clearing-up began. Wise bullied, bamboozled, nagged and bribed his way into Watts-Dunton's ménage, and bought the lion's share of the Swinburne manuscripts direct from their home. He was not without competitors: he had various tricky members of both Swinburne's and Watts-Dunton's families to contend with, yet he carried the affair off brilliantly. From the manuscripts thus obtained, he printed 16 pamphlets in 1909, 13 in 1910 . . . a total of some 70, all from unpublished Swinburne letters or manuscripts. Theodore Watts-Dunton was by no means a fool and had been trained as a lawyer, but Wise did him down in the grand style.

His coup de maître was to get Gosse to edit the manuscripts, though the relationship between Gosse and Watts-Dunton (and between Gosse and the Swinburne family) was never at all cordial. The Wise-Gosse letters give a vivid picture of this bustling activity: buying from and bullying Theodore; rushing the resultant manuscripts off to Gosse for their literary explanation and gloss; choking off rival suitors; testing the market with trial series of 'limited editions' based on the manuscripts; always, Wise himself reaping a rich financial reward. It is a most impressive performance and it enabled Wise to exert a pernicious stranglehold on Swinburne studies which lasted for many years, since he made sure to buy copyrights as well as physical manuscripts . . . In the end, Wise and Gosse edited the standard collected edition of Swinburne – the Bonchurch edition, 1925–1927.

It is, in fact, not true that Gosse and Watts-Dunton had never been on cordial terms. Their relationship had been a friendly one in the days before he had taken Swinburne to the Pines. It was only gradually, when Gosse began to fear that Watts-Dunton had prejudiced Swinburne against him, that Gosse began to dislike him. 'If all the letters *to* me had been lost, Watts-Dunton would deny that Swinburne ever had any friendship or intimacy with me,' Gosse suggested. It was perhaps the feeling that Swinburne was afraid of Watts-Dunton, as well as the certainty that his sobriety had been at the cost of both his poetry and his essential character, that turned Gosse against Watts-Dunton. Gosse was also convinced, as he told Osbert Sitwell, that Watts-Dunton and Swinburne had made identical wills, each leaving everything to the other, though Swinburne had money and Watts-Dunton none. After Swinburne's death, Gosse took every opportunity to point out Watts-Dunton's frailties to Wise. Dating a poem convincingly as belonging to 1867, he said Watts-Dunton thinking it 'early' was 'but another example of his ignorance of Swinburne's mental history'. 'There are few who know how harshly he was treated,' Gosse wrote to Theodore Wratislaw in 1917.

It was when he became aware that Watts-Dunton was blackening Gosse's character to the Swinburne family that Gosse began to hate him and that he and Wise began to refer to the old man as Toad, Asp, Reptile and the old Philistine. 'What a dreadful old man,' George Moore wrote to Gosse – 'all composed of envy and egotism and jealousy! How did he ever continue to attract and retain the affection of a great poet?' After Swinburne's death, it infuriated Gosse the way Watts-Dunton immediately began to profit by his inheritance of the papers. 'This lining of the hole of the Asp with five-pound notes makes me sick,' he wrote to Wise. In October 1909 he wrote again: 'I only hope that you will succeed, some day, in wiping the slime of T. W-D off the pure marble of Swinburne's memory. You are surely going to prevent that he should go down to posterity as the Hero-Friend.'

It suited Wise much better to keep on good terms with Watts-Dunton and in public Gosse also was polite. In his article on Swinburne in the *Dictionary of National Biography* in 1912, Gosse referred to

Watts-Dunton as the poet's 'devoted companion'. But this article caused problems all the same. Wise had happened to notice some poems in old copies of *Fraser's Magazine* above the initials A.C.S. The earliest was dated 1849, when Swinburne was just eleven. Gosse was hesitant about Wise's attribution: 'I am unable to guess what induces you to attribute them to Swinburne.' But he overcame his doubts and included in the original version of his *DNB* article the rash words: 'He was, in fact, now writing verses, some of which his mother sent to *Fraser's Magazine* . . . but of this "false start" he was afterwards not pleased to be reminded.' Wise printed the poems in a pamphlet: *Juvenilia* by Algernon Charles Swinburne.

But the poems unfortunately were not written by Swinburne. The feeble verses turned out to be the work of one Anthony Coningham-Sterling, KCB. Swinburne's sister Isabel was furious with Gosse – and Gosse wondered in a letter to Nellie whether Watts-Dunton was behind the fuss. A few days later he said 'Wise is off today to tell Watts-Dunton he must stop the conspiracy. But that is the last thing he will consent to do. It has upset me a good deal.' Isabel Swinburne eventually turned against Watts-Dunton for beginning 'the £.s.d. part of his dead friend's business before he was cold in his grave'. But she was never reconciled to Gosse. And her opposition and that of Swinburne's cousin, Mrs Disney Leith, made Gosse's work as Swinburne's biographer peculiarly difficult.

At first he did not really intend to write a full-scale life. His *DNB* entry was privately printed by the Chiswick Press in an edition of fifty copies. He wrote to Henry James on 11th October 1912:

> You crush me by the wit of your comparing my little Swinburne thing to a pincushion! But, remember, that a pincushion was all I was asked, or allowed, to make. And I modestly venture to think you would not be so sarcastic if you realized that the work had absolutely to be done from the egg, that no memoirs of Swinburne exist, and that this had to be built up with an infinitude of labour out of all sorts of material. But if you will be patient, I may yet give you a portrait of the creature not entirely inadequate.

In 1911 he had told Sidney Lee, editor of the *Dictionary*, that he had read hundreds of letters and cross-examined everyone he could think of and was in a condition to write 'a fat biography in 2 vols 8vo', but would soon forget it all. It had given him more trouble than anything he had ever written. He warned Lee that 'in the present particularly delicate case' no alterations should be made without his consent. Eventually the reference to Swinburne's juvenilia was expunged, but the damage to Gosse's reputation was again considerable. Churton Collins's attack was recalled; Gosse's notorious carelessness was again common gossip. And although Gosse's biography would eventually be attacked for its discretion, the *DNB* entry, in which Gosse had chosen his words with such care, was attacked for its scandalous suggestions. In the *Daily News* of 15th April 1913, James Douglas wrote: Gosse 'alone can strew the thorns of candour with one hand and the roses of devotion with the other. He alone can put his friend on a hook as if he loved him . . . The critic who stated that the poet was not pleased to be reminded of verses which he never wrote cannot be accepted as trustworthy in regard to other, far more injurious, insinuations.' Douglas had another go at Gosse eleven days later in *London Opinion*: 'There in cold print,' he declared, 'were things that even the Yellow Press would have hesitated to publish . . . How can Sir Sidney Lee justify the publication . . . of an unsavoury chronicle of unverified scandal.'

Douglas had certainly been reading between the lines. There were, of course, worse things that Gosse could have said. Isabel Swinburne had brought the article into the public eye by denunciatory letters in *The Times*. She went so far as to deny that Gosse had ever communicated with her, though a letter he quoted from in the entry was certainly in his possession. 'It has been the most violent storm in a tea-cup I recollect,' Gosse wrote to his wife. He wrote to Wise that he had just heard from Colonel Prideaux who says 'of our revered Isabel, "She reminds me of the malevolent old women in the Arabian Nights, who try to blind you by hurling a melon-pip in your eye!"' For two nights it destroyed Gosse's sleep. 'I feel the thing extremely,' he confessed.

The whole business discouraged him from continuing to work on Swinburne's life in 1913, though he had had his own copy of the Chiswick Press pamphlet interleaved 'with a view to constant correction and addition . . . It is meant as a sort of stock on which to graft exact biographical information.' He had been asked by Macmillan to do Swinburne for the English Men of Letters series but in April 1914 he decided he could not go on with it, 'or at least that I cannot publish it until some of these difficulties are removed . . .' 'The attitude of Watts-Dunton is perfectly comprehensible . . . He wants of course to defend his own position, and he cannot be blamed for that. On the other hand, the attitude of Miss Isabel Swinburne suggests to me that her mind is unbalanced.' He said he would put away what he had written already, together with all the notes and letters. 'They may be useful to some future biographer of Swinburne when *all* of us have passed away.'

477

As it happened, both Watts-Dunton and Isabel Swinburne 'passed away' very soon after this was written: Watts-Dunton in June 1914, Miss Swinburne in November 1915. But there was still Mrs Disney Leith, the beloved cousin of Swinburne's childhood, who saw herself as the original of his Dolores and could not bear Gosse's suggestion that Adah Menken was his inspiration. 'Algernon was far too well-bred a gentleman ever to *speak* to a woman of that class!' she told Lord Redesdale, who told Gosse with some amusement. They had, after all, both seen the photographs of Swinburne and Menken together.

Gosse decided to go ahead, even before Miss Swinburne's death. In January 1915 he told Wise that he had 'flung himself, head over heels, into Swinburne', but that he was 'carefully concealing . . . the nature of his peculiar moral aberration'. He was advising Wise, who was still busily producing Swinburne pamphlets, that they should 'try to prevent the world from ever knowing what a pig he sometimes was'. He was also groaning at the sheer quantity of material: 'It is terrible news that Miss Watts has "thousands of letters"! I wish they could be burned in one great heap. The world is infinitely too full of such documents.' It was hardly the view of a conscientious biographer.

Macmillans agreed to set the book up in type in July 1915, with the understanding that they were not expected to publish it until after the war. In fact, it was eventually published on 3rd April 1917. Gosse was at Sandbanks in Dorset with Heinemann when it came out. He wrote to Haldane: 'I have no pleasure in the thought or hope of success. In these dreadful times – growing more dreadful every day – who is going to give a thought to Swinburne? I am dreadfully upset at the destruction of St Quentin . . .'

He wrote to Robbie Ross: 'Bringing out a book involves pain like that of bearing a child. However this is the last that I shall ever publish.' There would, in fact, be numerous pamphlets and no fewer than seven collections of essays in the remaining years, but this was indeed Gosse's last original book. The first edition of 1500 copies was sold out within a few days; it was reprinted the same month. There was an 'admirable' review in the *Times Literary Supplement* ('the truth is even better than the dreams,' Gosse commented) and a 'simply magnificent' one in the *Telegraph*. A. E. Housman wrote, pointing out a few minor errors, but saying how much he had enjoyed the book: 'It is a great comfort to have it done by someone who knows chalk from cheese.'

But the general feeling, both in England and America, was of disappointment. In the *New Statesman*, Desmond MacCarthy said that the book was 'as easy to read as it is to drink when one is thirsty', but the failure came from Gosse's heeding the 'voice of that old Dame, Discretion, to whose warnings Mr Gosse in writing *Father and Son* was so fortunately deaf'. The American reviewers also spoke of Gosse's Victorian squeamishness. In *Poetry* (Chicago) there was a violent attack from Ezra Pound, who obviously pitied Swinburne for having been born into a world of Gosses. 'Gosse has written one excellent book, *Father and Son*,' Pound wrote, and he paid tribute obliquely to his having helped Joyce in 1915, but went on:

> Apart from that he resembles many literary figures of about his age and generation, who coming after the more or less drunken and more or less obstreperous real Victorians, acquired only the cant and fustiness. . . . We do not however wish a Swinburne coated with a veneer of British officialdom and decked out for a psalm-singing audience.
>
> Gosse in the safety of his annual pension of £666, 16 shillings, 8 pence, has little to fear from the slings of fortune or from the criticisms of younger men. If he preferred to present Swinburne as an epileptic rather than as an intemperate drinker, we can only attribute this to his taste, a taste for kowtowing.

Pound seems to forget, if he had ever known, that Gosse was himself one of the 'Bohemians' from whom Watts-Dunton had sought to separate Swinburne. In describing Gosse's *Life* as 'merely the attempt of a silly and pompous old man to present a man of genius', Pound had very little idea of the real problems.

Gosse wrote to Dobson, with understandable exasperation: 'The reviews of the American edition of my *Life of Swinburne* are now pouring in; and there is not one which would not disgrace an English provincial newspaper! Such ignorance, such absence of literary feeling, such vulgarity! It is really very serious for the Americans to possess such a contemptible press. Praise and blame alike, what they say is as worthless as the blame or praise of a boy scout would be. It surely was not so 30 years ago when we had so much to do with the U.S.A., you and I?'

But Benson in England was similarly disappointed, remembering the stories about Swinburne he had so often heard Gosse tell in the years when they were friends.

> I thought Swinburne . . . exactly the right subject for G. – but nothing comes of it at all. Swinburne becomes a gifted invalid, romantic and dignified . . . It is the life of a fearless and ebullient little man, written by a man in an armchair who is afraid of everyone and everything – the shadow of fear lies over the whole book – fear of critics, fear of relations, fear of readers, fear of press-cuttings.

The result is that S. is buried – and buried by the only man who might have made him live . . .

Gosse himself was disappointed. He declared dramatically when he discovered the book was not selected as one of 'The Books of the Year': 'My life . . . has been a failure.' He wrote to Maurice Baring soon after publication:

> I suffered from a number of severe disadvantages. 1. The extraordinary hostility of the family. 2. The embargo laid on any mention of drunkenness. 3. A still heavier sexual embargo. 4. The weight of the Watts-Dunton legend, which I had to break down without seeming to do so. 5. The fact that I was obliged to keep the Correspondence for another publication. I think no biographer ever had more to contend against. If I could, I would withdraw the whole book, and rewrite it from beginning to end. I ought to have been more daring, less reserved; but if you knew the difficulties you would see how cramped I was – particularly until the deaths of Watts-Dunton and of Isabel Swinburne.
>
> But I think the numerous other publications, – the 'Posthumous Poems,' the 'Letters,' the 'Triameron,' etc will give me opportunities to complete the picture.

There was one other way in which he could complete the picture. In 1920 Gosse lodged in the British Museum the *Confidential Papers*, which supplemented his biography. He said he was not moved by the 'mere curiosity' of any of the readers of his book, but by 'the censure of certain friends, expressed in private' which persuaded him he had a duty to posterity to tell the whole truth. Swinburne's 'moral irregularities' – his taste for flagellation and his alcoholism – 'existed, as it were, outside his morality'.

Gosse explains in this paper the pressures put on him by the family to disguise the truth. Mrs Disney Leith declared to Gosse that Swinburne 'was never intoxicated in all his life'. Not only would the family not help Gosse, they told him that if he published anything 'unpleasant', they would denounce the book as 'a pack of falsehoods' – an unenviable position for any biographer, and most of all for one with Gosse's reputation for inaccuracy. Gosse consulted a number of friends (Wise, Lord Redesdale, Lord Houghton); they all advised him to write nothing that would give the family the chance to carry out the threat.

The *Confidential Papers*, on which I drew in Chapter 6 of this book, were circulated to a number of Gosse's friends, including Beerbohm,

Housman and William Rossetti. Housman was particularly fascinated but Beerbohm thought 'how dreary and ghastly and disgusting the whole thing becomes. Why should anyone in posterity *know* that Swinburne did these things?' The general opinion, however, among the very few who were in the secret, was that Gosse had done the right thing.

18

Stifled in Roses

EDMUND GOSSE CELEBRATED his sixty-eighth birthday on holiday in Wales with Nellie. The Gosses always had 'birthday tables' – a collection of small presents. On 21st September 1917 Gosse's table was laid with:

i. 1 packet (large) marked 'Hughson's Soap Powder' for the bath.
ii. 2 packets Patience cards
iii. 3 boxes matches
iv. 6 India rubber bands
v. 1 writing pad
vi. A few peppermint creams
vii. Some sweet peas
And all the post that came.

There was one reason to be particularly cheerful. Philip was out of the European battlefield and would soon be on his way to India. 'How much we are all affected by our own affairs,' Gosse once truly said. With Philip no longer in such daily danger, 1918 became easier to bear, though in May Gosse felt 'Peace or any end to the war seems more remote than ever.' At last it came. Nellie – always enterprising, as Gosse said – struggled down to Buckingham Palace and saw the King and Queen receive the crowd, while Gosse himself went more comfortably to the House of Lords to hear the terms of the Armistice. Early in December he had severe bronchitis and wrote to Philip: 'It is funny that *I* should have the bronchitis this year which Mother usually has! I much prefer this arrangement as I am always so anxious about her, whereas in no circumstances does it ever occur to me that I shall not get well.' He had recovered sufficiently by December 21st to read both lessons at a service at All Saints, Ennismore Gardens, in memory of writers who had given their lives in the war. Hardy read the news item in *The Times* and remembered how, long before, he had himself read the lessons in his brother-in-law's Cornish church. 'I hardly thought that G. knew about such things – I mean such old-fashioned doings,' he wrote to Mrs Henniker.

The years of peace were not years of retirement for Gosse. It seems he worked harder than he had ever worked, and he had always worked hard. In March 1919, the *Daily Chronicle*, for which he had written regularly for some years, said it no longer required his services. 'I have been dismissed without a day's warning,' he told Drinkwater. 'I leave you to think how pleasant it is at my age to be treated like this.' Fitzmaurice Kelly commented: 'I suppose that they need the space for another column to the glorification of Mr Lloyd George. I am afraid that literature is less appreciated than ever. Very likely each generation thinks that.' Gosse thought the space would more likely go to Arnold Bennett, 'who, no doubt, will suit their public ten times better than I do'. But Gosse could not feel unappreciated for long.

'I was instantly snapped up,' he wrote to Evan Charteris on April 3rd, 'by the *Sunday Times*, in whose columns I make my bow next Sunday. If you choose to do so, you may commune with me in your dressing-gown, between your bloater and your sausage, at the cost – I believe – of twopence . . . I learnt a lesson in not making a contract with the *D.C.* and have bound over the *Sunday Times* to put up with me for a year, at the end of which I may probably be as tired of them as they can be of me.' In fact, the contract would be renewed over and over again; Gosse contributed his regular articles for the rest of his life, making his name an even more familiar one in households all over the country. He told J. C. Squire in July 1919 that he would have a long signed article every fortnight, and generally an unsigned one in the weeks between. 'It is quite a new experience for me, but I enjoy having a platform from which I may address a (supposititious) crowd exactly as I please.'

In 1923 Gosse was able to write to the editor, Leonard Rees, 'For nearly four years I have not missed a single Sunday in writing for the *Sunday Times*. I think this – you will agree with me? a remarkable record.' He was now seventy-three and was beginning 'to feel the strain considerably'. 'Would it interfere seriously with your arrangements if I were to be silent through the month of September? . . . If you will let me have a little respite, I shall return refreshed, and ready to work better than ever.' A new contract was drawn up which included four weeks' annual holiday. Up till then Gosse had taken holidays but had always stockpiled his articles ahead of them. He asked Rees while he was away 'to drop the rubric "The World of

Books'' altogether. I don't want anyone to occupy my pulpit!' He was disturbed when the following year the paper began to use E. V. Lucas regularly. 'It will be intensely disagreeable to me to find Lucas at every turn trying to dislodge me,' he wrote in a letter marked 'Strictly Confidential'. 'His talent for push is irresistible and you will find you have invited a very dangerous ally into your camp.' But on the whole his relations with the *Sunday Times* were extremely good, during the nine years he wrote for them, though he would be exasperated from time to time by the standard of the printing. On one occasion, he said his article was 'barely readable, with its blurred and blotted types, its broken letters, its disjointed lines'. It compared very badly, he thought, with the *Observer*. The *Observer* would try to tempt him away from the *Sunday Times* from time to time, but he remained loyal. Right at the end of his life, he wrote hesitantly to Rees (suggesting he could tear up the letter and say nothing about it, if he liked):

Of late, largely through your loyal and unfailing kindness, my 'stock' has very much risen in the market! I am pestered with offers of work, which I invariably refuse because I consider myself more than ever bound to the *S.T.* This very week a highly-reputed American magazine has – for the second time – offered me £100 an article if I will write for it . . . Don't you think Sir William Berry could afford to pay me rather more? It is a very unbecoming thing to ask anyone who has always behaved generously to me to raise my wages. But look what other people get. Arnold Bennett receives £50 each time for the tosh he contributes to the *Evening Standard* . . . If I chose to be disloyal I could double my income.

There! If I don't hear from you I shall know that nothing can be done, and I shall go on as cheerfully as ever. And be, always, whatever happens
    Your devoted
    E.G.

He had started at 8 guineas and then gone up to £10 a week, with an extra £20 each quarter day. Now his salary was raised to £800 a year.

Gosse was always a little mocking about his own influence. Early on, he wrote: 'The *Sunday Times* keeps me absorbingly busy. Rees says I cannot send him too much. It is a very wholesome occupation for me – I have not the illusion that it all has any effect. I don't think that at present anyone is influenced by printed opinions, but it is a pleasant way of spending my time.'

Other people put a higher value on his *Sunday Times* articles. Forty years before, E. C. Stedman, the American critic who had long since died, had said, 'There is no man in England whose critical opinion, all things considered, I value more . . . I do not except Matthew Arnold's.' Now those critical opinions were more widely disseminated than ever. Another American, Van Wyck Brooks, was able to write in the *New York Herald Tribune* in 1928, when the last book of pieces appeared:

> Edmund Gosse is on the verge of eighty but there is nothing in *Leaves and Fruit*, his new collection of essays, to suggest any diminution of the catholicity of mind, the alertness of intelligence, the sureness of taste that make him the most generally satisfactory of living critics. Indeed he has gained rather than lost with the advance of years.

Gosse remained faithful to the hero of his youth. In 1924 he wrote to an enquirer: 'I am the disciple of one man, and of one man only – Sainte-Beuve. No-one else has been my master.' Sainte-Beuve's method, he wrote in 1911, 'is the best which has yet been invented for the parallel examination of a literary figure, biographically and intellectually, the works illuminating the life, the life supporting and determining the works'. Raymond Mortimer, who eventually succeeded him at the *Sunday Times*, said on the centenary of Gosse's birth that if his discourses could be 'too insubstantial to be compared with the *Causeries du Lundi*, they display in miniature the same virtues – wide learning, disinterested curiosity and exquisite urbanity'.

Gosse's criticism has been dismissed by some as pleasant gossip, and of course he could gossip pleasantly. Some would suggest that he was always safe, that he praised only those 'who had been dead sufficiently long to have passed through the fire of ample posthumous criticism'. But, in fact, Gosse, as Osbert Sitwell saw, could take very strong lines on the living. He could be quite wrong, over Forster, Joyce, Eliot, but he could speak out with early courage and enthusiasm as he did for Ibsen, Hardy, Gide, Sassoon. 'His opinions were prejudiced,' Osbert Sitwell wrote, 'as I like an author's to be. His writings upon modern authors were biased and fiery, both in denunciation and praise, but he never endeavoured to play for Safety First by balancing both in the same composition.' There were always the recurrent charges of inaccuracy but, by the end of his life, the general opinion was that he had proved there were other qualities he possessed in abundance that were rather more important than accuracy. His essays may be enjoyed by some who will take the trouble to seek them out, long after the current structuralists and deconstructionists have been replaced by still newer approaches to literature.

Edmund Wilson once said, 'If we are reluctant to grant Gosse a high place in literature, it is simply because that does not seem to be precisely the kind of high place at which he himself has aimed.' This was certainly so. Gosse never made any great claims for himself. He said he had tried to see what writers were doing, that he had never rejected 'the rose because it was not a jasmine', nor indeed orchids because they were not daisies. He would claim, towards the end of his life, that he had always been 'consistent in the pursuit of what I feel to be excellence in every field of writing, without regard to prejudice or fashion'. The object of his life, he said, was not to teach or establish standards but to share with others 'the infinite pleasures which literature has afforded me'. 'We must fight in the last ditch,' he once said, 'for the aesthetic view. Beauty and entertainment, we must be bold enough to insist that these come first. And that literature is an art, and not a science.'

It was at the age of seventy, his obituaries would say, that Edmund Gosse became the most influential literary critic in England. New books would be made or broken by the power of his pen. 'At a good word from him,' Osbert Sitwell said, 'and at this time from him alone – the sales of a young author's books mounted higher.' Walter de la Mare and A. E. Housman were two poets who had particular reason to be thankful for his Sunday articles. Gosse rarely wrote about new novels. Old books he praised would gain new life. His words would be quoted everywhere. He cared nothing about popular appeal. If he wanted to write for four weeks on classical French literature, he did so, Raymond Mortimer said, 'not caring a rap about the agonies of devoted, but uninstructed readers in Newcastle or Stow-on-the-Wold'. His following was enormous. Letters poured in from friends and strangers, saying how much his articles enlivened their Sunday mornings and stayed with them during the week.

Thornycroft said how much they meant to him. 'Yours last Sunday on Max's book was quite delightful,' he wrote in December, 1920. Maurice Baring told him Hilaire Belloc had said: '"The English nation doesn't realize what it's being given" – a weekly bouquet of pearls.' Robert Lynd said, 'The miracle is not that you keep up your wonderful level, but that you make every Sunday seem better than the last.' The Regius Professor of Physics at Cambridge called him 'our Sunday friend'. Someone called Paul Faraday wrote extravagantly from Ruskin Road in Carshalton in Surrey: 'My only compensation for Sunday is the *Sunday Times*. It comes like the tabernacle into this weary desert. The very cycle boy is like a son of Levi with the tabernacle which enshrines your Article, which of course is the golden candlestick – and a light which will last when the oil lamps and the gas and the electric are no more!'

The Ranee of Sarawak wrote: 'Every Sunday its *Times* comes to me like some beautiful bird, laden with lovely messages from your pen.' Lucy Clifford, Henry James's old friend, was moved to write by a piece on Hardy's poetry: 'I think your searching Sunday morning criticisms are not only splendid but a *blessing* to the reading world. I love the old ones – for I was brought up on the old writers . . . but last Sunday you surpassed yourself. It was so understanding – I felt that you had walked beside Hardy's soul – tho', as you said, he has always been isolated. It is a fashion to say his poetry isn't good – that it's rough; and so it is, rough hewn and stark; but the real thing. You ought to be given the O.M. for that article – and . . . for all those before it that came crying into the literary wilderness of these days!'

There were many, not least Gosse himself, who felt it was time he was honoured. Haldane did his best. On 7th August 1919 he told Gosse, 'I had an hour and a half at Downing Street with Lloyd George and Bonar Law this morning . . . As they professed gratitude, I asked for a fee: – a K.C.B. for one Edmund Gosse, who had done so much. L.G. was friendly and knew something of your work and at once summoned Davies. But one cannot reckon on these people, so you must for the present take the will for the deed.' The next day he wrote, 'I wish I had some confidence in Lloyd George and his list. All I can say is that he instructed the appropriate secretary.' But it came to nothing at this point.

In the meantime there were still the rewards of friendship, though many friends had gone and many more were to go before he did. On 11th March 1919, Lady Londonderry had Gosse to dine, but she was taken ill that night and died on the 15th. Lord Haldane, sending Gosse his sympathy for the loss of 'the friendship of thirty years', commented that 'one does not at this time of life make new friendships easily'. Mountstewart still welcomed him. He sailed that Whitsun on the lough with young Lord Londonderry, as he had sailed so many times before with his mother. Mountstewart seemed more beautiful than ever with 'pyramids of scarlet rhododendrons' burning like pyres against the dark trees and the sea.

But, as early as 1912 when Andrew Lang died, Gosse had talked of the way the deaths of friends increased 'that sense of growing loneliness which invades an ageing man'. Haldane would say that their talk was becoming like exploring a cemetery, so many of their old friends were gone. Reading Lang's poems in 1923, Gosse said: 'They have rather saddened me, for they are like a bunch of flowers which seemed delightful once and now have faded and have lost their perfume. How volatile talent is – only genius lasts.' He knew he was not a genius. 'How thankful you and I ought to be,' he wrote to Edward Marsh, lamenting a little some unpredictable behaviour from Sassoon, 'How thankful you and I ought to be that we are not geniuses.' When an enthusiast called Norman Gullick began making a bibliography of Gosse's work, he wrote, 'You hold me out a plank to which I can cling a little before the waters of oblivion swallow me up.' He hoped someone might still read his poems from time to time. It was always poetry that really counted.

He was delighted when Ernest Benn included a selection of his poems in the series the Augustan Books of Modern Poetry, along with Bridges, Sassoon, Graves and Edith Sitwell. The biographical note said that his eminence 'as a critic, as well as a poet, and his services as a pioneer in the study of modern European literature are too well known to call for any note here'. The poems Gosse chose included 'The Prodigal' written long before:

> But ah! time slowly strips the vain illusion,
> And decks the fairy prince in common clothes;
> The breathless ages prove a boy's delusion,
> And naught so faithless as the Muses' oaths . . .
> Success may come, yet cropped and tame and partial,
> And joys, – but life has faded ere they come.

Certainly Gosse's success had been far beyond anything he could have imagined as a boy coming to London on the dusty velvet cushions of the train from Devon. But it was not as a poet that any would remember him, and his greatest success came in these last years – and with it, of course, failing health and the deaths of friends.

Gosse did make some new friends in these years: Sir Frederick Treves, the surgeon, with whom they holidayed at Evian-les-Bains and heard stories of the Elephant Man, and J. C. Squire, who had just started the *London Mercury*, and young Edmund Blunden, whom Sassoon would bring to lunch at Gosse's club. Treves was influential in getting Philip a job at the Radium Institute, when he returned from India, but Nellie found he made her feel extremely plain. When he died in 1923, Gosse said, 'I lose the best and warmest of friends.' In 1917 Gosse had written of Squire to Marsh, 'He hates me, I don't know why,' but in 1919, trudging home from the *New Statesman* during a general strike, Squire took one of Gosse's letters out of his pocket to cheer himself as he trudged. Gosse soon found him 'a pearl of a man', 'an awfully good fellow' and 'monstrously clever', even as he chided him for 'enjoying the Revolution' and for calling Conrad our 'greatest living novelist' when Hardy was still alive. In 1922 Gosse dedicated *Aspects and Impressions* to Squire. This was a collection of pieces *not* from the *Sunday Times*, including articles Gosse had written for Squire and his new *London Mercury*, and also the Taylorian lecture Gosse had given at Oxford in 1920. Squire had already dedicated a book of his poems to Gosse. 'You can't imagine what your friendship has been to me,' he wrote in 1922.

Before meeting Edmund Blunden, Gosse told Sassoon: 'I want very much to know him. I think he has the root of the matter in him.' After their first meeting in 1923 at the Marlborough Club, Sassoon commented on how the club atmosphere added an extra mellowness to Gosse's manner, 'like a coat of varnish to a fine old picture. It was one of E.G.'s special occasions and he made it entirely delightful.' Gosse was certainly delighted with Blunden. He wrote, 'He looked like a chinchilla, with his grey clothes, sharp nose and wonderful eyes. What eyes! Those of Keats must have had that expression.' Gosse was always inclined to bring in Keats when he was moved on meeting a young poet. But he was worried that Blunden had had too much early success for his own good. 'It will be a keen disappointment to me if you allow yourself to be fooled into indolence,' he wrote, pointing out one 'outrageously bad' line. But there is another indication of how much Gosse was attracted by him. When Blunden set off to teach in Tokyo, Gosse gave him a barometer to take with him, just as he had given one to Robert Louis Stevenson when he left for Samoa thirty years before. In the year *The Waste Land* was published, Gosse wrote of Blunden, 'No more interesting star has appeared of late in our poetical heavens.' 'Good old Gosse,' Blunden commented to Sassoon in a letter from Tokyo. 'E.G. being sensitive about old age made me doubt the safety of showing this,' Sassoon noted in his diary. 'But it was a triumph. "Good old Gosse," he beamed, adding, "Good old Blunden."'

The new friendship with the Sitwells also flourished, in spite of some reservations about their tastes. 'What perfect dears the Sitwells are,' he said, while distrusting the Picassos and Modiglianis hanging on their walls. Osbert Sitwell, long after Gosse's death, wrote the most vivid memoir of him in existence. It is from him, directly or indirectly, that many people who never knew Gosse have their knowledge of him, illustrated perhaps by some of the Max Beerbohm cartoons. When Sitwell published *Noble Essences* in 1950, he knew that Gosse was much mocked by 'the young critics of the present day' and he felt that Gosse deserved better than mockery. Sitwell himself, of course, knew Gosse only as an old man – he was sixty-eight, Sitwell twenty-four, when they first met. He gives a picture of Gosse ready to tear off his top hat and frock coat and rush into any fray that was going. 'In addition to his obvious integrity or rectitude, could be detected also an air of gaiety and dash, most attractive and seldom to be met with in one of his age.' Sitwell described this 'true fighting spirit – a nature perhaps a little feline, but most certainly daring and even aggressive . . .' and an 'impalpable aura of power that emanated from him . . . His stature, as it were, had increased of itself year by year, until now he was a prince of professors.' There was what Sitwell called a 'special collector's interest attaching to him, as the sole representative of many great men now dead . . . Only through him was it still possible to catch a glimpse of the Victorian giants, while, in *his* voice, as he related what they said, you could for the moment catch the very echo of *their* voices speaking. And his sense of the ludicrous – and that I think is what he possessed more than humour or wit – played even round such semi-sacred objects as Swinburne or Rossetti'.

Sitwell described the Sunday afternoons at Hanover Terrace: the pattern was much the same as it had been in the humbler ambience of Delamere Terrace over so many years. Sitwell would pause, he said, under the colonnade, 'lingering with mingled feelings of pleasure and trepidation', for the visit would be certain to prove both treat and ordeal. 'At last you knocked and with a scrupulous promptitude Parker, the celebrated parlour-maid, opened the door.' Sitwell portrays Parker as 'tall, thin, unobtrusive', a parlour-maid of genius, at her most superb as she announced the guests in exactly the right tone of voice. As she said 'Lord Haldane!' the name carried 'a ponderous and stately thunder all its own', containing whole volumes of philosophy and many councils of state. 'Siegfried Sassoon!' brought with it 'the sound of a poet kicking in vain against a horse-box, together with a suggestion of irregular political opinions'.

Ezra Pound had visited Hanover Terrace and had actually 'presumed to PUSH PAST PARKER,' Gosse told Sitwell, damning Pound once and for all. Parker was certainly a remarkable character, but not always such an exemplary pillar of the establishment as Sitwell suggests. Her moods were of constant concern to the Gosses. For instance in 1922, Gosse wrote to Nellie, 'Parker is in perfectly furious high spirits and joined almost too freely in general conversation. But this is a thousand times better than her being cross.' Even at her best she was fierce. 'I am extremely comfortable,' Gosse once reported, 'for Parker looks after me with fierce solicitude.' His only sadness at that time was the sustained unkindness of Caruso, the current cat. 'How I should welcome the slightest tenderness and how little it would cost him! He snaps at me even when I feed him with bits of fish.' He was nearly always 'a hard-hearted brute'. Once, during the war, Gosse had even gone so far as to tell Sassoon that 'the Germans are like Caruso, impervious to moral impression'. Buchanan, Caruso's successor, was equally proud but more charming. Edith Sitwell told a story of one occasion when Buchanan 'left the room after dinner in a marked manner' and the Gosses worried terribly about what had offended him.

Cats and servants were both vital parts of Gosse's life. It was not Parker but a housemaid at Hanover Terrace who provided Gosse with four lines of immortal verse. It was quite unusual, even in the Gosse household, to have a maid who wrote poetry. Unfortunately she neglected her other duties in the service of the muse and eventually had to be dismissed. She took most of her MSS with her, but when the room was made ready for her more prosaic successor, there was one piece of paper remaining. It was an Address to the Moon:

> O Moon, lovely Moon, with thy beautiful face,
> Careering throughout the boundaries of space,
> Whenever I see thee, I think in my mind,
> Shall I ever, oh ever, behold thy behind.

'It is bathos,' said Gosse, 'of purest ray serene, and incidentally it contains the statement of a profound astronomical problem.'

Parker, one feels, would not have had much time for that poetic housemaid. It was she who showed Sitwell upstairs to the drawing-room. He described the scene:

It was not, perhaps, exactly pretty, for it was too crowded, but it had a sort of glint about it, a threading of gold from picture-frames and furniture and objects, and offered a charming air of detailed late-Victorian domesticity. Moreover, it faced Regent's Park and, as you entered, you obtained a lovely vista, green and watery, of pool and weeping willow and stretches of grass, and distant depths of shadow between the taller, further trees. The tea-table stood, as a rule, between the windows, and Mrs Gosse sat with her back to them, between them, with a glistening silver tea-equipment in front of her. Gosse would be sitting facing the window, glaring back at the light with his blue eyes, or looking down from time to time, as he stroked with a rhythmic motion his black and white cat, Buchanan. (Buchanan was an important member of the household, and had adopted Gosse a year or two before. Though a common, he was a proud cat and would never consent to come up to tea unless called or carried by his master in person. Moreover, to secure his continued attendance, he had to be bribed with a saucer of milk, first

poured out by Mrs Gosse, and then served to him by her in a
kneeling position.) Behind Gosse, in the other part of the room –
which he used also as a study – stood, rank on rank, the tall
bookcases of his remarkable library.

Mrs Gosse, a most kind, charming and courteous woman,
understood perfectly her husband's character, comprehended his
fiery nature, his nervous irritability, no doubt aggravated by half a
century's hard work and also by the many vexations and jealousies
inseparable from a literary career – incidents exemplified at their
worst by the Churton Collins episode. She tried to pad the corners
for him, so that neither he nor others should be hurt.

Sassoon called Nellie Gosse 'one of the least fussy people I had ever
known. Her voice was richly subdued and reassuring, and there was a
sense of security in all she did. Like all the best women, she had an
element of masculinity in her.' It complemented, of course, the
element of femininity in Gosse himself. Nellie managed to maintain
her own individuality, in spite of her devotion to her famous husband.
He could never have managed without her. 'Mother is really quite
wonderful,' Gosse wrote to Philip at this period. 'She has the gift of
perfect calm, especially in an emergency.' Gosse continued to create
his own emergencies, his own tiny storms. He was by now reconciled
to Arthur Benson, who noted in his diary in July 1923 that on their first
meeting after the long rift, Gosse said, 'kindly and generous things. I
was quietly grateful and thankful that the absurd cloud had melted. I
don't now even understand the rupture – except that I think I was in a
very morbid state of inner irritability, probably drifting fast into
illness – and G. was trying and irritable too; but it was mainly my
fault, I confess.'

There were now other quarrels – with Margot Asquith, with E. V.
Lucas, with Desmond MacCarthy. Perhaps it was partly because, as
he said, his life had been so static, that Gosse seemed to need such
excitements – though how can one describe as 'static' a life so full of
agitation? Gosse wrote self-mockingly to Squire in 1925:

My own life has been extraordinarily static – I have only lived in two
houses in more than fifty years – largely from timidity and that
dread of change that makes me such a timorous conservative. But I
think it is a mistake not to live more 'dangerously' and most likely I
might with advantage have been more boldly nomadic.

Certainly his travels, though extensive, had been those of the tourist
and not of the nomad. He still continued to spend a great deal of time
away from home.

On 21st September 1919, the Gosses celebrated Edmund's seventieth birthday at the Black Lion at Llangurig, 'the highest village in Wales'. Gosse was presented with a letter of greeting and congratulation, with the promise of a portrait-bust of himself to be carried out by Sir William Goscombe John, RA, one of Thornycroft's former pupils. Gosse wished that Thornycroft himself might have done it, but there was otherwise no cause for regret, and every feeling of gratitude. The letter was signed first by Lord Crewe and then by an extraordinary galaxy of friends, more than two hundred from Archer and Asquith and the Balfours, Baring, Barrie, Beerbohm, Arnold Bennett, Sir Jesse Boot, Lord Bryce, the Burghcleres, Sir Philip Burne-Jones, the Vice-Chancellor of Cambridge and the Archbishop of Canterbury, G. K. Chesterton, Joseph Conrad and Lord Curzon, through Galsworthy, Sir Israel Gollancz, Haldane, Hardy and Heinemann, of course, Kipling, Compton Mackenzie, Lord Montagu of Beaulieu, Lord Morley and Pinero, to Bernard Shaw, the Sitwells, the Spencers, Arthur Symons, Thornycroft, Walpole, Arthur Waugh and the Archbishop of York.

'What fun it all is!' Gosse wrote to Beerbohm, signing himself 'the Notorious Septuagenarian' and thanking him for his promise of a caricature of the presentation of the bust. 'Do bring in the two Archbishops with their mitres and their croziers . . . I can't take it seriously. I shake with hysterical laughter. What has possessed you all to make such a painted pagan idol of poor old third-rate me? . . . We have buzzards here and ravens, but no shops.' Letters poured in and told him that 'England's Independent and Majestic Press rings with me today', but he could not get hold of the papers. *The Times* printed Lord Crewe's letter and a full list of the signatories. The *Observer* published an interview with Gosse.

If at the end of seventy years of life I have the good fortune to hold any special position, it is due solely to the fact that all through my life I have cared for literature and for nothing else . . . I have been very fortunate and very happy, and that happiness endures. Literature is so great, so constant a comfort, and it never fails. All my life I have been a spectator in the world, merely looking on at what others were doing, and yet the world has been very kind to me . . . I never hoped or tried to be a popular writer and yet there are so many faithful friends – there is so much kindness.

The English papers said they doubted 'if a greater tribute to a living man of letters has ever been paid'. They spoke of 'universal esteem', 'a rare gift for friendship', his 'encyclopaedic knowledge', his 'sympathy with the work of younger writers'. 'It is hard to associate Mr Gosse with any thought of age . . . He has never lost the capacity of enthusiasm.' The French papers talked of 'un grand ami de la France et grand ami de la littérature française'. On September 25th, Nellie reported to Tessa, 'Father is still in high spirits and enjoying the letters that are still arriving in great quantities.' There were thirty one day, twenty-five the next. He wrote dozens of individual replies, but also a collective one in which he thanked the 'list of admired and beloved' names:

> You have wished to make me happy. All my life through, happiness has flowed in upon me, through two channels, literature and my friends, and it is precisely through these, on this culminating occasion, that I am made fortunate and rich. I feel in myself . . . no flagging yet in my life-long passion for letters, nor in my eager curiosity regarding the immediate present and the probable future of the art of writing . . .
>
> You have added a word which connects my wife . . . Your sweetness would have lacked for me almost all its savour if she had not been here at my side to share it, as she has shared all the joys and sorrows of the long years gone by.

On September 30th, Nellie wrote: 'Our month is up now – but we must wait to see how the strike lasts – and when it is over, E.G. says, we must wait for the "rush" to be over.' On October 7th, they were still at the Black Lion, reading books from the London Library. 'I hope we shall keep up our good spirits when we get home,' Nellie wrote, 'But there's bound to be a reaction.'

The bust was finished in time to be shown at the Royal Academy in 1920 and was finally presented to Gosse in a ceremony on November 9th at A. J. Balfour's house, 4 Carlton Gardens. By this time, William Heinemann, one of those primarily responsible for the scheme, was dead, but there was a tremendous crowd to hear the eulogies. In his speech, Balfour said he was honoured to speak on behalf of so many friends: 'All of us in this room have had experience of his personal charm, all of us have rejoiced in his wide learning, in his ripe experience, in his gifts of insight, in his seriousness which is never heavy, and his humour which is never thin . . .'

Gosse, replying, said, 'I am stifled in roses, like the guests of a Roman Emperor, and if it were possible I would say nothing at all, but that would be ungracious and might even seem ungrateful . . . I indulge in no conceited illusion about the ceremony of this afternoon. It is on your part an evidence of friendship, of pure indulgent friendship and nothing else . . .' Thornycroft, in moving a vote of thanks to the sculptor, recalled that he had 'seen Mr Gosse under all circumstances', even 'wrecked on the shores of France'. He thought it 'a good test when the subject has to stand beside his bust'. In fact, Gosse looks much less 'craggy' than the bust, his hair is smoother, his moustache less bushy. Beerbohm's cartoon of the occasion loses nothing by its impossible assumption that the bust (now in the London Library, with casts in the House of Lords and the Savile Club) was a surprise to the sitter.

There was more celebration and excitement in June 1920, when Gosse was awarded an honorary degree at Cambridge. The degree of Doctor of Letters was conferred on him at the time of the installation of A. J. Balfour as the new Chancellor of the University. Gosse was one of several 'distinguished persons with whom the Chancellor in his various activities has been associated'. The citation pleased Gosse enormously:

Hic Johannis Donne et Thomae Gray ex antiquis fortunas revocavit et epistolas edidit, e recentioribus Henrici Ibsen et Algernoni Swinburne mores depinxit et animis fideliter illustravit. Ad hunc epistolas vel lepidissimas dedit Robertus Ludovicus Stevenson. Duco ad vos virum eruditum et ingeniosum,

Edmundum Gosse.

He wrote to Beerbohm just before the ceremony:

I am to walk, a new-plumaged Doctor, in a strange procession of quasi-celebrities, such as Bonar Law, M. Bergson, the Prime Minister and Lord Burnham. Imagine this file of flamingoes, in scarlet and rose, flinging down our harps on the jasper floor of the Senate House and singing 'Holy! holy! holy! Erudite and mighty Arthur James Balfour, we thy lost opportunities salute thee!'

There were pleasant social occasions of every sort. At one family lunch party, Helen, aged twelve, listened eagerly to her grandfather reading Mark Antony's great speech. Gosse continued to enjoy Grillions; on one occasion in 1927 the assembled twenty included Austen Chamberlain, the Earl of Oxford and Asquith, Lord Londonderry, Lord Haldane, both the Archbishops and the editor of *The Times*. Gosse wrote out the list with evident satisfaction. There was a reading at Hanover Terrace of John Drinkwater's new play *Cromwell* to a crowded drawing-room, including a great many lords and their ladies. 'Everybody was moved, exalted, carried out of himself. Even such "difficult" people as Siegfried Sassoon and Maurice Baring were enthusiastic,' Gosse reported to Drinkwater. Nellie's report to Tessa was slightly different. 'Everyone liked and admired it – nearly everyone took a little nap during some part of it.'

There was a quiet evening when Percy Lubbock came and read aloud some of Henry James's letters which he was editing. Another evening, George Moore loved 'a 3/9 chicken with green peas like buttons down its waistcoat'. He was publishing *Avowals* and *Conversations in Ebury Street* which, with convincing aplomb, made Gosse say lots of things he had never actually said. Gosse was a little worried, but agreed 'the thing will be great fun if you only do it properly'. 'My unfortunate memory, oh my unfortunate memory,' Moore makes Gosse groan. Moore defined the differences between their two lives. 'A gulf divides the man that marries in the beginning from the man who decides in the beginning that he will remain a bachelor . . . You owe a great deal to your wife and daughters. You will never know how much . . . It never happened to you to rush out after dinner to see a friend, or even to desire to do such a thing.' Moore shows Gosse sitting on his great balcony, 'as large as a parlour, reading, a shawl wrapped round his knees'. 'I am sure this is true, Gosse,' Moore said to him, 'that the best things we do are those in which we have not sought any compromise.' He was thinking, of course, of *Father and Son*.

There were happy visits to Sylvia, who was living and painting near Dieppe. They had meals on an open balcony 'two hours at a time', watching everything going on: a steam ferry, great coal boats taking coal along the coast. And always cats. In England there were continually visits to the country. One spring he wrote: 'it seems so disappointing to be old when the whole world is so brilliantly young'. The Thornycrofts now lived on the Evenlode, and he and Hamo revived a forgotten pleasure by borrowing a young Thornycroft's canoe and paddling along the river together, forty years after their expedition to the source of the Thames. Country hotels (for instance, the Bell Inn at Malmesbury in 1925) would continue to be 'the most charming hotel we ever struck'. Motoring was a pleasure. Nellie was as accommodating as ever: 'I kept to the "dicky" seat as I really did not think it would be easy to get E.G. into it – and less easy to get him out. But, with practice, I became quite nimble myself.'

There were the usual occasional visits to Hardy at Max Gate and regular visits to Haldane at Cloan. Gosse sometimes imagined Haldane 'sailing out far beyond my reach'; he would stand on the shore, he said, and watch him with a telescope. But in fact their friendship was as close as ever. Gosse continued to deny he was interested in politics, but continued to enjoy knowing what was going on. He would offer advice to Haldane, for instance in an undated letter which seems to have been in the turbulent summer of 1922, when he urged Haldane to offer himself to Lloyd George as a conciliator. When Haldane finally joined Ramsay MacDonald's cabinet, at the beginning of 1924, Gosse was cheered rather than dismayed; he trusted Haldane to act as a restraining influence. He had had moments of agitation about the way things were going.

'We are passing through dreadful days, in which the pillars of the world seem to be shaken, all in front of us seems to be darkness and hopelessness,' he wrote to Gide in the summer of 1920. 'It is much harder to bear than the war was, because there is no longer the unity that sustained us, nor the nobility which inspired hope and determination.' And there were disquieting stories about what had really gone on during the war. Lady Newton wrote from Marienbad full of indiscreet reports of Lord Carson's stories about the cabinet during the war and how 'hopeless and inept everyone seems to have been. Why we ever pulled through I cannot think. Kitchener said to Carson "French is losing the War every day" but nothing was done about it'.

'What is to come of the angry, distracted world?' Gosse asked Gide. 'I feel very old and helpless.' But it was a passing feeling. He continued to be in demand for advice of every sort. Charles Scott-Moncrieff, translating Proust, thanked him for his 'charming counsel'. He gave Sassoon useful and detailed advice over *Memoirs of a Fox-Hunting Man*. Work sustained him. He used it as a drug, he said, taking it every morning after breakfast so he could 'forget the world for a couple of hours'. But even work could lead to complications. An article on the new Romain Rolland brought a response from the translators who predicted Gosse would be an early victim of 'the avenging spirit of the multitude' and sent him a copy of a book called *Creative Revolution*. 'It makes my hair stand on end,' he wrote to Haldane.

Friendship was more precious than ever. At Cloan even Haldane's black dog was eager for his company. Whenever a car arrived, Haldane reported, he rushed out. 'He thinks it may be his own Gosse.' Nellie was not so happy at Cloan. She would often feel rather 'out of it'. Indeed both she and Lord Haldane felt 'out of it' on Gosse's birthday morning in 1926. She wrote to her daughters:

Elizabeth H. and he himself were in wild spirits . . . A splendid cake with the full number of candles. A large, wonderful bouquet made by Williams (the butler-valet) himself, with appropriate inscriptions. The Black Dog walked solemnly into the room and straight up to E.G. himself. Black Dog wore a large bow of pale blue satin at his neck and suspended from it a cake of Parma violets soap! My gift was a poor *pour rire*! I was going to get for Edmund a small hand-bag to replace the shabby one he always carries en route. But E.H. (always kind and rather masterful) ordered it right away for me from Perth. And, what do you think? There arrived a large bright green canvas travelling uniform trunk! It will be most useful; but it did look so horribly prosaic amidst the surrounding delicate attentions. (Elizabeth H. gave him two exquisite Perth-glass small bowls, for ashes).

Gosse continued to lecture. Two thousand people listened to him in Glasgow. He addressed the Royal College of Physicians on 'Literature and the Medical Profession'. The Curators of the Taylorian told him he had delivered many wonderful lectures in his time, but never a more wonderful than the one he gave when he was seventy-five. He cared as much as ever about the Royal Literary Fund. The speech he gave at the annual dinner in 1920 could be given now with hardly any alteration, quoting as he did a French satirist of two hundred years before:

> Aux petits des oiseaux Dieu donne la pâture
> Mais sa bonté s'arrête à la littérature,

which, if not quite true, he said, has a semblance of truth.

Gosse would attend Anglo-French luncheons and Anglo-Danish dinners and royal afternoon parties at Buckingham Palace. Rider Haggard saw him at one in October 1923, and recorded that he 'looks younger than he did ten years ago', whereas Winston Churchill was looking worn and much older. Gosse dined with the Queen in June 1922 at Lord Salisbury's, asking her (when no one could overhear, as he knew it was not etiquette): 'Do you, ma'am, follow with interest the intellectual developments of your subjects?'

'I am afraid I do not,' Queen Mary replied. 'I have so little time. I am absorbed more and more by political affairs. I used to read a great deal more than I do now.' Gosse reflected smugly that he thought it would not do her any harm to be reminded of other things than society and politics.

Gosse also attended other people's lectures. Virginia Woolf saw him in the well-dressed audience which heard Paul Valéry lecture on 1st November 1922. She shuddered at the atmosphere, full of feathers and white gloves. She shuddered too when Gosse took the chair at a lecture by Victoria Sackville-West at the Royal Society of Literature. She called him 'the ornament on the tea-pot'. Vita looked 'very ancestral like a picture under glass in a gallery. She was fawned on by the little dapper grocer Gosse, who kept spinning round on his heel to address her compliments and to scarify Bolshevists, in an ironical voice which seemed to ward off what might be said of him; and to be drawing round the lot of them the red plush curtains of respectability . . . Gosse will survive us all. Now how does he do it? Yet he seemed to me, with his irony and his scraping, somehow uneasy. A kind of black doormat got up and appeared to be Lady Gosse, so home . . .'

Virginia Woolf had had *Books on the Table*, one of the collections of *Sunday Times* pieces, for review in 1921 and had hated its effect on her. 'How low in tone it all is – purred out by the firesides of Dowagers.' She knew of Gosse's friendships with dowagers – not only Lady Dorothy Nevill, Lady Londonderry and Lady Desborough, but now with Lady Newton and Lady Airlie. (There were ninety letters, cards and notes from Lady Airlie in 1920 alone.) But no, she thought more fairly, 'that is not quite true, seeing that he has some sturdiness, some independence, and some love of letters. The peculiar combination of suavity, gravity, malignity and common sense always repels me'. She would portray one aspect of him as Sir Nicholas Greene in *Orlando* – Orlando has to reject Nick Greene after their first encounter, but needs him again later. In the end she seems to accept his function.

Virginia Woolf's feelings about Gosse were very mixed. She knew he thought she didn't sufficiently respect the memory of her father, his friend. Someone had reported he thought her 'a nonentity'. She knew Lytton Strachey, who himself was rather ambivalent, thought her 'narrow-minded about Gosse'. 'I say I know a mean skunk when I see one, or rather smell one,' she told him. She wrote to Edith Sitwell: 'Did that little grocer Gosse write about you? In a rage, I cancelled his paper: but I wish I had seen what he said', the common predicament of people who cancel papers in a rage. After his death, she called him 'a crafty, worldly, prim, astute little beast', in a letter to Ethel Smythe, and then had a change of heart: 'Gosse is dead,' she would write in her diary, 'and I am half reconciled to him by their saying in the papers that he chose to risk a dangerous operation rather than be an invalid for life. This kind of vitality always gets me.' She admired *Father and Son* too, and that would indeed survive.

In August 1921 Gosse told Philip: 'I shall try to live seven years more, if I can.' The Hanover Terrace house was on a seven-year lease, and he did not want it to be a burden to the family after he was gone. At times, in spite of his continually youthful appearance, his springy gait, his zest, on which people often remarked, it looked as if he might not live as long as he wished. 'How I wish time would go backwards, instead of forwards,' he wrote on his birthday in 1923.

In February 1920 he had been knocked over by a car in Maida Hill. No bones were broken, 'but I am a mass of bruises and my nerves much shaken'. Nellie too was ill that winter. As early as 1915 Gosse had called himself 'an afflicted old cripple'. From time to time, he had been hampered by sciatica or lumbago, and now was becoming deaf and his lungs, his heart and his eyes were all causing problems. The doctor would send them away for 'sea air' or 'to the south'. There seemed to be a great belief in the restorative powers of a change of air or more southerly climes.

In January 1923 Gosse wrote to Sassoon after a visit from him and Blunden: 'The excitement of entertaining two fiery bards must have been too much for my aged frame, for while I was dressing next morning, I had a cardiac seizure and fell on my back among the furniture.' But he made a good recovery. It was not until February 1924 that the *Sunday Times* appeared without an article by him for the first time in four and a half years. He was in bed for over a fortnight, but eager to resume once he was better. In March he wrote, 'I am getting used to having only one eye and don't barge into lamp posts and people too much.' Osbert Sitwell commented that the patch he was obliged to wear afforded Gosse 'a tactical advantage, because though he saw at all times at least twice as much with his one good eye as anyone else did with two, nobody suspected it. And it imparted to him something of the rakish air of a pirate chief – crafty but indomitable. You could perceive that he sailed the seas under his own flag . . .' 'No account of Gosse,' Sitwell insisted, 'should omit the sheer quality of fun which he possessed in the highest degree, and which his presence never failed to impart to any occasion or gathering, large or small.'

That this fun could sometimes make lesser spirits feel uncomfortable is illustrated vividly by an account Sitwell gives of a Robert Louis Stevenson celebration, at which, without the two men realizing it, the organizers had invited both Sidney Colvin and Edmund Gosse to speak. There was certainly some rivalry between them. They both claimed Stevenson as a close friend. Gosse had a slight advantage in that Stevenson's last letter, as we have seen, was written to him – but then Colvin had edited the letters and was inclined to pat himself on the back. Benson once described him as 'a pompous fool, in whose veins runs the blood of a fish', and even kindly Dobson had been known to suggest that there would be no need of ice on a sultry evening 'if Colvin puts the beverages against his person'. On this particular Stevensonian occasion, Sir Sidney was called on first and made a long and detailed speech. When Gosse's turn came, he rose at his most sprightly and said, 'Ladies and gentlemen, I came here with a few platitudes prepared for your edification, for I had not been aware that Sir Sidney was to speak to you this afternoon. But, sure enough, he has delivered them all, so I shall say nothing.'

He then sat down. That was Sitwell's story and it could well be true, but the letters between them suggest a perfectly amiable relationship between Colvin and Gosse. Gosse was apparently delighted by the edition of the Letters and told Colvin they 'give a beautiful impression of *yourself*'. He also wrote as one ardent Stevensonian to another about the aspersions cast on their friend by one Leonard Woolf, whom Gosse had not met and who he thought, for some reason, must be 'a perverse, partially-educated alien German, who has thrown in his lot violently with Bolshevism and Mr Joyce's *Ulysses* and "the great sexual emancipation" and all the rest of the nasty fads of the hour'. Gosse allowed himself to sound for once like the very man Blooms-bury thought him to be, moved as he was by the thought of Stevenson being attacked. 'What he hates in R.L.S. is radically what we love – the refinement, the delicacy, the beauty.' It is easy to imagine what Stevenson himself, or indeed the young Gosse, would have thought of that description of his qualities.

1925, the year in which Gosse became seventy-six, was a particularly exciting year. It began, so to speak, in December, 1924, when Gosse received a longed-for letter from Lord Curzon: 'I have had the pleasure of recommending you to the PM for a further honour.' Gosse had been given the CB in 1912. 'I heard from him this morning that he was prepared to submit your name to the King either for a CH (Compan-ion of Honour – a very notable distinction enjoyed only by a few) or for a Knighthood, whichever you would prefer.' Gosse, unsurpris-ingly, plumped for the knighthood. When the announcement was made in the New Year Honours, there were some who thought the recognition tardy and inadequate. There was, of course, another enormous pile of letters. The family laid bets. Nellie wrote to Tessa on January 5th, 'E.G. says the number you are backing of 300 ("Knight-hood") letters is nearly accomplished.' In the end there were nearly four hundred. 'I am determined to answer each one with my own hand,' Gosse declared. Only Nellie seemed rather less than enthusias-tic. She did not in the least want to be her Ladyship, unlike the first Mrs Hardy, who was furious when Hardy accepted an OM so he did not have to share his honour with her. 'Why can't men keep their honours to themselves?' Nellie asked Benson.

Gosse enjoyed the visit to the Heralds' College. 'It was slightly thrilling,' he told Elizabeth Haldane, 'to write one's name in the Roll which comes down more or less unbroken from the reign of Richard II. Garter King of Arms, a gay old soul who reminded me of Old King Cole, informed me when I signed that I was now "A Knight in the Sight of God." Isn't that a beautiful thought?' But of course Sir Edmund was rather more concerned with being a knight in the sight of the world. He went with a particular spring in his step, in spite of the icy weather, to the House of Lords to see Asquith take his seat as the Earl of Oxford and Asquith. 'The House was thronged tight, but I was made a Privy Counsellor for the nonce, and stood on the steps of the throne.'

There was further excitement and yet another enormous pile of letters in August, when Nellie and Edmund celebrated their Golden Wedding. There was much to celebrate. 'You are the most delightful companion in the world,' Edmund had written to his wife a few years before, 'and the only one of whom I never get tired.' 'The "stunt" about our Golden Wedding astonished us very much, for we had done nothing whatever to encourage it,' he told Elizabeth Haldane. The telegrams of congratulation included one from Winston Churchill at the Treasury. The *Daily Graphic* the following day had, under a banner headline GREAT CRITIC'S GOLDEN WEDDING, a photo of the happy couple, looking extremely solemn at a table full of presents. Arthur Waugh recorded a family dinner-party, 'bathed in golden light', and said Gosse seemed 'completely happy'. Young Evelyn had been dispatched to buy a present from Chapman and Hall, his father's firm. He had no enthusiasm for the task. Indeed he had despised his distant relative ever since he was eight or nine. Gosse had foolishly greeted him, 'And where do you carry those bare knees?' '*They* carry *me* wherever I want to go,' the boy replied. 'Ah, the confidence of youth!' Gosse exclaimed. 'To be able to envisage an attainable destination!' Evelyn thought this 'highly absurd and offensive' and never forgot it. Later he confirmed his dislike with an inaccurate summing-up, but admitted that 'better judges than I relished Gosse's company'. (His father always returned from Hanover Terrace having enjoyed 'a capital evening', however much he had worried about it beforehand.) To Evelyn Waugh, though, Gosse epitomized 'all that I found ignoble in the profession of letters. He was not, as I soon learned from investigating the quarrel with Churton Collins, a genuine scholar. He had written only one book and that anonymously. His eminence sprang from his sedulous pursuit of the eminent, among whom he was more proud of his intimacy with people of power and fashion than with artists . . . I saw Gosse as a Mr Tulkinghorn, the soft-footed, inconspicuous, ill-natured habitué of the great world, and I longed for a demented lady's maid to make an end of him.'

Evelyn Waugh's brother, Alec, on the other hand, was 'very proud to have so distinguished a relative' and listened with avidity to Gosse's tales of Balfour and Asquith and Lord Salisbury. When the schoolboy produced *The Loom of Youth*, Robert Graves reported Gosse 'rather alarmed at first' but 'enthusiastically converted by the three editions in a month the book went into'.

The last major event of 1925 was a visit to Paris to receive an honorary degree at the Sorbonne. In 1921 the University of Strasbourg had similarly honoured him and his presence and speech had been acclaimed by an audience of 2000. An admirer called William Bellows accompanied Gosse to Alsace for eight days; they stayed with the Comte and Comtesse de Pange. The Comtesse prepared a translation of his speech for him, as he still distrusted his ability to be impressive in French. Gosse was awarded six honorary degrees altogether – from St Andrews, Gothenburg and Oslo as well as Cambridge, Strasbourg and Paris. Of all his foreign orders and honours, it was the Sorbonne degree he valued most, he told Philip.

On the way to Paris, William Bellows, who was again his companion, watched the effect of the Legion of Honour, the very effect Gosse had suggested to Henry James. At the *douane*, 'the chalk was manipulated by a matronly old woman. As I was able at a critical moment to point to the bouton of Commandeur de la Légion d'honneur on my friend's coat, she whisked the chalk over the whole pile of luggage and we were free.'

An old friend, Mabel Robinson, described the ceremony at the Sorbonne to Nellie:

> He was most enthusiastically received and the honour done to him was much more personal than to any other of the Doctors . . . Edmund, like Kipling a few years back, is chosen for himself alone – 'le Sainte-Beuve de l'outre manche'. Fortunately the Dean of the Faculty of Letters has a voice and took the trouble to use it, so that the *thousands* of people who were packed into the large theatre of the Sorbonne heard what he said, . . . whereas the life work of the six eminent men of science who were doctorated with him remains wrapped in mystery. It was really an impressive sight . . . the vast platform occupied by rows and rows of shiny satin robes – plain red or yellow. Order was kept by the magnificent Garde . . . and the flags of all the Allies were draped over the doors and behind the platform. This colour and an audience of between three and four thousand spectators gave a certain grandeur to the ceremony. Of course all the new Doctors were acclaimed but Edmund had a quite special clapping. He looked extraordinarily well and young . . . He was splendid.

1926 was a much quieter year, overshadowed by the series of strikes culminating in the General Strike in May. In early February Gosse was in Bournemouth and wrote to Philip, 'What a hell of a time you all seem to be having in London! I expect to come back, if the strikers allow, on Monday.' When he got back, he found London 'beginning to be really frightened at last'. He heard alarming stories when he called in, as he often did, to see his friends in the House of Lords. 'The great people who live in the various colliery districts are all gone down to their country houses and are getting in firearms in case of plunder and riots. I hear of people losing their heads altogether. For instance, Lord Savile is not merely fortifying Rufford, but fitting his town house with guns and bars! . . . You must not be alarmed at all this,' he wrote to Nellie. 'There is generally a compromise to be discovered.'

Percy Lubbock celebrated Gosse's first broadcast this year in some rather uninspired lines:

> . . . his laurel acquires a new gloss
> Now we've heard his voice 2 L O'd,
> And we're all of us grateful to Gosse
> For the breadth of his cast of the ode.

Life was still interesting, but Gosse was beginning to feel old and tired. He told Wise that the reception he had had in Paris the previous December was 'magnificent but overpowering. It was beyond my strength'. He told Gide in August 1926, though it was not true: 'I shall certainly never come to France again.' Not many criticized Gosse these days, at least not in public. Virginia Woolf and Evelyn Waugh might be muttering away in their diaries but little reached Gosse's ears. 'Poor old man,' Harold Nicolson would write in *his* diary, thinking of the way Bloomsbury scoffed at Gosse, and himself enjoying the vivid talk of the past. Austen Chamberlain, whose eager face Gosse had enjoyed at Trinity thirty-five years before, wrote as Lord Privy Seal with the sort of criticism Gosse could also enjoy:

Oh Great Man,
On your honour tell me: did Zoffany paint Governor-Generals as you allege? Fie, fie, Mr Gosse; I protest they were Governors-General. The Great Cham of Literature must not make such mistakes.

> Your faithful friend
> and very humble admirer
> the latest of the Lords Privy Seal

(not of the Lord Privy Seals who could only be found in the Zoo.)

There was one minor poet who realized Gosse was not backing the eventual winners. William Kean Seymour wrote:

> May we not have – from Mr Edmund Gosse –
> A sad confession that he's at a loss
> Quite to account for Mr Ezra Pound,
> Lamenting that his head is going round
> With T.S. Eliot's sweet and simple muse?

Another, Douglas Goldring, in 'The Post-Georgian Poet in Search of a Master', suggested that there was still some chance of useful guidance from the aged critic:

> Now all is chaos, all confusion.
> Bolshes have cast E.M. from his high throne:
> Wild women have rushed in, and savage Yanks
> Blather of Booth and Heaven: and T.S.E.
> Uses great words that are as Greek to me . . .
> Are Sitwells really safe? Is Iris Tree
> A certain guide to higher poesy?
> Can Nichols be relied on for a lead;
> Or should I thump it with Sassoon and Read? . . .
> Oh mighty Mr Gosse! Unbend, I pray!
> Guide one poor poet who has lost his way.

Sitwell recorded Gosse on Pound. He once heard him call him 'that preposterous American filibuster and Provençal charlatan'. Gosse had hated his review of the Swinburne biography; he had hated him pushing past Parker. He hated Pound's poetry. As for Eliot, he had hated him being late for the reading at Lady Colefax's. Four and a half years later, on 6th June 1922, Sassoon wrote the following account of an evening at Hanover Terrace.

I came home feeling grateful to Gosse. He always sends me away with a desire to excel in the honourable craft of literature. He is a faithful servant to the distinctions and amenities of decent writing. He upholds delicacy and precision in the art of letters. And for that, as Johnson would say, 'he is to be applauded'. But I am always slightly self-conscious in our conversations. There are little occasions when I find it impossible to avoid insincerity. An instance of this occurred this evening; Gosse referred to 'an American poetaster named Eliot who has been making himself ridiculous by his condemnation of *Hamlet*'. I found myself incapable of defending Eliot. I actually concealed my slightly bewildered but quite genuine admiration for his intellectualities in verse. And T.S.E. was dismissed as a ninny – a conceited literary humbug. Yet I know quite well that T.S.E. is nothing of the kind, in spite of his too-intelligent perversities.

In the *Criterion* of September 1927, Eliot wrote on 'Sir Edmund Gosse on French Poetry':

Of the books with which Sir Edmund Gosse usually concerns himself, in his weekly causeries, one usually prefers to accept Sir Edmund's opinions, along with his copious information, rather than bother to hold an opinion of one's own. But in a recent essay on 'Symbolist Poetry,' Sir Edmund seems to have gone seriously wrong.

Some protest ought to be raised first against his dismissal of Jules Laforgue and Francis Jammes and Tristan Corbière as 'eccentrics' . . . and second against his statement that 'the interesting French poetry of the end of the last century . . . has had practically no influence at all on English metrical writers.' The latter assertion goes to suggest that Sir Edmund Gosse is completely out of touch with modern poetry.

Gosse was now seventy-eight. It is a measure of his unusual staying-power that Eliot should have expected him still to be in touch. In fact, as Eliot's comments appeared in the *Criterion*, Gosse was convalescing from being seriously ill with typhoid. As Eliot would write later, Gosse had really outlived his function:

The place that Sir Edmund Gosse filled in the literary and social life of London is one that no one can ever fill again, because it is, so to speak, an office that has been abolished . . . I will not say that Sir Edmund's activity was not a very useful activity, in a social-literary world which is rapidly receding into memory. He was, indeed, an amenity, but not quite any sort of amenity for which I can see any great need in our time.

Gosse recovered completely from the typhoid. In August 1927 Haldane wrote: 'No news of you for two days, but probably no news is good news', which shows how very closely they were still in touch. In September, Nellie wrote to Tessa, 'What a wonderful man E.G. is! He seems to be twenty years younger, at least, since his illness . . . What a darling you have been here with your father! And how you have trained him to fetch and carry – and, *almost*, to hold doors open!' She needed these attentions for, as Gosse said, 'My devoted Nellie has broken down under the strain of my six weeks' illness and the great anxiety of the first ten days.' She would never wholly recover. But Gosse himself was full of energy in September, apologizing to Rees at the *Sunday Times* for having let him down and promising to be 'an exemplary contributor again'.

Before Gosse's illness, in June 1927, there had been a final series of visits to Max Gate. Nellie told Tessa and Sylvia that 'True Thomas' was very 'Wessexian' and very chatty and very kind. 'I was given one red, but very sharp little strawberry to eat . . . They have a fluffy grey kitten, very spirited and playful – but its claws are sadly sharp and long.' It can be seen on Gosse's knee in the photograph William Bellows took of the old friends on the garden seat. On the day of the last drive over from Swanage to Max Gate, Gosse, indefatigable, had been up at 5.20 in the morning to see the eclipse. 'Between you and me and the post,' he wrote to Philip, 'I thought it a poor affair!' As for Hardy, 'He is a wonder if you like,' Gosse wrote to Grierson. 'At 87½ without a deficiency of sight, hearing, mind or conversation. Very tiny and fragile, but full of spirit and a gaiety not quite consistent in the most pessimistic of poets. He and I colloqued merrily of past generations like two antediluvian animals sporting in the primeval slime.' To T. J. Wise he wrote that Hardy, 'as we all get to do, finds himself lonely'.

In November 1927 Gosse wrote to Sassoon, 'I have been receiving letter after letter from Max Gate, as eager and energetic as the effusions of a youth. What a wonderful old man!' The last letter from Gosse to Hardy, the last of so many, was written on Christmas Eve 1927. It gives a picture of the Gosse family sitting round the breakfast-table at Hanover Terrace listening as Gosse read aloud a poem of Hardy's, 'Christmas in the Elgin Room', published in *The Times* that day, while outside there was 'dark rain falling through a pea-soup-coloured fog'. 'Accept both of you our fervent wishes for your happiness in 1928,' Gosse wrote to Hardy, but before the year was half over both men would be dead. Hardy pencilled a brief reply to Gosse's letter. 'He has written no other word than these since he went to bed three weeks ago,' Florence wrote to Gosse.

Thomas Hardy died on 11th January 1928. On the 13th Gosse received a reply-paid telegram from Macmillans:

WE HAVE BEEN REQUESTED TO ASK IF YOU WOULD ACT AS PALL–BEARER AT MR THOMAS HARDY'S FUNERAL ON MONDAY AFTERNOON NEXT AT TWO O'CLOCK AT WESTMINSTER ABBEY. AN EARLY REPLY WOULD FACILITATE ARRANGEMENTS.

There was no question of refusing. Gosse shared the honour with the Prime Minister, Stanley Baldwin, with the Leader of the Opposition, Ramsay MacDonald, with Kipling, Shaw, Housman, Barrie and Galsworthy and with the Masters of the two colleges which had made Hardy an Honorary Fellow: the Queen's College, Oxford and Magdalene College, Cambridge.

Sassoon hated 'the vulgar uproar' which attended Hardy's death. Gosse took no part in the dispute about the 'medieval butchery', the decision, urged on Florence by Barrie, that Hardy's heart should be buried in Dorset and the ashes of the rest in the Abbey. Gosse was asked to intervene but said 'I would say nothing in public which could give distress to Sir James Barrie, who was the devoted friend of the departed.' Helen Gosse, Philip's daughter, reported that in Westminster Abbey 'Grandpa looked splendid and held himself like a guardsman!' William Rothenstein, the artist, was immensely moved by the scene: 'They all looked pale and dignified . . . a really noble galaxy. As they stood round the opening, draped with violet, they looked so tense, the scene impressed itself vividly on my mind. I thought, what a fine composition these men, standing together, would make and I made a rough drawing of what was in my mind. I spoke of this to Gosse and showed him my drawing . . .'

Gosse was immensely co-operative, sitting for his likeness with an 'undefeated look in his eye . . . vital and sharply alert'. But there were endless difficulties. Baldwin's sitting was interrupted by a band playing 'God save the King' outside 10 Downing Street, so that Rothenstein had to stand up 'dropping about me pencils, chalk and rulers'. In the end Barrie refused to sit, which made Housman refuse too, as he had said he would only do so if everyone else did. Rothenstein decided to drop his idea and Gosse was indignant. He wrote:

> This is your picture, not Barrie's or Housman's. Anybody may look at a King, and make an impression of a public scene . . . Why indulge the vanity of Barrie? If you proposed to paint a monumental picture of Barrie alone, at night, in Poets' Corner, gazing down pensively on Hardy's tomb and a ray of moonlight falling on that broad white Scottish forehead, Barrie would sit till you were tired of the sight of him . . . You should only think of your picture and never mind what other people say.

So wrote the man who had so often minded what other people said, who had thought far too often about what people thought of him. But

Rothenstein could not be persuaded: 'The project had become distasteful.'

In the Chapter House, waiting for the funeral to begin, the pallbearers had eyed each other with interest. Gosse had the pleasure of introducing Shaw and Kipling who, amazingly, had never met before. Shaw and Gosse had met over the years mainly on committees and as Gosse was 'a most combative man and had a sense of humour which he could never control' they 'sparred and chaffed rather than communed on these occasions,' Shaw said. They had had more chance to talk at Cloan in 1924, and Shaw had pleased Gosse by discussing the condition that Restoration criticism had been in when he started ('silly tales about Etheredge and the like') and the difference Gosse's studies had made. After that meeting, Gosse had sent Shaw a copy of his *Life of Congreve* with a friendly inscription.

Now, in January 1928, as they walked away from Hardy's funeral together, Shaw pleased Gosse even more. Shaw had just been staying with the Astors at Cliveden and had found a copy of *Father and Son* at his bedside. He had read it straight through.

'Had you not read it before?' Gosse asked.

'Yes, of course: I read it when it first appeared; but this second time was the test; for I could not lay it down until I had been right through it again; and though I had always sworn by it I found it even better – more important – than I thought. It is,' Shaw said, 'one of the immortal pages of English literature.'

Gosse stopped in the roadway. 'Oh, my dear Shaw,' he said, 'You are the *only* one who ever encourages me.' This was not quite true, of course, but Gosse really did not think that anything he had written had a real chance of immortality. He would be remembered mainly, he knew, for the people he had known. For a man who sometimes seemed so arrogant, he was modest about his own achievement. Writing an introduction to the catalogue of his library in 1924, Gosse said, 'When ambition sinks to a close, and we are left with so many presumptuous hopes unrealized, so little done of all we gaily started out to do, I am not sure that much will be more consoling than to have at hand the proof that those who passed us in the race regarded us, while the race was being run, with esteem and sometimes with affection.' Reading the inscriptions in his lifetime's collection of books, he saw the association copies as 'precious memorials of friendship'. At least his children would know, he said, that he had 'possessed the confidence of men and women whose praise is better than rubies'.

Hardy was of course one of these. 'To my long-time friend Edmund Gosse,' Hardy had written in a volume of *The Dynasts* in 1906. In a broadcast tribute, in February 1928, Gosse spoke of the fifty-three years of their friendship and of Hardy's unchallenged predominance. 'The throne is vacant, and Literature is gravely bereaved.' He said, 'It is the fashion to over-estimate his poetry . . . It is the fashion to underrate his novels . . . Criticism will hold the balance more evenly and will show that this remarkable man was equally distinguished in the two arts of prose and verse.' Edmund wrote to Nellie in her nursing home: 'Alas! my broadcast lecturing was a dismal failure. What brought on my spasms of coughing was the dry hot air of the sound-proof studio. I never felt so ashamed and disgusted.' But, in fact, Gosse's recorded voice can be heard down the years, indomitable, splendid, the voice, one might think, of a fine Victorian actor.

Nellie's illness was causing Gosse grave concern. She was getting weaker and weaker. He wrote to Elizabeth Haldane: 'Her wonderful courage and optimism sustain her and in her weakness she is perpetually thinking of the happiness of others. Tomorrow, another specialist is to come . . . We all say to one another, "It will certainly be all right" and in our hearts expect it to be all wrong. There are occasions when the old formula "We leave it in the Lord's hands" would be a comfort.' Sylvia, 'dearest of intelligent companions', was keeping house for him, but he found the time hard. 'I find my best relief in absorption in my work for you,' he told Rees at the *Sunday Times*.

In February he wrote an impatient letter to a man who wanted to hear his recollections of Rossetti. 'You tell me,' he wrote, 'that you have "little leisure" and much "pressure of work". You suppose *me* to sit before the fire with nothing whatever to do but to help other people to write books.' A few days later he wrote again, apologetically. The letter had arrived, he explained, 'at a most unlucky moment when I am extremely worried with other things and I see I was unfairly impatient'.

In March Gosse spoke at the Ibsen centenary celebrations in London. He felt strong enough to be determined to take on the task of editing a selection of Hardy's letters, which Florence pressed on him. At least, he would like to do it, he said, if he could have a younger colleague to help him. He thought of Sassoon who had loved Hardy too. Florence had written to say that, in Hardy's will, Gosse was named as literary executor after Sydney Cockerell. 'Your name would have stood first, as it did once, but he fully anticipated, as did I, that he would live to be over ninety, and he thought that, by that time, you would have found the very arduous duties of a literary executor beyond your strength.'

On March 27th, Cockerell called to try to dissuade Gosse from taking advantage of Florence's 'rash request' to edit the letters. 'My object was to impress upon him that I would be damned if anyone else should,' Gosse wrote to Sassoon. 'The Gods admired how much we both dissembled. Each of us was very polite, and each very firm . . . And we parted, with many expressions of radiant amiability, each hating the other with the hate of Hell.'

Nellie was still in the nursing home when Gosse wrote to Elizabeth Haldane on April 15th:

My life of late has been so monotonous – empty, with such a strain of work, that my spirits have been affected by it. I seem stranded on the last end of life, no longer an object of interest or affection to anybody. This, I know, is morbid and ungrateful. Your dear letter breaks the spell and has cheered me.

The weather in London over Easter was 'radiant' but Gosse did not have much chance to enjoy it. 'I was working all day and every day. I was rushing on in order to have a free fortnight later on.' He was planning a final visit to Paris with William Bellows. When they left London he told Bellows 'he was now on the right side of three articles for the *Sunday Times* and could breathe freely'.

'Even when one is not feeling strong, Paris is exhilarating,' Gosse said. In his black cloak, André Gide came to tea at the Hôtel de Bourgogne. Another day, Gosse and Bellows dined on *sole au vin blanc* in the same old-fashioned little room, looking over the misty river, where he and Hamo Thornycroft had eaten so often together forty years before. Gosse and Bellows visited Barbizon, on the edge of the forest of Fontainebleau, now with a line of petrol pumps in the village street, so different from how it had been when Robert Louis Stevenson had stayed at Siron's Hotel in the summer of 1875. Bellows and Gosse lunched in the inn courtyard and Gosse fed crumbs of his lunch to the birds on the sunlit gravel and spoke of Stevenson. Stevenson had long been dead and now Thornycroft too was dead. Telephoning the news of that death to *The Times*, he had found himself, in his grief, speaking to someone who was 'quite indifferent and rather insolent . . . We old people are all coming nearer and nearer to the edge of the cliff,' he had written to Norman Gullick.

On 3rd May 1928 he wrote: 'I go back to England tomorrow as I have to give the toast of Literature at the Royal Academy next night . . . A chill no bigger than a man's hand is rising and may cover my sky, but I hope for the best.' Gosse never gave the speech at the Royal Academy dinner. That day he went into a nursing-home at 50 Weymouth Street, London W1, for a minor operation. A more serious one would follow. He was suffering from prostate trouble. He knew there was a risk in having the operations but he was prepared to take it.

He wrote to Rees at the *Sunday Times*, his firm clear handwriting at last deteriorating towards the end, almost into illegibility:

The first (or minor) operation has been so successful, that the surgeons wish to proceed at once. I am therefore to have the major operation tomorrow morning. My general strength is so well sustained that they are in great hopes I shall be able to bear it, and I am quite calm.

You speak of the article which was sent you on Saturday – of course it was written before my operation. I would suggest (subject to your approval) that it should be kept back for the moment, and used when I am recovering. Next Saturday, if I survive, I shall be at my worst, and therefore it will doubtless be best to admit my illness in the 'S.T.'. I leave it to you. The surgeon thinks that, if I have no relapse, I may begin the work for you again before I leave my bed. Accept my most affectionate thanks for your goodness. Will you tell Sir W. Berry how ashamed I am of behaving so badly! He will think me an 'unprofitable servant'!

Always your Edmund Gosse

He wrote to Bellows: 'There seems good reason to believe that I shall survive the shock. In any case I am perfectly calm, and able to enjoy the love which has accompanied me through such long years and surrounds me still.' Messages of comfort and consolation arrived hourly in Weymouth Street.

Gosse died on 16th May 1928. Sylvia wrote to the Haldanes: 'He had such a love of life, but only of a life crowded with work, friends and activity, that it would have been intolerable to him to have had to live on, suffering and inactive.' Sylvia registered his death, its cause 'acute bronchitis and retention of urine'. She described him as 'Knight, C.B. Author and formerly Clerk to Board of Trade'. In his simple will, in which he divided everything equally between the three children on their mother's death (she would survive him for only fifteen months), Gosse described himself as 'late Librarian to the House of Lords'.

At the funeral in St Marylebone Parish Church, the anthem was Tennyson's 'Crossing the Bar'. 'I hope to meet my Pilot face to face,' they sang. We cannot know whether Edmund Gosse did have a faint hope that there might after all have been some truth in the faith of his childhood. But certainly, after a life of agitation, he faced death with the same tranquillity, 'the serene and sensible resignation', he had observed at the awful hour when his mother had died seventy years before.

Bibliography

(This Bibliography is of first separate editions only and excludes publications in foreign languages, publications merely edited or introduced by Gosse and those in which he is one of several contributors.)

Madrigals, Songs and Sonnets. London: Longmans, Green, 1870. (Contains 32 poems by Gosse and 30 by John Arthur Blaikie.)

On Viol and Flute. London: Henry S. King, 1873. (Expanded edition published by Kegan Paul in 1890.)

The Ethical Condition of the Early Scandinavian Peoples. London: Robert Hardwicke, 1875. (Paper to be read at the Victoria Institute. Another edition *'to which is added the discussion thereon'* reprinted from *Journal of the Victoria Philosophical Institute*.)

King Erik. London: Chatto and Windus, 1876. (Actually published at Christmas, 1875. A 'remainder' of 250 copies was issued by Heinemann in 1893, with new title page and binding.)

The Unknown Lover: a drama for private acting. With an essay on the chamber drama in England. London: Chatto and Windus, 1878.

Studies in the Literature of Northern Europe. London: C. Kegan Paul, 1879. (Revised edition, *Northern Studies*, published by Walter Scott, 1890.)

New Poems. London: C. Kegan Paul, 1879.

Memoir of Samuel Rowlands. 1879. (This essay, written as an introduction to the Hunterian Club edition of Rowland's Works, 1880, was issued privately in an edition of only 6 to 8 copies.)

Memoir of Thomas Lodge. 1882. (This essay, written as an introduction to the Hunterian Club edition of Lodge's Works, 1883, was issued privately in an edition of 10 copies.)

Gray. London: Macmillan, 1882. (English Men of Letters series. Revised 1889.)

Seventeenth-Century Studies: a contribution to the history of English poetry. London: Kegan Paul, Trench, 1883. (Reprinted from *Cornhill Magazine*.)

Cecil Lawson: a memoir. London: Fine Art Society, 1883.

A Critical Essay on the Life and Works of George Tinworth. London: Fine Art Society, 1883.

An Epistle to Dr Oliver Wendell Holmes on his Seventy-fifth Birthday, August 29, 1884. Privately printed, 1884.

Six Lectures written to be delivered before the Lowell Institute in December, 1884. [London]: Privately printed . . . at the Chiswick Press, 1884. (The precursor of *From Shakespeare to Pope*, 1885.)

The Masque of Painters: as performed by the Royal Institute of Painters in Water Colours, May 19, 1885. Privately printed, 1885. (Programme for the performance of the masque, also distributed separately.)

From Shakespeare to Pope: an enquiry into the causes and phenomena of the rise of classical poetry in England. Cambridge: At the University Press, 1885.

Firdausi in Exile and Other Poems. London: Kegan Paul, Trench, 1885.

Raleigh. London: Longmans, Green, 1886. (English Worthies series.)

A Letter to the Editor of the 'Athenaeum'. [London: Chiswick Press, 1886.] (Privately reprinted from *Athenaeum*.)

Life of William Congreve. London: Walter Scott, 1888. (Great Writers series. Revised and enlarged edition published by Heinemann in 1924.)

A History of Eighteenth-Century Literature (1660–1780). London: Macmillan, 1889.

Robert Browning: personalia. Boston, New York: Houghton, Mifflin, 1890. (Reprinted from *Century*, December 1881.)

The Life of Philip Henry Gosse F.R.S. London: Kegan Paul, Trench, Trübner, 1890.

Poetry. Philadelphia: J. B. Lippincott, 1891. (Reprinted from *Chambers's Encyclopaedia*.)

Gossip in a Library. London: William Heinemann, 1891. (Articles reprinted from various periodicals.)

Shelley in 1892: centenary address at Horsham, August 11, 1892. (A few copies of this address were issued as a pamphlet for private distribution, 1892.)

The Secret of Narcisse: a romance. London: William Heinemann, 1892.

Wolcott Balestier: a portrait sketch. London: Privately printed for John W. Lovell, 1892. (Reprinted from *Century*. 100 copies, 90 on handmade paper and 10 on Japanese vellum paper.)

Questions at Issue. London: William Heinemann, 1893. (Articles reprinted from various periodicals.)

The Rose of Omar: inscription for the rose-tree brought by Mr W. Simpson from Omar's tomb at Naishapur and planted to-day on the grave of Edward Fitzgerald at Boulge, 1893. (40 copies printed for private distribution.)

The Jacobean Poets. London: John Murray, 1894. (University Extension Manuals.)

In Russet and Silver. London: William Heinemann, 1894.

Critical Kit-Kats. London: William Heinemann, 1896.

A Short History of Modern English Literature. London: William Heinemann, 1898. (Frequently revised; the edition of 1924 has two additional chapters. First appearance actually 1897.)

Henry Fielding: an essay. London: Privately printed, 1898. (Written as an introduction to an edition of Fielding's works published by Constable. 12 copies only, separately.)

The Life and Letters of John Donne Dean of St Paul's. Now for the first time revised and collected. London: William Heinemann, 1899. Two volumes.

The Character of Queen Victoria. New York: Leonard Scott, 1901. (Reprinted from *Quarterly Review*.)

English Literature. Edmund Spenser. Philadelphia: J. B. Lippincott, 1901. (Reprinted from *Chambers's Cyclopaedia of English Literature*.)

English Literature. Elizabethan and Jacobean. Philadelphia: J. B. Lippincott, 1901. (Prepared for *Chambers's Cyclopaedia of English Literature*.)

Hypolympia or The Gods in the Island: an ironic fantasy. London: William Heinemann, 1901.

The Challenge of the Brontës. Printed [for T. J. Wise] for private distribution, 1903. (Lecture at the Brontë Society.)

English Literature: an illustrated record. London: William Heinemann, 1903. (Volume 2 by Edmund Gosse and Richard Garnett; Volumes 3 and 4 entirely by Gosse and reprinted in 1906.)

Jeremy Taylor. London: Macmillan, 1904. (English Men of Letters series.)

French Profiles. London: William Heinemann, 1904. (Articles reprinted from various periodicals.)

Coventry Patmore. London: Hodder and Stoughton, 1905. (Literary Lives series.)

Sir Thomas Browne. London: Macmillan, 1905. (English Men of Letters series.)

British Portrait Painters and Engravers of the Eighteenth Century: Kneller to Reynolds. Paris: Goupil, 1906. (400 numbered copies.)

Ibsen. London: Hodder and Stoughton, 1907.

Father and Son: a study of two temperaments. London: William Heinemann, 1907.

A History of the Library of the House of Lords. London: [Eyre & Spottiswoode], 1908. (Gosse's introduction to the Catalogue of the Library was printed in an edition of 40 copies for private distribution.)

Biographical Notes on the Writings of Robert Louis Stevenson. London: Privately printed at the Chiswick Press, 1908. (Reprinted, with additions and corrections, from the Pentland edition of Stevenson's works.)

The Autumn Garden. London: William Heinemann, 1909. (Spine dated 1908.)

Swinburne: personal recollections. [London]: Reprinted from *Fortnightly Review* for private circulation, 1909.

A Paradox on Beauty. [Cambridge]: Reprinted from *Fasciculus Joanni Willis Clark dicatus*, [1909]. (An off-print of only a few copies. Gosse's own copy dated 1910 on the spine.)

The Collected Poems of Edmund Gosse. London: William Heinemann, 1911.

Two Visits to Denmark, 1872, 1874. London: Smith Elder, 1911.

The Life of Swinburne, with a Letter on Swinburne at Eton by Lord Redesdale. London: Privately printed at the Chiswick Press, 1912. (Gosse's contribution to the *Dictionary of National Biography New Supplement*, issued separately in an edition of 50 copies.)

Portraits and Sketches. London: William Heinemann, 1912.

Lady Dorothy Nevill: an open letter. London: Privately printed at the Chiswick Press, 1913.

The Future of English Poetry. [Oxford: Oxford University Press], 1913. (English Association pamphlet, 25.)

Two Pioneers of Romanticism: Joseph and Thomas Warton. London: Oxford University Press for the British Academy, [1915]. (British Academy Warton Lecture on English poetry, 6. Reprinted from *Proceedings of the British Academy*, Volume 7.)

Catherine Trotter: the precursor of the Blue-stockings. [London]: 1916. (Reprinted from *Transactions of the Royal Society of Literature*, Volume 25.)

Inter Arma: being essays in time of war. London: William Heinemann, 1916. (Reprinted from *Edinburgh Review*.)

Reims Revisited. Privately printed, 1916. (Reprinted from *Fortnightly Review*.)

Lord Cromer as a Man of Letters. Privately printed, 1917. (Reprinted from *Fortnightly Review*.)

The Life of Algernon Charles Swinburne. London: Macmillan, 1917.

The Novels of Benjamin Disraeli. Privately printed, 1918. (Reprinted from *Transactions of the Royal Society of Literature*.)

Three French Moralists, and the Gallantry of France. London: William Heinemann, [1918].

A Visit to the Friends of Ibsen. Cambridge: At the Cambridge University Press, [1918]. (Reprinted from *Modern Language Review*. 20 copies without advertisement for private distribution; a few more for sale with advertisement.)

Some Literary Aspects of France in the War. [London: 1919]. (Reprinted from *Transactions of the Royal Society of Literature*, Volume 37.)

The First Draft of Swinburne's 'Anactoria'. Cambridge: At the Cambridge University Press, 1919. (Reprinted from *Modern Language Review*. A few copies with *MLR* pagination; 10 copies for private distribution with pages numbered 1–7.)

Some Diversions of a Man of Letters. London: William Heinemann, 1919.

Malherbe and the Classical Reaction in the Seventeenth Century. Oxford: At the Clarendon Press, 1920.

Books on the Table. London: Heinemann, 1921. (Articles reprinted from *Sunday Times*.)

Byways round Helicon. [London: William Heinemann, 1922]. (Reprinted from *Sunday Times*, as an advertisement by the publishers.)

Aspects and Impressions. London: Cassell, 1922. (Articles reprinted from various periodicals.)

The Continuity of Literature. [Oxford: Oxford University Press], 1922. (English Association pamphlet, 54; Presidential address 1922.)

More Books on the Table. London: William Heinemann, [1923]. (Articles reprinted from *Sunday Times*.)

A Review of 'The Life of Lord Wolseley'. [London: William Heinemann], 1924. (Reprinted from *Sunday Times*, as an advertisement by the publishers.)

Silhouettes. London: William Heinemann, 1925. (Articles reprinted from *Sunday Times*.)

Tallement des Réaux or The Art of Miniature Biography: the Zaharoff lecture. Oxford: At the Clarendon Press, 1925.

Swinburne: an essay first written in 1875 and now first printed. [Edinburgh]: Printed [by the Riverside Press] for private circulation, 1925.

Poems. London: E. Benn, 1926. (Augustan Books of Modern Poetry.)

Leaves and Fruit. London: William Heinemann, 1927.

Selected Essays. London: William Heinemann, 1928. (Travellers' Library.)

Two Unpublished Poems. [Winchester: Printed by E. H. Blakeney at his private press, 1929].

An Address to the Fountain Club. [Printed by William Bellows], 1931. (Edited by Philip Gosse.)

America: the diary of a visit, winter 1884–1885. Edited with notes and an introduction by Robert L. Peters and David G. Halliburton. Lafayette: English Literature in Transition, 1966. (Special series, 2.)

A Norwegian Ghost Story. Edited by W. M. Parker. St Peter Port: Toucan Press, 1967.

Thomas Hardy, O.M. Edited and annotated by Ronald Knight. With an introduction by Lois Deacon. Bulphan: Knight & Knight, 1968. (The broadcast of 1928.)

Sir Henry Doulton: the man of business as a man of imagination. Edited by Desmond Eyles. London: Hutchinson, 1970. (Written 1899.)

The Unequal Yoke (1886): a novel. A facsimile reproduction with an introduction by James D. Woolf. Delmar, New York: Scholars' Facsimiles and Reprints, 1975.

Acknowledgments and Sources

I must first thank John Gross, whose suggestion in *The Rise and Fall of the Man of Letters* (1969) that Gosse deserved a new biography was certainly one of the factors responsible for this book. In 1974 he encouraged me to tackle it, though he warned me it would be a 'tough assignment'. One of the things that made it tough was the mass of available material: the thousands and thousands of extant letters and the hundreds of references in printed books.

There are a number of important books to which I must acknowledge a natural debt:

Evan Charteris: *The Life and Letters of Sir Edmund Gosse* (1931)
Paul Mattheisen: *Edmund Gosse: a literary record*, unpublished PhD thesis, Rutgers University (1959)
Linette F. Brugmans: *The Correspondence of André Gide and Edmund Gosse* (1959)
Elias Bredsdorff: *Sir Edmund Gosse's Correspondence with Scandinavian Writers* (1960)
Michael Millgate and Paul Mattheisen: *Transatlantic Dialogue: selected American correspondence of Edmund Gosse* (1965)
R. B. Freeman and Douglas Wertheimer: *P. H. Gosse: A Bibliography* (1980)

I was also particularly glad to be able to read:

Edward Marsh: *A Number of People* (1939)
Osbert Sitwell: *Noble Essences* (1950)
Phyllis Grosskurth: *John Addington Symonds* (1964)
Kathleen Fisher: *Conversations with Sylvia. Sylvia Gosse: painter* (1975)
Fayette Gosse: *The Gosses: the story of an Anglo-Australian family* (1981)
Elfrida Manning: *Marble and Bronze: the art and life of Sir Hamo Thornycroft* (1982)

I have no space to acknowledge here more of the hundreds of relevant printed sources; a few more may be found in the Notes. I must thank Nicholas Warren for providing me with copies of James D. Woolf's annotated bibliography of writings about Edmund Gosse, and the bibliography he made for his own Master's thesis, and for some insights of his own. And at this point I should acknowledge the marvellous services of the London Library, which allowed me to borrow for years on end some of Gosse's own books, which I was not able to buy, and many other books with references to Gosse.

But most of my material comes from unpublished sources. Jennifer Gosse, Edmund's granddaughter and literary executor, was as trusting and co-operative as I could have wished. She allowed me to keep for years a great box of family letters, diaries and other manuscript material, as well as the family's annotated copy of *The Life of Philip Henry Gosse* and the recording of Gosse's voice. She also lent me many photographs from the family albums. I am most grateful to her for her confidence and kindness.

I have borne in mind John Gross's suggestion that every quotation and phrase does not need a reference, 'as if it were applying for a job'. Where the source of a quotation is not given in the Notes, it will almost certainly come from one of the three great Gosse archives – in the Brotherton Collection at Leeds University, in the manuscript section of Cambridge University Library and in the Alexander Library at Rutgers University, New Brunswick, New Jersey. There are also substantial holdings in the British Library, mainly among the Ashley MSS. I am grateful to the staff of all these libraries, who were unfailingly helpful. In particular, I must mention C. D. W. Sheppard, the third librarian in the Brotherton Collection under whose aegis I worked. He has helped me in many ways, as did his predecessors (H. G. Tupper and David I. Masson), but above all in the preparation of the bibliography. It is more his than mine, and I must thank Dennis Cox, Brotherton Librarian, for allowing him to devote university time to it.

I must also thank the librarians, keepers and archivists of the following institutions: City of Aberdeen Art Gallery; Associated Newspapers Group Ltd; Lockwood Memorial Library, University of New York at Buffalo; Boston University; British Museum; British Newspaper Library, Colindale; University of Bristol; Magdalene, Newnham, Pembroke and Trinity Colleges at Cambridge; Dorset County Museum; University of East Anglia; Fitzwilliam Museum Print Room, Cambridge; Houghton Library, Harvard University; Hamilton and Kirkland Colleges (Clinton, NY); William Heinemann Ltd; the House of Lords Library; Huguenot Society; Huntington Library (California); University of Iowa; National Library of Ireland; King's School, Canterbury; University of Liverpool; the British Library of Political and Economic Science at the London School of Economics; the University of London Library (Senate House) and Westfield College, University of London; the *New Statesman*; the Berg Collection, New York Public Library; the Alexander Turnbull Library, Wellington, New Zealand; the Bodleian Library and Merton College, Oxford; Princeton University; the public libraries (special collections) of Hackney, Haringey and Torquay; the Public Record Office; the Royal Academy of Arts; the Royal Literary Fund; the Royal Society of Literature; the Savile Club; the National Library of Scotland; the Society of Authors; the Humanities Research Center, the University of Texas at Austin; *The Times* and *Sunday Times*; the USAF Academy; the Beinecke Library at Yale.

I remember with particular pleasure my week at Rutgers with its extraordinary treasures (sold to them in 1948 by the man who built up Lord Brotherton's collection, J. A. Symington). I was given free accommodation and trusted to have piles of the material around me and to do my own photo-copying without form-filling. Fellow-researchers will realize how appreciative I am of that confidence. I also remember with great pleasure long days in the Pepys Library at Magdalene College, Cambridge, reading the manuscript volumes of Benson's diary. I am grateful to David Newsome. Without the index he had had made to the entire four million words, my task would have been impossible.

Most biographies nowadays seem to have university departments behind them. Without any such, I relied a great deal on my friends, most of them old ones, some made in the course of my research. I am glad they share in the dedication of this book and I name many of them here. Most valuable of all was Alistair Elliot, then of Newcastle University Library, for many patient and amusing answers to queries and for a meticulous reading of the entire typescript. Four specialists, as well as giving me much other help, were kind enough to read some of my pages – my old tutor Helen Gardner (Donne), James McFarlane (Ibsen and other Scandinavian studies), Michael Millgate (Hardy), and Richard Ellmann (Wilde and Ross). Roy Fuller sent me so many Gosse references over the years that he dubbed himself 'Gosse Information Services'. Dorothy Edwards, who died too soon to read this book, early put me on to some references and gave me her own copy of Sassoon's *The Weald of Youth*; Charles Causley gave me George Moore's *Confessions of a Young Man* and Philip Gosse's *A Naturalist Goes to War*.

Other individuals I must thank by name include Alan Bell (who, as well as much else, took great trouble in checking the Gosse holdings at Texas for me), Victor Bonham-Carter, Malcolm and Elizabeth Bradbury, Jo Charlesworth, Dan Davin, Christopher Dobson (Austin Dobson's grandson), Evelyn and Mary Ebsworth, Leon Edel, Ann Farr, Ian Fletcher, Paul Fussell, Robert Gittings, Regina Glick, Edmund Barr Gosse (Edmund's godson), Geoffrey Grigson, Bryan Healing, James Hepburn, Michael Holroyd, Eric Homberger, Clinton Krauss, Raymond Lister, Penelope Lively, George MacBeth, Elfrida Manning (Hamo Thornycroft's daughter), Tom Maschler, Rayburn S. Moore, Janet Morgan, the late Raymond Mortimer, D. J. Palmer, Anthony Powell, Jonathan Raban, Christopher Ricks, May Roberts, D. C. Rose, J-P. B. Ross, Stanley Scott, Brocard Sewell, Diana Shine, Marc Simpson, Janet Adam Smith, Claire Tomalin, Margaret Vallance (Gosse's great-granddaughter), Martha Vogeler, Douglas Wertheimer, Susan Wheeler and Barbara Yaldwyn.

I must also thank with special warmth Rupert and June Hart-Davis and the many friends with whom I stayed on research trips: Karl and René Gay at Buffalo; Jan and Richard Hanna and Sue and Sanford Sacks in New York; my parents-in-law and Marion Maitlis and Nancy Hill in Yorkshire; Lydia and Chris Curtis in Bristol; Anne Harvey, Gill Frayn, Peter Porter, Felicity Taylor and John and Hilary Spurling in London; Joyce and Jonathan Price in Oxford – and, above all, because the Cambridge material involved more visits than they could possibly have imagined when they first invited me, Marni and Alan Hodgkin at Trinity College, Cambridge. All my hosts did far more than provide accommodation. They kept me going by their interest and enthusiasm and often put me on to new trails as well. I did a great deal of my Gosse reading, summer after summer, while staying in Tuscany with Marie and Ronald Ewart. I thank them for many hours of uninterrupted peace.

I must also thank my patient and intelligent typist Hilary Tulloch, and her husband Dick, who helped her produce an impressive typescript from my 260,000 words of difficult longhand. I was very lucky to have such conscientious help so near at hand. I have also been lucky in my publisher, Tom Rosenthal, particularly in his agreeing that the final length was the right length, in spite of the economic problems involved.

My greatest debt is to my family who have lived with Gosse for nine years. Alice is named in the dedication because she was at home all the time and was always supportive and enthusiastic. Supportive too, though less involved, were Lucy, Caroline and Emily. So too were my mother and mother-in-law, who at times thought they would not live to see the book finished, but happily did; they both read it in typescript and made many helpful suggestions. My husband, Anthony Thwaite, besides helping me through the long years of research, read the complete text at four different stages. I could not have written it without him.

Finally, I must put on record the help of the Leverhulme Trust, which gave me a one year research award, without which this whole enterprise would have been even more financially disastrous than it has proved. I thank them warmly.

Ann Thwaite
Low Tharston
Norfolk 1983

Abbreviations used in Notes and Index

ACS	Algernon Charles Swinburne
Aspects	*Aspects and Impressions* by Edmund Gosse (1922)
Benson	The diary of A. C. Benson at Magdalene College, Cambridge
Berg	The Berg Collection, New York Public Library
BL	British Library
BL Ashley	Ashley Library in the British Library
BM	British Museum
Bredsdorff	*Sir Edmund Gosse's Correspondence with Scandinavian Writers* ed. Elias Bredsdorff (1960)
Buffalo	Lockwood Memorial Library, State University of New York at Buffalo
CUL	Cambridge University Library
DNB	*Dictionary of National Biography*
EC	*The Life and Letters of Sir Edmund Gosse* by Evan Charteris (1931)
EG	Edmund Gosse
F&S	*Father and Son* by Edmund Gosse. The page references refer to the 1983 edition in the Penguin English Library.
Huntington	Huntington Library, San Marino, California
JAS	John Addington Symonds
Leeds	Brotherton Collection, Brotherton Library, University of Leeds
Life of ACS	*The Life of Algernon Charles Swinburne* by Edmund Gosse (1917)
Life of PHG	*The Life of Philip Henry Gosse F.R.S.* by Edmund Gosse (1890)
LSE	British Library of Political and Economic Science at the London School of Economics
Matt. and Mill.	*Transatlantic Dialogue: selected American correspondence of Edmund Gosse*, ed. Paul F. Mattheisen and Michael Millgate (1965)
Nat. Lib. Scot.	National Library of Scotland
NG	Nellie Gosse

Abbreviations used in the Notes

NY	New York
PG	Philip Gosse, Edmund's son
PHG	Philip Henry Gosse, Edmund's father
PMG	*Pall Mall Gazette*
RLF	Royal Literary Fund
RLS	Robert Louis Stevenson
Rutgers	Alexander Library, Rutgers University, New Brunswick, New Jersey
Some Diversions	*Some Diversions of a Man of Letters* by Edmund Gosse (1919)
Texas	Humanities Research Center, University of Texas, Austin
TLS	*Times Literary Supplement*
Turnbull	Alexander Turnbull Library, National Library of New Zealand
Yale	Beinecke Library, Yale University

Notes

Chapter 1: Messages Human and Divine

p. 7   EG describes himself as 'a helpless and unwelcome apparition' in his *Life of PHG* (1890) p. 223. Much of the information about PHG comes from this book.

p. 8   In a speech at a dinner given for him in Paris in 1904, EG said, 'Mes ancêtres étaient bourgeois de France, de respectables drapiers de Bordeaux et, avec beaucoup d'autres Huguenots, à la révocation de l'Edit de Nantes, ils durent fuir en Angleterre.' A copy of the speech is in CUL. The Huguenot Society can find no record of either Gosses or Corbins among the refugees.

There is a copy of the unpublished journal of Thomas Gosse in Poole Central Library. Thomas Gosse was admitted to the Royal Academy Schools on 8th October 1779 aged '14 6th last July'. The family tradition was that Reynolds had taught him; certainly he would have listened to his discourses as President at the annual distribution of Premiums. EG writes about Reynolds in *British Portrait Painters* (1906).

PHG's MS recollections are in CUL.

Thomas to William in his last surviving letter (CUL), 4th November 1844: 'My mind is firmly stayed on the Rock of Ages.'

p. 9   PHG's memories of his schooldays, written in 1869, appeared posthumously (1889) in *Longman's Magazine*.

See Lynn Barber's *The Heyday of Natural History* (1980) pp. 115–117. PHG actually describes the invention of an aquarium in *A Naturalist's Rambles on the Devonshire Coast* (1853).

p. 11   In his *Life of PHG*, EG records a disapproval of the drama which 'would have swept it out of existence had he possessed the power to do so'. But PHG did pay one visit to the theatre, on the first night of a revival of Byron's *Sardanapalus* at Drury Lane. The attraction was the set, a careful reproduction of an Assyrian court, based on the recent discoveries at Nineveh.

It was Thomas Bell (1792–1880), President of the Linnean Society in 1858, who made the unfortunate observation that the past year 'has not indeed been marked by any of those striking discoveries which at once revolutionize, so to speak, the department of science in which they occur' – of the very year that Darwin's paper on the origin of species by natural selection was read to the society. It was not quite as stupid a remark as would appear. The impact of Darwin's argument, as J. S. Mill noted, was cumulative rather than immediate. See J. W. Burrow's Introduction (1968) to the Penguin edition of *The Origin of Species*. Bell wrote the reptile section of Darwin's *Zoology of the Voyage of the Beagle*.

p. 11   In Alec Waugh's *My Brother Evelyn* (1967) the first portrait is of 'Cousin Edmund'. V. S. Pritchett's *The Living Novel* (1946) includes a chapter called 'A Plymouth Brother'. Alec Waugh's grandmother, Ann Morgan Waugh, was the granddaughter of John Gosse, younger brother of PHG's father Thomas. Her mother (born 1811), the 'Cousin Ann' of this quotation, is the 'paternal cousin from the west of England' in *F&S* (p. 83) who carried Edmund off to Clifton. See page 33. EG's great-grandfather, William Gosse of Ringwood (see page 8) was therefore Evelyn Waugh's great-great-great-grandfather.

EG spells the Moravian house Blewfields in *F&S* but not in *Life of PHG*.

p. 12   In F&S, EG identifies the Brethren (p. 37) with the Plymouth Brethren, but PHG (22nd Feb 1868 CUL) denied the connection. 'I fear the latter clause of 1 Thess. ii 15 too correctly describes them.' ('They please not God, and are contrary to all men.') On 3rd March 1868 he wrote 'In not a few things I differ from them. I am quite content that you should . . . call yourself a Baptist.'

p. 13   In *F&S* (p.36) EG does not specifically mention gambling, but writes of 'reckless expenditure . . . ruin' and 'penury'.

p. 13ff Much of the information about Emily Gosse comes from two memoirs published after her death: *A Memorial to Emily Gosse* by PHG (1857); *Tell Jesus!* by Anna Shipton (1863).

These family archives are almost all at CUL, although Emily's and Edmund's diaries and many other papers are at Leeds.

p. 19   The description of the cockle's progress comes from PHG: *A Year at the Shore* (1865), p. 94. Darwin shared PHG's interest in infancy and published a 'Biographical Sketch of an Infant' in *Mind*.

p. 21   PHG's own account of the decision to go to Devon (with 'the little naturalist in petticoats') is in *A Naturalist's Rambles on the Devonshire Coast* (1853).

p. 24   For EG's letter to Hardy 18th January 1920 see EC p. 461.

p. 25   In *Aspects and Impressions* (1922) EG has an essay on 'Rousseau in England' which draws attention to the 'amazing influence' of the evangelical Charles Simeon (1759–1836) during the period when young PHG and Emily Bowes were most open to influence. 'Simeon boldly proposed three tests to be applied to any species of literature. When confronted by a book, the reader should ask, "Does it uniformly tend to humble the sinner, to exalt the Saviour, to promote holiness?" A work that lost sight of any one of those three points was to be condemned without mercy.'

p. 28   The vivid experience of the young Edmund on the beach at Barricane is not in *F&S*. See *The Life of PHG*, p. 258. The subsequent quotations are from PHG: *Seaside Pleasures* (1853).

Charles Kingsley's 'Happy truly is the naturalist . . .' is quoted by Eliza Gosse in her 'Reminiscences' attached to *The Life of PHG*, p. 365.

p. 29   The emblem of the bog-myrtle is from PHG: *Tenby* (1856), p. 205.

In *Abraham and his Children* (1855) Emily wrote 'We can scarcely exaggerate the importance of a little child . . . That immortal being will largely be just what we make him.' Her tracts were published in one volume, 1857.

p. 30   EG's presentiment of disaster is described in *The Life of PHG*, p. 260. B. W. Newton's book was published in 1846.

p. 31   Mr Elliott is Edward Bishop Elliott (1793–1875) whose *Horae Apocalypticae* appeared in 1844.

p. 33   'The narrow stream of death' is Charles Wesley's phrase. Letters are at CUL.

p. 34   Alec Waugh's grandmother's memories are in *My Brother Evelyn* (1967).

p. 35   The 'acidulated women' are in *Leaves and Fruit* (1927), p. 229. They would 'plant themselves in a family and exercise a fantastic tyranny over every member of it'.

The house is now the Sandhurst Hotel, Manor Road, Babbacombe, Torquay. It was easier to get an idea of the house EG lived in from a neighbouring one, which remained almost unchanged in 1975.

p. 38   *Actinologia Britannica* (1860). PHG's bibliographers say the book is still useful today because 'no other book covers and illustrates the British corals'.

p. 39   The ladies who cited PHG as their authority are in *The Life of PHG*, p. 288. EG's new genus is claimed in *F&S*, p. 127.

p. 40   One of the Miss Willses was presumably 'that serpent Miss Wilkes' *F&S*, p. 140.

p. 43   For Eliza Brightwen's 'Reminiscences' see *The Life of PHG*, p. 353.

p. 44   The description of PHG's smile is from *The Life of PHG*, p. 207.

Of Eliza, EG writes in *F&S*, p. 181 that she had been 'brought up hitherto in the so-called Church of England' but all other evidence suggests she was a Quaker. Tessa Gosse (MS notes, Leeds) wrote 'She was a Quaker by birth and up-bringing. I remember how she and her sister "thee'd" each other.'

p. 45   The 'hearty welcome' is in *The Life of PHG*, p. 357.

p. 46   PHG's aspersions on the Greek gods are in *F&S*, p. 204.

I am indebted to Douglas Wertheimer (*Notes & Queries*, Jan 1976) for the *Revival* advertisement.

p. 47   In the 1861 census there were seventeen boys resident at Trafalgar Villa, aged eleven to nineteen. But there were obviously also dayboys, including Edmund, who is listed at Sandhurst as a 'scholar' aged eleven.

MS of review of Augustus Hare: *The Gurneys of Earlham* (1895) is in the Walpole Library, King's School, Canterbury.

p. 48   Edmund's essay CUL.

In *F&S*, EG echoes the biblical phrase from Matthew 12, verses 43 and 44. 'When the unclean spirit is gone out of a man,' he returns to his house 'and findeth it empty, swept and garnished'.

p. 49   The passage about *Coelebs* comes from *Leaves and Fruit* (1927), p. 145.

PHG quotes 'Hark! Hark! the lark . . .' in *Land and Sea* (1865, but much of it written earlier). It is on p. 383 in the 1879 edition.

p. 51   EG's memory of the Carlyle conversation is in *Books on the Table* (1921), p. 302.

'I, too, will be a poet' comes from an autobiographical sketch written for K. A. Winter-Hjelm in January 1875, for a piece which appeared in *Ny Illustrerte Tidende*, 14th February 1875.

See EG *Critical Kit-Kats* (1896), p. 172.

p. 53   The information about Elise Otté comes from EG's obituary of her, in a cutting at CUL from an unknown paper.

p. 54   PHG's attitude to pain and distress: *F&S*, p. 231.

Thomas Brightwen worked for Gurney, Birkbeck and Brightwen, Hall Quay, Yarmouth; his brother George for Overend and Gurney in London. The suggestion that 'no excitement in commercial circles ever exceeded' the collapse of the Gurney bank comes from *The Life of a Century* by Edwin Hodder (Newnes. 1901).

p. 55ff   In *English Literature: an illustrated record* (1903), EG would describe Kingsley as 'an inglorious professor of modern history at Cambridge', and write of him as 'a delightful companion, the soul of wit and capricious humour and bubbling over with enthusiastic information'.

p. 56   The speaker Henry Soltau did not actually use the phrase 'a lost soul in hell' of Shakespeare as EG suggested in *F&S*.

Chapter 3: The Assassin behind the Tree

p. 60   Mary Ann Baker 'fell asleep in Jesus June 18, 1884 in her 89th year' according to an In Memoriam notice at CUL. But the 1871 census puts her age as only 73.

   For PHG's attitude, V. S. Pritchett: 'A Plymouth Brother' in *The Living Novel* (1946).

p. 62   Quotation from Tract No. 52 *A Happy Family*.

p. 63   Introductory essay to *The Library of Edmund Gosse* by E. H. M. Cox (1924).

p. 64   For Marzials' behaviour, see EC p. 19.

   J. A. Symonds on Marzials comes from his autobiography in the London Library, at long last published in 1984.

p. 65   In his novel *The Secret of Narcisse* (1892), EG would symbolize the need of the artist for release by talking of Narcisse's 'crazy wish' 'to walk out upon the black night air . . . from roof to roof'.

   As for the fireworks from Cremorne, Madox Brown would tell a story of Turner taking a house at Chelsea specifically to be able to watch the fireworks from Cremorne Gardens without paying the shilling entrance fee. See *Ford Madox Brown. A Record of his Life and Works* by Ford Madox Hueffer (1896), p. 103. The Butler essay is in *Aspects*.

p. 67   PHG's attitude to poetry: *The Life of PHG*, p. 351.

p. 68   'Puseyite cross': Edward Pusey (1800–1882) was one of the leaders of the Oxford Movement, which sought to bring the Church of England closer to Rome.

p. 69f   References to Swinburne are from *Portraits and Sketches* (1912), p. 6. *Books on the Table* (1921), p. 63. In *More Books on the Table* (1923) EG refers (p. 40) to 'the unparalleled sensation and scandal of Swinburne's *Poems and Ballads*'. In *Some Diversions* (1920), p. 235, he says ACS 'succeeded in his revolution' and prepared the way for an ultimate appreciation of Thomas Hardy.

   The reference to Mrs Grundy also from *Some Diversions*, p. 235. See note to p.116.

p. 70   'laureate of a pack of satyrs' from John Morley in the *Saturday Review*, quoted by John Gross: *The Rise and Fall of the Man of Letters* (1969), p. 102.

   'pagan, suffering persecution' from Clara Watts-Dunton: *The Home Life of Swinburne* (1922), p. 19, quoting Winwood Reade.

p. 71   The two accounts are in *The Life of ACS*, p. 178 and *Portraits and Sketches*, p. 18.

   EG had presumably seen one of the photographs of ACS and Adah Menken, the actress Rossetti had procured for ACS. On 17th April 1868, ACS wrote 'There has been a *damned* row about it; paper after paper . . . assuming or asserting the falsehood that its publication and sale all over London were things authorised . . . by the sitters: whereas of course it was a private affair to be known (or shewn) to friends only.'

   Jean Overton Fuller in her biography of ACS also quotes his letter of 22nd July 1868 to John Nicoll.

p. 72   See 'Arthur O'Shaughnessy' in *Silhouettes* (1925), p. 173ff.
       EG in his obituary of Richard Garnett in *The Author* (1906).

p. 73   Letter at time of Barnardo's death in September 1905. EC p. 296.
       Conversation from a letter from someone in Marychurch to Philip Gosse, junior, after EG's death. This could refer to a visit long after this period. CUL.

p. 74   A. H. Clough, 1819–1861, from *Dipsychus* Sc. v. 1.82.

p. 75   EG's comment on Jean Ingelow from *More Books on the Table*, p. 140.
       Religious phases: EG referred to his own occasional 'flare up of piety'.
       Booth preached 'very noisily and badly'. EC p. 297.

p. 77   See EG to Blaikie on p. 84 for the suggestion that he had learnt not to care.

p. 78   The 'aromatic plant' is the bog-myrtle. PHG *Tenby*, p. 205. See also my p. 29.

p. 79   'It will be remembered': see p. 69.

p. 80   'Meeting angels in the street' from *Critical Kit-Kats* (1896), p. 222.
       Walter Pater: *Critical Kit-Kats*, p. 253.

p. 81   'Andromeda': EG refers to Charles Kingsley's poem.

p. 82   'The Poetry of the Period': l. 5 refers to Newman and Aubrey de Vere, l. 6 to Buchanan, l. 7–8 to Swinburne, l. 9 to G. Massey, Bennett etc, l. 10 to Walt Whitman, l. 11 to 'the Misses mathematical'. (EG's own annotation.)

p. 83   But on 25th March 1875 EG warns a Norwegian poet, Kirsten Hansen, against religious poetry. 'There is little new to be said on this august subject and poetry, to be good, should be also new.'

p. 84   Fairford: I can find no record of any poet of this name. EG's annotated copy is in the library of Trinity College, Cambridge.
       'Cecilia' is one of Blaikie's poems.

p. 86   'Four years later' EG wrote in the autobiographical article in *Ny Illustrerte Tidende* (1875).
       MS note about May Johnson at Leeds.

p. 87   See p. 20 for their earlier financial position.

p. 88   'Watch ye therefore': Luke 21, v. 36.

Chapter 4: Our Youngest Poet

p. 91   The description of Stevenson is from *Critical Kit-Kats*, p. 276.
       EG called RLS 'the most fascinating human being . . .' in a speech at the RLS Club in Edinburgh in November 1920.

p. 93   William Bell Scott, 1811–1890.
       Joachim de Patinir, 1485?–1524.
       'blaze of colour': EG in *Modern English Literature* (1897), p. 381.
       Information on Scott and Swinburne from EG's essay on ACS in 1875 for Brandes' journal, *Det Nittende Aarhundrede*. (Reprinted by the Riverside Press in 1925). See p. 115.

p. 94   'too easily successful': letter to W. D. Howells, 30th November 1886. See Matt. and Mill. p. 197.
       'lurid tragedies': *Modern English Literature*, p. 119.

p. 95   'Algernon took to you at once' is confirmed by W. B. Scott on 19th September 1878: 'He took to you from the first time he met you at Chelsea, and he does not do so to many.' Scott obviously thought they had first met at *his* house, not at the Madox Browns.
       The description of 37 Fitzroy Square and of Madox Brown is from *Ford Madox Brown* by Ford M. Hueffer (1896).
       EG used the more scandalous material about ACS which he could not include

in his *Life* in the *Confidential Papers* he circulated privately, which were eventually published in C. Y. Lang's edition of the *Letters* (1959–1962).

p. 96   In spite of EG's word to 'Mr Franks of your Museum' and a letter from Rossetti to the Home Secretary, Sidney Colvin got the job.

The description of the evening in Fitzroy Square comes from EG's *Life of ACS* (1917), p. 200.

p. 97   The note about the meeting with Rossetti is in Trinity College, Cambridge.

For Sainte-Beuve, see 'The Prince of Critics' in *More Books on the Table*, p. 13.

p. 98   Ford Madox Ford (Hueffer) tells the story, *op. cit.*, of Rossetti's wombat dozing in the épergne in the centre of the dining-table and eating the entire contents of a valuable box of cigars unnoticed, during a post-prandial discussion. This wombat is said to have been the original of Lewis Carroll's dormouse.

Christina Rossetti from *Critical Kit-Kats*, p. 158.

p. 99   *The Nightside of London* was published in 1857.

p. 100   John Morley's attack on Swinburne was in the *Saturday Review*. See also p. 70, though it should be remembered that Morley would publish Swinburne regularly when he became editor of the *Fortnightly*.

See William Gaunt: *The Pre-Raphaelite Tragedy* (1942).

p. 101   The Scott story comes from Oswald Doughty: *A Victorian Romantic, Dante Gabriel Rossetti* (1949).

The meeting with Tennyson first appeared in the *Cambridge Review* in 1911. The full text is in *Tennyson: Interviews and Recollections*, edited by Norman Page (1983). In it EG dates the encounter as in 'the early summer of 1871' but it may well have been much later. In a letter to Scott on 28th August 1874, EG wrote 'Did I tell you I was presented by Ralston to Tennyson, who was very affable?' I have kept it at 1871 because EG ties it up with his Norwegian visit. Tennyson visited Norway in 1858, which fits in with 'some dozen years before' if it is 1871. It remains odd that Ralston should have *twice* presented EG to Tennyson and it seems likely that EG is conflating two occasions.

p. 103   *Tristram Jones* is in CUL.

p. 105   Eliza Brightwen's character from a letter to George Armour 24th June 1887.

p. 106   *Consuelo* (1842–3) by George Sand.

p. 107   Article on the Lofoten Islands was in *Fraser's Magazine* (1871). Reprinted in *Studies in the Literature of Northern Europe* (1879).

H. G. Ollendorff had marketed a quick method of learning languages.

p. 108   'the first time Ibsen's name had been written in English'. In fact, it was the first time in *England* but one poem had already been translated by Johan A. Dahl in *Norwegian and Swedish Poems*, published in Bergen the same year (1872).

EG refers to Ibsen's letter in a letter to Scott 26th February 1873.

p. 109   William Allingham (1824–1889) poet, later editor of *Fraser's*.

p. 110   Charles Edward Appleton (1841–1879) founded the *Academy* in 1869.

Eirikr Magnusson (1833–1913) Icelandic scholar and Librarian, Cambridge University, 1871–1909. He collaborated with Morris on *Three Northern Love Stories and other Tales* reviewed by EG in the *Academy*, 17th July 1875.

The description of Morris at the lecture is from a MS in Leeds.

'after Morris's death': the letter is to Maurice Baring 12th August 1899. See EC p. 264.

p. 111   But as early as 26th October 1874 EG had identified himself with *The Examiner* in writing to Brandes: 'We are atheist and republican and I write on poetry every week, do dramatic criticism etc. and the paper has become the vehicle for my poetry too.'

'the flaming creature': *Books on the Table*, p. 63.

p. 112ff Later quotations about Swinburne come from letters in 1886 to T. Watts-Dunton and E. C. Stedman, from the *Confidential Papers on A. C. Swinburne's Moral Irregularities* in the BL (see note on p. 95), from the *Life of ACS* and from *Portraits and Sketches*.

p. 113 Henrik Wergeland (1808–1845) Norwegian poet, well known as a radical.
Arthur Waugh in 'The Book of Gosse' in the *Fortnightly Review*, September 1932. See note to p. 325.

p. 114 The undated MS note is inside the Trinity College, Cambridge, copy of *Life of ACS*.
Morris's story comes from a letter to EG from Sydney Cockerell 28th March 1915 (B. L. Ashley).

p. 115 The Bothwell reading according to EG's diary was on 6th April 1874, a Bank Holiday Monday. Madox Brown, Marston, Austin Dobson and Theo Marzials were there with EG. The quotation comes from the *Confidential Papers* and it is interesting to compare it with the account in *Life of ACS*, p. 219.

p. 116 Grundyism, much used by EG as shorthand for prudishness, comes from the character Mrs Grundy, the symbol of conventional propriety, who does not actually appear, in Thomas Morton's *Speed the Plough* (1798).
Censorship comments come from *Books on the Table*, p. 259, *Questions at Issue*, p. 20, *French Profiles*, p. 266 and A. C. Benson's diary, 1911.

p. 117 EG to Georg Brandes 11th January 1912, looking back to their youth. 'You used to hate Icelanders in the old days; you have forgiven them as I have forgiven kings!'

Chapter 5: Northern Studies

p. 118 EG sent *A Norwegian Ghost Story* to *Blackwood*'s in Nov 1871. In Jan 1873, he wrote to ask what had happened to it. It was not published until 1967 by W. M. Parker at St Peter Port, Guernsey. It has some interest in its vivid picture of Norwegian fishing wives, one of them called Fru Ibsen.

p. 121 Ibsen to EG 30th April 1872: 'I have written requesting him to call on you. Mr Løkke has a thorough acquaintance with our literature.'
'for the purpose of reporting': 'A Visit to the Friends of Ibsen' in *Aspects*.
'via Hamburg': Isabel Becker may have accompanied him on this part of the trip. See p. 53.

p. 123 In a letter to Andersen (23rd July 1872) from Dr Fog's house, EG wrote: 'I cannot tell you what a delight it has been to me to see and speak with you; when I was a little child, and first began to love your writings, I used to wonder whether I should ever see yourself.' There is no other evidence that EG read Andersen as a child. In *F&S*, it will be remembered, EG specifically says he had no fiction and 'had never heard of fairies', p. 49–50.
The occasion in the *Chambers's* article is also referred to in *Leaves and Fruit*, p. 187.

p. 124 *Two Visits to Denmark*, p. 123.

p. 125 Bjørnstjerne Bjørnson (1832–1910).
Brandes letter is to Hans Brøchner. For EG's interpretation see *Aspects*, 'A Visit to the Friends of Ibsen'.
Ibsen wrote to Brandes, 4th April 1872: 'The Liberals are the worst enemies of freedom'.

p. 126 Brandes' reply (26th Aug 1879) is rather disloyal to EG. It was true they had seldom met but there are 30 letters from Brandes to EG up to this point (Leeds) and many more afterwards. In 1874 they performed the ceremony 'at drikke dus' – a pledge of friendship, drinking from wine glasses with their hands coiled. EG thought that, after Dean Fog, 'Brandes is the warmest friend I have in Denmark'. See p. 144.

'Ibsen's Danish champion' – Michael Meyer's phrase for Brandes in his biography of Ibsen. Brandes' essay on Ibsen in 1866/7 was at a time when Ibsen was unknown, even by name, outside Scandinavia. By the time EG reviewed *Digte* in England, Ibsen had had some continental acclaim.

EG's phrases about Bjørnson are from *Fraser's* Feb 1874 and the *Academy* Nov 1877.

p. 127   EG's article on J. L. Runeberg, Swedish-Finnish poet (1804–77) in the Oct 1878 issue of *The Cornhill* was reprinted in *Studies in the Literature of Northern Europe*.

EG's criticism of himself was in the *Saturday Review*, 12 April 1884.

Brandes was known as an iconoclast, a republican, an extreme individualist. Danes were offended both by his interest in German literature and the fact that he was a Jew. Like Ibsen, but in a very different way, he wanted 'to wake the people', to use Ibsen's own phrase.

p. 130   The description of the *Fortnightly* is from John Gross: *The Rise and Fall of the Man of Letters*, p. 99.

The 'tantalising letter' is from G. A. Simcox, 16th Dec 1873 (Leeds).

p. 133   'possible death': see also p. 143.

R. L. Nettleship (1846–92); his *Philosophical Lectures* were edited by A. C. Bradley and G. R. Benson in 2 vols in 1897.

p. 134   On Hepworth Dixon's death in 1879, EG wrote to Stevenson: 'I take it as a good omen, they evidently want the bad writers, not the good ones, up there.'

For Horne, see *Life of ACS*, p. 264, *Portraits and Sketches*, p. 97ff, *Leaves and Fruit*, p. 171/2.

p. 135   EG to Wise in 1907 dates his earliest Browning letter as 1872 but the first exchange seems really to have been early in 1874 (Huntington).

Hugh Walpole is quoted in the biography by Rupert Hart-Davis, p. 287.

In *Two Visits to Denmark*, p. 136, EG records his travels with Fog as simply 'a delightful journey'.

p. 138   *On Viol and Flute* was praised by E. C. Stedman, the American critic, in a letter to EG, 29th Nov 1875. He commended 'the natural and modern feeling of such poems as "Sunshine before Sunrise" and "Lying in the Grass". Your pre-Raphaelite friends too often . . . forget that there is a live world around us'.

p. 139   Augusta Webster (1837–1894), poet and translator of Aeschylus and Euripides.

PHG's lines are at Rutgers.

p. 141   Dobson's poem seems to have been the *rondeau* called 'Footpath'. EG recalls the occasion in the *Quarterly*, Jan 1922, reprinted in *Austin Dobson: Some Notes* by Alban Dobson (1928).

p. 142   Comments on Dobson from A. C. Benson's diary and Edward Marsh: *A Number of People* (1939), p. 106.

p. 143   See also p. 133 for EG's feelings when faced with death.

p. 147   'his income': In 1874 EG's literary earnings were £112 2s 11d; from investments he had £1 19s 9d. The Museum paid him £160 and PHG gave him £40.

'Editors were not always interested . . .' EG to K. A. Winter-Hjelm, 22nd Feb 1875: 'I hope you will realize how difficult it is for me to get a hearing when I write on Scandinavian matters and so, if I am sometimes silent . . . put it down to the wilfulness of editors . . .'

p. 149   Rowland Hill: not the founder of the penny post.
   Her father's hero was Dr C. F. S. Hahnemann (1755–1843), the German physician who founded homeopathy and was forced to leave Leipzig because of the hostility of the apothecaries.

p. 154   Article on Alma-Tadema in *Illustrated Biographies of Modern Artists* (1883).

p. 155   Alma-Tadema's temper: EG to W. B. Scott, 8th April 1875. 'Don't talk much to Tadema about the etchings. We had a great quarrel yesterday, he and I, loud high words on both sides, and then he became exceedingly amiable . . .'
   The story about his Dutch comes from Edward Marsh: *A Number of People* (1939), p. 112.
   His daughter's memories were published in the *Cornhill*, Dec 1929. TS at Leeds, dated from Versailles, 7th May 1929.

p. 156   The description of the Lamb dinner is from a speech EG gave on 10th Feb 1912 at the University Arms, Cambridge. In *Cambridge Review*, 2nd May 1912. See also *Portraits and Sketches*, p. 53.

p. 157   'Dinner at the Stephens' from F. W. Maitland: *Life of Leslie Stephen* (1906), p. 158. In 1905, Maitland wrote to EG 'I guess that he was more frightened of you and Stevenson than you were of him.' Noel Annan in his biography of Stephen refers to his 'cheerless obmutescence'.
   Mallarmé: *French Profiles*, p. 179, *Leaves and Fruit*, p. 285.

p. 158   'other supporters': a letter from Rev. G. W. Kitchin, in the BM archives, pays tribute to 'a most charming, modest young man, of most ingenious abilities, fresh and full of literary tastes and feelings – an excellent linguist . . . He is at present in a Dept. of the Museum which gives no scope to his real abilities'.

p. 159   PHG and London. When Nellie wrote to invite them to London in Jan 1876, PHG wrote: 'I fear it is quite hors de question. I do not expect that I shall ever see London again, while I am in this body.'

p. 160   'out of a Hardy novel': so much like a Hardy story did it sound that John Drinkwater's memory played tricks with him. He tells the story in his *Book for Bookmen* (1926), transferring it to Hardy. (Letter from EG to Drinkwater, 21st Oct 1926 Yale.)
   Robert Stephen Hawker (1803–75). Drinkwater edited a selection of his poems in 1925.

p. 161   EG's letter of thanks to Norway is in *Norsk Folkeminnesamling*, Oslo. (See Bredsdorff, p. 74.)

p. 162   Marzials' later letter: on 20th Nov 1875, he sent a photo to replace one he had torn from EG's album. 'I especially thought of you while it was being taken, but no-one need know that but you . . . Do forget and forgive the nasty Theo of the past with his jealousies and caprices.' The Gosses continued to entertain Marzials and a succession of his lovers. (e.g. 8th Oct 1878 TM to EG 'You were so sweet and nice to him . . .')
   In fact, it would seem that EG did eventually have to take an examination. 3rd Jan 1876 PHG to EG: 'I must say I await with some solicitude the verdict of your Examiners', though this could refer to the forthcoming reviews of *King Erik*. There is an undated letter to Dobson: 'I am summoned to appear before the Examiners next Thursday morning' but this may be 1884/5 when EG was trying to get back to the BM.
   Arthur Waugh: *One Man's Road* (1931).
   'shockingly dull stuff': EG in *TP's Weekly* 2nd June 1928 (i.e. just after his death).

p. 163   The stories about Thomas Farrer (1819–1899) come from EC p. 77.

p. 164 Frederick Locker (1821–1895) added the name Lampson in 1885. *London Lyrics* had first appeared in 1857.

p. 165 Yeats's *Letters* (ed. Wade), p. 259. 23 Nov 1895. He recalls *King Erik* scene 2, Act 4.

29 Delamere Terrace no longer exists. It seems to have been destroyed during the Second World War.

'Browning . . . is almost my next-door neighbour': EG to Stedman, 28th April 1879.

p. 166 Comments on EG's conversation from A. C. Benson's diary, E. F. Benson's *As we were* (1932), p. 203, and EC, p. 277.

EG has an essay on John Leicester Warren, Lord de Tabley, in *Critical Kit-Kats*, p. 165.

p. 169 Swinburne extract from *Confidential Papers*.

Emily Teresa Gosse was called after her aunt Emily and Nellie's great friend Theresa Thornycroft (Siegfried Sassoon's mother). She was usually called Tessa.

p. 171 EG's essay on George Eliot begins *Aspects*.

The portrait of her was presumably Laura Alma-Tadema's 1877 drawing now in the National Portrait Gallery (No. 1758).

The phrase about Lydgate being George Eliot comes from a letter to Elizabeth Haldane in 1925. (Nat. Lib. Scot.)

p. 172 George Saintsbury's memories of EG in *London Mercury*, July 1928.

MS account of quarrel at Leeds.

p. 176 All references to EG have been expunged from Collins's son's version of his diaries, published in *Life and Memoirs of John Churton Collins* (1912) and there is no explanation of the situation described in the 4th Nov 1878 letter.

p. 177 Lunch with RLS: EG to Graham Balfour (Nat. Lib. Scot.) 26th Feb 1900. Information also from script of broadcast on Stevenson 3rd Dec 1926. Yale. EG's essay on RLS is in *Critical Kit-Kats*, p. 273.

p. 178 James on RLS to T. S. Perry 14th Sept 1879. EG on James to E. C. Stedman 28th April 1879.

The Queen-Mother; Rosamond had been published in 1860. RLS's last letter was 1st Dec 1894.

p. 180 Symonds's gift: *Books on the Table*, p. 154.

p. 181 'with every respect paid to "states"': *Gossip in a Library* Introductory. Heywood: *Books on the Table*, p. 46.

'folio Beaumont and Fletcher': letter to RLS 1st July 1884.

'revealing sexual memoir': see note to p. 64.

p. 182 But on 19th Sept 1884 EG was to write to Symonds: 'I so abhor the undignified modern system of arranging beforehand for the reviews of books that I will have nothing to do with it and always refuse requests of this sort from my friends which are pretty frequently made to me.'

Chapter 7: 'Something better than a brother'

p. 184 Kegan Paul printed, published and advertised *Studies in the Literature of Northern Europe* for EG 'on a royalty of 3s 6d per copy (reckoning 13 as 12) after the sale of 300 copies'.

p. 187 For EG's interest in art: EG to Thornycroft 3rd May 1881: 'I began two years ago by taking a violent interest in the Academy all for your sake, but now I begin to do it for my own. One lives doubly by being all alive in the march of two professions.'

p. 190   'A more recent critic' – Paul Mattheisen: *Edmund Gosse: a literary record* (1959), unpublished PhD thesis at Rutgers.

    R. H. Stoddard described E. C. Stedman's *Victorian Poets* as 'the most important contribution ever made by an American writer to the critical literature of the English poets'.

p. 193   John Addington Symonds: *Studies of the Greek Poets*. 2 vols (1873–76).
    'clubbishness' – by Nov 1879, EG was on the committee of the Savile Club.

p. 194   Hart-Davis recorded Sassoon's conversation in a letter of 28th Sept 1958 to George Lyttelton. (*Lyttelton–Hart-Davis Letters* vol. 3 1980).

p. 195   'a very fortunate life': EG first wrote 'a very *happy* life'. The letters from EG to JAS are in the library of the University of Bristol.

    Leon Edel, biographer of Henry James, quite rightly sure that EG 'was too cautious and too worried about his rôle and reputation to take any large homosexual risks' (letter to me, 6th June 1982), denied altogether in his book the interpretation of this passage by Phyllis Grosskurth in her biography of Symonds, which (picked up by Gross in *The Rise and Fall of the Man of Letters*, by Gittings in *The Older Hardy*, by Jenni Calder in *RLS: A Life Study*, and by Ted Morgan in *Somerset Maugham*) has widely established the idea of EG's homosexuality. I have found the conviction of it even among A level students of *F&S*. It seems to me that the confession of strong feelings at one period for one person of the same sex does not qualify EG as 'a secret homosexual', as he has constantly been called in recent years. See also pp. 320–321.

p. 197   Lines from 'Our wood in winter', *Collected Poems,* p. 220.

p. 199   Philip Gosse: *An Apple a Day* (1948), p. 20: 'most indulgent of parents . . .'

p. 200   'sixth birthday': cf *F&S* p. 65, and his running away p. 76.

p. 201   Philip's memories of RLS are in *My Pirate Library* (1926). There are others in *Go to the Country* (1935) and *An Apple a Day* (1948).

p. 202   James on English children: letter to Grace Norton, c. 4th Jan 1888. Harvard.
    Browning's pigs – in *An Apple a Day*, Philip says they were for him, but the BL pigs are annotated in Gosse's hand, 'drawn by Mr Browning, the poet, to amuse Teresa when she spent an afternoon at his house, April 6, 81'.

p. 202   *The Century*: in 1881 Roswell Smith had bought out Scribner and started the new magazine.

p. 203   *The Ring and the Book*. Nineteen-year-old EG wrote in his journal on 2nd Dec 1868: 'A new poem by Robert Browning is out . . . about 20,000 lines. It is a powerful but ugly and repulsive study of human nature.'

    EG described his reception in *Robert Browning. Personalia* (1890).

    See Edel: *The Life of Henry James,* vol. 1, p. 848 (Penguin) and A. C. Benson's diary for 1900: 'He was a strangely uninteresting man . . .'

p. 204   EG on E. B. Browning: see *English Literature: an illustrated record* (1903).

    Thomas Raynesford Lounsbury (1838–1915) was professor of English Language and Literature at Yale. One of his books was on Browning.

    F. J. Furnivall (1825–1910) founded the Browning Society and compiled a Browning bibliography in 1881.

p. 206   EG borrowed the box again, after Browning's death, from Robert Barrett Browning, for his edition of the letters for Elkin Matthews. The box was returned but when R. B. Browning died, no trace of it was found. EG's final work on Beddoes, the Fanfrolico Press edition of 1928, was published after EG's death. According to F. L. Lucas, it perpetuated many of the 'errors and corruptions and mutilations' of the old edition.

    Strachey's essay was in Desmond MacCarthy's *New Quarterly*, autumn, 1907. See Michael Holroyd: *Lytton Strachey: The Unknown Years* (1967), p. 367.

Chapter 8: Playthings

p. 207   The spring trips to France were from 1884 to 1894, but not in 1888.

p. 208   William Bellows: *Edmund Gosse. Some Memories* (1929).

p. 211   Meeting Wilde – from EC p. 145.

p. 215   EG's poem 'Firdausi in Exile' was first published as an introduction to Helen Zimmern's *Epic of the Kings* (1883).

Mrs Cecil Lawson. Hubert Herkomer to EG: 'She absorbed him wholly, even to the last – was at her post sucking his life out.' EG was a pall-bearer at Lawson's funeral, 17th June 1882 and wrote a memoir of him (1883), illustrated by Herkomer and Whistler.

p. 217   See *Biographical notes on the Writings of RLS* published by Chiswick Press (1908).

EG's essay on 'Cummy' is in *Leaves and Fruit*, p. 327.

p. 218   Of *Treasure Island*, Fanny Stevenson to Nellie, 16th March 1882: 'I am glad Mr Gosse likes 'Treasure Island' [in *Young Folks*]. I don't. I liked the beginning, but after that the life seemed to go out of it . . . [I] don't like Louis' name to go before the public with any but the best work . . . What does the Poet think honestly?'

p. 219   Jenni Calder: *RLS: A Life Study*, p. 155 commends EG's 'balance and generosity'. Fanny Stevenson's letter at Yale.

p. 220   *Cornhill* article reprinted in *Memoirs and Portraits* by Robert Louis Stevenson (1887).

'Thirty-five years later' – W. A. Sim quotes EG in a letter to Philip at CUL on 22nd Oct 1917. EG typically remembered the year as 1879 not 1881.

p. 221   The complete poem is in *Collected Poems*, p. 186. It is inevitable for post-Freudians to think of Yeats's 'his rod and its butting head'. Gosse, of course, refers to fishing rods.

p. 224   'Three years later': Barnes's deathbed is described in a letter to Coventry Patmore.

p. 226   'Stretched on the sofa' from 'Henry James' in *Aspects*, p. 27.

James's biographer, Leon Edel, suggests James, at the beginning of their relationship, found EG 'amiable but secondrate'. I can find no real evidence of this. More important, Edel suggests that posthumous publication has betrayed EG's apparent duplicity, when telling Hardy that James admired *Tess*. But James did talk of the book having 'a singular beauty and charm' in spite of its faults, when writing to RLS on 19th March 1892 (letter in Lubbock's selection; not in Edel's). It was a year later James used the word 'vile' and had apparently forgotten the beauty and charm he had felt on first reading it.

p. 227   For Patmore, see mainly EG's biography *Coventry Patmore* and 'the Laureate of Wedded Love' in *More Books on the Table*, p. 147.

p. 229   In 1886 EG wrote important articles on Patmore in the *Athenaeum*, *St James's Gazette* and the *Saturday Review*.

p. 230   At the Newcastle Literary and Philosophical Society in Dec 1882, 250 people turned up to hear Gosse lecture, in spite of 'a most fearful night, snow falling, slosh on the ground'.

'Playthings' is on p. 15 of *In Russet and Silver*. 'The Wallpaper' is on p. 62 of *In Russet and Silver*. EG reprinted neither in his *Collected Poems*.

p. 232   In a letter to Humphry Ward (17th May 1880) about his *English Poets*, EG said, 'Dowden and I flatly contradict each other about Lodge, and I am afraid he is right and I wrong.' Philip Harwood was editor of *Saturday Review*.

p. 233   The letter to Emilie Marzials (25th Dec 1883) is at Texas.

p. 235   EG to K. A. Winter-Hjelm 20th Jan 1875. (Bredsdorff, p. 81.)

p. 236   EG's essay on Matthew Arnold is in *More Books on the Table*, p. 379.

p. 238   EG's essay on Leslie Stephen is in *Silhouettes*, p. 319. See also F. W. Maitland: *Life of Leslie Stephen*.

The 'bigger person' was presumably Stephen, but could have been A. C. Bradley (1851–1935), later Professor of Poetry at Oxford, who was also standing, though he told F. W. Myers he did not wish it to be known.

Getting back to the BM – EG said his fate was decided at a meeting of the Trustees of the BM on 8th Nov 1884. Richard Garnett told him in September that his appointment over the heads of internal candidates for promotion would have caused much bad feeling. 'If you succeed, you will soon be wishing you had failed,' though there was no man he would rather have as a colleague on personal grounds.

p. 239   *Silhouettes* essay on Stephen.

For 'the letter Z', see *To the Lighthouse*, Virginia Woolf, section 6.

Letter from Hamo Thornycroft to his wife on 8th May 1894 tells of EG meeting Hardy at the Academy. Hardy said, 'I have been cheered up by seeing the most beautiful woman in England, or rather her whom I think the most beautiful woman in England, her on whom I thought when I wrote *Tess of the d'Urbervilles*.' (Elfrida Manning: *Marble and Bronze: the art and life of Homo Thornycroft*, 1982.)

p. 240   'The birthday of your life' is Christina Rossetti's phrase: 'Because the birthday of my life is come, my love is come to me.'

Chapter 9: America and After: the outer cliff of fame

p. 241   Publishers of the *Century*: EG to Gilder 18th March 1887: 'It is a great comfort to me to have Mr Unwin instead of Warne. There is all the difference between them that there is between butter and oleomargarine.'

p. 242   W. E. Norris (1847–1925), novelist. Henry James's Christmas letters to him (Yale) regularly contained an assessment of EG, their mutual friend.

Alphonse Daudet (1840–97) and Frédéric Mistral (1830–1914) were both French Provençal writers.

'there can be no patriotism': EG to Clinton Scollard 25th March 1887 (Yale).

EG did procure *The Silverado Squatters* by RLS for the *Century* in 1883. RLS was paid $200 (£40).

Christina Rossetti on Dante appeared in Feb 1884 and does not seem to have been reprinted.

p. 246   The poem for Holmes first appeared in *The Critic* (US), commissioned by them as part of a tribute on Holmes's birthday. 40 copies were privately printed; it was in Pope's manner, with spelling and punctuation of the period.

p. 246   Dr Benjamin Cotting was manager of the Lowell Lectures from 1842 to 1897!

p. 247   The title was originally 'From Shakespeare – to Waller', not Pope, but was changed on Howells's suggestion. 'He thinks that nobody knows who Waller was,' EG to Gilder 8th March 1884. (Matt. and Mill. p. 134)

p. 248   H. A. Beers (1847–1926), Professor of English at Yale, author of two histories of English Romanticism. E. C. Stedman told EG that 'any long established and successful author would decline its hack-work and obscure and ill-paid routine'. (Matt. and Mill. p. 151)

'£300 a year'. In fact, according to EG's accounts, he received £292 10s. from Cambridge in 1885 and 1886 and £200, annually, on the renewal of the contract, in 1887, 1888 and 1889.

p. 249   EG to Sir Thomas Farrer at the Board of Trade, 8th Sept 1884: 'Although I am not a member of that university, I was unanimously elected a little while ago, without having applied for the honour, to the Clark chair of English Literature at the University of Cambridge.'

p. 250   Matthew Arnold: *More Books on the Table*, p. 386.

'the discoveries of Huxley and Häckel'. Both T. H. Huxley (1825–1895) and the German Ernst Häckel (1834–1919) were convinced evolutionists and separately formulated similar theories – that the first primal organisms were formed spontaneously through abiogenesis – and that all living matter thereafter was created solely by earlier living matter. Häckel's own particular field, like PHG's, was marine zoology.

p. 251   They actually sailed on SS *Germanic*.

p. 252f   Boston visit: *W. D. Howells. The Friendly Eye* by Edward Wagen (1969) and *Glimpses of Authors* by Caroline Ticknor (1922).

p. 253   *PMG* 6th Jan 1885. EG's essay on Howells: *Silhouettes*, p. 193.

p. 254   'My mind was just like': interview with EG in *The Critic* 24th Jan 1885.

The New York lectures earned EG $700. The first was in the house of his American publisher, Henry Holt, on East 54th Street.

p. 255   'The Perrys': Thomas Sergeant Perry (1845–1928) critic and scholar at Harvard.

'The President of Harvard' from 1869–1909 was Charles William Eliot (1834–1926).

p. 256   Ralph Waldo Emerson had died in 1882.

'attention': I am indebted to William White in *Victorian Studies* (Dec 1957) for pointing out this example of EG altering, deliberately or by chance, the facts of his own biography.

'passionate discipleship' – But he wrote to Howells 7th Jan 1885 'I am going to begin admiring Walt all over again, his person is so attractive.'

p. 257   Mary Pearsall Smith's reactions are quoted in *Remarkable Relations* (1980) by Barbara Strachey. See also Logan Pearsall Smith: *Unforgotten Years* (1939) and Kenneth Clark: *Another Part of the Wood* (1974).

p. 258   General Condé, defeated in Spain in 1647.

p. 259   Chester Alan Arthur (1830–86), who had succeeded Garfield on his assassination, was shortly to leave the White House himself. Grover Cleveland had already been elected.

p. 260   Gwen Raverat: *Period Piece* (1952).

p. 263   There is a copy of the Gray memorial in Johns Hopkins University in Baltimore.

p. 264   But a review by EG of Howells's *The Rise of Silas Lapham* appeared in the *PMG* on 11th Sept 1885.

p. 267   Sargent's portrait of Madame Gautreau is now in the Metropolitan Museum, New York, with an unfinished variant in the Tate Gallery, London.

Sargent's Patmore is in the National Portrait Gallery in London (see illustration no. 27). Patmore wrote to EG in 1894: 'As you were instrumental in getting the portrait done, I ought to tell you . . . it will be, simply as a work of art, the picture of the Academy.'

It is difficult to sort out details of the different visits to Broadway. Leon Edel says James was in Broadway in 1885. It would have had to be in the first week of September, before he went to Paris, but Sargent was in Broadway then, and James says on 10th Sept that he has had no tidings of Sargent till that day. EG was certainly in Broadway in Sept 1885, though Edel says it was 'on a later occasion'.

EG's birthday: in Benson's diary in 1908, when they were visiting Broadway together, we read that EG told Benson he was 'led about in a large hat (called a Gosse!) decorated with daisy chains'.

p. 268   EG's MA: the Vice-master of Trinity wrote: 'It does not confer a vote, but gives the use of the library as well as the gown and status of an MA.'

p. 269   Theodore Watts-Dunton. Watts added the name Dunton in 1896.

p. 270   Howells wrote regularly from his 'Editor's Study' in *Harper's Monthly*.

p. 272   Mildred (Pilla) Howells, b. 1872. EG had reviewed her *A Little Girl Among the Old Masters*, a book of drawings in *PMG* (20th Dec 1883).

     Our hundred days in Europe by O. W. Holmes (1887).

     'his new American friend': George Allison Armour (1856–1936) devoted much time to travel and books. He was in contact with EG from 1885; his son Edmund was EG's godson. EG's letters to him at Princeton.

p. 274   Swinburne's article appeared in the *Nineteenth Century* in June 1886.

Chapter 10: The Scandal of the Year

p. 278   John Gross on Morley in *The Rise and Fall of the Man of Letters*, p. 103.

     Collins's articles on Tennyson appeared in *The Cornhill* in Jan and July 1880 and July 1881.

     Tennyson's complaint was recorded by W. F. Rawnsley in *The Nineteenth Century and After* (xcvii) 1925.

     I am also indebted to Phyllis Grosskurth: 'Churton Collins; Scourge of the Late Victorians', *University of Toronto Quarterly* xxxiv (April 1965).

     Robert Greene's birth date: Collins's searches must have been in vain. My edition of the *Oxford Companion to English Literature* still has a question-mark.

     'article after article' – for example, 'Your two invaluable papers on the Educational Crisis, which appeared in the *Pall Mall Gazette* . . .' Swinburne to Collins, 16th June 1886.

p. 279   'the examination . . . of the classics of the nation': EG in *Aspects*.

     'Dickins' is Bruce Dickins (1889–1978) who would become Elrington and Bosworth Professor of Anglo Saxon at Cambridge.

p. 280   The Dr Fairbain in the list of familiar names is A. M. Fairbain (1838–1912), author of *The Place of Christ in Modern Theology* (1893).

     The London Letter quoted was in *The Critic*, 20th Nov 1886.

p. 281   Collins quoting Dr Johnson, see 'Log Rolling and Education' in *Ephemera Critica*, p. 135.

p. 283   Arthur Sidgwick (1842–1920), later Reader in Greek at Oxford.

p. 284   EG's jottings of quotations from Collins are at Rutgers.

p. 288   Richard Watson Dixon (1833–1900), poet, clergyman, friend of Gerard Manley Hopkins.

p. 291   Macaulay was reviewing Croker's edition of Boswell's *Life of Johnson*.

     PMG reference to attack, 15th Oct 1886.

p. 294   'a Gosse of himself': EC, p. 196.

     W. R. Ralston's letter to the *Athenaeum*, 6th Nov 1886.

p. 295   Swinnerton could also be inaccurate. In *The Georgian Literary Scene* he wrote that EG was 'pilloried *at the beginning of the twentieth century* by Churton Collins for writing about *eighteenth* century literature' (my italics).

     'biographies of Tennyson' – Robert Bernard Martin in his (1980) was wise to call the anecdote 'probably apocryphal, but the tenor of it is accurate enough'.

p. 298 Harris and Henley. EG to Coventry Patmore 26th Nov 1886: 'Frank Harris oppressed me like a nightmare, for I was conscious of his extreme prejudice directly our eyes met . . . I conjecture that it was to leave himself quite free to publish Collins' new diatribe in the *Fortnightly*'.

Colvin to EG 11th Jan 1887: 'I shall try to induce Henley to say no more about it and if he says anything more to say it on the right side and tell Collins the time has come to have done with his persecution'. Colvin said Henley might be unreasonable but did not think Gosse justified in calling him 'treacherous'. 'Prejudiced, tough and blundering he may be and is.'

Letter to Gilder, 17th Dec 1886. In a comment (unsigned, undated) attached to this letter at Yale, some latter-day librarian has attempted to put Collins's case: 'This letter deals almost exclusively with Churton Collins' criticism of Gosse in the *Quarterly Review*, Oct 1886. Collins, a great scholar, disgusted with the Clark Lectureship at Cambridge being thrown to Gosse through pull, log-rolling, and the ganging-up of his crowd of literary journalists, finally rebelled, and unearthed Gosse's sloppy and ignorant work, *From Shakespeare to Pope*, and took it apart . . . Collins' word was the word of a real scholar – and Gosse suffered bitterly; but his gang still log-rolled for him, and stood behind him.' It is odd to see Colvin, Browning, Arnold and Tennyson, who alone had supported EG's application for the Lectureship, described as a 'crowd of literary journalists'.

p. 300 Mary Robinson (later Darmesteter, later Duclaux) 1857–1944. She and her sister, Mabel, were life-long friends of the Gosses. She published her *Collected Poems* in 1902 and was also a prolific writer of prose.

'Fame and money': *Questions at Issue*, p. 117, p. 133.

p. 301 Stevenson 'in real life': letter to G. Armour, 21st Aug 1887.

'South Seas like the Hebrides': EG to Rupert Brooke 7th Sept 1913.

p. 302 Newspaper quotations from EG to RLS 13th Nov 1893.

p. 305 On Dostoievsky, in Jan 1900 diary of A. C. Benson. In letter to Gide, 22nd Aug 1926.

Biography of Patmore, p. 83.

p. 306 Clinton Scollard (1860–1932). His letters are in the library of the Hamilton and Kirkland Colleges, Clinton, New York.

Life of PHG, p. 376 and Harold Nicolson's 1927 diary, recording talk with EG.

p. 308 EG's last lecture, in June 1889, was the final one of a series on 'Naturalism in English Poetry at the beginning of the present century'.

p. 310 Lady Dorothy Nevill: see *Some Diversions*, p. 182.

p. 311 Mallarmé's praise: 'Ce sont d'exquises pages où l'évocation, sans surcharge, est toute conduite par un subtil et fluide sentiment d'un tour si delicat!' From Roger A. Lhombreaud, 'Deux Lettres de Mallarmé à Edmund Gosse' *Revue de littérature comparée* xxv (July 1951).

Rebecca West: *Ending in Earnest* (NY 1931), p. 93.

p. 312 Sir Arthur Blackwood's speech 15th Dec 1887. *Star* 3rd Aug 1888.

p. 313 J. S. Little, secretary of the Society of Authors.

'disappointed journalists' from EG to Mrs Verrall 1st Dec 1887.

p. 314 Tennyson material: see p. 297 (letter to Nellie at CUL).

EG's note on *The Throstle* reads: 'In September 1889, the poem was given to the public by the Associated Literary Press,' the agency of which EG was European Editor.

p. 315 *Life of PHG*, p. 351.

PHG's death: Harold Nicolson says EG told him 3 am but Eliza Gosse in her memoir written at the time has I am. The 'official' version of his death, in *Life of PHG*, was: 'He was very restless nearly the whole of that night, but towards midnight he became quiet. He said, "It is all over. The Lord is near! I am going to my reward!" At one o'clock in the morning he passed in his sleep to be with his expected Lord.'

p. 317   'fluttering in the network': *F&S*, p. 232.

p. 318   'his American friends': E. C. Stedman to EG, 18th Sept 1884. 'There is a good deal of the American about you', perhaps referring to his drive and ambition.

Henry James on *The Life* in a letter to RLS in Samoa, 12th Jan 1891.

p. 319   'the Savile on Saturdays': EG's 'Corner' included Walter Besant, Andrew Lang and Rider Haggard, but it was certainly not what it had been in RLS's day.

p. 320   Moore's story was given to EC by Moore himself. The date would seem to have been 1896, eleven years before *F&S* was published. 'Everything is to hand – nothing can stop you if your courage does not fail you,' Moore to EG, 27th Nov 1896 (Leeds).

'It is cancer'. In *F&S*, EG records his mother's words as 'He says it is ——', not naming the disease. He probably did name it to Moore, but, surely, even with his culpable memory, he could not have forgotten that his mother always called his father 'Henry' not 'Philip'. This version is probably the fault of Moore's memory. EG's side of the 'vivid correspondence' is in the library of the University of Bristol.

Symonds's sonnets were in *PMG* early in 1890.

p. 321   'ingratitude, disloyalty . . .' Letter to Heinemann, 12th May 1900 (CUL).

Janet Vaughan, b. 1899, daughter of Margaret née Symonds, was then a medical student in London. She was eventually Principal of Somerville College, Oxford. In a letter to the editors of Symonds's letters (23rd Sept 1967) she wrote that EG 'said he knew how glad I should be to hear what he had done to preserve the good name of my grandfather . . . It was not safe to let myself speak as I thought of those two old men destroying, one could only guess, all the case histories and basic studies of sexual inversion that JAS is known to have made, together no doubt with other letters and papers that would have thrown much light on JAS's work and friendships. Gosse's smug gloating delight as he told me, the sense that he had enjoyed to the full the honour fate had given him, was nauseating. There was nothing to be said. I walked out and never went back.'

p. 323   'taking furtive looks': the suggestion is made by Phyllis Grosskurth in her biography of JAS and picked up by John Gross in his *Rise and Fall of the Man of Letters*. See notes to p. 195.

'sehnsucht': longing, yearning.

p. 324   EG's description is in the BL and was published in *T. J. Wise. Centenary Studies* (1960) as EG gave his M˙ to Wise.

Chapter 12: Sunday Talk

p. 325   Arthur Waugh's article (Sept 1932) eventually appeared as a small book *The Book of Gosse* (1932). Also see his *One Man's Road* (1931).

p. 326   'You won't have much to do': MS note in EG's hand (Leeds). 'Old boy' is omitted in biography of CP . . . In 1897, EG wrote to Alice Meynell: 'I remain convinced that my account of the disappearance of *Sponsa Dei* is substantially correct. He told me, with gravity and reiteration, that of *Sponsa Dei* every MS, every fragment, had been destroyed at Christmas, 1887. The papers he showed you in 1892 . . . were certainly other than *Sponsa Dei*, though of course of cognate character, and sometimes, perhaps, nearly identical in subject.' (Texas).

p. 327   Lady Dorothy Nevill: *Some Diversions*, p. 188.

Beerbohm on Sundays with EG. See David Cecil: *Max* (1964), p. 155, and Rupert Hart-Davis: *A Peep into the Past and other Prose Pieces by Max Beerbohm*. 'Two Glimpses of Andrew Lang' (1972).

p. 328   Clark: *Another Part of the Wood* (1974).

Trevelyan: letter to EG 1916.

Maugham: *The Summing Up* (1938).

Some of Gosse's stories are passed on by Osbert Sitwell; others come from Benson's diary and EC. 'He could grumble . . .' from Harold Nicolson in an unidentified magazine cutting quoted by Fayette Gosse in *The Gosses*.

p. 330   *On Viol and Flute* had been re-issued in 1890, with twice as many poems as in the original 1873 edition, all that EG wished to preserve from his books, up to and including *New Poems* (1879).

p. 331   The Kipling verses are at Rutgers. Angus Wilson in *The Strange Ride . . .*(1977), p. 140.

p. 332   International Library: one of the first volumes was *Footsteps of Fate* (*Noodlot*) by Louis Couperus, trans. from the Dutch by Clara Bell. EG's introduction suggests a wide acquaintance with Dutch literature and literary history, but a letter from a young Dutch writer, F. van Eeden, 5th April 1891, among EG's papers, reveals he got most of his information secondhand rather than from the books themselves. Wilde thought highly of this novel. JAS saw its homosexual undertones: 'What a number of Urnings are being portrayed in novels now.' JAS to EG (Leeds) 22nd June 1891.

EG wrote Balestier's obituary in *The Times* 8th Dec 1891 and a memoir, which was in the April 1892 issue of the *Century*, was privately printed in an edition of 100 copies and later appeared in *Portraits and Sketches*. James criticized EG's comments on Balestier's appearance and his 'secretiveness' ('To the young, the early dead, the baffled, the defeated, I don't think we can be tender enough . . .') though EG had in fact written with a warmth and sensitivity which makes his later judgment seem surprising as well as crude.

Barrack Room Ballads: 49 reviews recorded in the Book Review Index.

p. 333   Kipling's illness: EG to Nellie 27th Feb 1899, 'Every other subject seems blotted out by the news about Kipling. Isn't it miserable, miserable? I am afraid before you read this, we shall hear that the end has come. It does seem the most cruel, purposeless waste of a valuable life one ever heard of. I can think of nothing else.'

Photos: the one of Hardy with EG seems to be missing.

p. 336   Jock Haggard's death. In Tessa's 1891 diary, on February 10th she wrote without comment: 'Jock died this week.' Philip, Sylvia's brother, certainly knew something in adult life – but perhaps only from published sources, as Sylvia's friend did. One of Nellie's letters to Tessa referring to Jock is annotated in Philip's hand, 'Died from measles caught while stopping with us.' Philip would, of course, not have seen his father's letter to Armour, now at Princeton, which said so specifically that Jock had been in contact with measles before arriving at Delamere Terrace. Haggard's nephew recalled a 'super-taboo' on the mention of Jock's name at Ditchingham. Medical information from Dr Richard Jupe.

p. 336   Haggard's journal: *The Private Diaries of Sir Henry Rider Haggard* ed. D. S. Higgins (1980). Sylvia's friend was Kathleen Fisher: see p. 518.

p. 337   Baring's essay: EC, p. 240.

Arnold died in 1888, Browning in 1889 and Tennyson in 1892.

p. 338   EG's letter to Le Gallienne is at Texas.
James letter to RLS, 18th Feb 1891.

p. 339   'Ibsen as a commercial proposition'. It was not until 1897 that Yeats could
write in a letter to Lady Gregory: 'Ibsen makes money.' (17th November 1897).

p. 339f   The March 1898 Archer letters to EG and EG's article in the *Sketch* are
published in Bredsdorff pp. 182/5.

p. 340   *The Wild Duck* in *F&S* p. 246.

p. 341   Gosse obviously thought he had acted correctly over *Hedda Gabler*. There is a
note in his hand at Rutgers, which says simply:
'Made a definite proposition to Ibsen   Sept 1889
                            told Archer   Oct 16 1889
                    Answer from Ibsen   Oct 30 1889.'

p. 342   While *Ibsen's Prose Dramas* was being published in Britain, an American firm
John W. Lovell Co. did their own edition in 1890–91, edited by EG, which also
included Archer's not Gosse's *Hedda Gabler*.
See Elizabeth Robins: *Ibsen and the Actress*. Hogarth Essay (1928).
'Art is art': W. B. Yeats. *Autobiographies* (1955), p. 279 (also p. 480).

p. 345   NG's article 'The Tyranny of Women', *The Century*, vol. x. No. 60.
EG and Pinero: Pinero always sent the Gosses tickets for his first nights. Of
The Second Mrs Tanqueray, he wrote to EG on 2nd May 1893: 'This is a play for
grown-up people and you are among the few grown-up people whose word I
care for.'
Shaw's criticism was in the *Saturday Review*, 26th March 1898.

p. 348   'my mind is absolutely idle'. EG was in good company. The legendary
Jowett, Master of Balliol, once said, 'When I say nothing, people fancy I am
thinking about something. Generally I am thinking about nothing.'

p. 349   'a marmot': the creatures at Stanmore were a perpetual interest. 'Try to be a
thoughtful friend to the mongoose,' EG had written to his daughters on one
occasion when they were staying there. Eliza Brightwen to Annie Varini: 'Sylvia
Gosse wrote and told me there was a marmot at Whiteleys and, wishing to secure
such an interesting pet, I telegraphed for it to be sent to Stanmore Station . . .
Please ask Mr Gurney what food is best for a marmot.'

p. 351   'some interest in art'. EG's article 'The New Sculpture' in the *Art Journal* in
1894 has given the title to Susan Beattie's 1983 monograph (Yale). Beattie writes
'Gosse's ideas have shaped posterity's view of mainstream sculpture in England
during the last decades of the nineteenth century'. She accuses EG of a 'fundamental misinterpretation of its character'. Soon after the 1894 article EG
'abandoned his position as the New Sculpture's chief spokesman and promoter
and wrote no more upon the subject'.
In the *Magazine of Art* (1895) EG wrote a series of articles on 'The Place of
Sculpture in Daily Life'.

p. 352   EG tells the Marlowe Committee story in a letter to *The Times* 29th Jan 1925.
He admitted in a letter to Thornycroft that he had intrigued to get himself on to
the Committee because he wanted Thornycroft to get the chance to do the
monument.

p. 353   Ernest Rhys: *Letters from Limbo* (1936).
McClure's Associated Literary Press was a syndicate devoted to providing the
literary press in England and America with contributions of high quality by the
best writers. EG, as European Editor, received £50 in 1889, £75 in 1890. Mrs
Burnett was called Editor of Youth's Dept. The London address was Heinemann's: 21 Bedford Street.
'overworked': in a letter dated 21.18.89 (sic), EG wrote to Eliza Lynn Linton:

'I see that you have never been an editor and have no conception of his miseries.'
In another letter, 19th Dec 1889, he wrote 'I find it engrossingly interesting but
the worry is very considerable'.

The Smale/Smart story comes from Philip Gosse: *Go to the Country* (1935), p.
182. In 1924, EG called a Lady Stewart, Lady Scott – 'not once but again and
again, like the Lady of Spain, who was sick on the train . . . My nights are
rendered sleepless by the sting of social remorse.' EG to Elizabeth Haldane, 4th
Oct 1924. (Nat. Lib. Scot.)

Chapter 13: Enough of Nightingales

p. 355   Olivia Shakespear would soon publish her second novel. She would become
a close friend of Yeats.

p. 356   Jean Moréas (1856–1910).

EG's later version of this letter, in his essay in *French Profiles* ('A First Sight of
Verlaine') gives us some alternative and some additional details. In the printed
version all twelve at the Café Soleil d'Or are poets. M. Verlaine flops out of the
darkness like an owl not a moth, though the moths appear earlier in the essay, and
we know the poems he reads are 'Clair de lune' and part of 'Mon Dieu m'a dit'.

Arthur Waugh's account is in *One Man's Road*, p. 250.

p. 357   A. C. Ainger (1841–1919) was a master at Eton (1864–1901). He sometimes
spent holidays with Gosse and Benson.

Beardsley's frequent visits to Delamere Terrace were in 1894 and 1895.
'Beardsley's wonderful, pure line' from *Aspects*, p. 269. EG attended a Requiem
Mass for Beardsley at Farm Street Chapel on 12th May 1898. Whistler on
Beardsley: *The Romantic '90s* by Richard Le Gallienne (1926), p. 174.

Protests over *The Yellow Book*: '. . . possibly, however, it may be intended to
attract by its very repulsiveness and insolence' (*Times*). Henley's *National Observer* spoke of 'the audacious vulgarity and the laborious inelegance of the cover'.

Baring's hoax was in Feb 1894. POOR MAURICE DIED TODAY took in EG
completely. He told Benson, who telegraphed a Cambridge friend for more
information. Baring was actually at tea with the friend when this telegram
arrived. His tutor wrote to EG: 'I am more vexed than I can tell you that you
should have been annoyed and distressed by so senseless a jest.' Amazingly, EG's
feelings for Baring remained warm and sympathetic.

p. 359   V. Woolf's review of EC (originally in the *TLS*) appears in her collection of
essays *The Moment* (1947).

p. 360   'You must come back': Ross was soon welcomed to Delamere Terrace again.
The next visit recorded in the Book of Gosse is on 4th Aug 1895. His name is
recorded 112 times between 1892 and his death in 1918.

'His biographer': William Freeman: *The Life of Lord Alfred Douglas, Spoilt
Child of Genius* (1948).

'high quarter': this was presumably Lord Haldane, the Lord Chancellor and
EG's very close friend.

p. 362   'as Leonard Woolf used to tell her' – *Sowing* (1960): 'I used to tell Virginia that
the difference between us was that she was mentally, morally and physically a
snob, while I was mentally, morally and physically a coward and she was inclined
to agree.' V. Woolf's essay in *The Moment*.

p. 363   'as Osbert Sitwell would tell everyone': *Noble Essences* (1950).

Mrs Dugdale, Sir George Trevelyan's sister, was organizing the lectures.

p. 364   Stories of Eliza Gosse from *Edward Marsh* by Christopher Hassall (1959).

p. 365   Bertha Newcombe, illustrator and painter, was a friend of the Hardys.

p. 366   'The Wounded Gull' is in *In Russet and Silver* and reprinted in *Collected Poems*.

p. 367   Philip's Aconcagua expedition: Philip had sent James his *Notes on the Natural History of the Aconcagua Valleys* (1899). EG had written to James (14th June 1896) 'We are conscious that your cordial words, spoken at the right moment, had a great deal to do with this happy arrangement . . . All must now depend on his own brain and character.' Before setting off for the Andes, Philip had some training in Switzerland, at the Royal Zoological Society and at Kew.

p. 368   The Lord Wolseley story Philip himself tells in the preface of *Memoirs of a Camp Follower* (1934) – later reissued as *A Naturalist Goes to War*.

p. 369   Tessa Gosse, some information from Newnham College, Cambridge.

    Sylvia Gosse was at the Royal Academy Schools 1903–1908. She exhibited 14 works at the RA between 1912 and 1948. Evelyn Waugh thought Sylvia 'much the most amusing of the family' but said her paintings were 'horrid – all iron bedsteads and Sickert': letter to Harold Acton, 18th Feb 1925.

    Philip's comment in old age: *The Gosses* by Fayette Gosse (Canberra 1981).

p. 370   'An American critic': I am indebted to *The Critic's Alchemy* by Ruth Z. Temple (NY 1953) for information in this section.

    EG on Mallarmé: *French Profiles*, p. 313.

    'defence of symbolism': *The Future of English Poetry*, presidential address to the English Association (1913), reprinted in *Some Diversions*.

p. 371f   Accounts of Verlaine in London: see Verlaine: 'My Visit to London' *The Savoy* April 1896. *North American Review* May 1915. G. Jean-Aubry: 'Verlaine et l'Angleterre' *La Revue de Paris* 1918. V. P. Underwood: *Verlaine et l'Angleterre* (Paris 1956). R. Speaight: *William Rothenstein* (1962). Roger Lhombreaud: *Arthur Symons* (1963). Cecily Mackworth: *English Interludes* (1974). On his return to France, Verlaine sent EG a drawing, showing a tiny Verlaine looking lost in an immense armchair, and a poem giving an account of the occasion, dedicated to EG, which he got published in the *Athenaeum* of 12th May 1894.

    Symons's account says the Crown visit was the following night when EG, Symons and Verlaine dined with Heinemann and some of them visited the Alhambra.

p. 372   Benson's connections: Arthur Benson's uncle Henry Sidgwick was married to Nora Balfour, niece of Lord Salisbury and sister of Arthur Balfour.

p. 373   E. F. Benson: in 1982 none of A. C. Benson's books were in print in England but six titles by E. F. were available from Heinemann.

p. 375   Marsh on Benson. Hassall: *Edward Marsh*, p. 90.

p. 376   'oozed drop by drop': EG is quoting Edward Fitzgerald's *Rubaiyat of Omar Khayyam*.

    'literary executor' – in fact, EG outlived Benson who died in 1925; Philip Gosse acted as his father's executor.

    Funerals: Tennyson died in 1892, William Gosse and Symonds in 1893, Pater and Stevenson in 1894 and Patmore in 1896. EG had contributed first £20 and then £60 per annum to his uncle's support for the last six years of his life.

p. 377   Graham Balfour wrote this biography of RLS (1901).

p. 378   Baring's parody is at Yale.

Chapter 14: Scribbling and Scribbling

p. 379   Wilde play: *An Ideal Husband* had opened on 3rd Jan 1895.

    Shaw attack: in *The Albemarle* Sept 1892 Shaw accused EG of ignoring Shelley the hardened sinner, republican and atheist in EG's address at the Shelley centenary celebrations that July, published in *The Author* Oct 1892.

In Aug 1898 James and EG cycled from Rye to New Romney to check up on Wells's circumstances for the RLF.

p. 380 EG's visit to James 6th Jan 1895. For EG's own account see *Aspects*, p. 34.

p. 381 'As twilight deepened': *Aspects*, p. 42.

William James's report. See Edel: *Life of Henry James* vol. 2 (Penguin ed. p. 260). James's letters to Norris are at Yale.

p. 383 'to her stepson, EWG'. This is what the will says. In a letter to Thornycroft, 4th Nov 1900, EG says: 'Her money is left to a brother-in-law and to a niece.' The suggestion I suppose is that EG felt the money that came to him was from his father.

p. 384 KING ITALY MURDERED: assassination of King Humbert of Italy at Monza in 1900.

Nellie's inheritance. Administration of the will was granted to her brother, Washington Epps, on 26th June 1907. Under this will, Nellie was supposed to receive only £500, though her brother Hahnemann had been left £20,000 absolutely. The actual effects totalled £735,387 10s.

Review of *Tess*. On 1st April 1897, referring to the review which 'annoyed us all so much', EG said that 'as soon as one found out that Mrs Andrew Lang had written it – what did it matter?'

p. 385 Catharine Trotter: see *Some Diversions*, p. 37.

p. 386 'writing verses': he wrote part of the masque *Hypolympia* in Norway.

p. 388 Hardy's poetry. He responded with pleasure to EG's comments on his poems. On 5th Dec 1901, he wrote 'It is striking that you should mention as your favourites three that I like best myself.'

p. 389 An edition of *Sonnets from the Portuguese*: one story has it that this edition of the Sonnets with Gosse's introduction (Dent, 1894) was withdrawn from sale, according to the illustrator, F. C. Tilney, because of the quality of the printing by a firm in Austria. (Information from a letter from Ralph Brown, who had been in touch with Tilney, to Fannie Ratchford, 18th Nov 1950; copy at Leeds.) But at the same period E. F. Bozman of Dent said his records showed the edition still available in 1910.

'new edition of *An Enquiry*': it is in two volumes with *A Sequel to An Enquiry* by Nicolas Barker and John Collins (1982).

'American collector': Mr Herman Liebert.

p. 390 Wise's mutilations: David Foxon of the BM wrote in the *TLS* in Oct 1956 of them as 'so coarse, so clumsy, so vulgar'. At least the forgeries showed some ingenuity and skill.

Iris Murdoch in an Open University broadcast, July 1982.

'more or less legally': forgeries were about 20% of Wise's output.

p. 391 Genesis comment. Quoted by Philip Gosse in his review of *Thomas J. Wise in the Original Cloth* by Wilfred Partington, in the *Cambridge Review* in 1947.

'a volume inscribed': it seems this may be the New York edition of *Portrait of a Lady* now in Nanzan University, Japan. It is signed by Henry James for Edmund Gosse.

p. 392 'imitations of books'. In his bibliography of Swinburne, Wise had actually written himself: 'The whole thing proves once more that, easy as it appears to be to fabricate reprints of rare books, it is in actual practice absolutely impossible to do so in such a manner that detection cannot follow the result.'

p. 393 '. . . careless about dates'. That EG's mistake about time and place was a genuine and typical carelessness, without ulterior motive, is shown by the fact that William Sharp in his *Life of Browning* (1890) uses EG's story long before EG had heard of the spurious Reading edition, which seems not to have been produced until 1893 or 94. In other words, EG's story *did* come first and cannot have been invented to support the forgery.

In *English Literature: an illustrated record* (1903), EG tells the story again: 'They settled in Pisa where, early in the year 1847, Mrs Browning showed to her husband the *Sonnets from the Portuguese* which she had written during their engagement; in 1850 these were added to the second edition of her *Poems*.'

p. 394   Buxton Forman. H. Buxton Forman (1842–1917) edited the *Letters* and *Works* of Keats and also Shelley's *Works* and *Notebooks*. Recent investigations show him even more involved with the forgeries than was originally thought. In fact, he seems to have been as culpable as Wise himself. EG never knew him well. 'I was never at any time intimate with him,' he wrote on Forman's death in 1917, and perhaps he never realized that, by an odd coincidence, they had been educated at the same small school in Teignmouth.

Last Tournament. As early as 1898, G. D. Smith in New York commented, 'Maybe *The Last Tournament* by Tennyson *is* worth $300, but it is curious that every Tennyson collector of note has been supplied with one lately.'

Strahan: presumably Alexander Strahan, publisher and editor of the *Contemporary Review*.

p. 395   'first honorary degree': the honorary MA from Cambridge was tied to his appointment and is hardly what is meant by an honorary degree.

Browne and *Marvell*. Both were in Macmillan's English Men of Letters series.

p. 396   The reference in this letter to Garnett (at Texas) is to Freeman's *History of the Norman Conquest*. The mistake is corrected in the 1898 reprint.

p. 397   'a fine piece of work': *Gossip in a Library*, p. 64.

'so huge an enterprise': Preface to *The Life and Letters of John Donne*.

p. 398   'breaking down': *Books on the Table*, p. 187.

'a more recent critic', Clement H. Wyke: *Edmund Gosse as Biographer and Critic of Donne: his fallible rôle in the poet's rediscovery*. Texas Studies in Literature and Language, vol. 17, pp. 805–819 (1976).

Augustus Jessopp (1823–1914) actually published three accounts of Donne. The first was in 1855 as a preface to an edition of *Essays in Divinity*. In 1888 he wrote the *DNB* entry and in 1897 a short book in the 'Leaders of Religion' series. On 25th Aug 1898 Jessop gave (or sold) to EG his 1633 ed. of Donne's poems. It later belonged to Richard Gimbel, of the Gimbel department store family, and has become part of the Gimbel Collection at the USAF Academy in Colorado, together with many aeronautical books. (Information from Lt Col W. E. McCarron, USAF.)

John Carey in *John Donne: Life, Mind and Art* (1981) says 'Sir Edmund Gosse's theory that the poems are autobiographical has been roundly derided – for the most part by persons with literary gifts smaller than Gosse's.'

Grierson is cited in EC. He also acknowledges EG's contribution in his introduction to the 1912 *Poems*.

p. 399   Helen Gardner in her introduction to *John Donne. A Collection of Critical Essays* (1962).

Bateman and Pelham: Sir Alfred Bateman KCMG and Hon. T. H. W. Pelham CB. Boyle: Sir Courtenay Boyle, Permanent Secretary to the Board of Trade. The rhyme is not in Dobson's *Collected Poems* but is included in *Austin Dobson. Some Notes* by Alban Dobson (1928).

p. 402   At *King John*: see *Aspects*, p. 283. EG says it was the night war was declared and quotes 12th Oct 1899. There is a suspicion EG was twisting the facts to make a better story. Wolseley's telegram of invitation for 'tomorrow night' seems to be dated 1st Sept 1899. EG's diary entry is on 20th Sept.

Scandinavian reaction to Boer War. See Bredsdorff, pp. 155/159.

p. 403 Maarten Maartens (1858–1915) was the pen-name of Joost M. W. van der Poorten Schwartz, who wrote in English, though he lived almost entirely on the continent. In his collected letters, large numbers are addressed to Nellie Gosse. In one to EG in 1913 he recalls a visit they made together to Swinburne in June 1895.

Sir Edward Clarke's lecture on 15th Nov 1902 and EG's reply were commemorated by Sir Henry Newbolt in *Le Byron de nos jours*.

Letters in *The Times* from Clarke and EG were reprinted in a pamphlet. Clarke wrote: 'The literature of England is a fair and spacious domain, and it does not belong to Mr Edmund Gosse'.

Chapter 15: On the Fringe of the Real Thing

p. 405 *Life of Donne*, vol. 2, p. 4.

Belvoir Castle: the Duke of Rutland. Taplow Court: the Grenfells (Lady Desborough). Temple Newsam: Lord Halifax.

Sisera's mother. See Judges 5, v. 29.

p. 409 17 Hanover Terrace. When I visited the house on a Friday early in 1981 I was, by an odd coincidence, just in time to see it very much as it had been in EG's day. It had been allowed to run down: the very next Monday it was to be totally gutted and renovated at a vast expense which would have amazed EG. The present leaseholders did not respond to my suggestion of a blue plaque to commemorate EG's residence.

p. 410 'Queen Victoria'. Lady Ponsonby gave her share of the fee to the Queen Victoria Fund for Nurses. When the King enquired whether she had *written* the article, she was able to say, 'Certainly not, but I thought it was very good.' 'Please burn this,' she wrote to EG several times, wishing to hide the fact that she had given him much intimate information. He burned none of her letters and they are now at Rutgers.

Lytton Strachey's reactions from Michael Holroyd's biography.

p. 412 'the American volume' (1903) was by William Petersfield Trent (1862–1939), Professor of English at Columbia University.

'a pamphlet': *Thomas Wentworth Higginson* was a reprint of the Editor's Table of the *New England Magazine* XXI (Feb 1900).

p. 413 EG on biography. *Anglo-Saxon Review* 26th Feb 1901.

p. 415 Biography of Patmore. Many people took a very different view from Benson. Pearl Craigie wrote (22nd Mar 1905): 'The Patmore is perfection – written with exquisite humour and justice.' She called it enchanting, brilliant, wise and kind though Patmore himself had made her ill and she felt for the three wives. 'He seemed to me a person who told wilful lies to himself because he would not face the plain crude facts of his own undisciplined temperament.'

p. 416 Visit to Paris. In *The Correspondence of André Gide and Edmund Gosse, 1904–28* (NY 1959) Linette F. Brugmans suggests the audience had some difficulty in following the lecture but this seems unlikely if, as Davray reported, there was such continuous applause. At the dinner, EG spoke in French. There is a bound copy of the speech in CUL. He apologized for his defective pronunciation and maladroit phrases.

p. 418 'the full diary' is in the House of Lords Library. It is unpublished.

p. 424   'on the fringe of the real thing': Benson felt he was also on the fringe. 'I stand on the outskirts and applaud,' he wrote in his diary at this time.

'a luncheon he gave': EG loved to show off Hardy in company, to have the most distinguished novelist in England as his guest. Hardy would generally prefer to see him on his own e.g. Hardy to EG 9th April 1901 '. . . Though to meet you for an unrestricted time, without the dinner, would perhaps suit me better, if a dinner is in order, let it be so and I will come.'

p. 427   Pentland Stevenson. On 18th Jan 1906 there was an offer from Cassell, Longman, Chatto and Windus, and Heinemann (signed by William Heinemann) that EG should edit the new Pentland Edition of R. L. Stevenson's Works for £200.

p. 429   Publishers' protest etc. Information from Derek Hudson: 'Reading' in Simon Nowell-Smith's *Edwardian England* (1964).

Chapter 16: The Masterpiece

p. 431   I am indebted to 'George Moore and *Father and Son*' by Charles Burkhart in *Nineteenth Century Fiction*, vol. 15, No. 1 (June 1960).

p. 432   EG's letter to Sydney Holland is in Berg.
The letter to Harrison is at LSE.

p. 433   The letters to Heinemann are in the archives of the publisher at Kingswood, Surrey.

The letter from EG to Benson escaped burning with the rest of his letters to him because it was inside his copy of *Father and Son*. By an odd chance, a friend of mine was staying with the owners of this letter at the time I was writing this chapter, and I was therefore sent a copy.

p. 434   'Heinemann's NY rep': Paul R. Reynolds to Messrs Charles Scribners Sons. 24th Sept 1907. (Scribner archives, Princeton.)

p. 435   In 1887. *Questions at Issue*, p. 243.

p. 437   Monument to his father: letter 29th May 1924. EG to David Lloyd. EC, p. 307.

Pound wrote of EG in *Poetry* (Chicago) XI, March 1918.

The linked quotations are from Lord David Cecil, Walter Raleigh, Gilbert Murray, Lady Dorothy Nevill, Harold Nicolson, Raymond Mortimer, Osbert Sitwell, Compton Mackenzie, Maurice Baring, Hamo Thornycroft, Virginia Woolf, Ernle Prothero, William Archer. The most interesting recent criticism of *F&S* is in *Guardians and Angels* by David Grylls (1978) and in the Introduction by Peter Abbs to the Penguin English Library edition (1983).

'among the Immortals': in 1918 EG would tell Haldane that *he* would be remembered 'when all the rest of us are forgotten'. Baring on *F&S*. 1908 review reprinted in *Punch and Judy* (1924).

p. 438   'the curiosity biography satisfies': EG's article on biography in *Encyclopaedia Britannica*.

Arthur Symons was now on the verge of insanity. EG had recently lent him £100 to help repair his cottage. On 21st Oct 1908 EG told Rhoda Symons: 'I shall work for poor Arthur as keenly as I should for my own son.' EG was instrumental in raising financial assistance for Symons, who was certified insane two weeks after EG's letter of support. Against the doctor's prognosis, Symons lived another 36 years and to regain his faculties. Symons paid no fewer than 84 visits to the Gosses' houses before his illness. EG acted as a trustee after that. Symons received an RLF grant in 1909 and a Civil List Pension in 1913, largely through EG's intervention.

p. 439 'translated into French': EG to Gide 7th June 1912 'It seems to me marvellously well translated, conscientiously, no difficulty skipped or slurred.'

Paul Desjardins (1859–1940) Sorbonne Professor. In 1911 EG had found it a great strain discussing 'tragedy' in daily sessions – 'the enthusiasm and the seriousness were so remarkable' (Benson).

'An English critic': quoted by Raymond Mortimer in his 1960 *Sunday Times* review of *The Correspondence of André Gide and Edmund Gosse*.

Edinburgh Review: the essays of this period on French themes were collected in *Inter Arma* (1916).

p. 441 Gide letter:

'What a fine letter I have from you, and how deeply I am moved by it!

'Why did I write this book? Because I thought I had to write it.

'What do I expect from it? I expect nothing but consequences painful to me (and not only to me, alas). And of course the moral obligation had to be more than a little imperious to make me persist; but really it would have seemed cowardly to let myself be stopped by contemplation of the distress, or of the risk. I had the feeling that I could not have died in peace if I had kept all this locked in my heart.

'My dear friend, I abominate falsehood. I can't endure having a share in the customary camouflage that deliberately belies the writing of X, Y, and many others. I wrote this book to 'create a precedent', to set an example of candour; to enlighten some persons, hearten others, and compel public opinion to reckon with something of which it is oblivious or pretends to be, to the immense impairment of psychology, morality, art – and society.

'I wrote this book because I had rather be hated than be beloved for what I am not . . .

'I am talking to you without strain and without fear, and I am indeed happy to be talking to you. Please do see in all I am telling you a testimony to my great respect and deep friendship.'

Virginia Woolf: in her Gosse essay reprinted in *The Moment* (1947), p. 76.

p. 442 'What can one do with such a friend?' My account of the quarrels between EG and Benson can be supplemented, if one has the stomach for them, by the details of different quarrels in David Newsome's biography of Benson *On the Edge of Paradise* (1980).

p. 448 Lis Escop. Originally called Kenwyn Vicarage, this was the house where Benson had lived when his father was Bishop of Truro.

Chapter 17: The Formidable Adventure

p. 450 Freya Stark: *Traveller's Prelude* (1950). The date was 23rd June 1912.

p. 451 Grillions was founded in 1812; EG was elected in 1912. A gathering might include, among the dozen diners, the Lord Chancellor, the Prime Minister and the Archbishop of York as it did on 6th June 1923. J. M. Barrie called it 'the most attractive of all clubs'. EG was Secretary at one period. There were normally dinners every Wednesday when Parliament was sitting.

Yeats to Lady Gregory 9th Dec 1909.

p. 453 Virginia Woolf on Joyce: see Quentin Bell's biography, vol. 2, ch. 2.

Yeats and *Ulysses*: see Yeats to Olivia Shakespear. 28th June 1923. *Letters* ed. Wade, p. 698.

p. 453 The Academic Committee was eventually disbanded in 1939. National

Portrait Gallery: on 1st Dec 1908 Asquith invited EG 'to accept one of the now vacant Trusteeships' of the gallery.

p. 454   EG against censorship and for the liberty of the press. See the last essay in *Leaves and Fruit*, p. 367, dated 9th May 1926 and reprinted from the *Sunday Times*.

p. 455   Bridges to EG 12th Dec 1913: 'You have been a very good friend to me throughout this affair . . . Cannot you get your friend the Prime Minister to tell Lloyd George to arrange that all "interviews" require a government stamp, say minimum value one or two guineas to be presented with visiting card of interviewer to his victim?'

p. 456   'full diary': revised and completed 16th Oct 1914. TS at Rutgers and Leeds.

p. 459   Haldane and Gosse. The letters from EG to Haldane in the Nat. Lib. Scot. and from Haldane to EG at Leeds form nearly forty fat and handsomely-bound volumes. Haldane died on 19th Aug 1928, less than 3 months after his friend.

p. 463   'hoping Gide would translate': Gide was keen ('Je les traduirais volontiers,' Gide to EG 7th July 1915) but for some reason the translation was never made.

A reference to Hamo Sassoon in *Goodbye to All That* was one of the contributory causes (with 'my resentment about your behaviour to Gosse') of the later breach between Sassoon and Graves. See Paul O'Prey: *Broken Images*, selected letters of Robert Graves (1982), pp. 197/8.

Sassoon's first sight of EG: *The Weald of Youth* (1942), p. 16.

p. 464   'more to guide and encourage me': Sassoon was writing to Philip Gosse (CUL). There is an unpublished Sassoon poem in the Imperial War Museum which begins 'I wish old Gosse were here to read that poem'.

p. 465   Graves/Sassoon breach: 'The first row we had, about Gosse.' Graves to Sassoon. 7th July 1933.

EG on Georgians: *Morning Post* 27th Jan 1913. Letter to Blunden undated, 1923 (Texas).

The article 'Some Soldier Poets' was reprinted in *Some Diversions*, p. 259.

p. 466   EG refers to his 'propaganda' in a letter to PG 30th Jan 1917. Stark Young in an obituary in the *New Republic* (6th June 1928) also referred to EG's war work. EG had apparently told him he had been on a committee for propaganda which the Americans swallowed 'beyond our wildest hopes'.

p. 469   Sargent portrait. The attack on it as it hung in the Royal Academy in 1914 increased EG's dislike of militant suffragettes.

p. 471   Tokyo University Library. In a letter to PG in Dec 1928, Nichols: 'I hope some day full justice will be done to him in that connection.' I have tried to find out more from Tokyo without success. For a scandalous account of Nichols's subsequent career, see Paul O'Prey: *Broken Images*, p. 319.

p. 472   Huxley to his brother Julian: *Letters of Aldous Huxley* ed. Grover Smith (1969). See also *Robert Ross, Friend of Friends*, ed. M. Ross (1952) and Sitwell: Laughter in the Next Room (1949), p. 33.

Madam Fan-the-Devil: Vandervelde.

p. 473   The *New Statesman*'s anonymous review was apparently by Edward Shanks.

p. 474   Nicolas Barker in *A Sequel to An Enquiry into the Nature of Certain Nineteenth Century Pamphlets* (1982).

'cordial terms': there is a warm exchange of letters in 1890, and again in 1893, when EG writes of their old friendship. In 1905 Watts-Dunton writes to Nellie, remembering 'those pleasant days when I used to see you by the canal'.

Swinburne afraid: 'I receive from strangers as well as friends dreadful stories of the way in which, of late years particularly, he bullied ACS.' EG to Wise June 1914. But Philip Henderson in his *Swinburne* (1974) refers to the devoted, much-maligned Theodore Watts-Dunton.

'harshly treated': EC, p. 411.

p. 476 Sir Anthony Coningham Sterling was Brigade-Major and Assistant Adjutant-General of the Highland Division in the Crimea.

EG wrote a clever letter to *The Times* (5th April 1913) . . . 'It has become universal to attribute verses in *Fraser* to Swinburne . . . For some time past however I have had my doubts and it is now proved we have all been mistaken.' He does not apologize for the error but presents the new information as 'a discovery which is of importance to bibliographers'.

p. 477 'How can Sir Sidney Lee': the Editor of the *DNB* stood by the article as 'from all just points of view, of great value to the Dictionary.' 16th April 1913.

Chapter 18: Stifled in Roses

p. 482 'read both lessons': I am grateful to Michael Millgate for tracking down the facts behind a reference in one of Hardy's letters to Mrs Henniker.

p. 483 'not missed a single Sunday': J. C. Squire, in his tribute in the *Observer*, 20th May 1928, spoke of EG's 'weekly critical essay'.

p. 485 Van Wyck Brooks: *NY Herald Tribune* 8th Jan 1928, p. 7.

Sainte-Beuve: EC, p. 478 and *Two Visits to Denmark* (1911), p. 328.

Churton Collins said EG 'can gossip pleasantly'. Malcolm Elwin: *Old Gods Falling* (1939) is full of dismissive comments on EG, including the charge that he praised only those long dead. But Elwin suggests that EG deserves 'to live by virtue of his letters as the Horace Walpole of his time'.

p. 486 Edmund Wilson in *New Republic* LIV (22nd Feb 1928), p. 21. For the American opinions I am indebted to Matt. and Mill.

'rose not a jasmine': Preface to Travellers' Library edition (1928) *Selected Essays* (first series).

'the aesthetic view': to Prof. Bliss Perry 3rd April 1906.

p. 488 Gullick bibliography: this appeared in EC, p. 511 and is the basis of the bibliography in the present book. EG answered Gullick's bibliographical queries patiently; their correspondence is in the Turnbull. EG always referred to him as 'the faithful Gullick,' according to PG. Gullick supplied the 'Edmund Gosse Literary Group' (which flourished in NY in 1928) with a memoir in which he praised EG's 'concern for one's private difficulties, whether a baby or a bank-balance'. (TS at Turnbull.)

Augustan Book. The 1927 royalty statement showed sales of 4108 on an edition of 5000 copies at a 12½% royalty. These were pamphlets rather than books and sold at only sixpence each. EG had had 118 free copies.

Frederick Treves (1853–1923) was born in Dorchester and as a small boy had attended a school kept by William Barnes. He was surgeon at the London Hospital and was the first person in England to advocate surgery in the treatment of appendicitis. In June 1902 he operated on Edward VII two days before the date fixed for his Coronation. His last book was called *The Elephant Man and other Reminiscences*; a film, book and play have recently revived his fame.

'pearl of a man': Osbert Sitwell misquotes a letter to Baring (22nd April 1920) as 'that peach of a man' and John Gross perpetuates this misquotation in *The Rise and Fall of the Man of Letters. Aspects* was dedicated to J. C. Squire. *Aspects* sold 2,800 copies in the first two months.

p. 489   Blunden's clothes: in his diary, Sassoon notes that 'EB was wearing a new soft tweed suit . . . of a rough lightish-grey material.'

p. 491   Edith Sitwell's Buchanan story is from *Taken Care of* (1965).
Poetic housemaid: story recorded by E. F. Benson. *As We Were* (1930).
Osbert Sitwell: *Noble Essences* (1950), p. 50.

p. 492   Sassoon on Nellie: *The Weald of Youth* (1942), p. 90.

p. 493   Asquith's signature was in fact added in a further list on 27th Sept 1919.
Letter to Beerbohm: EC, p. 458.

p. 494   'finally presented': the presentation was originally planned for 10th May and then for 5th Nov 1920, in the Steinway Hall, but was postponed and moved. Balfour had been Prime Minister (1902–05) and was now Lord President of the Council, a member of Lloyd George's coalition government. Balfour was given his earldom in 1922.

p. 497   Proust: Sassoon recorded EG's 'abhorrence' for Proust, but EG was a signatory to a tribute to Proust's memory in the *Nouvelle revue française*, 8th Jan 1923.

p. 498   Vita's lecture from V. Woolf's Diary. 27th Oct 1926 (Berg).

p. 499   Lytton Strachey and Gosse: EG dedicated *Leaves and Fruit* to Strachey in 1927 'with affectionate admiration'.
'a letter to Ethel Smythe.' She herself wrote to Nellie after EG's death: 'You know I loved your husband. I think his mind was as alive as any I know.'

p. 500   Sitwell: *Noble Essences*, p. 61.

p. 501   Knighthood. In one existing letter (at Buffalo, to someone called Fleetwood) EG wrote 6th Jan 1925: 'I was afraid my friends would think it ridiculous. I refused it twice before. This time both Curzon and Baldwin pressed it and I gave way.' There is no other evidence of any reluctance.

p. 502   Evelyn Waugh diary 13th Aug 1925 and *A Little Learning* (1964), p. 65.
Mr Tulkinghorn: see Dickens's *Bleak House*.

p. 503   Alec Waugh: *My Brother Evelyn and other profiles* (1967). EG handed over to Bellows £51 for the expenses of the Paris trip. He accounted for £32 8s 8d, and duly returned the balance, less 5s 6d for 'Parker's gift'.

p. 504   William Kean Seymour: *Voices* III (June 1920).

p. 505   Douglas Goldring: *Streets and other verses* (1921).
General William Booth enters into Heaven: Vachel Lindsay, 1913.
Sitwell: *Noble Essences*, p. 40, p. 52.
Sassoon: *Diaries 1920–22* ed. Hart-Davis (1981).

p. 506   Eliot 'later': in July 1931, reviewing EC in the *Criterion*.

p. 509   Shaw to EG at Hardy's funeral from Shaw's letter to PG 18th Jan 1929 (CUL). EC, p. 505.
Catalogue of his library: *The Library of Edmund Gosse*, compiled by E. H. M. Cox (1924).

p. 510   Hardy's letters. There was no systematic collection or even systematic selection of Hardy's letters until the Oxford edition began in 1978; though there were odd volumes – the letters in Colby College, Maine, and of Hardy's letters to his first wife and to Mrs Henniker.

p. 511   Thornycroft's death: letter from EG to Gullick 19th Dec 1925 (Turnbull).
'A chill no bigger': EC, p. 507.

p. 512   EG to Rees: Buffalo.
Nellie Gosse died on 29th Aug 1929. *The Times* described her as 'the widow of Sir Edmund Gosse, the critic and poet'.

Index

N.B.   Letters to individuals are grouped at the beginning of their entries where there are more than one, except in the case of letters to members of EG's immediate family, where they are too numerous to index. Otherwise the arrangement within entries is basically in numerical order of page references, with general entries being marked off from sub-headings by semi-colons. I have found it irritating when checking Gosse entries in literally hundreds of indexes to find the references not in numerical order. But it seemed cumbersome to have a sequential entry for EG himself here (see under separate entries—e.g. ancestry; inaccuracy; poet, EG as etc—and titles of individual books).
Page numbers following n. refer to notes; illustrations followed by a p. number refer to those in the text. Plate numbers of illustrations are italicized.

Index